W9-AQD-275

THE
MOON
MAN

THE MOON MAN

A Biography of
Nikolai Miklouho-Maclay

E. M. WEBSTER

UNIVERSITY OF CALIFORNIA PRESS
Berkeley   Los Angeles   London

University of California Press
Berkeley and Los Angeles, California

University of California Press, Ltd.
London, England

Library of Congress Cataloging in Publication Data

Webster, E. M. (Elsie May).
   The moon man.
   Bibliography.
   Includes index.
   1. Miklukho-Maklaĭ, Nikolaĭ Nikolaevich, 1846–1888.
2. Zoologists—Soviet Union—Biography. 3. Naturalists—
Soviet Union—Biography. 4. Explorers—Soviet Union—
Biography. I. Title.
   QL31.M56W43   1985   591′.092′4   [B]   84-16248
   ISBN 0-520-05435-0

Printed in Australia at Griffin Press Limited
Marion Road, Netley, South Australia 5037

1 2 3 4 5 6 7 8 9

For Peter Ryan
who probably wanted a different book

'Natives love stories'
Miklouho-Maclay

The author and publishers acknowledge the generous assistance
of the Utah Foundation towards the preparation
and printing of illustrations and maps.

Foreword

THIS IS A remarkable book about a
remarkable man. Probably most Australians who have heard of
Miklouho-Maclay at all have a vague idea that he was the first
ethnographer to do serious work in New Guinea, a Russian with a
warm human sympathy for 'native races'. Others, who have read C. L.
Sentinella's translation of his vivid New Guinea diaries, published by the
Kristen Press at Madang in 1975, will know more. But what are mere
outlines and hints in Sentinella—Maclay's family background, his
cultural and scientific formation, his work in Malaya and the East Indies,
the political aspect of his New Guinea activities—are here filled out
with a wealth of detail. In the process of putting flesh on the skeleton,
some of the gilding is scraped off the rather saintly image; but Maclay
emerges as a far more complexly interesting human being, alike in his
triumphs and his disasters, his joys and his frustrations. Some at least of
his failures were due to his own failings, and one may see him as a Rajah
Brooke *manqué*. *The Moon Man* is the real stuff of history.

Elsie Webster excels in the very difficult art of pulling together
discrete diary passages into a coherent and most readable narrative; one
must salute also the tactful way in which she conveys essential scientific
information, so often a stumbling-block, in crisp and lucid footnotes.
The transitions in the narrative, always the points at which less expert
writers fall down, are admirably handled, for instance at the end of
Chapter 11. Very rarely indeed does she miss a trick; perhaps only at
Maclay's conclusion that 'the great obstacle to progress in ethnology was
the frailty of women', which to me demands, irresistibly, the counter
that the potency of men has as much or more to do with it. But she
brings out, very skilfully, the extent of Maclay's misunderstanding of
the people whom he thought he knew so well, and who, however

dazzled by 'the Moon Man' and his tricks, took from him what they wanted and held their own secrets and their own ways.

There is comedy in Maclay's Sydney sojourn and his bizarre ideas on the proper running of a research institute, not to mention the delicious thought that the Australia Club *might* not be the right venue for anatomical research; tragedy in his tangled doings on the Papua-Koviai coast, culminating in the 'vile parody of his anatomical preparations ... the dismembered and headless, decomposing body of that pretty little girl, the daughter of Raja Aiduma'. And disillusion is almost a constant: what could be better than Webster's evocation of the 'improved' aspect of Russia on Maclay's return: 'The cities were bigger and busier, with more people making a living there or somehow staying alive without a living. More business was done. There were more factories, roads, railways. More bureaucrats drudged or yawned in more offices and more soldiers paraded around more barracks. There was more, in short, of all he hated and fled in modern Europe...'?

These extracts give some idea of the quality of Webster's writing; note for example the simplicity, but the telling cumulation of simple words, in the last passage. But for full enjoyment, one must read more continuously; subtle but not falling into the temptation of over-subtlety, Webster's style is admirably adapted to her theme. This is not an over-psychologized biography, yet it seems to me that Maclay's psychological problems, notably his unsatisfactory but not unique relations with his family, are analysed with as sure a touch as are his financial misadventures, which were plenty. Occasionally one may feel—as is almost inevitable in the critical evaluation of a myth—that Maclay might more often be given the benefit of numerous doubts. Any such feelings must surely be dissipated in the concluding chapters, where both author and subject mellow marvellously, and the darkening scene is lightened, briefly, by the touching devotion of Maclay's wife Margaret, Sir John Robertson's daughter, before the final shadow fell.

It is indeed more than saddening to find Maclay's idealism deteriorating to the point where, in a desperate search for Tsarist backing for a grossly impracticable paternalistic Protectorate (with himself as Protector) he seems little more than a self-appointed agent for Russian imperialism, and a failed agent at that, since official Russia was not interested.

The elements were indeed greatly mixed in Maclay, as in all of us; yet despite all his inconsistencies, deceptions and self-deceptions, he remains a man of exceptional gifts: an acute and enquiring mind, basic generosity of spirit, great powers of endurance and great courage. It is fitting that the last words of *The Moon Man* should refer to the simple inscription, that 'satisfied her belief without insulting his unbelief', placed by Margaret Miklouho-Maclay over his grave: '"Well done thou

good and faithful servant". She had found him faithful in all things ...
He had left only plans for a kingdom, only sketches for a crown, but
she kept them'.

We must be grateful to Elsie Webster for this fascinating, and
ultimately most moving, portrait of Nikolai Nikolaevich Miklouho-
Maclay, in all his generosity and his vanity, his littleness and his greatness.

O. H. K. Spate
Canberra,
January 1984

Contents

Maps

Illustrations

Miklouho-Maclay in Moroccan dress in Jena, 1867 (Mitchell Library)
The Red Sea traveller in Syrian dress (Mitchell Library)
In Jena in 1870 (Mitchell Library)
Oranienbaum Palace in 1870 (Mitchell Library)
The corvette *Vityaz*
Miklouho-Maclay's mission cottage, July 1871

FACING PAGE

BETWEEN PAGES 86 AND 87

The villages of Gorendu and Gumbu. Maclay Coast
The men's house in Tengum-mana, Maclay Coast
Astrolabe Bay, looking south from Bogadjim
A Bilbil *vang*
The commemorative plaque at Garagassi

BETWEEN PAGES 118 AND 119

Kema, Celebes, in 1873
Ahmad, the Papuan boy, in 1873
The Governor-General's Palace in Buitenzorg
The Loudon family and friends (Mitchell Library)
Umburmeta, Aiduma Island
The house at Aiva
The urumbai at anchor
Raja Aiduma, Maclay's protégé, in 1874
'Sassi, Kapitan Mavara—my prisoner' (National Library of Australia, Manuscript Collection)
Vuoucirau, inhabitants of Kamaka-Walla district, 1874

FACING PAGE

FACING PAGE

BETWEEN PAGES 246 AND 247

FACING PAGE

Spelling and Dates

The subject of this biography has been discussed in several languages, by many different writers, with the result that there are nearly as many spellings of his name. That adopted throughout this book, 'Miklouho-Maclay', is the version he most frequently used when writing in English or French. In the notes and bibliography, however, the spelling given in titles of works in languages other than Russian conforms to the preferences of the authors cited.

In transliterating other Russian names, an attempt has been made to retain the spelling most familiar to English-speaking readers. This, of course, raises as many problems as it solves, and in some cases it has been necessary to forgo a well-established spelling in order to be consistent with the usual transliteration of a name that is even better known. It is hoped that readers will find no more inconsistencies and irritations than are commonly encountered in English texts which include much transliteration from Russian.

Nineteenth-century Russia used the Julian ('old-style') calendar which was twelve days behind the Gregorian calendar used in western Europe. Russian ships at sea and in foreign ports, however, followed the Gregorian system, as did Miklouho-Maclay in his travel journals. The few precise dates mentioned in this book are given according to the Gregorian calendar. Those included in reference notes agree with the sources, and consequently may be either 'new style' or 'old style'.

Conversions

1d (penny)	0.83 cent
1s (shilling)	10 cents
£1 (pound)	$2
1 mile	1.60 kilometres
1 acre	0.40 hectare

Acknowledgements

Without financial assistance, I could not have hoped to complete this work for many years more, and indeed might not have dared to undertake it. I therefore owe fundamental acknowledgements to the Myer Foundation of Melbourne for the funds that made the project possible. Further financial aid came from a source whose identity is so well concealed that I can only trust my thanks will meet the right eyes.

In the course of research, I depended greatly upon the Mitchell Library, Sydney; the Public Library of New South Wales; the Fisher Library of the University of Sydney; the Archives of New South Wales; the National Library of Australia, Canberra; the La Trobe Library, Melbourne, and the Oxley Memorial Library, Brisbane. I gladly take this opportunity to thank the staffs of those institutions for their expert and courteous assistance. My thanks are also due to the Council of the Royal Geographical Society, London, for photocopies of correspondence from the Society's archives, and to the Archivist, Mrs Christine Kelly, for her thorough and imaginative search of the Society's records. Mrs Rosemary Seton, Archivist of the School of Oriental and African Studies, University of London, kindly investigated the papers of Sir William Mackinnon on my behalf. The British Library supplied photocopies of essential material from Gladstone and Stanmore Papers.

I am deeply grateful to Luciana Trojer for translations from Italian. For invaluable corrections to some of my translations from Russian I have to thank Nina Christesen, who also commented helpfully on my treatment of the Russian background. Over the years, Peter Ryan suggested many improvements in the text, and I am similarly indebted to Professor O. H. K. Spate for his close and thoughtful reading of the manuscript.

Permission to quote from Australian manuscript sources was granted by the Mitchell Library and the Archives Authority of New South

Wales. The solicitors for Lord Stanmore's executors authorized quotations from Stanmore Papers held by the British Library. Illustrations as individually acknowledged are reproduced with the permission of the Mitchell Library and the National Library of Australia. All other illustrations are drawn from N. N. Miklouho-Maclay, *Sobraniye sochineniy* (*Collected Works*), 1950–1954, published by the U.S.S.R. Academy of Sciences, which holds the original drawings and photographs; this material is gratefully acknowledged. For assistance in reproducing pictures from printed sources I am indebted to the Mitchell Library and the General Reference Library, State Library of New South Wales.

Preface

I<small>T IS NOT</small> unknown for a biographer to confess that after years of research and analysis the subject of study remains elusive, even rather enigmatic. In the case of the Russian scientific traveller Miklouho-Maclay, however, the confession entails a sense of isolation, for his is generally regarded as a life of exemplary clarity and consistency. For generations of his compatriots, and for many admirers outside Russia, he is the perfect humanitarian hero, a symbol of science dedicated to human welfare in the highest sense. He possessed great personal charm and the power to win admiration from people of the most disparate temperament and outlook. He copiously documented his own activities and character and clearly thought well of both. The only failing biographers have noticed in him is one to which he himself drew attention: an incurable tendency to place excessive trust in others. Thus the accepted picture remains as he painted it, and an attractive one it is, unshadowed by any suggestion of mystery, inconsistency or ambiguity.

Even on the basis of his own record I have been unable to see his career as an unwavering line determined entirely by moral and scientific principles. I quite early had to abandon any kind of thesis on his position in intellectual history and the effect of his actions in the public sphere. Why, then, write a biography? In the first place there was the fascination of a life story in constant movement, combining a multiplicity of scenes and themes, intimately affected by currents of the time. Then there was the fact that though the traveller spent many years in British colonies, involving himself in their public affairs, no comprehensive, reasonably up-to-date account of him existed in English. Finally there was the sense that someone would eventually break the pattern in which writings on Miklouho-Maclay had become set, and look at him in the more analytical spirit that marks, for example, modern studies of David

Livingstone. This book can be regarded as a first attempt to examine the available facts as they might be treated in the case of any other conspicuous figure.

A biographer with faith in our ability to psychoanalyse the dead would probably make more of the scientist's occasional self-revelations. Lacking that faith, I have merely tried to indicate without excessive emphasis some points that may be psychologically significant. If any general psychological interpretation could be applied, it would be that propounded in O. Mannoni's *Prospero and Caliban* (*La Psychologie de la Colonisation*, as translated by P. Powesland, London 1956). My own work was well advanced before I belatedly studied that classic essay, in fact I was led to it by what I had noticed in Miklouho-Maclay. There is, of course, no absolute 'fit'. Some readers will be offended by the suggestion that any aspect of the Russian traveller can be compared to the European character-type depicted by Mannoni. It nevertheless seems to me that enough similarities exist to invite consideration and perhaps provide an illuminating commentary.

On concluding this work, I am very conscious of how much I have been compelled to leave out. In some instances well-known episodes have given way to facts and actions less frequently described. The sheer number of events involving or significant for Miklouho-Maclay sometimes made it impossible to introduce them all if the tale was to remain coherent. Many readers will undoubtedly feel that I have sacrificed the greater to the lesser in some respects, and I have indeed given more attention than is usual to some phases of the traveller's career. For this I can only plead what seems to me an overriding reason: these matters were important to Miklouho-Maclay.

A Note on Sources

As I have not had the opportunity to visit Russia to investigate manuscripts as yet unpublished, I have concentrated on two bodies of information:

1. Writings by and about Miklouho-Maclay published from 1867 to 1984.
2. Manuscripts in Australian and British libraries and archives.

In the first of these categories, particularly in the examination of scientific books and journals, daily newspapers, and British and Australian official publications, 'new' information has come to light. The second has also yielded facts not previously used, or insufficiently examined.

Until the enlarged edition of Miklouho-Maclay's *Collected Works* appears in 1988, any account of his life must depend fundamentally upon the edition published by the U.S.S.R. Academy of Sciences between 1950 and 1954. This extensively annotated and illustrated edition (five volumes in six) includes all his extant travel journals, nearly all his published papers and reports, selections from manuscripts in Russian archives, a volume of correspondence, and a volume of reproductions from the traveller's drawings with photographs of objects from his ethnographical collection. It is supplemented by contemporary newspaper articles, reports by Russian naval officers, and 'specialist' articles on Miklouho-Maclay's life and work.

The new edition will no doubt include material that has already been published elsewhere. It will also draw upon Australian manuscript sources which were not utilized in the 1950–1954 *Collected Works*. It therefore seems probable that many writings to be added to the *Collected Works* have been taken into account in the present book.

Some material used here does not satisfy the highest standards of historical evidence. Miklouho-Maclay's letters to his family, for example, apparently exist only as copies made by his brother Mikhail, but it has been necessary, in spite of evident omissions, to treat these as primary sources. Similar considerations apply to what must have been an important correspondence with Prince A. A. Meshchersky, now represented only by a few letters edited for publication in 1912. The greatest problem is presented by the writings that Miklouho-Maclay himself prepared for publication or caused others to publish. Anyone who compares statements made at different times must notice that the traveller's accounts of events could differ substantially. Only one of his extant travel journals, that of the first Malay Peninsula expedition, appears never to have been revised for publication. It is therefore sometimes impossible either to reconcile the journal account with other statements made or authorized by Miklouho-Maclay or to determine which version is actually the earlier. In such cases one can only follow the final text of the journal. Where difficulties exist I have tried to indicate them without belabouring the point.

Little use has been made of secondary biographical sources, which in most cases are notable mainly for ideological purity and avoidance of unsuitable information. Among the longer general publications subsequent to the 1950-1954 *Collected Works*, the writings of N. A. Butinov, Dora Fischer and C. L. Sentinella are the most complete. I have relied upon them for some information on Miklouho-Maclay's family background and early years. All require, however, to be supplemented by the three articles of B. A. Valskaya, which include documents essential for any realistic view of Miklouho-Maclay's activities in the last five years of his life.

The first biography of Miklouho-Maclay in any language was the pamphlet published by his British friend and representative, E. S. Thomassen, in 1882. This short work, compiled under the traveller's supervision, can be read as accurately conveying the view of his career and character that he wished to establish. With information from Miklouho-Maclay's sons, it formed the basis of the second biography in English, F. S. Greenop's *Who Travels Alone* (1944). Now outdated in most respects, Greenop's was a pioneering work, and it remains interesting for the impressions he gathered from Sydney people who as children had known the Russian scientist.

English-speaking readers with no Russian are deeply indebted to the late C. L. Sentinella not only for his translations from Miklouho-Maclay's New Guinea diaries but for the biographical matter which links them into a complete narrative. Though a devoted and discreet admirer of the traveller, Sentinella was not hampered by the obligations of Russian biographers. Consequently he could depart somewhat from the orthodox view of Miklouho-Maclay's colonization projects and could mention, in appendix and annotations, the primary reason for the 1883 visit to New Guinea. A recent publication from Moscow (N. N. Miklouho-Maclay, *Travels to New Guinea*, 1983) does not supersede Sentinella's translations. While one must occasionally disagree with Sentinella, his remains the better of the two versions. It is used in the present book to provide English references alongside those to the Russian text. Sentinella's translations of Miklouho-Maclay's Papua-Koviai journal and that of the first Malay Peninsula journal (not included in the published volume) can be studied in typescript in the Mitchell Library, Sydney.

Miklouho-Maclay's scientific work has not been adequately treated in any biography, and specialist articles devoted to it have been much influenced by his standing as humanitarian. The essay by I. I. Pusanov in the *Collected Works* (vol. III, pt. 2) suggests tension between scientific appraisal and the obligation to maintain a national hero. It should not be read without the somewhat more critical annotations in the same volume. L. S. Berg's article on Miklouho-Maclay as geographer and traveller (in *Otechestvennie fiziko-geografy i puteshestvenniki*, 1959) does not actually mention contributions to geography. The essay by Ya. Ya. Roginsky and S. A. Tokarev in the *Collected Works* (vol. III, pt. 1) is gently critical of some deficiencies in Miklouho-Maclay's work as ethnographer and anthropologist. On the whole, I have found it best to return to the writings of Miklouho-Maclay's contemporaries and near-contemporaries, which are cited in the relevant reference notes.

Some of the works listed in Section 3 of the Bibliography to the present book, while adding little or nothing to the stock of information about the traveller, are interesting as examples of the development of the Miklouho-Maclay cult in Russia and elsewhere.

1: The Search for Solitude

Few visitors disturbed the hotel *Zum Rössle* in late summer 1864. Perched in the heights of the Schwartzwald, four kilometres from any village, it sheltered only the proprietors and their servants. For days on end no wayfarer climbed the mountain.

'Fine!' said the Russian student who wandered there from Heidelberg. It was beautiful, cheap, good for his weak chest and sore eyes. He could ramble as he pleased, climbing every peak and sketching the villages clustered round their churches. Above all, it was quiet, solitary, conducive to study and the inner life that was threatened by the chatter and bustle of the human herd. 'Here', he told his mother, 'here I can say that I am completely alone'.

Ekaterina Semyonovna Miklouho, a harassed woman somewhere in St Petersburg or Kiev, knew how much her son Nikolai Nikolaevich wanted solitude. She sometimes doubted his desire for uninterrupted work and strict economy. Nothing could be less practicable than the cautious dream she dreamed for the child she had borne at Rozhdestvensk, Novgorod government, on 17 July 1846, the second of five who were left fatherless in 1857. She saw him as one of the new technical élite, but not as a builder of the railways that in drawing Russia into the modern world had advanced her late husband in government service. He was to be engineer in a factory, devising better means for converting raw materials into saleable goods.

Indications of her mistake had come early in 1864. After education at home, a short time at the Lutheran school of Saint Anne, a course at the Second St Petersburg Gymnasium and two months as external student in the physico-mathematical faculty of the university, her second son had been expelled without right to enter any other Russian university.

1

There might or might not have been political reasons for his expulsion. The inspector's report referred only to the youth's having 'while in the university buildings, repeatedly broken the rules ...'. For himself, the ban on entrance to Russian universities seemed providential rather than punitive. Before long, his dossier was marked 'Gone abroad'. It was understood that he would obtain a technical training, but he thought it too early to put his name down for employment. Nor should Ekaterina Semyonovna worry about his weakness in mathematics. It was still necessary to 'study and study'.

He might have been expected to choose science or medicine, the subjects that had attracted him as a schoolboy. At Heidelberg he did not join the majority of Russian students. While his compatriots pursued the natural sciences, he concentrated on philosophy, languages and law.

His life in company with Kant, Schopenhauer and Goethe was sufficiently penurious. A decrepit black overcoat concealed a sketchy wardrobe. His new secondhand boots must be explained to Ekaterina Semyonovna, as must expenditure on tuition, rent, food and books. Hence his emphasis on remittances expected from Russia, the cheapness of Schwartzwald holidays, and the progress of companies in which his mother held shares. In this respect the pattern of his life was set before he was nineteen. Only in study or the solitude of a mountain peak could he forget that he was poor, unproductive, and totally dependent on others.

Otherwise the pattern remained unsettled, the one certainty being his determination to stay abroad. He could not visit Russia unless his return to Germany were guaranteed. He would not risk being forced into an engineering course, thence into a factory. Having begun at Heidelberg the studies his mother thought a waste of time, he wished to finish them there.

He nevertheless left romantic Heidelberg in spring 1865, to enter the medical faculty at Leipzig. German tradition encouraged a change of university. The times encouraged a return to his earlier interests. Perhaps his new start reflected his mother's pride in her grandfather, who had been physician to Prussian and Polish kings. Perhaps it was prompted by the spirit of a time when Russian youth learned to despise all but the 'practical', to count art superfluous, poetry a bore and philosophy an impediment to the liberation of the people. Nikolai Miklouho had had to defend himself against hints that he cared insufficiently for the poor and oppressed, political justice and the rights of women.

His earlier political interests did seem to have faded. At nineteen he was too much the intellectual aristocrat to give himself wholly to the 'practical', too solitary to be a politician, too much oppressed by women to work for their emancipation. Quoting Schopenhauer (who was quoting an admired mystic), he had let fall some words—'To me, everything is indifferent'—that he could neither disown nor frankly adopt. In medicine, his activity might provide its own justification.

At Leipzig he heard lectures only for the summer of 1865. The city was too large and noisy; he preferred the tranquil life of the smaller university towns. Little Jena offered more than semi-rural peace, as yet unbroken by the railway. Its university had become the centre of diffusion for the thought of Charles Darwin, with philosophical elaborations far beyond anything that modest naturalist imagined. There were reports of living things too simple to be true cells, dots of protoplasm that bridged the gulf between animate and inanimate nature. There were men prepared to say that 'all true science is philosophy and all true philosophy is science, and in this sense all true science is natural philosophy', ultimately to fashion from Darwin's theory a new religion of the uncreated universe. There were privately circulated essays on the descent of man, horrifying the orthodox and attracting by rumour a swarm of students to the university. For winter 1865–66, Nikolai Miklouho joined a virtual migration to Jena.

Again he enrolled as a medical student, following a condensed course in natural science, devoted to comparative anatomy under Carl Gegenbaur and zoology under Ernst Haeckel. By the end of summer 1866 he was an assistant to Haeckel, rather a favourite with both celebrated professors, one of zoology's coming men. Ekaterina Semyonovna considered comparative anatomy and experimental zoology as useless, expensive and unhealthy as philosophy. Their correspondence during this period was not one either party wished to preserve.

His teacher Ernst Haeckel, at thirty-two, regarded his own life as finished. The death of his wife two years before seemed a blow he could not survive. Amid tempests of sorrow and the struggles provoked by his extreme Darwinism, he had proposed to end his life as he originally meant to begin it, as a scientific traveller in distant lands. But his friend T. H. Huxley had discouraged his wish to join a British expedition. Huxley having further laid it down that the times required organization rather than increase of knowledge, the German professor decided to use his remaining days in one vast effort to organize knowledge. Hardly sleeping, living like a hermit, he expounded his thought in a 'last great work'. By autumn 1866 the *General Morphology of Organisms*, two volumes containing more than 1200 crowded pages, was with the printer. Its author, in a physical and mental state that alarmed his friends, asked leave to undertake his 'last voyage' after his 'last book'. He proposed to take with him medical students Hermann Fol and Nikolai Miklouho.

The young Russian now had prospects for which most students would give a great deal—a journey through France, Spain and Portugal,

followed by three or four months on subtropical islands. It would be
his first journey outside Europe, his first scientific expedition. Yet his
outward response was marked by the coolness with which he greeted
all prospects that were not positively disagreeable. He might have been
sixty years old when he dropped a note to his young sister, enclosing a
photograph and advising in two sentences that he was off to the Canary
Islands. But for a passing reference to Hermann Fol, he might have been
alone. But for his criticism of the photograph, it seemed that to him
everything was indifferent.

Haeckel and his senior companion Richard Greeff, a lecturer from
Bonn, made a pilgrimage to England to visit Darwin. The students went
direct to Lisbon, whence the whole party sailed for Funchal in
mid-November 1866. Brief inspection of Madeira sufficed for Haeckel.
Strengthened by talks with Darwin, the professor still thirsted for the
'powerful restorative' of Tenerife, of which another of his masters,
Alexander von Humboldt, had said that no place was 'better calculated
to banish sorrow and restore peace to an embittered soul'. A week after
they left Lisbon, a Prussian warship set the travellers down at Santa Cruz.

It was not for students to describe such events as the obligatory ascent
of the Pico de Tiede. Haeckel, the only one to struggle through snow
to the rim of the crater, would rhapsodize in print. Greeff planned a
book about their journey. The real business began for Miklouho when
a sailing vessel landed them at the capital of Lanzarote.

The advice that sent them there seemed to have elements of malice.
Lanzarote is the easternmost of the group, about seventy kilometres
long and forbiddingly barren. Winds from the Sahara sweep over its
chains of craters, lava flows, marching sand dunes and sparse vegetation.
At first glance, all life seemed concentrated on and in the sea. Quartered
in houses with unglazed windows, the visitors soon wished first
impressions were more reliable. Swarms of bloodthirsty insects made
life on Lanzarote a constant torment.

Yet more than nostalgia made the scientists look back on the place
affectionately. The lunar landscape invited Miklouho to use his pencil,
as did the stark little coastal settlements with their fishing craft and
windmills. The sea that had its place in almost every picture yielded its
own delicate beauties. From currents that were almost rivers of
plankton, the nets drew material for half a dozen monographs, quickly
overcoming Haeckel's sense of undertaking his 'last voyage' after his 'last
book'. Each naturalist concentrated on one or two departments of
marine zoology. Miklouho worked on two groups of animals almost at
opposite poles of marine life, the fishes and the sponges.

In the first department his physical activity was unadventurous; for
specimens he walked to Arrecife market. The mental activity inspiring
in verged on the grandiose. At twenty, after three semesters of formal

study, he contemplated an exhaustive work on the comparative neurology of the vertebrates, from the lancelet to man.

His second concern left more traces in memories of Lanzarote. On broken masses of lava about the harbour and on the reef below the old fort, he found a profusion of sponges, patches of yellow, red and violet revealed among seaweed at low tide. He recognized their beauty, but more than this attracted him. Haeckel contended that the natural history of sponges, especially the small calcareous forms, presented a 'connected and striking argument in favour of Darwin'. In winter 1866–67, after visits to Down and in anticipation of a furious reception for the *General Morphology*, such evidence was particularly desirable. When Haeckel incited his pupil to investigate sponges, he expected far-reaching results.

In spartan surroundings, the naturalists possessed the means of intellectual luxury. Haeckel could recount his conversations with Darwin, 'a venerable sage of ancient Greece, a Socrates or an Aristotle'. He might discuss the equally revered Goethe and Humboldt, or declare his acceptance of Lamarck's ideas on 'use and disuse' and the inheritance of acquired characters. He might expound his own extreme version of the 'biogenetic law', according to which animal embryos recapitulated the forms of their most remote ancestors. There were equally exciting possibilities in the branch of science Haeckel had recently defined and named 'ecology'. Haeckel's researches on the colonial nature of creatures like the Portuguese man-o'-war caused excitement. So did his discovery of an orange-red speck of jelly that appeared to have no nucleus. He declared this 'the most simple organism', and placed it among his 'Monera', the formless products of spontaneous generation, the hypothetical beginnings of life on earth.

If he cared to speak of personal matters, as he often did, Haeckel could describe his rapturous journey in Italy six years before, especially his stay at Messina, a place brought to mind by the local conditions and abundant marine fauna of Lanzarote. Reaching farther back, he could reveal his early ambition to become a scientific traveller in the tropics, dreamlike lands whose extravagance still haunted his imagination.

Much that was in Haeckel's mind found its natural way into his pupil's, sometimes modified in transit. Miklouho took Darwinism more or less for granted. He more consciously accepted inheritance of acquired characters as 'the law of inheritance', ready to apply it in sweeping ways. He was equally prepared to be guided by the 'biogenetic law' and to appreciate the importance of ecology. Talk of Italy and the tropics was the stuff that deeds are made of.

Meanwhile he trudged to and from the fish market, ranged the shores and reefs, made careful scientific drawings or sketched the flat-roofed houses and empty streets of Arrecife. Among the equipment and materials of their work, he and Haeckel posed for photographs, arms about each other's shoulders, the student rather lifted off his feet by the embrace of his tall, proprietorial master. When they faced the camera more formally, wearing careless neckties and high, soft boots, Haeckel sat relaxed but alert, ready to display the athleticism that had won a laurel crown in the long jump. Sombre and intense, Miklouho leaned on the handle of his net like some rebel mountaineer upon a rifle, an oilskin hanging cloak-like from one shoulder. Haeckel held a dried starfish as though it were a rose. Miklouho clutched what might have been a dagger. In their own persons, votaries of philosophy and science paid tribute to romantic art.

It became difficult to remain either romantic or philosophical on Lanzarote. After killing six thousand fleas, Haeckel conceded defeat, announcing that they would leave the island a month earlier than originally planned. Miklouho did not welcome the interruption. He had worked with growing interest on sponges, finding apparently new species and making observations on living animals. His attention fastened especially on what seemed at least three 'new' calcareous sponges—one a tiny, simple tube on a flexible stalk, the second a larger, stalked, pear-shaped body with many openings, the third an almost formless mass spreading over the rocks. He had decided that these different forms were specifically one, evidence of the extreme variability that caused Haeckel to doubt whether calcareous sponges ever formed 'good species', important for the natural history of colonial forms and for evolutionary theory in general. He had theories to test and experiments under way, reluctantly abandoned when the party left Lanzarote.

With time to spare they crossed to Morocco, a country that still represented adventure. The land was torn by rebellion and tribal war. Robbery and murder were a way of life. Hatred of foreigners became almost a religion as the populace struggled to preserve mediaeval ways against European encroachment. Along the coast foreigners controlled trade and customs revenue, ran postal services and voyaged between Moroccan ports on French and British steamers. Only two Europeans were known to live in the interior, and they lived in disguise.

At dazzling Mogador, the naturalists stayed just long enough for Miklouho to sketch the mosque and customs house and search unsuccessfully for his protean new sponge. The most cursory enquiry revealed that Europeans from the port ventured to the capital only at intervals of years, in strong armed parties. A glimpse of Marrakesh entailed a four-day journey on roads exposed to attack by bandits, where water was so scarce that each summer men and animals died of thirst. Holy Marrakesh, once a legend for wealth and culture, had become the home of barbarism and misery, fever and fanaticism. A visit was an undertaking from which a traveller might make half a book.

Nikolai Ilich Miklouho (d. 1857),
Miklouho-Maclay's father

Miklouho-Maclay with a friend in
St Petersburg, about 1862

In St Petersburg, about 1864

Olga, Miklouho-Maclay's sister

Olga as her brother saw her

Sergei Miklouho, Miklouho-Maclay's older
brother

Haeckel and Greeff took ship for Gibraltar. The students set out for Marrakesh, wearing Moroccan dress, well-mounted, and equipped with a large tent. Disguised effectively enough to remain a few minutes in one place, Miklouho sketched scenes along the way, the party's camps and animals, architectural details, a lonely shrine, a romantic bridge, a view of the Great Atlas. When he returned to the coast he had undoubtedly learnt much amid scenes that shook European faith in the need for sanitary laws and caused some doubt as to whether slavery was always an unmitigated evil. Not yet ready to use such material, he resumed the quest for sponges.

The travellers pursued their homeward way by steamer, calling briefly at those ports where the surf permitted a landing. At Mazagan the young Russian sketched the remains of centuries of Portuguese occupation, and searched the dreary shore in vain. The absence of that most interesting of sponges remained uppermost in his thoughts as he viewed tumbledown, fever-stricken Casablanca, passed through Tangier and crossed to Gibraltar. Around Algeciras Bay, where the reunited party spent some weeks, he again sought but did not find the humble organism that dominated his imagination. When they set out for Jena, the student had, like his master, theories enough to occupy him for years. Any energies left over from investigation of the vertebrate brain would be devoted to animals that had long been regarded as plants.

His first published research concerned neither sponges nor the brain. Returning to Jena bronzed, fit, bursting with scientific plans and ready to marry again, Haeckel found that his revolutionary testament had fallen remarkably flat. The silence might be that of impotent rage. Perhaps it showed that the controversy Haeckel meant to stir was lost among the technicalities of his masterpiece. He began the shorter, less technical work suggested by Carl Gegenbaur. To be presented first as a course of lectures, this 'popular' exposition was intended to provoke a sluggish enemy. But before opening his war, Haeckel had to mend his defences. As part of that operation, Nikolai Miklouho investigated the 'swimbladder' or 'air bladder', the gas-filled sac which in most bony fishes serves as a hydrostatic apparatus.

Assuming that the 'simple' swimbladder was more 'primitive' than the complex lung to which embryology related it, Darwin had suggested that vertebrates with lungs evolved from an 'ancient and unknown prototype . . . furnished with a floating apparatus'. Gegenbaur had shown, to Haeckel's satisfaction, that the unknown ancestor of modern fishes and air-breathing vertebrates was a sharklike animal. The great obstacle to uniting these two ideas was the fact that modern adult sharks have no swimbladders. Only the 'biogenetic law' could save all interests. Some investigator must find, in embryos of living forms, the evidence of an organ more necessary for the scientists than for sharks.

Miklouho was satisfied that 'undifferentiated' sharklike fishes were both 'the point of departure for other fishes' and 'the origin of higher vertebrates'. He found the evidence in embryos of the lowlier sharks, a forward-directed pocket of mucous membrane arising from the gullet, minute but consistently detectable. Gegenbaur thought this could be 'regarded as the rudiment of an air-bladder'. Haeckel unconditionally adopted it. If the little membraneous pocket existed as a rudiment in the ancestral shark, it could evolve as a swimbladder in one line of descent and lungs in the other. If it was, as Miklouho preferred, the vestige of an organ that had been functional in the ancestors, the theory remained intact.

The results so acceptable to the teachers (neither of whom cited Miklouho as authority for their statements) were quickly obtained in early summer 1867, and immediately printed in the scientific journal of which Gegenbaur was the moving spirit. In triumphant lectures and in the book evolved from them, his famous *History of Creation*, Haeckel spoke confidently of the swimbladder possessed by the ancient 'Proselachii'. Miklouho returned to medical studies and work on materials collected abroad. But not for long. He left Jena again that autumn to study sponge collections in European museums. In Sweden, the ultimate goal of the excursion, he applied to join an expedition led by Baron Adolf Nordenskiöld.

The explorer could count on three zoologists, seasoned by previous Arctic voyages. Miklouho returned with nothing to show but sketches of romantic Scandinavia and notes on sponges preserved in Berlin, Copenhagen and Stockholm. In a way this was fortunate. No man was less suited to life aboard the tiny, crowded vessel in which the expedition presently departed. He needed solitude and loathed noise, dreaded cold and secretly feared the sea. If his destiny demanded the heroic life, it could not be fulfilled by a voyage aimed at the North Pole.

He conceived the hero clearly, as 'an extraordinary person ... who' would wish to help everyone, to teach everyone'. This being was innately noble, perhaps self-disciplined by the kind of asceticism that Nikolai Chernyshevsky imposed upon the hero of his celebrated novel *What is to be Done?* Chernyshevsky, an early influence in the scientist's life, had been exiled to Siberia four years before. His characterization of the austere, fearless, didactic and totally materialist hero remained as a model for Russian youth. But when Miklouho looked into his own heart, he found nothing resembling that selfless revolutionary. He saw, or professed to see,

> ... a tiresome egoist, completely indifferent to the lives and aspirations of other, worthy folk, even ridiculing them; who obeys only his own desires, striving by one means or another to put an end to his boredom; who considers virtue, friendship, magnanimity to be

only fine words, pleasantly soothing to the eager ears of good people.

The self-portrait lost some confessional value in the context. In what he thought a 'quite original manner', his path had crossed that of a young German woman visiting Frankfurt-am-Main. Now she urgently summoned him to her side. His self-appraisal was ostensibly meant to dispel her illusions. Adding some advice—'When you wish to see people as splendid and interesting, observe them only from afar'—he seemingly did everything to repel a deluded admirer. Yet he took measures to preserve and strengthen this tie. Depicting himself as an empty cynic, he avowed a nature 'not quite made to the measure of ordinary worthy people', depths left unplumbed by a few hours acquaintance and two or three letters. Emphasizing his inability to save Auguste Seligman, he implied that he himself needed and deserved salvation. The challenge to redeem a lost soul, irresistible to any young woman worth her salt, concluded with promises of a sudden, pleasant and interesting meeting in the spring.

To enthral a troubled young lady, he posed byronically, much as he struck an attitude for the camera on Lanzarote or leaned, wearing Moroccan dress, upon a classical pillar in the studio of a Jena photographer. In his twenty-second year he tried on selves like garments—cool, objective scientist, romantic traveller, weary cynic or potential hero. Yet he truly was not made to the measure of ordinary people, nor was he easy to know, perhaps least of all to himself. In 1868 he symbolized his quest for distinctive identity by adopting a new name, adding to his Zaporozhian Cossack surname a further difficulty of pronunciation and spelling. Some believed the name 'Maclay' was that of Scottish ancestors who had migrated to Russia before the eighteenth century, distinguished themselves in military service and been ennobled by Catherine the Great. Others thought the name had been used by one of the scientist's grandfathers. Others still, on Miklouho-Maclay's authority, maintained that his grandmother had been Scottish-born. The new or revived name may have drawn him closer to his ancestors or to the fashion for things Scottish. It brought him no closer to living relatives, for his father's brother and his own elder brother never used it, and his mother's family remained content with the name of Bekker. The name Maclay or Macleay—popularly believed to be from the Gaelic 'Mac an Leigh', meaning 'Son of the Physician', further distinguished as the original family name of Livingstone the explorer—perhaps expressed determination for the future. For the present it identified his uniqueness, distancing him from both Russia and his relatives.

Additional distance hardly seemed necessary. The great phase of reform in Russia had been succeeded by one of reaction, but Nikolai Nikolaevich was still treated with an indifference that testified to the insignificance of his misdeeds. He was free to enter and leave his homeland as he chose. He nevertheless associated so little with compatriots that he believed his Russian was becoming incomprehensible. Sometimes he felt that no one tried to understand it, particularly when he wrote about money.

Money or the lack of it dominated his existence, perhaps one reason why he no longer lived alone. In 1868 he shared a flat with Prince Alexander Alexandrovich Meshchersky, an old schoolfriend who was studying law. A member of one of Russia's most aristocratic and erratic families, Meshchersky seemed born to represent his country's 'superfluous men'—talented, idealistic and wealthy, but directionless, vacillating, given to alternate enthusiasm and ennui. Sympathy formed one element in his relationship with the naturalist, whose poverty was plain to see. Admiration was clearly another. Miklouho-Maclay (as he was determined to be called) displayed all the energy and decision that Meshchersky lacked. Whether or not Meshchersky knew all about his friend—perceived, for instance, the traits sketched for the girl in Frankfurt—he displayed complete faith in one not made to the measure of ordinary people. For his part, Nikolai Nikolaevich felt there was hardly anyone more closely linked to him than this young aristocrat who personified the qualities least appropriate to the finished portrait of Miklouho-Maclay.

Between his scientific 'family' and the society of a friend he called 'brother', he rarely missed the family of his birth. He sometimes wondered whether his mother and sister lived in St Petersburg, Kiev or Samara. The doings of his older brother Sergei and the younger boys Vladimir and Mikhail were equally mysterious. As his letters remained unread or unanswered, it became clear that the distance separating the family from its most ambitious member could not be measured solely in kilometres or versts.

Perhaps Ekaterina Semyonovna and her other sons were not entirely to blame. Nikolai Nikolaevich tended to be perfunctory in expressing filial or fraternal concern. His letters conveyed nothing of the scientific work in which his mother was required to have complete faith, none of the excitement of study and travel in foreign lands. Brief and businesslike, they were written when his allowance failed to arrive or was needed before its due date. The ensuing silence left him to feel the precariousness of his position, or to suspect that, as 'the kind of person who needs a good deal', he placed an undue tax on his mother's resources. Such suspicions never noticeably influenced his plans. Constrained by personal needs or by her unpredictable will, by the influence of her brother or by hope that her son might be forced into the path she chose, Ekaterina Semyonovna could ignore two or three letters. Money, when it came, was accompanied by strictures on studies that cost a fortune, ruined the eyes and brought no tangible benefits. Money always came eventually.

Sometimes it came as the result of his sister's intercession. In earlier years Olga Nikolaevna had received occasional laconically playful notes, crumbs from the table of her brother's adventurous existence, accompanied by photographs for her album. His latest brief visit to Russia had introduced him to a new Olga, an attractive young girl, eager to learn, nursing aspirations as remote as his own from the limited aims their mother preferred. More than any other of the family, Olga resembled him. She also revealed a capacity for usefulness. As part of their alliance of kindred minds, Olga became her brother's agent, forwarding his books and comforts to Jena, passing on papers and photographs to scientific contacts in St Petersburg. She became the confidante in financial anxiety, the mediator when it was necessary to 'ask mother' about money.

Juggling debts and deploring the effect of uncertainty upon his work, Miklouho-Maclay looked ahead to a sojourn in Italy. His second scientific paper was published late in spring 1868, a description of the highly variable sponge discovered on Lanzarote, with remarks on its biological significance. He presented his results clearly and authoritatively. He displayed a comprehensive knowledge of the literature, except for the most recent publications in English. Systematists noticed the lack of a precise 'diagnosis' for the new genus, but his sponge was amply illustrated and thoroughly discussed in a rather unconventional style. The dearth of experimental details to support his more far-reaching statements was not exceptional for the time.

Up to a point, his work did not conflict with established opinion. Contemporary zoology recognized the liability of sponges to vary in form under the influence of environment, kept an open mind as to how sponge colonies were formed, and entertained more than one view of their affinities. The idea that sponges were best grouped with corals and sea anemones had prevailed among naturalists from Linnaeus to Cuvier, at least among those who did not regard these animals as plants. Respected scientists had recently revived it in modified form. Miklouho-Maclay claimed only to supply the proof that had been missing, while placing the sponges closer to the corals than his predecessors supposed. His basic propositions were that the sponge's internal spaces corresponded in both development and function to the digestive cavity of a coral polyp, and that the so-called 'osculum' through which water is expelled also serves as the sponge's mouth. But this was quite enough to bring about a revolution in the subject. Gentlemen who had studied these animals for forty years and more were told that their observations were inadequate, their ideas of sponge anatomy and physiology entirely mistaken.

The new views were not immediately attacked, a surprising outcome in a field where the placidity of the subject was equalled by the touchiness of its students. Ernst Haeckel had already welcomed the proof of the coelenterate nature of sponges. He promptly began work on sponges himself, obviously eager to abandon his earlier opinions. Critics of this theory had reason to save their ammunition for the weightier opponent.

Self-confidence also marked Miklouho-Maclay's next publication, a preliminary communication of work on the brain. In his opinion, this research left 'no doubt' that all other anatomists had mistaken the midbrain of sharks for the cerebellum. Established names for parts of the fish brain would have to be changed. By giving the sharks a cerebellum no better developed than that of the frog, his results also seemed to support the hypothesis that made primitive sharks the starting point for the evolution of bony fishes and land-dwelling vertebrates. Carl Gegenbaur decided to revise his textbook of comparative anatomy to agree with his pupil's interpretation.

Behind the poised young anatomist, the student was swamped by debts, rather frightened by his 'very unenviable position'. Alarm and testiness crept into his account of himself—constantly ill, suffering from bad eyes, showered with bills and left, 'thanks to the Russian post and a non-answering mother', in most uncomfortable uncertainty. The money that released him from Jena and his most pressing debts was a mere palliative. He would return 'as before, without a kopeck', in immediate need of more funds.

Ekaterina Semyonovna to some extent deserved the bitter overtones that accompanied her son's demands. Rejecting his vague offer to relieve her of the burden, she had undertaken to support him for five years abroad. When those years turned out to include extensive travels, she had neither the means to grant his wishes freely nor the will-power to refuse outright. The son who addressed her as '*Mia cara Madre!*', in anticipation of his new Italian identity, reacted with a mixture of pride and humility, pleading and ruthlessness, exhortations to be as candid as he, combined with evidence that no candour on her part could alter his decision. He knew the objections by heart: that he was wasteful, lived beyond their means, encroached upon the rights of brothers and sister. The answer would appear in his work, proof that he never wasted time or money. Meanwhile, his mother should prepare herself for the cost of his next journey.

Just as Ekaterina Semyonovna's attempt at control through the financial lever was probably unconscious, Nikolai Nikolaevich detected no self-interest in his self-imposed necessities or ruthlessness in his determination. His needs were those of science, his travels undertaken exclusively for research. Burdened with proof of more than scientific points, obliged also to justify the scientist in the eyes of his family, his work required his presence in Sicily. To Sicily he went in autumn 1868, betraying none of the elated uncertainty with which Ernst Haeckel had journeyed south eight years before.

Haeckel in Italy was as outdated as Byron's Harold. Biologists no longer rambled through the peninsula rhapsodizing over orange-blossom, seas and sunsets and getting drunk with painters. They came for specific purposes, stuck to their microscopes, and went home to publish reports on beauties inaccessible to the unaided senses. Italy did impress Miklouho-Maclay as a country where he could live. A soft sketch of a gondola on a Venetian canal revealed interests less uncompromisingly scientific than his letters allowed. Otherwise he seemed no more concerned with the face of Italy than with its politics and brigandage.

Apart from Mafia murders and an autonomist plot, the Sicilians stayed quiet that winter while mainland Italy rioted. The land itself was less tranquil. Etna erupted, thrilling the crowds as far away as Malta. Miklouho-Maclay slept through an earthquake that kept the populace alert all night.

For most of his stay he was the guest of his wealthy, cultivated colleague, Anton Dohrn. In a spacious, comfortable apartment, assisted by Dohrn's array of instruments and portable aquaria, he continued his research. Investigating the brain of the chimaera or rat-fish, he again obtained startling results which were for a time adopted by Gegenbaur. In the complex conditions of the Strait of Messina, an investigator might devote years to the effects of external factors on marine life. Yet Miklouho-Maclay regarded with dissatisfaction the superb view out-spread below the Palazzo Vitale. Like the celebrated Fata Morgana of the Strait, the sponges he wanted were always elsewhere.

It might already be too late to find these urgently needed animals. In a Paris museum he had seen specimens from Indo-Pacific waters, directly contradicting his published views on the structure of sponges. But he argued that these objects preserved in museums did not reliably represent living animals. He must observe the creatures in their natural state, then decide whether his opinions stood unchanged. Plans for a journey to the Red Sea emerged, half-recognized as preliminary to further travels. Meanwhile his endangered results were in the hands of the scientific world. Haeckel was preparing a monograph in which the opinions of Miklouho-Maclay would be used to support daring generalizations.

While Maclay awaited funds to leave Messina, his host was in a troubled state of mind. At no time since abandoning his academic career had Dohrn found satisfaction in his work. Benevolent domination by Haeckel and Gegenbaur was a thing of the past. Importunate students no longer kept him from original research. He remained a prisoner, dissatisfied with life and Europe, thinking of escape to the Tropics. Impulsive, imaginative and subject to nervous depression, Dohrn recognized his own 'many peculiarities' as clearly as did his guest, and as easily forgave them. He did not blame them for his disappointing results. Pondering the 'accident' that made him a zoologist, the question marks hanging over the future, he found concrete reasons for his frustration.

In Scotland it had been caused by weather that prevented his obtaining research material. In a Sicilian winter that behaved like spring, he was still beset by obstacles. Too much time was lost in obtaining and identifying, preparing and maintaining the materials for embryological studies. He believed his companion was equally oppressed by the sense of achievement falling short of expectations. These impressions led Dohrn back to an idea dating from his first field-work with Haeckel: the necessity for research stations where zoologists, finding everything ready to hand, could concentrate upon experiment and thought.

Miklouho-Maclay at the time complained only of the unsatisfactory fauna, his 'non-answering mother' and the state of his eyes, which required 'expensive' rest in a distant region. He agreed that zoologists needed convenient laboratories by the sea. He and Dohrn often discussed the matter, decided to leave their equipment as the nucleus for a station at Messina, attempted to collect donations to start the project. Within general agreement, they thought of a zoological station in different terms. To Miklouho-Maclay it would be a quiet, bare place, a hermitage where the researcher might delve and meditate, secure from the world's intrusion. For Dohrn it became a temple and showcase of science, where *savants* of all nations, relieved of drudgery by a staff of assistants, would work alone or co-operatively in their sanctum while the public visited the outer halls. Instead of presenting 'the ridiculous aspect of a man in child's dress', Darwinian biology would have institutional clothing equal to that worn by the physical sciences. It would become capable of progress 'even if all the universities were extinct at once'. The presence at Messina of an Austrian naval squadron, circumnavigating the globe with a scientific staff, led Dohrn to an ultimate vision, a chain of zoological stations around the earth.

When they left Messina (which had not financed one zoological station), both young scientists had finished with universities. Otherwise they parted to follow very different ways. In the idea of zoological stations, Miklouho-Maclay adopted a subsidiary ambition. Dohrn had recognized the gateway to his kingdom. He had also encountered, in the family at the Agence Russe, the girl he would eventually marry. He went home to reconcile Darwinism with the Hegelian maxim that the real is rational, and to find the means of building a zoological station at Naples.

Miklouho-Maclay sometimes doubted whether his own reality was rational. He admitted it as he prepared to visit the Red Sea. This would not be the first time he risked his poor health and bad eyes in a notoriously unhealthy region where trachoma prevailed. The dangers he expected—poor food, insalubrious climate, bad communications, the absence of Europeans, the presence of 'particularly fanatical' Muslims— were those he had surmounted almost casually in Morocco. 'He who risks nothing gains nothing', he told Meshchersky. He was grateful for the money that allowed him to take risks. Yet he wanted his mother to know that he might not return from this 'none too pleasant *partie de plaisir*', not to be worried unnecessarily, but 'sensibly' prepared to hear of his death.

He sent this warning from Cairo. When his elder brother passed it on, Nikolai Nikolaevich would be on his way to Suakin or Massawa or 'somewhere or other'. For a month or so, Ekaterina Semyonovna could feel remorse for the stubborn ignorance that denied value to his work, parsimony that questioned his expenditure and sent him abroad with dangerously inadequate funds. If he returned, he would prove the extent of her error. Until then she must be assured that he never paid a kopeck without extreme necessity. 'As to the way I spend this money', he insisted, 'I am convinced that in applying it to my researches I am *right*. And nobody will persuade me to the contrary'.

With half-acknowledged desire for risk, an unrecognized urge to chasten and an endless need to prove and justify, he combined more avowable reasons. Confident of publishing proof of his proposition, he still needed the sponges to settle the fate of his theories. New species might come his way to be described and figured. Beyond that he discerned a broader purpose. Regarding the Red Sea as 'almost entirely uninvestigated from the zoological point of view', he meant to do what he could to reveal its treasures.

He thought of them as threatened treasures, to be urgently appraised before they disappeared. The official opening of the Suez Canal was set for August 1869. He saw himself as 'probably the last naturalist' to examine the Red Sea fauna before marine inhabitants of the Mediterranean streamed through the canal to change the ecology of the southern waters.

He conceded the possibility of some migration in the opposite direction. Certain assumptions forbade him to imagine this predominating as it was to do. In disregarding the relative poverty of the eastern Mediterranean fauna, the connection of the Red Sea with a teeming ocean, the barrier of hypersaline lakes across the canal, and the strong northward current that was expected, he was not misled solely by lack of scientific information. The warm south symbolized ease, inertia, softness, its biological luxuriance unconsciously equated with luxury.

His thoughts were tinged with belief that vigour, aggressiveness, adaptability flowed from the north, from the direction of Europe. Concluding that the struggle for survival could have but one result, the 'last naturalist' prepared to sing a scientific requiem for what had been in the Red Sea.

He would not be the last in this rich field. He was right in feeling he must act quickly. Besides construction of the canal, a British military expedition to Abyssinia had drawn European political and commercial attention to lands bordering the Red Sea. Travellers and naturalists responded to the trend. An unprecedented number of books and articles on those countries came out in 1868 and 1869. While much of this topical literature concentrated on Abyssinia, there were important studies of the plant and animal geography of the Sudan and the western shore of the Red Sea generally. More significantly, from Miklouho-Maclay's point of view, a British naturalist had just spent a happy winter dredging in the Gulf of Suez, and a young Italian, author of a monograph on Red Sea molluscs, was preparing to return to the region. Everything indicated that to be the first investigator of phenomena south of Suez would become increasingly difficult.

With 200 roubles and an admitted 'ignorance of the Arabic language', he left Cairo for Suez late in March 1869. The Turks, who nominally ruled most of the Red Sea area, were particularly sensitive about possible designs on their territory. Where a European travelling openly might be accepted, a man in disguise was liable to be taken for a spy. But Miklouho-Maclay adopted all the precautions used by Europeans who had reached Mecca. His flowing chestnut hair was shaven, his beard cut short and dyed and his face and arms darkened. Instead of Moroccan dress, he chose Syrian costume, a disguise favoured by more than one famous traveller. To complete the effect, he relied on a remarkable facility in acquiring languages and a willingness to imitate 'in externals' the religious observances of Muslims. Much depended on whether Muslims believed in a co-religionist who travelled from Syria to collect reef animals and measure sea temperatures instead of going to Mecca. Much also depended on his meeting nobody from Syria.

Committed to 'all the abominations of Egyptian steamers', he visited Yenbo on the Hejaz coast, Jidda, Massawa and Suakin. At the mercy of trading dhows, he managed to see the less-frequented Yemeni ports of Hodeida and Luhaiya. He formed an extremely low opinion of Arab seamanship. He was safely conveyed to all the ports he could afford to visit. Adding some local excursions—to the inhospitable Dahlak group, to islands near Luhaiya and to reefs north of Massawa—he acquired in about six weeks a considerable experience of Red Sea travel.

The trials of the journey surpassed his grimmest predictions. 'Travelling in these parts is far from comfortable', he told his sister, 'and I have had a great deal to put up with'. And again, 'I in no way expected all the difficulties and inconveniences I had to meet'. His reports implied encounters with fanaticism and crime and with the hardships travellers must face in beggarly towns and barren islands. But some expected difficulties melted away. Europeans were present as consuls and businessmen in the larger towns. He often met 'good people who from honourable motives are ready to help the naturalist who gladly risks everything for marine science'. He stayed with the friendly and cultured Egyptian governor of Suakin. At Jidda on the return journey, he lived 'very comfortably for fully eighteen days, without paying a kopeck', in the home of a French commercial agent from whom he borrowed money to reach Suez. Weary but 'not sick and not with empty hands, only with empty pockets', he set out for Russia early in May.

As he borrowed his way homeward, he had gained more than the nine 'new' species of sponges to be described. He carried memories of the island-town of Suakin, a smaller, simpler Venice whose delicate cluster of coral-built houses and mosques seemed to float upon the sea. He remembered sunrise over waters so calm and transparent that the naturalist might 'clearly see the luxuriant life of coral reefs and pick up the very smallest thing'. He saw lithe divers working skilfully in submarine gardens to bring him, for a few small coins, great pieces of coral with all their inhabitants attached. Most vividly he re-experienced the beauty and animation of Jidda, its streets, coffee-houses and matting-shaded squares crowded with pilgrims from all quarters of the Muslim world. Faces thronged his mind—natives of the East Indies, Turks, Persians, Indians, Bedouin, Tartars from the Volga and newly converted Negroes from the shores of Lake Chad. He did not approve their faith, to him a fatalistic creed that imprisoned its followers in 'immobility and apathy'. It brought before him a greater pageant of humanity than he had yet surveyed, indirectly influencing his own fate.

His mental pictures included glimpses of Miklouho-Maclay the traveller. His disguised image leaned intently forward in a skiff propelled by a muscular Nubian. Despite the governor and the commercial agent, he saw himself defying hunger and scurvy as well as fever and oppressive heat. He saw the lone, embattled European, constantly compelled by Arab fanaticism and rapacity to fear for his life. In another mood he felt that danger of robbery added 'piquant variety' to a walk in the hills behind Suakin, or told how he outmanoeuvred and dominated a crowd of fanatics who sought to murder him aboard an Egyptian vessel. Whatever his mood, there remained no doubt that this journey was 'only preparatory to further travels'.

2: The Sea of Okhotsk

A SENSE OF URGENCY pervaded Miklouho-Maclay's plans as he returned to Russia. Travelling via Odessa, the Crimea, the Sea of Azov and the lower Don to Saratov on the Volga, he could stay nowhere for more than a few days. Having collected the fishes required for work on the vertebrate brain, he would settle for most of the summer wherever his family happened to be. He had a full programme of work, writing accounts of his travels and preparing for his book on comparative neurology. His sister was warned that she would spend the summer 'in harness' as his amanuensis. The urgency of these tasks probably arose in part from two matters he had not discussed with his family, the project for further travels and the fact that the five years for which his mother had promised to pay were almost over.

The opposition included all the authority of the family—worried, indecisive Ekaterina Semyonovna and her practical brother Sergei Bekker, the newly qualified lawyer Sergei Miklouho, cold to his scientist-brother's aspirations and to his determination to use a name that was not their father's. Miklouho-Maclay invested some hopes in his younger brother Vladimir, a cadet at the naval college. He could count only upon Olga and twelve-year old Mikhail. Olga loved music and study, nurturing artistic ambitions that Nikolai Nikolaevich encouraged. Mikhail was inclined to follow his advice and become a geologist or mining engineer. These two became their brother's spiritual children, ready to adopt his chosen name, looking to him for leadership and counsel. Before he left them, the second son had distinguished from the pedestrian Miklouhos a family of Miklouho-Maclays, of which he was the natural head.

Whatever authority said, he pushed forward. At a Moscow scientific congress he advocated zoological stations on all Russian coasts, speaking as a researcher who would shortly publish a work on the vertebrate brain and would himself visit remote regions. Arriving in St Petersburg in September 1869, he was introduced to the Imperial Russian Geographical Society as an 'indefatigable traveller' whose future journeys might make him useful to the Society.

Although he had not graduated and did not intend to do so, there was talk of an academic post, which he declined as incompatible with his tastes and objects. To him as to Anton Dohrn, the academic life was barren slavery, a vending of the soul for wretched kopecks. His ideal remained the aristocratic, rather outdated figure of the independent man of science, owing nothing to any institution. He did realize that funds from his mother could never suffice for the expeditions he had in mind. Seeking links with the Geographical Society, he hoped for material aid. When he delivered a report on his Red Sea journey, the new associate member felt encouraged to place his project before the Society.

The proposal was extremely attractive for geographers, a broad conception in the spirit of Alexander von Humboldt, with a touch of modern specialization. Arguing from the need to study living animals in their natural surroundings, he meant to investigate marine life of the western Pacific between the Bering Sea and the Equator. As well as studying a group of animals that had been 'little investigated', he would trace their distribution, determine questions of physical geography, and observe how animal forms changed in response to environment. To this programme—any part of it enough to occupy a group of researchers for years—he proposed to add the solution of questions in anthropology and ethnology. Finally, he was prepared to return to St Petersburg by way of Siberia, undertaking any research the Society might designate.

The presentation indicated that his plan followed naturally from the task then occupying him, examination of sponges in the zoological museum of the Imperial Academy of Sciences. Gathered by Russian scientists on both sides of the northernmost Pacific, these collections confirmed his beliefs about the variability of sponges. He was convinced that a sponge in widely differing conditions could assume such divergent forms that scientists unaware of its distribution might ascribe it to several species. Through these studies, which involved much reading on the physical geography of northern waters, he seemed committed to tracing sponges of north-east Asia throughout their range. The project approximately satisfied the Society's statute, which required that its funds be devoted to exploration in Russia and neighbouring lands.

Miklouho-Maclay was known in Russia as a zoologist whose work
on sponges might change fundamental ideas. He had the reputation of
a traveller who with slender means, in the face of privation and danger,
would successfully complete his investigations. There might be doubt of
his physical fitness. The good health he had enjoyed at Jidda was
superseded by the illness that was at once the burden and the *cachet* of
explorers. Young Prince Peter Kropotkin, scientist, explorer and future
anarchist leader, who met him at this time, saw 'a tiny, nervous man,
always suffering from malaria'. On the other hand, Miklouho-Maclay
no longer complained of the sore eyes and chest ailments that had
troubled him throughout his student years.

In an age that regarded conquest of personal limitations as a duty, ill
health never disqualified a born traveller. Some members of the
Geographical Society argued that the proposed journey held no
advantages for Russian science and lay to a great extent outside the
Society's proper field. Others complained that biographical details
supplied revealed too little about the young man's scientific standing.
Funds were scarce. Members could easily think of researches—their
own, for instance—on which money would be more suitably spent. The
Society supported Miklouho-Maclay's request for a passage to the Far
East on a warship, but the question of financial aid was left unresolved.

Back in Jena late in November, he found rooms equipped against
cold, remote enough from 'the uproar and singing of druken students',
and settled to live 'as before', preparing his work on comparative
neurology. Prince Meshchersky had left Jena, so the scientist's life was
rather solitary. It was also expensive. Renting two rooms more than he
needed, hiring furniture and servants, he soon had to borrow. He
seldom wrote home without news of a pressing need for money.

Insecurity did not deter him from arranging to publish a fastidiously
designed book. Nor did it cancel his plans for a trip to England, to make
useful friends and buy equipment for his expedition. But a letter from
Baron Fyodor Romanovich Osten-Sacken, secretary of the Geographical Society, gravely threatened the larger project. Miklouho-Maclay still
told his family that everything was being arranged as he wished. The
main news was that the Society found it difficult to give him financial
support.

Study of his communications had convinced influential people that
he would spend too much time too far from Russia. They noted that
instead of starting from the north he would begin in the tropics,
relegating to a 'secondary plan' the studies most interesting to the
Society. If he failed to complete his project, the geographers would get
none of the information they really wanted.

He returned a dignified answer. If the conditions were incompatible
with his chosen line of research, he would renounce the subsidy. 'I am

convinced', he explained, 'that the solution of these problems, even though incomplete, can yield no little profit to our knowledge, and I would not be false to them for the sake of a few kopecks, even if the kopecks were transformed into roubles'. He counted on overcoming any financial difficulties: 'For the sake of my task I declined, without regrets, more than one remunerative offer—and I will carry it out . . !'

Pointing out that the time to be devoted to any region could not be known beforehand, he suggested that his results, promptly transmitted during the years in the Pacific, would teach a '*Russian* scientific society' to see his work 'through the eyes of *scientific* Russian society'. He denied attaching lesser importance to research in northern seas. 'On the contrary', he insisted, 'I am definitely very interested in this region, and hope to have the opportunity to investigate it; my future efforts will accord with the Society's wishes'.

Needing the money more than he admitted, he made strong efforts to obtain it. He had not intended to publish results on sponge collections examined in St Petersburg. Now he sent a long article to his most influential supporter, Count P. P. Semyonov-Tianshansky, explorer, scientist and president of the Society's section for physical geography.

He described many 'new' sponges, eleven of them united in his new genus and species *Veluspa polymorpha*. Fascinated by this organism's variability, he emphasized the need to study it in its natural state. To discover how such forms arose, and compare them with tropical species—these were the great tasks. His remarks left no doubt that he would happily spend years studying, in relation to sponges, the tides, currents, temperatures, ice-cover and salinity of the Sea of Okhotsk and adjacent waters. Including with *Veluspa polymorpha* the problematic sponges of Lake Baikal, he suggested that these animals should be sought in other Siberian lakes. If they belonged to a marine genus, as he contended, their presence would support Humboldt's hypothesis concerning a former great Central Asia sea connected with the ocean. He made no explicit promise to carry out this investigation, but it seemed a most suitable project for his return journey.

A traveller investigating the lower marine animals must naturally obtain valuable knowledge of external factors on which they depend. With fuller information, and the implied promises, Semyonov-Tianshansky presented a stronger case. Opponents were silenced. Miklouho-Maclay felt he could 'almost count' on the Russian Geographical Society. Expecting the small subsidy of 1350 roubles, he incurred a heavy moral obligation to the revered elder who supported his cause.

As he wrote of that region of mist and tundra, bearing 'the imprint of the Arctic', the part of his mind that craved warmth, luxuriance, clear skies and seas, could not do otherwise than shudder. More seriously, he resented suggestions that he work in Russia and its borderlands. He knew the importance of research on Russian seas and lakes, advocating zoological stations on every shore. In his own case, the idea of studying 'Russian puddles and ponds' seemed to affront the magnitude of his design. Overlooking the need of world science for information about Russia's unexplored territories, he treated the wishes of a '*Russian scientific society*' as the carping of narrow nationalism.

Determined to follow his own wishes, he worked and planned, struggling with debt and the problems of future expenditure. He reported a few personal events—remission of his fever, being photographed in Syrian dress, meeting Turgenev the novelist, with whom he was 'quite soon thoroughly in harmony'. In general he deserved his sister's reproaches for revealing little of his thoughts and experiences. In words reminiscent of Schopenhauer's definition of genius, he explained:

> In the presence of great, indeed enormous, fields of observation and mental activity, interest in one's own personality is relegated quite to the background. The more the brain has work that is worthy of it, the less one wastes its activity on one's own person [...] This pushing aside of the personality ... however, goes parallel with the development of one's individuality.

He wrote in haste, leaving Olga to complete his remarks with what she found 'between the lines'. There was advice for his own family, for little Mikhail Miklouho-Maclay and for Vladimir who might become a Miklouho-Maclay. 'Read', he exhorted his sister, 'and vary your life, by any means and in any way you can—I am coming, I will help...'

He was not going immediately to Russia. In April he left Jena 'on the quiet, without having paid all the debts', for an indefinite stay in London. The Royal Navy's chief hydrographer showed him apparatus for deep-sea investigations. Thomas Henry Huxley saw a good deal of him, assessed him as 'a man of very considerable capacity and energy', and promised help in furthering the expedition. Alfred Russel Wallace, dining with him at Huxley's house, formed equally favourable impressions. Delighted by a visitor with whom he could discuss Russia, the land of his most exciting geological work, Sir Roderick Murchison, president of the Royal Geographical Society, undertook to use his influence. None of the helpful scientists, officials and instrument-makers who met Miklouho-Maclay guessed the insecurity of his position or the bitterness of his thoughts. With money for his trip to England, he had received from uncle Sergei Bekker the news that on returning to Russia he could expect no further support from the family.

He was still uncertain how to deal with this. But having despatched a calmly ruthless letter to his mother, he answered the family's 'rather

The castle at Cintra, Portugal, 1866

The port and harbour at Arrecife, Lanzarote, Canary Islands, 1866

Volcanic craters, Lanzarote

Ernst Haeckel and Miklouho-Maclay at
Arrecife in 1867

The mosque at Jedda in 1869

The second camp from Mogador, on the road to Marrakesh in 1867

Two views of Morocco in 1867

cunning' move with superior cunning. By the time fever and poverty compelled him to 'flee the place', he had produced in London some *faits accomplis* well calculated to baffle the opposition.

Back in Jena he produced more. Since Uncle Sergei's words were uncompromisingly clear, Miklouho-Maclay decided to treat money he could 'almost count on' as being quite his. He wrote to Baron Osten-Sacken requesting that half the subsidy 'promised' by the Russian Geographical Society should be sent to him at once, for purchase of scientific equipment.

Any weapon seemed legitimate in the fight for his project. Reporting Murchison's promise to mention him to the secretary of state for foreign affairs, he implied that he had obtained Lord Clarendon's 'open letter to all English consuls in the Pacific Ocean'. In fact he had not met his Lordship and had yet to negotiate for such help. When he mentioned that his work was 'better known in England than in Russia', he neglected to explain that it was known mainly by the opposition it aroused. He subtly but strongly hinted that if Russia did not grasp the opportunity he offered the English would.

Anxiety revealed itself in his feeling, after ten days, that this trivial business was 'protracted for a long time'. A fortnight later, it seemed time to convert the English possibility into reality. Huxley was asked to approach Lord Clarendon, and provide introductions useful in Australia and New Zealand. Huxley was also to hand Maclay's memorandum on his proposed journey to Sir Roderick Murchison, with 'a few convincing words' about the importance of zoological research in the Pacific, and a reminder that 'for these investigations there is a not entirely unfit person—myself'.

Experience with the Russian Geographical Society guided his approach to its British counterpart. Properties of seawater and the range of tides appeared prominently among subjects for research. Emphasizing studies of animals in their environment, he gave due place to meteorology and to the geology that he had not studied. He spoke of 'spending several years on the islands of the Pacific'. He did not mention Siberia or the Sea of Okhotsk. Maclay's thinking, like his signature, had become perfectly adjusted to British interests.

With no assurance of financial help, he prepared for his journey as though nothing stood in the way. While he could pay neither Jena debts nor his fare to St Petersburg, he ordered equipment and arranged his passage on a warship. He invited a dozen eminent scientists to set questions for investigation, sought advice and help from everyone with connections in the Pacific. At the same time he published, with the same disregard for 'such trash as money', the first part of his *Contributions to the Comparative Neurology of the Vertebrates*, dedicated to Carl Gegenbaur. With its wide-margined quarto pages of fine paper and seven lithographic plates, the volume made Gegenbaur's famous textbooks look shoddy. How the publication was financed, and whether anyone bought it, were questions to which the author seemed completely indifferent.

Less anxious to return to Russia than he appeared—on receiving the 'ridiculous kopecks' for which he frantically signalled he found it necessary to stay a little longer in Germany—he did not regret leaving Jena. Instead of occupying part of Professor Bruno Hildebrandt's comfortable house, he had been living in 'a little old pavilion in a luxuriant garden'. Because of 'stupid and absurd rumours', the Hildebrandts had dropped him in a 'not-quite-delicate' manner. He was no longer friendly with Haeckel, uncertain even how he stood with Gegenbaur. Without the least offence on his part, there were houses in which it was best not to mention his name. For sympathetic interest he depended on Academician Otto Boethlingk, the orientalist, whom he had once considered a great bore. Besides, he again had to disappear quietly, leaving some debts unpaid.

He predicted cholera, insisted he could come to Russia only if his mother rented a suitably located *dacha*. He nevertheless spent most of summer 1870 in the capital. From his little room in the dismal family flat in the Kolpakov building, Maly Prospekt, he enjoyed a view of nothing. Late in July he seemed to have reached a full stop. His mother could not provide 5000 roubles for his first year of travels. Meshchersky could not lend such a sum. At best, Miklouho-Maclay offered prospective lenders the hope of being repaid by one of these sponsors within two years. By pressing on with arrangements, he made it almost inevitable that someone must go into debt on his behalf. Money was found, and Ekaterina Semyonovna assumed the financial burden of her son's first year in the Pacific.

He was to travel on the steam corvette *Vityaz* ('Knight'), bound for the Far East as part of the rotation of vessels on that station. At first he was content to secure a passage, asking only the sailing date and ports of call. He soon became more exacting.

The experience of other naturalists did not encourage hopes for an untroubled voyage. Told that Captain Nazimov would welcome him cordially, he remarked, 'We shall see!' 'More or less satisfied' with his future travelling companions, he still thought it wise to 'take up a position' that minimized contact with the officers. For his convenience a separate cabin was partitioned off. Finally it seemed essential that *Vityaz*, instead of taking the usual route round Cape Horn, should visit Cape Town, Batavia and Australian ports. Orders were written to his requirements. He had the ear of the Grand Duke Konstantin Nikolaevich, brother of the tsar and director of the navy ministry.

For all his haughtiness and tendency to treat the navy as personal property, Konstantin was a liberal reformer and a friend of science. His fondness for accounts of exploration had been awakened by his first teacher, Admiral Count Lütke the circumnavigator. As president of the Geographical Society, he felt a lively interest in the first Russian to undertake extensive research in the Pacific since Lütke's voyage of 1826–29. So did his aunt, the Grand Duchess Elena Pavlovna, Russia's great patroness of learning and the arts, whose taste for science dated from her girlhood acquaintance with Cuvier. Miklouho-Maclay gravitated naturally to the grand duchess's *salon*, which attracted everyone of note in the arts, sciences and administration.

He fitted in well, a pale young man, handsome in a slightly irregular way, with bright blue eyes and thick, curling chestnut hair and beard. Though large men thought of him as very small, his height was almost average for a European of the time. His thin frame, though troubled from childhood by illness, housed what doctors called a 'strong constitution'. His manner pleased different people in different ways. Despite what some regarded as nervousness or shyness, he was never overawed by the surroundings or company. The family had fallen on hard times since his father's death. They always remembered what was due to the past. He took pride in ancestors who had distinguished themselves in military or medical service to royalty. Though he forgot which roll of nobility carried the family's name, he attached more importance to being a 'hereditary nobleman' than was common in Russia by that time. He belonged still more consciously to an intellectual and moral aristocracy that made him equal or superior to anyone in the room. Victorious in the fight to realize his ambition, about to satisfy his wish to see the world, he could relax, charming the exalted circles he entered only to leave.

He could discuss painting, music and literature as well as science, travel and social questions. He had stories of adventure to relate, sketches of exotic scenes to show. Among the intellectual ladies of Elena Pavlovna's court, he forgot his 'decided repugnance to all stages of development and differentiation of the genus "blue stocking"'. He became particularly friendly with Baroness Edith von Rhaden, lady-in-waiting to the grand duchess, and with Baron von Rhaden, who like Osten-Sacken worked in the foreign ministry. His sister was introduced into these circles, where the baroness and her daughter were inclined to befriend the lonely, depressed girl. Nikolai Nikolaevich advised on behaviour—on the need to listen and observe rather than talk, to avoid aloofness while always reserving 'a certain independence'. If the ideal he set up left little room for spontaneity in friendship, it did embody sound guidance for one who must learn and make her way in the world. Olga too could hope to escape the cramped existence to which she had seemed condemned.

The departure of *Vityaz* was several times postponed. In western Europe a great war raged. Great political questions hovered in the air, capable of cancelling the voyage. Impatient with delays, Miklouho-Maclay moved between the Kolpakov house and Mikhailovsky Palace, between museums and libraries and the Kronstadt naval base, completing arrangements down to choosing goods for barter with Pacific islanders. The geographers provided a letter of introduction, recommending him to the good will and aid of learned societies everywhere. He acquired a passport that described his journey as undertaken 'for scientific purposes to the islands of the Pacific Ocean and to East Asia', made his adopted name official, and prefixed it by the '*von*' and '*de*' that many upper-class Russians used abroad. Finally, on 19 October 1870, he read his detailed research programme to the general council of the Geographical Society.

His last few weeks in Russia were spent as the grand duchess's guest at Oranienbaum Palace on the Gulf of Finland. From his room in the family apartment, with its folding furniture, scientific equipment and walls hung with tools and weapons, he stepped into one of the most notable creations of eighteenth-century ostentation and fantasy. Before him stretched many years in regions that might belong to a different planet from that of the *Salon japonaise* or Catherine the Great's satin-lined bedroom. Amid delicate *chinoiserie*, bronze monkeys bearing offerings of Meissen china, silk hangings landscaped with millions of glass beads, he accepted these as he accepted all contrasts and incongruities in his life. For all the royal wretchedness it had seen, Oranienbaum embodied a belief in the possibility of happiness for some people. Its conscienceless extravagance formed a monument to the assumption that life is sweet. But Miklouho-Maclay's self-portrait at age twenty-four combined imperturbable courage and implacable will with disdain for 'this fine existence', a vast 'indifference to life'. As for the possibility of happiness, he simply did not believe in it.

Or so he thought. In reality he seemed almost happy, despite the fever he treated with 'a large quantity of quinine and small doses of patience'. As he sketched the palace and autumnal park, he might have been the only person at Oranienbaum. Certainly he found no one there to question his actions, no narrow-minded colleagues grudging him support, no Uncle Sergei to snatch opportunity away, no precariously-conquered mother or unsympathetic older brother. He invited Russian acquaintances to guess what he thought while using his microscope or studying the landscape. To distant friends he hinted at a further 'grandiose plan' to be undertaken when his official programme was completed. When so many difficulties had been overcome, obstacles that could block his path were unimaginable.

It was equally difficult to imagine an enterprise more grandiose than that he had described. For seven or eight years, he would investigate the western Pacific from New Guinea almost to the Arctic Circle. In the first of the departments into which he divided his work—'concerned mainly with the lower forms of animals in their natural surroundings'—he would be guided by 'the local fauna and local conditions'. In other fields, 'meteorological observations and researches in anthropology and ethnography', the authorities he consulted had produced some 130 questions. Most of these were large enough to occupy an investigator for life. When he added equally complex questions of his own, the list practically constituted an encyclopaedia of the unknown. As he emphasized, to answer many of these questions was unlikely to be within his power. He mentioned them as examples of 'the blanks which science has difficulty in filling', undertaking only to do his best.

The Society had reason to be pleased with his independent but accommodating approach to his task. Eminent authorities had supplied questions in meteorology and physical geography, some specifically concerning ice and snow. He added his determination, while 'working to the north, to the shores of the Sea of Okhotsk', to supplement knowledge of the northern Sea of Japan. Those who feared he would linger over southern sponges and corals were further reassured by his plan to spend only a year in the tropics and then 'to advance gradually to the north, to the shores of the Sea of Okhotsk . . .'

His travels must begin in the tropics in order to finish economically with a return through Siberia, so New Guinea seemed as good as starting point as any. His correspondence contained hints that the island was more than a starting point. The sketch of his den in the Kolpakov building was labelled, 'My room in St Petersburg before my departure for New Guinea', as though New Guinea itself were the goal. He evidently felt the Geographical Society wanted further explanations, for he promised, and drafted, a long account of his reasons. Some were prosaic enough, like his feeling that New Guinea, perhaps the most demanding part of the journey, should be tackled before he was 'weakened by other exertions'. Others verged on the romantic. He had been almost excited by the words of James Beete Jukes:

> I know of no part of the world, the exploration of which is so flattering to the imagination, so likely to be fruitful in interesting results, . . . and altogether so well calculated to gratify the enlightened curiosity of an adventurous explorer, as the interior of New Guinea. New Guinea! the very mention of being taken into the interior of New Guinea sounds like being allowed to visit some of the enchanted regions of the 'Arabian Nights', so dim an atmosphere of obscurity rests at present on the wonders it probably contains.

Little had changed since Jukes and the officers of H.M.S. *Fly* dreamed of following into the interior the great river they had detected almost thirty years before. In a book published in 1869, avidly studied by Miklouho-Maclay, Alfred Russel Wallace spoke of the bulk of New Guinea as 'the greatest *terra incognita* that still remains for the naturalist to explore'. The work of those who visited the island after Wallace had also been confined to coastal districts. The obscurity veiling the interior remained as dense as ever, and Miklouho-Maclay meant to dispel it. Departing so far from his official programme, he strayed farther with every line he wrote in explanation.

To account for the apparently anomalous distribution of lemurs and their allies, an English zoologist had imagined an ancient continent now vanished beneath the Indian Ocean. Using the 'Lemuria' hypothesis to explain far more than the originator intended, Ernst Haeckel had postulated more vanished continents. One of them, including Sumatra, Java, Borneo and the Philippines, was connected to Asia through the Malay Peninsula and southern Indo-China, and 'probably also with the Lemurian continent'. The second, including Celebes, the Moluccas, New Guinea and the Solomons, was joined to Australia in accordance with Wallace's views. Rounding off with another lost continent in the south Pacific, Haeckel had tidied up everything in the southern hemisphere. All islands were united either with existing continents or with each other, as remains of land masses otherwise covered by the sea.

Miklouho-Maclay disagreed with both his former teacher and A. R. Wallace. The geologist Jukes had remarked on the great difference in climate and vegetation between Australia and what he saw of New Guinea. The similarity of fauna in such contrasted countries seemed 'almost astounding' to Wallace himself. The much-travelled naturalist and independent author of the theory of evolution by natural selection saw the apparent anomaly pointing to a 'common origin' for the two faunas. Miklouho-Maclay read it as a sign that Wallace was mistaken. On grounds of climate and terrain, he thought of New Guinea as 'a unique country where entirely new organic forms may be concealed'. He did not mean to divorce it from all associations. 'By its position', he wrote, 'New Guinea is the central link of the chain in investigation of the organic nature of Polynesia, permitting us to complete our information about the hypothetical continent of Lemuria'.

The Russian geographers never meant to subsidize exploration of the New Guinea interior or a determination of the relationship between its fauna and that of Australia. Still less had they contemplated a search for lost Lemuria. Yet by comparison with the full explanation these seemed slight departures from the formal programme. Miklouho-Maclay's supporters had overlooked the potent germ contained in his under-taking to investigate, 'with permission, according to opportunity', the anthropological and ethnographical problems encountered.

When he first made that tentative proposal, he had not systematically studied the subjects. The report of his Red Sea journey nevertheless revealed a growing interest. Mingling his observations with information gained from books, he said as much of the people and their way of life as of geography. In the intervening year, reading in anthropology, ethnology and the literature of travel had left him impatient and dissatisfied. Everywhere he found 'very unsatisfactory descriptions of the natives in their primitive condition', a sketchiness he attributed to contempt or indifference on the part of European travellers. The authorities he consulted confirmed the ignorance, if not the suspected 'disdain for acquaintance with primitive races'. The encyclopaedia of the unknown compiled to guide his journey was filled mainly with questions on anthropology and ethnography. At some unrecorded moment, he had come to regard the study of primitive peoples as the object truly 'worthy of one's devoting to it several years of one's life'. The sense that he possessed what Huxley and Haeckel declared essential for this task—a background in zoology and comparative anatomy—made it his particular duty. Everything else was 'subordinated ... to anthropo-ethnographical goals'.

The first step was to find 'primitive tribes of people, beyond the influence of others who have been raised to a comparatively high level of civilization'. Again he was directed towards New Guinea, the land whose 'size and obscurity' gave it first place among the southern islands.

Practically everything about the people of New Guinea was in dispute. To some authorities the 'Papuans' represented the original population of all south-east Asia and the Pacific. Others maintained that the Papuans had been preceded by a different people, whose remnants survived in mountainous areas of other large islands. The same uncertainty prevailed in ideas of their distribution. According to Haeckel's fairly restrained interpretation, the Papuans spread eastward from Lemuria through the East Indies and New Guinea to reach Fiji, moving as far north as the Philippines, as far south as Tasmania. The map compiled by Miklouho-Maclay (combining older views with the most recent) placed Papuans or their relatives in Africa and Madagascar. In considering New Guinea itself, the imagination was unrestrained. Travellers had found among the islanders characteristics varied enough to relate them directly to half the peoples of earth. Miklouho-Maclay believed that New Guinea was probably inhabited 'not by one but by many races'.

From the mass of disagreement he extracted two fundamental problems for investigation: 'Firstly, to explain the anthropological relationship of the Papuans to other races ... Secondly, ... to determine, by personal observation, the dispersion of these races in comparison with the rest of the tribes of the Pacific Ocean'. To answer these questions, he was prepared to spend many years among the Papuans and the peoples who might be closely related to them.

Stupendous vistas opened from the line of thought he faintly sketched. According to Haeckel, it was in Lemuria that mankind had evolved from a long-extinct anthropoid ape. On Haeckel's map of hypothetical migrations, all currents of humanity streamed out of the lost continent. If New Guinea had been linked with Lemuria rather than Australia, as Miklouho-Maclay suggested, the great obscure island might be a remnant of Haeckel's *'single primaeval home'*, the 'probable cradle of the human race'. By the same argument, the inhabitants of the unknown interior might include the most primitive of men, the nearest to the hypothetical *'Homo primigenius'*.

The new object explained the urgency with which Miklouho-Maclay approached his task, the anxiety that seemed excessive when he spoke only of physical geography or the variability of sponges. As when he hastened to study the Red Sea fauna, he had dedicated himself to what must shortly disappear.

Something of the same feeling always coloured his attitude towards peoples who aroused his interest. The first such race were the 'Guanche', regarded as the original inhabitants of the Canary Islands, generally believed to have been exterminated by European invaders and North African slavers. Unaware that the Canaries had supported two early populations, who had both left descendants, Miklouho-Maclay had named his first 'new' sponge *Guancha blanca*, to commemorate the vanished race.

Similar preoccupation with change and disappearance marked his thoughts on the future of the Red Sea littoral. It seemed to him that European humanity, like marine animals of the Mediterranean, must surge through the new canal to collide with the peoples of Arabia and Sudan. Here he had reservations about the outcome, suggesting that climate might defeat Europeans as he believed it had defeated the natives. He reserved his sympathy for what was native to the place. The poverty, slavery, fanaticism and crime he described as prevailing on the shores of the Red Sea were always lesser evils than those bound to follow the arrival of Europeans.

Spreading through the Pacific, the European plague must inevitably destroy the native peoples. When he accused science of 'disdain for the study of primitive races', he found it the more deplorable since 'these races . . . because of collision with European civilization, are disappearing with every year'. In the New Guinea interior he would find peoples not yet contaminated by Europe, untouched even by the lesser plagues of Malays, Chinese, Indians and Arabs. His mission was a race against time, to be the 'last naturalist' to observe these tribes in their primitive state.

Some of his beliefs were debatable. Any 'disdain' evident among ethnologists seemed to be directed at Europe and neighbouring lands. When systematic study of European anthropology and prehistory had hardly begun, travellers were ever eager to investigate Africa or the Pacific islands, corners of Asia or the Americas. The largest and most influential textbook of the time dealt exclusively with 'primitive' peoples. Science was deluged with facts on the customs and character-istics of distant tribes. The study of man had come to mean the study of 'primitive' man.

The fascination of the distant and unfamiliar helped to establish this bias. Many another man with severe scientific aims privately responded, like Miklouho-Maclay, to a simple desire to see the world. There was the continuing search for the 'pure race', isolated from all others, which would endow the science of man with something like laboratory conditions. New impetus came from the acceptance of evolutionary theories that with increasing boldness were applied to man and his institutions. Much effort was expended in pursuit of 'atavisms' and, as Haeckel said, 'the discovery of tailed men was long anxiously expected ... in order to establish a closer relationship between man and the other mammals'. Embryology answered many questions, including that of the human tail. It did not exclude the possibility that somewhere the total human atavism might be walking about.

Yet at the same time as the search for the most 'primitive', there went forward a less obvious quest for the more nearly perfect. Behind the façade of confident power, modern Europe was prey to gnawing doubt. Thoughtful people reflected that material wealth and comfort and growing command over nature brought no corresponding growth in virtue or happiness. In this time of public optimism and faith in progress, Schopenhauer's pessimistic teachings reached the height of popularity. Quotation marks often surrounded the word 'civilization'. People became ironical about the process of 'improving away'. Many meditated upon the ultimate instance of 'improving away', the actual or expected obliteration of other peoples, other modes of life, before the advance of Europe.

Men like Haeckel, ultra-Darwinists and atheists, satisfied that their own race was fittest to survive, regarded that prospect with equanimity, as part of the process that had decreed the extinction of trilobite and dinosaur. At most they urged scientific study of such doomed peoples as the Australian Aborigines or those Asian tribes who, according to Baron Nordenskiöld, must soon disappear before Russian conquest and settlement. Others, no less numerous and vocal, demanded on humani-tarian and religious grounds the protection and civilization of 'inferior' peoples. Still another school of thought rejected both extinction and civilization for contemporary primitives. Its unorganized ranks included the traveller who found among the natives of the Nicobar Islands a 'chastity, honesty, cleanliness and kindly bearing towards each other' that Europeans should emulate. The same spirit more coarsely informed the naval officer who wandered through Patagonia admiring the Indians' physique, endurance and instinctive 'decency', noting that in their horse-racing 'foul play is unknown and all debts of honour are scrupulously paid on the spot'. To the uneasy eyes of many Europeans, remote and despised tribes proved that 'a people deemed by us uncivilized and savage may yet be in possession of all that makes life happy and contented, and present moral and industrial qualities of no mean order'. Haeckel himself felt obliged to put the phrase 'blessings of civilization' in quotation marks.

Perhaps the meaning of it all came most vividly to light in the fame that nineteenth-century Europe accorded the Guanche. Whether derived from wandering Vikings or from survivors of lost Atlantis, the Guanche became an example, peaceable, honorable and innocent, representing the unspoiled humanity of the Golden Age. Their patriarchal and aristocratic society appealed to critics of bourgeois democracy. Their needy pastoral way of life, described as at once feudal and 'communistic', was contrasted with the obsessive greed of modern Europe. The Guanche were declared extinct, memorialized with compassion and indignation. There remained other peoples in whom the same exemplary force might be found, living evidence that the moral nature of man was warped rather than improved by a problematic 'civilization'. Born in the Rome of Tacitus, matured in eighteenth-century *salons*, the Noble Savage haunted the meetings of scientific societies. He was still encountered in the world's archaic corners by those who sought to cure or escape from Europe's ills.

The young Russian held no conscious belief in the primitive virtue of mankind. His favourite pronouncement on the subject was that of Count Arthur de Gobineau, theorist of aristocratic racism: 'Man is the wicked animal *par excellence*'. His notebooks and memory contained many such pronouncements, expressing a settled misanthropy. Yet he was not without hope of a kind. Occasionally he met people who pleased him—idealistic youngsters like his devoted sister and little brother, who accepted his authority and guidance, or sympathetic elders who fostered his ambition and supplied his needs. He was prepared to believe that a 'joyless planet' concealed lands where existence was 'still bearable' for the untainted few, places as glowing and innocent as childhood, where nothing would discourage or disgust. With rational scientific aims, he was bound for the pure well-spring of existence, a country too long lost to be corrupt. Ernst Haeckel had provided the map, with the vanished continent playfully labelled 'Paradise'.

3: To the Blessed Isles

ON ATLANTIC or Mediterranean shores, Miklouho-Maclay had often surrendered to an overpowering experience. Classical coastlines lost their attraction. The open sea seemed to draw him out of himself, 'somewhere into the distance'. He forgot fear of drowning, forgot intentions, forgot where he stood. He wished only to go farther and farther, in a disembodied voyage towards an unreachable horizon.

If he looked seaward from the island choked by the 'Kronstadt slum', circumstances crippled spiritual flight. The real voyage involved a very solid vessel, 2225 tons, 350 horsepower, nine guns, sailing almost in company with three other warships. Instead of travelling alone, a liberated spirit, he was an inconvenient passenger, dependent on a commander he hardly knew and a crowd of officers who might or might not be respectful and co-operative after a harangue from the grand duke. And he was tied to a mountain of luggage. *Vityaz* loaded more than a hundred cases of his possessions, a revelation of what a civilized man needs in his search for the primitive.

Much of this would accompany him everywhere, capped by its intellectual equivalent—counsels from Goethe, Kant and Schopenhauer, inspiration from Italian, Indian and Spanish sayings, world-weariness from Byron and acid thoughts from Molière. And with the weight of civilization he bore responsibilities distinct from his stated programme. The correctness and importance of his choice must be demonstrated. He had to prove that detailed investigations on the spot were worth more than collections sent back to museums. Chauvinists must learn from his example that science could not be restricted by national interests. Foreigners must be disabused of the notion that Russians began well but never finished everything. Most demanding of all was his duty to prove that the right kind of European could live peaceably among 'savage' peoples, neither damaging their way of life nor exploiting them for any gain but knowledge.

The load included more personal responsibilities to those he left behind. His mother must be convinced that while strictly conserving time and money he would do all he undertook. She must be persuaded, too, that for health's sake she should move to Italy, where he might eventually live with her. Olga must take off the dark glasses of boredom and melancholy and seize her new opportunities. She must draw, read, travel, expand her life in every way, while awaiting the day when her brother would build her a new existence. Young Vladimir must prepare to follow Miklouho-Maclay to New Guinea. Meshchersky should detach himself from the Russia in which he found no future, have done with hopeless Europe, and join his friend in the tropics. For the time being, Miklouho-Maclay was forced to take a great deal, with only promises and advice to give in return. He pioneered the way for those akin to him. In time, he would repay them with a new world.

Meshchersky saw him off from Kronstadt on 8 November 1870. Farewells to the family were completed by a terse note: '*Au revoir* or goodbye. Keep your promises, as I will keep mine'. The possibility of death was faced in a one-sentence will, leaving to Olga all that her brother possessed or might possess. Then he became an inmate of a 'floating barracks'. Cold bit into his bones; damp and frost hindered his work; his legs ached and he felt the beginnings of a chill. For comfort he had a folding armchair given him by the grand duchess, portraits of his mother and sister, and plans too grandiose to be revealed.

While *Vityaz* sailed from Copenhagen to Plymouth, Miklouho-Maclay was ashore, completing his equipment and arrangements. The eyes of Europe were on the German siege of Paris. He hardly noticed that he traversed a country at war. In German cities he conferred with scientists, bankers, booksellers, instrument-makers. He visited libraries and scientific institutions and added to his equipment until cash ran short and bills were being sent to St Petersburg.

Everyone confirmed the importance of his undertaking. Some could help with information and advice. German business firms and mission societies had great and growing interests in the Pacific. German naturalists had visited the western end of New Guinea. In recent years geographers had strongly supported proposals that the island should become a German colony. The 'worthy, practical persons' Miklouho-Maclay consulted never failed to envy him. Their admiration always ended with a 'significant ooh!!, *ach*!! or *aber*—'. They were not going to New Guinea, not they—too risky.

Hugging his satisfaction, he bustled through Europe, practising for hardship by taking only one meal a day, sending home a faithful stream of promises, advice and personal news. In the Netherlands he obtained letters to potentially helpful people in the East Indies. In England, his arrival stirred up the scientists and caught the attention of newspapers. Though English biologists disagreed with his views on sponges and fish brains, scientific dissent never prevented friendly co-operation. Huxley and others provided letters to smooth his way in Australia, claiming for him the assistance due to a leader of science. Many things were his for the asking.

But much of his preparatory effort had been wasted. Lord Clarendon had died. The sympathetic, russophil Murchison was dying, taking with him any hope of support from the Royal Geographical Society. The acting president, Sir Henry Rawlinson, was a prophet of the great British bogy, the Russian threat to India. And for all the courtesy, times had never offered less encouragement to a Russian seeking English official assistance. The world had just learned that Russia, taking advantage of European upheavals, was abrogating treaty provisions that had closed the Black Sea to her navy since the Crimean War.

What Huxley called 'the Russian row' had erupted—outcry in parliament and press, men-of-war making ready for sea, Woolwich arsenal working day and night. Englishmen almost forgot the Franco-Prussian conflict in the prospect of their own war with Russia. Four Russian warships, calling at Portsmouth and Plymouth, were more significant than welcome.

Arrangements for an international conference had begun to blunt the crisis when Miklouho-Maclay joined *Vityaz* at Plymouth. He personally had met with nothing but kindness. He was nonetheless glad to leave 'cold, northern' England, where rumour claimed he travelled on the grand duchess's money, or even as an official emissary of Russia. The politics he ignored had not finished with him. When the corvette sailed on 18 December, she was unexpectedly bound for Madeira.

He understood the reasons, and reconciled himself to delay. A recent decision made him joyful as he welcomed 1871.

After objective consideration, he had decided not to stay away for seven years. Three years in New Guinea, Australia and 'about the tropics generally' would do for a start. Then he would live for a year or so in his mother's Italian villa. With scientific results partly worked out, he would turn refreshed to the second stage of his travels—east Asia, northern seas and the breadth of Siberia. Olga and his mother could live by the certainty that within four years he would return.

The warships left the vantage point closest to Gibraltar and anchored at St Vincent, Cape Verde Islands. Miklouho-Maclay welcomed the chance of three weeks alone in a tent on the desolate shore. 'My health is good', he reported, 'and there is enough work. *Summa* = all's well!' His one care was that outsiders—the Russian Geographical Society, for instance—should learn nothing about his change of plan.

Threats of war faded out while *Vityaz* lay at St Vincent. Late in January 1871 she sailed at last for Rio de Janeiro. Miklouho-Maclay knew by now that he would never voluntarily associate with Captain Nazimov. He suspected that the grand duke's preaching had done more harm than good among the officers. And the voyage in this company was going to last a long time; like most warships of the period, *Vityaz* used her engines only occasionally. But thus far shipboard life had been bearable. He had weathered a storm in the Baltic, disturbed more by shrieks and groans from the cabin partition than by wind and waves that damaged the corvette. While *Vityaz* pranced and rolled between Madeira and St Vincent, he had learned to catch a flying breakfast or a waltzing dinner and tie himself into his bunk or armchair. These experiences made breezy paragraphs for letters home, a breath of salt air and danger sweeping into the family's stuffy apartment. He preferred not to mention the seasickness he endured almost all the way to Rio, and the fact that Nazimov made a point of doing so could not improve their relations.

In spite of seasickness, he finished a paper on Red Sea sponges. He also began work on the study of the seas. Some of his advisers' questions in this department had already been overtaken by the progress of science. Others presupposed a large expedition with a ship of its own. He nevertheless meant to do something about the topic of the hour, the measurement of deep-sea temperatures and the revived theory of a general oceanic circulation. In recent years entrenched errors had been cleared away, techniques developed to the point where he could buy the most advanced deep-sea thermometer for £2 2s 6d. He had two such thermometers from Casella of London, with a thousand fathoms of special line from the Royal Navy's chief hydrographer and plenty of expert advice. Nazimov was not going to emulate commanders who kept their ships stationary all day for 'serial' readings from surface to bottom, but he agreed to lend assistance and loiter for three hours in the doldrums. Miklouho-Maclay was able to take the first measurement of deep-sea temperature in that part of the Atlantic.

He wrote up the result at Rio de Janeiro, with an historical and theoretical introduction to make a substantial article. But Rio was a plunge into the real business of the journey. Each step in this ethnologist's paradise brought him face to face with different races and mixtures of races. He visited hospitals and examined specimens of both sexes. In streets and markets he pounced on interesting subjects and took them to be photographed naked from three different angles. He did not seek the aborigine, reduced to a shadowy influence in a few people of mixed descent. The fascination lay in the 'lowest neighbourhoods', where African blood ran pure or predominant.

Meetings with representatives of 'every possible African tribe, from Morocco and Guinea as far as Mozambique', made a perfect introduction to studies meant to settle, among other things, the question of links between Pacific peoples and Africans. But he sought especially the African natives who had spent many years in Brazil, and their children born in that country.

As a follower of the most extreme environmentalism, he expected the Negro 'type' to change quickly in new climatic and social conditions. He took it for granted that the difference between Africa and Brazil could bring this about. Everywhere he found the expected changes 'leaping to the eye'. A long life in a 'more temperate climate' made an old African's skin dull, even pale, by imaginary comparison with the glossy black that must prevail in his native land. When another old man seemed as glossy and black as he should be, the comparison was with his adult son, 'born in a much cooler country'. Exactly as reported from the northern United States, these blacks were turning white.

The widespread idea that transplanted Negroes became more like Europeans had served various purposes. For some early nineteenth-century advocates of human unity, it confirmed the Negro's 'degeneration' from an ideal white Adamic stock. To later writers, it made him a primitive forerunner, capable of becoming a white man if placed in the right conditions. For many it brought racial differentiation comfortably within a Biblical time scale. Miklouho-Maclay gained his satisfaction in contemplating the power of environment.

Change of living conditions, then, could produce 'complete transformation'. Yet the evidence had its disturbing side. Behind the influences he mentioned—time spent indoors, a settled mode of life and work that was presumed unknown in Africa, association with other races—there lay the single great fact of slavery.

The slave traffic to Brazil had ceased eighteen years before. After centuries of manumission, the majority of Afro-Brazilians were as free as Miklouho-Maclay. With emancipation certain, a visitor could concentrate on prices charged for the remaining slaves—'enormous' by comparison with those paid in Nubia and Abyssinia—and the legal conditions governing their treatment. However he communicated with them, whatever questions he asked, he saw in every African a slave or a product of slavery.

So the apparent evolution of Afro-Brazilians caused mixed feelings. After half a lifetime in Brazil, a slave could still match the white man's image of the Negro—shiny black, with a 'naively-stupid visage ... grinning at every trifle'. A new style of behaviour marked his

Brazilian-born son. The influences that faded the complexion seemed to suppress the thoughtless good nature born 'in Africa, in freedom'. When reserve and self-control replaced primitive simplicity, the observer's sense of what the black man should be declared it a poor exchange. It was pointless to regret an inevitable process. He understood that Afro-Brazilians without 'a drop of European blood' were already indistinguishable from mulattos. Confirmed and strengthened by heredity, the effect of using different muscles would re-shape the Negro face.

The Brazilian summary of Africa perhaps took the edge off disappointment when he learned that *Vityaz* would neither call at the Cape of Good Hope nor help test the 'Lemuria' hypothesis by soundings in the Indian Ocean. When changed orders sent the corvette south, he could no longer count on visiting Australia or even being taken to New Guinea. 'I am alive, healthy, and have more than enough work', he summed up, 'but I don't know where I'm going or how to get to the Papuans'.

On the shores of Magellan Strait he was too engrossed to fret about the future. Those shores, where he very consciously walked in the footsteps of the young Charles Darwin, were not quite as Darwin had seen them forty years before. The world's most southerly township now occupied Punta Arenas on the Brunswick Peninsula. Forest and snow-streaked hills formed the background for more than two hundred houses, with church, school, barracks and sawmills. Perhaps misled by English and Irish names and a British steamer service, Miklouho-Maclay took this part of Chile for an 'English colony' mainly populated by Chileans. In fact the settlement was a Chilean Siberia, built by transported criminals and political exiles. Whatever its materials, civilization had come to stay.

Ascending a mountain on trolleys pushed by human 'locomotives', a party from *Vityaz* inspected coal mines and gold diggings. On excursions from the town the naturalist followed a road that seemed at first 'too good for Patagonia'. The minimal clearing of forest, settlers told him, had already improved vegetable gardens by altering the rainfall. But the settlement amounted to a fingernail scratch in the wilderness. A few minutes on horseback, and he entered a primeval world.

The road shrank to a faint path between a wall of forest and the moody expanse of the strait, completely disappearing at high tide. He could ride forty kilometres in either direction along cobblestone beaches without meeting a soul. In the sodden gloom of beech forests he plunged among mossy rocks and decaying wood, between columnar trunks thickly studded with fungi, wrapped in a silence that might have reigned since the world began. He stood on the windswept threshold of the continent, asked what lay ahead, and was told, 'The Pampas'.

Massawa, Abyssinia, in 1869

A souvenir of Suakin: from the title page of Miklouho-Maclay's notes on Red Sea sponges

Miklouho-Maclay in Moroccan dress in Jena,
1867

The Red Sea traveller: Miklouho-Macla
Syrian dress

Miklouho–Maclay in Jena, 1870

Oranienbaum Palace, the
Salon Japonais, 1870

The corvette *Vityaz* which took Miklouho-Maclay to New Guinea, 1871

Mangareva, Tuamotu Archipelago, with the mission cottage in which
Miklouho-Maclay lived, July 1871

Freedom, fine weather, a willing horse, an unspoilt country—all was excellent as on the first day.

Darwin had discovered in Patagonia that there was nothing like geology. Miklouho-Maclay, regretting his ignorance of the subject, caught a touch of his predecessor's enthusiasm. But elementary observations on coastal uplift and the action of streams soon took second place. As though it had been arranged for him, the village filled with Patagonians, Tehuelche horsemen who crossed the isthmus to Punta Arenas once or twice a year.

Everywhere, tall figures swathed in guanaco skins rode silently through the streets or lounged about shop doorways. He studied their rugged features, long black hair and clumsy garments, admired their highly efficient harness, copied their decorative designs, and watched a demonstration with the bolas. In these hardy, intelligent, taciturn hunters, he saw a people equal to Patagonia. He was hardly surprised to find among them, as Darwin had, a fugitive from civilization, an Argentinian who had long before exchanged Buenos Aires for primitive freedom.

Yet sadness shadowed the meeting. Darwin had found the Tehuelche 'half civilized and proportionally demoralized' by their strange fondness for Europeans. Now they were half civilized and wholly ruined. When they traded guanaco skins and ostrich feathers to the settlers, what interested them most was rum. Within three hours most of the Indians were too drunk to stand. They drank until they lost consciousness. The only consolations came from the rarity of the event and the proof that Patagonians were never too drunk to ride.

Miklouho-Maclay left facts to speak for themselves: women drinking themselves as insensible as their husbands, guns offered as freely as liquor, the friendly, well-informed governor making money from this trade. He could not entirely condemn a settlement where a regular steamer delivered, along with alcohol and firearms, a sheaf of letters from home. Before leaving Punta Arenas, he sent off a long report to the Russian Geographical Society, again reminded his mother of his careful regard for time and money and his promise to live with her in Italy.

Then *Vityaz* left the strait, past untouched shores of snowpatch and forest, peaks rising tier beyond tier, sombre channels that Darwin had imagined leading to 'another and worse world'. By the end of April, Maclay might indeed have entered another world. He stood in a courtyard at Talcahuano, while the British consul explained the brainchild on which he had spent a fortune, a 'solar machine' for smelting copper. If the old visionary did not die or beggar himself before he perfected it, the traveller concluded, the invention would be 'immensely powerful'.

Somewhere in Chile—in the arid surroundings of Talcahuano or Valparaiso, on a up-river trip from Concepción, in the streets and museums of almost-Parisian Santiago or on the road to Aconcagua—Miklouho-Maclay managed to catch a fever. Or perhaps he relapsed into the malaria he had suffered in Europe. Either way, he became and remained so ill that Nazimov doubted his chances of surviving in New Guinea. Illness was the least of Maclay's worries. At Valparaiso the captain received orders to make direct for New Guinea, without calling at any Australian port.

So much for the grand duke's promises. With calm restored between England and Russia, political storms blew up from the south Pacific. British colonists in Australia, always nervous about their exposed position, had lately seen too many Russian warships. While *Vityaz* was at sea between Rio and Magellan Strait, yet another Russian corvette had appeared in Australian waters. And while the colonists chewed over their surmises, they had heard of Miklouho-Maclay's impending arrival in the Pacific. Moreover, the scope of his plans and enquiries had convinced German and English scientists that he led an official expedition. As Australians heard it, the Russian government was sending New Guinea a 'scientific mission' that would spend two years in 'complete examination and survey of the island'.

Soothing but improbable hopes were put forward, suggestions that Australian scientists, missionaries and prospectors could work in New Guinea under Russian 'protection'. Friends of civilization were told to rejoice that the interior was to be explored from end to end. Miklouho-Maclay was introduced as a potential 'Rajah Brooke' to bring the great island out of primeval darkness. But the general reaction was hostile. Optimists took it for granted that Russia had 'an eye to New Guinea'. Alarmists saw the Russian scientific mission 'establishing a footing for annexation'. Australians, always interested in obtaining New Guinea for themselves, or at least in keeping others out, were urged to be 'up and doing if they would not have the Russian empire extending to their very doors'.

While *Vityaz* lay at Valparaiso, the Australian alarm reached London. Others began to take steps. The Dutch nominally held western New Guinea through their vassal state of Tidore. For thirteen years they had ignored it. Their only real interest, the exclusion of other powers, had recently been threatened by the ideas of Germans, Italians and Australians. Now Batavia started to organize its own long-postponed expedition to the island. The sight of the Dutch, 'startled out of their apathy', seemed to confirm Australian fears, and Australian agitation further alarmed the Dutch.

It would take time to convince this South Seas hornets' nest that the great Russian expedition consisted of one young man, travelling at his mother's expense. Meanwhile, alarmists caused him more trouble than he caused them. He had rather fancied making his way to New Guinea without Nazimov's 'floating barracks' and its mindless inhabitants. But his funds had been sent to Australia, where only he could draw them. He had nothing for current expenses, purchase of supplies and building materials, or payment of the servants he must find as substitutes for men engaged at Sydney. In this extremity he overcame distaste for dealing with Nazimov. He obtained 1000 roubles from the captain, covering the loan by a bill drawn on Meshchersky. This faithful friend would understand the position and say, 'He is right!'

Six months away from Russia, Miklouho-Maclay often thought of those he had left behind. He found decent folk in Chile, especially a little girl of fourteen, one of the rare people who pleased him. But he many times wished he could seel Olga and his mother. He regretted that Meshchersky was not sharing his adventures and alleviating the miseries of shipboard life. As an antidote to this sense of loss and loneliness, Darwin had recommended 'the exhaustless delight of anticipating the long wished-for day of return'. Miklouho-Maclay thought more of the day when those he needed would come to him. Vladimir must join him, 'even in New Guinea'. This brief separation meant nothing, he comforted Olga: 'I will come soon, and perhaps (I speak very seriously) I will take you away with me'.

The future he desired for this beloved sister did not include an Olga who grew older, married some suitable man, became a mother. At times he seemed almost to wish her changed to stone until his return. As he passed beyond reach of her letters, beyond the possibility of guiding her life, he insisted on the duties she owed him: 'Keep your diary, and don't do anything without my advice' ... 'Write more to me, and don't undertake anything without my advice'. Their shared future was to resemble the past, with Olga as his companion and handmaiden, but in some better place.

He was bound for islands that to generations of Europeans had formed the very image of the better place. Approaching New Guinea from an unplanned direction, he had only to reverse the order in which he studied the relationship of Papuans to their Polynesian neighbours. And the change of route brought unexpected opportunity. *Vityaz* carried letters for Easter Island, Rapanui, most fascinating island of them all.

Adolph Bastian, the president of the Berlin Geographical Society and vice-president of the Society for Anthropology, Ethnology and Pre-history, had especially urged study of Easter Island. One of those who took Miklouho-Maclay for leader of a scientific mission, he even hoped to see excavations carried out. In any case he wanted information about smaller objects than stone platforms and enigmatic colossi. He had received rubbings of wooden tablets found on the island, showing rows of incised symbols that he declared a form of writing. Other eminent scientists disagreed. But the original tablets in the Santiago museum had convinced Miklouho-Maclay. These were true hieroglyphs, the first writing found in the Pacific islands. He had enthusiastically prepared for Rapanui, studying works of art brought back by a Chilean frigate and official reports available at Santiago. He roundly condemned most of his predecessors, ignorant or indifferent travellers who had allowed themselves to be prematurely driven from the island by famine, bad weather or native hostility.

As *Vityaz* approached Rapanui, Miklouho-Maclay began to tackle a problem set by one of his advisers: to determine whether Humboldt's 'law' on the decrease of sea temperature near land held good for the Pacific islands. He gained nothing else, for there was no going ashore. He saw only the island's rolling profile, a stony beach pounded by surf, and some white buildings against reddish-dun slopes. The people whose history he wished to unveil were a few half-clad figures bobbing about in two European sloops. According to white men who came aboard, the missionaries and most of the islanders had gone to Tahiti. The remaining natives would probably leave when the Tahiti vessel returned.

The resident Europeans impressed the officers as three embittered castaways, almost unhinged by monotony and isolation, re-fighting the Franco-Prussian War in the middle of nowhere. Nobody recognized the voluble Frenchman as a future king. Jean-Baptiste Dutroux-Bornier and his native allies had ousted their rivals, priests and flock. He had their cottages, gardens and animals, even their church for use as a wool store. He could turn to developing a prosperous pastoral concern. And he wanted more. He would marry a native 'princess', proclaim her queen, and rule in her name. He would enjoy wealth, women, power, and see a child born to continue his line. Then he would be killed by his enraged subjects. But no forebodings disturbed the man who would be king.

He told the Russians the necessary lies, but made no attempt to dissuade them from landing. Unable to deliver the missionaries' letters, Nazimov refused to linger at an unsafe anchorage. Disappointment sharpened Miklouho-Maclay's criticism of predecessors who had wasted the privilege of visiting Rapanui. It did not prevent his writing up everything learned from books and museum study. Others might test his theories. Besides, he was bound for places where most of the Rapanui people now lived.

Illness prevented his going ashore at Pitcairn. The officers went, and returned in raptures. The earth's abundance, closeness to nature, an enchanting simplicity, peace, harmony—it was the Pitcairn of children's books, the idyll that helped shape the restless European's vision of the South Seas. These exemplary people knew nothing of Europe's frenzies and alarms. They were not like the hysterical trio on Rapanui, hungry for newspapers to feed private hatreds. They no more needed wine and cigars than that other poison, the money that 'civilization' made essential. They wanted only their own simple ways, true Christian faith and mutual love. Admirers preferred to overlook the quantity and variety of European goods that the descendants of the *Bounty* mutineers wanted from *Vityaz*.

It did not satisfy Miklouho-Maclay's idea of the 'primitive', this half-Polynesian community that clung to European furniture and respectability, taught its children in English and kept a more-than-English Sabbath. He carried away only some sketches, more temperature measurements contradicting 'Humboldt's law', and an impression that the islanders' Polynesian inheritance was overcoming the 'English type'. A week later he was established beside a lagoon at Mangareva. His cottage steps led straight on to the beach. A few paces from the back door, a rich tangle of vegetation began. Beyond, a green-clad mountain rose to a vibrant sky. He had entered the Pacific of legend. His own Pacific was still far to seek.

Wearied by illness and a 36-day voyage from Valparaiso, he gladly stayed under the roof provided by the mission. Mangareva had been dominated by missionaries for almost forty years, part of a French protectorate since 1844. From his veranda he saw all he wished to see. Natives were sent to him in satisfactory numbers, brought from the other side of the island on request. Several times a day, people gathered on his veranda. He inspected them from the comfort of his armchair. They conformed to his silence and immobility, only occasionally talking and laughing among themselves. He noted facial characteristics, drew portraits with the aid of the *camera lucida*, and gave thanks for ideal conditions. Surrounded by strangers whose talk he did not understand, he felt safe from the influence of sympathy and antipathy, able to determine the 'general type' quite objectively. When he found it 'far from beautiful', this conclusion seemed as objective as the rest.

The visitors whispering who-knows-what about the stranger included many people from Rapanui. They displayed the same features as the Mangarevans, yet Miklouho-Maclay easily picked them out. Their 'frowning, sad expression and thin faces' spoke to him of recent upheavals on their island and sufferings on the way to Mangareva. They spoke, too, of what these people had earlier suffered at the hands of white men. A string of population estimates, and some idea of South American politics, made him cautious about Chilean claims that Peruvians had killed thousands of Rapanui. But many islanders had been violently or fraudulently carried off, nine years before, to work in Peru. The few who returned had brought smallpox to the island. He was examining survivors of the destruction he expected to find wherever Europeans had been.

He nevertheless concluded that native wars and a 'scanty and unreliable food supply' had helped reduce the number of Rapanui. The principal cause of depopulation seemed to be a 'huge numerical disproportion between the sexes'. Europeans had always remarked on it. Now there remained, for four hundred Rapanui men, only one hundred very thin and sickly women, and the few little girls were married at about ten years of age.

Perhaps disproportionate numbers of women had died from smallpox, as the men explained. But reliable records of Mangareva's declining population showed a similar imbalance. Ever fewer girls were born alive, and more of them died in the first year of life. As on Rapanui, many married young, died young and left no offspring. The dutiful survivors bore four children on the average, yet the rising generation contained twice as many boys as girls.

Miklouho-Maclay answered the standard question about the condition of women. He refrained from interpreting the figures. Faced by two peoples without a future, he retrieved what he could of their past. Authentic Mangarevan artefacts could still be purchased. One man, incapable of felling trees with his father's stone axe, donated it to science. Rapanui tablets obtained by the missionaries had been sent to Tahiti or Chile, but the refugees still held two or three of these *kohau rongorongo*. Their past was in those beautifully-inscribed symbols, they explained, all the important events of the island. Their fathers had been able to engrave and read these signs, but nobody understood them now.

Some Rapanui customs could be ascertained almost directly. Former warriors bore vestiges of tattooing that in the great days had covered even the lips of the war-leaders. Children of eleven remembered meals of human flesh. Confirming reports that men in their early twenties were smaller and less robust than their elders, Miklouho-Maclay traced this decline to the abolition of cannibalism. He left European readers to judge whether missionaries should tamper with such practices. He regretted only that these zealots did so little to record what they destroyed.

He might as reasonably have criticized a sailor's neglect to study marine life as the ship went down. The brief, discontinuous evangelization of Rapanui had begun and ended in turmoil. In between, death and departure had halved the mission. Père Hippolyte Roussel had nevertheless stolen time from religion and island politics to copy rock engravings and examine fallen statues. He had collected eight inscribed tablets and confirmed the existence of more, compiled vocabularies, recorded some customs. But on Mangareva in 1871 he could tell a visitor hardly anything new. Other investigators had questioned him and published the results.

With Roussel as interpreter and principal informant, Miklouho-

Maclay confirmed English and Chilean reports that were still news in Russia. He learned more about events as yet unknown to the outside world. Dutroux-Bornier claimed to have bought the mission's buildings and sheep. Lies, said the missionary; the pirate had simply taken everything. Thinking of that desolate island, so poor in 'means of existence', the scientist almost believed that its inhabitants had emigrated of their own accord. Not at all, said Père Roussel. Dutroux-Bornier had incited his allies to destroy the Christians' houses. He, not the rats, had dug up the sweet potatoes and forced the people to choose between flight and starvation. Now those on Rapanui were held by terror, while those in safety pined to go home. Only authority and guns could recover the graveyard that meant so much to them, and so far nobody with the power had the will.

Rapanui problems provided an education. Nobody denied that the refugees had undertaken to work a set time for Dutroux-Bornier's partner in Tahiti. The missionaries accused that respected planter and trader of using intrigue and violence to get the island for his sheep and its people as plantation labourers. Not. so, said John Brander. He had bought the island. To save his sheep from hungry islanders and the islanders from starvation, he had arranged to resettle the Rapanui, at one stroke doing good deeds and good business. Now he complained that the exiles on Mangareva were prevented from keeping their agreement. The priests claimed to have rescued the remnant from slavery. With one party French and Catholic, the other mainly British and Protestant, Tahiti tradition brewed a dispute in which even the Rapanui would take sides.

The officers of *Vityaz* had already taken sides when Brander welcomed them to Tahiti. Miklouho-Maclay accepted the missionaries' account, but saw no reason to refuse the predator's hospitality. With the officers and most of local 'society', he attended a party at Brander's house. With Brander and the officers, he visited the southern districts for a native festival and witnessed dances that no missionary approved. The trip gave him his first acquaintance with close relatives of the Papuans, plantation workers from the Solomon Islands and New Hebrides. It allowed him to study the ruins of the great *marae* at Mahaiatea, for comparison with other Pacific island religious monuments. It also introduced him to the man who had completed the destruction begun by nature. Against Tahitian protests, William Stewart had salvaged masonry from the temple for use in another extravagant dream. On his cotton plantation, the sacred stones had helped to build a settlement that he represented as a working man's paradise and his enemies condemned as hell on earth. Now he was sliding into ruin, soon to die, deposed and penniless. Vegetation would smother his kingdom's foundations as though they had remained in the *marae* Mahaiatea.

For Miklouho-Maclay, the most interesting man in Tahiti was neither the despoiler of Rapanui nor the magnate whose agents were ravaging other islands for labourers to prop up doomed fortunes. The time he could spare from excursions and business was spent with Tepano Jaussen, Bishop of Axieri *in partibus infidelium*, first vicar apostolic of Oceania, who held most of the Rapanui tablets thus far obtained.

Monseigneur Jaussen could claim priority in recognizing the importance of *kohau rongorongo*—'speaking wood', as he translated the name. The lay brother who had spent nine hair-raising months on the island in 1864 had seen many such tablets, whose owners seemed to care very little for them. But European scientists had cared no more. His discovery forgotten, the discoverer had died on Rapanui in 1868, without mentioning the subject to his colleagues of the new mission. Then the bishop had come across the neglected report. A missionary from Rapanui had brought a gift—braids of human hair wrapped round a board bearing engraved signs. The hunt was on for pieces of wood that the people of a treeless island were said to be feeding into their cooking fires.

The bishop had five, all affectionately named, and spent his spare time trying to extract their meaning. Thus early in his task, he never doubted that the speaking wood must speak to him. Neither he nor his visitor imagined that these symbols would baffle scholars a century later.

Miklouho-Maclay chose for description the largest and best-preserved tablet, made from a European ashwood oar that proved both the inscription's modernity and the island's lack of wood. By the time he finished with the bishop's collection he had seen ten of these relics—boards in all shapes and sizes and a variety of timbers, some marked by ill-treatment, fire, worms or long immersion in the sea. Without discovering anything the bishop had not, he could give European scientists a vivid picture of objects they knew only from two paper copies. His good luck was completed by the possession of specimens. The bishop donated one of his finest tablets 'to the Russian warship *Vityaz*'. In Miklouho-Maclay's collection it made a splendid companion for a smaller, odd-shaped, defective tablet that he had perhaps obtained at Mangareva.

His last word about Rapanui was written in mid-August at Apia, the capital of Samoa. He was counting the days to New Guinea, sure that even Olga could not imagine his eagerness. The officers speculated on their reception among savages who did not expect visitors. The carpenters were dressing timber for Miklouho-Maclay's New Guinea home. Yet his enterprise still suffered from uncertainty. He easily resisted Nazimov's argument that a man so sick and weakened should abandon the undertaking and go on to Japan. He could not ignore the difficulties of trying to live alone in New Guinea. Nobody in Chile or Tahiti had wished to join the expedition. Apia seemed equally unable to provide two servants. He faced the prospect of leaving the corvette and making his own way to the goal via unpredictable detours in search of men.

Help came from Theodore Weber, consul for the German Empire and local manager for the great Hamburg firm of Godeffroy. One of Weber's finds was a Niue Island youth, probably conscripted from among imported labourers on Godeffroy plantations. The other, a Swede named Will Olsen, had been a seaman on a merchant vessel.

Miklouho-Maclay could not afford to be too particular. Olsen seemed cheerful and obliging, fit to keep house and manage a boat. His prospective employer, who wanted a servant not a companion, never asked how this talkative fellow would adapt to a life of isolation and silence. The young islander should at least be able to cook native foods and the dried beef brought from Chile. By some aberration Miklouho-Maclay imagined that a Polynesian, born on a small island more than four thousand kilometres from New Guinea, might act as 'guide' among the Papuans. He neither found out whether this waif had any name but the condescending 'Boy' nor noticed his deep-seated cough.

Olsen understood German and could sign his name. 'Boy' understood no language but his own. Both accepted a written agreement pledging them to do whatever their master required and follow wherever he went. As to their expectations, the record was less clear. Olsen seemed to think he might better himself in New Guinea. Boy was too scared and ignorant to expect anything.

They sailed from shabby little Apia, with its bars and billiard tables, native power-struggles and European intrigue. European influence was not left behind. Samoans solved the religious problem by impartially attending both Protestant and Catholic churches, balancing the double dose of sermons by dances that the visitors found even more indecent that those of Tahiti. On Rotuma, native factions made war on behalf of imported creeds. *Vityaz* delivered a letter there, assuring the Catholic missionaries that a French gunboat was on the way. For a couple of days the Russians provided the frightened fathers with company guaranteed to overawe the Protestants. These were their last dealings with white men in the south Pacific. On 12 September they anchored in Port Praslin, at the south-west tip of New Ireland, and knew they had entered a different world.

Nazimov did not like the looks of the 'Papuans' who wandered about the deck, exclaiming in amazement at everything they saw. They appealed no more to the literary-minded officer who rhapsodized over the primitive idyll of Pitcairn. It was not merely the sight of sticks and bones thrust through nostrils and ear lobes, teeth blackened by betel-chewing, harsh, bushy hair dyed red or daubed white with lime. These wild men punctuated their torrential talk by alarming shouts and bursts of laughter. Their eyes were 'knavish', their whole expression disagreeable and disturbing. For the first time, the Russians felt they were meeting savages.

Yet these men, dressed 'entirely in the costume of Adam', were ready for business, very clear about what they wanted in exchange for garden produce. Along with a few words of English, they had picked up some of the low-grade civilization dispensed by whaling vessels. They stole nothing, threatened nobody. When *Vityaz* sailed, a flotilla of canoes gave her a gala farewell.

Along the south coast of New Britain the wind played the kind of tricks that had prolonged the voyage across the Pacific. Then calms and light, capricious breezes gave way to squalls and thunderstorms. Clouds blotted out the sun and hurled masses of water on to the deck. Lightning slashed the gloom of sea and sky and Saint Elmo's fire tipped the masts. Everything increased the travellers' sense of approaching a special place.

It filled the horizon on 19 September, an immense, brooding unknown. Mountains rose to view, half-hidden in cloud, half-revealed as steep slopes dark with forest. The light-coloured strip at their feet took shape as a series of terraces clad in grassland and isolated thickets, slashed by jungle-filled clefts. As *Vityaz* followed the coast north-west, the trees seemed to close ranks until their sombre mass stretched from shore to mountains. Here and there, columns of smoke signalled the presence of men. Just before nightfall the corvette passed a small island where roofs appeared among coconut palms. The Russians saw no other evidence of human life in that secretive land.

Their destination, still uncertain while *Vityaz* lay at Apia, had been settled before they sighted New Guinea. They had reached the north coast near William Dampier's 'Cape King William', and were making for Dumont d'Urville's 'Cape Rigny'. The islands to their right had been labelled by Dampier. The mountains looming to the left had received from the French explorer the name of 'Finisterre'. Next day, the Russians would land on one of those stretches of coast that mapmakers indicated by broken lines. Dampier had seen this bight or gulf, the only large indentation in more than 1000 kilometres north-west from Cape King William. In 1827 Dumont d'Urville had laid down its southern and northern limits and named it after his ship—'Astrolabe Bay'. No European had entered it or formed more than a vague idea of how far it bit into the bulk of New Guinea. None, that is, unless one believed the rumour that a Captain Edgar had recently sailed up the gulf for more than 300 kilometres without sighting its termination. With or without the rumour, Astrolabe Bay promised a sheltered anchorage for taking on wood and water. For Miklouho-Maclay, it formed a possible gateway to the interior.

On deck at dawn to study the mountains without their veil of cloud, he expected to see a series of peaks, gaps that might lead to the heart of the island. Instead, he faced a 'high, unbroken wall' that looked no more encouraging when sunrise resolved it into three or four parallel ranges 'piled up one on top of another'. When *Vityaz* reached the middle of Astrolabe Bay, one glance showed that this bight had few inlets of any size, no evidence of a large river. The mountains decreased in height towards the north and stood farther from the coast, yet still they formed a stubborn barrier with no immediately discernible gaps. The shore, studied through the telescope, had a closed, unwelcoming look. Miklouho-Maclay saw no houses, no canoes, not a break among the trees that grew to the water's edge. Only smoke and some patches of coconut palms on the hillsides proved that people lived there.

And where, Captain Nazimov asked, would he like to be set down? He chose the southern side, which looked less 'unhealthy' than the rest.

A sandy hook, halfway into the bay, protected a fairly good anchorage. As *Vityaz* drew in, the first officer noticed figures on the sand, running and stopping, running and stopping. When the corvette rounded the spit the natives reappeared on the inner side, creeping down to watch as a boat put off to take soundings, fleeing when it came towards them. *Vityaz* anchored between the sandy cape and a shore of coral rock where giant trees, laced together by creepers, dropped their branches to the sea.

In that dark tangle nothing moved. The people on the opposite shore could not afford to lurk out of sight. A great floating thing had nosed into the cove and settled as though to stay. It looked like a canoe, a canoe large enough to carry the ancestors of all living men. Most of its bulk was dark and dull as a charred log, yet here and there it billowed with white or glittered with mysterious brilliance. Unknown objects pro-truded from the upper surface. It gave off smaller versions of itself. It was full of voices, swarming with pale, misshapen beings like visitants from another world. It was impossible, but there. The men had to do something about it.

They came out of the jungle, keeping close together. They talked until there was nothing more to say. Then the boldest left them and went down to face the apparition. He placed a coconut on the sand and tried to show by signs that it was a gift. Perhaps the spirits would take it and go away.

4: First Contact

Every educated sailor knew what could occur when white men first appeared among savages. Through their outlandish looks and equipment, manifestations of European power, or peculiarities of native thought, the newcomers were often received as something more than men. Drake and Raleigh had tasted this experience in the New World. As late as 1860, on the fringes of the East Indies, A. R. Wallace had met people who seemed ready to take him for a demigod. An ignorant and destitute castaway could become god-king of a South Seas island, provided he was first. The officers of *Vityaz* hardly doubted what was happening when a larger group of natives appeared on the beach to the north, bringing coconuts, taro and yams. They were practically sure when the Papuans displayed two small yellow dogs, brained them against a log, and laid the carcasses on the pile. A sacrifice was offered. The gods accepted.

Tossing about in a boat behind the cape, Miklouho-Maclay felt less godlike. The men on the beach raised their weapons and motioned him away. When he cast gifts on the waters and withdrew a little, the natives seemed pleased with the strips of red cloth that drifted to the shore. But still they shook their weapons, and signalled 'Go away!'

Heavy surf prevented his landing. Aboard the corvette, they formed the impression that threats had driven him off. Everyone acknowledged the scientist's right to contact the natives first, without interference, but the day was almost gone. Nazimov felt justified in spying out the land, at least from the sea.

The commander's expedition located several villages. At one point natives seemed to invite the Russians to land. Miklouho-Maclay and his servants set out again, with red cloth, beads, nails, fish hooks. He must be first to meet these people, and he must do it before dark. When he

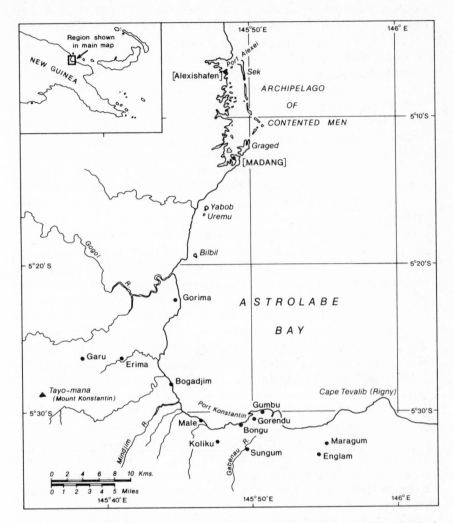

Astrolabe Bay and surroundings, north-eastern New Guinea, with principal places visited by Miklouho-Maclay. Names of modern towns are shown in square brackets.

noticed a track leading into the jungle, he could not wait for the servants to secure the boat. Alone he leapt ashore and hurried along the path.

From the first glimpse of the village, he sensed its perfect rightness. Coconut palms shaded a dozen huts around a small 'square' of beaten earth. Dark jungle and groves of fruit trees set off palm-leaf thatch silvered by time and sunlight, crimson hibiscus flowers and the leaves of multicoloured shrubs. The place welcomed him—neat, pleasant, entirely strange yet somehow homelike. And it was quiet, wrapped in a dreamlike stillness. The cry of a bird confirmed the silence.

Suddenly as he had come to them, the people had seen or heard him first. A fire smouldered and flickered in the square; opened coconuts lay where they had been dropped in flight; two huts stood open, gaping evidence of hasty departure. He peered through one doorway and inventoried the contents—bamboo bed frames, a few loose stones containing a smoulder under a pot, bunches of shells and feathers on the wall, a skull dangling from the roof. He was moving towards the other open hut when a rustle behind him broke the trance.

A man stood there, paralysed. Their eyes met for a moment. Then the savage dashed into the jungle with the white man in pursuit.

The fugitive soon looked back, saw white hands bearing only a piece of red stuff, gestures that seemed to mean no harm. He stopped and allowed the apparition to approach, took the cloth and tied it round his head. But when a hand touched him his whole body trembled so much it seemed he must fall. The ghostly hand that felt like flesh stroked his arm. A voice spoke unknown words. Resisting, but afraid to resist too much, he let himself be dragged back to the village.

Olsen and Boy were in the square, looking for their master. Seven or eight more natives emerged from the jungle and watched from a distance until Maclay pulled them one by one into his 'circle'. Exhausted, he sat on a stone, observing his new acquaintances and distributing gifts.

They avoided meeting his gaze, but uneasily submitted to its scrutiny. Though they did not understand the nails and fish hooks, nobody refused what he offered. Finally they assembled their own gifts—coconuts, bananas and two squealing piglets—and accompanied him to the shore.

They balked at following him to the corvette. He persuaded four or five men to board a canoe, and masterfully took it in tow. Others followed in another vessel, as though hypnotized. But halfway out the men in the second canoe woke up and fled. Those in the craft under tow tried to release the line. Olsen and Boy had to row hard to bring them alongside *Vityaz*, then bundle them up the ladder while the sailors dragged them on to the deck. The Papuans shook with terror and looked ready to collapse.

They stayed upright nevertheless, small, dark figures in breech-cloths and armbands, barefoot on a wooden expanse as wide as the village square. Unknown shapes loomed or gleamed in the dusk. Indefinable beings crowded round, speaking, but not in the speech of men. As the leader of the visitants examined them and their possessions, without doing any harm, their minds grew a little easier.

Captain Nazimov still disliked black teeth in mouths reddened by betel chewing; on the whole he found these faces pleasant compared with those of New Ireland. The natives were marched off the quarterdeck and into the floating village. In the lamplit wardroom they became almost calm. Though they squatted on the benches in their own fashion, they drank tea like gentlemen and seemed to enjoy it. They were gratified by presents and displays of new things, not at all alarmed by the sound of the piano. But they could not bear the hard, smooth, shining surface in which faces—their own faces—appeared as though imprisoned. Allowed to go, they scrambled down the ladder in great haste.

So far everything promised well. Nazimov noted that he had seen no natives carrying arms. The officers rather relished the idea of being gods. Miklouho-Maclay experienced a deeper contentment. He had found his ideal primitive village, the tranquil, unspoiled place where he could feel at home. Its inhabitants, though not exactly beautiful, and clearly subject to interesting diseases, looked neither wild nor fierce. They were quiet, timid, manageable if taken by surprise. In particular he thought kindly of Tui, the small middle-aged man with a 'quite engaging' face, who had surrendered so easily in the jungle. He sensed that Tui would *obey*.

Early next morning the same men returned with friends. They came aboard when invited and inspected the corvette, still timid, less intense or more restrained in their curiosity than the New Irelanders. When leaving, they indicated that food would be brought to the ship, and sure enough, the supplies arrived. A 'chief' came first, spear in hand, followed by three men waving palm leaves. Behind them, two stout fellows carried a large pig tied to a bamboo pole. Auxiliaries with baskets of coconuts, fruit and taro brought up the rear. They piled the tribute on the beach and departed in the same ceremonious manner. The gods showed approval by collecting the gifts and leaving a basket of useful articles.

The second day at anchor coincided with an important birthday. The inlet was named 'Port Grand Duke Konstantin'; the ship was dressed, privileges arranged for the men. But the celebration could not be limited to these peaceful gestures. To honour the grand duke properly, *Vityaz* must treat the jungle to a 21-gun salute.

No sign-language could prepare the people for an event so far beyond their experience. Miklouho-Maclay felt it within his power to reduce their fear. As the time approached, he took up his post in the village, with Tui and his other new friends.

At each explosion the villagers tried to run, threw themselves to the ground or cowered trembling, hands over ears. Helpless with laughter, Maclay made none of the reassuring gestures he had imagined. Yet he felt that his presence, and his laughter, had helped them through the crisis.

The women hidden in the jungle, and all the inhabitants of other villages, had to cope with the grand duke's birthday as best they could. And between the midday salute and the evening illuminations all the natives, protected or not, decided they wanted nothing to do with the corvette. Nazimov preferred not to connect this with the grand duke. Relations changed, he suggested, when the Papuans realized that some of the visitants intended to stay.

He and his officers disliked the place Miklouho-Maclay had chosen for his dwelling, a small promontory on the southern side of Port Konstantin. In that position, he could not sight vessels passing Astrolabe Bay, nor would his house be noticed from the sea. Strategists assessed the place as a death-trap. The surgeon reported that it shrieked of malaria. Maclay inspected the 'better' places, and stuck to his choice. The little cape lay about ten minutes walk from his ideal village, near a clear stream and a native path. Its virgin forest suggested ownerless land, where his unauthorized presence would offend nobody. It suited his need for quiet and isolation; closer to a village he might be annoyed by crying children and howling dogs. He did not find it particularly malarial, or otherwise dangerous; and he was not anxious to see European ships.

Over the next five days up to 110 men at a time worked for him. A space 77 metres square was hacked from almost impenetrable jungle. They surrounded the clearing with a barricade of tree trunks and thorny bushes, built graded paths to the beach and the stream. A cabin took shape, just over four metres long and two metres wide, raised on piles and divided into two rooms, with a separate shed for use as a kitchen. Then Maclay's possessions were brought ashore, load after load. He had left some luggage in Samoa, to be collected in a few years time; clothing and equipment needed for his northern travels stayed aboard *Vityaz*, to be taken to Japan; still the cases, sacks and baskets filled the cabin and the space beneath and overflowed into the clearing. There was no room to sit down.

He felt as exhausted as if he had felled each tree and carried every box. Everything required his planning and supervision. When a chance of sleep occurred, worry kept him awake. Most of all, perhaps, he was worn out by haste and tumult, desperate for them all to be gone so that

Port Konstantin, Astrolabe Bay, after the chart drawn by officers of *Vityaz*. Position of Maclay's house at Garagassi as indicated by him on a copy of the chart.

he might know peace in his new surroundings. The wish lost nothing by the knowledge that while practical concerns imprisoned him the officers explored the coast, met the inhabitants, bought up the skulls and artefacts he needed for scientific work. Under his eyes, they were stealing New Guinea.

The natives kept away from the building site. Parties sent out with gifts to establish friendship 'in Mr Maclay's interests' found that people were withdrawing from the villages. The women and children had been taken away, towards the foothills, and the men who met the Russians opposed any progress in that direction. No clash took place. The white men always gave way. The officers managed to present gifts and make exchanges. But the villages stood deserted, and the canoes disappeared from the shore.

Maclay's friend Tui came once to the clearing, and raised hopes by spontaneously helping the workers. He accepted a knife, promised to come again, then failed for some days to return. Parties from *Vityaz* met him and urged him to go to Mr Maclay. He always indicated by signs that he would come soon but first must have a bite to eat. The Russians grew tired of this. Next time they saw him, they brought him to Maclay.

He really was obedient. The trouble, apparently, was that he had to obey fellow villagers who forbade him to work on Maclay's house. And he told the Russians more in his expressive mime. With a sweep of the hand he wiped the corvette from the sea. He indicated Maclay and his servants as those who would stay. Gestures showed how men from the villages would converge on the clearing, wreck and burn the house and spear its occupants to death.

It might be bluff. Travel literature had taught Maclay that the white man must never show fear. In his own principles he went further, resolved to meet all threats with impenetrable calm. He answered with feigned incomprehension. When Tui repeated the performance, Maclay waved a hand and offered him a nail. The account he gave aboard *Vityaz* seemed serious enough, and when the gunnery officer outlined suitable precautions Maclay agreed.

Lieutenant Chirikov installed six land mines or *fougasses* in a semicircle facing the jungle. The basic device had stopped enemy assaults at Sevastopol. Recent improvements allowed it to be fired almost instantly from a distance. One of Maclay's tasks, after another sleepless night, was to study this simple system for blowing his neighbours to kingdom come.

He might spring the mines, defend the house to the last with rifles, revolvers and 'rapid fire' gun, but what then? In such extremes he could not stay; nor could he leave, since he had no boat. Even if peace were preserved, Nazimov pointed out, Maclay needed a boat to investigate the sea and islands, yet he had made no effort to obtain one. The solution was to leave him the smallest of the ship's boats, with all its tackle. Maclay accepted. As he had shown when engaging a sailor-servant, he had always expected something of the kind.

Another point worrying the officers, who worried about him more than he liked, was the meagreness of his provisions. He had brought some beans and dried beef from Valparaiso, but at Apia, the last port where European food could be obtained, he had seemed indifferent to such things. 'There are people in New Guinea', he replied when the officers nagged, 'and I can eat whatever they eat'. True, the New Guineans cultivated gardens and kept pigs. But what if they refused to feed him? Maclay would hunt in the jungle and cultivate the fruit and vegetable seeds brought from Tahiti. In any case, staying in New Guinea for an indefinite time, he must be independent of European food. When Nazimov insisted on giving him biscuit and canned goods from the ship's stores, and the officers sacrificed some of their rice, tea and sugar, Maclay acquiesced again. After months at sea he could not look at canned food himself, but it might be acceptable to his servants.

Spare supplies and equipment were stored in 'cellars' under the house. The flag of the Russian merchant marine flapped from a tall mast where it might be seen if a ship happened to pass. Astrolabe Bay had been surveyed as far as time allowed (with closer attention to Port Konstantin) and a number of Russian names appeared on the map. Amid chaos, Miklouho-Maclay wrote his last letters to Europe. So weary that he could hardly stand, he accompanied Nazimov to the sandy point opposite his new home. Here he was to bury, from time to time, special canisters containing his journals and scientific notes. Some Russian vessel might retrieve his work if he and his servants should die.

All that foresight suggested had been done, except for one thing. If all went well, Miklouho-Maclay would stay for a year or two. In emergency, he could use the small boat to escape. Nobody mentioned the question of how he might leave New Guinea peacefully, with his luggage and specimens. It seemed that neither he nor anyone else expected his survival.

Perhaps this occurred to Olsen, who knew no Russian but had seen the mines installed. The situation became real to him on 27 September, when the corvette's anchor rose, when his master sent him to dip the flag in salute, when he knew beyond hope that the men with whom he had lived and worked were going. After a few minutes, Miklouho-Maclay noticed that nothing was happening with the flag. Annoyed, he hurried to the flagpole and saluted the ship himself. Olsen was crying.

Maclay reclined on a fallen tree, listening to the murmur of waves, wind among leaves, the occasional cry of a bird. He was really resting.

Without dregs of the past or care for the future, his mind lay open to enjoyment of the moment. It thankfully embraced all he saw and could not see in this new world—the splendour of jungles, sparkling sea, cloud-wreathed mountains, the hidden life of reef and forest. Joy and responsibility were one: to observe and understand all this unknown land might reveal. He felt his powers expanding to the task. Felt, too, the expansion of a naturally serene temperament that had too often been disturbed by tiresome people. It was pleasant not to hear arguments, quarrels, nagging, advice, rarely a human voice. World without men.

Now that everything depended on his 'energy, work and will', he found himself equal to the lonely responsibility. He had quickly recovered from tottering exhaustion to sort out the chaos in and around his hut. He was in good health and meant to preserve it—to dress warmly after dark and avoid wet clothing, never to go outdoors without a hat, to drink only boiled water. With plenty of rest and a regular life, he hoped to fend off malaria. Olsen, by contrast, had satisfied Nazimov by suffering a fever attack before *Vityaz* left. Hands and faces lumpy with insect bites suggested that both servants were physically less suited to New Guinea than their master. As for their moral strength, he preferred to say nothing. That incident at the flagpole had shown what could be expected from Olsen's boasted courage. Though Maclay had demonstrated that in worrying circumstances one should have a good night's rest, Olsen and Boy insisted on keeping watch all night long.

That the situation was dangerous Maclay readily admitted. Just after *Vityaz* sailed, he had seen a crowd of men on the opposite shore, running and leaping in something like a dance. Then Tui had come, with something suspicious in his manner—the word 'spy' occurred to Maclay—inspecting everything, wanting to enter the house. But the gesture that accompanied the unknown word '*Tabu!*' made him keep his distance. When he asked by signs whether the corvette would return, Maclay gave him to understand that it would. Even when he came back, with companions who watched Maclay's every movement, renewed study of the minefield taught him nothing. He could stare all day at levers and plungers and the lines leading to the house, without divining the hidden physics and chemistry. There was something in the ground, perhaps a dangerous magic. After Tui's inspection, a group of natives came very cautiously, bringing coconuts and sugar cane.

Considerable ceremony accompanied the next visit. Twenty-five men brought gifts, including a sucking pig, laid them on the ground before Maclay, and individually presented their offerings. They behaved quietly, keeping away from the house. All their attention centred on Maclay, at least until Boy began to play the mouth-organ. Then Maclay proved his willingness to suffer for the cause. Despite his cultivated musical taste and sensitivity to noise, he had bought some of these little instruments, so popular in Samoa. When he distributed them, the delighted Papuans all began to blow at once.

Maclay endured it, for the sake of a foot on the ladder to his goal. He already made progress in observing physical characteristics, dress and ornament, weapons, implements of wood, stone, bone and bamboo, equipment for smoking and betel-chewing and other oddments the natives carried in neat bags slung round their necks and over their shoulders. He began to recognize individuals, to pick up some of their words. He dared not predict how long it might take to penetrate beyond appearances.

He early realized that he was unique in their perceptions. While he remained calm and passive, they could not meet his eye or bear his gaze for long. If he frowned and looked at them hard, they ran away. With a glance he could make them obey, while his servants, walking amid the same magic, were of no account in the visitors' eyes. They called Olsen 'Vil'. They knew the young dark one as 'Boy'. But one of these mysterious beings was master. Everything belonged to him; all gifts came from him. The name going through the villages was 'Maclay', and all his visitors knew it before they arrived.

They would never manage to pronounce 'Miklouho'. In any case, the family name had fallen into such disuse aboard *Vityaz* that even Nazimov rarely remembered it. Now this establishment of the chosen name in New Guinea increased its bearer's sense of becoming completely himself.

He did not renounce vital ties—portraits of his mother and sister stood on his work table—yet everything induced 'forgetfulness of the past'. He had entered a country new to his race, as a stranger even to those he brought with him. The last representative of outside authority, interfering, critical, full of stupid advice, had disappeared with *Vityaz*. And no portrait of Nikolai Ilich Miklouho looked up from the table, no image of that handsome man in uniform, alert, clean-shaven, with a soldier's bearing and a scholar's eyeglasses, dead of pneumonia at the age of thirty-eight. The sons remembered an ideal father, strict but just, attentive to their education, artistic and intellectual as well as practical. The early influence of such a man could never be lost. Yet his name slipped out of the second son's life as naturally as a beard and moustache concealed the lips inherited from Nikolai Miklouho. If a name was left on the map on New Guinea, it would not be the Miklouho name. This new world created 'Maclay', a unique being, of whom nothing was known and everything might be expected.

Exploring and expanding his powers, he still did not know what to expect of himself in relations with Papuans. While they clustered before him, talking together, sometimes addressing him as though they thought he understood, he noticed the weapons they kept handy, their uneasy glances to all sides. Their distrust worried him, as did their way of staying only until they received gifts. The behaviour of some, inspecting his possessions, suggested envy. A few approached him with something like malice and hostility in their faces, as though they would bare their teeth. He could not confidently describe these expressions in terms of the questionnaire Charles Darwin had sent out. Nor could he be sure that his calm manner and authoritative glance would always prevail.

One thing certain was that he would never understand their lives by staying on his own ground. Four days after *Vityaz* left, encouraged by two rather formal calls and the natives' familiarity with his name, he decided to visit a village.

He took it for granted that he should go alone. The question was whether he should go armed. By the loaded guns in his house, and the mines surrounding it, he assumed the right to kill any number of men in self-defence. Indifference to life raised no serious doubts about the need for survival. What seemed questionable at that moment was his ability to meet provocation with unshakeable calm. Even if it brought no other consequences, one untimely bullet could destroy all hope of winning the natives' trust. If it came to a fight, he could kill six men without attaining safety. Fear might keep his neighbours at bay for a time; in the end their numbers and thirst for revenge must prevail. The only safe weapons were those of the mind. In the interests of safety, he left his revolver at home.

He meant to revisit Tui's Gorendu, the homelike village of first contact. He took the wrong path, and found himself among strangers who had been warned of his coming.

All the women and children were in hiding. The men awaited him in the square, weapons at the ready. Convinced that he must not retreat, Maclay walked slowly towards them, seeking a familiar face. Before he reached the group, two arrows flew dangerously close to his head.

Voices seemed to reprimand those who loosed the arrows. Men near by explained by signs that the bowmen had aimed at a now-invisible bird. There were people here with whom he might have reached an understanding. But the longer he stood among them, disciplining his face to express no more than a mild curiosity, the more futile he found his position. Nobody here recognized Maclay, his wonderful gifts or his commanding glance. The crowd grew, and the hostile party seemed to prevail. One of the loudest talkers almost struck Maclay's eye with a spear.

While the villagers discussed this, Maclay congratulated himself on being unarmed. He might have shot the hunters of the non-existent bird or the uncouth fellow with the spear. Instead, he discovered a secret weapon.

He was far from home, and desperately tired. Without long search, he might have found a quiet place for a nap. He chose to rest here, in this unfriendly village, unconcerned whether death caught him standing, sitting or lying down. Before the inhabitants' eyes he took a clean new mat, found a shady place, and composed himself to sleep.

No man in New Guinea came silently to a strange village, refused to see that he was unwelcome, openly appropriated other people's belongings and completed his transgressions by falling asleep. None of the noisy, generous ghosts from the great spirit canoe had behaved like this. He was as large and hairy as a man, as white and strangely covered as a ghost, yet he acted like a child. And even the most ignorant child would be afraid to do such things where he did not belong.

They discussed the situation, looking at him and what he had removed when he lay down. At first he seemed to have taken off his feet, but the man who had waved his spear too close discovered that the black objects were hollow. Moreover, two peculiarly-coloured, foot-shaped appendages remained in the place of feet. Convinced there was nothing to be done, the men sauntered off and put their weapons away. They squatted in the shade, a few paces from the sleeper, talking and chewing betel. They did not call the women and children home. These days they always had to wait, to see what outrageous thing would happen next.

When Maclay next chose a village for investigation, he made an obviously dangerous experiment. Gumbu, the large settlement northeast of Port Konstantin, was the home of those who had threatened him when he first tried to land. He did have the advantage of surprise. This time nobody met him on the path and raced ahead to warn the village.

He glimpsed a pleasantly animated scene—men at work on the roof of a hut, girls preparing palm-leaf thatch and handing it up to the builders, women nursing children. Then someone noticed him, a scream tore through the chatter, and in an instant there was turmoil. The women shrieked and snatched up howling babies, grabbed the children's hands and streamed into the jungle. Even the dogs and pigs ran away.

The men ran too—towards him, seizing makeshift weapons on the way. They surrounded him, scowling, evidently unafraid. Perplexed by the commotion, Maclay noted his own perfect calm. He was tired after the long walk, but sleep, however useful as a psychological weapon, did not profit science. He climbed on to one of the wooden platforms on the perimeter of the square, seated himself comfortably, and began to take notes and make sketches.

Nobody accepted his invitation to join him. They kept their distance, ignoring his thirsty glances at a pile of fresh coconuts. Again he was defying the rules, assuming rights he did not possess, asserting a kind of power. The villagers did not hide their wish that he should go, or their resentment under his inspection. In London that intense scrutiny could have brought him a punch on the nose or the attention of a policeman; in Sicily he might have received the last services of a priest. In Gumbu they simply walked away muttering. The enormity of his behaviour left them helpless.

He went when staying seemed unprofitable, and kept away for months. These visits had proved that by self-control and surprise he could impose himself. He could not regard them as otherwise satisfactory. He had seen only sullen hostility, a tension that hardly relaxed until he prepared to leave. Faces seemed to ask why he had come, out of nowhere, to disturb and embarrass them. He had no words to answer their unspoken question. When forced to ask it of himself, he had no satisfactory reply.

Results were little better when he dropped in on Gorendu, the village that possibly owed him something. The women and children ran away. The men, though less hostile than those elsewhere, still met him with weapons in their hands, too excited to sit for portraits or teach him words. Since they did not accept his right to be there, cases of what he called 'insolence' occurred.

For the time being, he found it best to let the natives come to him. Staying at home, he had all his drawing materials at hand. He avoided carrying an assortment of gifts. He had no need to question himself about taking a revolver. All the guns were there, behind the semicircle of mines.

Patience. Non-interference. Maclay let matters take their course. Villagers came readily to 'Garagassi', as the promontory was called, treating it as his territory, where 'insolence' was inappropriate. Men who had behaved churlishly at home soon joined in the examination of his belongings and the exchange of ornaments and small utensils for European goods. They learned to mix trade tobacco with their own, to sit down and stay, instead of wandering about uneasily or 'sneaking off' as soon as they were given something. They came by twos and threes and in parties of twenty or thirty. They might arrive early on a chilly morning, carrying burning brands that they piled together to make a comfortable glow, or quite late at night, elaborately decorated and on their way to a feast. Whenever there was nothing else to do, the men of the neighbourhood visited Maclay, source of inexhaustible wonder and gifts.

Sometimes they reciprocated with gifts of food; sometimes they brought nothing. Maclay treated givers and takers alike. Coconuts were supplied often enough for him to adopt the 'milk' as a regular luxury. He did not otherwise rely upon the natives. He asked for nothing, allowed them to do the asking, and in this dependent role they became quite 'tame'. Some began to fetch and carry for him, accepting this relationship as naturally as he did.

The importance he assumed in their lives was revealed by more than their increasing docility. When men from other localities paid visits, Maclay's neighbours brought them to Garagassi. While the local men displayed him and his possessions, Maclay observed the inhabitants of places he meant to visit. There were men from coastal communities farther to the north, mountain dwellers from the ranges behind Gorendu, canoe parties from the islands of Bilbil and Yabob in the northern part of the bay. Wherever they came from, their astonishment confirmed that they had never seen a white man. Saucepans in the kitchen, a table, a folding chair, Maclay with his boots and striped socks—everything overwhelmed them. The festive crowd from Bilbil shrieked with wonder at every revelation. The lone, wild-looking little man from the mountains tried to run away, then burst into laughter and jumped up and down on the spot. He had bravely come to investigate an improbable rumour. A reality so far beyond his imagining almost unhinged him.

So while Maclay stayed home a variety of ethnological material came to him, and his spreading fame prepared the way for future journeys. He concentrated on mastering the 'Papuan' language, looking forward to the day when friendly speech would prevent misunderstandings and gain his neighbours' trust. Then he would learn customs, legends and songs, become familiar with every detail of these doomed lives.

He had underestimated the difficulties of acquiring a language entirely by signs. Most of his new acquaintances did not understand or 'wish to understand' what it was that he wanted to know. He learned some expressions by constant attention and fortunate chance. Otherwise, he could discover words only by pointing at objects. After two months in New Guinea he knew names for some birds and a variety of ornaments, foods and utensils. He could name heavenly bodies and parts of the human body. He could not say 'yes' or 'no', 'good' or 'bad', 'hot' or 'cold', or employ any verb of motion. The meanings of the words most often used eluded him, and he could devise no way of finding out.

Without words, he learned something about his neighbours' minds and characters. None of the things lying about Garagassi had been stolen—an 'unthinkable' result in any civilized place—and though he saw advantages in isolation he gave full credit to the natives' honesty. He found them 'a practical people'. All European goods were new and welcome, but the Papuans preferred useful articles—knives, hatchets, nails, bottles—to merely decorative items. They quickly discovered uses for strange things. Nails that would never be hammered became engraving tools. Tui picked up broken glass, ground it sharp and expertly shaved himself, immediately creating a market for broken glass. Pocket mirrors, at first frightening, became valued aids in the removal of facial hair, an operation that took up much of the young men's time.

By relating the new to the familiar, they helped themselves through the shocks. The unknown nature of metal did not disturb them; it performed more quickly the work of shell or stone. Glass, too, merely took the place of local materials for several purposes. At first much afraid of books and pictures, the villagers soon came to terms with them, calling all the strange marks *negrengba*—'drawing'. They had never before heard the word *tabu*, but they had similar magical prohibitions and soon used this term for everything forbidden by Maclay.

They accepted that the recent visitors were *tamo-Russ*, 'men from Russia', whatever that might mean. Yet Maclay had to realize that they did not accept him. Three months after his arrival, he still sensed distrust and 'a kind of fear'—'tiresome', 'ridiculous' and always present. Men who had visited him a dozen times still avoided his eyes and misunderstood his intentions. Even his quiet, intelligent 'old friend' Tui, the most constant caller at Garagassi, betrayed a veiled but persistent uneasiness.

When he noticed that visitors always came armed, Maclay too exclusively connected this with their attitude to him. These men seldom went anywhere without the weapons that might be needed for hunting or a skirmish with traditional enemies. To its bearer, a spear or bow was as ordinary as his knife, comb or lime spatula, almost part of himself. To Maclay it signified fear or hostility, particularly when half-concealed. When a few men approached without weapons, he knew their well-armed friends were watching from the bushes.

Prepared for something, but for what? Though Maclay believed they feared him, he never forgot the mimed warnings of destruction, the 'insolence' in villages, the envious appraisal of his possessions. More than once, when visitors concluded that he carried no weapons, they tried to learn what was hidden in the house. They asked by signs whether he had spears and bows. If he had none, perhaps he would like some of theirs. Maclay answered with a laugh, and rejected the proffered weapons with all the scorn he could express. Contrary to the prudent white man's usual practice, he preferred not to demonstrate his gun just yet. Let them live in ignorance as long as possible.

Life at Garagassi was hard enough, without the need to be 'forever on one's guard'. The cramped hut, the upper halves of its walls filled in by canvas, had to be extended and protected by a veranda on two sides. The shaggy palm-leaf roof began to leak, and many hours were spent on unsuccessful repairs. The boat had to be rescued when it drifted on the reef, hauled ashore for scraping and painting, returned to the water. The garden involved days of back-breaking work, chopping through tangled masses of roots, constantly striking coral rock, before Maclay could plant the seeds that he did not expect to sprout.

Proud and fond of the first estate he had owned, he never grudged time and effort expended on his house and land. The boat allowed him to test and expand his physical powers, and to reflect on the one-sided European education that developed the mind but neglected the body. Just as he had left behind that unworthy self who in St Petersburg had been hungry every two hours, he was escaping the intellectual who in civilized surroundings depended on the muscles of others. Cuts and callouses from such labour were honourable scars, proof that he met the demands of this primitive life.

Heavy rain came more and more frequently, in crashing, blinding thunderstorms that tore the night apart. When water poured through the roof, Maclay rescued books and papers and spread a waterproof coat over his bunk. When wind put out his lamp too often, he stoically went to bed. Mildew ruined his clothes. Mosquitoes gave him no peace. Wasps attacked him, ants ate his butterfly collection, and dogs or sharks took the few birds he shot. Nature always compensated for the trials she inflicted and helped him to look upon his troubles with 'complete detachment'.

A series of earth tremors, some strong enough to jolt books from the shelves, stimulated curiosity and the sense of nature's power. The storms that plunged him into damp discomfort rewarded him by their grandeur. In the clear mornings the world seemed renewed, and Maclay wandered through the jungle entranced by the variety of sparkling foliage, the overnight growth of fantastic fungi and the brilliant insects that emerged to dry themselves and join his collection. On fine evenings he swung in a hammock under giant trees, admiring the moonlight, listening to the concert of frogs, insects and night birds accompanied by distant thunder. In his best moments he was lost in 'contemplation of the magnificent, mysteriously-fantastic surroundings'. His vilest mood could be cured by a sudden vision of beauty. When he stumbled and slid in darkness down the path to the stream, soaked by rain, chilled by wind, stabbed by the thorny bush he accidentally grasped, one flash of lightning restored his 'normally good state of mind'. He loved everything revealed in that ecstatic moment—waves breaking on the beach, individual leaves etched by a bluish light, even the thorn in his hand. Living in and for such beauty and illumination, he wanted nothing more.

He often wished for something less. To flourish, his natural serenity required not only beautiful surroundings but freedom from 'tiresome people'. And even here he had not escaped them. Troublesome people. Boring people. Sick people.

A fortnight after the corvette's departure, his hut had become 'a regular hospital', with all its inmates laid low together or by turns. Maclay hardly considered his own malaria an interruption to peaceful study of nature. The fever paroxysm, headache and pains in the back, days lost to weakness and lassitude—these were accepted as part of the life he had chosen. He counted on resilience and determination to drag his body upright and move his shaky legs. But he could not bear the illnesses of his servants. His plan of life had excluded the possibility that those engaged to save him drudgery might become dependent on him.

On most days, little remained of his satisfactory routine but a 5 a.m. rising, meteorological observations morning, noon and night, and the bedtime inspection of guns. When he could hardly move, he had to act as doctor and nurse to two sick men. While he hungered for his proper work, he found himself carrying water, chopping wood, cooking meals, a servant to servants.

He might have borne the drudgery and frustration had these men been capable of suffering quietly. But the 'delightful silence' that had reigned immediately after *Vityaz* left was a thing of the past. Olsen moaned as he shivered under his blanket or staggered about glassy-eyed. Boy emitted heart-rending groans or 'bellowed like a calf'. The 'concert' drove Maclay out of the light, airy veranda room where he had enjoyed the view of the sea or entertained the natives without coming down among them. The outdoors became his home. One tree in the clearing shaded his 'study'; another marked his 'dining-room'; a third space was set aside for 'receptions'. Though he still heard groans, these arrangements were satisfactory, even pleasant, in fine weather. At night and on rainy days there was no escape. Often, as he was falling asleep, groans from the other side of the canvas partition dragged him back to consciousness.

He blamed himself to some extent. He should not have settled under one roof with others, and would never do it again. He should have paid more attention to the young Polynesian's health before engaging him, for Boy confessed that the ominous cough had troubled him for years. Perhaps it had been a mistake to bring these cast-offs from Samoa. Perhaps it would have been a mistake to bring anybody. Maclay often thought how free and serene he would be without these useless servants who stole his time and strength and tied him to the house.

Alone, he would have avoided cooking, the domestic task that annoyed him most. Though the natives showed no inclination to provide for him, he imagined himself going to the village and allowing them to serve him taro and yams. Olsen and Boy barred the way to that solution. He even more bitterly resented them when he thought of the journeys he wished to make. Had he been alone, he would have left the house to itself and gone exploring, regardless of what the natives might do. At the same time, he dared not leave Garagassi in Olsen's hands. Olsen had no control over the natives, could not check them with a glance as Maclay did. And he was a coward through and through. Far from committing rash violence, he would surrender his master's property without a shot.

Rational or irrational, consistent or not, it added up to one thing: 'tied to these two individuals', Maclay could not be truly productive and happy. Early in December, he knew he would soon be free of one of them. Boy had hardly moved for more than a month. Some complication or new illness produced swellings of the lymphatic glands and an enormous abscess. His temperature remained high; his cough grew worse; he suffered abdominal pain. Week after week he lay in bed, eating next to nothing, rarely speaking, sometimes groaning, sometimes silenced by morphia. Just once more he managed to rise and stagger along the veranda. Maclay caught him as he was falling down the steps, and dragged him back to the room. Boy was too far gone to recognize his master.

Maclay still found it 'very unpleasant' to sense distrust and fear among his neighbours. He no longer encouraged them to stay and make themselves at home. He became bored, sitting in front of a crowd of men with whom he could not talk. Or he merely wished, for unspecified reasons, to be rid of them as quickly as possible. As the situation deteriorated, one of his most trying tasks was that of receiving 'uninvited, inquisitive and sometimes importunate visitors'.

The white man and those belonging to him must never appear to be sick. However wretched he felt, Maclay showed himself to the natives, did his best to create the impression that all was well. His efforts were frustrated from the start. Visitors never saw Olsen delirious or vomiting, but they surely heard him moaning in the hut. In the recent past they had seen him carrying wood and water, working on the house and boat or digging in the garden. He had learned some of their words, given them presents, played the mouth organ. Now they perhaps glimpsed a haggard creature sitting about listlessly, with swollen eyelids, lips and tongue. As for Boy, he had been six weeks out of sight, with only groans from the hut to prove he existed. Garagassi stank of death.

Tui raised the subject in his matter-of-fact way. Boy would die soon, he pointed out. Then Vil would die and Maclay would be left alone. Men would come from Bongu and Gumbu, he showed by gestures, in numbers expressed by all his fingers and toes. They would spear Maclay *here* in the throat, *here* in the stomach, and *here* in the chest. Then, it went without saying, the Bongu and Gumbu *tamo* would have his house and all it contained.

'O Maclay, O Maclay ...', Tui repeated in a melancholy sing-song, searching for something in Maclay's face. No longer able to pretend he did not understand, Maclay decided to treat this second warning as a joke. At the same time he tried to make it clear that nobody at Garagassi could possibly die. Tui looked slightly sceptical, and went on moaning, 'O Maclay, O Maclay ...'. A little later he asked again whether a ship would come. Maclay told him it would.

Garagassi had experienced false alarms. Olsen awakened his master one night, imagining he heard signals for attack, but Maclay identified the shrieks as the natives' greeting to the rising full moon. A few nights later he himself had been alerted by a commotion at the landing place, lights on the track from the beach. Olsen shouted, 'They're coming!' Maclay went out and found men near the house, all armed and carrying torches, calling his name. What did they want at midnight? Olsen thrust a gun into his hand, muttering 'Don't let them come any closer!' Maclay invited them to approach—six acquaintances, holding out gleaming fish. Olsen, who had been wanting fish for a long time, was suitably ashamed.

All the same, the villagers evidently discussed the 'old subject' of killing Maclay. Expecting the enemy every night, Olsen suggested leaving while there was time. Maclay planned to bury his notes and scientific equipment. The fishermen had shown how vulnerable Garagassi was to attack by sea. A landing party would remove or destroy the boat, the white men's only means of excape. No mines guarded that side, and the steps of the house faced the water.

Perhaps these thoughts helped to prompt an experiment Maclay made on the still, dark night of 7 December, when he noticed two lighted canoes off the cape. On a sudden inspiration, he lit one of the signal flares supplied by *Vityaz*, just to test the effect.

For half a minute a fierce blue aura surrounded Garagassi, driving night from the face of the sea. The fishermen threw away their torches. When the flare died down, the canoes had gone.

Maclay counted the demonstration 'very successful', bound to make a strong impression. The news was slow to reach some of those he wished to impress. Crowds of visitors came from Bongu. Fishing canoes again appeared off the cape at night. Through four days in which Maclay experienced nothing he wished to record, the events Tui predicted seemed to draw near. On 13 December Maclay began to prepare his notes, journals and sketches for burial, not at the appointed place—that was too far away—but under a marked tree at Garagassi. He decided to bury blank paper as well, in case he survived.

Though he resented Olsen's calling Tui a spy, Maclay himself was not immune to impressions. The removal of beard and moustache had revealed something unpleasant in Tui's face. And this morning Tui behaved like a spy. He inspected the house from all sides. Droning 'O

Boy, O Boy …', he tried to look into the servants' room. He importuned Maclay to let him take Boy to Gumbu, where the sick man would surely be cured.

Maclay put an end to this by going inside. Shaking with fever, he dared not lie down. He still had to cope with more of the same—men from Gorendu, asking whether Boy was alive, proposing to take him away to be cured. Unable to guess their motives, Maclay assumed they meant to use Boy against him.

No possible asset to the natives, Boy was a dangerous liability to Maclay. His protracted dying taught the whole neighbourhood that those at Garagassi could die. The white men could neither abandon him in his helplessness nor allow him to impede their escape. And he seemed as incapable of dying as of living. That evening he twice fell out of his bunk. In his master's arms he weighed no more than a child. Coldly sweating, writhing in pain from suspected peritonitis, he still grasped Maclay with terrible strength and tried to deliver an inaudible message.

Down on the beach, where Olsen was busy with the boat, Maclay announced that it was all up with Boy. This was no news to Olsen, but Maclay for once needed company in what he had to do. They found Boy writhing on the floor again, a pitiful sight, no longer to be borne.

In a hospital this bag of bones, with his weak, faltering pulse, white lips and cold extremities, might not have been considered fit for anaesthesia. Maclay poured chloroform on cotton wool and held it to the bloodless nose. By the time Maclay had convinced Olsen that digging a grave was too difficult and risky, superintended preparation of the boat, and helped gather stones to sink the body, Boy was certifiably dead.

While Boy lived, his fellow servant had said nothing but ill of him. Now Olsen professed to mourn, and solemnly spoke of God's will. Maclay found himself speaking softly, as though he could wake the dead. Often driven out of the house by groans, he now seemed to remember that Boy had suffered as silently as he died. But he wasted no time on talk or ceremony. He took it for granted that a servant's remains became the master's property. Against Olsen's protests, he prepared to obtain a Polynesian brain for science.

An annoying discovery. He had no container large enough to hold a human brain. While Olsen held a candle with one trembling hand and the cadaver's head with the other, Maclay removed part of the forehead and scalp. Then he fulfilled a promise given Professor Gegenbaur—to obtain a dark man's larynx, with tongue and related muscles.

When he cut through the nerves, the dead arm moved slightly. Olsen took fright and dropped the candle. The job was nevertheless successfully finished. The young Polynesian who had come to New Guinea only to die, more useful dead than alive, was packed for disposal.

Olsen tripped and fell on the descent to the beach, allowing the corpse to roll far down the sand. They had to search for it in darkness, lug it into the boat, fill the enshrouding sacks with stones and drag the whole weight out to launch it on an inconveniently low tide. Just as they shoved off, a procession of lighted canoes entered Port Konstantin.

Maclay thought of a festive party visiting Garagassi, or a war party about to attack. Quite simply, not all the flares of the Imperial Russian navy could keep the Gumbu men away from their grounds when the fishing was good. They paddled on serenely—eleven canoes, thirty-three men, with enough torches to reveal everything Maclay had to hide.

Olsen, a simple, ignorant man, easily imagined what other simple, ignorant men would think of Boy's scalped head and opened throat. Maclay thought it too late to jettison a hundredweight of stones and hide the body. As they crossed the path of the canoes, trying to row at full speed without making a sound, he assessed the odds. Thirty-three spears and bows against two revolvers. Twelve bullets would probably break the attack. Then let come what might. But the natives neither saw the boat nor meant to attack anything but fish. Maclay relaxed and admired the scene—the line of canoes, the long reflections of torches hardly wavering on a calm sea. His one regret was that he had not brought a dipper to collect plankton.

With a kind thought for the sharks, they pushed the body overboard and rowed home leisurely. The fishermen had moved away. At Garagassi all was peace. While Olsen made tea, Maclay recorded the day's events. He could not repress all pride. Despite mishaps and the unforeseen, he had managed well. In emergency he had converted a liability into a scientific asset. Cheerful and comfortable, he marvelled at the speed with which one mood replaces another.

Olsen was cheerful, too, as he served the tea. He had done everything required, and in shared danger and labour become almost friendly with his master. Now he would live like Maclay's equal, in a quiet room of his own. Much as he feared death in New Guinea, he had one comfort. As a European, he was not interesting. His master would never cut him up.

Early English settlers in America had been warned that any death among them must be hidden from the natives. Almost three centuries later, the same rule applied in New Guinea. In case visitors looked inside, Olsen had to keep his room exactly as it had been when shared with Boy. If he talked to them, he must avoid mentioning his late companion. Maclay's policy stood several tests in the next few days, when a succession of visitors raised the subject he wished to forget.

The cabin at Garagassi, Port Konstantin, New Guinea, 1872

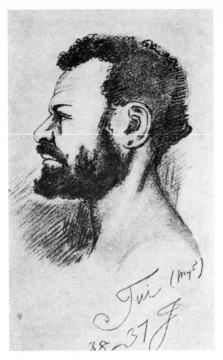

Tui of Gorendu, Maclay's first
acquaintance in New Guinea

Kain of Bilbil Island

Tui came first, with a party including a stranger who stood high in the medical world. If Maclay let Boy go to Gumbu, Tui insisted, this practitioner would effect a cure. Maclay inscrutably repulsed all arguments. He did not like this individual from Gumbu. Drinking his morning tea, he decided it was time for another 'test of impression-ability'.

Behind his half-wall, he poured a little alcohol into the saucer, which he placed where the visitors could see. After demonstratively sipping water, he added some to the saucer. Then he lit the alcohol.

The visitors jumped back, wide-eyed and open-mouthed. When Maclay completed the demonstration by splashing fire towards them, on to the steps and ground, they left in a hurry.

By all the rules, he should have been rid of them for a long time. Instead they returned with a crowd of highly-decorated sightseers, and Tui begged Maclay to show everyone how he burned water. The second demonstration went as well as the first. Most of the newcomers fled. The rest stood immobilized by fear, imploring Maclay not to burn the sea.

When they calmed down, he acquired a new function. Some of them had suppurating wounds, to be disinfected and bandaged, or fly-blown sores to be cleared of maggots. Next day there were more patients, with fever, sores, rheumatism. Since they distrusted all unfamiliar substances, and refused to take anything internally, Maclay could do little for their ailments. He nevertheless gave the attention that helped win trust and encouraged dependence. They were pathetically grateful. Maclay was the medicine man now.

With all the excitement and magic, his neighbours refused to forget. Three days later they were back, asking after Boy. 'No Boy', Maclay tried to explain, 'Boy's not here'. Then they naturally wanted to know where he had gone, an appalling question for one who loathed falsehood but dared not tell the truth.

Not knowing how these people disposed of the dead, Maclay avoided pointing to the earth or sea. He waved his hand towards a region somewhere above the horizon. The questioners seemed to conclude that Boy had 'flown away', and within a few days this theory completed itself. All the villagers thought that Maclay's magic had sent Boy far, far across the sea, to mysterious Russia. Astonished and amused by their simplicity, Maclay never knew their language well enough to ascertain exactly what they believed or to correct such helpful errors.

In all his reading of travel literature, no story had impressed him more than George Keate's romanticized account of events in the Palau Islands, where the noblest savages had treated ordinary English seamen as gods. Yet he drew no discernible inspiration from evidence that primitives frequently made such mistakes. He had detected no religious overtones in the ceremonial delivery of gifts to *Vityaz*, never joined in the officers' theorizing. When he provided, within that single fortnight, an eerie, unprecedented illumination, the miraculous ignition of water, and the mysterious flight of a sick man to a distant country, there were reasons of science or expediency. He meant to test the Papuans' psychological reactions, or to conceal his servant's death, never to pose as anything more than man. Nobody could be more surprised than he, when it dawned on him that his neighbours took him for 'some kind of supernatural being'.

5: Prospero's Island

As the hands of his watch came together on the hour, Maclay raised his double-barrelled revolver. He welcomed 1872 with twelve solemn shots, drank a toast in coconut milk to family and friends, and went to sleep.

He ran no risk of disturbing the neighbours—New Year came in with thunderstorms and torrents of rain—but perhaps this celebration seemed rather juvenile. He later preferred to forget it. If he chose this traditional time to review his actions, he had little else with which to reproach himself. He sometimes let his den become untidy, an unavoidable failing in such cramped quarters. Through days of fever and weakness, he could not maintain his routine. He often feared his mind might prove unequal to the problems presented by nature and man in New Guinea. Otherwise he felt content with his chosen life and the way he met its challenges.

He still checked the guns at night, still went to the door, ill as he was, to show himself to the natives. Olsen was useless in these circumstances. No matter how roughly he spoke, the Papuans acted too familiarly with him. They feared only Maclay, who was always kind and patient. Only Maclay had the eye that subdued.

For his part, Maclay noticed how quickly he had become accustomed to constant danger. 'Indifference to life', or simple fatalism, dispelled any shadow of fear. Stoic fortitude overcame sickness, hunger, hard labour. Nature repaid him for everything, filling the most ordinary day with beauty and stimulation.

He often thought he had been wise to settle well away from villages. In silence and solitude he attained the deep peace that he came to equate with happiness. While he welcomed the lightning flash, he gladly embraced the routine of observing the temperature of water, air and

73

soil, barometric pressure, the heights of tides, wind strength and direction and rates of evaporation. He collected on the reef or wandered in the rain forest admiring the endless variety of vegetation. In the evenings he relaxed in his hammock, listening to jungle sounds, or sat on a tree overhanging the water, watching the waves and the luminous movements of a myriad living things. Studies at the microscope, preservation of specimens, writing up his notes and journals—everything fell into a soothing, strengthening pattern that never became stale.

After nights of fever and storm, his ears ringing from heavy doses of quinine, he followed the alternation of sunshine and shadow over sea and jungle, finding all things peaceful, all things good. Millions, no doubt, shared his belief in perfect peace as ultimate happiness. He alone was living it. Lost in contemplation, he almost escaped the deceptive world of individuality. The true Self of which the Indian sages taught reached out to the Eternal All.

These were the best days, when 'noisy people did not interrupt—nobody came'. All the same, the visitors were the reason for his presence. Upon their unpredictable arrival, he gave all his attention to the natives.

The externals of Papuans, in all their variety, had become almost as familiar as his own. He had seen dark brown skins and skins as light as those of Samoans, youngsters of quite 'African' type and men with comparatively thin lips and great hooked noses. He knew the thickness of fingernails and the dexterity of toes, the breadth of the foot and the frequency of use for right hand and left. He had compared the well-developed leg muscles of mountain dwellers with the thin calves of islanders who spent much of their lives in canoes. He could correct those writers who ascribed to Papuan skins a roughness sufficient to form a racial characteristic. He had investigated the texture of Papuan hair, knew how much its 'typical' appearance owed to teasing and combing, and could refute the belief that it grew in small separate tufts. In this department, his great disappointment was that the natives' suspicion of any physical manipulation still made it impossible to measure heads.

The nearest approach to a 'general type' among his neighbours did not meet his standards of beauty. This people who made an art form of the human body nevertheless provided many memorable images. He would not forget the gala travellers from the offshore islands, or Tui's eldest son, balancing bow in hand on a canoe platform, with hibiscus flowers in his hair and long, coloured leaves fluttering from girdle and armbands. In the midst of crisis he had admired the dramatic crowd around his hut—men from distant Karkar Island whose black-smeared faces and bodies contrasted powerfully with the flaring red of their Bongu hosts. Painted faces, waving plumes, coronets of flowers and streamers of leaves, high decorated combs, ornaments of boar tusks, dog teeth, shell and bone—at times a pageant swirled around him, the human counterpart of this magnificent land, savage, proud, completely male. Since the Gumbu women ran away, he had not seen a woman.

He realized that the tension in the villages was connected with the women's flight. Papuan men seemed inordinately jealous of their females, an attitude he explained by their knowing 'no pleasure other than sexual'. Or perhaps he represented some less commonplace menace. Whatever the reason, the men received him sullenly, with weapons in their hands. He had never seen a village in its normal state, never spent an hour watching its ordinary activities. At times it seemed impossible to overcome 'the mistrusting nature of this race'.

Patience. Non-interference. Without leaving Garagassi, he was acquiring a working knowledge of one dialect and beginning to realize that there were others. Tui had given him an account of local geography, amazing him by the detail in which the inhabitants named every natural feature. He had seen visitors making cigars of native tobacco, plaiting bracelets and decorating lime-tubes. He had noted their minimal greetings, their favourite postures and their mania for plucking every grey hair from the head. Sitting by the shore in his own domain, he had watched Tui skilfully catching fish with his toes. Tui and a friend had staged a mock fight with bows and spears, and others had demonstrated, less successfully, a native method of counting. The villages could wait.

Gorendu reminded him of itself by loud drumming at full moon. Almost-inhuman howls—Papuan singing—sometimes mingled with his fever until he could not tell the music from the illness. But after one hallucinatory experience, when in 'a kind of deadful dream' he had almost collapsed on the track, he did not try to witness the festivities. He visited this 'clean, green and pleasant' place only to get coconuts, and left when he saw that his presence was burdensome.

The situation had nevertheless improved. It had occurred to him that mistrustful people who spent most of their time outdoors might regard his sudden, silent arrival as an attempt at spying or surprise. He found that by blowing a whistle as he approached, then waiting a few minutes outside the village, he had a better reception. The women and children made a quiet departure. The men met him unarmed and soon resumed their ordinary activities. He still sensed uneasiness, anxiety for him to leave, but elementary consideration did much to relieve the strain.

His second visit to the larger community of Bongu, three months after its bowmen had greeted him with arrows, made a very formal occasion. When he arrived by boat with Olsen, villagers were waiting waist-deep in the sea to carry him ashore. He was led from one club-house to another, greeted at each by a group of men in all their finery. After distributing gifts, including some for the absent women, he was able to inspect the village at his leisure.

Bongu made a good impression—solid, comfortable, pleasant enough even under drizzling rain. And it offered special attractions. Maclay paid less stately visits over the next few weeks, to copy drawings found on the rear wall of one 'men's house', and to sketch the carven figures that his hosts called *telum*, the first large examples of art he had seen in New Guinea.

The company of Tui and other Gorendu men smoothed his way. Instead of running into the jungle, the Bongu women hid in the huts. He could barter for fish and bananas, stroll about as he pleased. Tui was equally helpful in Gumbu, where one lucky day Maclay obtained six well-preserved skulls to compensate for those lost to *tamo-Russ* in other villages. In every way the Gorendu connection proved its worth. By discounting those days when Tui's behaviour seemed suspect, Maclay had found the white man's essential helper, the faithful, trusting native whose knowledge and influence made this strange world manageable.

He was therefore doubly disturbed when a Gorendu man stole a knife from Garagassi. He could not afford to ignore this first theft. Any attempt to obtain restitution and prevent further pilfering carried a risk of falling out with Gorendu. Then Tui accidentally came to the rescue, by standing in the wrong place while felling a tree. Badly wounded in the head, he called the doctor.

At one stroke, Maclay could help a valued friend, prove his general good will, and deal with the theft. He gave preliminary treatment, then mentioned the stolen knife. While he went home for more equipment, the villagers settled things in their own way. The knife was handed over at the first request.

Maclay was never again troubled by theft. For weeks he struggled with a bad patient. Tui grew bored and lonely in the hut, needed fresh air and sunshine, talk and activity. Maclay had to follow the patient to the gardens and hunt him home. He applied poultices for hours on end, visited Gorendu twice in a day, dragged himself there when almost too ill to move. He could not breathe freely until linseed poultices, or basic toughness, had pulled Tui out of danger.

Tui was no useless servant but a personal friend, an essential key to the general friendship. And visits to Gorendu brought many rewards. Maclay inspected the gardens, admiring sturdy fences formed from branches and growing sugar cane, well-cultivated raised beds separated by neat paths, flourishing plots of sweet potatoes, sugar cane and tobacco. He watched the villagers at their meals, marvelling at the amount of vegetable food they had to consume just to maintain life. He saw them preparing *kéu*, a drink he thought the same as the Polynesian *kava*, not previously known to be used in New Guinea.

The great progress came early in these medical visits, when Tui mentioned the warning whistle that sent the women into hiding. It was wrong for them to run away like that, he suggested. Maclay was a good man, of whom nobody need be afraid. He was enlarging on this when a woman's voice interrupted, and Maclay saw his first Papuan female at close quarters.

Tui's wife was old, hideous, with flat, pendulous breasts and wrinkles all over her body. She had a good-natured smile, and to Maclay she seemed the most important person in the world. When he pressed her hand, to noises of approval from the men, all the women and girls appeared as if at a signal, bringing gifts for Maclay. In a matter of minutes, with grace and humour, the village shook off the tension and inconvenience of months.

Maclay inspected the Gorendu women, some of them quite pretty and well-rounded, while they did the same by him. He watched their work in the gardens, concluding that economic as well as sexual services made Papuan women 'more necessary' than those of Europe. Above all, he felt he had won the natives' complete trust. He celebrated by digging up the notes and journals he had buried in expectation of being killed.

He refused invitations to live in Gorendu. There was no disputing his friends' statement that his roof was in a bad way—the moon shone through the thatch. It was equally true that the large trees shading Garagassi might fall and kill him. One of them had come down, with a fearful crash in the night, narrowly missing the hut. But he valued quiet and solitude too much to accept the new, safe house Gorendu promised. He preferred not to mix in village affairs. Ideally he would remain the lone spectator, observing without taking part in events. Distance preserved the sense of his uniqueness, a certain mystery surrounding his ways. Besides, the Gorendu and Bongu men were always a little too proprietorial when displaying him to visitors. When he wished to find out how to reach mountain villages, his neighbours evaded his questions. They did not want him to know other communities, he concluded. They were trying to own him.

This impression was confirmed when he decided to visit Koliku-mana, his first excursion away from the coast. Reconnaissance by sea had shown him smoke-columns marking villages in the hills, but he had no intention of tackling the paths alone. Overnight, the promised Gorendu guides had 'forgotten' him and gone elsewhere.

They must not make a fool of him. He whipped out his compass and announced that it would show the way. The villagers stepped back from the magic needle. With a display of self-sufficiency he strode off, hoping to have better luck in Bongu.

Within a few minutes two Gorendu men caught up, trying to

dissuade him from the journey. When they had turned back, another man appeared, ready to take Maclay to Koliku. Another quarter of an hour and the first pair were again shouting behind, eager to visit the mountains. Some change of mind had occurred—desire to keep faith with him, fear of his anger, a feeling that if his trip could not be prevented it should be supervised. Maclay met their shuffling with the indifference that kept him master of every situation.

The walk proved how much he needed company. On to the beach by a ladder of roots, in and out of the jungle, across streams, down to the floor of a deep ravine and up the other side—the track hardly kept the same direction for five minutes. For the first time he crossed an area of head-high grass, realizing how nearly impossible this would be without guidance. By the time he set foot on the steep black path leading up the bare ridge to Koliku, he felt he had ventured to the interior.

Koliku had not expected him so soon. He was received by two men, a boy and a very ugly old woman. But the Gorendu men set to work as though impressing multitudes, extolling his character and powers and the wonderful things he owned. Any possessiveness flavouring the praise was lost on him.

Apart from its setting, this first upland community offered nothing very different from the coastal villages four or five kilometres away. The excitement came from the narrow path leading up the range, the view of mountains stretching into the real interior. Some day he would take such a path and conquer the ranges one by one, to reveal the heart of the island. But not yet. First he must visit mountain villages his new friends had pointed out. He had standing invitations to coastal communities and islands to the north. And when he reached home, after a bout of fever on the way, he was almost immediately confronted by crisis.

He saw no reason to doubt that men from the mountain village of Maragum-mana had attacked Gorendu and killed several people. For weeks Gorendu had kept weapons ready for such an emergency. In Gumbu, where he happened to be visiting, they seemed to believe the news, beating the great wooden slit gong, bringing out their weapons. The enemy was supposed to have gone to Bongu. Then the mountain men would descend upon Gumbu and Garagassi.

Maclay hurried home and prepared the guns. Admitting the possibility of defeat, he allowed Olsen to ready the boat for escape. He did not intend to stand guard. While the agitated Olsen kept watch, Maclay stretched out and enjoyed his almost-superhuman powers of sleep.

He nevertheless heard the approaching noise before he was called. He directed the barricading of the entrance, stationed himself on the veranda with the armoury within reach and Olsen behind to load the guns. He was first to sight figures among the trees, first to notice they were armed with bananas and coconuts. They had come to tell him it was all an absurd mistake.

All the same, strangers seen that morning could have come from Maragum-mana. Bongu and Gorendu continued to fear attack. When Maclay's neighbours praised his preparations, they asked that in case of need the women and children should be given protection at Garagassi.

Dozens of frightened women and children in a flimsy, flammable little hut—the idea invited disaster. Yet Maclay could not reject his friends' pathetic faith. To confirm his ability to defend them, he demonstrated the power of firearms.

There was nothing to shoot, and the connection between loud noise and possible death was often obscure to people whose weapons killed silently. Maclay's occasional shots at birds had almost certainly been heard in the nearest village. The Bongu men nevertheless clapped their hands to their ears and looked ready to run. They begged Maclay to hide the gun and fire it only against the men from Maragum. But they wanted to handle it. Maclay said *'Tabu!'* so many times that the new word for prohibition became the local name for a gun.

At last they had some idea of his weapons. Next day visitors came from Gumbu, with Tui and representatives of Koliku. They made no bones about what they wanted—an attack on Maragum, with Maclay to direct operations and use his *tabu*. They predicted that the first news of his approach would make the Maragum people take to their heels.

Maclay betrayed no suspicion that the panic might have been stage-managed to this end. Nor did he noticeably question the morality of attacking people who had done him no harm. He rejected the proposal because mixing in their quarrels could bring him nothing but trouble, because these 'capers' threatened his tranquillity. Far from being flattered by this 'widespread notion' of his power, he found it distasteful. As time went on, however, he began to feel that his reputation was an asset to his neighbours. In the end he believed that only fear of Maclay had prevented an attack from Maragum.

His friends did not seem upset by being denied their preventive war. That night a feast began at Gorendu, attended by most of the men from neighbouring villages. For more than twenty-four hours, Gorendu, Bongu and Gumbu lay helplessly open to attack.

Invited to his first Papuan feast at half-past four in the morning, Maclay was too enthralled to think of defence. He was witnessing 'the life of savages at their most primitive', the wild harmony of nature and man that repaid a traveller for hardship. In a clearing by the shore, he observed the poetry of muscular, decorated bodies in every possible attitude and grouping, in a setting of dawnlight, firelight, sea and jungle. When he went home, with a huge basket of food, and a violent headache caused by Papuan music, he had collected all the details of festive food preparation, cooking and eating utensils, procedure and etiquette. He was familiar with the instruments whose 'excruciating sounds' reached Garagassi at night and with the sight of his friends stupefied by *kéu*. He had sensed the ritual nature of this male feast, in a place from which women were strictly excluded. He never suspected it might have political significance.

The feast was nominally Tui's, perhaps the first sign that this unassuming man was becoming a power in the land. With fewer than thirty adult inhabitants, Gorendu had no individual of outstanding wealth and prestige to give feasts, organize economic and religious life and impress friends and enemies. Tui had only one old wife and one grown son, no large network of helpful connections, no crowd of followers to sit before his hut and rush to do his bidding. He must have needed much help from Bongu and Gumbu before he led the procession carrying festive supplies, called each man for his share of pork and farewelled the guests with baskets of food. By the old standards, he had nothing to make him eminent. But he seemed to have Maclay, whose presence changed everything.

The first to meet this strange, powerful being, Tui was the most frequent visitor at Garagassi, the only one who sometimes ascended to Maclay's veranda. He had actually received permission to spend the night there once, though silence and isolation had soon driven him home. He was Maclay's favoured companion on excursions. He taught Maclay words and the names of places, and learned the names of distant, unknown places that Maclay pointed out on a large drawing. When Tui was ill Maclay had come at his call, and shown more concern for Tui than for himself. It was Tui's little boy whom Maclay wished to take away, perhaps to Russia. At this rate, Tui might share the secrets of Maclay's magic. It was fitting that the principal mediator between the villages and the power of Garagassi should become a leader, expressing his status in the only way he understood. It seemed equally fitting that Tui should be called 'Maclay' and Maclay addressed as 'Tui'.

Maclay had been interested to find the custom of name-exchange practised in New Guinea. He appreciated the esteem inherent in the explanation—that since the healing of his wound Tui would do anything for Maclay; that they two, almost close enough to be regarded as one, should bear each other's names. He had not authorized this and never would. With proposals for an aggressive alliance fresh in mind, he could not relish the implication that he should be ready to do whatever Tui wanted. He had made it clear that Tui was not Maclay, that the name of Maclay must never be applied to any other.

Tui had had his moment, when he called, 'Maclay *tamo-Russ!*', and presented Maclay's share of pork. Next day he hung the empty basket on a tree at Garagassi, explaining that if anyone asked about it Maclay must reply, 'Pork and yams from Tui of Gorendu'. He pressed no claim to be called 'Maclay'. But his friends had shown surprise and resentment at this prohibition. Talk of war went on until Maclay almost wished the enemy would come. He showed his opinion of the war scare by sailing with Olsen for the island of Bilbil, the sanctuary the white men spoke of when they discussed escape.

When they reached it, rowing, after a sleepless night, the place repaid them. It was magically beautiful, a dream of a South Seas island, with magnificent views of the mainland coast and ranges. A crowd of men greeted Maclay with extravagant joy, competing for the honour of helping to beach the boat, thronging round to escort him into the village. With the help of Kain, a highly influential person who had visited Garagassi, he quite easily persuaded the Bilbil men that their women need not remain in hiding.

Strolling about the island, he realized that this community could give him months of profitable study. Its houses were more elaborate, its carvings more numerous and varied than those of his mainland neighbours. It was a centre for canoe-building, and made enormous quantities of pots, which its seafarers distributed along the coast. Its lively people seemed easier in their manners than the suspicious folk of Gorendu and Bongu. When he took a walk they did not ask where he was going or why. Nobody ran after him to watch. He was noticing something he might have observed in Europe, the psychological difference between small peasant communities and a relative metropolis, devoted to manufactures and trade.

Maclay foresaw difficulties, even as he felt 'at home'. There were too many people, or too little space. It might be unsuitable for a man who needed quiet and a certain distance between himself and others. Besides, the island had not much cultivable land. As well as making all those pots, the women tended gardens on the mainland, sometimes staying there overnight. Despite this kind of overseas agricultural colony, food supplies depended largely on the yield of trading voyages. This tight little island might soon resent extra mouths.

When he lightly suggested that he would live there, he detected a false note in his hosts' enthusiasm. Of course they longed for him to come. They told him many times that Bilbil was much better than Bongu and Gorendu. But when rain forced him to stay overnight nobody offered a hut or a place in the men's house.

Maclay imperturbably sheltered on the covered platform of Kain's canoe, a seagoing house that accommodated six or seven men comfortably in any weather. He was no more put out when his hosts' faces betrayed the wish that he should leave. He often felt like that himself. As soon as a breeze came up he gave the signal, and thirty men put the boat in the water as willingly as they had hauled it out.

He did not abandon all idea of living on Bilbil. The island had several nooks suitable for his house. Though the language differed greatly from that of his neighbours, he need not start again from nothing, and many islanders spoke the Bongu tongue. If he lived among them, these urbane, courteous people would take his presence for granted. Ambitious Bilbil parents already understood that they must not name their children 'Maclay'. Admirers would learn that he wanted no such tribute as the unfortunate dog that had been smashed against a tree and laid at his feet. As for food, when his trade goods gave out—as they soon must among such a crowd—he might draw on other resources. The islanders' sores cried out for ointment.

Having travelled halfway round the world to experience the primitive, he was tempted by a place where personal life faintly resembled the privacy and anonymity of European cities. Bilbil promised to be valuable even if he never made it his home. His 'good friend' Kain was a real force in the region, a leader whose prestige rested securely on ability and wealth. Maclay foresaw the time when Kain's twelve-metre sailing canoe would take him exploring along the whole coast, while Bilbil linguists helped him contact people throughout their trading sphere.

Meanwhile he had business in the mountains, perhaps beyond the gaps he had sighted from the sea. And he was truly attached to Garagassi. Approaching the cape, he felt the pleasure of home-coming. He hastened to see how the house had fared, unguarded for almost two days.

The Papuan-style door fastenings of poles, rope and palm leaves were untouched. Apparently his cabin might have stood like that for weeks. The neighbours had imagined he was visiting Russia.

Even before establishing satisfactory relations with the natives, Maclay had thought of staying in New Guinea, 'never returning to Europe'. There were precedents—naturalists disgusted by civilization or European politics, who settled in the South American jungle or wandered the South Seas with no intention of going back. Nowhere in Europe had he known such beauty and solitude, peace and freedom. He felt more at home every day. When he followed a path in the dark, without suffering bruises or lacerations, or pounced on a crab and ate it raw, he imagined himself becoming 'a little bit Papuan'.

The single great impediment was sickness. 'Not the natives, not the tropical heat, not the dense forests' repelled intruders from New Guinea. Before he could make the island his home, he must reckon with the 'pale, cold, shivering then burning fever'.

The gender of the Russian word for 'fever' is feminine. But in English Maclay still thought of malaria as a merciless female. She was on the watch for him at dawn. Her talons closed on him in the heat of noon and in the day's last glimmer. Chill, stormy nights and soft, moonlit evenings were all the same to her, and precautions never saved him from her fury. She sent the giddiness, the leaden feeling, the shivering fits and 'dry, endless heat'. She persecuted him with monstrous images and processions of sad visions that dissolved in a kaleidoscopic dance. She tricked his perceptions, making his body grow until it threatened to fill the room, thickening his fingers until they equalled his arms, enlarging his head until it almost touched the roof. Harpy, fury, vampire, she attacked him five and six days in a row, two and three times in a day, tearing his life to pieces, leaving him too weak to sit in his chair or hold a book.

With no idea what went on in his bloodstream—it would be years before men in Europe studied the right microscope slides—he might as well symbolize fever by the consuming female. His more precise explanations were no more real. He had stayed too long outside in the evening. A wind had chilled him when his legs were wet. Some physiological shock had occurred when he passed from blazing sunshine to cool, moist shade. Just as he imagined his European or North African fever abandoned in Europe and his Chilean fever left aboard *Vityaz*, he saw each bout of malaria in New Guinea as an isolated event. At the same time, he could not always distinguish between fever and the effects of 'almost eating' quinine. But he did not blame his weakness entirely on fever. He had not eaten the raw crab to prove his New Guinea manhood. He was hungry.

Always convinced that he must live on local foods, he had made only minimal provison for three months. The sugar had lasted less than six weeks. After a long battle with grubs, the stock of biscuit had been thrown out. Though Maclay never touched it—the mere thought disgusted him—Nazimov's canned meat and fish had quickly disappeared. The simplicity and monotony of meals—rice and curry for breakfast, beans and a little dried beef for dinner—had rather pleased Maclay. But he never regarded dried beef as real meat. When he first noted the decline in his physical powers, he had attributed it to three months of vegetable diet. Now nothing remained of the imported stores but tea and a small daily ration of rice and beans, consumed without salt.

The pork he had expected to be plentiful turned out to be a rare and solemn privilege to Papuans. Dog meat, far less palatable, was just as scarce. Fowls seemed to be kept only for plumage, and Maclay tasted neither their flesh nor their eggs. Once or twice the natives provided fish. They had no idea of bringing a regular supply.

After three months at Garagassi, Maclay had still imagined the problem of animal food would be solved once relations with the neighbours allowed him to hunt. When he did go out with his gun, he experienced all the disadvantages of the Australian faunal region without its benefits. Wild mammals in this thickly-populated district were few, small and nearly all nocturnal. He knew most of them only as a squeak and scuttle in the dark.

The delightfully ignorant birds improved his diet and eked out his trade goods with plumes to give the natives. Yet some days there seemed to be none, and though he gladly ate anything with feathers he had to weigh the cost in shot against the unreliable gains. His garden grew nothing but coconut palms that would not bear for about six years. The natives' gifts of vegetables could never be relied upon, and in any case he tried to avoid dependence. He was not Papuan enough to eat reptiles and insects or confident enough to persevere with fishing. His strength was failing. His teeth and gums became sore from chewing sugar cane to sweeten the tea. He began to dream about food.

As long as no ship dropped in, the question about leaving New Guinea remained theoretical. He assumed that some vessel must appear, with a captain willing and able to give him supplies. One thing certain was that if he stayed he would be alone. The first ship, whatever its destination, would take away his servant Olsen.

Unless there had been something wrong with Olsen, he probably would not have been available at Apia. He showed none of the vices expected of a white drifter in the South Seas. He neither complained of lack of alcohol nor broke into the medical supplies. He did not steal, or offend by dirty habits, bad language or boisterous behaviour. Though he regretted not seeing the women during the first visit to Bongu, he never caused trouble by chasing native females.

Olsen recognized his own inferiority. His faith in his employer's knowledge was sometimes absurd, as when he asked Maclay whether there would be another earthquake. When attack seemed imminent, he begged to be told what to do, sure that without Maclay's instructions he would be helpless. At the height of crisis, he remembered to call Maclay 'master'.

Yet they would never get on together. The qualities that might have made Olsen an acceptable member of some mediocre European community were hopelessly inadequate here. Maclay's basic problem was that of all heroic adventurers: any assistant must be totally devoted and subordinate, yet equal to him in courage, intelligence and endurance.

Olsen never approached that standard. He was, or had been, capable of great physical effort. There were intermissions in his cowardice, since he could be left alone to receive the natives' gifts in Bongu or to guard the boat while Maclay explored Bilbil. He was not entirely a fool; he and Maclay sometimes had the same idea at the same time. But in general Maclay regarded him as cowardly, stupid, lazy and dependent.

Once 'cheerful and obliging', Olsen had become irritable and querulous, constantly complaining, shirking his work. He was always hungry, without the decency to keep quiet about it. He was always ill, shameless in his fear of death. When Maclay found Olsen 'ready to collapse as soon as he felt slightly off colour', he naturally suspected sham. There was no simple devotion to compensate for faults. When Olsen flung himself down, sobbing, at Maclay's bedside, imagining his master about to die, Maclay knew the man was thinking of his own subsequent fate.

As Maclay's character strengthened and expanded, Olsen's deteriorated. He had no sustaining self-image, no store of knowledge and interests to help him forget his troubles. Except when ordered to hold the head of Boy's corpse, he took no part in scientific work. He was not permitted to join Maclay's excursions by land, go hunting or fishing, or visit the villages on his own account. He sometimes came to life, as when he handled the boat or helped remove a fallen tree from the stream. His usual work, when he was on his legs, consisted of cooking and washing, carrying fuel and water, with such diversions as sorting out grub-riddled beans or airing Maclay's mildewed clothes. No wonder he was bored.

On top of that, he was disappointed. His master had not promised to make him governor of an island, but Olsen had somehow expected to better himself. His deterioration had become apparent when he decided there was nothing to be gained here.

It became more obvious as he learned how he must exist. Perhaps sociable, perhaps merely weak, he could not live without talk. Egotistical and ignorant, he had limited subjects of conversation. At first he had bored Maclay with 'endless anecdotes about his past life'. But not any more. Maclay found it difficult to tolerate chatterers at any time. He refused to have his time in New Guinea wasted, a precious experience ruined, by 'society' that he felt as an intrusion. Three months after their arrival, the only known European residents of mainland New Guinea hardly spoke to each other, and never took meals together.

Olsen tried talking to himself. Maclay still had to hear monologues about sickness, starvation and the danger of native attack. He pointed out that he had not asked Olsen to come to New Guinea—literally true, since Consul Weber in Samoa had done the asking. He gave reminders of that moment beside the flagpole, when the man had been offered a chance to leave with *Vityaz*. When he made Olsen aware of his contempt and resentment, he never imagined that such a creature might hate in return. Not even when Olsen let him lie five days ill without offering him anything to eat.

That was just an aspect of Olsen's uselessness. His usefulness was more subtle. Maclay took scientific interest in observing the effects of such living conditions upon a European. Olsen's presence made it possible to compare reactions.

Olsen had grumbled when the sugar ran out. Maclay, though he later found sugarless tea unacceptable, had not felt the change at first. The way Olsen tore into a piece of meat, when he could get it, confirmed the carnivorous nature of man and the sustaining quality of Maclay's detachment. Day in, day out, Maclay's busy contentment contrasted with Olsen's fretful listlessness. The contrast was never more marked than in their response to solitude. Maclay found human society 'almost superfluous'. Olsen needed it desperately. The man who achieved his ambition remained active and serene. The disappointed man became peevish and indolent. The silent man thrived on silence. The talkative man, deprived of talk, began to disintegrate.

In facing the possibility of attack, Maclay's calm had always shown up clearly beside Olsen's trembling terror. With friendly relations established, Olsen still feared the natives. But he raised no more false alarms. He spent days and nights alone at Garagassi without causing specific annoyance. Among the Papuans he seemed solid and responsible, neither becoming rattled nor giving them offence. The worst to be said was that he lacked the sense of privilege. To Maclay, any gift from Papuans was sacred, a bond uniting them to him. Olsen criticized tough fish and green bananas as though they had come from Europeans.

Maclay always noticed how the Papuans differentiated between the two white men. When gifts of different meats were sent, the pork was for Maclay; Olsen got dog flesh. Tui might sit with Olsen in the kitchen, but only while waiting for Maclay. The demonstrative welcome at Bilbil had been for Maclay, not Olsen, and nobody wanted to name children 'Vil'. When Maclay noticed that the natives thought him a 'supernatural being', he had realized they only 'to some extent' ascribed that status to his servant.

That did not mean they expected nothing of Olsen. When Maclay sailed away from a village, Olsen, at the tiller, had to shout the farewell 'E aba! E meme!'—'Goodbye brothers! Goodbye fathers!' Never called upon to burn water or lead a military expedition, Olsen was sometimes asked for a tune on the mouth-organ, or a Swedish song. As the fame of Maclay's magic spread through the country, so did that of the mouth-organ.

The 'music' lacerated Maclay's ears. But he himself tried to fulfil the natives' requests. He must allow his servant to do the same. For the general safely, it was best that on his own level Olsen got along with them fairly well. Maclay showed no curiosity about what happened at Garagassi during his absence, or what Olsen might experience when left alone in a village. For him, at such times, his servant ceased to exist.

Gorendu village, Maclay Coast, New Guinea, February 1872

Gumbu village, Maclay Coast, February 1872

The men's house in the mountain village of Tengum-mana,
Maclay Coast, 1872

Astrolabe Bay, looking south from Bogadjim

A Bilbil *vang*

The commemorative plaque at Garagassi

In his seventh month in New Guinea, he received notice that Olsen's loneliness, and the neighbours' idea of him as a lesser being than Maclay, might endanger correct relations. Since Tui's first unsuccessful attempts to spy or to prove his trust, no Papuan had set foot in the house or thought of staying overnight. Now, after a trip to the mountains, Maclay found the magical barrier broken. Tui had stayed at Garagassi, to keep Olsen company.

It never happened again, at least not to Maclay's knowledge. In fact Olsen had little chance to establish over-close relations with Papuans. Maclay stayed two or three times in nearby villages. He recorded only one more expedition to the mountains.

Illness and weakness restricted his movements. So did his neighbours' reluctance to help. He would happily have gone alone, with his lightest blanket and the old rucksack used on student rambles in Germany and Switzerland. Instead, he needed guides on the capricious paths, interpreters to introduce him in new places. Obtaining them involved tedious negotiations, particularly since the coast villages were at odds with some mountain communities. The guides grumbled at being required to carry his small table and folding chair and other items of white man's equipment. Though he invariably travelled with more followers than he wanted, the youths who came along to protect their friends, or for the fun of it, were decorative rather than useful. They entertained and informed. They carried nothing but their weapons.

Bongu or Gumbu guides refused to take him beyond the first mountain community. Everyone insisted—and Maclay's observations seemed to confirm—that no villages or tracks existed in the dense forest rising towards the veil of cloud. Other villages in the same belt were enemies, forever unapproachable. A visit to the mountains never lasted more than three days, and Maclay had to abandon hope of penetrating the interior.

He experienced many fine moments—when a gap in the trees opened an inspiring view of coast and ranges, when he witnessed a brief magical rite in a forest grove, when in deepest secrecy he was shown a great wooden mask. He studied 'hieroglyphs' on a fallen tree. He acquired highly-valued carvings. Mustering all his knowledge of the Bongu dialect, he made, to general approval, a halting and strictly practical public speech. The mountain villages were full of fascination. Yet he was never sorry to be back at Garagassi. Exhausted on difficult tracks, he felt unable to rest because of his crowd of followers. When he wished to enjoy the surroundings, he had to watch where he put his feet. He suffered from sunburn and lacerations to feet and legs, incurred in crossing rocky streams. Then there were disturbed nights in villages whose inhabitants never seemed to stop talking and moving about, days full of 'tiresome' people who followed him everywhere. With relief he sank back into soothing routine, happy 'not to see or hear people about from morning to night'.

Birds in great variety contributed their flesh to the pot and their plumage to his collections or the natives' head-dresses. A few small marsupials came his way for dissection and drawing. He enjoyed rearing a young cuscus that spent its days sleeping and nights trying to gnaw through its box. His collections grew to the point where it became haru to cram more into the hut. And there was always more to learn about his neighbours, either from visitors to Garagassi or in almost-daily trips to the nearest villages.

Sometimes, going to Gorendu or Bongu at an hour when the people were in the plantations, he had the place to himself, strolling among the huts with only a dog or a pig to supervise him. Sometimes he took meals there, the centre of attention for the whole community. He constantly observed new facts about the practical side of life. He attended feasts and collected details of songs and dances. He noted tokens of social relations, without learning anything about their significance. He never saw a wedding or a circumcision, and witnessed a funeral only as an uninvited and not particularly welcome guest. But he could wait. He was ready to spend 'several years' on that coast.

No 'culture shock' occurred in Maclay's New Guinea, at least not to Maclay. In mountain villages he saw 'savage' faces, a wildness of expression rather than features. He might reject food after a well-meaning friend had taken it in less-than-clean hands and blown on it to cool it, or refuse the only water the mountain people could offer. He witnessed no disturbing rituals. His primitive world contained prohibitions but no known punishments. It echoed with war and the cult of warriors, but he saw no fighting. Surrounded by magic, sometimes told of its use for revenge and malice, he observed only its benevolent side. He lived in a world without crime, anger or competition, an accusing contrast to the Europe he hoped to abandon.

Physical isolation fostered this impression. So did the language barrier, his command of the neighbourhood dialect being limited to the concrete. Living above the villagers rather than among them, he seemed content to believe that in his absence their life went on exactly as in his presence.

In any case, his detached, enquiring attitude prepared him for anything. Early in his stay, when the natives provided some unidentified meat, he had shocked his servants by suggesting they had enjoyed a meal of human flesh. Though he saw no proof, he continued to expect cannibalism, regarding it as a natural response to scarcity of animal food.

After a year, his one complaint was that he found Papuan music 'excruciating'. He noticed that people defecated close to dwellings, leaving the excrement to be eaten by dogs and pigs. He was much impressed by their personal cleanliness, and in Maclay's New Guinea there were no bad smells. Though he never forgot the sight of his friends after a feast, so stuffed with food that they could not move, he knew their condition had nothing to do with greed. Any religious significance in the drinking of *kéu* escaped him. Nobody pretended to enjoy the taste. But Papuan drunkenness was a brief oblivion, with no noisy, quarrelsome prelude or evil after-effects. Like everything here it was natural, wholesome, a ceremony that helped bind the community together.

The more he saw of this life, the more he liked its kindly morality. He often saw children on the beach, imitating the sexual activities of their elders. He learned to appreciate the freedom with which women and girls discussed the sexual functions and young people exchanged jokes that would be 'filthy to European ears'. It was an important day in his investigations when he discovered that peculiar exercises with the pelvis, practised by little girls for hours on end, were part of every girl's upbringing, a highly-valued preparation for coitus. And with all their freedom from false shame, their assumption that sexual relations were the same as other physical needs, he found Papuan girls in no way loose. They were more truly chaste than European women 'brought up in hypocrisy and pretended innocence'.

The men were 'distinguished by strict morality'. Late in his stay, he heard of fights involving acquaintances who had made too free with other men's wives. Perhaps the rarity of extramarital intercourse owed something to fear of a husband's weapons. Maclay saw nothing to change his opinion. Most men married early and had only one wife at a time, polygyny being a rarely-attained ideal. Where women were in the minority, and tended to die young, the men had to be jealous. On the other hand, there was none of that over-valuation of women, so wittily exposed by Schopenhauer. Relations between the sexes here confirmed both European artificiality and the philosopher's view, shared by Maclay, that woman was the natural 'number two of the human race'.

Papuans seemed to make little fuss about marriage and none about divorce. If they could not manage polygyny, they improved on Schopenhauer's recommendations in one respect: women worked for men, rather than the other way round. Maclay quite pitied them when they staggered home, bowed under loads of vegetables and infants, with bundles of firewood on their heads and children dragging at their hands. While the men ate the best food, seated on their platforms, the women sat on the ground among dogs and pigs, consuming what their husbands discarded. But they were seldom beaten or required to work beyond their strength. A man who could easily rid himself of a disabled wife and take another might go to considerable trouble to obtain magical medicine. On the whole, Maclay considered the position of women fairly good.

It was as good as they seemed to deserve or desire. Economic value assured every female of a husband, so these women neither indulged in unproductive sentiment nor bothered to make themselves attractive. Though they suckled infants for years to avoid more frequent pregnancies, they rarely showed the tenderness for children that was so pleasant in the men. Hard work and hard commons contributed to the early loss of their few charms. Custom perhaps decreed that women's bodies should be less ornamented than those of men. There was no mistaking their indifference to elegance and art. Seeking fine objects for his collection, Maclay asked why cooking pots were not decorated. The Bilbil women, making hundreds of fragile articles that might never reach their destination, replied, 'What for? It's not necessary'. These natural females proved Schopenhauer's contention that the European woman's supposed interest in art was mere pretence and coquetry.

The men were instinctively artistic. All Maclay's friends exercised skill and taste in embellishing their bodies and every article they owned. Though he never regarded their productions as more than 'rudiments of art', he greatly admired the patience and dexterity with which they used their primitive implements. Time was essential to higher achievements here as elsewhere. These men who otherwise possessed so little had plenty of time. Their heaviest work, the clearing and fencing of gardens and the breaking of the soil, occupied a few weeks each year. Hunting and fishing were sport and adventure rather than work. The building or repair of a hut or canoe formed islands of interesting activity in oceans of pleasant idleness. The men were dandies, conversationalists, warriors, musicians, artists, custodians of the sacred. Maclay had never seen, and never would see, a society that more clearly illustrated the benefits of feminine industry and masculine leisure.

This paradise for men seemed equally blessed for children. They were few in the first place, and those who arrived were sure of being cherished. They rarely cried, never seemed to be punished. A four-year-old who sought the breast might be unwillingly received, but not deprived. Sexual play was never discouraged. Yet these indulged children were far from spoilt. Like women, they ate only what the men rejected, and youths of twenty dared not touch the pork that was safe only for grown men. The little fellow who ran to his mother's breast had to help with domestic tasks. Later, while girls shared the women's work and practised the gyrations meant to please future husbands, he would learn the use of weapons, accompany his father to the gardens and on hunting and fishing trips. Cheerful, friendly, free to exercise their instincts, these youngsters presented a picture of happy childhood while painlessly gaining the knowledge and skill to fit them for adult life.

Well-loved, satisfied children; leisured, dignified men; women who knew their place and accepted it. Had Maclay imagined a truly harmonious society, enjoying every necessary freedom but honouring every necessary restraint, this might have fulfilled his ideal. Wealth was expressed, as far as he could make out, entirely in weapons and the beautifully-fashioned wooden dishes that were handed down from generation to generation. Each man owned one stone axe of the small kind. One large axe, greatly treasured, might serve a whole village. Most mainland villages boasted only two or three canoes, and some had none at all. Maclay could not imagine a dwelling that contained less than a Papuan hut. It was simplicity and sufficiency, not poverty, the natural state of men who knew neither money nor commerce, with all their wants supplied by the earth and sea or the exchange of gifts between friends.

The world he described for future European readers was on the whole a sunny, simple place, little disturbed by the breath of sorcery and almost devoid of mystery. The many things he did not know—for instance, the Papuans' ideas of spiritual beings, the origins of this world and the possibility of any other—would all be revealed by time and perseverance. When he sketched *telums* and noted their names, he wondered whether they could properly be called 'idols' and what relationship they bore to the oddly-shaped stones that received similar veneration. For the time being, these static, burdened-looking figures, as remote from his own aesthetic as the eldritch music of moonrise, were classed among 'rudiments of art'. As soon as he could investigate myths and legends, he would pry out any mysteries behind the grave, stylized, chinless faces, sunk deep in the shoulders, and those animal heads on human bodies.

Maclay was determined not to change the material he studied. Despite curiously 'Semitic' names, evidence for a smallpox epidemic eight or ten years before, and cases of influenza directly observed, he was satisfied that these people had never met outsiders. Although they remembered smallpox coming 'from the north-west', and told how their grandfathers had received tobacco and the knowledge of its use from the same direction, he understood that until the arrival of *Vityaz* they had thought themselves the world's only inhabitants. He found this situation as desirable for the humanitarian as for the anthropologist. He could wish the Papuans nothing better than the chance to remain forever ignorant of the world beyond their horizon.

Missionaries in the South Seas had discovered with horror that the measles they inadvertently brought killed the people they meant to save. Maclay had never imagined that the fever he suffered during the voyage, or the chest complaint of his Polynesian servant, might endanger the natives. He did not associate the influenza cases with the visit of *Vityaz*. Like most people of conscious rectitude, he assumed that bad things came only through bad men. Knowing his good intentions, he was satisfied that neither he nor those connected with him could harm the Papuans.

By the same token, he did not believe that these people could be corrupted by European goods received from the right hands. Though annoyed by 'rubbish' with which the naval officers bought New Guinea skulls, he confidently gave similar articles for what he wanted. He developed some idea of native principles of equivalence. There was no recognized equivalent for what he brought. The usual introductory items of South Seas trade—cloth, beads, tobacco—all figured in his system of exchange. He established a small mirror as the 'standard price' for a pig. When he insisted on having a revered *telum* in exchange for nails and bottles, he did not feel this upset traditional values. Realizing that religious feelings made Papuans reluctant to part with the lower jawbones of their dead, he obtained specimens, at last, by irresistible appeals to greed.

His ideal being observation with minimum interference, he never intended to teach. The Papuans showed enough didactic spirit for both parties. Even small children, noticing that he did anything by methods different from theirs, would demonstrate the one correct way. He learned native techniques and sometimes picked up knowledge—like how to obtain salt from driftwood—that was immediately useful to himself. But his teachers could not help learning. Their readiness to use things that other Pacific islanders had bought from Europeans for generations always surprised Maclay. Just as they discovered uses for nails, glass and hoop iron, they learned by observation the relative values of axes, knives and bottles.

If Maclay wanted to test their adaptability, he had to provide the means to be adaptable. He fondly expected that European knives would encourage more freedom and originality in an art whose formal straight lines spoke to him of technical limitations and human laziness. Wishing to see how easily these people learned new words, he had to give them names for the things that interested them most. They had been calling *Vityaz* a *korvet* before she was out of sight. Now the Russian words for 'axe', 'knife', 'bottle', 'nail', very well pronounced, had passed into daily use. When his neighbours grew *tikva* from seed he donated, Maclay had to show them how to cook pumpkin, and prove its wholesomeness by eating a dish he disliked. It was only a short step to explaining how to obtain coconut oil, a tropical product previously unknown to the villagers.

He became a teacher, because his very presence was a lesson. He could no more avoid assuming authority. On principle he rejected the European tendency to dominate among 'primitive' peoples. He belonged by birth and temperament to a class accustomed to command. In any part of the world the requirements of scientific progress, inseparable from those of personal safety and convenience, obliged him to give orders. At Garagassi a native who began to climb the steps must be ordered down. Travelling companions must be told what to do. When village chatter kept Maclay awake at night, he naturally demanded quiet. If the interior of a men's house was too dark, it became necessary to have the *telums* carried outside. Sometimes considerations of justice restrained him. He knew the Gorendu people would not 'dare to oppose' his taking an animal they had captured, but he preferred negotiation to force. Sometimes he was hampered by lack of words. He could not tell the mountain men who trod on his heels that they were a nuisance. He never doubted his right to restrict their movements as well as their conversation.

He saw no native authority to clash with his, not a single formal chieftainship. In almost every village, however, he identified at least one individual with whom he came to associate the expression *tamo-boro*— 'big-man'. Kain of Bilbil was one of them, as was Saul in Bongu. Nothing happened at Bogadjim without a sly old fellow named Kodi-boro. In one of the mountain villages everything revolved around a certain Minem. Neither age nor ornament nor visible occupation distinguished them from fellow-villagers. Able men and strong personalities, they had no monopoly on intelligence. Yet they seemed to preside over the most elaborate club-houses. Followers sat around them, awaiting their word. They made the speeches, gave the most effective orders. However they came by it (a point Maclay never really understood) they possessed the only power he could see.

Rather than encroaching on this vague authority, he wished to study it scientifically and perhaps use it to further his objects. He naturally tended to attract and be attracted by the most important people. Apart from being a fine fellow, Kain had the best sailing canoe on the coast. Friendship with Saul helped put Bongu at Maclay's disposal. When the mountain people objected to parting with a *telum*, Minem talked them down. Kodi could obtain a rattle so treasured by his village that he had to smuggle it into Maclay's hands. This made an ideal situation for a European—surrounded by friendly men whose prestige supported his own, influential enough to help him but not pedigreed or powerful enough to expect homage. The one danger was that of falling into the vacancy at the top.

His friends had nowhere else to place him. Until he came, this had been an orderly, charted world. The great gods and heroes who made it had retired, leaving humans to run their creation in prescribed ways. Every component, man or tree, occupied a known place from birth to death and beyond. Men lived in the villages like their ancestors. The ancestors lived near by, in much the same way, on another plane of being but always able to intervene on this one. As long as everyone obeyed the rules, living men and the spirits of the dead managed well. If something went wrong, they found out which deity or ancestor had been offended, and the appropriate ritual set life on its proper course. All possible events, good and ill, had already been experienced and explained. Nothing fundamentally new could enter a world that had been filled and fixed for all time. Now this scheme of things had to accommodate Maclay and all that came with him.

His mere appearance defied understanding—features that were humanlike yet subtly unhuman, unearthly pallor, unnatural eyes that seemed to open on another sky inside the skull. When he looked at them, people still felt an impulse to run. If a baby's cry brought a frown to Maclay's face, the mother hurriedly took her child to safety.

What people saw formed only a fragment of the mystery that had suddenly entered the world. They called Maclay *tamo* and invited him to feasts, but nobody could be sure that he was male. Trying to settle this, the Gumbu people had broken the rules by sending a girl into the club-house where Maclay slept alone. She had lain beside him and grasped his hand, only to be told: 'Go away! Maclay doesn't need women!' In the morning he had acted as though nothing had happened, leaving the plotters to think what they chose.

Age became just as unfathomable. Often he seemed old, slow, staid, heavy with knowledge beyond human understanding. But he denied having children, and sometimes he seemed as ignorant as a little child. He had to be taught words for the commonest things and the way to do the simplest tasks. He had to be told not to throw food scraps into the fire or leave them on the ground for sorcerers to find. Nothing could make him understand the dangers of long journeys among the malignant spirits of the bush. At a funeral, with the token 'battle' about to begin, he had almost to be pushed from the path of spears and arrows.

Like a child he knew no fear, treating weapons as though unaware of their meaning. And it truly seemed that he need fear nothing. No sorcery had been able to kill him or dislodge him from Garagassi. Somehow he paralysed the will of warriors. Giant trees fell close by and did him no harm, as though his spiritual force repelled their bulk. He had said that he would not die. Now it was easy to believe. Looking vulnerable when those disquieting eyes were turned away, yet indifferent to every danger, Maclay perhaps could never know death.

Mortal or immortal, he was the force with which men must come to terms. The *korvet's* arrival, with its awesome sights and sounds, had led only to his establishment at Garagassi. The busy *tamo-Russ*, not unlike him to look at, apparently existed only to do his will. From the start he had calmly exercised power over men. Apart from his terrifying magic and his attempts to obtain the bones of the dead, he seemed harmless, even benevolent. Nothing revealed the purpose for which he came, the ends to which his power might be used.

Such an upheaval must have an equally great purpose. It must concern the people, who stood at the centre of all things. They would perhaps learn immense mysteries, the origin of Maclay and the wonderful things he brought, the secrets of his power and wealth. He might grant them, at last, the gift of living forever.

Meanwhile, practising patience and obedience, they held together the fabric that his presence threw into question. Admit new knowledge, and all knowledge became suspect. Admit an unexplained being, and the whole structure was thrown out of joint. To keep existence going while awaiting the new order of things, they must find a place for Maclay within the old.

Unable to die, and above the need for women, he could not be a man. He could not be an ancestor, since he had no descendants. The one possible precedent was found far back. Maclay's neighbours owed all they had and all they were to Kilibob, the great creator, who had completed his work long, long ago and retired to a distant island in the south-east. They had not expected him to come back. Now all the evidence—an enormous canoe from the right direction, a powerful, otherwise inexplicable being, a sudden accession of novel objects— suggested that Kilibob had returned, with a new name and a new dispensation. They were ready to believe. They could never be quite sure.

They possessed no precedents for dealing with a visibly-active god. Women and children, who must not look upon any musical instrument lest they be harmed by its sacred power, saw Maclay almost daily without detriment to themselves. Uninitiated boys, unfit to view a *telum* or an ancestral mask, were familiar with his look and voice. Yet no revolution occurred. Like other people, Maclay's neighbours kept contradictory ideas in separate compartments. And another protective habit of thought preserved tranquillity. Where spiritual beings lived in almost social relations with humans, taken for granted unless directly invoked, the tentative identification of a deity imposed no constant burden of awe. People asked Maclay about his doings as they would ask any neighbour. When he took off some of his coverings to cross a stream, his companions felt free to make humorous remarks. It became a regular joke for young followers to screen him from view, then step aside to reveal him suddenly to some unsuspecting girl. When it seemed expedient to deceive him, his supposed divinity never made it impermissible.

Maclay was satisfied that they thought him a 'quite extraordinary being'. At first he became indignant when Bongu guides told the mountain men how he burned water, killed at a distance with fire and made people fall ill by the power of his gaze. They added to the terror of his new acquaintances, caused his research material to run away. Yet a few weeks later, in another mountain village, he listened serenely to equally terrifying stories, including 'trifling' incidents that he had forgotten. His friends were welcome to any advantage they gained from spreading the sense of his dangerous power.

He did not personally reject the advantages of a godlike reputation. Half his mind insisted that he had won friendship and esteem by purely human qualities. The other half remained open to the thought that his friends, given incentive, opportunity and courage enough, would try to kill him.

When he noticed that travelling companions feared to walk ahead of him, he could not blame them. He too sometimes thought how easily the man behind might spear him in the back. When Bongu men reported that some distant people wished to attack his house, he felt that no such thing could occur without help from neighbours who 'wouldn't mind sharing the loot'. It did no harm to drop hints about the disaster courted by anyone who attacked him. But his best defence was a general belief that men were simply powerless to do him injury.

In explaining his success, he emphasized qualities admired by Europeans—strict adherence to his word, invariable kindness and justice, unshakeable self-control and indifference to danger. He sensed that some of these meant even more to the Papuans. Indifference to their actions told his friends that he had no need to fear them. It had brought him through the test of spears and arrows. Now he applied it automatically in every situation. When his guides' refusal to lead the way inconvenienced him, he did not comment or try to make them go ahead. When Tui gave him the slip during an excursion, perhaps to find out whether the magic needle could guide him home, Maclay neither reproached him nor demanded explanations. Over and over, people learned that nothing they did affected this being who stood an immense, irreducible distance above them.

This moral ascendancy seemed to him far more significant than a few simple tricks. Perhaps there were further trivial pieces of magic that he forgot and others remembered. After guides had lauded his powers to the mountain-dwellers, for instance, he publicly performed a miraculous 'cure' on his own imaginary stiff leg. Otherwise he was not obliged to add to his magical reputation. Neither contradicted nor confirmed by him, it rolled along of its own accord, gathering many amusing exaggerations and distortions. He never ceased to marvel at how imagination fed on next-to-nothing, belief upon belief.

He constantly saw how the native mind transformed and connected fortuitous events. As an honoured guest in Gumbu, he had been questioned about life on the moon and stars, which his hosts apparently confused with Russia. The indifference with which he treated the girl-in-the-bed episode was meant to emphasize that 'such little things could not interest a man from the moon'. He noticed how the account of his extra-terrestrial travels became distorted when Gumbu men passed it on. But he was mystified when the name *Kaaram-tamo*, the Moon Man, began to reach his ears. Discovering at last that it referred to him, he found that its origins went far back. Those who witnessed his early experiment with the blue flare had thought he commanded light from the moon.

He liked the title *Kaaram-tamo*, the very description he had casually used. There might be advantages in association with a heavenly body that seemed important to the natives. He felt no responsibility for the error, or need to arrest its progress. The more unearthly they thought him, the less the likelihood of attack. For their sake as well as his own, he acquiesced in useful misunderstandings.

It might have been impossible to correct them. Those who had exaggerated his feats to frighten potential enemies now seemed to believe every word themselves. Normal behaviour, as 'European, scientist, investigator', made him strange enough. Imagination supplied the rest.

He appreciated the simplicity and comfort of being some kind of god while remaining completely himself, never obliged to pose or pretend. He overlooked the risks of such a reputation among a practical people. Burning water and releasing private moonlight had rather suggested divine wrath. Apart from their use in warning enemies, they could not be said to do any good. Papuans, on the whole, expected worthwhile deities to serve the humans who acknowledged them.

They were patient with Maclay. Eyes that could make people fall ill were evidently powerless or unwilling to give them health. Every-where he looked impassively upon elephantiasis, fever, skin diseases. But people said nothing, gratefully allowing him to treat sores and wounds, relying on Saul to deal with fever by whispering his old magic into a piece of sugar cane. Maclay's *tabu* provided feathers, a thrilling entertainment, and a lesson to those who might threaten his neighbours. But he refused to lead the villages to war, never used his powers to smite their enemies at a distance. They could no more look to him for better crops. When giving seeds of new plants, he supplied no incantations to make them grow. His own garden showed that he either knew no special magic or never bothered to use it.

If only they had proper ritual. Neither the old creator nor the problematic resurgent god had taught means for his own invocation. Men were forced to approach without the sustaining forms that won co-operation from other superhuman beings. And this haphazard business gave unsatisfactory results. People who lost valuable fish-traps, carried away by the sea, were told that Maclay did not know where to find them. When prolonged rain began to damage the gardens, he insisted he could not stop it.

Surely he could manage such simple, useful things if he wished. Yet he met their accusing disappointment with indifference, as though he did not realize how unfriendly his attitude seemed. The usual man went on performing the usual magic; the rain eventually stopped, without leaving them the prospect of famine. They did not understand Maclay and never would. The one thing clear was that any good action must be of his own choosing.

Unless he relented, or someone learned the necessary ritual in a dream, there was no hope of harnessing Maclay's full potential. Meanwhile, he made satisfying material return for goods and services. When he received pigs from the mountains, his friends shared in the meat. Prestige accrued to those he favoured. Protection might be gained by spreading his reputation. And most of these benefits came to villages near Garagassi. Wherever his restlessness took him, Maclay returned to the house on the point.

Kodi-boro, the big-man of Bogadjim, found this unnatural. Bongu and Gorendu were backwaters, poor in women, pigs and coconuts, places where nothing much happened or could happen. Maclay had shown his opinion of them by refusing to live in either. The wanderings that mystified everyone could have but one object: Maclay was looking for a better place to live.

Bogadjim was the largest and richest village on the bay, the scene of all really brilliant events. Its people acted as middlemen, trading Bilbil wares to the hinterland. It bought or invented stories, songs and dances that the mountain dwellers transmitted far inland. It set the fashion, set the pace. Kodi confidently promised plenty of everything, a fine house, two or three wives to be chosen from a far greater range than that available at Bongu. At Bogadjim Maclay could manifest himself in circumstances worthy of his greatness and Kodi-boro's.

Yet he refused. Kodi and his followers went home puzzled, still hopeful of adding Maclay to the public and personal assets of Bogadjim. Maclay did not speculate on the motives for this 'pressing invitation'. Nor did he connect events when another deputation came with a 'strange request'. Bongu, Gorendu and Gumbu could neither quarrel with Bogadjim nor ignore Kodi's machinations. Their leading men implored Maclay not to think of leaving. They offered houses in every village, an unlimited number of wives. All they asked was his promise to stay with them.

Touching as the proposal was, Maclay could not quite agree to it. He was not sure whether he would go away, he told them, but if so he would certainly return. As for women, he did not need them. They talked too much, made too much noise, and he disliked that.

His friends' disappointment was partly soothed by gifts of tobacco. For the time being, they had nothing to fear. He had dropped all idea of exploring the interior or living elsewhere on the coast. Sometimes he toyed with the thought that Olsen's death might allow him to move to the mountains, where malaria was less prevalent. On the whole he found it best to stay at his original base, in case a ship should call.

Life at Garagassi had been more secure in one respect since early June, when the neighbours had made peace with their old enemies in the mountains. In other ways, Maclay's position constantly worsened. He could still dip into his bag for tobacco, beads and scraps of cloth, and produce the occasional knife or mirror for really important transactions, but his stock of trade goods was running out. At the same time, the need for them increased. At the end of March he had measured out very small rations of rice and beans for five months, confident that he could avoid depending on friends who experienced seasonal food shortages. By August he was thoroughly dependent, not merely for the meals he took in villages whenever he decently could. Hunting brought in too little. The natives, left to themselves, provided a 'luxurious meal' one day, then nothing for weeks. The white men obtained taro and yams by almost daily barter, yet never felt adequately fed.

Weakened by undernourishment, and worried by the depletion of his quinine, Maclay suffered more than ever from malaria. Out hunting, he collapsed and lay for hours before he could drag himself home. Through July and early August, bouts came nearly every day. Illness consumed as much as twelve days in a row. In pain from spreading tropical ulcers, he no longer celebrated the tranquillity that had cast a golden glow over the early months in New Guinea. But his remaining time could not be spent passively at home. When his strength sufficed, he used it for strenuous action.

Little more than a week after receiving Maclay's qualified promise, those who feared he would leave them found his house deserted. Maclay was on Bilbil, waiting for a wind.

A view from the mountains had shown him a group of islands in the north, just beyond Astrolabe Bay. Now he wanted Kain to take him there. He waited three days, finding plenty to investigate, rather suspicious of dangerous winds that did not prevent canoes from going elsewhere. Finally he woke in the night, decided the weather was as helpful as it ever would be, and dug Kain out of bed. They sailed at three in the morning, leaving Olsen on Bilbil to guard the boat.

Kain's friendship and good nature quietly bore treatment that a man of his standing might have resented. His big canoe, a *vang* as the natives called it, proved nearly as comfortable afloat as ashore. Maclay relaxed, enjoying the voyage north through the narrow channel between Graged and the mainland and among the isles he had glimpsed from afar. In Kain's company he was sure of a friendly reception. His own fame had spread among the islanders, several of whom had visited Garagassi. He recognized acquaintances, charmed them by reading their names from his notebook. The men he distingushed sat at his feet and hardly left him, outdoing each other in services to Maclay.

He found the villages less clean and pleasant than those near home, yet he sensed an even more attractive quality in these communities. A special harmony marked relations among the inhabitants. Wives and children were treated even more gently here. These men loved their surroundings, their neighbours and themselves. In a part of the world where everyone seemed reasonably satisfied, these reached the pinnacle of content. Maclay named the group the Archipelago of Contented Men.

An arc of islands protected a sheet of quiet water where the rest of the archipelago lay like coral eggs in an over-sized nest. Gaps in the outer reef gave safe entrance to the great sheltered harbour. So far as Maclay could judge—he lacked means to take soundings—deep channels and anchorages abounded. A considerable river entered the bay. The climate seemed good, the food supply abundant. The people said that fever rarely visited these blessed isles.

Maclay had found Paradise on earth, and was considering what to do with it. He did not regard it merely as a possible home for himself. As he noted its advantages and made a rough sketch map, his thoughts ran ahead to a proper survey, ships using those convenient channels, mariners buying pigs and vegetables from the friendly inhabitants. It seemed an ideal port of refreshment for European vessels, and perhaps something more. He showed no doubt that others could share this Land of Content without impairing the contentment of its present owners.

Back at Garagassi after a five-day absence, the longest period for which he had left the house unguarded, he found all safe. Various signs told him the natives had been there. They had not disturbed the 'cobweb' of string and white thread that entangled the doors. He supposed they imagined a touch on the string would cause guns to fire from all sides. Or perhaps the frail barrier suggested some magical prohibition, threatening infinite evil to those who broke it. He never asked what they thought. Such trifles could not concern a man from the moon.

Three days later, he cobwebbed the doors again and set out with Olsen on another voyage. Months of bumping on reefs had left the boat in bad shape. The trip to Bilbil had depended as much on the bailer as on oars and sail. Intending at least to visit the eager folk at Bogadjim, he had to do it quickly.

Kodi-boro renewed his invitation more urgently than ever. The first inducement was a 'rather pretty' young girl who looked upon Maclay with favour. Next came a 'not bad-looking' and even younger maiden, equally well disposed. Everywhere there were attractive, healthy girls—Kodi pointed them out with his tongue—all of them suitable wives. But this 'bride inspection' merely irritated Maclay. He could not actually dislike any inhabitant of this coast where he felt beloved and at home, but he came close to antipathy for Kodi-boro. He disciplined himself to express nothing, shake his head, change the subject. Feminine whispers in the night made him suspect that Kodi was trying to repair the day's 'fiasco'. He again managed to ignore the episode.

They parted good friends, Kodi satisfied with the knife that rewarded him for stealing a sacred object on Maclay's behalf. The 'irksome' experience never affected Maclay. Sexual relations between white and black, regarded as an offence against the latter, were contrary to his principles. Besides, Papuan girls fell short of the male standards in style and cleanliness. At their youngest and prettiest, they never equalled the sensitive beauty that quite often appeared among the boys. And apart from morality and aesthetics he had to think of policy. His heavenly origin now seemed established. On Bilbil he had to answer questions about life on the moon and the stars. He must remain on his guard against behaviour inconsistent with a superhuman reputation, inscrutable, free of entanglements, above the cares and needs of men. No Papuan, male or female, should enter Maclay's house or testify to his merely human nature.

Life in the *tal-Maklai* safer as well as quieter without women, had included few excitements over the last three months. Maclay attended village feasts. He took part in an important seasonal event, the burning of the long grass and the hunt for animals driven out by the flames, covering himself with ash, blood and glory. Before his eyes, another great tree crashed to earth, two paces from the hut. After the visit to Bogadjim he could undertake no more sea voyages. The boat, taking in eighty buckets of water a day, was finally placed high and dry. To the neighbours who assisted, the beaching of the boat must have seemed direct proof that Maclay would never leave them.

He almost thought so himself, as he celebrated the anniversary of his arrival. With the ground prepared for 'many years of investigation' in New Guinea, he forgot about researches in northern seas. Assured of the natives' 'complete trust' and willing help, he would gladly stay on this coast. Three things gave him pause: the dangerously low stock of quinine, the shortage of ammunition, and the fact that he was wearing his last pair of boots.

He might have added to the list, for misfortunes came in crowds. The food supply caused constant anxiety. The stock of trade goods, on which it largely depended, presented an equally ominous picture. He was now forced to reserve tobacco for the old and important men, gratifying the young ones only if they were handsome. Then September began with disaster—'violent fever' that never really left him, a deep axe-cut in the knee that crippled him for weeks. Unable to hunt or to visit the villages, forced to save the scanty stores, he was reduced to dreams of dining in luxury. When he again went out with his gun there were no birds. The villagers were clearing his hunting grounds for gardens.

Decay surrounded him—the derelict boat, the hut quickly falling into disrepair, the clearing where bushes and saplings stood shoulder-high. He saw signs of collapse in himself. He became giddy from hunger. His weakened muscles hardly dragged him over level ground, and an insignificant slope represented defeat. When his will demanded action, his worn-out body tended to refuse. He could not describe the state of mind that sometimes overcame him, a vagueness, an absence, a sense of living in a dream. Holding his gun carelessly, he shot himself in the hand.

Gaps in his journal became longer and more frequent. The days he chose as samples were harrowing enough. Gentlemen in Europe, he imagined, would not envy him those times when he went to bed exhausted, ill, with a night of hunger before him and the thought that the hut might collapse. But he reminded himself that worse situations existed. Though he meant to show that a traveller's life was no round of pleasures, he remembered the compensations. Except when headache tortured him, he could never be really wretched in the 'peace and solitude' of Garagassi. He might have remained entirely at one with these surroundings, had he only been free of Olsen.

The servant had continued unwell and 'very tiresome'. When Maclay lost a week through sickness, he could remind himself that Olsen was much more often ill. Olsen, it was true, had sometimes risen from lethargy and despair. In July he had had enough life in him to persuade Maclay to let him attend a festival at Gorendu. In August he had played the mouth-organ for visitors, rowed to Bilbil, apparently quite enjoyed the trip to Bogadjim. For weeks he had been 'shopping' in the villages, a fact Maclay mentioned obliquely when Olsen was unable to go. But early in September Olsen had directed the Gorendu men in hauling the boat ashore. For the sailor, the funeral of the boat seemed to symbolize the end. That vessel had once been considered good enough to take them as far as Ternate in the Moluccas. Now Olsen had no hope of leaving New Guinea.

He collapsed in mid-September, complaining of pains all over the body. Whenever Maclay needed him, he was groaning in bed 'getting ready to die', or lounging about 'pretending to be very sick'. When he rose to cook meals or wash clothes, he was 'sullen and bad-tempered' He really talked to himself now, not only spoke aloud but listened for an answer. Maclay sometimes thought the man was deranged.

Completely disgusted with 'this lazy coward', Maclay no longer deigned even to give him orders. He felt he made concessions enough by feeding a useless mouth and tolerating the man's presence, instead of turning him out to fend for himself. His tolerance was stretched to the limit. Olsen incommunicado still disrupted the peace with mutterings of misery and doom. Maclay had pointed out the solution: there were trees all round and the sea a few steps from the door; Olsen was free to hang or drown himself. Too craven to take the hint, Olsen stayed on, a wretched intruder who could not live and would not die.

He still had uses as a subject of psychological observations. Maclay sometimes devoted a journal entry to Olsen, satisfied that his remarks would be worthy of publication. Olsen's collapse had its good side. The sound of the mouth-organ no longer assailed Maclay's ears. He no longer had to worry about what Olsen did or said in villages. There was no more risk of the natives' becoming over-familiar with a white man who failed the tests of divinity or cheapened its outward signs.

Maclay's own memory easily slipped where his servant was concerned. Before long, he would forget that Olsen had accompanied him on voyages and visited the villages alone. He could expect something similar of the Papuans. He thought highly of their intelligence and morality, but gave them little credit for powers of recollection. And it was becoming important that they should not remember mere incidentals of his sojourn, that Maclay alone should be impressed upon their minds.

He had had one unpleasant experience early in his stay, when the Gorendu people complained that *tamo-Russ* had felled some coconut palms. This was serious in itself, since Gorendu possessed few coconuts, and mentioned this incident when unable to send him supplies. Annoyed by being associated with such thoughtlessness, Maclay lived it down. But nearly fourteen months after his arrival he had proof that *Vityaz* was not forgotten.

The trip to Male, a large village between Bongu and Bogadjim, was his only excursion in almost two months. The place was interesting, the welcome friendly. Though the people offered only broken *telums* and skulls without lower jaws, they fed him well and insisted on his staying the night. The distasteful moments came when villagers complained that *tamo-Russ* had broken into huts and stolen a valuable drum and a particularly good spear, removed fish from a trap and taken or lost the trap itself. They wanted compensation.

Maclay offered payment and suggested they collect it at Garagassi. From all sides he heard, 'Maclay is a good, good man!' But it had been a disturbing surprise. These people remembered every detail of the Russian visit and connected it with him. For them he remained a man, however wonderful, associated with men who did wrong, and liable for their actions.

On one side the dangers of being human; on the other, those of being a god. October and November 1872 were cruel months at Garagassi. The stock of food was exhausted, the quinine almost gone. So few gun caps remained that Maclay had to ration his hunting. No alcohol was left for preserving zoological specimens; many of the old ones had so deteriorated that he threw them out. For hours at a time, Olsen muttered and listened, muttered and listened. Maclay tried to work in the shaky, sodden hut full of piled-up collections and human hostility. 'Rain and still more rain' poured down, trickling through the roof on to table, bed and books. The side veranda fell with a crash in the night.

On the morning of 3 November Tui plodded through the rain for a serious talk with Maclay. Their conversation revealed many interesting details of native life, but Tui refused to be side-tracked. The deluge was ruining the gardens. Bongu and Gorendu had done everything possible to drive it away. If Maclay would use his powers, it would stop at once.

Sheltered beside Maclay's door, Tui could see the collapsed veranda, water streaming through the roof of the inner room. Had Maclay been capable of improving the weather he would have done it weeks before. He was able to silence these importunities for the moment. But when he went to Gorendu next morning—there was nothing to eat at Garagassi—the whole village 'pestered' him to stop the rain. The discussions allowed him to see how the Gorendu rain man, now reduced to sullen despair, normally went about his business. No diversions fended off the dangers of inflated reputation. All Gorendu said that Maclay did not want to save the gardens that fed him.

For forty-three days nothing happened. That, at least, was the impression conveyed by Maclay's journal, which neither recorded events nor explained why none were recorded. When he resumed it, everything seemed normal to the point of tediousness. It was no longer raining. A feast at Bongu had just run its usual course, and Maclay had spent the night of 18 December in the men's house. As he lay in bed in the morning, making up for rest disturbed by yells and 'excruciating music', more noise broke through his drowse. Somewhere they were shouting 'Fire! Fire!'

A large steamer, still hull down, was approaching from the north. He had to hurry home by canoe, find the flag and raise it. The news threw Olsen into such incoherence, such mingled laughter and tears, that Maclay thought the man was out of his mind. The ship came into view, heading for Port Konstantin. Maclay wanted to make a decent appearance before these Europeans. When he went to change, however, he realized that the clothes he might put on were as bad as those he was wearing.

Aboard the steam clipper *Izumrud* ('Emerald'), one of the ships that had left Kronstadt with *Vityaz* in 1870, hardly anyone expected to find Maclay alive. Alarm about his position had begun in March 1872, a mere six months after his landing at Astrolabe Bay. The Russian Geographical Society, ill informed about New Guinea communications, had appealed to its British counterpart. The English geographers had written to governors of Australian colonies, requesting that ships visiting New Guinea waters should try to find and assist Maclay. Then, in July, Russian newspapers had published a vague message from Hong Kong, reporting Maclay's death from fever. In September rumours current on the China coast had reached St Petersburg via London. It was said that some colonial vessel had called at Astrolabe Bay, without finding traces of the white men, or that Olsen had been rescued, or that both Europeans had been killed. Despite the mysterious source and changeable content of the stories, Grand Duke Konstantin had caused action at Vladivostok. *Izumrud*, about to return to Europe, had been diverted to New Guinea.

The officer who first discerned Maclay's flag was almost too excited to tell the captain. As the clipper lost way, a canoe laboured towards it, with a European seated on the platform. Olsen, the watchers surmised. Then they recognized their countryman. On the commander's order, the crew lined the rails to greet Maclay with three cheers and a flourish of caps.

He looked 'a real Robinson Crusoe' as he came aboard—in threadbare clothes and a battered straw hat, with a satchel full of 'trade' over his shoulder, knife and revolver at his belt. Those who had met him two years before found him greatly changed, aged by suffering and a hermit's life. And as he shook dozens of hands, listened to congratulatory voices, he felt weary, confused, already rather disaffected. He had come from the noise and crowd of a Bongu festival, yet it was only now that he really experienced the pressure of humanity. All unprepared, he faced the people he had escaped fifteen months before—Europeans, with their questions and advice, their torrents of trivia and their looming authority. They meant well, but 'the sound of voices all around' exhausted him. Their very kindness threatened his independence. At the first opportunity he returned to the hut, to think out his position alone.

He had never managed to penetrate the interior of the island. He had no more penetrated the minds of its inhabitants—it would take more years than he could estimate to grasp their 'way of thought and way of life'. His knowledge of the local language, much as it impressed his countrymen, did not allow him to understand a conventional speech at a feast, much less discuss traditions and beliefs. He had never witnessed a wedding or an initiation, or discovered what rites, if any, surrounded the birth of a child. He did not know how power was attained in New Guinea or whether these people had other gods besides him. The path of duty and inclination was clear. He should stay in New Guinea, using the trust he had gained as the key to further discoveries.

He assumed that the navy would repair the hut, provide him with necessities for an indefinite stay, take charge of his papers and collections and remove the 'completely useless' Olsen. He found the commander making different assumptions. Captain Kumani and his officers reacted doubtfully when Maclay explained his plan. They suspected that hardship and solitude had affected his brain.

At any rate, he won time for further thought. News of the outside world clarified his thinking. While he lived in isolation, naturalists had been busy in other parts of his island. On the south-east coast a missionary society had established stations. Missionaries and traders had moved into surrounding islands. European intruders were drawing closer to his people. But this activity opened more welcome possibilities. The Dutch 'political' expedition was now to be followed by a scientific one. He could perhaps join this undertaking and use it to return to his coast with 'new strength and new supplies'. Return he must, and at the first opportunity. He needed no pressure or invitation to realize that.

Everything was settled next morning, with equal regard for necessity and honour. Captain Kumani could not wait while Maclay wrote scientific reports for Europe. He was anxious to leave a coast where men of *Vityaz* had contracted fever. Maclay undertook to be ready to go within three days.

The time became a fury of packing and carrying; even the materials of the hut were to be removed. Maclay chose to stay as long as possible in the familiar hut, sleeping on the makeshift bed (two large baskets of different heights) that had often kept him awake in the last fifteen months. No matter how he insulated himself everything revolved around him, everyone worked for him—the officers supervising the removal of his belongings, the boat crews rowing to and from the clipper, the craftsman engraving a copper plaque to commemorate Maclay's sojourn and the names of the ships that would be forever associated with him.

He also occupied the centre of the natives' thoughts. All along the coast they knew he was leaving. People came from Bilbil, from Male, from mountain villages, to say goodbye and join in whatever was happening. Gumbu was organizing a farewell feast. But while they prepared for his departure his friends did not despair of keeping him. Men from the nearest communities, with representatives of other places, visited him one evening in force. Close associates again begged him to stay, offering houses in every village, with a wife or two in every house. Maclay naturally had to decline the immediate proposal. Having reached his own decision, he could promise only to return 'in due course'.

However their accounts differed from his, the officers agreed that Maclay enjoyed the natives' perfect trust. He told them how this was achieved—by guarding his neighbours' women and children when the mountain prople attacked, tending the men wounded in battle, and giving the coast villages the protection of his fame. They saw the result in the way natives clung to him aboard the ship, constantly appealing to him for information and protection, in the honour paid him everywhere, in the general grief at parting with the 'beloved white man'. His influence was obvious wherever his compatriots went.

After a little alarm, the first people seen ashore came forward boldly, shook hands with the strangers, felt them, smelt them, and asked for tobacco. The Gorendu men surrounded the Russians trustfully, even affectionately. The women, who at first ran away, soon returned to examine and discuss the newcomers. But the officers' self-esteem was quickly deflated. The Papuans found the white men far less fascinating than the small South American monkey that accompanied them, and the big black Newfoundland dog Izumrudka.

One officer, transferred from *Vityaz* to show where Maclay's papers might have been buried, took an interest in comparing the situation with that of the previous year. From the start, he felt sure these people no longer regarded white men as supernatural beings. They brought no 'sacrificial offerings'. No trace of awe appeared in their behaviour. They seemed more knowing in every way. They gladly accepted tobacco, clothes and gold braid as presents, but gave nothing in return. When they offered articles in barter they tried to make a profit, demanding axes and knives for the poorest foodstuffs. He actually got the impression that those who offered Maclay a house (and a pretty girl without any clothes) required two axes in return. Maclay had taught the Papuans a scale of values that might save them from exploitation. The young man from *Vityaz*, as well as witnessing the beginnings of Russo-Papuan friendship, dimly recognized the end of innocence.

Maclay's possessions had been transferred to Izumrud. The commemorative plaque, set on a stout red board, was affixed to the tree he

chose as most imposing. He and some officers went to the feast at
Gumbu, a splendid affair attended by more than four hundred people.
Everywhere the Russians were made welcome and asked to come again.
One distressing episode marred a memorable occasion. Having stayed
overnight in Gumbu, Maclay was too exhausted, and too crippled by
his injured leg, to get back to Garagassi. He himself told how the natives
made a stretcher and carried him to Port Konstantin. The officers were
under the impression that one of them had found him lying down,
alone and helpless, and had him brought aboard the clipper. At any rate,
he received medical attention and was allowed to go home. More
powerfully than ever, the Russians appreciated the fortitude that had
brought him through his long ordeal.

Nobody had much time to spare for Olsen, a servant and a foreigner.
Maclay told the officers, as he was to tell many others, how much his
servant's shortcomings had added to his difficulties. They admired the
humanity with which Maclay, himself 'on the brink of the grave', had
given this man the best of care and saved a useless life. They inspected
Olsen—along with the overgrown clearing, the decaying roof, and the
rooms so crammed with boxes that one could hardly turn round—as
part of the test Maclay had passed. Then someone decided the man was
'in the most deplorable condition'. He was carried aboard *Izumrud* and
into the sick bay; out of Maclay's life, but never out of bitter memory.

When the anchor rose and the propeller began to churn, the canoes
hovering round the warship hastily retreated. Voices calling to Maclay
were lost in the rumble of engines. As *Izumrud* moved slowly out of
Port Konstantin, the clamour of slit gongs began in Gorendu, spread to
Bongu, to Gumbu, and northward round the bay. All along the coast
they signalled Maclay's departure, an end to the era of marvels, the start
of indefinite waiting. They had no idea how long it would be before
he returned. Unable to say 'many months' in the Bongu dialect, he had
always fallen back on the expression he believed meant 'in due time'.

He recorded no emotion on leaving the country he now considered
his home, the people he looked upon as his own. The last word in his
New Guinea journal concerned the name 'Izumrud Strait', by which he
distinguished the channel between Karkar and the mainland. On his map
it balanced 'Vityaz Strait' at the other end of his domain. Many more
new names appeared in between. He had named the highest summits
seen to the south-east, Mounts Kant and Schopenhauer. He had
dedicated peaks to Meshchersky, Grand Duke Konstantin, the Grand
Duchess Elena, Peter the Great and Prince Gorchakov, the foreign
minister. A mountain chain farther inland had been called after one of
his advisers, the biologist, Karl Ernst von Baer. Elsewhere, native names
were to be substituted for those that appeared on the maps—
Mana-boro-boro for the range known as Finisterre, Karkar for the

island called after William Dampier. But just as the natives had no designation for themselves as a people, they apparently had no name for this coast as a whole. For convenience in speaking and writing, he intended to call it the 'Maclay Coast'.

6: Sans Souci

THE MEN WHO WERE on their way
home paid dearly for rescuing Maclay. *Izumrud* became a sick ship
within a few days. When she reached Ternate three weeks later,
eighty-four of the crew and nearly all the officers were down with
fever.

Not Maclay. Thanks to the 'strong-nerved, elastic and robust'
constitution inherited from his mother, he had come through 'in good
health and ready for anything'. During the voyage he had worked on a
general report for the Russian Geographical Society. He was writing up
anthropological and meteorological results, planning several zoological
papers. Journeys stretched ahead, new tests for the vigour he claimed to
have gained from acclimatization.

He remembered the promise to visit his family between his tropical
travels and those in eastern Siberia. It made uncomfortable news to hear
that Olga constantly thought of him, always awaited his return. But
Olga must throw off melancholy and faint-heartedness, mobilize the
resolution she shared with her brother, and prepare herself to bear a
longer separation. Letters received at Ternate assured him that his
mother did not insist on his coming home at once. As he pointed out,
it would have been almost unpatriotic for her to ask him to abandon
the task begun. It would have justified the common belief that 'a
Russian begins well but doesn't have the staying power to finish the job'.

Free to disprove this notion by successfully completing his research,
he wrote at once to the governor-general of the Netherlands Indies,
asking permission to accompany the Dutch expedition. He would spend
a year or so in the Indies, then move to Australia, then to Japan, where
his brother Vladimir must join him. After that, it would be time to think
of return to Europe.

He did not have to waste six weeks aboard a motionless vessel full of sick men. Accompanied by guides who feared that some European insult to guardian demons might start an eruption, he climbed the volcano of Ternate. He crossed to the north-eastern peninsula of Celebes to visit localities celebrated for their beauty. As guest of the sultan, he spent eight days investigating the small but important island of Tidore. Everywhere he tasted fame. For the past year, people had been 'chattering' about his journey and his supposed death. Now they chattered about the man who had survived and succeeded. The sultan of Tidore commemorated his guest by naming his newborn son after 'Sultan Maclay of New Guinea'.

Maclay acquired at Tidore the very thing he needed, a youngster to fill the position once intended for Tui's son. When the sultan gave him away, Ahmad the slave boy was eleven or twelve years old and small for his age. Though frequently disobedient, and not consistently keen on work, he made on the whole an intelligent, good-natured servant. His most important quality was that of being Papuan. With Ahmad at hand, Maclay could directly compare an undoubted New Guinean with representatives of possibly related races.

Ahmad had four months aboard *Izumrud* to learn Russian and his duties. When enough men were fit for work, the clipper headed for higher latitudes, where Captain Kumani hoped to rid his ship of fever. Maclay was bound for the Philippines, to meet a people who might be allied to the Papuans.

The venerable K. E. von Baer, who had written about the Papuans without seeing them alive, had wished him to concentrate on the Philippines in the first place. Several writers declared the Aeta or *Negritos del Monte* to be Papuans. The German naturalist A. B. Meyer, just come from the Philippines, had joined Maclay in examining New Guineans at Ternate, and reached the same conclusion. But Meyer had not measured heads in the Philippines. The two Aeta skulls available to Baer were broad in relation to their length, while Papuan skulls presented the opposite condition. For Baer, everything depended on measurements of the living. If the Aeta always showed a significantly higher 'cephalic index' than Papuans, it would dispose of the relationship between the groups and cast doubt on the Papuan position as original inhabitants of the whole region.

Discussions in England and Germany had satisfied Maclay that ethnology no longer attached such importance to the form of skull. Nowadays they talked about microscopic study of hair and skin, or the overall 'habitus' of a race. He nevertheless had to answer Baer's question: 'Are these negritos of the Philippines brachycephalic?' The morning after *Izumrud* reached Manila, he crossed the bay in a fisherman's canoe, ready to penetrate the mountains.

Two hours walk with guides from a coastal village brought him to a seasonal camp of negritos. For the first time he gauged the heads of the living, using an improvised device to mark the length and breadth on paper for later measurement. As to the twenty men who paraded before him there was no doubt: all were brachycephalic. Whereas all the Papuan skulls he had measured had been less than four-fifths as broad as they were long.

He could not resolve the greater questions as Baer expected. One glance told him these people belonged to 'the same race as the Papuans'. Two days among them deepened the impression. They were Papuan in everything—'customs, attitude to women and children, facial expressions, manner of speaking, posture, dance and song'. The shapes of heads seemed relatively insignificant. In any case, Maclay argued that some New Guineans might prove to have broader heads than others, while some Aeta might incline towards the Papuan form.

He had to discount more than the negritos' discrepant heads and small stature. As wandering hunters and food gatherers, they contrasted sharply with the settled gardeners of the Maclay Coast. They had no pigs or fowls, canoes or pots. They elaborated no club-houses, produced no art they could not carry on their persons. Compared with their flimsy little shelters, the most scantily-equipped Papuan home was a furnished mansion. Maclay did not speculate on what historical or environmental forces had reduced the negritos to poor relations of the people he called the 'most primitive'. To him, New Guinea had become the navel of the world. While he could still speak of 'pure-blood Papuans', his now-settled opinion that the race exhibited many different types was broad enough to include any dark-skinned people he met.

Others must establish his point by research on negrito customs and language. Maclay looked forward to the next stage of the problem he had chosen as most important, his second visit to the island that represented his destiny. Aboard *Izumrud* he was still 'the most vigorous and healthiest *of all*'. At Hong Kong a telegram from the Dutch governor-general assured him of being a 'most welcome guest' in the expedition to New Guinea.

Fame preceded him, opening all doors. Along the China coast, Europeans had chattered and scribbled about his adventures. Now they wanted to offer hospitality and hear his story. News of his supposed death and dramatic resurrection also reached the best-informed Chinese. On a trip to Canton he had audience with the governor, and this great mandarin, almost beyond the world of ordinary men, returned the visit with full ceremonial. It became boring to have so many people seeking his acquaintance, but the fuss was not entirely distasteful to Maclay. He appreciated the kindness, the honours and opportunities. His letters to

Europe sounded exultant. He wanted to know what Russian papers had said of him when he was believed to be dead.

A brilliant return to civilization, with a public image to be maintained, perhaps began to colour his memories of New Guinea. When he completed reports at Ternate, his mountain journeys had seemed in retrospect both longer and more numerous. As he saw himself struggling on while Olsen 'lay 11 months sick', his solitude became complete. Magical events arranged as tests of native impression-ability began to seem like fortunate accidents, owing nothing to his will. He was satisfied, now, that the Papuans truly believed his gaze could heal the sick as well as strike down the healthy. For the first time, he recorded potent titles conferred on him—*Kaaram-tamo*, the Moon Man, and *Tamo-boro-boro*, Big-big-man. He was sure that only his presence had saved the coast villages from their enemies, that his friends' desire to keep him proved their need for his protection. And he wished the world to know him as more than the patient investigator who had 'entered deeply into the life of these interesting savages'. Once he had been content to describe how the Papuans vacillated for three or four months without deciding to kill him. 'In spite of five long months of almost daily attempts to murder me', he told a German geographer a few weeks later, 'I became ... so much their master that they were not only convinced I was a higher being but firmly believed and still believe I am a kind of god'.

'Master' ... 'a higher being' ... 'a kind of god'. For Europeans, Maclay embodied the ultimate fantasy of power. By mind alone, he saved, restrained, instructed and protected. His quelling eye transformed Caliban into Ariel. Under his moral dominion, the cannibal gladly became Man Friday. Europeans honoured not only the devoted scientist and hardy adventurer but the ideal white man whose innate superiority made him divine in the black man's eyes.

The sense of mastery still sustained him, though in a different form. 'My destiny is *decided*', he told Meshchersky.

> I am moving on—I do not say by a known road (the road is a matter of chance), but in a known direction. And I am going *to everything*, prepared *for everything*. This is not the fancy of a youthful enthusiasm, but a profound consciousness of the strength that is growing in me ...

At the same time, he became terribly vulnerable, not merely through renewed fever and rheumatism. Return to civilization threw him back into the toils of money. Amid generous hospitality, innumerable things had to be paid for—clothes, excursions, materials for work, photographs of himself in bush dress, seated on a studio rock with his Papuan servant at his feet—trivial things in the face of destiny, yet a constant drain on scanty funds. He had months to wait for the Dutch expedition, no means to support himself while waiting or to finance a second sojourn in New Guinea. He disliked asking help from strangers in a world that praised but failed to nurture. And his mother's encouragement to continue his travels left him the problem of how to do it. His first triumphant letter had warned her that he must soon ask for money. The next contained instructions for sending at least 1000 roubles. He needed, besides, assurances for the future, relief from the fear that he cost more than his share of family resources. He could neither plan his life nor enjoy peace of mind until Ekaterina Semyonovna disclosed her total income and approximate annual expenditure.

World-famous and twenty-six years old, he had no resource but the maternal breast that might be withdrawn or dry. Celebrity already bored him. With memories of godlike power, and a new sense of spiritual strength, he found himself powerless against a world dominated by 'stupid kopecks'. With one hand it gave admiration and sympathy; with the other it stole his independence, the right to shape his life. Yet it could be escaped if not overcome. A few days before describing his surge of spiritual power, his henceforth steady march towards his goal, he had been absorbed in the opposite experience. As *Izumrud* steamed towards Batavia, he celebrated not the triumph of the will but its annihilation.

One afternoon in Hong Kong he had dressed in Chinese trousers and Turkish tunic and stretched out on a couch in the Chinese club. In two and three-quarter hours he had smoked 107 grains of opium. An English doctor stayed by him, recording pulse-rate, respiration and temperature, asking questions, observing responses to stimuli, the state of eyes and skin, the decline of motor control, speech and hearing. The medical man's notes formed the basis for an interesting physiological report.

More than describable physiology made the experiment important for Maclay. His slow tongue had summed up the attraction towards the end: 'I want nothing and aspire to nothing'. What he described in retrospect—profound peace, obliteration of memory and thought, will and self—merely enlarged upon this blessing. He had discovered the state from which 'one would never wish to be released', understood the multitudes who sought this 'foretaste of non-being'. Yet there were weaknesses in his reiterated conviction that with opium he had wanted 'nothing, absolutely *nothing*'. After the fourteenth pipe he had wished to hear Schumann's incidental music to Byron's 'Manfred'. As long as consciousness lasted, he had always wanted another pipe.

Tied to 'self', Maclay visited Singapore and made many useful acquaintances. In June 1873, nearly six months after leaving New Guinea,

Izumrud landed him at Batavia and resumed her voyage to Europe. With nothing to depend upon, he now had two dependants, Ahmad and the little South American monkey from the clipper.

After a short, unhappy stay in a Batavia hotel, he moved to the hill station of Buitenzorg (Bogor), a favourite resort of Europeans and the real administrative centre of the colony. His fever and rheumatism persisted. In the sublime surroundings of the colonial *Sans Souci* his cares and irritations increased. His villa's rooms were small and low-ceilinged, stuffy and dark. Attended only by Ahmad (who went into hiding when work displeased him), he had to send out for breakfast and dine at a hotel. Instead of too much social life, he had none. He did not present his letters of introduction, and the Dutch concluded that he wished to be left alone.

Rescue came in the form of a tactful invitation from the governor-general. Maclay could choose an apartment in the great, rambling palace and live there as in his own house, restricted in nothing, under no obligation to see the other inhabitants. When he inspected the vice-regal residence, his choice fell inevitably on the 'simplest and most remote rooms, in a completely separate pavilion'.

Comfortably housed, daintily fed, waited upon by many servants, he was freed of all care about daily existence. In the opulent beauty of Buitenzorg, protected from intruders and given every facility for study and leisure, he worked or rested as the fancy took him. But all this, he emphasized, would count for nothing had he not found the governor-general and his family surprisingly congenial people.

There were seven in the family: James Loudon, his wife, and five daughters ranging in age from eight to seventeen years. Loudon was the son of an Englishman who had migrated to Java in the days of Stamford Raffles and become a Dutch citizen when the colony was handed back to the Netherlands. In colonial councils, at gatherings of the civil and military establishment, or among his children at Buitenzorg, he radiated authority. Visitors soon heard that he was extremely strict in official business, feared throughout the colony. To Maclay he was 'a man of justice and energy' whose public severity never conflicted with private kindliness. These qualities were magnified for a young friend, almost one of the family, fatherless from childhood and neglected, as he felt it, by his own distant family. Strict but just, sensitive but practical, always sympathetic despite his differing temperament, Maclay's governor-general strongly resembled the ideal father who had been absent from the adolescence and perhaps from the whole life of Nikolai Nikolae-vich. He also possessed in abundance the essential attribute of ideal fathers—power. Maclay repeatedly mentioned that the governor-general played 'the role of king', with 'more absolute power than the king of the Netherlands'.

Disillusionment was bound to come. The viceroy had neither the absolute power his admirer imagined nor the will to use power as Maclay eventually desired. While Maclay invested him with a state approaching that of the tsar–autocrat, Loudon struggled with advisers, appealed to The Hague for support, waited upon the decisions of cabinet ministers and parliamentary chambers. Maclay had wandered into the colony at a crisis in its history and the life of James Loudon.

In a tangle of treaty obligations, rumoured foreign intervention, intrigue, stubbornness and confusion, the governor-general had declared war on the ramshackle, piratical old state of Atjeh in northern Sumatra. While sensation boiled in the Netherlands, almost incredible news had come from Atjeh. In its first serious engagement the expeditionary force had suffered a stunning defeat, with the loss of its commander-in-chief.

The force had been withdrawn, arrangements set in train for a larger expedition. Everyone knew the Dutch must win in the end. But long-range views brought little comfort to James Loudon. While he awaited reinforcements, the voting of war credits, the survival or fall of the government that gave him rather bewildered support, Dutch prestige, and his own, suffered blow upon blow.

The less secure the governor-general's position, the more dramatic and uncompromising were his attitudes. As minister for colonies he had pushed through important reforms that he meant to see thoroughly carried out. He must also produce improvements in the native states under Dutch suzerainty. Thwarted in plans for supporting rebels against the sultan of Atjeh, Loudon had decided that this 'Asiatic despot' must be removed by a short, sharp war. He had wanted a sense of emergency. Now he had it. No European nation could stomach defeat by a barbarian rabble. A satisfactory 'war mood' had arisen in the Netherlands. Unfortunately an even more vehement war mood was born in Atjeh, where an incurably independent, fanatically Muslim population would follow any native leader rather than submit to the dubious intentions of Batavia.

European governments assured the Dutch of their sympathy. Private persons everywhere sided with the lawless Atjehnese. The situation was full of significance for an observer like Maclay. In one frame of mind, he might sympathize with the 'traitors', as Loudon called them, who defied a Dutch sovereignty they had never accepted. The predicted imposition of European power and ways might, in another time and place, have roused his indignation. Yet Maclay refrained from passing judgement. Brought to Java by a Russian war vessel, he had acquired almost official standing, backed by recommendations from Grand Duke Alexei and Admiral Possiet, earlier visitors on another Russian man-of-war. Dutch fear of Russian designs on New Guinea had apparently subsided. Russia was the one great power not rumoured to be ready to intervene in Atjeh. The naturalist remained a kind of guarantee for his country's good behaviour. While a guest of the governor-general, he mentioned Atjeh only as an obstacle to the New Guinea expedition he had hoped to join.

He spent six months in his pavilion, working up the results of his observations and considering the future. 'Inborn laziness ... and pain in the finger joints' prevented his doing much writing himself. Nobody in Buitenzorg or Batavia could write the Russian language, or render French to his satisfaction. When he found an amanuensis who wrote German 'almost without mistakes', he worked through his notes, deciphering crabbed handwriting and obscure abbreviations and translating aloud as he went. He expected criticism for excessive brevity, 'angular' style, failure to provide interpretations. He nevertheless sent off his notes, satisfied that their rough form was best for science.

To Russia and Germany he sent letters and articles on New Guinea anthropology and ethnology, on the meteorology of the Maclay Coast, and on his own activities. J. C. Galton, an English surgeon attached to the second Atjeh expedition, translated and summarized the longer ethnological writings for British readers. When Maclay gave most of his papers first to Batavia scientific journals, he assumed that some of his compatriots would be shocked. Explaining that he feared loss of manuscripts in transit to Europe, or misprints in articles not published under his own eye, he insisted that no 'intelligent person' could reproach him.

No reproaches reached him at Buitenzorg, where diplomacy and gratitude quite justified giving his work to the local learned society. Scientific circles had received him warmly. He awaited the chance to join a Dutch expedition, or Dutch help in what he undertook alone. Under Dutch auspices he began work on the comparative anatomy of the human brain, using Malay brains obtained from the prison hospital, and carried out craniological measurements in the Batavia morgue. The curator of Buitenzorg botanic garden was examining Maclay's plant specimens from New Guinea. Above all he lived at Buitenzorg, thanks to the fatherly viceroy, something like the life of a king's son, without its tiresome duties.

When tired of work and piles of books from the Batavia library, he walked in the extensive park of the palace or the adjacent botanic garden, called for a carriage to take him to the city, or went riding on one of the horses at his disposal. Illness forced or permitted him to lead a 'quiet and sedentary life', his world temporarily bounded by the palace, the park and the governor's family. Almost effortlessly he picked up the Dutch language and the native tongue. He sketched the palace façade, the skyline of volcanoes and the features of the milk-white, amplebrowed Loudon daughters. Relaxing in the garden, he let the monkey caper to entertain the children, or posed with the rest for a family photograph.

A special position as the governor's friend, a sick man and a foreigner freed him from most conventions of local society. No guest at Buitenzorg was entirely exempt from formality. If he wished to dine with the governor-general, he must wear the tail coat, white tie and gloves that protected European standards.

Maclay swallowed this prophylactic against tropical rot as 'the price of a very good dinner'. It was also the price of something he valued more. After the ceremonious meal, he escaped further ceremony by retreating with the ladies to the drawing-room, where he exercised the soft, veiled tyranny of the pampered only son and brother.

To extend the girls' competently performed piano repertoire, he sent to Europe for copies of suitable works, including the 'Manfred' music that had haunted his opium trance. When the ladies were inclined to make conversation, he put an end to this by introducing the custom of reading aloud from worthwhile literature. His evenings thus passed 'tolerably well', with the music for which he famished in his wanderings, sufficiently intelligent discourse, and the company of an indulgent 'mother' and substitute sisters. Given better health and more money, he might have contrived to be happy.

Illness made real tranquillity impossible. His fever and rheumatism continued in the reputedly healthful air of Buitenzorg. Sores developed on his legs. The doctors feared an ulcerated liver, urging him to leave as soon as possible for Europe or Australia. 'My health has suffered *severely*', he told Meshchersky, 'and it could not have been otherwise. I would wish mother and sister to be prepared for *all eventualities*'. At the same time he avoided warning the family himself, leaving them to suppose he still enjoyed the vigour he had boasted during the voyage from New Guinea. It was the old story: learning from a third person that her son was likely to die, Ekaterina Semyonovna must be pierced by remorse for the neglect that left him without support. She must assure him that wherever he might be, whatever he might undertake, he need not fear destitution.

At Buitenzorg he received one letter each from his mother and sister, from which he found that they no longer breathed 'the rotten air of Peterburg'. Where and how they lived remained a mystery. He had no answer to enquiries about the family finances, no sign of a remittance, no assurance that he was never a burden to the distant women whose portraits stood on his work table. Silence committed him to the judgement of conscience, which as ever confirmed that he was right.

Conscience also acquitted him when Olga's reaffirmed longing for his return brought to mind his excited promise of New Year's Day

Kema, Celebes, in 1873: Maclay acquired land in this district

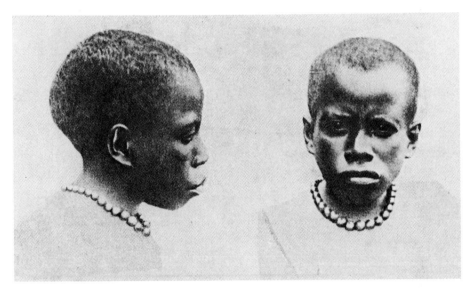

Ahmad, the Papuan boy, Maclay's servant, in 1873

The Governor-General's Palace in Buitenzorg, Maclay's home during his first sojourn in Java

The Loudon family and friends, Buitenzorg, 1873

Umburmeta, Aiduma Island, Papua-Koviai

The house at Aiva, Papua–Koviai, 1874

The urumbai at anchor, 1874

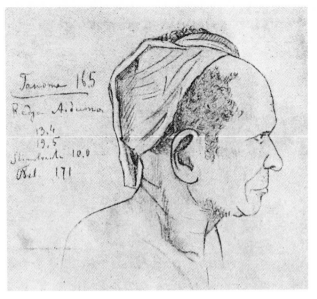

Raja Aiduma, Maclay's protégé, Papua-Koviai, 1874

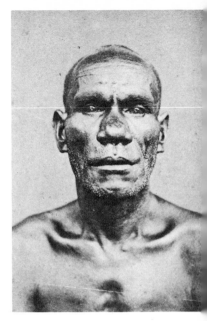

'Sassi, Kapitan Mavara — my prisoner': photograph taken at Ambon

Vuoucirau, inhabitants of Kamaka-Walla district, Papua-Koviai, 1874

1871. His motto was *'Tengo una palabra'*— 'I keep a promise'. After his years in the tropics he would come to her. But reunion was postponed to some unpredictable moment when his work should be complete. He wrote more frankly to Meshchersky. Given the most favourable circumstances, he would perhaps 'take a look at Europe', but this would be impossible for several years. It became clearer every day that he could not live there. 'Nature, air and conditions of life in the tropics', he explained to Meshchersky (but not to Olga), 'are definitely more in accord with my character and tastes'. Beyond that, he saw the difficulty of attaining an 'independent and comfortable life'. A substantial fortune would not provide what he called a tolerable existence in Europe, let alone satisfy the 'demands and caprices' with which he surprised himself. 'Well', he concluded, 'I shall settle somewhere here in the blessed tropical lands . . .'.

So it was decided, unless—. He wavered between predictions of death and the likelihood of a penniless future, between the allure of the tropics and hope of a bearable life in Europe. To Meshchersky he broadly hinted that they should meet at Sorrento, Capri or Ischia, to share a view of sea or mountains from a villa planned by Maclay and paid for by Meshchersky. He sketched a similar project for his sister. While awaiting him, Olga should deflect Ekaterina Semyonovna from her obsession with owning 'some of the steppe' to the purchase of a villa on Ischia or Capri or near Sorrento. 'This would be a glorious surprise for me', he suggested, 'and perhaps I, departing a second time for New Guinea, would not wish to go there a third time but would settle for a long while with you!'

In his heart, perhaps, he knew the futility of such persuasion. Meshchersky now followed the traditional career of the bored Russian landowner, that of travelling for his health. Desiring both a country home and an income, Ekaterina Semyonovna would inexorably prefer a slice of the steppe to a romantically-dilapidated Italian villa. Without abandoning hope of a satisfactory life in Europe, he scanned the tropics for a permanent residence. It seemed impossible to settle close to Europeans—'near them, everything is terribly expensive and boring'— equally impossible to live entirely without what Europe provided. His home must be a land without tail coats and white gloves, where money was unnecessary and his will supreme. At the same time it must have communication with science, with the sister who might still be rescued from her fate. New Guinea waited in the background, at once a duty to be shouldered, an 'intractable thing' to be mastered and a promised homeland as yet unattainable.

All naval resources were required for the Atjeh war. No Dutch expedition could reach New Guinea within any time that he could afford to wait. Maclay took up on his own account the challenge of the country with which he identified himself.

This time he chose the Dutch half of the island. The north coast, distantly ruled by the vassal sultan of Tidore, was relatively well known. In constant touch with the Moluccas, it enjoyed or endured the presence of two or three missionaries, fairly frequent visits from European ships, and the attention of naturalists from Alfred Russel Wallace onwards. Two Italians, Luigi D'Albertis and Odoardo Beccari, had recently spent some months there, and A. B. Meyer intended to investigate another part of the same region.

The prevalence of naturalists in the north-west no doubt had something to do with Maclay's decisions. He himself emphasized the prevalence of traders. In truth both coasts had been frequented for centuries by *prahus* from various islands, though the south had seen fewer Europeans and no Chinese. Both received the benefits of civilization—metal tools, cotton cloth, firearms, firewater, the casual begettings of sailors and a sprinkling of 'rajas' and 'kapitans' with Dutch flags and slightly superior guns. Both had suffered visitations by *hongis* or tribute-collecting fleets from Tidore, thinly-disguised pillaging and slave-taking expeditions now prohibited by the Dutch. Northerners and southerners alike bore such reputations for savagery that it was difficult to choose between them.

Maclay favoured the southern folk. Their recent record was less impressive than that of their compatriots, who in November 1872 had slaughtered half a ship's company. A long-established character for ferocity nevertheless seemed to guarantee their racial integrity. On the south-west coast, in the region known as Papua-Koviai, he expected to find pure-blooded Papuans.

For all their stories of murder and torture, Malay traders still visited that coast. When Maclay tried to learn more about their voyages he faced a barrier stronger than mere ignorance. Nobody in Java knew whence the *prahus* departed, when they sailed or by what route. In all probability nobody wanted to know. With their lawful purchases, the traders often brought back a strictly-illegal cargo of slaves.

Maclay based his first plans on sailing with the traders. Taking no servant but Ahmad, he would go to Banda or Ambon and find a vessel bound for southern New Guinea. He thought first of destinations beyond Papua-Koviai—the mouth of the Utanate River, or even the southern end of Princess Marianne Strait, where uncharted coast stretched far towards the east. If he escaped death from fever and 'the bloodthirstiness of the Papuans', his return was assured. Six months after his departure, a steamer sent by the governor-general would seek him out and bring him back to Java.

Nothing about his project was less certain than its financing. His original letter of credit had been spent, as had a donation of 2000 roubles

received through the Russian Geographical Society. But 'miserly
incidentals' would never obstruct his expedition. Since 'one there
doesn't need that money which evaporates so quickly here', poverty
itself became an argument for retreat to New Guinea. There remained
the problem of how to live if he returned. He heard nothing from his
mother to determine the future, his mind rejecting the obvious
interpretation of her silence. Sometimes he spurned the idea of asking
anything more from the Geographical Society. Sometimes he felt that
the promise of his ethnological collection might induce the Society to
provide an annual stipend. If the patriots were open to influence, they
might consider another possibility. 'Really', he warned, 'they are forcing
me to offer my work and researches to the Dutch or some other
government!' For the present, money was 'not worth thinking about',
however prominently it figured in his correspondence. 'Whatever is to
come, let it come!' he told Meshchersky. 'I set off for New Guinea as
though I had the prospect of complete material prosperity on my
return!'

He was sure he could extricate himself from any difficulty. He did
feel compelled to take strong measures. Without awaiting replies to his
offers, appeals and threats, he told a Batavia business house to expect
money from Russia, and obtained a substantial advance. Meshchersky
was left to find the 2000 roubles that would convert hope into fact.

Maclay was again going 'to everything, prepared for everything',
escaping the over-civilized self that was sometimes capricious and
demanding, sometimes 'utterly indifferent to everything, to the point of
complete, weary apathy'. His feelings were summed up in a quotation
from Otto Boethlingk's collection of Indian sayings: 'He who knows
well what he must do, he it is who tames destiny'. Then his new
encounter with destiny suffered a postponement. Ten days before he
was to embark, he went down with dengue fever. While the monthly
steamer sailed for Ambon, he lay in bed, racked by pains in the joints,
unable to move his legs or hold anything in his hands. When he rose
for the last few days of correcting articles, collecting and packing
equipment, his feelings were more mixed than he dared admit. He had
become so accustomed to the Loudon family, increasingly reluctant to
leave 'this dear, peaceful Sans Souci'. But more than the tendrils of peace
and comfort attached him to Buitenzorg. Leisure and proximity, shared
tastes and affectionate care in a family of substitute sisters had done their
work. He had fallen in love with one of the governor-general's
daughters.

7: Pray Tomorrow

O<small>NE</small> <small>DECEMBER</small> <small>MIDNIGHT</small> the carriage left the park at Buitenzorg, its passenger hoping that his half-asleep state would soften the parting into dreamlike unreality. Just after dawn he was in Batavia, watching his luggage start for the wharf in a cart drawn by a broken-down nag, presently whisked there himself in the resident's carriage. He noticed people bathing and defecating in the canals, discussed the cholera that had taken more than two thousand lives in Batavia. Among the throng of travellers he was fascinated by the little girls of a wealthy Chinese family, gorgeously dressed, glittering with jewellery, their faces white masks of rice powder. He meditated upon anthropological problems presented by mixed races, questioned the belief that in the islands European families inevitably died out after three generations. He noted everything useful for an article he hoped to sell to a Russian magazine. But neither waterfront diversions nor the bustle aboard the *König Willem III* dulled the sense of separation. In his cabin with no company but Ahmad and the monkey, and lying dead-tired in his bunk, he thought of Buitenzorg.

The steamer coasted northern Java, past intense cultivation resembling one vast garden, or low, swampy shores that seemed untouched by man. The horizon of mountains, occasional headlands or the beauty of isolated volcanic cones broke through the sultry monotony. In his softened mood Maclay almost ceased to be irritated by tiresome fellow voyagers, seasick ladies and boisterous children who inconvenienced him on deck. With other male passengers he talked of the islands. They told him of Javanese precautions against offending the spirits that inhabit volcanoes, of strange sexual customs among the Dyaks, of how Malay boys were circumcised and of the impossibility of discovering how the corresponding operation was performed on girls. He heard tales of murder by cumulative or slow-acting poisons, and of bizarre revenge. The ports slipped behind—Tjirebon, a ghostly place in darkness—Semarang, where cholera was taking its toll, high surf prevented a landing and there was no ice for drinks. At Surabaja the sightseers admired public gardens and an opera house, a dry dock and workshops making castings and boilers for the navy. Maclay spent most of his time on a divan at a friend's house, discussing native customs, writing to James Loudon, feeling ill. The doctor declared the explorer's health would not stand another visit to New Guinea. Maclay 'decided otherwise'. A parcel from Buitenzorg brought him a moment of 'great joy', for it contained, besides a raincoat as evidence of practical solicitude, the portrait of his beloved.

Illness, love and separation brought his spirits to low water during his two days in the governor's residence at Makasar. He visited a redundant king, was bored by this amiable relic of a vanished power, was bored again and again by garrulous representatives of the present power. Just before he left, he enjoyed a rare, heartening encounter with another member of the brotherhood of travelling naturalists.

He and the botanist Odoardo Beccari took an immediate liking to each other. The shared fascination of New Guinea gave them endless matter for conversation. Their past travels in many ways complemented each other. Still barely thirty, Beccari could describe a long expedition to Borneo, whence he had been invalided home while Maclay was a student, his travels in the Red Sea area a year after Maclay's visit, or his recent sojourn in north-western New Guinea. He could tell of meetings with the White Rajah of Sarawak, of Egyptian hostility at Massawa, of the absurd suspicion with which the Dutch had greeted his return from Papua-Notan. He was less likely to mention his ambitions for Italian power in Abyssinia, his part in his country's acquisition of territory on the Bay of Assab, or his growing belief that New Guinea should belong to Italy. Beccari belonged to a less brotherly group of naturalists, those who travelled with one eye on imperial opportunity. A breath of these interests could destroy his harmony with Maclay, the supporter of native rights. As it was, they parted firm friends, Maclay charmed by the Italian's lively manner and interesting conversation, Beccari feeling he had known the young Russian for years. Their one regret was that they followed different paths.

While Beccari was sending his patron an appreciative description of his new friend, Maclay shuddered with fever between Flores and Sumbawa. Great and petty things swarmed through his mind—plans for his journey, dreams of Buitenzorg, annoyance at learning that a talented woman had wasted her time and desecrated the Italian language by translating Captain Nazimov's 'silly, ignorant letters'. A woman passenger to whom he was called had cholera—had cholerine—was getting better—survived past Kupang, to die before they reached the capital of Portuguese Timor. 'Headache. Lassitude. The blues'. Little Dili was buzzing over an attempt to kill the governor. Aboard the *Willem III* they were bringing out champagne and fireworks. Maclay met New Year 1874 alone in his cabin, 'with a high fever'.

Staying with the Dutch resident at Ambon, he revised his plans. Instead of searching for trading vessels, he now meant to charter a ship as Beccari had done, and be taken direct to his chosen destination. Instead of visiting the swampy coast of the far south, he would make for higher ground near Triton Bay, where the Dutch had once attempted settlement. He believed it safer to live and travel alone among primitive peoples than to take a retinue of servants. He came to recognize the peril of a sick man on a probably hostile shore with no assistant but a twelve-year-old boy. At Ambon he engaged two men of Portuguese-Malay descent—David Houkhoum, an experienced hunter who had worked with several naturalists in New Guinea, and Joseph Lopez, a younger man, recommended by his honest face. Houkhoum was regarded as second-in-command of what was becoming a considerable expedition.

Maclay bustled about the old city of spices, below hillsides dotted with white-walled Chinese graves and mountain forests patched by bright green clove trees. He made many acquaintances, sorted out equipment, inspected vessels that were beyond his means. He wrote letters and an article on Papuan customs, collected a number of interesting sponges, and attended the medical inspection of prostitutes, finding among them three Papuan women to be measured and sketched. All his activity ended in prostration. Fever was joined by pains in the side, sores on the legs, periostosis, colic and pain in the liver. Pain and sleeplessness brought him to a state of mind in which no duty seemed more urgent than that of making a bequest to the Dutch couple who were so kind in his illness.

How long he lay immobilized was not recorded, nor what reflections occupied his mind. If it occurred to him that his condition might justify cancelling a journey, the thought was suppressed. He never sought medical advice without deciding 'otherwise' himself, never advised friends of his state without reiterating his determination to carry out the expedition. Nor did he ask whether a man with so many ailments should go among people who might be free of them. Europe had learned that gravely compromised health could never prevent Maclay from grappling with the challenge of New Guinea.

All questions were swept aside in mid-February. With a vessel and crew lent by the authorities, he and his followers made a midnight departure. For five days they struggled against high winds and rough seas towards the islands of Ceram Laut, battered by waves breaking over the deck and persecuted by the biting ants and large cockroaches that infested the cabin. Then they were at anchor off the chief village of Geser Island, and Maclay was presenting his demands to the headmen who came out to meet him.

In the names of the governor-general and the Ambon resident, he ordered a vessel with a crew supervised by one of the notables. In the name of the government, he kept the headmen aboard the official vessel, badgered until they promised all he wanted. He had never before exercised such power over men so abjectly anxious to obey. By the end of the day he had an *urumbai*, a two-masted vessel, capable of being rowed in a calm, with a fairly roomy deckhouse amidships. He had a crew of fifteen men, chosen from different communities to reduce the risk of plots against the white man, and led by the ill-favoured but intelligent brother of the 'mayor'. Confusion developed regarding the time for which these conscripts would serve. In his journal Maclay mentioned their engagement for five months. To the Russian Geographical Society, he indicated that as soon as a hut had been built for him in New Guinea the *urumbai* would return to Geser. His new employees believed the latter version, so from the start there was potential for dispute between master and men.

By 23 February the *urumbai* was laden with baggage, provisions, and palm-leaf mats for constructing a house. Maclay called the roll of his Malays, Papuans and men of mixed race from half-a-dozen islands, and had the anchor raised. They sailed via Goram and precipitous, green-clad Watu-Bella, from whose high cliffs he glimpsed the peaks of Papua-Koviai.

The fourth day out from Geser, wild weather buffeted the vessel, swamped the cabin, tore the jib to shreds and carried away a small boat Maclay had bought for local voyages. In tumult and darkness he noticed that one of the helmsmen was on his knees petitioning Allah instead of struggling with the helm. The situation resembled that encountered by a favourite traveller, James Bruce, on the Red Sea in 1769. Maclay reacted like James Bruce. Plunging towards the helm he dragged the man's head up and presented the revolver. 'You can pray tomorrow', he shouted above the uproar. 'If you don't steer properly now I'll put a bullet through your head!' A shot beside the helmsman's ear convinced him this infidel's revolver was more dangerous than Allah's winds and waves. It set the keynote for Maclay's relations with his men, the process by which they became 'accustomed to obey'.

Next night the *urumbai* lay between Adi Island and the New Guinea mainland, in a great stillness where the only tokens of life on land were cries that might come from either humans or birds. In dead calm they rowed towards the shrouded mountains, towards a solitary fire that was covered at their approach. The beauty and strangeness began to grip

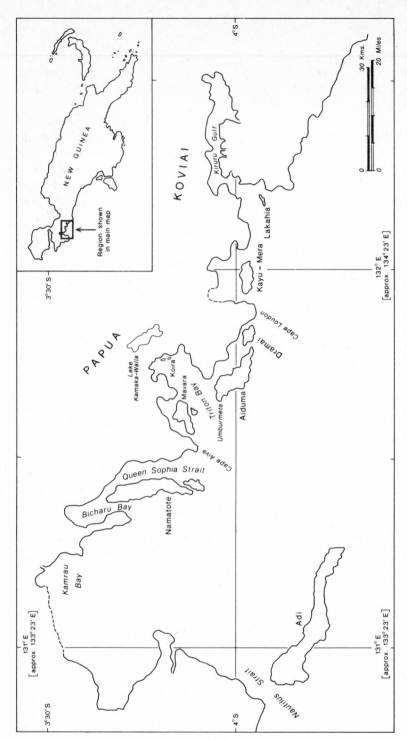

Papua-Koviai, south-western New Guinea. From a Dutch map, with Maclay's discoveries of 1874. Approximate latitudes and longitudes according to modern maps are given in square brackets.

Maclay. Deserted shores, moonlight on cliffs swathed in dense growth, huge echoes roused by the drums, gongs and singing that encouraged the rowers—these were foretastes of the ecstatic moments for which he endured. He was not disappointed by the occupants of canoes that met his vessel. These timid folk needed his reassurance, his protection. He was back in New Guinea, among his people, without a pain or a misgiving.

When he landed on Namatote Island he nevertheless carried a revolver as well as notebook and umbrella, and was escorted by two armed men. Impressions were less pleasing by daylight. Apart from a few youthful 'specimens of Papuan beauty', the inhabitants were nearly all of mixed race and neither healthy nor handsome. Their village hardly deserved the name, beached canoes and two or three huts being all it had to show. Maclay was no more favourably impressed by the dignitaries. Raja Namatote, whose 'government', according to the map, embraced half of Papua-Koviai, was an athletic but ugly young man in a state of unease. The face of Sassi, 'kapitan' of Mavara Island, aroused immediate dislike. The chieftains evidently took Maclay for a representative of the mysterious government whose flag decorated Namatote's canoe. Hearing that he wished to learn all about the country, people and local events, they lodged complaints of warfare and depredations.

These tale-telling men, with their Malay and Arab garments and their enquiries for rum and gin, were not his people. He could not stay on that small, dry island, in Raja Namatote's repulsive hut. Ignoring their report that the Aiduma people had been driven away by attackers, he sailed for the island whose raja supposedly governed the other half of Papua-Koviai.

He found Aiduma exactly as they said—not a glimpse of a human being, not a human sound to be heard. The abandoned huts were too decrepit for repair. The island was even smaller and less productive than Namatote. Maclay sailed for Mavara. The fires went out; the shore was silent; the people fled.

When the *urumbai* turned into Triton Bay it met a canoe containing two women, two children and a thin old man who identified himself as the Raja Aiduma whose title covered so much space on maps. In tones of tragedy and pathos he told of the fall of Aiduma, how without reason the islanders of Adi had hired mercenaries from afar to attack his villages and drive Aiduma forth, a dispossessed wanderer in his own land. Maclay was not entirely satisfied with the history. He believed enough in the end. However the old man came to such misfortunes, he was incontestably unfortunate now. Maclay presented him with rice and sago and attached him to the expedition. Aiduma remembered exactly where the Dutch settlement had stood forty years before.

Merkusoord, or Fort du Bus as it was commonly called, had been built beside a deep, placid basin within an amphitheatre of mountains. Maclay's men cut a track through jungle that crowded down to the beach. They came first upon a stone plinth bearing remains of a heavy wooden pillar. Then there was artificial smoothness underfoot, a metallic sound beneath Maclay's studded boot. His men cleared layers of growth and decay from a great iron slab, turned it and revealed the corroded, earth-encrusted Royal Arms of the Netherlands. Around them jungle surged over the graves of hundreds who had futilely died. In breathless heat where it seemed 'easier to die than to live', trees towered within the crumbling foundations and rose from stumps cut forty years before. The Russian had the fallen symbol cleaned and set upright against the rotting pillar.

He could not live at Fort du Bus. He followed Raja Aiduma through a mangrove swamp and up a scorching hill. Almost at the end of his strength, he looked at the wretched huts, last refuge of Aiduma's people, and knew he could not live there. Nor could Raja Aiduma. With a fresh burst of lamentation he threw himself upon the visitor's protection, begging to be allowed to live with his followers wherever Maclay might settle. Maclay saw how useful it would be to have subjects for research constantly available. 'And of course', he reflected, 'Aiduma's people would soon become my servants, and could act as guides ...'. When he resumed his voyage, the dispossessed of Aiduma were close upon the wake of the *urumbai*.

Another day's search revealed the place where he could live. The natives called it 'Aiva', a cape on the mainland between Triton Bay and Bicharu Bay, high and dry, with easy access to the fauna of coast and foothills. As Maclay looked seawards from the rock ledge chosen for his dwelling, there lay to his left a meandering strait bounded by rocky islands that apart from Mavara were uninhabited. The Grand Duchess Elena Pavlovna had died a year before, but he named in her honour, in memory of his weeks at Oranienbaum, this cavern-bordered waterway traversed only by canoes. To the west, between Namatote and the mainland, there was an equally gracious and undisturbed channel, named in due time for Queen Sophie of the Netherlands. Between royalty and royalty he gazed upon the sailless Arafura Sea, from a promontory where no one had ever lived. Yet his sanctuary already became less secluded. Aiduma's people put up shelters along the beach, mingling with visitors from Namatote, Mavara and surrounding inlets. While Maclay's house rose on Cape Aiva, a lively village grew in all too intimate proximity.

On 7 March the house was finished—an anteroom, a smallish room for Maclay and a large one for his three servants—and Maclay again called himself 'a resident of New Guinea'. His comfortable establishment was not without hints of trouble to come, from more than the termites that promptly invaded the house.

The new settlement threatened to become something other than a handy source of servants and anthropological material. The natives would accept only gin as a reward for their work. Reluctant to pander to their vices, Maclay had to give them the gin brought for preserving specimens. Almost on his doorstep, they emptied one bottle, shouting and singing so lustily that he invited them to leave. Their voices still carried from the beach, augmented by shots from ancient flintlocks. The sailors visited the shacks in search of women. Wild men from the mountains prowled about at night. In the Eden of Aiva the powerful newcomer's presence created a little waterfront, complete with sins and dangers.

He heard of murders committed the day of his arrival. Strange cries at night sent him to the arms chest. There were endless tales of raids and payback killings, attacks on trading vessels and warfare between coast and mountains. The natives boasted that 'Orang-Papua' would kill any man to get his possessions. Maclay recalled that while declaring the Namatote people untrustworthy a Dutch traveller had praised others whom the sailors called bandits. 'I myself', Maclay noted, 'am convinced they are all untrustworthy'. In particular he learned to distrust his client Raja Aiduma. The old fellow was no victim of unprovoked attack, but the object of long-invited revenge. Papuans told how he had accompanied a Tidore *hongi* to plunder Lakahia Island and massacre its inhabitants. Malay traders knew him as the greatest swindler in Papua-Koviai, repeatedly obtaining goods and absconding to hiding-places inaccessible to his creditors. Now he wore the mask of aggrieved virtue for Maclay's benefit, but he should be watched.

Maclay watched as well as he could while measuring and sketching, collecting vocabularies and struggling to adjust his tongue to the dialect. He explored Elena Pavlovna Strait, where waves fretted the coral limestone into fantastic shapes, collapsed cliffs left scars among the greenery and old landslides could be traced from high on mountainsides to the water's edge. He visited the spring where his men drew water, and the beautiful, crocodile-haunted pool that received the stream. In a cave hung with stalactites he gathered fossils and human bones. On the shore he found a profusion of sponges. His huntsmen were successfully at work, helped at times by Raja Namatote, a skilful bird-catcher. Maclay's hands were full of work, his head full of ideas. He had never dwelt in a lovelier place, or one he loved more.

Yet he felt restless, even somewhat depressed, doubtful about the value of staying there. The sparse local population included few uncontaminated Papuans. An apparently pure-blooded Papuan couple would present as their children a row of infants whose hair ranged from frizzy to almost straight, with skins in equally varied shades. Maclay rapidly approached the conclusion that the great obstacle to progress in ethnology was the frailty of women. He must search elsewhere for the pure race, as far east as Lakahia, where explorers had reported a people so fierce and unpredictable that they were almost bound to be pure. He also wished to see the strange lake of which he heard from visitors calling themselves 'Vuoucirau', whose home was on its shores.

Again he was ill, first with pain in the legs and a feeling of sickness from head to toe. His left arm became 'entirely useless'; then fever laid him up for days. His followers proved that servants can be as sick as masters and twenty men fall ill as easily as two. David Houkhoum had a badly swollen hand and a significant fever. Ahmad's paroxysms seemed capable of shattering his childish frame. Some of the sailors living in the beached *urumbai* were as sick as the gentry on the hill, but with them Maclay was not concerned.

He had to concern himself with them when he announced plans for exploring. Whether he originally intended to keep the vessel and crew for five months or to send them back almost immediately with his despatches, his actions were now determined by the loss of his boat. Without a vessel of his own, distrustful of the natives, he could not explore unless he kept the *urumbai*. So the ship lay beached at Aiva, retained by Maclay's will and the name of the Netherlands Indies government. The sea-lawyers claimed that having built his house they were entitled to go home. Others were prepared to stay, provided they need not visit Lakahia. One way or another, many of the crew preferred not to go with him.

Maclay refrained from calling it mutiny, attributing the whole situation to fear of the natives. It was neither here nor there, since he must leave a guard over his house. The cowards could stay behind while he went to Lakahia with a crew of volunteers.

Ahmad became alarmingly weak. Joseph Lopez fell ill. Maclay doctored the sick, fought white ants, listened to Raja Aiduma's stories—especially the hints of a pygmy people in New Guinea—and endured a visit from the Namatote ladies. When annoyed by 'troubles of daily existence', he often forgot them in the view from his window. A fortnight of this wonderful scene still seemed too much. He pitied Ahmad, who seemed unlikely to recover. Other considerations settled his conflict. 'I have been much out of spirits . . .', he noted. 'Kamaka and Lakahia will divert me with fresh impressions.' He had the *urumbai* launched. Ahmad would be nursed back to health or buried by Joseph.

Only five men were to stay under Joseph's command. There were enough volunteers, adventurous, loyal or afraid of the Dutch, to work and defend the vessel. But the result owed something to Sangil, the brother of the mayor of Geser. Without the headman's consent, the ship would never have entered the water to go to Lakahia.

Maclay disposed of the native rulers, ordering Raja Namatote to stay at Aiva. Raja Aiduma could neither be trusted with first place at Aiva nor subordinated to young Namatote. On the other hand, Sangil and Namatote advised against taking him to Lakahia. If Aiduma appeared on the scene of his former exploits, they predicted, the natives would either avoid the expedition or attack to revenge themselves on him. Finally Aiduma was taken along to help find guides. Some of his strongest men went ahead to await the expedition, for which they would act as porters.

Maclay enjoyed Aiduma's company, mainly because the old man enjoyed himself so much. Aiduma's great days came again, greater than ever under Maclay's patronage. Dressed in a yellow robe and full of consequence, he sat beating a little drum and pointing out the sights. He was so rich in information and entertainment that Maclay forgot the reputed villainy. Maclay also forgot about returning him to his people.

The expedition for the mountains landed on the eastern shore of Triton Bay, a party consisting of Maclay, David Houkhoum, Sangil and Raja Aiduma, with five or six of Aiduma's men and some Vuoucirau guides. Maclay liked the Vuoucirau, quiet, respectful people whose chieftain bowed when greeting the white man. Apart from possessing firearms, they seemed gentle and unspoiled.

Their country proved a tough place. After half an hour on steep up-and-down tracks under a broiling sun Maclay was weak in the legs, blistered by new boots and in increasing pain from his swollen left side. Then came headache and giddiness, vestiges of an aborted fever attack. There was nowhere to rest, nothing to do but keep walking. For the last three hours of the journey it poured rain. Exhausted, soaked and starving, they reached the Vuoucirau village at sundown.

The hut Maclay occupied was so low that he could not stand, its door so narrow that he must squeeze through. It was nevertheless substantial, with partitioned living space, incised decorations on the walls, and beams carved to represent crocodile heads. Though there seemed to be only about forty Vuoucirau, they lived settled lives, visiting the coast but securely apart from its turmoil. In their company Maclay escaped that poignantly beautiful, ruined Papua-Koviai, where trickery, robbery, murder and enslavement were a way of life.

He was equally pleased by lovely Lake Kamaka-Walla, with its thought-provoking populations of molluscs and sponges and its evidence of great and mysterious changes of level. He could have spent profitable weeks on its shores or canoeing on its waters. Instead he had barely half a day to investigate the lake, to measure and sketch its proprietors and throw them into fits of laughter by his attempts to pronounce their words. Relying on hospitality, his party had brought very little in the way of provisions. The Vuoucirau had art, peace and beautiful surroundings, but no surplus food.

Without hard feelings, hosts and guests set out for the coast. As though they had not a care in the world, the Vuoucirau decorated themselves with multicoloured leaves and sang their way down to the landing-place. Nine canoes full of people followed the *urumbai* out to its anchorage at Koira Island. On each of the open vessels, carrying only men, a warrior leapt and shouted in his war dance, chastized the air and loosed arrows at the sky. In the covered canoes women and children sang and yelled, each party trying to drown out the others. That night there was a general dance on Koira—crescendos of movement that over and over reached the point of frenzy and suddenly stopped. Clouds gathered and discharged their rain; Maclay retired to the *urumbai*; but deep into the night the dance went on.

Refreshed by new impressions, or by old expectations given new life, Maclay sailed out of Triton Bay. Nothing tarnished his memories of the Vuoucirau sanctuary, the courtly Vuoucirau chief, or a young girl whose eyes would please 'the most exacting connoisseur of feminine beauty'. The singing procession down the mountainside, the firelit dance on the shore, a sacred vine-curtained inlet where the water splashed in constant, mysterious agitation—these were true pictures of Maclay's New Guinea. They did not come again as the *urumbai* passed eastward between Aiduma and the mainland, coasted south of Dramai and entered Kayu-Mera Bay. Everywhere he found scenes so beautiful they must be called sublime, in a land so empty that it must be called unpopulated. Kayu-Mera village had been burned down by attackers just before his arrival in Papua-Koviai. The other islands and the mountains behind seemed equally deserted. Maclay doubted whether all the people from Namatote to the western shores of Triton Bay would number more than a hundred. Between Triton Bay and Lakahia he saw nobody. Only the occasional clump of coconut palms showed where people had lived beside some secluded inlet.

He had read that the way of life here was largely nomadic. A family would use its covered canoe as a shelter for a short stay in one locality, then move on to fish and gather food at another little beach. He had met one floating household whose leader, asked where they were going, replied: 'I am looking for something to eat'. Contrasting this existence with that of gardening communities on the Maclay Coast, he attributed it wholly to fear and persecution. Granted peace and security, these people would live like the villagers of Bongu and Gorendu, cultivating the soil and bringing up generations of children in one place. At least they would live like the Vuoucirau, growing nothing much to eat but enjoying leisure and tranquil minds for the cultivation of art and song and the collection of zoological specimens. Maclay saw much in the emptiness, and formed far-reaching ideas.

Perhaps because of Raja Aiduma's presence, he made no attempt to explore Lakahia or contact its inhabitants. Past low, mangrove-covered shores as deserted as the cliffs to the west, the expedition entered Kiruru Gulf. Once, a group of natives ran down the beach, waving their garments and tossing handfuls of sand. On seeing the white man and a cake of tobacco they cautiously brought their canoes up to the *urumbai*. When Maclay demonstrated that the cabin curtain concealed no armed men, they ventured on deck, shouting, laughing and hugging the sailors. Maclay had time to ascertain that they were darker and more robust—more Papuan—than his neighbours at Aiva, and to taste the drink they made from the shoots of a palm. He sensed uneasiness behind their extravagant delight. Their older memories told of Tidore *hongi*. Fresh memories included the devastation of Kayu-Mera. He did not wonder that to them all strangers were enemies. On the other hand, he remembered their reputation. When not acting as victims, these people were fierce and indiscriminate in revenge.

He went to view a waterfall shown on Dutch charts, only to find that the long dry season had reduced it to insignificance. He looked for a purported village and found a single decaying hut. Three canoe-loads of people approached the *urumbai* closely enough for him to conjecture how the custom of piercing the nasal septum might result in noses 'resembling the Hebrew'. He saw no other inhabitants on the way up the silent, windless gulf.

At the eastern limit of the waterway he led a party into the mountains, camped on the seaward slope of the first ridge and climbed to the crest. He was in the area where the maps showed western New Guinea narrowest in its north-south direction, the point on the south coast apparently nearest to the head of vast Geelvink Bay.

He saw nothing from the heights but trees and mountains. Yet the trip convinced him that an inland expedition from this point— perhaps an attempt to cross the island—would not be impossibly difficult. The forest looked relatively open. Only tracks and cut branches revealed the presence of inhabitants on the ridge. Beyond, the land seemed as empty as the Vuoucirau asserted.

The sailors nevertheless feared attack. Even Maclay, in that stillness, could imagine mountain people gathering with 'not the best intentions'. That same day he rejoined the *urumbai* and turned back for the open sea.

No natives had visited the anchored vessel. The land party had been disturbed only by a hornbill's screech or the pre-dawn prowling of a cassowary. Now, just as the explorers were about to collect some skulls from a cleft in a rock, five canoes appeared, crowded with armed men.

The sailors began to load their guns and the natives to handle their weapons. The canoes came on, their occupants chanting and shrieking. Maclay ordered preparations for defence, stationed himself on the cabin roof with rifle, revolver and 'rapid fire gun', and had his vessel rowed straight at the canoes. There was no question of a warning volley. His men had orders to aim well and waste no ammunition. One canoe maintained a dignified position, the rest retreating as fast as their crews could paddle.

In reply to Maclay's shout, a headman explained in broken Malay that the warriors only wanted to see the white *tuan*. They hesitantly came alongside. After reassurances the leaders climbed aboard and accepted tobacco. Nobody was quite at ease. While Maclay noted native words and place names, his visitors slipped back to their canoes. The last man, alarmed to find himself alone, leapt over the side without taking his tobacco.

The sailors were sure that the Papuans came only to see how many men were on the vessel and what weapons they carried. Now they would hide until nightfall and the best moment for attack. Maclay preferred to believe that piles of weapons in the canoes proved the natives' fear of strangers, rather than their own warlike intentions, yet he could not feel wholly satisfied with this. He was persuaded to abandon further exploration of Kiruru Gulf. The sailors rowed so hard that by dawn they were back on the open sea.

Strong winds and high waves made it too dangerous to take the small, ill-equipped vessel farther along the exposed coast to the south-east. Maclay decided to investigate the large bays west of Aiva. In rough seas they rowed across to Kayu-Mera Bay for a day's rest. Again they rowed 'with all their might' to pass a grand cape that Maclay named after the governor-general. At an anchorage off the north coast of Aiduma, a native in a canoe gave Maclay the worst news he could have received.

Mountain men from Bicharu Bay had attacked the Aiva settlement. A wife and child of Raja Aiduma had been killed, captives taken, and Maclay's house plundered. Through the confusion of the story and its interpretation, Maclay made out the general course of events. The business of the mountain men was with Aiduma's family and followers. But Aiduma's people had fled to the white man's house for protection. There the killing had been done, and pillage had followed as a matter of course. Something was saved, for Joseph Lopez had reached a large trading vessel anchored off Namatote, returning to Aiva with an armed party in time to interrupt the division of spoils. Now Maclay's men and his rescued chattels were aboard the Makasar *paduakan*. The raiders were back in their mountains with their booty, captives and trophies, the heads of Aiduma's wife and child.

Anger acted on Maclay like a stimulant. Weary and afraid, his men were forced to row all night. But he never intended to confront the

Maclay and Ahmad ready for the jungle, 1874

The maharaja's palace, Johor Baharu, where Maclay stayed in 1874 and 1875

Maclay's *yalo* at Bukit Kepong, Muar River, Johor, 1874

warriors of Bicharu Bay. For reasons he did not explain—beyond the fact that he 'never liked' the man's face—he had identified Kapitan Mavara as the chief culprit, with Raja Namatote sharing the guilt.

The one person he did not blame was himself. Knowing how well Raja Aiduma was hated, he had risked attracting enmity by extending protection to Aiduma's people. Then he had withdrawn most of the protection, while weakening his clients by taking their leader and strongest men on the voyage. Left to defend the followers of a man who was hated and feared, Namatote and his friend Mavara had shirked the task. Maclay could not allow himself to see this. Raja Aiduma understood. Amid his tears and wailing, he heaped recrimination on Maclay.

After visiting Mavara, where he found nobody home but frightened old women and howling children, Maclay made for the anchorage of the Makasar trader. The shattered Joseph Lopez gave a slightly different but not entirely unexpected account. Certainly the Bicharu men had descended on Aiva to settle old scores. Deeming it safer not to defend their neighbours against a force said to be larger than the entire population of the two islands, Namatote and Mavara had stood aside. When the invaders had gone, with all the booty they could carry, these friends had swooped to appropriate the remainder. Joseph was convinced that Maclay's employees, nearly all Papuans or half-Papuans, were in league with the raiders. When he served out ammunition, the guards had fired only blanks.

The only good news was that Ahmad had recovered. Maclay waited aboard the *urumbai* while his remaining possessions were transferred from the Makasar vessel. Somewhere in the Bicharu mountains, they could now work great magic with his meteorological equipment, or operate on each other with instruments from his large dissecting case. While he claimed to be indifferent to the loss of clothing, linen and food, he worried about the disappearance of his medicine chest and most of the quinine. Eight of the sailors had fever.

The atmosphere aboard the *urumbai* was enigmatically disturbing. Raja Aiduma stopped accusing his failed protector and strenuously tried to please Maclay. This might be explained by Aiduma's having other wives and daughters and hoping still to gain something from the white man. Raja Namatote's behaviour was less comprehensible. As though he knew no reason to stay away, he arrived to co-operate or compete with Aiduma. Together they besieged Maclay, clung to his garments, pressed his hands and outbid each other in assurances of devotion. All they wanted was to follow him. Let Maclay give the order and they would collect the people wherever he chose to live. The Ceramese sailors told him not to believe a word. In their opinion, Aiduma meant to pay back someone for the deaths in his family and the wounding or capture of his followers. If he could not reach the murderers, he would revenge himself upon Maclay. Later, both rajas spoke to the sailors, promising that whatever happened no harm would befall the crew. Unable to digest the implications of this, Maclay turned his suspicion and contempt upon the Ceramese, who cared less for his life than for what the Dutch would do to them if he were killed.

He ordered them to return to Aiva. They proposed to sail for home. Even David and Joseph refused to live on the cape again. What Maclay required was that fear of Dutch prisons should make his men risk death to support him in purposes they did not understand. It was not enough. Nor was he entirely successful with threats to shoot them. The revolver argument drove them only as far as the beach, where Maclay was landed with his baggage and the men withdrew to the *urumbai*.

He never explained what he proposed to do at Aiva. Before Papuan ferocity and Ceramese cowardice, he acted as he believed a superior being should, exerting his will without much regard for purpose. Despite the men who lacked his superhuman self-confidence and indifference to life, Maclay must live in his chosen domain, assert his power and find means to punish the transgressors. Anything less would give the triumph to his inferiors and to the unworthy self he had left behind. So he went up to Aiva to prove what must be proved. He was prepared to find chaos in the house on the promontory, for the absence of his possessions and the ruin of what remained. He expected the patches of dried blood on walls and floor, since here murder had been done. But he found something against which he was not fore-armed. Across his work table, like a vile parody of his anatomical preparations, lay the dismembered and headless, decomposing body of that pretty little girl, the daughter of Raja Aiduma.

Back on the *urumbai*, he told himself he would have stayed at Aiva had the enemy not poisoned the water supply. In his memory the bodies of fishes floated belly-up, hiding the submerged ghastliness of the murdered child. He would nevertheless maintain his authority and bring to justice those who stole his goods, killed his followers and profaned his only altar. The question was how to accomplish this, surrounded by enemies, with an openly mutinous crew. Promises of 'handsome remuneration' persuaded some of the sailors to return with him, strip the matting from the house for use in a new dwelling and set the rest alight. Otherwise the position for some days remained uncertain.

While Maclay pondered his moves and did some desultory anthropological research, the Makasar captain reached his own decision. This conscientious seaman had rescued Maclay's servants and goods and spent nearly two weeks in idleness and danger on Maclay's behalf. Trade was bad. The situation on the coast made him afraid to stay any longer. He proposed to take his valuable ship and cargo to more peaceful markets.

The news had a disastrous effect on the men of the *urumbai*, nearly all suffering from fever. Maclay still seemed to have the upper hand, his threats evoking promises of loyalty and obedience. He did not believe these men really regarded him with devotion or would willingly risk their lives so that he might risk his. While preparing boxes of specimens for despatch on the *paduakan*, he wrote to James Loudon, giving 'a brief account of events and of my decision to stay here'. To the captain of a government vessel said to be visiting Geser, he wrote a terse note:

Very urgent
On 28 March the Papuans robbed my hut. I find myself in a difficult position and I have the honour to request you to come to me at Aiduma without delay. Only in the case of extreme necessity would I decide to return with the urumbai to Geser.

The words preserved his freedom of action. If the government vessel came, he could demand help to stay in Papua-Koviai. He might also yield to persuasion and leave. One thing unambiguously revealed was that he felt less than usual confidence in his ability to dominate the surroundings.

The supposed proximity of a Dutch ship added another twist to the sailors' predicament. They were sufficiently reassured or intimidated to obey when ordered to sail for Aiduma. There Maclay chose a place if possible more sublime than Aiva, commanding a full view of Triton Bay, with the Kamaka Mountains, Mavara and Aiva itself. A good water supply lay close at hand; the island vantage point seemed relatively safe; but his men refused to sleep on shore. Maclay announced that he would live there alone, while they remained on the *urumbai*. The sailors built another hut, just large enough to accommodate his table, chair and bunk. Obliged to work ashore during the day, and to come to his aid in case of attack at night, his employees were hardly safer afloat than on the island.

Umburmeta, as the place was called, became as animated as Aiva had been. Aiduma's people settled there. Survivors from Kayu-Mera and a large party of Vuoucirau mysteriously joined the community. From his veranda Maclay watched the doings of the whole shore—men and women at work and leisure, youngsters practising for war. Though the material was restricted by the absence of Namatote and Mavara people, he resumed his scientific work. As he inspected a newborn Papuan baby, or followed racial traits through the results of female promiscuity, he would not have changed places with scholars who presumed to classify the human species without leaving their armchairs in Europe.

Yet he never knew a peaceful day at Umburmeta. The hut, true product of unwilling labour, admitted every breeze to keep him cold at night and prevent his lighting a candle. Anyone who believed Maclay might be dislodged by discomfort was mistaken, but he could not ignore other assaults on his nerves. Now it was a canoe arriving at night with news that mountain men had visited Aiva in the hope of killing Maclay and picking up any neglected booty. Next it was said that Namatote and Mavara planned to attack in force. One community after another seemed to be hatching mischief against Maclay. Some of his followers found traces of unknown men about his hut. Others sighted strange canoes in suspicious manoeuvres. Aiduma's people pointed out this one and that one as enemy spies or infiltrators posing as subjects of Aiduma. In the deepening confusion it became impossible to say who waged the war of nerves, or for what purpose.

Maclay made his men laugh by asking how mountain warriors could reach Aiduma without canoes. Argument and laughter broke down when the reports concerned invasion from other islands. 'Fear has big eyes and ears', he reflected. 'The worst thing is that it is infectious.' Still looking for outside assistance, he thought to check the disease by dismissing the *urumbai* and its sullen, terrified crew. But his Ambonese servants were frankly afraid of this. The Papuans, they said, would kill a man for an empty bottle or a cracked plate. If they three and the boy stayed there without means of escape, the affair would end badly for them and for the wives and children in Ambon. The result of their talk was perhaps not what David and Joseph hoped. Instead of deciding to return to Geser, Maclay felt compelled to keep the *urumbai*.

In defiance of rumours and entreaties, he spent each night in the sievelike hut, binding his men as firmly to his will as if they had been shackled beside the door. Sometimes events of broad daylight seemed to take place in a dream. He had little opportunity to dream at night, the time of whispers and mysterious activity. One visit to the island, that of a Goram trader, caused an early-morning alarm. One definite incident—the appearance of a fleet of canoes and their swift retreat at sight of the trading vessel—lent substance to the sailors' attacks of 'imagination'. David and Joseph made their own contributions to the uneasiness. Among the belongings of a half-Papuan sailor, they saw articles supposedly stolen by the raiders. Many of Maclay's possessions, they reported, had been bartered to natives for New Guinea produce.

Maclay was tired of alarms and evidence that he could trust nobody. It was 'irksome and tiring' to be constantly armed and alert. He had almost exhausted the anthropological materials, and on zoological excursions dared go no farther than the nearest reef. The government vessel clearly was not coming, had probably left Geser before his message could arrive. He could not take retribution to his enemies. With his quinine perilously low, and the monsoon in the offing, he could not wait for the enemy to come to him. He must accomplish some act of justice and leave Papua-Koviai.

The necessary act and the means to it were revealed on 23 April, as he sat drinking coffee and admiring the sunrise. While waiting on his master, Joseph Lopez mentioned an alarm caused in the night by a canoe arriving from Mavara. The vessel had moved away when hailed, but Joseph was sure that one of its passengers was Kapitan Mavara himself.

Maclay regretted the absence of Raja Namatote, whom he had not seen for almost three weeks. Still, Kapitan Mavara was equally guilty of permitting the killings and had always been regarded as 'one of the leading participants in the robbery'. He must be taken 'dead or alive'.

Joseph brought David from the *urumbai* and made sure that the enemy was actually in the covered canoe. All the guns were loaded, everything in the hut collected and packed. Outside, dispositions were in order. Instead of having breakfast on the ship, some of the sailors were flirting with girls on the beach, keeping hold of their weapons as they paid their addresses. But Maclay saw three times as many natives as Ceramese. These were his friends and *protégés*—Aiduma's followers, Vuoucirau and men of Kayu-Mera—yet he feared they would misunderstand his motives and rush to defend Kapitan Mavara. Then memories of a blood-spattered room, that poor child's body on his table, overcame any hesitation. To avenge these crimes upon his chosen enemy, he was prepared to kill relatives and friends of the victims.

Accompanied by Lopez and a Papuan sailor named Moi-Birit (noted for unquestioning obedience), he set out to capture and execute Kapitan Mavara. He still did not know exactly what action to take, depending on the inspiration that sometimes came to him in moments of crisis. He nonetheless enjoyed the picture of Maclay, strolling down the beach, armed with a revolver, flanked by Joseph with a rifle and Moi with a stout rope, but looking, he imagined, as though nothing unusual was afoot. Without speaking to anyone, they passed the flirtatious couples and the groups cooking and gossiping. Near the strange canoe they stopped, and Maclay, in the quiet, even voice on which he prided himself, called out for Kapitan Mavara.

Kapitan Mavara did not answer the first call or the second. With a third summons, Maclay tore the awning from the canoe and exposed his paralysed enemy. Rifle in hand, Joseph confronted the gathering crowd. The amorous sailors worked their way to the front. Maclay gripped Kapitan Mavara by the throat and held the revolver to his mouth while Moi-Birit tied the captive's arms. When Sangil took charge of the prisoner, everything was over except the explanations.

Kapitan Mavara was a miserable capture. From first to last his only utterances were a mechanical 'Greetings, *tuan*', and a sickly denial of any knowledge of Raja Namatote's whereabouts. His only action was a violent trembling. The danger loomed from another quarter, combining with the prisoner's abject state to make Maclay abandon ideas of a summary execution.

The crowd did not understand why Maclay treated Kapitan Mavara thus. He told them he was taking the prisoner because this man had failed to protect Aiva, permitted women and children to be killed in the master's house and 'looted everything in it'. Yet they did not recognize the agent of justice, their friend and protector Maclay. They saw a white man and his servants dealing roughly with a Papuan, binding a man's arms and dragging him off to a ship, and they wondered where it would end. Scowling men began to handle their weapons. The women ran off to hide. Surrounded by his own armed men, Maclay faced the prospect of shooting down people whose interests he meant to defend.

He talked them into docility at last, explaining that he was not angry with anyone but Kapitan Mavara and Raja Namatote. His friends were made to understand that they would not be shot or taken away and that by laying down their weapons and carrying Maclay's boxes to the beach they could earn some tobacco. The main thing was to keep them busy, allow them no time to recover from surprise and discuss these events among themselves. While his servants made ready for departure, and his watchmen prevented any canoe from leaving the shore, Maclay created diversions that absorbed surplus attention and ensured that only he should speak.

Followed by the crowd, he went to assure the women that there was no danger. He offered a passage on the *urumbai* to Kapitan Mavara's wife, who either failed to understand or preferred not to starve alone in a foreign country while something or other was done to her husband. He also offered transport to one of Raja Aiduma's older daughters, just married to a man from the *urumbai*; but she preferred to stay and comfort her old father, and perhaps be sold to another sailor. By the time Maclay had finished with speeches, diplomacy and the distribution of tobacco, his vessel was ready to sail.

He did not forget scientific interests. He had long coveted an 'interesting anthropological object' displayed on a structure near his hut. While forced to stay on the island, he had hesitated to offend his friends by taking what science required. Now he could not abandon the prize to time and weather. By a stratagem that caused him considerable pride, he stole the skull of a former Raja Aiduma.

That was something for them to ponder when they discovered it—why the white man who pursued a thief should filch the relics that held life convulsively together in Papua-Koviai. But Papuan collective wisdom had much to consider when relieved of Maclay's overpowering presence. There were small but disturbing matters, like the question of how Kapitan Mavara's wife happened to be on Aiduma, the stronghold of her enemies. There was the problem of exactly what her husband had done, his fate, and how his absence would affect the future. There were mysteries in why the white man had not pursued thieves and murderers at Bicharu Bay, and why he pretended not to know where

Raja Namatote was. Above them all loomed the ungraspable question of who was really to blame for the disaster at Aiva. Probably the whole puzzle could be solved only by that Allah of whom a foreign teacher had told the ancestors.

At least one knew where one stood with the men from Bicharu Bay. They had not done harm by ignorance, vanity or accident but deliberately, after the ways of the coast. And according to the ways of the coast they should now be defending themselves against those who sought to kill them in revenge. Numerous as they seemed to Maclay, fewer men than usual were on the beach at Umburmeta. With the Vuoucirau as his principal allies, Raja Aiduma had launched his attack on Namatote and Bicharu Bay. While Maclay sailed away, his friends awaited the war news. It would be a long time before he learned that Raja Namatote was dead.

8: Disillusion

APART FROM a navigational error
that took the *urumbai* far south of its proper course, the homeward
voyage was almost uneventful. Maclay sometimes threatened the sailors
with gaol, showed his revolver, or fired a shot 'as a last resort'. On the
whole, he considered them fairly well tamed. When they wished to
replace the admittedly low and noisome water supply, he refused to
land; but next day he called at Goram to buy himself a fowl. As they
approached Geser, he allowed the men to hoist flags, beat gongs and fire
guns to signal and celebrate their homecoming. Then he ordered them
to sail for Kilvaru instead. Thus they learned what it is to serve a man
of power. They learned more when he dismissed them. In a few weeks
they would have to return to Kilvaru. Maclay could not pay them until
he received funds from Batavia.

He handed over his prisoner to the raja of Kilvaru and settled to wait
in the heir-apparent's palace. The 'rustic Venice', as A. R. Wallace called
Kilvaru, seemed to rise directly from the sea, its pile dwellings
completely hiding the islet. As in Wallace's day, it remained an
important trading centre dealing particularly in New Guinea produce.
Its gloriously mixed population, placed at Maclay's disposal by *raja-muda*
Muhamed, supplied perhaps the richest field of investigation encountered in his journey. Examining specimens of mixed race, he could
compare them with both parents. He inspected examples of 'atavisms'
—children with remarkably hairy bodies, or a woman with two pairs
of breasts—and observed cases of incomplete albinism. He heard of the
grandest atavism of all, a race of people with tails, but these lived
elsewhere and had never quite been seen by his informants. There was
dancing to watch in the evenings, much to be learned of customs and
beliefs. The island itself, a sandbank over which the highest tides

occasionally flowed, showed more interesting features than might be expected. But Maclay was pestered by people with ailments and grievances. His stocks of wine, sugar and coffee were almost done; he had no biscuits or money, and no hope of release until the Dutch resident's steamer arrived from Ambon.

Kapitan Mavara, hitherto a model prisoner, provided some excitement. On the night of a lunar eclipse he contrived to escape. There being nowhere else to go, he ran into the water and stood throwing stones at his pursuers. Maclay was again temped to shoot him, but refrained out of consideration for the raja. Thenceforth the prisoner's legs were chained to a block. During the voyage, it appeared, he had offered large bribes in New Guinea produce for a chance of freedom. Since similar temptations might confront the Kilvaru gaolers, Maclay the more impatiently awaited the resident.

'Talking very confusedly' before the authorities, Kapitan Mavara seemed to declare himself innocent. The raja, a staunch adherent of Maclay, affirmed both the prisoner's guilt and that of the Ceramese sailors. In the attitude of the Dutch official, Maclay found something so unsatisfactory that he decided to take the case to the governor-general.

Other matters were to be laid before the governor-general. Maclay had learned that Tidore *hongis* still visited New Guinea to collect 'tribute'. Regardless of the effect on his admirer, the sultan of Tidore, he meant to expose this persistence in forbidden ways. Regardless of consequences for the dignified old raja and the engaging Muhamed, he would also report aspects of life at Kilvaru. The traders there still dealt in human beings.

He was not so much concerned with adult or adolescent slaves, often purchased from Papuan tribes who specialized in taking captives for the purpose. The Ceramese highly valued their Papuans, the girls as concubines and the youths as industrious, obedient workers. What made his gorge rise was the treatment of children two or three years old, sold for next to nothing by their parents. These 'wares of small price' were so starved and neglected that they only by chance survived to reach full market value. At the case of one little child, emaciated and covered with sores, crawling about among goats beneath a hut, Maclay so trembled with anger that he could hardly stand. He delivered his reprimand on the spot. He meant to cause more lasting action from Buitenzorg.

James Loudon was a man of his word. On the way to Ambon with the resident, Maclay met the steamer despatched to bring him from New Guinea. But he had no thought for the colony's useless trouble and expense. On arrival at Ambon, suffering from fever and neuralgia, he entered hospital under the care of Dr Huseman, a 'decent fellow' he had met during the outward journey.

He still thought of expeditions—to New Guinea with a Dutch

acquaintance, to the Kei and Aru islands or to Halmahera, where the little-known interior sheltered a people said to be related to Papuans. Such hopes were abandoned as he lay week after week, with erysipelas and partial paralysis added to his sufferings. The doctors regarded his case with great anxiety. Visitors from H.M.S. *Basilisk* were convinced that he could not live, a belief they spread by word of mouth and correspondence. Yet Maclay listened intently to accounts of *Basilisk's* voyage in New Guinea waters, noted that her officers had not set foot on the Maclay Coast, and obtained a copy of Captain Moresby's map. For the present he said nothing about an ominous piece of imperialism, Moresby's proclamation of three islands off eastern New Guinea as a British possession.

By the end of June 1874, thanking his hardy constitution and the efficient hospital, he had recovered well enough to resume his journey. The wandering twenty-day voyage aided his recuperation. It allowed him to confirm that Dutch officials at Ternate were as ignorant as their Ambon counterparts about the despatch of *hongis*. It also renewed his acquaintance with the northern peninsula of Celebes, a district he regarded as a possible home.

The home he re-entered was no longer the safe haven he had left in December. The government that supported James Loudon had fallen. Having sent in his resignation, Loudon acted as governor-general only until his successor's arrival. This made no immediate difference to Maclay. When the family moved to the rather modest country residence, their guest went with them. But something in Maclay resisted these changes, preventing any admission that his patron had ceased to be all-powerful. He acted as though no such thing had occurred.

On the case of Kapitan Mavara, the governor-general requested written particulars. He received a statement fit to evoke both mirth and anguish. Without access to Maclay's journal, Loudon could not guess that the original charge against Mavara had been that of 'permitting' murders, not of committing them. He could not question Maclay's account of how men from the *urumbai*, immediately after the attack, had found stolen goods in the chieftain's hut. Nor could he be aware that upon arrest Kapitan Mavara had made two useless remarks rather than the full confession that Maclay now described. There was no such difficulty in perceiving that Maclay had no first-hand knowledge of any significant event. Moreover, he discredited his informants and potential witnesses by suggesting that their personal interests made it 'impossible to attach great importance to the word of these people'. After that, the governor-general would hardly bother to explain the worthlessness of a paraphrased confession, allegedly obtained from a man with a hand on his windpipe and a revolver held 'almost to his teeth'.

One surprising aspect of the statement was Maclay's anxiety to discredit the headman of his crew. Sangil figured in the explorer's diary as an interpreter whose translations, sometimes doubted, were never actually proved wrong. He appeared as a serious adviser, as one of Maclay's bodyguard, as member of the Kamaka-Walla expedition, finally as master-at-arms taking charge of the prisoner. He seemed a reliable officer against whom Maclay made no particular complaint. Yet almost as much of Maclay's testimony was devoted to Sangil's short-comings as to the crimes of Kapitan Mavara. Far from rendering service, Sangil had caused 'many annoyances and difficulties'. Ignorant of the 'Papuan' language, lazy and cowardly, he had done nothing but smoke opium and skulk in the cabin of the *urumbai*. His was 'a character full of falsehood and deceit', in all things untrustworthy. It almost seemed that Maclay was afraid of Sangil.

After tendering his statement, Maclay brought forward evidence from unidentified traders who had told him that Kapitan Mavara frequently 'robbed Makasar and Ceram *prahus*, in this committing murders'. It appeared in the end that he had removed the prisoner from New Guinea to prevent further crimes and allow the government to make a 'salutary example', which would then, presumably, be publicized in Papua-Koviai.

Time passed, and no witnesses were called. Maclay learned that his captive, a subject of the sultan of Tidore, accused of crimes committed in the sultan's territories, had been sent to Tidore and there imprisoned. Finally he heard that Mavara had been deported to New Guinea—in other words, sent home. Kapitan Mavara was never tried. But then there would have been no trial had Maclay carried out his original intention of shooting the prisoner on the spot.

The additional charges appeared in a memorandum presented soon after Maclay reached Buitenzorg. He described what he had learned about *hongis* and the treatment of Papuan children at Kilvaru. In more general terms, he discussed the 'deplorable state' of Papua-Koviai. He did not in this report lay the blame so exclusively on Malays as he had in writing to Russia. He placed more emphasis on local warfare as a cause of depopulation, terror and nomadism. He mentioned murder of traders, theft of cargoes and non-payment of debts as factors in the decline of New Guinea trade. But he made it clear that his sympathy lay with the natives in their 'sad lot'. He advocated a Dutch settlement 'strong enough to maintain justice and punish wrongdoers'. Thus protected, the Papuans would abandon fighting and nomadism and settle to cultivate the soil. Trade would revive; Papua-Koviai would attain the prosperity foretold by its natural wealth; the Netherlands would be justified at last in claiming the territory as its own.

The experience of Fort du Bus, which in six years had made no impression on Papua-Koviai, did not encourage hopes of transformation. But Maclay envisaged a purely military colony, with suppression of 'lawless acts' as its sole aim. The natives wanted such an establishment, he insisted. In any case, he expected no trouble in maintaining a military post, since 'the sparsity of the population and the weak influence of chiefs would greatly facilitate such an undertaking'.

He seemed unconscious of addressing an official whose authority survived only from day to day. He also revealed how little he understood James Loudon and the Dutch East Indies. Traditionally the colony existed for the sake of Java, with interests in Celebes and the Moluccas. Elsewhere, Dutch control was exercised through native rulers. Year in, year out, Loudon insisted that Netherlands power should not be asserted in any more territories. Even while invading Atjeh, he had not contemplated direct rule. Holding that Netherlands resources were over-extended, he was justified by everything in the Indies. Every residency outside Java reported chronic piracy, slave-trading, insurrection and anarchy.

Over it all hung the spectre of Atjeh, straining colonial resources and heartening all rebels. In December 1873 a larger Dutch army had landed in Sumatra. Within a few weeks the recalcitrant sultan was dead, a successor installed and a treaty signed. Then came the blow from which Batavia never recovered. No sultan had authority to bind Atjeh to the Dutch. Real power belonged to a dozen chiefdoms, jealous of their own independence. The war was extinguished in one district, reborn in another. Native leaders were killed or imprisoned, and new leaders took their places. The Dutch parliament and people demanded quick victory in this unforeseen war. The troops plunged through Sumatran swamps and jungles, hunting and hunted by an enemy who was everywhere and nowhere. With the best intentions, James Loudon had created a war that would virtually halt development of the Indies for a whole generation, and cost the lives of Dutchmen and Sumatrans yet unborn.

Oblivious to the older man's despair, Maclay was ready to become a reformer. Despite his confident tone, he did not regard the pacification of Papua-Koviai as easy. Success required a leader free of self-seeking ambition, familiar with the land and people, and moved purely by 'humane and sympathetic feelings'. It seemed to him that one man combined the knowledge, compassion, moral influence and will to save that tormented country. As for the natives, he recalled, or thought he recalled, the respect they showed him, the eagerness with which they began to cultivate the soil near his house, their reiterated wish for a protector. They might well have used the words in which ninth-century Russians had addressed the Scandinavians: 'Our land is great and rich, but there is no order in it. Come and rule over us!'

Entering a sequence of events with no known beginning or foreseeable end, he had thrown in his lot with the party that flattered him best. He had failed to protect Aiduma's people, failed to prevent Aiduma's revenge, and slipped perilously close to becoming its object. Impervious to his influence, the Vuoucirau abandoned peace for a share in other people's quarrels. Yet Maclay saw no weakness in his authority or error in his judgement. To regulate affairs in south-west New Guinea, he needed only physical power to match his moral force.

In private conversation with Loudon, he indicated the need for a few dozen Javanese soldiers and a gunboat. With these, he undertook to uproot in one year the evils of centuries. Since '*only* the wish to be useful to this part of the human race' prompted his offer, he felt justified in imposing further conditions. There must be no other European involved. He must not be recompensed or fettered by any kind of payment from the Dutch. He must have complete independence of action, 'going as far as power of life and death over my subordinates and the natives'.

Loudon did not bother with much explanation of his refusal, stating only that the Netherlands intended no further settlement. He could hardly help feeling uneasy. Maclay seemed unaware of demanding personal power that no civilized government could confer. His naivety and confusion were almost touching when he rejected all European assistance, yet required a gunboat with its inevitable officers and crew. The same qualities became frightening when he demanded that he, as dictator answerable to nobody, should have 'power of life and death' over Netherlands soldiers and sailors. Combined with attitudes displayed in the case of Kapitan Mavara, the proposal revealed that his idealistic consciousness might breed monsters.

He continued to live with the Loudons, his friends apparently no less respectful and affectionate than of old. He had shown himself muddled, impetuous and ignorant of the restraints upon respectable governments. He had given a glimpse of the moral arrogance and breathtaking self-confidence of which he was capable. But these need never be exercised in James Loudon's jurisdiction. Loudon saw no evidence that his friend was ever less than honest, every reason to respect the humanitarian who reported the secret despatch of *hongis* and the fate of little Papuans in the slave-dealing islands.

Maclay still thought Loudon a just, well-meaning man, though unexpectedly hidebound. He declined to admit that his patron lacked the power to authorize a dictatorship. Feeling that conditions attached to his offer had influenced the refusal, he was prepared to believe that in this Loudon fell short of ideal justice. He argued that the decision resulted largely from his being a foreigner. The suspected prejudice did not change his regard for the family at Tjipanas.

No more did he abandon hope of pacification for Papua-Koviai. His report to the Russian Geographical Society was an *exposé* of violence, misery and dislocation. For a Batavia scientific journal, he prepared a summary of his semi-official memorandum, including the news that he had proposed 'a sure and simple way to reform the situation' and a plea that his report should not be 'merely consigned to the archives'. Late that year he wrote again to St Petersburg, describing his personal offer. While he hoped that appeals to the Dutch would not 'remain without effect', his strongest feeling was resigned pity for 'the poor Papuans of Koviai', who for decades more would go on 'starving, plundering and killing each other, stealing and selling each other into bondage'. He evidently looked for some Russian intervention; more than a year later, he was asking what had been done; but whatever happened to his report in Batavia, his inviting letter was promptly buried in the archives of the Russian Geographical Society.

He professed himself content with a rejection that allowed this year, unexpectedly offered 'out of humanitarianism to practical activities', to be given to pure science. His second stay in Java produced little scientific work. Apart from his report to the Geographical Society (written mainly at Kilvaru), a brief account of the expedition for a German journal, and a correction to matter previously published, the articles that appeared that year had been sent to press before he left for Papua-Koviai. These last months of 1874 passed mainly in recuperation and in planning a new journey.

The peaceful family life, now that of a prince in exile, went on as though it could never be disrupted. Maclay read and meditated, sketched and listened to music. He could entertain friends with a wealth of exciting anecdotes, some of them—like those of his journey 'alone and unarmed' in the Kamaka Mountains, and his virtually single-handed arrest of Kapitan Mavara—becoming more heroic as time passed. His love for the little sister who was developing under his eyes and influence made steady though uncharted progress. Their initials, entwined and decorated, appeared in the margins of his writings. The symbol of her name floated above his landscapes. Promises were exchanged, though how far these went was never revealed. He nevertheless imagined journeys—to the Malay Peninsula, to Europe, to Australia—in which his beloved had no apparent place.

All plans, as ever, depended on money. Meshchersky had paid for the Papua-Koviai expedition, allowing a reasonable sum for Maclay's support on his return. Maclay found himself 'placed under the necessity of *borrowing*' to provide for further travels. 'It is even possible that this money will not suffice', he warned his mother, 'and that on my return (?) I will be forced to resort to further borrowing'. Hoping that the tax would not inconvenience her too much, he requested despatch of funds without delay.

He had reason to believe that no such remittance would arrive. Before leaving for Papua-Koviai, he had learned that Ekaterina Semyonovna's obsession with landed property had led her to purchase an estate in the Kiev district. At the time he had limited his comment to the hope that she would not repent a decision he personally found 'far from cheering'. Lying ill after the expedition, he had received almost with surprise her confirmation of the news. For months he could not trust himself to reply. Then, shortly after regretting that she had tied herself to this property, not even situated in a good climate, he began to feel that 'Malin', as the estate was called, might be put to use.

The outcome was a series of numbered questions requiring Ekaterina Semyonovna to state, firstly, whether her wandering son was entitled to share in the property. If he was, she must advise whether he could expect an income from that share or had, as he obviously preferred, the right *'to turn it into money'*. Assuming that questions 1 and 2 were answered in the affirmative, he asked: 'Approximately when can I, *with justice to all*, receive my proper share?'

He could not be expected to live permanently in Europe. Within a few years he might be forced to go to Australia for his health. But his mother could expect him fairly soon. 'My tasks are approaching their conclusion', he pleaded, 'and in two years I will be able to return to Europe. But will it be possible for me to live *independently* there? Will I just have the means to be entirely free to continue my scientific work, without depending on any kind of salary or assistance?' He needed so little. He would be more content with 'a trifle' than if he sold time and thoughts 'for thousands'. All he asked was a candid answer confirming his right to whatever he contemplated spending, assuring him that he might always count on her support. 'I ask you very urgently', he concluded, 'to answer me at once and quite frankly, *if* you still love your son a little and have not quite forgotten him'.

The answer was silence. As Olga had explained when Meshchersky asked about money on her brother's behalf, the purchase of Malin had involved great financial sacrifice. Then came the time of drought, dying cattle, desiccated crops, negotiations for an emergency loan. Nikolai Nikolaevich's share, if it existed, would be a share of debt.

The silence that protected him from this knowledge also saved him from knowing how deeply his sister was hurt. With almost religious faith, Olga believed that he could not die before they met again and his research was laid before the scientific world. She learned of his survival only by a telegram from Meshchersky. To her, his work remained 'a right and just cause' which must prevail, but she faced a pressing task of her own, the fight for mental survival amid a host of dreary worries. She hardened her thoughts and suggested that Nikolai Nikolaevich's needs might be met by the Russian Geographical Society.

Maclay had considered that possibility for himself. He had asked financial help from the Society, '*not* as a gift, but as a temporary loan', by which the organization might justify its existence. 'I have already said that for my researches I am prepared to sacrifice all', he told Baron Osten-Sacken, 'but it is a difficult circumstance when this *all* does not suffice'. Osten-Sacken found this letter 'quite strange', but passed it to the finance committee. Semyonov-Tianshansky received a more persuasive appeal. While awaiting replies, Maclay depended heavily on Hendrick-Jan Ankersmit, head of Dummler and Co., Batavia. Mynheer Ankersmit was a gentleman and a friend. He nevertheless lent money to make money, and he would ask for it back, principal plus interest.

Regardless of love or money, Maclay planned a new expedition. For reasons of health, he could not return immediately to New Guinea. It seemed that his health might benefit from a visit to the heart of the Malay Peninsula, where a note on his world-map indicated another race possibly allied to the Papuans.

The European powers that had squabbled over footholds on the Peninsula since the days of Albuquerque had never done much to explore the interior or investigate its inhabitants. Nevertheless by 1813 the armchair anthropologist James Cowles Prichard, in a book whose latest edition Maclay had studied, had been able to assert: 'Most of the mountainous districts in the peninsula of Malacca are peopled with tribes of black savages, who closely resemble the Papuas, and are evidently of the same stock'. More recent descriptions of these people only confused opinion, eminent men arguing strongly against what had been accepted as fact. The disputants in Europe had never seen a native of the Malayan interior. But equal confusion appeared among those who had met these tribes, some describing them as 'negritos' while others maintained that the 'Sakai' or 'Semang' did not differ significantly from Malays. Maclay proposed to settle the disagreement by seeking out the pure-blooded aborigines who must live in areas never visited by Europeans.

He restricted his aims to 'finding and observing, from a purely zoological point of view, this interesting variety of the human race', proposing to complete the task in a matter of days. The country, population and means of travel all being unknown, he could plan nothing beyond the purchase of a steamer ticket. But the undertaking must not be postponed. He must push forward, 'not thinking much about the future', to do what his failing strength permitted. He also believed himself in search of a race whose language, customs and very

Mkal, the Jakun girl,
Lobo-Loondan, Johor,
1875

On the Keratong River, Johor, 1874

Bivouac on the Madek River, Johor, 1875

The title page to the journal or sketch book of the second Malay
Peninsula expedition

Pekan, the capital of Pahang, July 1875

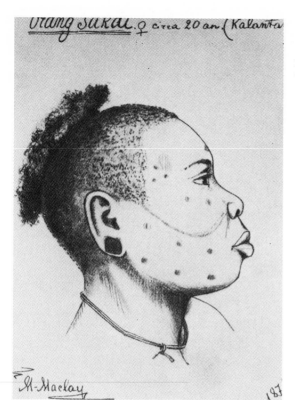

A negrito woman,
Kelantan, 1875

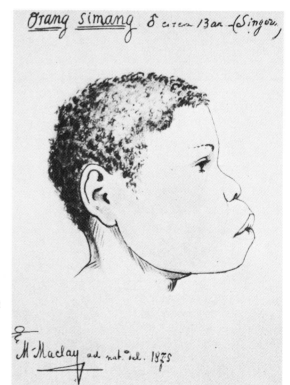

'A real chimpanzee profile':
one of Maclay's drawings
of typical negritos, 1875

form must soon vanish before the advance of stronger peoples. Again he was 'the last naturalist', the recorder of what had been.

Thoughts of the future resulted, before he left Batavia, in the drawing-up of a new will. In concrete terms, the chief beneficiaries were Meshchersky, who would have all books, manuscripts and drawings, and the Russian Geographical Society, which would receive all collections with the exception of craniological specimens. The skulls were to go to the museum of the Imperial Academy of Sciences, with an addition that aroused interest when the news became public: Maclay intended to have his own head preserved and sent to the Academy. Ahmad was allocated 1000 silver roubles that the testator did not possess. Olga, once sole beneficiary, became residuary legatee, inheriting all her brother's 'property estate and rights not mentioned above in this Will'. For his mother and brothers there was not a memento or a word. Nor was there a remembrance for anyone in the Loudon family.

Things had fallen apart at Buitenzorg. Perhaps for reasons of love or money—his dealings with James Loudon's daughter or his dealings with Ankersmit—perhaps because of more public actions, Maclay was no longer an honoured guest in the Loudon household. The reasons remained locked in the breasts of those concerned. From magnanimity, from embarrassment, or from deeper than ordinary hurt, neither party decried the other to outsiders.

Preparing to leave Java, Maclay wished only to forget Buitenzorg. The home in which he had lived as son, as brother, as prince, had become the symbol of betrayal and humiliation, from which he drew the bitterest of lessons: 'Don't become attached to anyone. Don't believe in others'. He did not renounce his love, though what he might do about it remained a mystery. But when the steamer was under way for Singapore, he realized he had forgotten to hand over the letter for his beloved.

9: Pages from an Old Book

MACLAY NEVER ADMIRED Singapore's favourite music, a Chinese orchestra of bank tellers ceaselessly counting dollars or testing for counterfeit by pouring coin from hand to hand. His mood late in 1874 did not respond to the motley immigrant population or the placid waters embroidered at night with the multicoloured reflections of lanterns. In the dark little rooms and draughty corridors of the single men's quarters at the Hôtel de l'Europe, he ate poor food, winced at loud voices, slamming doors, the tramp of Europeans on their way to or from China, Japan, the Indies or Australia. Surrounded by 'respectable members of the rabble', he could neither rest nor work.

He inspected ethnological collections brought in by H.M.S. *Basilisk*, and renewed acquaintance with local friends of science. In the governor's absence, he called at Government House and listened to the chatter of his excellency's attractive wife. But the hotel became unbearable. The gossip—like the story of a wandering Hungarian nobleman, said to be hopelessly in love with the governor's lady—set him brooding on his own lost love. He repacked his bags and fled to Johor Baharu.

For once there were no other guests in the unpretentious palace overlooking the waters between the mainland and Singapore Island. The capital that had grown up on the site of a saw-milling village was far enough away. Maclay read and wrote, admired the view, investigated ways and means for his expedition. On an excursion with officials, he met the local tribe of '*Orang-utan*', the wild 'men of the forest', living in their normal miserable conditions while felling timber for the government. With his host, the maharaja Abu Bakar, he talked about the roads and railways, schools and hospitals the ruler meant to build and the European ideas he hoped would benefit his country. He liked the maharaja, but sometimes preferred to dine alone. Memories of Buitenzorg tormented him. Rainy days brought on the 'blue devils'. Solitude that edged towards loneliness when he reproached his forgetful sister was too peopled for a mood that became 'constantly more misanthropic'. His shaky tranquillity came to an end with the arrival of four Englishwomen who chattered and sang half the night. From the respectable rabble there was no escape but the jungle.

When he visited Singapore again, he found the governor could contribute little. On taking up his appointment in 1873, Sir Andrew Clarke had been unable to obtain maps or up-to-date facts about lands next door to the British colonies. It was said that no European and very few Malays could give the names of all the peninsula states, their geographical positions or the titles of their rulers. To the British, the sole reliable informant was Abu Bakar, who had no map of his own territory.

Maclay filled his place at the Government House table and sat through the play to which he accompanied the vice-regal party. His bitterness and desolation, welling up with thoughts of letters that did not arrive from Buitenzorg, was not betrayed to his host. His state of mind was no more apparent to Luigi Maria D'Albertis, who met him late that night. Superficially they had little in common—the swashbuckling, opera-singing D'Albertis and Maclay, the would-be contemplative. Yet the Italian explorer was captivated by Maclay's enthusiastic talk of past adventures and those he hoped to have. In 'very lively French', his eyes shining and dancing, Maclay described his expedition to Papua-Koviai and sketched future travels. D'Albertis understood why Maclay had used his gun in Papua-Koviai. He shared Maclay's indignation over the misbehaviour of the Ceramese sailors, the real cause of the trouble. They agreed about everything, D'Albertis reported, particularly about New Guinea, the land that obsessed them both. When the Russian spoke of the Maclay Coast, 'you would think he had found the earthly Paradise'. To the Italian, the whole island was paradise, degraded to Purgatory where other white men had set foot. But while they praised Papuan customs and virtues, with comparisons much to the disadvantage of Europeans, the travellers looked to the day when 'those happy savages will become civilized human beings'. Both, though they might differ about the means, believed they knew how to accomplish this apparently inconsistent end.

D'Albertis left again for New Guinea, to besiege the natives with confident love that in a moment crumbled into fear and hatred, benevolence that favoured a little salutary terror. Maclay already planned a third visit to the island, and a fourth expedition in which his brother Vladimir would join. He still seemed no closer to his object in

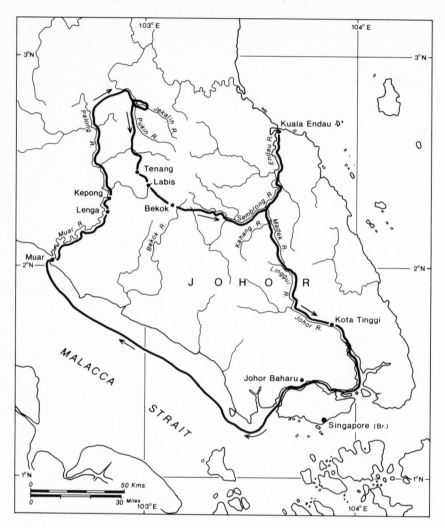

Maclay's journey in Johor and southern Pahang, 1874–75

the Peninsula. Meetings with *Orang-utan* of Johor ('Jakun' as they were called more precisely) had assured him that 'Papuan' characteristics would be found among inland tribes. Reaching these people was more difficult than expected. Johor's one road ran in the wrong direction. Elsewhere, tracks were so narrow that a porter's load must be very small. At best, a man could carry no more than his own provisions for twenty days. Amid counsels of despair, Maclay began to think the undertaking 'almost impracticable'. Then came a sudden opportunity, a police foray in borderlands of the north-west, and within three days the new adventure began.

The excursion meant to last twenty days eventually took fifty, traversing Johor from the Straits of Malacca to the South China Sea and from northern border regions to the tip of the peninsula. Deposited by the gunboat at a settlement on the Muar River, Maclay, Ahmad and a Javanese cook named Sainan took to the river again in a *yalo*, a partly-covered, flat-bottomed boat with four rowers. They covered much of the distance by similar means. Rivers were the true roads of the country, the tracks mere temporary links between streams. Swollen by rains, the waters spread wide, travellers often navigating a forest rather than a river.

Maclay at first regarded this style of travel as 'comfort', feeling that he saw more of the country than was visible from a jungle-walled track. As river voyages extended and multiplied, he grew cramped and tired in the narrow belly of a canoe or balanced all day on the baggage. On narrow streams, overhanging vegetation must be cut away. Where banks were undermined, the boat's awning was removed and the occupants lay flat to creep beneath fallen trees. Maclay noticed how little freeboard kept his heavily-laden craft afloat, how easily an incautious movement brought water pouring in. Along the watery highways, the primal fear of drowning kept him company.

He still preferred the rivers to the tracks. When the party was divided the porters, not Maclay, took the land route to their meeting-place. Between voyages they faced innumerable crossings of the same sinuous rivulet, knee-deep swamps or flooded hollows where water reached the waist. Here Maclay tried to negotiate a slippery log and tumbled into the stream. Elsewhere the men towed him on a hastily-built raft or raised a makeshift bridge that might be crossed with safety but never with dignity. On overgrown paths, half the day might be lost in chopping through spiny entanglements. In more civilized places Maclay walked 'infernal structures' of poles laid lengthwise, envying the barefooted porters their coolness and agility.

By night he shook with fever or wrote by the light of dammar-resin torches in a variety of places. He spent poetic nights afloat in a moonlit forest. He found shelter at encampments of the western Jakun and in the communal dwellings of more settled eastern tribes. In villages he shared a Malay headman's house, took over a humbler dwelling, or claimed the hospitality of a lone Chinese. Nowhere did he feel so much at home as in the jungle bivouacs that he sketched and described with particular pleasure. Sometimes his followers merely built him a platform of branches above the reach of sudden floods. Sometimes they raised a hut on piles. Maclay was often content with an arrangement tested in Papua-Koviai, a hammock slung between trees and roofed with a rubber sheet. The bivouac symbolized his existence, a nomad's life in which home began wherever the day's journey ended.

He wandered northward well beyond the ill-defined frontier, south again and eastward to the sea, plotting his course for a progressive maharaja whose country had never been mapped. On featureless wooded plains rising to an almost equally featureless wooded plateau, he found little to indicate but rivers and rare settlements. With his eye for enlivening detail, he was never bored. Though he hailed the first mountains seen in his journey, he did not strike out for the ranges. For the time being he sought neither the sublime nor final answers to his questions.

He met no great perils once despatch of baggage by the land route let his vessel ride higher in the stream. He saw tiger tracks, traps for tigers, people who feared the beast and people who bore its claw marks, but never a tiger. He floundered in the water-filled tracks of elephants, but elephants never appeared. The one great snake to cross his path was instantly gone, leaving only an impression of speed and elegance. Nor did he contend with the savagery of man. Johor had long been free of the chiefly power-struggles, brigandage and gang-warfare that made life cheap farther north. On the frontier, where neighbouring Pahang sometimes pressed territorial claims, the travellers found barricades across streams, communications at a standstill. Following the murder of a Johor official and the appearance of a strongman from over the border, many people had fled and the remainder lived in fear. The expedition passed through as though the conflict were one of shadows. Maclay was apparently right when he told his followers that a white *tuan* need not fear the squabbles of Malays.

Afterwards he was inclined to recall the sufferings more vividly than the compensations. He told of finding his boots full of blood after a day in company with leeches, of attacks by mosquitoes and the agony of centipede bites. He spoke of wearing wet boots for more than a month and of seventeen days without a dry stitch of clothing. In retrospect he seemed to have spent too many overlong days in the jungle, all of them filled by weariness and pain. At the time, he did not feel the journey an unrelieved martyrdom. Hardships faded in dawn splendours, the beckoning gleam of rivers, shafts of sunlight in treasure-caves of vegetation whose riches he could not describe. In moments of solitude he listened to the silence. 'But in the jungle it is never silent', he corrected himself; 'only there is not that insistent hubbub of humanity, so often distasteful to me'. In the muted sounds of wordless life, the plash of water on leaves, the distant, reverberating fall of trees, he heard the voice of the tropical lands and pledged himself anew to them. He found himself 'perfectly well in this way of life', more than ever resolved to continue it.

His life in the jungle included much of an ingredient essential to his freedom, the servitude of others. Arriving at a settlement, he would present an open letter from the maharaja, ordering the headmen to do everything Maclay required. Where respect for authority was strong but the art of reading somewhat neglected, the sight of the princely seal was enough. If too many excuses were made, Maclay had the ruler's letter read out and threatened recalcitrants with the maharaja's anger. He might still be irritated by people who talked more than they acted, by the eternal 'a long way' or 'I don't know' of men evading his questions. But Johor was a law-abiding country, and the maharaja's will was law. If Maclay intended to stay overnight, the best hut was cleared for him. Should he wish to move on immediately, porters must be found within an hour. Boats were requisitioned; people whose crops barely satisfied their needs brought him supplies; men who never went farther than their own ricefields left their homes and occupations and shouldered loads for destinations where they had no business.

Maclay exercised the kind of power he had known in the Nether-lands Indies, the authority granted a white *tuan* by a government with an arm long enough to inspire fear. He sometimes coupled threats of his own anger with invocation of the maharaja. He never had to depend on personal prestige or resort to bribes. He also came to feel that Europeans were more highly esteemed here than in the Indies. In reaction against a half-formed allegiance, he was prepared to attribute this to some difference in character between the English and the Dutch. Or perhaps it resulted from the comparative rarity of Europeans in the Peninsula. As either a fascinating novelty or a supposed representative of Singapore, he could rely on his right to command.

The same half-official, half-magical power that secured supplies and transport brought him material for research. At first, having politely waited for Jakun who failed to appear, he attracted suitable crowds by promises of tobacco and rice. He soon discarded such tactics. Jakun on the move were ordered to turn back. When Maclay reached one of their encampments, the tribal leader had to assemble the people. In Malay settlements, it was the headman's duty to collect all Jakun in the neighbourhood. Maclay noticed that Malays often treated these people

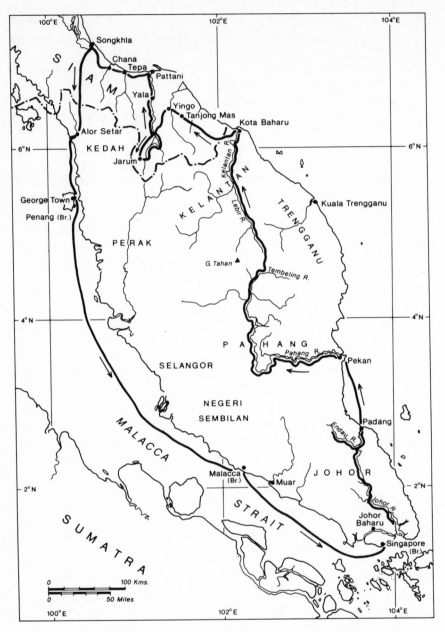

Maclay's journey in the Malay states and southern Siam, 1875

cruelly. He did not ask how his orders were fulfilled. Finding terrified women and children huddled in a windowless hut, he did not question the manner of their imprisonment. Their temporary fear and discomfort, perhaps their pain, were insignificant beside his object. He wished only that they would not hinder him by covering their faces and turning to the wall.

With his right to obedience established, he was kind to all ranks and races. Malay notables became quite friendly and communicative. A Chinese might of his own accord welcome the traveller and offer the fruits of his garden. Among the Jakun, Maclay found intelligence, energy and courage, 'quite pleasant faces' and girls who were not bad-looking by any standards. He shared his quinine, listened to Jakun grievances and tried to allay fears. His men, often hard-driven on the march, were treated well as long as they worked and obeyed without question. Delighted by tropical nature, falling into the rhythm of travel, he stopped asking 'What next, and how much farther?' With red wine, more biscuits and an inexhaustible stock of quinine, he could contentedly spend longer in 'these backwoods'.

Yet he was always in a hurry. Those who served the restless white *tuan* never wished to travel so far or so fast. Usually they did not want to travel at all. As the maharaja had predicted, the first crew of Jakun Maclay requisitioned ran off into the jungle, to be retrieved by the headmen threatening death from the white man's gun. They were doubtless afraid of the work, as Maclay decided, since the loads were heavy and the Jakun very small. They were strangers to discipline, living semi-nomadic lives and hardly acknowledging any authority. But once in harness they seemed cheerfully resigned, clearing the track and bearing loads for ten or eleven hours a day. They did not need to be told that the day wasn't over, or that the night would be spent at a certain place because Maclay willed it so. He was always glad to exchange the lazy, argumentative Malays for quiet, obedient little Jakun.

He did so with particular pleasure towards the end of the journey. Rowing back from the east coast, along the Endau River, the men shouted and laughed until he let them know the noise was intolerable. When after a day of deadly silence the roof of the shelter caught fire, he suspected the blaze was not entirely accidental. The Malays were as anxious to leave the white master as he was to be rid of them. At their suggestion, he stopped a clan of travelling Jakun and forced them to return to their old camp.

For some reason, only three Jakun could be obtained. Day after day, they struggled through swamps, bowed under loads that had seemed excessive to much bigger men. Rain poured down; barricades caused labour and delay; deteriorating rice was sorted grain by grain to obtain a scanty meal. Giving way to pity, weariness and something in the atmosphere, Maclay at last called an early halt and sent the Jakun to a village to find more men of their own stamp.

Days passed and no Jakun appeared. Feeling the approach of fever, Maclay thought of going to the village, but stayed and unpacked the baggage. All his remaining followers set off to find provisions and the Jakun. With fever, swollen legs and painful sores, he sat alone in the jungle.

He was pleased with solitude, reminded of his peaceful isolation on the Maclay Coast. Listening to the murmur of the forest, he thought of past and future, considered ethnological results and sought less banal adjectives to describe his surroundings. He had never felt more content in his way of life or more enchanted by the tropical lands. But he had no quinine, dry blankets or clothing. The little food remaining could not be cooked, for rain doused the fire and there were no matches. After two days poetry and philosophy fled before brute hunger. When against the odds his Jakun reappeared, he was frankly glad to see them, still more pleased with the rice they brought and the fire they kindled. When his short-handed party thereafter proposed an early halt, Maclay himself explained that the men were slightly built and the loads very heavy.

Apart from these concessions, which hardly mattered so late in the journey, he never had to relax the will of the white *tuan*. Among the learned and humane in cities, he scorned the white man's pretensions and condemned European absorption of the world. In the jungle, at once the slave and master of a myth, he sustained almost flawlessly the burden of European superiority and power. Malays and Jakun procrastinated or malingered, argued or played tricks. They bent to the white man's authority in the end, never forcing him to use a stronger weapon than his voice. It was not until he re-entered civilized areas that Maclay made the ultimate wager in the game of rank and race. The lower Johor River was plied by large, peculiar vessels. Marching past plantations of pepper and *gambir*, new-felled forest and busy sawmills, he heard a language as foreign to the country as his own. The enterprise of this district was owned and worked exclusively by Chinese.

Maclay admired Chinese industry. The best European workers, he guessed, could not equal 'these yellow men'. He distinguished their position from that of Malays, never treating the Chinese settler as a man whose labour could be requisitioned. Some of the richest and most influential people in Singapore were Chinese. The humblest Chinese immigrant was encouraged by the colonial administration. Behind them stretched the vast, disdainful empire where Maclay had been flattered to have audience with a lofty mandarin. Yet in southern Johor he found himself increasingly annoyed by their attitude towards a white man. Mostly it was an indefinite something in the way people spoke or looked at him. Then came a clearer instance. Without so much as a reply from the deck, the junk he hailed kept on its course for Singapore, leaving him standing on the river bank with the letter he wished to send. A dozen Malays had seen him treated as disrespectfully as their own headman.

The lone Chinese sawyer working in the forest knew nothing of this. When Maclay called him to show the way, there was no response. At a second summons the workman neither raised his head nor altered the rhythm of his saw. Malays were watching this contest of race and station. Incivility that might earn a European workman a stroke of the gentleman's cane assumed the proportions of dangerous revolt. Raising his gun, Maclay told the Chinese to come at once or be shot.

It was well for the white man that the the yellow man decided to obey. Johor's ruler had certainly never authorized his friend to shoot the people who provided the state's only revenue. Anxious to establish the rule of law, he could not permit Maclay to shoot anybody. Anger also blinded Maclay to further complications. Many Chinese workers in Johor held dangerously influential papers. One moment more, and Maclay might have shot a British citizen.

Maclay was not the first white man to cross Johor. That had been done accidentally a year before, by an Englishman pursuing elephants. But he had seen and charted much territory never visited by Europeans. He had also looked into the question of boundaries and gathered alarming political information.

Applying their own names for rivers, the Pahang people claimed territories extending as much as twenty kilometres south of the boundary recognized by Johor. Fear of Pahang disrupted life well beyond the area in dispute. Assured on the Pahang side that the state had no warlike intentions, Maclay had nevertheless found villages full of armed men, an atmosphere of preparedness and secrecy. On the other hand, he heard evidence that Pahang's ruler was not necessarily responsible for this. People along the frontier complained of an ambitious local chief who used the border question to his own advantage, terrorizing Johor and Pahang alike. Curious to interview a person who reportedly combined great boldness and determination with almost monstrous ugliness, Maclay had visited the warlord's village. The tyrant did not choose to meet the white *tuan*, but the attitude of his followers matched the stories.

Whether or not he was asked to investigate, Maclay was bound to report, for the people had begged him to tell the maharaja of their sufferings. He could no more withhold his observations on the weakness of Johor's defences and the low morale of the defenders. Taken for an emissary of Singapore, he had also used this misunderstanding to impress Pahang minds with the Johor version of political geography. His findings were neither new nor conclusive, but his enquiries had been conducted with the coolness and skill of an experienced political agent.

He would soon be going back to Pahang for further scientific work. Among the Jakun he had seen enough dark skins, broad noses and frizzy hair to satisfy him of a 'Papuan' presence. But these traits appeared sporadically in an extremely mixed population, where the majority resembled undersized Malays. He often wavered in his interpretation. Sometimes exceptionally dark skin and curly hair were read as signs of a Papuan 'infusion'. His latest opinions moved far in the opposite direction. Comparing some Jakun with Ahmad, he found them matching feature for feature. When he told people that formerly all *Orang-utan* had hair like Ahmad's, Malays and Jakun politely agreed. Instead of finding a Papuan strain in basically Malay tribes, he had come to regard the exceptional individuals as 'retrograde instances', 'reversions to the main aboriginal type'. All the Jakun had once been Papuans.

He felt he had begun to read 'an interesting old book, of whose half-effaced pages some were missing'. The book was not such a simple story, and he was trying to read it upside-down. The Jakun were primitive Malays whose ancestors had lived in the Peninsula long before the arrival of their modernized relatives. When Maclay found them, they were adopting the Malay way of life, exchanging their language for the modern version, and marrying incalculably distant cousins. The absorption he deplored was more a kind of family reunion. But the Jakun intermarried with other groups who shared the wild interior. In north-west Johor they showed the influence of the Senoi, a people of the great mountain ranges, who mixed with negrito tribes known as 'Semang'. Where Maclay found them most interesting, they had mingled more directly with negritos.

Engrossed in the search for Papuans, Maclay never realized the significance of the Jakun majority in whose features he found 'nothing particular'. The very existence of the Senoi was lost in the over-abundance of names by which Malays described primitive tribes. Preliminary results nevertheless showed the direction his quest should take. He had heard of people called 'Semang', all with hair like Ahmad's. Other reported characteristics—like feet three hand-spans long—belonged to an interesting body of fiction. In essence the reports were sober enough to send an investigator farther north. His attention was drawn especially to the jungles of the Tekam River in Pahang, where an informant had seen those mighty footprints.

Soon after Maclay's return, Sir Andrew Clarke, leaving on an urgent mission to Bangkok, suggested that a cruise might benefit the scientist's health. Maclay seized the opportunity to see the Siamese capital, and perhaps buy some material for comparative neurology, an elephant. The trip also promised well for his next expedition. The Malay states north of Pahang were vassals of Siam. Should he wish to travel through them and cross the Siamese frontier, his way would be smoothed by official letters.

He saw King Chulalongkorn (Rama V) only from a distance. He felt no interest in talking with a monarch who 'aped Europeans', no sympathy for the young king who had abolished slavery and relieved his subjects of the obligation to fall on their faces in his divine presence. Maclay tolerated Abu Bakar's taste for tweeds, *Punch* and English horse-racing. He never forgave the 'European barracks-like style' in which the Bangkok palace was being rebuilt, the 'unsuitable' uniforms of Chulalongkorn's officers and un-Siamese decorations worn by 'lackeys and princelings'. He became possibly the only man in history to refuse the offer of an audience with the king of Siam.

While he wandered round the city in search of what was native, incidentally collecting lurid gossip about the king, momentous affairs were discussed. Others besides Maclay were displeased by Chula-longkorn's efforts to ape Europeans. After an angry reaction that threatened to split the state, the conservative and redundant 'second king' had taken refuge in the British consulate. Sir Andrew was trying to mediate the situation while making sure that Chulalongkorn retained supreme power. Someone nevertheless found time to tell the king that the Russian naturalist wanted an elephant. Chulalongkorn sent a written promise that at the next royal elephant hunt the youngest captive would be reserved for Maclay. The king also heard that Maclay thought of visiting territories under Siamese dominion. The result was an open letter commanding all vassals of Rama V to assist the traveller and provide men and supplies.

Maclay never received the elephant, but such thoughtfulness from an absolute monarch gave him further reason to feel he had 'learnt much' in Bangkok. He might have learned more by meeting the king. Chulalongkorn took great interest in the little black people of the far south. Eventually he would write an edifying and popular play with a negrito hero as Noble Savage. Had he known how much they shared, Maclay might even have felt sympathy for Chulalongkorn. The counsellors had decided that the king must bow to the conservatives. Reforms were to be rescinded, modernization postponed. Quiet was restored, French intervention staved off, and a warship remained at Bangkok to protect British interests.

Maclay returned to Singapore more unwell than ever, blaming the heat and long walks in Bangkok for the renewal of his fever and spreading sores on his legs. In this state he went to stay with the vice-consul for the Russian Empire, the Honourable Ho Ah Kay, member of the Legislative Council, occasional member of the Execu-tive Council, shortly to become a C.M.G.

At first sight Maclay seemed to have landed in another earthly Paradise. 'Mr Whampoa', as his host was called, after his birthplace near Canton, was intermittently Singapore's wealthiest citizen and always its most popular, esteemed for tact, fair dealing and liberal outlook as well as profuse hospitality. The creations of Whampoa's kitchen sent visitors into raptures. His garden was famous throughout the East. With all this at his command, Maclay did not live in the big white house where Mr Whampoa entertained all Singapore. While resting his wounds and dictating further notes on Maclay Coast ethnology, he occupied a separate pavilion in the grounds.

The situation might have been uncomfortable for a man who threatened to shoot a disobedient Chinese. Mr Whampoa became quite heated over affront to his countrymen. But Whampoa's 'national taste' rather than national pride upset his guest. The Chinese pavilion bridged one of the lily-ponds that some people thought the garden's most charming features. Maclay thought it unhygienic. By day he sometimes forgot damp timbers and stagnant water. At night he fell helpless victim to the pool's inhabitants. Whining mosquitoes filled his workroom; a sonorous chorus of frogs struck up below. When numerous watchdogs joined the 'unbearable concert' he was beaten. 'All connected thought' fled from his mind. He could no more live with the animal rabble of the Villa Whampoa than among the human herd. As soon as his sore leg permitted, he left for Johor Baharu.

And there it was no better. The maharaja had a large and noisy staff of servants. He was also reconstructing the palace in a style worthier of Johor's ancient glory and his own wealth. Dozens of workmen were replacing brick floors by marble, adding rooms and opening doorways. And to the normal din of the building trade they added a doleful accompaniment. All the workers were convicts, whose chains clanked at every step.

'I am positively suffering. . .', Maclay wrote in agitation. 'For many months I have not had one really peaceful day. Here in these luxurious houses I enviously recall the tranquillity of life in my hut on the Maclay Coast'. Some scientific work, for instance his experiments on cats and dogs with the poisons used to tip Jakun blow-gun darts, was not much affected by noise. He was as little able to read and think as amid the frogs of the Villa Whampoa. In the 'absolute necessity' of finding 'a quite sanctuary' with no interruptions, no need to ask favours, he remembered the old idea of zoological stations.

Anton Dohrn's efforts had resulted in a 'great establishment', being opened while Maclay suffered at Johor Baharu. Maclay conceived nothing like the temple of science at Naples. His 'Tampat Senang' (Place of Repose) was to be 'an isolated abode for *one* student of nature', in the first place for himself. With his own requirements as standard, he chose a high, jungle-covered promontory in Johor Strait, commanding 'a fine view and very complete isolation'. He planned a house and made rules for those who in his absence or after his death might control or occupy the place. European scientists were informed. Similar proposals went to Batavia. But Maclay was not through with asking favours. The site belonged to the maharaja, who after approving began to retreat. Abu Bakar's agreement with the British (designed to prevent other powers from obtaining a foothold at Singapore's back door), pledged him not to sell land to foreigners. After weeks of discussion, and some comment in the press, he felt unable to part with the cape outright. It could be occupied only on lease, the maharaja retaining certain rights over the land. Dissatisfied with this, Maclay dropped his scheme for the present. There was no escape but the jungle.

He spent a wretched four months between expeditions, persecuted by man and beast. Not least of his distress was that loneliness amid crowds that he sought to cure by complete solitude. He attended meetings of the Straits branch of the Royal Asiatic Society. He maintained relations with Government House and with people like the archdeacon, who appreciated his joke in the Malay language likening white-men to 'white ants'. He had no closer friends than those universal providers, the maharaja and Mr Whampoa.

His correspondence was almost as impersonal as his life in the European enclave at the tip of the Malay Peninsula. There were reports to the Russian Geographical Society and letters that acquaintances might see in Russian newspapers. He wrote to Otto Boethlingk on Jakun dialects, to Dohrn and Huxley concerning the 'Tampat Senang', to the Singapore press complaining about reports of his activities. To Baroness von Rhaden he sent a long, much-improved account of his adventures in Papua-Koviai, intended for publication. He had no one to whom to write more intimately. Meshchersky's whereabouts were unknown. Olga did not respond to pleas, playfulness or reproaches. Maclay was probably the only famous explorer who repeatedly asked a geographical society for his mother's address.

In a world that seemed to detach itself from him, his resolve to attach himself to no one was never tested. Much of that chagrin was already dispelled. Early in his journey through Johor, memories of Buitenzorg had filled him with 'very bitter feelings'. When later he thought of his lost beloved, the bitterness had drained away. So had most of the reality. She became a pair of initials entwined with his, a vision as insubstantial as the imagined music that surrounded it. He had come close to forming a more corporeal attachment.

Among the crowd in a Jakun long-house, he had noticed an attractive young person whose sex was hard to determine at first sight. When the expression his gaze evoked had convinced him this was a girl, he took the usual measurements and drew her portrait. Mkal was about thirteen years old, without a physical sign of the early sexual maturity Europeans expected to find among girls of the tropical lands. Maclay depicted hardly perceptible breasts, straight shoulders, a strong young neck beneath a cap of short curls. As he saw them, her features were almost European.

Mkal enjoyed this admiring attention, as frankly drawn to the strange visitor as he to her. That evening she sat near by and watched him writing. As he prepared to leave, depressed by rain and a lowering sky, exasperated by procrastinators and malingerers, Mkal was there, never taking her eyes off him. She was not like the affected, calculating young ladies of Europe, he told himself. He had only to make the parents a present and bid her, 'Come with me'. She would follow as confidently as she carried a heavy box along the slippery causeway, smiling gently at his unsteady progress. Maclay said nothing, boarded the canoe and set off down the brimming river, leaving her to wonder.

Afterwards he thought it strange that he would so gladly have taken this girl with him. The strangest thing was that he found it strange. Though he forgot the date of his birth, he was only twenty-eight years old. For years he had lived like a monk but without a monk's defences, surrounded by the frank sexuality of others, insisting from pride and policy that Maclay did not need women. He had spent months in the same house as the girl he loved, could not marry and could not (without outrage to family and society) invite to share his bed. Then in the jungle he had met or imagined all the world's ideal lover—fresh, beautiful and guileless, submissive and tender as a girl should be, strong, brave and comradely as a perfect boy, intelligent enough for a companion, humble enough to be a willing slave. She was a little sister, a younger brother, a spirit of the wilds. But he had not taken her, and that was the end of it.

Maclay left Johor Baharu in June 1875, again attended by Sainan the cook, who was nothing but a servant, and Ahmad the travelling standard of Papuan ethnology, a far from perfect boy. His followers included twenty men donated by the maharaja, and a 'minor official' who would requisition whatever was needed and transmit Maclay's orders. Plans announced to the Russian Geographical Society promised nothing beyond a visit to the wild tribes of the Tekam. When he spoke of going farther, people had laughed and predicted he would turn back from Pahang.

A government vessel took the party up the Johor River, whence they followed northward the route by which Maclay had returned in January. The 'war' between Johor and Pahang did not prevent his ascending the Endau River for about 130 kilometres. Combined with

The palace of the sultan of Kelantan, Kota Baharu, August 1875

On the Pattani River, Siam, 1875

The residence of the *raja-muda*, where Maclay stayed at Songkhla, Siam, 1875

The palace of the sultan of Kedah, 1875

impassable rapids, it did compel him to turn back without seeing the mountain-dwellers. Having followed most of the disputed river's course, and climbed a mountain previously unknown to Europeans, he returned to the coast to take ship for the capital of Pahang.

Parting from the minor official and everything Johor provided, he entered an area of risk. In Pahang the rulers often behaved like pirates. But Maclay cared less about this, or the wholesale lopping of heads he knew to be fashionable, than about his reception as bearer of letters from the maharaja. Despite the ancestry they shared, Abu Bakar and the *bendahara* of Pahang had long been enemies. The *bendahara* Ahmad had won Pahang from the recognized ruler by force of arms. Attempting to prevent it, Abu Bakar had done everything short of leading his army to war. Ahmad would never forget the arms and mercenaries that had delayed his installation, or the price offered for his head by Abu Bakar. No more could he forget that Johor had acquired much Pahang territory, of which the compromise arranged by the British had returned only a small fraction. The *bendahara* believed that Abu Bakar and others coveted the rest of Pahang. Most of all he feared the British, who admitted his capacity to rule but deplored the way he did it. The unprecedented arrival of a European bearing Abu Bakar's letter, fresh from inspection of the frontier, and proposing to travel through Pahang, was bound to cause deep suspicion.

Maclay met a contrast to the ruler south of whatever river might truthfully be called the 'Endau'. Abu Bakar was *bon vivant*, with figure to match. Ahmad had a lean and hungry look, attributed to illness that might carry him off at an early age. But for all the symptoms he described to visitors, he was, and looked, both tough and dangerous.

Maclay may or may not have carried letters from the British governor—his statements on the point were contradictory. Whatever he presented would meet with the same reception. The British officials who came to know the *bendahara* best described him, in Byron's words, as

> ... the mildest mannered man
> That ever scuttled ship or cut a throat.

Even if Maclay felt compelled to mention the border dispute, he would meet with nothing worse than the frustration suffered by Sir Andrew Clarke, who when seeking punishment of a murderer had received a talking myna-bird.

After some surprise and embarrassment, the *bendahara* became friendly enough. Maclay was invited to stay in the palace, assured of all assistance. Rivalry between neighbours actually worked to his advantage, Ahmad declaring that if Johor gave twenty-five men for the expedition Pahang could give forty. The *bendahara* did have reservations. He had heard of beings who left footprints three hand-spans long, and of a beautiful aboriginal princess who enjoyed the privilege of immortality. The expedition sent to bring these marvels to the ruler had returned with only a few miserable little blacks, having lost four men to tigers. Moreover everybody knew the wild people were cannibals whose poisoned arrows killed men instantly, no more within a ruler's control than the tigers and elephants. The *bendahara* begged Maclay to write to Singapore and Europe, absolving Pahang of blame for what might happen among the savages. By complying, Maclay placed himself entirely in Ahmad's power.

Pahang and its capital, the ancient town of Pekan, had been coveted and fought over by every power that rose in the Peninsula. When Maclay saw it, Pekan consisted of two or three streets of houses that looked incapable of resisting a stiff breeze. The gold and tin mines were in decline, as were agriculture, trade and population. The state was none the less interesting for a visitor. In Johor, Maclay could admire the maharaja's combination of 'almost European' outlook with desire to preserve the best of traditional ways. Pahang appealed to him by its absolute rejection of Europe. He believed he was observing 'the pure Malay character and customs'.

Some customs originated in Ahmad's character rather than the traditions of his people. His predecessors had not practised quite such arbitrary rule and imaginative cruelty. Maclay had little time to distinguish tradition from innovation. In Pekan he met the experience that recurred throughout his journey, convincing him that however warmly he was welcomed he would be still more cordially encouraged to leave. His presence disrupted the largely nocturnal life of the palace, where the removal of opponents was often urgent business. Moreover Ahmad was preparing to receive a new governor of the Straits Settlements. He would have to fend off requests for freer trade, stricter respect for agreements and greater regard for life and property, as well as questions about the frontier. He made a sacrifice in sending his chief military adviser with Maclay, but when the governor arrived the *bendahara* could report that Datu Maclay had left for the interior under the best protection.

Well protected, and well watched, Maclay set off along the Pahang River. Knowing that the wild people feared slave-hunters, he had hoped to approach them 'alone', with only his personal servants and perhaps a few porters. Instead he had a retinue of forty, plus the commander-in-chief. Several boats carried the party and a pile of baggage that included a fair-sized table, an object unknown in the interior and a cause of amazement all along the way. This grand progress did not matter for most of the river journey. Some distance to right or left, he might have found tribes like the Jakun, with the same sprinkling of negrito traits. The riverside plains were inhabited only by Malays, whose ricefields and hamlets made this the most civilized part of the state. About three hundred kilometres of the Pahang's wandering course were traversed before he entered more varied country along the Tembeling, Maclay was free of the military magnate and from most of the forty porters and boatmen. He could still count on a fresh relay into the Tekam jungles.

Advancing into the wild, densely-forested region of the upper Tembeling, Maclay was free of the military magnate and from most of the forty porters and boatmen. He could still count on a fresh relay of servants after almost every day's journey, and the company of some official as far as the next centre of authority. He never had to pay for supplies or transport. Whatever the state of his finances he would not have paid the porters, whose 'Malay laziness and dishonesty towards white men' made them too dear at any price. Instead, funds were eroded by what he called 'baksheesh', the assistance given by officials being proportional to the bribe.

From the upper Trembeling he deviated westward through the jungle to sight Gunong Tahan, reputedly the highest peak in the Peninsula. He neither climbed it nor explored its flanks. No native would approach this fount of legend. It was said to be the home of spirits inimical to man. Its summit bore a house built entirely of gold, guarded by unseen powers and strange beasts. One of the latter came to Maclay's notice as a great ape called the *bru*, taller than a man and extremely fierce. The task of observing this animal was left to future zoologists. Maclay's time was absorbed by people he found in the vicinity, negritos of tribes ranging north-central Pahang and the southern interior of Kelantan and Trengganu. In them, he believed, he had discovered a 'pure-blood Papuan tribe'.

He again met negritos in the ranges where the vague Pahang boundaries joined those of the northern states, again hailed them as 'pure-blood' Papuans. Beyond the low watershed, long search in the jungle that was their element revealed other groups of nomads. After his first enthusiasm, Maclay admitted that these hidden people showed much admixture. The Malays divided the 'Sakai', as negritos were locally called, into the categories of 'wild' and 'tame'. Maclay's direct communication was only with the latter, people who frequented villages, acted as intermediaries in trade, gave their daughters to Malays and sometimes accepted a job. The 'wild' negritos were either ignorant of the Malay language or so stupefied by their first sight of a white man that they lost the use of brain and tongue. Helped by the 'tame', he persuaded a few uneasy jungle people to undergo inspection, measurement and portraiture. Notes on their language and way of life were gathered from the 'tame', careful informants, modest enough to consult the 'wild' for facts that they themselves forgot or had never known. By these means he collected, along with much hearsay and sensation, the first substantial information about negrito tribes of the eastern Malay Peninsula.

He felt that he advanced 'very slowly' in this part of his expedition, conducted mainly on foot, but the impression perhaps arose from the general speed of his progress. Rowed upstream on the meandering rivers of Pahang, he was almost out of that state within a fortnight. Shooting towards the sea on the Lebir and Kelantan rivers, he passed through most of Kelantan in less than a week.

For this he had to thank, besides geography, the wish of local authorities to be rid of him. He tried to avoid causing too much consternation. As he approached some rustic palace, heralds went ahead to announce Datu Russ Maclay. There were standard answers to possible questions, explaining that Datu Maclay came from the domain of such-and-such a magnate and was on his way to the next. If a chieftain asked what Datu Maclay was doing in these countries, the reply was that he wished to learn 'how people live ... how the princes live and the poor people, people in villages and those in the forests, to become acquainted not only with the people but with the animals, trees and plants in the forest'. Arriving at court, Maclay presented his letters from the Siamese king and the British governor. He nevertheless encountered 'no little anxiety and amazement'. He also sensed 'great suspiciousness and pretended stupidity', apparently aroused by the very letters meant to secure help and confidence.

The notables wanted nothing to do with any outsider, much less a *protégé* of Siam. In peaceful times Siamese suzerainty was undemanding, but Kelantan, with the most peaceful history of any Peninsula state, had felt a heavier hand. Some of the men with whom Maclay was dealing surely remembered the last attempt to oust the ruling sultan, who had retained his throne by calling on Siamese power. Lately, alarmed by French conquests in the east and British expansion in the south, Bangkok asserted itself more strongly. The time might come when the overlord demanded more than tribute of gold and silver flowers, and feudal chieftains might regret the information gathered by a wandering friend of Rama V.

The British were known mainly as the faithless ones who had repeatedly thrown rebellious Kedah back under Siamese domination. In almost everything concerning the vassal states, Singapore spoke only to Bangkok. Yet the British had imposed themselves on three troubled west-coast states within a few months. Their officials were interfering with the rulers' prerogatives, subverting such institutions as debt slavery, forcing open the way for foreign enterprises. Should local chieftains in the northern states ever succeed in freeing themselves from Siam, they would almost inevitably fall into British hands. Maclay was probably right in feeling that by not being an Englishman he enjoyed an advantage. He perhaps reaped some benefit from being Russian. Of Russia, the Malay notables knew only that it was very large and far away. Like most Muslims in out-of-the-way places, they believed that twenty years earlier the Turkish sultan had thoroughly conquered the Russian Empire and converted its people to Islam.

Despite these advantages, Maclay grew weary of lies, suspicion and feigned ignorance before he reached Kota Baharu, capital of Kelantan. Here he stayed with old Sultan Muhamed II, regarded by Europeans as a harsh but reasonably just ruler, known to his subjects as 'Red-Mouth'. Maclay investigated the town, famous for silk sarongs and elegant metal-work, bull-fights, ram-fights and a shadow play inherited from the first Indianized kingdom of south-east Asia. He sketched the pleasant, rambling palace, and the monumental triple gateway leading into its great sand-floored courtyard. He also learned of 'peace-loving, friendly and sweet-sounding speeches' that had recently aroused suspicion. While Maclay travelled through the interior, the British governor, with naval escort and inquisitive officials, had enjoyed a brilliant reception at Pekan, called at Kota Baharu, and gone on to the coastal centres of southern Siam, leaving a backwash of conjecture and fear.

After two months of wandering and diplomacy, Maclay felt he had been travelling for three. He believed he had a 'definite and satisfactory answer' to his scientific problem. From this busy port he might have returned comfortably to Singapore. Instead he resolved to press on, perhaps as far as Bangkok. Apart from occasional giddiness, his health was 'comparatively good'. The sultan, not forthcoming with his elephants, agreed to provide mere men. Given the usual enthusiastic farewell, Maclay took the road into Siam.

He knew by experience that negritos were not found outside the upper river valleys and the foothills of important ranges. Nowhere else was there space and security for nomads who lived by hunting and gathering food. To present himself to the authorities, however, he travelled some way north, through populous agricultural districts, before returning to the ranges between Siam and the Malay sultanates.

The journey was fascinating from political and social points of view, taking him through a civilized land of which Europeans had seen only the coast. This had been the Malay state of Pattani, once so rich and powerful that its pride became insufferable to the overlords. Through centuries of war and insurrection, Pattani had at last been thoroughly suppressed, carved into seven little provinces under rajas subordinate to a Siamese governor. Greatly reduced by the flight of defeated rebels, waves of executions and deportations, the Malays lived comfortably, practised Islam and followed the old ways. They felt themselves as doomed as the aborigines in the forest. Even twenty years before, it had been estimated that the majority of Pattani's inhabitants were Siamese.

Maclay still concentrated on that other doomed remnant, and the Malays were mainly aid or hindrance in his progress. Presenting the orders of the Siamese monarch, he did not sense what divided feelings they must arouse. He saw only evasiveness and duplicity, a desire to do nothing at war with an urge to send him packing. By 'baksheesh' or superior willpower, he invariably got his way. There were always porters to take him further. Sometimes there were elephants.

He doubled back southward and advanced two-thirds of the way across the Peninsula, skirting the frontier ranges. To meet the third raja on his list, he had to visit a village near the head of the Pattani River and the borders with Kedah and Perak. This fortunate necessity, bringing him again to the haunts of negritos, also led him to a potentially dangerous area. With or without Bangkok's approval, the raja of Raman had taken advantage of a collapse of authority in Perak to extend his territories at his neighbours' expense. But Perak had lately received a British resident. Complaints had gone to Singapore. The raja of Raman, watching his newly-acquired interests from a 'temporary residence', was the one vassal of Siam with immediate reason to fear the British, of all rulers the least likely to welcome a European.

Regardless of politics, Maclay measured negrito heads, observed skin colour and hair texture, ornament and weapons, and with much pains discovered a few words of the dialect. Encounters were necessarily brief. Within a fortnight of entering Siam he had left this centre of negrito population. Travelling north along the Pattani River, he heard of other tribes in the hills to right and left, but the journey now had an object quite unrelated to his earlier aims. He meant to compare the Siamese way of life and 'political situation' with those of the Malay states.

The British governor, doing something similar, had preceded him at the old port of Pattani. The same was true at Songkhla, seat of the Siamese governor, which Maclay reached by way of coastal provinces inhabited almost entirely by Siamese. Here he again saw negritos, two captive boys in an official's house. He learned that wild tribes lived to the north. After three weeks on elephant back in the beginning of the rainy season he no longer felt inclined to go farther. Obtaining fresh elephants, he turned southward.

The broad, well-kept road from Songkhla to Kedah had never before been traversed by a white man on an elephant. Its traffic of market-bound peasants, buffaloes and consignments of Pattani tin had often enough been interrupted by frightening sights. Time and again it had taken Siamese armies south to crush revolt in Kedah. Once, military traffic had moved in the opposite direction, as victorious rebels burst out to carry war to the gates of Songkhla. But the Siamese had recovered; the British had imposed a naval blockade, cutting off the Malay army from sources of men and arms. The retribution had been frighful. After this, the road had decayed on the Kedah side. Visitors viewing it from the south could not believe in this supposed highway from Songkhla. As it approached the capital of Kedah, however, it became again a broad smooth road.

No uninformed stranger entering Alor Setar in 1875 would guess that Kedah had been laid waste and its capital totally destroyed. Europeans admired the little town's regularity and neatness. The countryside breathed peace and wealth. An English official, visiting Kedah a year before Maclay, had found it more advanced, orderly, humane and prosperous than any other Peninsula state. The sultan was esteemed for justice, integrity and intellect. To all appearances he faithfully observed the agreement that had allowed his grandfather to return to Kedah, living in submission to the Siamese crown. Maclay could not know whether the command of Rama V was received by the obedient vassal or by the man whose family, through twenty years of exile, had plotted and fought against the Siamese.

When he settled in the palace to await a ship for Singapore, Maclay had wandered for 112 days. No more than three weeks had been spent with the people he originally wished to study. The tribes encountered in southern Siam also ranged the Kedah mountains, sixty kilometres from the capital; quick ethnological results could have been obtained by taking ship for Alor Setar in the first place. Instead he had completed a journey which from central Pahang ran almost entirely through lands never previously visited by Europeans. He had seen negritos in their eastern stronghold and near their northern limit, establishing that these widely separated groups belonged to the same race. He had gained extensive geographical knowledge. With unprecedented opportunities to observe society and politics in southern Siam, he had also seen Malay life in lands never penetrated by European influence. The Peninsula journey, he felt, had taught him more about Malays than all his months in the East Indies.

This did not mean that he liked them better. He had come from Java convinced that Malays were by nature indolent, cowardly and procrastinating. For all he had learned of the political situation, he still condemned the suspicion and mendacity of rulers and officials. Despite what he saw of their position as mere property, subject to forced labour, debt slavery and dispossession at a ruler's whim, he did not excuse the laziness, timidity and dishonesty he found among the lower classes. Knowing he was not English, all classes had still obeyed reluctantly, without trust. Maclay, who adopted 'Don't believe in others' as a principle, needed trust as he needed obedience.

10: Return to Paradise

THE LARGE VILLA near Buitenzorg, once the seat of one of the native princes through whom the Dutch ruled Java, was still called 'The Regent's House' long after its glory had passed. When Maclay occupied it in November 1875, naming it 'Tampat Susah' (Abode of Unease), the old house had 'holes in the roof and holes in the floor'. He valued it for size and isolation and perhaps for a rent adjusted to its decrepit state. For almost two years not a kopeck had come from Russia. His travels in the Malay Peninsula, and now his stay in Java, were financed by borrowing from Ankersmit.

Increasing debt was the price of pride, his ideal of scientific independence, and his determination to stay in the tropics. He had earlier received a half-promise of financial support from the Russian Geographical Society. But Semyonov-Tianshansky's news was accompanied by advice that he should suspend ethnological research and return to publish his results. The *doyen* of Russian geographers also regretted that Maclay's planned research 'on the marine fauna from the tropics to the Arctic current of Japan and the Sea of Okhotsk' had proved impracticable. 'And we regret it the more', he pursued, 'because precisely this part of your programme introduced your travels as long ago outlined to the Society . . .'. The traveller who felt at home only in the tropics was urged to return to Europe. The man who prided himself on keeping every promise was told that in the Society's eyes he had broken his word. No assurances of sympathy and admiration could make this palatable. Attributing advice and reproaches to the machinations of 'patriotically-inspired men', Maclay had refused the proffered funds.

He sat under a tattered roof in the rainiest district of Java, preparing articles for publication. There was an expanded report on Papua-Koviai,

174

with supplements describing Lake Kamaka-Walla and the mixed population of the eastern Moluccas. He completed a substantial second instalment of 'Ethnological Remarks on the Papuans of the Maclay Coast of New Guinea', polished the account of his Johor travels, and added a fairly long article on the second expedition in the Peninsula. These, with a short paper on 'rudiments of art' among the Papuans and some notes on Dyak sexual customs, kept Maclay and his amanuensis busy through the last two months of 1875, one of the most productive periods in his scientific career.

At the same time he worked out schemes for zoological stations, pressing the idea at meetings of the Royal Society for Natural Sciences in Batavia. Before leaving Singapore, he had obtained from the British authorities a lease of the small island of Sarimbun in Johor Strait. In Java he applied to purchase about two and a half hectares in the Minahassa Peninsula of Celebes, the district whose beauty had first impressed him three years before. Inexpensive in themselves, these acquisitions formed a considerable burden for a man with nothing but debts. He nevertheless secured two sanctuaries where he might eventually find rest.

For the present he had no intention of living anywhere permanently, though his friends must often have wondered where he meant to go. Olga had been told that he would spend the (northern) winter of 1875–76 in Australia and return to Europe in 1877. Meshchersky and Dohrn were asked to find a suitable house in Italy. Olga was to arm herself with patience, good handwriting and three foreign languages, in order to act as her brother's secretary. Maclay spoke of attending a congress of naturalists in Moscow. He spoke of personally founding a zoological station on the Sea of Okhotsk. Early in the year he had thought it essential to visit Europe and put into shape his 'large accumulation of materials'. After Semyonov-Tianshansky suggested exactly that, Maclay refused to 'waste time on deviations to Europe'. He must continue to travel while strength sufficed. '*Mein Cadaver*', he explained, 'will perhaps soon refuse to carry out so submissively the superior orders of my quite demanding brain'.

He would soon be 'on the road', spurred by stronger feelings than the resentments that gnawed him in the Abode of Unease. As he had told D'Albertis a year before, he was returning to the Maclay Coast.

Late in 1874 the Australian campaign for British acquisition of eastern New Guinea had been renewed. Captain Moresby, whose creeping annexation had been unfavourably viewed by the imperial government, had warned that the Russians were 'in Astrolabe Gulf'. In April 1875 the Royal Colonial Institute had approached the government with the case for annexation, and certain official enquiries were being made. Maclay had written immediately to St Petersburg, requesting Russian action, perhaps a proposal for an international protectorate, at least official support for the protest he intended to make. Semyonov-Tianshansky was to lay this matter before the tsar.

While Maclay traversed the Peninsula, public meetings in Australia had demanded eastern New Guinea. One colonial legislature passed a resolution in that sense. Another sent to London a proposal for annexing almost all the islands of the south-west Pacific. Schemes for colonization were put up and put down, and London remained unmoved. On the other hand, scientific expeditions visited south-east New Guinea. Missionaries were active there. To Maclay, Australian propaganda was indistinguishable from 'English designs'.

Again he wrote in agitation, '*not* as a Russian but as *Tamo-boro-boro* (highest headman) *of the Papuans of the Maclay Coast*', to appeal for the tsar's protection of '*my* country and *my* people'. For the moment he asked only a one-word cable indicating what might be expected. It must come quickly. 'Because of the *pressing* requests of the people of that coast', he explained, 'I promised to return whenever they should be in *trouble*. Now, knowing that . . . great danger threatens them . . . I *wish* and am *obliged* to keep my word; although given to Papuans, although given perhaps to cannibals, it was given *by me*'.

When his people asked how long he would be away, Maclay's limited vocabulary and uncertainty about future movements had forced him to answer non-committally. Nobody had mentioned 'trouble', though he guessed they wanted his protection against traditional enemies who might have attacked any number of times since 1872. But no such uncertainty touched his belief that 'English colonization will end with the destruction of the Papuans'. Sometimes he felt he had promised to return whenever it would benefit his people. By the end of 1875 he knew what should be done. 'I attained great influence over the natives', he told Semyonov-Tianshansky, 'and I hope to have still more when I return'. Through this influence he meant to defend 'their true interest: their independence', or at least to prevent European colonization from having '*too disastrous* an effect'. The first step would be a native federation, with Maclay at its head. How a leader with an extremely limited vocabulary would explain this to a multilingual people who had never conceived such an idea was a question for the future. The imminence of danger did not allow him to wait for general enlightenment and agreement. By the ship that took him there, he would send a declaration 'that the *Papuan Union of the Maclay Coast* wishes to remain independent and will, to the limits of possibility, *protest* against European invasion'.

Waiting to return to his own country, Maclay still thought of other oppressed and endangered peoples. He never campaigned on behalf of the negritos of the Malay Peninsula. He saw them as victims of displacement and exploitation, robbed of their identity and traditional life by intermarriage with other races and the spread of Malay and Chinese settlement, but that process seemed inevitable. His only duty was to record what he knew and exhort other scientists to follow his path before these tribes became extinct. He did not view with such resignation the plight of Papua-Koviai, where the Dutch still did nothing. As well as publishing an article on social and political conditions, he urged the colonial authorities to action on his earlier report. His advice remained unchanged: abolition of slave trading and establishment of law and order by means of a Dutch military settlement. That this represented drastic interference with the traditional ways of Papua-Koviai, Ceram and Tidore was of no consequence to Maclay. He was no more deterred by belief that the 'tactless policy of the Dutch' had caused the continuing war in Atjeh. In Papua-Koviai he had looked upon the face of evil. He wanted it erased.

He took a different attitude towards the third endangered group to win his sympathy. In the Malay Peninsula he had emphasized his struggles with distrust and deceit. Three months later he recalled that some of his hosts, assured he was not English, had found it unnecessary 'to withhold their confidence or to dissimulate'. Their frankness had given him 'a true understanding of the political situation in the countries of the Malay rajas', knowledge that might have 'no little importance' in British designs upon the Malay states. Forbidden by principle to abet 'the invasion of the country of a coloured race by whites, interference in the affairs of the natives, finally either the enslavement or the extermination of the latter', he had been compelled to move hastily to Java, where he could not inadvertently betray his friends to the English.

What he had seen of British rule and influence in the Peninsula could not justify predictions of enslavement and extermination. In Singapore they talked about reforms similar to those he advocated for Papua-Koviai, without the military settlements. His compassion seemed directed less to the Malay lower classes, who were already slaves, than to the rajas, threatened with loss of their absolute power. It was not to be expected, however, that Maclay should distinguish between conscientious British officials in the Peninsula and the Australian colonists who demanded New Guinea. These latter, having exterminated the native Tasmanians, almost wiped out the Australian Aborigines and begun upon the Fijians, were about to invade the Maclay Coast. To Maclay all men of their race were damned, 'irreconcilable future enemies' of coloured peoples everywhere.

He perhaps overestimated his importance to the British, who as yet had no designs on the states he had traversed. The silence he maintained lest the rajas accuse him of 'espionage' was tantalizing for the Russian Geographical Society. A few days after he returned to Java (not prematurely but six months later than he had planned), the world's

attention had been drawn to the Malay Peninsula. The British resident
in Perak, a righteous, inflexible man, determined to free the slaves and
impose European ideas of law and order, had been murdered by
chieftains who saw their prerogatives slipping away. As troops were
called from Hong Kong and India, Maclay rewrote his half-finished
letter to St Petersburg, substituting for remarks on Dutch tactlessness a
prediction that 'tactless policies on the part of the English could bring
upon them something like the Atjehno-Dutch war'. For once, the
Russian geographers might have preferred a confidential report on the
Malay Peninsula to a zoogeographical treatise on the Sea of Okhotsk,
but there was no time to request it.

The common people of Perak were not enthusiastic in defending
their rulers' privileges. The 'war' in the Peninsula was over before
Maclay left Java. So was the immediate danger to the Maclay Coast. The
British government had decided against a move useful only to colonists
who declined to pay for it. Maclay knew nothing of this as he waited in
a wretched hotel at Tjirebon for his ship to New Guinea. He knew no
more about the effect of his appeal to St Petersburg, though he
understood a letter was on the way. 'Whatever the contents of that
letter', he pointed out, 'the *nature* of my undertaking ... could *not* have
been changed. I would *not* be able to act *otherwise*, being bound by my
word!'

He realized that travels undertaken largely from philanthropic
motives might be dubiously regarded. He tried to ensure that the
Geographical Society should not withdraw its support because '*completely disinterested concern* for the natives' welfare' forced him to mix
political action with scientific research. Sacrificing time, health and
means, he could not help worrying about the future. Meshchersky had
been asked to find someone ready to lend 3000 or 4000 roubles to a
man in poor health and circumstances on the other side of the globe. In
Batavia Maclay left a debt of about 6000 roubles, accumulating interest
at 9 per cent and secured on his ethnological collection. His principal
creditor was friendly for the time being. Maclay had undertaken to use
influence with Baron Osten-Sacken (deputy director of the Asiatic
department of the foreign ministry) to have Ankersmit appointed
Russian vice-consul.

With these matters unresolved, he had ordered supplies, trade goods
and a prefabricated house from Singapore, as well as a vessel to take him
back to his people. Another ship was to call at Astrolabe Bay in
November 1876, bringing letters and supplies and taking anything he
wished to send. With that vessel he might leave New Guinea, in time
to return to Europe in 1877.

Late in February 1876 the schooner *Sea Bird*, carrying trade goods,
supplies and six European traders to the western Carolines, the Palau

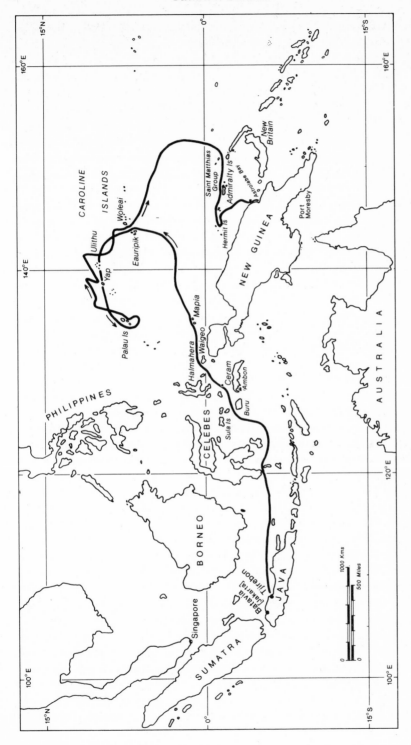

Voyage of the *Sea Bird*, Java to New Guinea, 1876

Islands and the Admiralty group, collected Maclay at Tjirebon. His agreement entitled him to alter the route, extend the ship's time at any place, and direct the course of the voyage once the cargo had been discharged. First acquaintance with the captain of the *Sea Bird*, David Dean O'Keefe, probably disabused him of such notions. Captain O'Keefe called no man master, least of all aboard an O'Keefe vessel.

This brawny red-bearded adventurer was said to have fled the Irish famine at the age of twenty, working on American railroads while educating himself in seamanship and the classics of literature. He was believed to have run the blockade for the southern states during the Civil War. As captain of American steamers he was accused of killing two mutinous seamen with his own hands. The story went that he had fled to the Pacific to escape arrest, survived shipwreck, gone into partnership with a Chinese merchant, and sailed in a junk to found a trading empire. Whatever the truth, nobody could doubt O'Keefe's determination to live by no authority but his own. One of those ambitious misfits for whom the great ocean became a promised land, he prowled the seas for the wealth and dominion that civilization held beyond his reach. When Maclay fell into his hands, the captain was on the course that eventually let him style himself 'King of Yap, Sovereign of Sonsorol and Monarch of Mapia'.

Together and infinitely apart, the future emperor of the isles and the future *Tamo-boro-boro* of the Maclay Coast sailed for Celebes. Then the *Sea Bird* struck north-east on a route almost entirely new to Maclay, betwen Buru and the Sula islands, through archipelagos south and east of Halmahera and along the north coast of Waigeo. From Mapia (not yet part of O'Keefe's dominions), they crossed an ocean of few landfalls.

Through weeks at sea, with nothing to watch but waves, clouds and the life of the ship, Maclay was still concerned about his own position. For publication in Russia he sent Meshchersky a long explanation of his intentions, a plea that friends should not forsake him, imagine his decision lightly taken or his scientific work neglected for philanthropic aims. To enlist 'the public opinion of *all honourable* and *just* people', extracts from the same letter were prepared for an Italian geographical magazine. Similar information and instructions went to Osten-Sacken, who surely agreed that 'only weakness of character or cowardice in the face of obstacles and dangers' could prevent Maclay's fulfilling his pledge to the Papuans.

Conscious that the only aims of his life were 'the *profit and progress of science* and the *welfare of humanity*', he trustfully appealed to those who shared his beliefs. His approach to the family from whom he had heard nothing for almost three years was less confident. When he wrote of returning to Russia, he doubted whether his arrival would cause pleasure. Ekaterina Semyonovna, he suspected, had forgotten the existence of a son who still loved and respected her. He was forced to remind her by more than a recent photograph. If Meshchersky obtained a loan to keep Ankersmit quiet, Maclay would still be liable, as soon as he reached his coast, for the expenses of the journey and his establishment there, including a house and a boat. Should this bill remain long unpaid, his Singapore creditors might decline to send another vessel to New Guinea. He had already warned his mother that he would be asking help. From the ocean north of New Guinea he begged her to send, without delay, 1000 silver roubles to the creditors in Singapore.

Among the islands of Micronesia, he forgot wretched kopecks and the opinions of Europe. As the *Sea Bird* wandered north via Eauripik and Ulithi, followed a great arc west and south-west to Yap and the Palau Islands and returned on a zig-zag course, the scientific harvest hardly left time to watch for opportunities of sending letters. He used the briefest call at any island for routine research—measurements, classification of skin colour, observations on hair texture, facial features, dress and ornament. Where the schooner remained longer at anchor, he lived ashore and sought to enter into native life.

The experience could be disconcerting. Gathered round Yap he found an empire, acquired by naval expeditions, paying tribute to the dominant island and ruled by governors sent from the capital. On Yap itself he observed a strictly hierarchical society. A paramount chief and a high priest occupied the top of the pyramid. At the bottom stood a slave caste, forbidden to own land, living in segregated villages, their dress and mobility restricted, their lives, possessions and offspring entirely in the rulers' hands. He noticed that the aristocrats and freemen were comparatively tall, handsome, light-skinned people, while the slaves were smaller, darker, less attractive. Marriage across the caste barrier was prohibited.

Another poison had entered the system of Yap. According to textbooks, the inhabitants of this almost unspoiled island were innocent of the use of money. Maclay found four types of currency, from huge, quarried pieces of aragonite shaped like millstones, usually communally owned, to polished pebbles and rare shells, obtained from distant islands and used only by chiefs. And for these objects of purely conventional value the natives ran risks, performed heavy labour, even paid white men to take them to the source of supply and bring back cargoes of what was indubitably money.

When he examined and sketched ancient squares paved with heavy stones, or stepped-pyramid tombs which by the number of their levels disclosed a dead man's rank, Maclay found nothing to regret in legends of how teachings from a distant country had set Yap 'on the path of non-European civilization'. He was there to observe the native society, not to judge it. To him the one true oppression was European oppression, the only real corruption was European. The legend of how dark, robust people from the south had treacherously acquired the Palau Islands, slaughtering and driving out the previous inhabitants, was 'interesting, as showing the manner in which not a few islands ... were probably populated'. The white man's exploitation of the natives proved 'the melancholy old truth: "Man is a wolf to man" '. Maclay intended to take this matter up in the future.

In the Palaus he learned enough to confirm his anger, but much to confuse him. Constantly as he advocated long, patient investigation, he sometimes believed first impressions could be most reliable. Here, first impressions were bad. He landed on Koror to find the painted warriors relaxing after an all-night dance to honour the taking of enemy heads. When he wished to see the trophies, he found they could not be shown, having become too offensive during their tour of numerous villages.

He never understood the war that caused or satisfied the desire to take heads. To him it seemed a series of wars, conducted on the most trifling pretexts. In fact it had lasted for untold generations and required no pretext at all, being fundamental in the Palauan way of life. Most Europeans in the archipelago adapted to a state of affairs they found immutable. Maclay remained troubled. While he collected legends and vocabulary, studied social structure, customs, religion, architecture and pictographs, he asked indiscreet questions about military affairs. He found 'all ruses, deceptions and ambushes considered permissible'. Wondering whether it was not degrading for strong parties of warriors to hide all night and take the heads of unarmed men or women and children, he was assured it did not matter what head was taken—'A woman can bear many children, and a child grows up'. The warriors would be rewarded, the head paraded through festive villages, whether it had belonged to an enemy chief or an enemy infant. For such reasons, Maclay suspected, the islands were becoming depopulated, as a steady stream of Palauans was despatched to an afterworld as hierarchical as this, where aristocracy and commoners occupied separate heavens.

As well as forming unfavourable impressions of their wars and politics, Maclay found himself disliking the Palauans as individuals. They struck him as 'deceitful, secretive and extremely mercenary', petty in enmity and cruel in revenge. It took ingenuity to conclude that without the influence of a few whites the Palauans would display the 'carefree spirit', openness and trustfulness natural to unspoiled humanity. But natives who spoke a little English told him how white traders sold inferior goods, broke promises and abused native trust. When a white man was killed or fighting became too dangerous, traders terrorized the islanders by threatening to call a warship. The Palauans nevertheless continued to trade with resident Europeans and vessels that called fairly regularly. Cloth and glass beads were eagerly sought. Steel tools had

The *ibedul*, paramount chief of Koror, Palau
Islands, 1876

A girl of Yap, 1876

The interior of a club-house, Yap, 1876

The *pai* (club-house) in Koror, Palau Islands, where Maclay lived

Mira, the Palauan girl, Maclay's servant 1876–78: portrait drawn in New Guinea

The house at Bugarlom, near Bongu, Maclay Coast, 1877

Tayo-mana (Mount Konstantin), Maclay Coast, New Guinea

replaced stone. Almost every man carried a gun, be it a superannuated muzzle-loader or the latest repeating rifle. Nobody blamed Europeans for the war, but they supplied what a highly-militarized society valued most. In any case, Maclay felt the nature of the trade hardly mattered. 'All these useful foreign things and superfluous baubles', he concluded, 'produce discontent in the natives, contempt for their own products. They direct all their thoughts towards one object: to obtain these useful and attractive things.' Played upon by envy and 'unpleasant sensations', dissatisfied with old circumstances and embittered by feeling dependent on whites for what was new, the native character was warped beyond recognition.

After solving this problem, Maclay remained troubled. He could not quite reconcile such 'base' traditional methods of warfare with the natural honesty and openness of primitive man. Convinced that white men killed by Palauans deserved the penalty, he recoiled from physical details of these executions. He found his host, the *ibedul* or paramount chief of Koror, both kind and courteous; but he had difficulty in believing that only orders from a British naval commander had caused this man to shoot his brother and grasp power. In principle he opposed visits by warships, whose officers and crews behaved arrogantly towards the frightened natives. Yet he could not think it good policy for European governments to leave murder and robbery uninvestigated.

A strange nostalgia mingled with these moral questions. Just as the natives had been contented and open-hearted, white men had once been as gods on Palau. In those days islanders had bowed before the white man in the streets, laid aside their axes on entering his dwelling, and removed the combs from their hair in token of respect. Now all was rough and tumble, equalized by the chicanery of trade, the distribution of firearms, the increasing number of European visitors and the experience of islanders in Manila and Hong Kong. Something in Maclay yearned for the time before disillusionment, when Europeans were taken for 'beings of a higher order'. The money-grubbing skippers and traders had not known how to be gods. He would never forgive their failure.

Despite bewilderment and bitterness, he thought of the Palaus as a place where he could live. Moving to the large island of Babeldaob, he chose two parcels of land in the district of Ngetelngal, bearing the musical names of Komis and Oraberamis. A document was drawn up in French, the paramount chief and three lesser dignitaries affixed their marks before European witnesses, and on the spot the land changed hands. Maclay did not realize that he himself had changed hands. As guest of the *ibedul* in Koror, he had been regarded as the 'property' of the federation gathered round that paramount chief. Buying land in Ngetelngal, he became a subject of the *reklai*, leader of the alliance that confronted Koror in perpetual war. To the *ibedul* he became a traitor. To the *reklai* he was a politically valuable acquisition. Like other Europeans, he would eventually be asked to give more than the undisclosed price he paid for the land.

Knowledge of pitfalls might not have changed his actions, for in the Palau Islands a spirit of recklessness possessed him. It led him, when he watched youths training for war, to set himself up as target in less boring exercises. The boys used light bamboo practice spears, and he did not think they could hit a mark at such a distance. But the spear flying close to his face might have cost him an eye. The shaft that struck his hand left pain and swelling as a 'memento'. Something was proved to himself and the delighted onlookers, perhaps that Maclay remained indifferent to life, perhaps that some white men were still as gods, above concern with pain or danger. If it did nothing to restore native respect for Europeans, the test, at once self-glory and self-punishment, to some extent relieved the tension in Maclay.

In the Palau group he lived in the large club-houses, the *pai*, among the warriors and their communally-owned concubines. He took great scientific interest in the lives of these girls, the most attractive and accomplished of their sex, purchased for high prices from their fathers and available to the whole club. But when he asked, in the most impersonal manner, whether the chief might lend such a girl to a European guest, he was told that even the paramount chief would not dare thus offend the politically-powerful military societies. Several times a day he passed through the club-house doorway, beneath an almost-lifesize female figure in an attitude of changeless receptivity. Each night he tried to sleep in the womb of the *pai*, amid activities for which the exterior carving formed an appropriate 'signboard'. Other possibilities were offered, but in women as in all things Maclay could tolerate only the best. On Palau the 'best', under the same roof, were inaccessible as the stars.

Maclay thought of a 'temporary wife', who would live with him in New Guinea and go home when no longer required. Besides being comely, submissive and discardable, she must be fresh, unspoiled, embodying the innocence that he sought vainly through the inhabited world.

In the *pai* at Koror he had seen little girls, below nubile age but bought and paid for, obviously 'waiting their turn'. In Ngetelngal he found Mira, about twelve years old, whose uncle the *reklai* was willing to bind the white man's loyalty by such a gift. With enormous eyes and full, pouting lips, a sultry little face framed by long hair, she did not look a strong, boyish girl like Mkal of the eastern Jakun. But though undoubtedly female she was physically undeveloped. Maclay need not decide immediately, and Mira, waiting her turn, could learn to be what he desired. She joined his staff of servants, the company of Saleh the new Javanese cook and Mebli the Palau man who was to act as hunter and oarsman. In place of Ahmad, from whom Maclay had parted, she would serve as housekeeper and valet.

Maclay's nerves had been severely tried during the first half of the voyage. To write letters, articles and journal, he struggled against uncomfortable conditions, the rolling of the ship and the uproar of a small vessel crowded with robust, unintellectual men of several races. And the *Sea Bird* brought him more than the normal sufferings of travelling naturalists. He soon discovered in Captain O'Keefe 'a man of cruel and brutal character', a thoroughgoing scoundrel. Fearful stories were told of the crimes that accompanied the captain's voyages. Three out of five Malay sailors, preferring any dangers to the treatment received from O'Keefe, had deserted at Yap or Palau. The European passengers, in Maclay's eyes hardly better men than the skipper, quarrelled loudly with O'Keefe, came to blows, threatened to throw him overboard. As Maclay experienced it, each day at sea was filled with violence and terror.

The *Sea Bird* sailed on. Men from Yap replaced the runaways and formed a strong armed guard for the rest of the voyage. The traders continued to argue and shout, and did not hurl the tyrant into the sea. With beads and trinkets, knives and hatchets, cloth, firearms, gunpowder and a neat new line in little brass cannon, the schooner flew south towards the Saint Matthias group and westward again to the Admiralty and Hermit islands. The traders were set ashore, one by one, to start trading posts, to exchange European goods for trepang and turtleshell, to make money or meet death.

Urgent as was his return to his people, Maclay had thought of directing the schooner to New Britain, New Ireland and the Solomons, perhaps choosing a fresh field of research. Before reaching the Admiralty Islands he knew the project was absurd. He doubted even seeing New Guinea again. In agitation he half formed a plan for being set down with his followers somewhere among the islands, to await the chance appearance of a ship that might take him to his destination. Anything was better than remaining in the power of O'Keefe.

He found some pleasant resting places. His desperate scheme never came into effect. Wherever possible he escaped to study the natives in their villages, explore by boat or relax in a hammock by the shore. Aboard the schooner he stayed in his cabin, hemmed in by the pandemonium of trade, the bellowing of native salesmen abusing their rivals, the barking of a huge Newfoundland dog let loose to clear the crowded quarterdeck, heartless laughter from the skipper and traders. On deck he was sickened by the spectacle of greed and degradation, filled with anger at 'so much human baseness, injustice and malevolence'. He intended to write a comprehensive report.

Impressive precautions were taken aboard the schooner, but Maclay never witnessed violence against the islanders. The natives saw the white men's revolvers, the rifles of the Yap guards, the small cannon in readiness, and fought each other to reach the deck. In evident terror of the dog, they climbed the shrouds or flung themselves into the sea. Two minutes later they were back, shouting as lustily as ever, intent upon nothing but trade. The slow match smouldered but the cannon never fired; the dog chased the natives but never caught them. Feeling contaminated by proximity to such events, Maclay nursed his neuralgia alone in a world he did not understand.

His moral revulsion was compounded where white faces were familiar and trading less tumultuous. On some of the Admiralty Islands, women and children did not flee from Europeans, and native men stayed aboard the schooner the first night after its arrival. In the Hermit group, where O'Keefe had lived while trepang fishing, the familiarity was of another order. Islanders came aboard at dusk, greeted the skipper as an old crony, talked loudly among themselves and tramped about as though they owned the ship. Maclay concluded that these people, meeting only a 'very low class' of white men, had never had the chance to learn respect for Europeans. Nobody ordered them to stop shouting, or reproved 'the impudence of their demands'. They settled into the skipper's cabin, a partition's thickness from the man who could have taught them better, and spent the night carousing with O'Keefe and the traders. Maclay felt that what he heard summed up relations between white men and black in that part of the world. At the top of his voice, the man O'Keefe called 'the king' demanded brandy. A half-drunk trader, unsubtle by nature and with no charming little girl awaiting his will, as loudly asked for 'a woman for the night'. The time was past, if it had ever been, when a white man in the Hermit Islands might have walked as a god.

Maclay used his 'last reserves of patience' to endure the short voyage to his coast. He had no personal reason for fear. He had never shouted at the captain, struck him or threatened to throw him overboard. Saving himself for the trials ahead, he had kept to his cabin, leaving the task of remonstrance to men with the necessary violence and crudity. Perhaps that was why the skipper regarded him kindly, glad that the famous traveller had been in good health throughout the voyage and was now to land safely in New Guinea. O'Keefe willingly undertook to send Maclay's packet of mail. Maclay was sure these letters, some of them damning to O'Keefe, would never reach their destination. By the time he landed at Astrolabe Bay he was beyond caring. He had survived. He was exhausted. At last he could rest.

11: No Ships Call

MACLAY'S NEW DOMAIN, 'Bugar-lom', occupied a promontory near Bongu, far enough from the noise of the village, close enough to the native labour he expected to need. The excited villagers gave him an estate ten times as large as Garagassi. Directed by his servants and the ship's carpenter they built his dwelling, supplementing the ready-make sections with foundations and roof of local materials.

The house measured some ten metres long by five metres wide, containing one large room and a veranda, raised on piles and enclosed below to form a laboratory and store. In accord with Maclay's determination not to live under the same roof with others, the kitchen and servants' quarters were in a separate building. With a boatshed added, the land selectively cleared, and a broad road opened from the house to the beach, Bugarlom formed an attractive property. The Bongu people must have thought that Maclay would never leave them.

He did intend to leave, had resolved to sail by the vessel expected in November, join a warship and land in Europe early in 1878. Requests for his passage had gone to Russia, with the additional requirement that the warship spend some time in African ports for scientific purposes. But through July 1876 Maclay was absorbed in home-making. He arranged folding furniture, chests and gun-racks, covered the floor with Chinese carpets, set out his books on shelves improvised from packing cases. Meteorological instruments were positioned, the laboratory made ready for anatomical work. In the garden prepared by the natives, he planted maize, coconuts and a selection of fruits and vegetables. He had enough servants to relieve him of daily details, supplies for about six months, including 'a very fair Bordeaux and champagne'. Escaped from brutality and degradation, he rested and refreshed himself for tasks ahead.

The face of the land had suffered violent change since his first visit. Mountain tops, once thickly forested, were now partly bare. The outlines of Port Konstantin were altered. Along the shore stretches of forest had been destroyed, sandbars changed the courses of streams and paths were closed by fallen trees. It was the *tangrim-boro*, the people told him, severe earthquakes followed by great waves. Men had been killed by falling trees and houses; huts had been swept away.

There were more changes among his people, old men dead and children almost grown up. The youths were men, and among the mothers-to-be Maclay found some he had last seen as little girls. Their reverence for the *Kaaram-tamo*, their zeal and obedience in his service, remained as he had willed it. With the serious, blue-eyed being who perhaps was immortal, they ventured no shouting or familiarity. A simple gesture kept them at a respectful distance. Once work on the new *tal-Maklai* was finished, no native attempted to set foot in the sacred dwelling. They remembered Maclay's magic as they remembered the Russian words he had taught them. Nothing had occurred to lessen their awe. In the three and a half years between *Izumrud* and *Sea Bird*, no Europeans had called at Astrolabe Bay, and Captain O'Keefe seemed to make no impression. The *tamo-Russ* and their ships were vaguely remembered, ghostly presences accessory to Maclay. If the people recalled 'Vil', with his marvellous musical instrument and strange songs, they did not remind Maclay, who believed himself the only white man who had lived among them.

Not everything was perfect. Maclay had not grasped the complexity of native land tenure, and the Bongu people had given him what was not entirely theirs to give. Men from other villages appeared, claiming part of the land or rights over its natural products. Obliged to compensate them all, Maclay was never sure they knew they had parted with the land forever.

Scientific progress also encountered difficulties. 'Secretiveness and superstitious fear' still caused people to conceal customs or change their behaviour in his presence. Where his command of the language allowed him to ask questions, he got misleading or 'fanciful' answers. Researches that had been 'unthinkable' during the first visit were again postponed. Months passed before trust sufficiently overcame fear of magic, allowing him to take anthropological measurements.

The greatest disappointment was the collapse of his ultimate project in New Guinea, to be the first white explorer of the interior. Sometimes he believed he relinquished this ambition from lack of funds, or from distaste for the crowd of foreigners who would form a barrier between him and the Papuans. In reality, he clung for a time to the hope of using natives in place of the Malays he could not afford. The unknown interior still beckoned. Maclay still struggled to respond to the call.

His first journey was undertaken less for his purposes than for those of his friends. In his absence, the coast villages had again quarrelled and made peace with the mountain folk of Maragum-mana. Both sides still feared treachery, hesitating to ratify the agreement by visits. If Maclay went with them, his neighbours would feel perfectly safe. So Maclay went, an incongruous figure in sun helmet and white jacket, borne along by a wave of more than a hundred warriors decorated for feasting or war. They wished, he supposed, to dazzle the former enemy by splendour and numbers. They also wished to show, by more than the array of weapons, that the mountain men should stay on their best behaviour. The coast again possessed its *Kaaram-tamo*, whose magic outmatched any mountain sorcery.

Maclay soon planned another expedition, intended to try out natives as porters for longer journeys. He chose the three Bongu men who seemed most enduring and reliable and completed the party with his servant Mebli. The test showed the limits of his authority. Nothing persuaded the men to accept rice and dried venison in place of their familiar taro, food that by its bulk and nutritional inadequacy must severely limit the journey. Despite this and the open reluctance of his helpers, Maclay distributed loads of seven to ten kilos each and led them into the mountains. It seemed to him that by shouldering a pack himself, giving them so little to carry, and limiting the daily march to eight hours, he made every possible concession.

For two days the men plodded on, chafing against a steady, meaningless effort never before experienced, their fear of the mountain people never dispelled by Maclay's presence. Sometimes he felt that at any turn of the track they might drop their loads and disappear. It was no surprise when on the third day, with the taro nearly finished, one man refused to go on.

Maclay did not argue against a catalogue of fears and complaints delivered 'in a whining voice'. He silently placed the rejected load on top of his own and strode off. Within an hour there was another 'invalid', Mebli complaining that fever had left him too feeble to walk. Maclay could neither abandon Mebli's pack nor carry a third load himself. Incomprehensible as he often found Papuan facial expressions, he recognized the looks of the other porters as unmistakably sour, boding ill for any attempt to increase their loads. The Bongu men had no prince or governor to fear. If Maclay was not king on the Maclay Coast nobody was, and as far as his friends were concerned the expedition was over.

He did not waste time pondering the meaning of this incident for his future ascendancy. With his gift for making the best of things, he found other ways to conduct his expeditions. Afraid of unfamiliar territory, where every bush might conceal human or ghostly enemies, the coastal people also feared the unknown consequences of his anger. They dared not refuse to take him as far as the nearest mountain village and see him provided with new burden-bearers. Then they were dismissed or ordered to await his return, depending on his estimate of the time he would be away.

In practice, he never walked in the mountains for more than two or three days. The expedition always came to an end among people more afraid of those in the next village than of the *Kaaram-tamo*. Efficient and obliging guides in their own districts, the Papuans became 'completely useless' when they stepped outside, fearful of everything, ignorant of everything, declaring all Maclay's wishes impossible. There were long discussions before men used to carrying only their weapons submitted to different loads, helpless as women under the white man's protection. When they travelled in their own style, seeking safety in numbers and treating the journey as a festival, it seemed to Maclay that every stick and bottle required its own carrier. He recognized the advantages of being introduced where his name was hardly known, learning about native politics, receiving answers to questions on the spot. He grew tired of adjusting himself to their customs, character and 'rather tiresome' demands. He often wished for a supply of concentrated food. Carrying his own provisions, relieved of the insufferable 'coaxing and persuading' and of all these troublesome presences, he would set off alone for the interior.

Denied this ideal freedom of action, he made the best of what he had, alternately imposing his will and bending to the wishes of others. Through August and September he was almost constantly on the move, visiting nearly all the villages about Astrolabe Bay. Between land journeys he explored by sea, here and there in the bay, northward to the Islands of Contented Men, eastward around Cape Rigny. Much as he fretted against the restrictions imposed by his retinue or by the small size and inadequate equipment of his boat, he had reason to be satisfied with the sum of his travels. By the end of September 1876 he had seen more than 100 kilometres of the coast and raised a canvas banner on Mount Grand Duke Konstantin, nearly twenty kilometres inland. Only the mountains south-west of Bongu, where every village was at war with its neighbours, remained outside the widening boundaries of the Maclay Coast.

Sometimes he returned to his base alone, almost stunned by heat after days at sea in the open boat. Sometimes he led a procession, arriving by torchlight with hundreds of villagers who had added themselves to his party for a sight of the *tal-Maklai*. To reach his own domain was always satisfying. Whether at Bugarlom or in the second house he acquired on Bilbil, the traveller insatiable for a life of movement as greedily sought a life at home.

When he tried to express what pleased him most in this life, the first word that came to mind was 'tranquillity'. Days at Bugarlom were regularly patterned: a 5 a.m. rising, about half an hour for each meal, an hour's siesta in the early afternoon, another hour for conversation with the natives and instructions to his servants, bedtime at nine in the evening. He found infinite variety in this monotony, a calm invaluable for intellectual work and 'beneficial to the character'. With twelve hours free for scientific activity, a day on his coast still seemed too short.

He owed his tranquillity to his servants, essential supports of intellectual and spiritual progress. This did not mean he found the service flawless. Saleh the Javanese, 'a very decent man', competent as cook and occasional tailor, sometimes made his master regret bringing a Muslim chef to a country where the commonest meat was pork. Mebli proved far less of a marksman than Maclay had been led to expect, and in heavy work his indolence offset his strapping physique. The men from different countries and cultures were soon at odds, united only in superstitous fears and a tendency to succumb to what Maclay called 'laziness and malingering' rather than fever. It was mostly on Mira's account, however, that the servants totalled two-and-a-half rather than three. The little girl from Palau was naturally unused to waiting on a European gentleman, keeping his house in order and presiding over such mysteries as the laundering of shirts and socks. Considering her purely as a servant, Maclay felt that given a week's trial he would never have engaged her.

His peace was never threatened by the need to carry wood and water or struggle with the fire. When Mebli's erratic marksmanship, and successful fishing, saved Saleh from touching an unclean animal, meals appeared as though of their own accord. Mira learned enough to become useful about the house and as an attendant on expeditions. For Maclay this marked the limits of her functions. Concerning Mira, his diary contained nothing he would not wish his mother and sister to read. But if she never became a temporary wife or an efficient house-keeper she apparently saved him from one hazard of celibacy. This time, he was spared offers of wives from the villages.

For Maclay, living with these people was almost like living alone. They needed little, stayed under their separate roof, talked to their master only when it suited him. Their occasional shirking could be treated tolerantly. Their fears, sometimes ethnologically interesting, never caused disgust. They did not bore Maclay with complaints or reminiscences, and if they found life miserable he need not know it. With them he endured neither importunate pleas for companionship nor the sight of a white man disintegrating from sheer loneliness. Relieved of such threats to his inner security, he forgot that Olsen had ever existed.

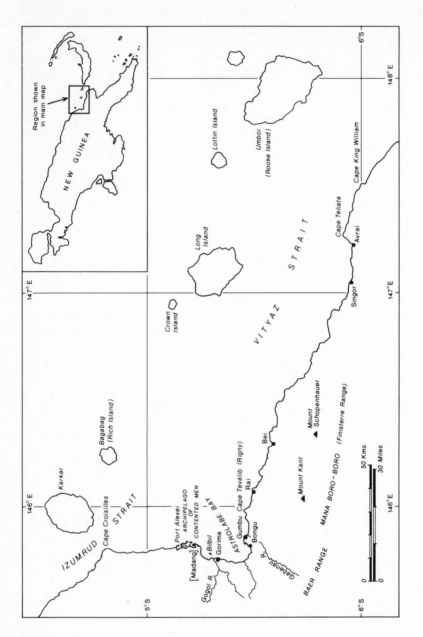

The Maclay Coast, north-eastern New Guinea, as defined in 1877

Great obstacles still hindered scientific progress and the expansion of a temperament he considered naturally serene. Fever first attacked him on the journey to Mount Konstantin, causing a dangerous fall. Thereafter his work was often interrupted by 'a few days of fever', anaemia, neuralgia, sudden attacks of giddiness. Nothing oppressed him more than the ulcers that appeared on his legs. Precious hours were lost in attending to these painful sores. For weeks on end he was confined to the house, sleeping only with the aid of chloral. Repeating his favourite maxim from Schopenhauer, 'Every evening we are poorer by a day', he set to work on the comparative anatomy of the vertebrate brain.

Through housebound weeks in October and November, he worked at dissection, description and drawing, hampered less by neuralgia and aching legs than by the scarcity of material. As it become possible, he carried out measurements upon the natives who almost every day visited him singly or by twos and threes. He kept up meteorological observations, made many sketches, and began a watercolour album of reef fishes. The four-month voyage had yielded a mass of notes to be put in order for despatch by the vessel expected within a few weeks. And writing, for reasons he never explained, became increasingly troublesome for Maclay. Combined with illness and the difficulty of describing a life that was regular to the point of monotony, this distaste for writing made his journal a meagre record, a few lines often accounting for a whole month. He still responded to the dramatic moment, as when lightning fantastically illuminated the dancers at a feast. There were no more rhapsodies on the loveliness of his surroundings, no marvelling attention to every detail of primitive life. Maclay was five years older, and the Maclay Coast had ceased to be a new world.

The first crop of maize was harvested and another sown; his coconut palms were growing well; in his plantation and the gardens of natives to whom he distributed seeds, the foreign fruits and vegetables flourished. While cultivating his new estate and reclaiming the over-grown land at Garagassi, however, he looked anxiously towards the sea. He wanted letters, scientific journals, an opportunity to send papers to St Petersburg and Berlin. He was oppressed by thoughts of the future, scientific reputation, mounting debts, possible misunderstandings with friends and supporters. Over his tropical paradise, the cares of the European formed an ever-present cloud.

Besides ordering a ship from Singapore, he had made known in Australia his hope that vessels trading with New Britain and New Ireland might look in at Astrolabe Bay. Before the end of the year, his request had been more than once published in Sydney. But no trading skipper would sail so far out of his course, and risk a ship in little-known waters, for the sake of a man who had 'marooned' himself. November passed into December, 1876 into 1877, and not a European sail appeared. Maclay awaited the schooner with as much fear as impatience. Its arrival might settle some problems. Others would become acute, in particular that of his return to Europe.

When he deplored the shortness of the days and dreaded being torn from his work, he thought first of the principal scientific undertaking, the collection of information on native society and its customs. He had expected much from this second stay on his coast, when old acquaintance with the natives would combine with his philanthropic purpose to help him understand their ways. As the months passed, the most he could claim was that his neighbours did not always conceal their customs. The expression 'step by step' overstated a rate of advance that seemed more like a quarter of a step at a time. Enquiries still brought evasive or 'fanciful' answers. Convinced that the only reliable information was that given by his own eyes, he found that a warning of his arrival or a request that he be called for some event could change the whole procedure. He adopted the policy of appearing indifferent to his neighbours' doing, 'lying in wait' to observe significant moments in their lives, employing stratagems to witness ceremonies 'accidentally'. Becoming a spy for science, he recorded fragments of a way of life he believed must soon disappear. They were often dubious fragments, destined to be thrown out as 'lumber'. He was rarely able to claim a verified discovery, never in a position to interpret what he saw. Of the natives' thoughts and beliefs he learned next to nothing. His own were frequently 'melancholy thoughts' about the inadequacy of the human mind.

He described his relationship with these people mainly in terms of mutual trust and friendship. It seemed to him that they became less constrained in his presence, that eventually they would grant him the perfect confidence essential for his purposes. He learned more details of ritual circumcision. He managed to take a census in Bongu and Gorendu. Not long after the men first submitted to his craniometer, husbandly jealousy was sufficiently overcome to allow him to measure the heads of women. The gulf remained, almost imperceptible when the *Kaaram-tamo* theorized, yawningly evident in his daily life. It revealed itself to Maclay in his inability to interpret a gesture or a facial expression, to frame the right question or understand the answer. It came to light in his personal feelings. Just as he was still struck by the ugliness of his neighbours' faces, he continued to feel a certain helplessness before the ways of a people 'so remote from us'. He never wrote more or longer letters to Europe than during this second sojourn in his earthly paradise, among the people he called his own.

The relationship remained a delicate equilibrium: aloofness, mystery and the assumption of authority on one side, balanced by imagination, incomprehension and obedience on the other. Practical details had been explained to an Italian trader aboard the *Sea Bird*. Maclay in New Guinea would never live in a village. While he bartered European goods for his requirements, the natives never saw the contents of his house. Since a trader, apart from other considerations, could not conceal the potential profits of murder, Maclay believed Signor Paldi would be killed in the Admiralty Islands.

He remained conscious that he himself might be killed on the Maclay Coast. He no longer thought his neighbours would dare attack him openly. He never ruled out the possibility of receiving a spear in the back, being ambushed in a village or shot down by an unseen bowman. At the height of his power, practising all he preached, he felt how little separated this tranquil existence from the disasters of Papua-Koviai.

He always remembered what he owed to the imaginations of his friends. He was the magician who burned water, luridly illuminated the night and caused a man to fly away to Russia. They believed that the *Kaaram-tamo's* gaze could heal the sick or strike down the healthy. Strange lapses occurred in their faith. He was never trusted to deflect the mountain-dwellers' spears and arrows. There were lingering questions about his nature, origin and intentions towards the people. But on the whole Maclay found his myth self-perpetuating. 'Once they had raised me to the position of *Kaaram-tamo* and given me that heavenly origin', he explained, 'my every action and word, interpreted in that light, apparently confirmed their opinion'.

Spectacular feats of magic were no longer necessary. Sometimes the same effect was produced accidentally, as in the incident of the *bulu-ribut*, a musical instrument first heard on the Maclay Coast early in 1877. At that time Maclay slept badly, plagued by worrying thoughts. He believed he might rest more peacefully if he heard the 'plaintive music' that had lulled him to sleep in the Malay Peninsula. So Saleh made a *bulu-ribut*, long pieces of bamboo with the internal divisions removed, pierced here and there by longitudinal slits and fastened upright in nearby trees.

At first the sounds were startling, even for Maclay. In the village they caused alarm. When he asked why visits suddenly ceased, he found the neighbours afraid of *tamo-Russ* who talked loudly round his house at night. Laughing at such fears, he led half the village to Bugarlom to see that there were no *tamo-Russ*. He did not show the *bulu-ribut* or attempt to explain what happened when the wind blew. By day the strange sounds were suppressed. At night aeolian music filled the air, confirming that *tamo-Russ* flew over the sea, convincing the Bongu people that Bugarlom was a dangerous place after sunset. For a time the penetrating notes disturbed Maclay, but he grew used to them. They sounded 'like the voices of guards at their posts'.

He was similarly guarded by imagination on every side. His 'hermit-like' life conformed to the distance and self-sufficiency of a superhuman being. The useful and attractive objects that came from his house, as mysterious in origin as their proprietor, might be fresh created every day. From the *Kaaram-tamo* inconvenient questioners received enigmatic answers or evocative silences, to be interpreted as imagination might suggest. There was no need to lie, he emphasized. But it was neither necessary nor safe to undeceive. Maclay believed that an end to his magical reputation meant the end of his peace. He must live in his country as a god or not at all.

He might impulsively echo enthusiasm for civilizing happy savages. He could not seriously entertain such ideas on his own account. He had scientific and moral reasons 'to interfere as little as possible with the doings of the natives, in order not to change their habits or customs'. Little as he understood their beliefs, he could not wish to alter a way of thought essential to his security. Yet in many ways he changed his neighbours' lives. The villagers were broken-in to being summoned at three o'clock in the morning to prepare for his journeys. They grew used to his assumption that they must shoulder his belongings and trudge, their fears and reluctance ignored, along tracks they neither desired nor needed to travel. It was established that 'good men' were those who followed Maclay and 'bad men' were those who did not. It was recognized that when Maclay sounded a gong on his veranda people must leave their own business and attend to his.

Their work was rewarded by an honourable acquaintanceship, useful plants, occasional medical attention, and lingering hope that his powers might stop excessive rain or find drifting fish-traps. They again obtained European goods, the otherwise harmless articles that Maclay blamed for the cupidity and discontent of the Palauans. Gradually they learned a new set of values, a new idea of authority. If they had not acquired a god, they had a white master, and Maclay was gaining a kingdom.

Thinking about the power and knowledge attained through his friendship with the natives and his status as a being unique in their experience, Maclay was often depressed. It seemed to him that a world of brutes and scoundrels must be eager to exploit his information and influence in order to penetrate his country. At its worst, the coming of Europeans would bring enslavement and extermination to his people. In its mildest form it meant the destruction of a way of life he sought to preserve. He already foretold the day when scientists would search the interior for pure-blooded Papuans, when the vanished coastal tribes would be known only from his writings. Again he was the recorder of what must pass away, finding both duty and solace in research. For more positive action he needed a distant and lofty word. In solitude he formed one clear resolve. Neither directly nor indirectly would he aid 'the establishment of relations between whites and Papuans'.

The decision always had a certain unreality. Europeans rarely waited for knowledge of native customs and language before intruding on other peoples. While Maclay agonized, any flag could be raised a day's sail from Bugarlom. Some Captain O'Keefe, with the slow match burning, might be offering cloth and beads at an anchorage just out of sight. A white-clad, book-bearing figure could be on the way to announce that the mission was extending its care from the south coast to the north. Maclay never discussed what he would do in such cases, his silence adding to the unreality of his position.

Most of the substance of his vow had already been eaten away by his actions. The results of his first visit to New Guinea had been published in several languages. By bringing three vessels to Astrolabe Bay, and inviting more, he had probably done as much as one man could to introduce Europeans to the natives. But if this rose to consciousness among the 'sad thoughts' from which he found refuge in work, it was suppressed. Without Europeans, he could not travel to and from New Guinea, receive or send letters or replenish his stores. Perhaps he would eventually become as independent as his coast, his people free to forget all other white men as they seemed to forget Olsen. Until then, ships must continue to call, purified, as it were, by service to his cause.

No ship had called by February 1877, and the rice supply was finished. In March, when the shot ran out, Mebli began to spend much time in a canoe, trying his luck wherever there might be fish. Nearly all imported food was gone by the end of April. Believing his provisions need last only five or six months, Maclay had not been much upset by the discovery that sacks of biscuits and beans shipped from Singapore were far from full, other foodstuffs poor in quality or spoiled by bad packing. When he found himself 'punished' for trusting the supplier, he refused to worry, treating his predicament as another 'opportunity to observe the effect of Papuan food on white people'. Only shortages of such items as pens and ink, writing paper or microscope slides could hamper his activities. Here too, he took the philosophical attitude, 'There are many things I do not need'. As he explained, it was not in his temperament to regard these deficiencies as a great misfortune. Living the life he had chosen, he looked upon its hardships 'with the greatest indifference'.

It also occurred to him that he was 'punished' for his impractical approach to 'a member of the commercial classes'. When such people received orders for goods and services, he now realized, they usually required some guarantee that they would not be out of pocket. He had not deposited cash or a promissory note against the cost. Perhaps no ship would call. Again he could not feel seriously perturbed. The days were too short for all he must do. He made plans as though he need never leave.

As his health improved, he resumed trips to villages on the coast and in the foothills. In February he stayed a while at 'Airu' on Bilbil, where the islanders had built him a native-style hut, dark but cool, with a wide view of coast and mountains. He studied the manufacture of pots, learned much about Bilbil trading voyages. In Kain's big *vang*, sheltered from the weather and freed from the toil and anxiety of managing a boat, he cruised among the Islands of Contented Men and visited mainland villages at Cape Duperrey. Suspecting that cannibalism was practised on the coast—Bongu people described the taste of human flesh—he still had no concrete proof. At Cape Duperrey he found many villages of cannibals, shocked by their first sight of a white man but ready to tell him, through Sek Island and Bilbil interpreters, exactly how and when they enjoyed such interesting repasts. He saw no cannibalism, since it depended on the results of war. Nor did he add anything to his osteological collection. After being thoroughly gnawed and broken, all bones were thrown into the sea.

The Sek people occasionally visited the large island of Karkar, about 45 kilometres farther north, and Maclay hoped to join such an expedition. He intended to use the experience and palatial vessels of the Bilbil traders in a voyage to the east. Negotiations over these projects soon took him back to Bilbil and the islands just beyond.

They were not his only business. Even without the effects of the latest earthquakes, Port Konstantin had never been a really satisfactory anchorage. Sailing north again in April, he concentrated on larger and safer harbours.

One sheltered anchorage, 'quite convenient for small ships', came to light between the mainland and the islands of Yabob and Uremu. By planting a dozen coconut palms and telling his companions to remember this act, Maclay took possession of Uremu, an uninhabited islet which served as overnight refuge for thousands of pigeons. Then he cruised thoughtfully among the homes of the Contented Men, improving his sketch map and taking occasional soundings.

Everywhere good anchorages and 'a considerable depth of water' confirmed the impressions formed in 1872. He discovered a fine strait, 'deep enough for large vessels'. Behind Sek, the northernmost of the chain, there lay exactly what he wanted, a harbour good enough for a fleet. His most important geographical discoveries could be useful only to the owners of large vessels, the Europeans whose coming he dreaded. He did not intend to keep them secret.

Insecta

Crania

Bugatira 1876

corner in the house at Bugarlom

Saul of Bongu, 1877

In the middle of 1877, with no idea when or whether the schooner would arrive, Maclay prepared for an indefinite stay. His house was in bad condition, its timbers attacked by white ants, its roof too roughly fashioned to withstand the rainiest months. Bugarlom again became a busy place, as his servants directed the Bongu people in adding a new structure, about the same size as the first, with timbers allegedly resistant to termites. Eventually he was delighted by a 'European-Malay-Papuan' house, its two halves joined by a veranda serving as a corridor. It was a long time a-building, and he had cause to doubt he would ever occupy it.

For the first eleven months, he had recorded nothing ominous. With faith in his own precautions and the respect inspired in his neighbours, he saw no further need to keep loaded guns in the house or to stay on the alert in the villages. In June 1877 he discovered a threat to his security. Some people were not awed by the *Kaaram-tamo*'s powers, guessed that his house contained treasure, and believed he could be killed.

He learned it when his foxy old friend Kodi-boro of Bogadjim warned him not to visit Gorima, a village about twenty kilometres to the north. Kodi and his son discussed the matter while Maclay sat between them. They never meant to give details. Pressed for explanations, Kodi admitted that Gorima was plotting. With or without Bongu's help, Gorima men would kill Maclay and loot his property.

Gorima was bad; Bongu might also be bad; the only reliable friends were at Bogadjim, where Kodi still wished to win Maclay for his village. Taking the story at face value, Maclay was 'surprised' that some still thought his death possible and desirable. Worse, ideas discussed at Gorima or Bogadjim could easily reach his closest neighbours. To stop this talk, he set out for a village he had not intended to visit.

Few Gorima people had seen the *Kaaram-tamo*. Ignorant of their dialect, Maclay could do little to quieten their agitation. Pantomime requests for food and a sleeping-place, methodical attention to the meal and arrangements for the night, nevertheless went far to produce an uneasy hush. Maclay ordered the fire built up, took his place before the crowd and scrutinized the apprehensive faces. He called for the men whose names Kodi-boro had given, and made them sit opposite him in the full light of the fire. Considering their guilt proved by their 'obvious reluctance' to come forward or to meet his gaze, he accused Abui and Malu of wishing to kill him. This was very bad, since he had done nothing to anyone in Gorima. Now he was going to sleep, so those who wished to kill him would have every opportunity.

He slept badly, waking often to hear discussions in which his name recurred, but this restlessness, he explained, was caused by a heavy meal. In the morning the villagers were docility itself. Abui presented Maclay

with a large pig. Both the accused insisted on escorting him back to
Bugarlom. Satisfied with the effect of his action, seeing the desire to
appease as final proof of guilt, Maclay considered the matter closed.
What happened between Gorima and the Bogadjim people, whom he
had named as informers, was not his business.

While this incident was making its impression, he left Mebli and the
bulu-ribut to guard the house and started on the long-planned voyage
with the Bilbil traders. They sailed by night, Maclay and Mira in the
leading *vang*, Captain Kain, with Saleh and his kitchen installed in a
second vessel.

Maclay would gladly have travelled thus for weeks, amply accommodated with his table, bunk and armchair on the sheltered platform,
secure in the skill of Kain and his assistant. Gliding through the night on
the strength of the land breeze, he slept peacefully, watched the dark
coast slip by, or wrote by the light of a kerosene lamp. By day, when the
south-east wind opposed them, they beached the vessels and Maclay
wandered through the jungle or visited settlements. The Bilbil connection and his companions' fluency in all languages allowed him to work
in an atmosphere of calm and confidence. It was in many ways the most
comfortable and profitable voyage he had undertaken.

It also provided opportunity to extend his influence. Along this
populous coast he found many dialects, but no marked physical or
cultural differences among the inhabitants. Already enclosed in the
Bilbil economic sphere, they were all suitable members for a political
entity he meant to extend to Cape King William, about 200 kilometres
from his base. He had some reason to doubt their ignorance of
Europeans. Kain told a confused story about a country far south-east of
Bilbil, where people wore clothes, built large houses and used metal
tools. But all the villagers were astounded by the sight of a white man
and his equipment. Even at busy, dirty Singor, people who specialized
in charging dear for imitation boar's-tusk ornaments made from
clamshell were awed by Maclay's table and chair, his cooking and eating
utensils and the light that he increased or diminished at will. Apart from
the value they placed on their work, they were as unspoiled as any
well-wisher could hope.

Maclay was not careful of feelings in Singor. Merely to rouse his men,
he fired his double-barrelled gun. When the villagers came running to
discover what caused this thunderous reveille, Kain addressed them in
his best 'big-man' style, naming Maclay as '*Tamo-boro-boro, Kaaram-tamo,
Tamo-Russ*', berating the listeners for failing to bring gifts to such a
visitor. The people retreated as fast as they had come. They reappeared
with chickens, sucking-pigs, yams, bananas, bags of *Canarium* nuts. For
the first time, Maclay had been formally awarded all his titles. For the
first time, tribute had been demanded and received in his name.

As Maclay half expected, Kain's idea of a 'long, long way' did not match his own. Three days' sail from Bugarlom, they sighted the agreed terminus of the journey. He spent two days about Cape Teliata, inspecting villages, plantations and handicrafts. He struggled with Kain, offering untold wealth in axes, knives, cloth and beads as payment for a longer voyage. Kain would venture no farther, stubbornly contending that beyond that point they would be killed and eaten. Maclay showed the revolver. Kain believed but did not believe, feared the magic weapon yet insisted on its uselessness against the cannibals beyond the cape. 'They will kill', he repeated, clinching the argument with, 'Maclay is one. They are many'. Unable to counter such fears with worse threats, Maclay gave up. A brass plate bearing his monogram was nailed to a tree, and the expedition turned homeward.

His only recorded emotion was annoyance. Yet the incident signified more than his immediate frustration. His scheme of things included no more necessary man than the *tamo-boro* of Bilbil, whose seamanship, trading connections and linguistic talents must form a cornerstone of Maclay's Papuan Union. Now Kain, a perfect Grand Vizier in public, had shown himself recalcitrant in private, without real faith in his leader's power and immortality. To him, Maclay was *Tamo-boro-boro* only for the purpose of extorting tribute.

Maclay experienced the limits of his authority again during the homeward voyage, when the Bilbil men insisted that accompanying mountain excursions was not the duty of seafarers. At Bugarlom he had no time to analyse the unsatisfactory side of a generally successful trip. A strong young man had suddenly died at Gorendu. The people were wild with grief and dismay. And the agitation would outlast the mourning. The death was seen as the work of sorcerers. There was talk of war against the mountain men.

What Maclay knew of native warfare convinced him that it seldom caused much bloodshed. These so-called wars were nevertheless apt to last a long time, drifting into private feuds and payback killings that kept the villages in upheaval for months or years. Apart from humanitarian concern, the situation aroused purely personal misgivings. War meant constant commotion in a village five minutes walk from his house, rupture of communications with the mountains, the country unsafe for miles around. It meant an end to his tranquillity and the pursuit of his chief goals. At its worst, it could force him to leave Bugarlom.

Arguments that had restrained Bongu a few weeks earlier would not work in this case. Then, the death had been that of an old, childless woman. In the loss of a vigorous young male, the people had clearer evidence of sorcery, stronger cause for fear and anger. Everybody agreed that sorcerers had caused Vangum's death. His family demanded war. Delay arose from their inability to fix on the guilty party, but this was overcome by a proposal to attack each suspected village in turn. Finally a deputation came to request Maclay's alliance.

He never knew exactly what his refusal meant to his friends. They still talked of a march against the mountain people. There was no response to his arguments of peace, a measure of resentment in his reception. Vangum's father, building a fire beneath his dead son's new canoe, hardly gave Maclay a glance. In all Gorendu, the white man seemed to have no friends but Tui and perhaps Vangum's young wife, whose flashing smile as she watched over the dead suggested she was bored by 'her role as inconsolable widow'. For a full week, the week of Vangum's funeral, Maclay experienced no event he wished to remember.

The quiet was broken by news that Vangum's little brother had been bitten by a snake. The boy had died before Maclay could reach the village with his medical equipment. The slit gong was being sounded. The square was a scene of terrible excitement as women shrieked and wailed and armed men rushed about shouting. Stunned by this eruption in a place that had always seemed the very heart of tranquillity, Maclay saw the uselessness of soothing words. Every individual in Gorendu felt threatened. All but grave, silent Tui were hostile to Maclay, seeming to blame him for their misfortunes.

Cooler than their afflicted neighbours, the Bongu people were no more swayed by Maclay's arguments. Instead, Saul tried again to persuade him of the need for war and the rejected alliance. Even at home Maclay found no peace. His servants knew all about events in the villages. Though they called it by different names, they firmly believed in the danger of sorcery.

A silent, absorbed spectator at rites he did not understand, he attended the boy's funeral. The people, though calmer, remained sullen and hostile. But afterwards Maclay was included in the group when one of the men spat into their hands a magical preparation to shield them from evil. With the others he went to wash his hand in the sea and returned to the village, protected from the sorcery of their enemies. Then he was asked for something in return. Tui begged him to prepare his own magic, to cause an earthquake that would destroy the mountain villages and leave the coast unharmed.

Somehow Maclay escaped, leaving his friends to their conclusions about his inability or unwillingness to save them, leaving Tui to cope with the blow to his faith and prestige. That evening the slit gong sounded in Gorendu. Late at night, Mebli woke his master to report that the people had resolved on war. The one sign of regard for Maclay's opinion was their wish to conceal the decision from him.

Maclay had much to trouble him, waiting for dawn in his half-finished house, surrounded by the guardian voices of the *bulu-ribut*. He always assured himself that he did nothing deliberately to foster his superhuman reputation. There was no denying that it had grown uncontradicted, to become the foundation of his safety. Now the structure of illusion threatened to collapse. In his neighbours' eyes, he was either no deity or no friend. If his supposed divine powers were real, he clearly would not use them on Gorendu's behalf. Despairing of a god who refused to help them, his people were taking traditional action to help themselves.

There must be no war. But Maclay lacked the confident authority to forbid it outright. Nor could he argue against the reality of sorcery. With his 'limited knowledge of the language' he could not discuss such subjects, much less convince a frightened, angry audience. Besides, though he did not face the fact, an argument against sorcery became an argument against himself. If no such powers existed, they could not be attributed to him.

He worked out a scheme worthy of any minister for foreign affairs. Bongu had never seemed as fiery as Gorendu—nobody had died in Bongu. The villages had disagreed about the identity of the enemy, evading the question by a plan too ambitious for their strength. The need for Maclay's assistance had been most felt in Bongu, where his refusal produced a telling effect. He concentrated on Bongu. By opposing to fear of the mountain men an even stronger fear, he could play upon misgivings, heighten disagreement between the allies, and win a delay for 'cooling-off'.

He strolled to Bongu at the usual time and waited for his friends to raise the question. When asked, he repeated that there should be no war, and sat in silence as impassioned speakers tried to change his mind. When they had finished he rose to go, announcing calmly: 'There must be no war. If you attack the mountain people, disaster will fall upon everyone in Gorendu and Bongu'.

'What will happen? What will it be? What would Maclay do?', a dozen questioners demanded.

'If you go', said Maclay, 'you will find out for yourselves'.

As he left the village he could feel imagination beginning its work. At the gates of Bugarlom he heard the first results.

'If the Bongu men go to the mountains', gasped the old man who came running after him, 'will there be an earthquake?'

'Maclay did not say that.'

But he had said there would be a disaster, and an earthquake was a great, great disaster, dreaded by everyone. 'Well', the old man pleaded, 'will there by an earthquake?'

'Perhaps', said Maclay.

For a week or so Maclay kept away from the villages, superintending the completion of his house, attentive to rumours brought by his servants. He learned that dissension had arisen within and between the communities, that warlike preparations had stopped and debate subsided into repetitious bickering. Something was nevertheless decided. No further deaths stuck Gorendu, but every man, woman and child was daily expected to die from spells breathed over remnants of Gorendu's taro and yams. Then they noticed the leaves of coconut palms turning red. Mountain men had buried spells in the soil, to starve out those not killed directly by sorcery. 'Gorendu is finished', Tui had said, and Maclay learned that Gorendu had lost the will to live. Once the taro was harvested, the villagers would disperse among other communities. The prettiest, cleanest, quietest little place on the coast would be nothing but a name on the white man's map.

Maclay felt no duty to argue against it when Tui came to confirm the rumour. Nor did he protest when the recital of misfortunes and fears developed reproachful overtones. 'We wanted to beat these mountain men', Tui said despondently, 'but we're not allowed. Maclay doesn't want us to do it. He says there will be a disaster. The Bongu people are afraid of an earthquake. If there is an earthquake all the villages will say: "It's Bongu's fault. Maclay said there would be a disaster if Bongu went to the mountains". All the villages will attack Bongu if there is an earthquake. So the Bongu people are afraid . . .'.

Maclay listened patiently and let the old man go without contradiction. He could truthfully say he had never predicted or threatened an earthquake. The whole rigmarole was a growth of fantasy around a few vague words, a misinterpretation 'quite typical' of his relations with the natives. It prevented the war—all that mattered for the present. Yet Tui's account contained a warning. Apparently neither Bongu nor Gorendu now believed that Maclay could foresee or cause earthquakes. They feared that others would believe it and hold them guilty should defiance be followed by such an event. If an earthquake occurred in spite of their obedience—. But that was a possibility Maclay dared not consider.

He resumed visits to Bongu in full consciousness that his prestige was at stake. Within a few days he had to defend it. Slanting red through the doorway of the men's house, the rays of the setting sun fell on personages from Bogadjim and Bilbil as well as Bongu and Gorendu, in animated talk that ceased abruptly when Maclay appeared. He sat in the midst of an awkward silence, aware that his presence hindered their discussions. At last Saul advanced, looked straight in the *Kaaram-tamo*'s eyes, and put the question that troubled them:

'Maclay, can you die?'

So were still in doubt, six years after his legend had first taken root. All his heroic self-discipline had failed to prove his immortality. In the frame of Saul's question, several events formed an illuminating pattern. When Maclay had fallen on Mount Konstantin, giddily clutching at a vine that broke and deposited him unconscious half-way down a slope, his companions had sat a little way off, debating whether he was dead or merely asleep. Then there had been the equivocal behaviour of Kodi-boro, warning Maclay not to visit Gorima and at the same time almost sending him there, as though experimentally. The Gorendu people had experimented in a way, by offering magical protection to one who theoretically need fear no sorcery. Most significantly, there had been a strange conversation some months earlier, with Saul trying to discover something definite about Maclay's age, hinting at what he might have seen or done near Bongu several generations before. Their talk had left Saul very dissatisfied. He was still dissatisfied as he asked, 'Can you die? Can you be dead like the Bongu people?' His pleading voice proclaimed his wish to hear that Maclay would live forever.

Maclay paced back and forth, studying the rafters. The question could not be dismissed with a 'Perhaps'. He could not pronounce a plain 'Yes', for the truth would be fatal to his prestige. Nor could he answer 'No'. Accident might at any time reveal that the *Kaaram-tamo* could both die and lie like ordinary men. Oppressed by care for reputation, present and posthumous, he found nothing safe to say. He searched the roof for inspiration. Among the pig jaws and fish skeletons there hung a collection of weapons. He took a sharp, heavy spear and handed it to Saul. Facing Saul as he had faced the boys on Palau, he removed his hat so that no shadow hid his calm, serious look, his unblinking eyes.

'Let's see if Maclay can die.'

Saul, the hunter, warrior, husband of three wives, Bongu's nearest approach to a chieftain, was broken from the start by a challenge so foreign to his experience. Without raising the spear, he stood irresolutely, muttering 'No! No!' Maclay maintained his position a little longer, pressing home the lesson of his invulnerability. The intervention of those who rushed in as though to shield him was never necessary. Calling Saul an 'old woman', albeit jokingly, he sat down amid an outburst of relieved chatter.

It seemed to him that the question had been dealt with satisfactorily. But the answer had closed quite different questions. It confirmed dramatically that Maclay never feared death. It showed that Saul, more trusted than the others, admitted to the privilege of conversation on Maclay's veranda, could not in cold blood spear a friend whose prestige increased his own. Beyond that, all was confusion, humiliation, an indecisive struggle between scepticism and the will to believe, taking place in a mythological context of which Maclay had no inkling. At least they would never again ask if he could die. His answers were unbearable.

As with most of his actions, he never knew the real effect in the villages. All danger seemingly past, strengthened by another demonstration of his poise and power, he returned to peaceful solitude and increasing adversity. Scientific work was impeded by fever, the weakness and giddiness of anaemia and the nag of tropical ulcers. Only a little coffee, tea and wine remained in his store, he and his servants subsisting entirely on Mebli's fishing, their garden produce, and barter with the natives. He lacked the very materials of his work, 'trifles' he had underestimated, forgotten, or lost between Java and New Guinea. Every day he looked out for the ship that was almost a year overdue and might never come. Yet he still dreaded its coming. There was still so much to do.

Through September and October 1877, the natives almost disappeared from the outward life of the hermit at Bugarlom. Bogadjim held a festival, but Maclay either failed to attend or did not find the event worth describing. When news from Gorendu convinced him the people intended to leave, he made no attempt to dissuade them. When a death occurred at Gumbu, the first village to recognize the *Kaaramtamo*, he was neither consulted nor informed about possible consequences. There were no more triumphs of will and diplomacy to set beside the subjection of Gorima and the prevention of war, hardly anything worth preserving in his journal. The people who had faded into the background were nonetheless present to his mind. In the face of his difficulties in writing, and a severe shortage of paper, he wrote a great deal during these months. In long letters to Europe he described his work, adventures and way of life. He examined his relationship with the natives, their strange ideas about his nature, his consequent power to live safely among them, dominating them in their own best interests. He spoke of his fears for their future and the precautions he must take to prevent, or at least postpone, their encounter with other white men. He did not report on their political organization, which remained what it had been, a resounding phrase in a letter to Europe.

November brought signs that Maclay, for all his seeming indifference, could not afford to ignore. The earth began a faint but definite trembling. On still nights he heard a muted rumble like the sound of a distant bombardment. They would be listening in Bongu and Gorendu, dreading the *tangrim*, asking who was responsible for this. If the earth became too restless, there might be emissaries seeking mercy for an obedient people, or magical intervention on their behalf. Maclay was more preoccupied with a different phenomenon, a river of corruption flowing into Bongu from a source in the kitchen of the *tal-Maklai*.

He had never paid much attention to relations between his servants and the natives, or been particularly impressed by the ease with which Saleh and Mebli learned the dialect and reached an understanding with the Papuans. Visitors sought a chat in the kitchen almost as often as an audience with the *Kaaram-tamo*, but Maclay accepted the situation without misgivings. He saw no reason to prohibit his servants' nocturnal visits to the villages. Saleh and Mebli brought information, including news meant to be kept secret from Maclay.

Congratulating himself on having no white employee—nobody to make the natives suspect 'the earthly origin of the *Kaaram-tamo*'—Maclay seemed to fall into the European error of lumping all dark men together. The matter could not be so simple for his neighbours. Saleh and Mebli came from countries too distant to be distinguishable from Russia, where beings like him were commonplace. While the Javanese and the Palauan did not look like *tamo-Russ*, they were as different from each other and from the people of Bongu. As adjuncts of Maclay, they walked confidently in and out of his house and handled his wonderful property. The darker of the strangers even used the '*tabu*', the weapon sacred to Maclay. In many ways, these two were as inexplicable as a man from the moon.

But Mebli often failed to kill the birds at which he aimed the '*tabu*'. Though he and Saleh wore clothes, they were less covered than Maclay. They could be seen to consist of flesh, the same colour all over, neither black nor white. Their minds, too, were less remote than Maclay's. Mebli was haunted by ghosts from Bongu, spirits of the dead who came by night to strangle him, like those of his native land. He and Saleh believed as strongly as their neighbours in the power of sorcery. For all their outlandishness, they were closer to men than the *Kaaram-tamo*. Familiar, confidential, something betwixt and between, they bridged the magical distance separating Bongu from the *tal-Maklai*. Now they secretly brought beautiful and useful things to exchange for food.

The Papuans kept secrets better than Mebli and Saleh. When Maclay learned that his servants were stealing his goods for barter in the villages, the revelation emerged from their own feud. Each accused the other. Maclay found both guilty. He did not make allowance for their hunger, or excuse them as victims of European corruption. He condemned their 'conscienceless behaviour', as though they had been white.

Whatever happened to the thieves, the damage was done. Either the villagers knew, and did not care, that the things they bought were stolen, or they fancied Maclay's companions as rich and powerful as he. However they decided, the result looked fatal for his ascendancy. While he wrote of the deep friendship and perfect trust he had inspired, the godlike authority with which he was invested, his servants cast doubt on his power to frustrate wrongdoers, undermined his security, corrupted his people. There had been no greater threat to the illusions on which his reputation rested. But there was no time for the urgent, exemplary action. Early in November, while the ground continued to shiver and distant artillery rumbled, a ship dropped anchor in the bay.

12: Descent into Hell

WHILE MACLAY IMAGINED a distant bombardment, or watched from the ship the origin of that ominous sound—volcanic activity on the islands of Manam and Bam—guns had been thundering in Bulgaria and Asia Minor. The skipper of the *Flower of Yarrow* was wrong in reporting that Russia had taken Constantinople. Only British power, the British believed, could thwart that age-old ambition. As the Russo-Turkish war drew to a close, the world feared war between Russia and Britain.

The news was merely interesting to Maclay. His English acquaintances were not the kind of people who roared, 'We don't want to fight, but, by Jingo! if we do . . . !' The vulnerable trading port for which he was bound could not afford warlike enthusiasm. Any hostility in Singapore would come not from inflamed patriots but from enraged creditors.

Landing there in January 1878, he was suffering from fever and anaemia. During the two-month voyage via the Exchequer and Anchorite groups, Mindanao and north Borneo, he had developed scurvy and beri-beri. But Schomburg of Singapore was on the doorstep, demanding the costs of Maclay's outward voyage and his stay in New Guinea. When news of his return reached Batavia, Ankersmit began to write dunning letters. Civilization confronted Maclay with fiercer enemies than any he found among wild beasts and savages.

He wrote at once to the mother who had not responded for years. Another cry for help went to Semyonov-Tianshansky. In these early days, Maclay felt able to refuse anything that smacked of 'relief' or 'donations'. By borrowing half the sum he owed, he would preserve his independence, free himself from creditors and from Singapore. Already granted his passage, he would make his way to Japan and await a warship for the Baltic. At times he believed himself 'on the way to Russia'.

He was condemned to spend four months in Singapore, his creditors unbearably importunate, his mind shrill with persecution, his physical state causing grave fear. A 'chronic catarrh of the stomach and intestines', chronic diarrhoea and the threat of dysentery increased his suffering. Hyperaesthesia tortured him into 'extreme nervous irritability'. Confined to bed for months on end, he sank beneath anaemia and general exhaustion, 'almost constant giddiness' and 'frequent, sudden bouts of unconsciousness', until it was again time to prepare his mother 'for the *worst* (or the best)'.

From his letters to St Petersburg, he seemed utterly alone. Humanity haunted the background, source of the footsteps and voices that brought him to an 'almost hysterical state'. All hearts were dead or inaccessible to Maclay. Delivered over to Malay servants from whom he expected nothing, he endured without comfort or care. It was plain to distant friends that without their immediate aid he must die wretchedly, abandoned by the human race.

At the same time, he lived in the house of a medical friend, where other doctors visited him quite frequently. His own servants had accompanied him to Singapore, Mebli and Mira remaining there for three months. Mr Whampoa and one of the doctors lent him enough for immediate needs. People came to discuss things in general and the international situation in particular, predicting war now that Russia had imposed on Turkey a treaty unacceptable to the great powers, and Maclay was concerned enough to feel he must see Russian newspapers. He enquired about the situation at Sarimbun, annoyed to hear that nothing had been done about a zoological station. He enjoyed a talk with Odoardo Beccari about New Guinea plants. He heard accounts of a volcanic eruption on New Britain, observed at almost the same time as the display at Manam. The Straits branch of the Royal Asiatic Society elected him an honorary member.

None of these diversions relieved him of the sense that his last days were passing, under the shadow of the duns. Then, almost incredulously, he had proof that he was not forsaken. Money from the Russian Geographical Society released him from Schomburg. He could send Mebli and Mira back to Palau, move to Johor Baharu. He almost enjoyed the thought of Ankersmit, 'incensed because he was not made Russian vice-consul', impatiently waiting to be paid.

Sickness and despair never prevented him from planning a future. The basic scheme was that for returning to Russia and paying his debts from the proceeds of his book of travels. He soon added an intention to visit the Maclay Coast again in 1881. But then the future took a new direction. Having regained his health and published his work, he would spend a few years in Africa, clearing up the relationship between its tribes and the Papuans.

All these plans foundered on news that no warship would return to the Baltic that year. Yet Maclay could not stay in Singapore. He agreed with the doctors that the only cure in his case was a change of climate. He refused to waste his remaining funds on buying a passage that the Russian navy would eventually provide free of charge. Japan, close to naval headquarters and the Sea of Okhotsk, was suggested and rejected. There remained a country that had been often in his thoughts over the years, a land of interesting animals whose brains had never been properly investigated and native tribes whose relationship to the Papuans was not finally determined. Its climate was kinder to Europeans than that of Singapore, and its principal communities lay farther from Ankersmit's Batavia. Towards the end of June 1878, he left for Hong Kong, to join a steamer for Australia.

Maclay felt he was received 'very kindly' in Australia. From the first colonial port of call he attracted journalists, as 'a devoted martyr to science' and an informant on New Guinea. He was recognized well beyond the scientific community as a dedicated naturalist, a fearless and unwearied traveller. He was known as one who went alone and unarmed among savage tribes, brought criminals to justice, forced hostile warriors to lay their weapons at his feet, and received homage as divine *Kaaram-tamo* of the Maclay Coast. All manner of men wished to help and honour a visitor who combined with the prestige of science an almost-legendary heroism and power.

The voyage to Sydney had so improved his health that he no longer thought it necessary to enter a hospital. Living at the Australian Club, the stronghold of the upper classes, he quickly got to know everyone interested in science. Within a week of his arrival he had been elected an honorary member of the Linnean Society of New South Wales, perhaps the most active scientific organization in the colonies. He began to use his powers of leadership and persuasion to improve what he found. Alert to the possibilities of a wealthy but raw community that was determined to be inferior to none, he immediately opened a campaign to establish a zoological station near the city.

Maclay had already experienced the need when he told the Linnean Society how science had gained from stations in Europe and North America. The Australian Club provided no facilities for anatomical research; he suspected that using the rooms for that purpose might infringe the rules. The same might be true in a rented apartment, and he could not afford to set up in a cottage. After nine months of enforced abstinence, impatience to start work in comparative anatomy added fervour to his advocacy of a zoological station. That project depended on the conclusions of the inevitable committee, and the public support obtained. Maclay's situation was eased by an invitation from William Macleay, guiding spirit of the Linnean Society and member of the Legislative Council of New South Wales.

William Macleay could fairly be called a 'self-made man', having come to the colony as a well-born but impoverished youth to make his fortune from sheep. His background and intellect exempted him from the crudities by which colonial self-made men grated on fastidious visitors. Having shed nearly all other interests, he was approximately what Miklouho-Maclay wished to be, a wealthy, independent man of science. His life centred on his private museum and the learned society he had founded. Its most important and only desired events were the receipt of specimens from collectors, the arrival of journals and correspondence from Europe, and the meetings at which he read zoological papers.

Yet five years before he had been dissatisfied with his life and uncertain how to change it. It had been temporarily changed, at the age of fifty-four, by the words that had inspired the twenty-four-year-old Miklouho-Maclay, J. B. Jukes's evocation of enchanted New Guinea. William Macleay had bought a ship and equipped an expedition with everything foresight could provide. And he had spent many hours in regret. There had been sickness, mistakes and mishaps, never a chance to approach that magical interior. Entangled with the annexation fantasy, the expedition was declared a failure because it found no mineral wealth or fertile lands with vacant possession. William Macleay consoled himself with a cargo of specimens, the real object of the journey. There was no denying that he, so impatient with ignorance and incompetence in others, had been publicly treated as a fool.

He kept up his interest in New Guinea, though he would certainly never go there again. Since he regarded non-scientific conversation as a waste of time, he found in Miklouho-Maclay the perfect guest, a quiet, solitary man who lived and breathed science, with the added advantage of a famous name. Besides, it was believed that Miklouho-Maclay's Scottish ancestors belonged to the same stock as those of William Macleay.

Living together still called for tact. A religious man, and in all things conservative, William Macleay inclined to the anti-Darwinian side. It seemed to him that with evolutionary theory biology was attempting to pass 'the utmost range of the human intellect'. A comprehensive distrust of 'barren theories', and a taste for the Scottish legal verdict of 'not proven', helped to soften the outlines of his opposition. He co-operated with scientists whose Darwinism made that of his new friend look faint and tentative. The Linnean Society of New South

Wales welcomed men of the most advanced opinions. But they had to leave their opinions outside. Under William Macleay's influence, the Society adhered to a biology that described and classified without attempting to explain.

Miklouho-Maclay had long been out of touch with the masters whose exuberant Darwinism had dominated his student years. His only scientific correspondent in Germany was Professor Rudolf Virchow, whose attitude approximated William Macleay's. At any rate, he had seen enough of theorists to favour principles like those his host advocated—exact observation, patient collection of facts, resistance to any kind of speculation. He found himself at home in the Linnean Society, and would never seriously deviate from its ideals.

Physically, he seemed well placed. Elizabeth Bay House, quiet and secluded, commanded a splendid view down the harbour to Sydney Heads. Its grounds, almost a botanic garden, ran down to the water's edge. When he considered the accommodation, the outlook, the interesting museum and fine zoological library, he felt able to spend months there 'very comfortably and with advantage for science'. At first, his one complaint was that a body habituated to the tropics proved 'remarkably sensitive' to the chilly end of a Sydney winter.

He converted part of Macleay's museum into a laboratory. Fishermen employed by his host brought sharks and rays that had never been available elsewhere. He arranged to receive the brains of Melanesians and Polynesians who died in the hospitals. He sought the brains of Australian Aborigines and such lower forms as the platypus, spiny anteater, dugong and Queensland lungfish. Not everything he wanted was obtainable in Sydney. 'Regulations, traditions, superstitions, etc., etc.,' made it difficult to receive human corpses in a private house, and the hospital dissecting room proved quite inadequate. But enough material arrived on his table to keep him busy from dawn to dusk. He was writing papers for presentation to the Linnean Society, ethnological notes to be sent to Berlin, a communication to the Russian Geographical Society. Days in Australia, organized like those at Bugarlom, proved as much too short for all he had to do.

Much effort in these early months was aimed at establishing a zoological station. For the Linnean Society, he wrote a detailed exposition of the objects and advantages, published first in newspapers to enlist public interest. He guided a committee that seemed to approve all his ideas. Little that he said could be new to a scientific community that for six years had seen reports of Anton Dohrn's undertaking and evidence of its influence. The idea of Australia as a place for zoological stations had been put forward in Dohrn's first communication to the British scientific press. The new factor was the presence of a distinguished visitor with strongly-felt personal needs. Maclay still wanted a refuge for the solitary student of nature. He first proposed a small cottage on the shore, close to the museum and library of Elizabeth Bay House and supervised by William Macleay. Time and discussion altered the plan to something more like a public institution. The rules remained true to the 'Tampat Senang'.

Maclay's influence followed naturally from his fame and his standing as a full-time researcher in a community where 'professional' scientific workers were numbered with digits to spare on the fingers of two hands. Had his reputation been unknown on his arrival, his name would have drawn attention. It headed the passenger list, as that of the only titled traveller.

The habit of calling him 'Baron Maclay' had developed in Singapore and Johor, where neither the press nor the highest authorities could accept that a Russian 'hereditary nobleman' bore no particular title. Maclay had thought such errors unworthy of correction, permitting himself to be introduced as 'baron' to guests at Goverment House and the maharaja's palace. He also made allowance for the problems of port officials. Since the Russian '*dvorianin*' became awkward in trans-lation, and the '*Monsieur*' and '*Herr*' on other leaves of his passport were disregarded, he had allowed the use of the simple 'baron'.

In Australia, the press unanimously used the title, varying it only by the 'doctor' that was current in European scientific journals. He was 'baron' to the consul for the Russian Empire, colonial officials and the compilers of passenger lists. He eventually received the title from the commodore of the Royal Navy's Australia squadron, the British high commissioner for the western Pacific, and the successive governors of New South Wales. Nothing could eradicate the habit in the scientific community. Nobody was more determined to call him 'baron' than his closest associate, William Macleay.

He thought it unnecessary to issue a public correction, once he had tried to make matters clear to friends. In any case, he considered the rank of 'baron' in no way superior to that of 'hereditary nobleman'. Since early 1875 he had used, for certain letters, a special writing paper bearing his monogram surmounted by a coronet. His visiting card displayed only the name 'de Maclay'. He no more claimed to be a baron than to be a god, but in colonial cities, as on the Maclay Coast, silence and symbols went far to confirm an established belief.

The respect and consideration he received never influenced him in favour of Sydney and its inhabitants. Like any visitor, he admired 'vast and beautiful Port Jackson'. The surrounding country lacked everything that made nature lovely in his eyes. The city itself, smothering its ridges and promontories with a crust of industry and commerce, raw ostentation and premature decay, won from him, at best, a forbearing

The *telum* in the men's house, Bongu, 1877

The men's house in Bongu, Maclay Coast

Bilbil Island, with beached *vangs*

William John Macleay, the traveller's principal associate in Sydney

Miklouho-Maclay, aged about thirty

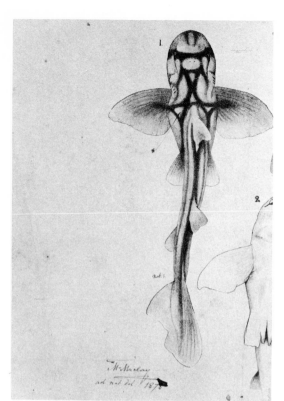

A Port Jackson shark, 1878

The *Sadie F. Caller* at Prony Bay, New Caledonia, 1879

silence. In winter it was cold and boring, in summer 'hot, dusty and boring'. It swarmed with a money-grubbing European population whose presence in that country offended his principles. Their political attitudes also repelled him. Among his acquaintances—mostly wealthy conservatives who might have formed a local aristocracy had their fellow colonists allowed it—he discovered real or pretended 'democrats' who coloured his view of the whole society. Altogether he gave thanks that through absorption in scientific work he was 'saved from close acquaintance with the worthy "Australians" '.

For the man who called himself 'the white Papuan', white 'Australians' could only be enemies. Despite rebuffs from the British government, many colonists still talked about annexation of eastern New Guinea. Would-be exploiters desired the move as a key to the idle land, labourers and resources they imagined to exist there. Missionary societies favoured it as a means of excluding such people and preserving the natives uncontaminated to receive the gospel. Another school of thought emphasized the island's strategic position, insisting that if Britain did not claim it some other power would, with consequent danger, in time of war, to colonial trade and communications. This accidental coalition of the greedy, the godly and the uneasy had room for the arrogant idealism that cloaks a lust for power. There was no lack of voices to proclaim Britain's duty to protect and civilize New Guineans. Even William Macleay, who derided the idea of white colonization, believed some European country would assume the civilizing mission, and preferred that it should be Britain.

To Maclay, the aims of missionaries were as pernicious as those of traders, and other stated Australian purposes merely disguised the will to grab his country and enslave his people. He recognized no other threats. While discussing botany in Singapore, Odoardo Beccari had been inwardly preoccupied with moves for Italian annexation of eastern New Guinea. German traders were moving into surrounding islands in sufficient force to revive the old idea of a German colony. In France a Breton nobleman planned settlements proportionate to his self-bestowed sovereignty over a realm that included the Maclay Coast. Maclay saw only the enemies before his eyes, the brazen annexationists of Australia. He had never felt more strongly that man is the wickedest of animals.

He was nevertheless lucky to meet no more direct and personal 'unpleasantness'. From his first day in Australia, he declared his opposition to white incursions into New Guinea. He was still widely regarded as an agent of Russian imperialism. And recent news combined these apparently incompatible ideas. Maclay's proposed 'Papuan Union' had been commended in the *Journal de St Pétersbourg*, mouthpiece of the Russian ministry for foreign affairs. The fact had been transmitted to Australia, where anything approved by that ministry was automatically suspect.

The times were uncomfortable for a Russian in a British colony, with war constantly on the horizon, sombre editorials in newspapers and anti-Russian speeches at public meetings. The alarming Russian moves occurred in Central Asia, not the Pacific. The Russian press talked of invading India, not Australia. But transplanted Englishmen in Australia felt as strongly about India as did those at home. Events of 1870 had taught them that Europe's wars could disrupt Pacific Ocean trade and shipping. Looking at New Guinea and surrounding islands, they more than ever feared a hostile neighbour.

If Maclay knew they suspected him of trying to establish Russia in New Guinea, he could not blame the Australians. The same mistake had been made in Russia. A letter almost two years old, received on his arrival at Singapore, had informed him that the tsar rejected his appeal. The official reason—the remoteness of New Guinea from Russian interests—was accompanied by Semyonov-Tianshansky's reflections on the non-success of Russian colonization nearer to home. As well as reminding his countrymen that 'enlightened and humane governments' should place 'the general interests of humanity' above purely national concerns, Maclay had to point out that he did not advocate colonization. 'What appeared . . . desirable to me', he explained, 'was a "protectorate" over part of New Guinea, whose inhabitants would be, through my mediation, the subject of some international guarantee, having legally powerful protectors in case of violence on the part of whites'.

Since the highest decision was 'No', Maclay could only watch events and explore possibilities. There was no better observation post than Sydney, where he proposed to spend five or six months. Materials for research continued to flow to him and openings for investigation constantly appeared. He collaborated with William Macleay in work on sharks. Preparing for the ultimate fifth part of his work on vertebrate neurology, he studied Melanesian and Polynesian brains. At the Australian Museum he found Aboriginal skulls and skeletons, and important collections in Melanesian ethnology. Without the occasional attacks of fever, his days would still have been too short for work and his nights for rest.

He nevertheless began to practise another time-consuming skill. In New Guinea he had decided that photography was essential for ethnological research. In Sydney it proved equally necessary to illustrate the comparative study of the brain. Maclay obtained the use of studio, equipment and photographer at the museum, and from this moved to learning the art himself.

Trips between Elizabeth Bay and the museum, about twenty minutes each way if he walked, soon seemed an absurd waste of time. He had also discovered, after the first delight wore off, that William Macleay's premises were unfit for serious scientific work. Noisy servants caused 'constant interruptions and inconveniences'. The private museum, a temporary building with sheet-iron walls, became unbearably hot. And bad as it was, William Macleay and his museum curator worked there. The guest needed a place to himself.

More complex reasons also impelled him to leave Elizabeth Bay. To live in a private house rather than an official palace placed him in a 'dependent position', contributing to fits of depression that hindered his work. William Macleay, a kind but rather dominating man, perhaps imposed a strain on an independent and dominating guest. Maclay accepted an invitation from Edward Ramsay, curator of the institution, to occupy a room at the Australian Museum. He continued to collaborate with William Macleay in the friendly but distant fashion both preferred.

Nothing could be less congenial to Maclay than life in a great, echoing building, open to the public six days a week, bounded on two sides by streets and situated next door to a large school. The very best view from the museum embraced the eastern fringe of the business district and the untidy acreage of half-formed parks. His workroom was a 'cold, badly-ventilated *basement*'.

He had never before been expected to work in such a place. The advantages—space to himself, a bedroom under the same roof, proximity to specimens and photographic studio—did not compensate for bad air and the chill that damaged his health in the middle of summer. When fever attacks seemed more frequent and violent, he did not hesitate to blame the wretched quarters. And the basement broke the one promise a basement could make. Instead of being quiet, it resounded with voices—cows, dogs, people and cockatoos.

When annoyed by cockatoos on his coast, Maclay simply shot them. He could not adopt that solution here, much less slaughter the rest of the 'zoological garden' that robbed him of thought and reduced him to a 'very nasty state of mind'. The 'good people' clucked and fluttered, astonished to find he had '*such* weak nerves'. He was obliged to be grateful for what amounted to torture and insult.

He had to stay, for the reason that had made him dependent on William Macleay. Sydney matched his idea of European colonies by being expensive as well as boring. He had very little money, with no prospect of getting more, and a strong distaste prevented his asking help from 'these democrats'. Not least among the costs of independence was the increasing difficulty of keeping alive.

With all this worry and distress, he probably suffered blows to his scientific prestige. For seven years he had published nothing in zoology,

a silence that might have put paid to that side of his career. His fame, in
the event, had been maintained not only by his travels and ethnographical work but by the controversies he left behind in Europe. Maclay had
never shown the slightest interest in the outcome of these disputes, but
the effect of his early zoological contributions must have been nearly
inescapable in Sydney.

It was obvious in 1878, if not before, that he had wasted the pages in
which he insisted on a homology between the 'gastro-vascular apparatus' of sponges and the digestive system of corals. In a quiet footnote
to his monograph on calcareous sponges, Ernst Haeckel had settled for
mere analogy. It had also turned out that supposed radially symmetrical
segments·in sponges, discovered by Maclay and enthusiastically confirmed by Haeckel, were no real counterpart of 'antimers' in corals and
sea-anemones. On top of that, Haeckel had subjected his former pupil
to criticism amounting to attack. Partly unfair, partly less than honest, it
contained enough truth to be damaging. While the general tendency of
Maclay's work was miraculously preserved, its details were demolished.

The 'coelenterate theory of sponges' survived in modified form, kept
going by Haeckel's imaginative agility. Nothing could sustain Maclay's
version of the fish brain. He had carefully examined the brains of
thirty-seven species of 'primitive' fishes. He had studied the works of
more than two dozen authors, finding much confusion and error. Yet
his conclusions embodied a mistaken approach, some failures of
observation, and a misinterpretation verging on eccentricity. Huxley
and several prominent German anatomists had rejected them. An
embryologist had shown that Maclay 'misinterpreted the facts of
development' in sharks. By 1878 Gegenbaur had been persuaded to
abandon his lonely position. The interpretation of the fish brain was put
back where Maclay found it, enriched by the new research that
accompanied opposition to his views.

He had continued to collect and study sponges, but he published no
more on that subject. His opinions on the fish brain had not changed
when he reached Sydney. In collaborating with William Macleay, he
had seen their joint work as an 'illustrated catalogue' of sharks, to
accompany an expansion of his earlier book. But the contents of Sydney
libraries left no doubt that his theory had fallen. He published nothing
further on fish brains, and became noticeably less enthusiastic about the
catalogue of sharks.

Somehow he struggled into 1879, oppressed by doubts concerning
the future and certainty that his Batavia debt continued to grow. His
days, when thought was possible, were passed in dissection and drawing
and the tedious processes of wet-plate photography. He studied the
museum's ethnological collections or inspected Pacific islanders visiting
Sydney. With visitors from the outback he discussed Australian

Aborigines, converting hearsay information on sexual customs into articles for publication in Europe. He joined the museum staff for some dredging trips about the harbour, but could not spare time for their longer voyages. The free pass entitling him to travel anywhere on New South Wales railways remained unused, a symbol of concentration and self-denial.

He sometimes escaped in thought to Japan, to Russia, to an Italian villa where he would live harmoniously with his sister. There was no closer prospect of relief. His colleagues agreed about the desirability of a zoological station, but saw its urgency less clearly. Other worthy causes cried out for support—an underequipped and understaffed museum, a university without a biological laboratory. Some felt reservations about an establishment intended purely for the rare scientific visitor. Others raised questions about its ownership and control, points 'of no moment for science', as Maclay put it, but real enough to those contemplating a permanent financial responsibility. Six months of discussion and caution left Maclay no nearer to occupying a Tampat Senang.

His third appeal to the Linnean Society called for immediate action supported by '*every friend* of biological science in Australia'. The time required to carry out his proposal became 'a good test of the degree and intensity of scientific life in Australia—at least in Sydney'. But discussions had taken a dangerous turn. Some people wanted a smaller version of Anton Dohrn's establishment, research facilities associated with and supported by an aquarium open to the public.

Nothing could be farther from Maclay's mind than an institution built in the botanic garden for 'popular instruction and amusement'. Faced with this proposal, he could not await the result of any test. He drew up plans for a building, found a suitable site, and took steps to obtain the land from the government. Finally he began to collect subscriptions, on the understanding that if half the necessary sum were raised the government would provide a matching grant. The land selected had been ear-marked for military use. The donations hurriedly obtained amounted to less than £100. The proposed building, if practicable, threatened to be expensive. But the project was set in motion, by Maclay's initiative and in tolerable harmony with his ideal.

He had recently seen more important proof of his power to influence events, an official letter from Batavia advising him that the Dutch were moving at last to abolish slavery in the Moluccas. He had no such encouragement in his struggle for the Maclay Coast.

All the news about New Guinea reached him. He could follow the comings and goings of explorers, missionaries and official visitors to the island. He saw the proposal and rejection of annexation schemes, the rise and fall of colonization societies, and the collapse of a miniature gold rush to the Port Moresby area. But the most powerful moves for annexation were made in London. The syndicates were organized in Queensland, Victoria and New Zealand. The expeditions sailed from Cooktown, Melbourne or Wellington. Though always interested in New Guinea, Sydney people did not actively threaten the island. By the end of 1878, Maclay had found that his most dangerous enemies were beyond his reach.

News published in Sydney on the first day of 1879 illustrated his near-helplessness. The barque *Courier* had returned to New Zealand after a brief visit to Astrolabe Bay. Without finding the trading opportunities they sought, her company had met with friendly, intelligent natives and fertile country. They had also seen, carved on a tree, the name of the schooner *Dove*, which had left Melbourne in August. In the course of two months, Maclay's unguarded people had met two groups of white men and, as it turned out, had got on well with both of them.

Maclay's mind raced ahead to what he considered the inevitable outcome—introduction of liquor and firearms, confiscation of the land, finally the extermination of the people. In imagination he saw the massacre of women and children, 'murder and war *without end*', as the coastal people, driven from their villages, were caught between the rifles of invaders and the spears of mountain-dwellers. He saw less clearly the steps he must take to prevent these horrors. His one appeal for official intervention, addressed to the emperor whose honoured viceroy in Turkestan had ordered the extermination of recalcitrant tribes, had been misunderstood and rejected. The British government bore responsibility for the disappearance of Australian Aborigines. He thought it equally ready to permit destruction of other peoples. Yet he was prepared to believe this government might try to be a 'just adversary', to shield natives against extremes of oppression. In the faint hope that for once action might be taken in time, Maclay decided to appeal to London.

He remembered a passing acquaintance of nearly four years standing. When they met at Singapore, Sir Arthur Hamilton Gordon had been on his way to Fiji, as first governor of that new British possession and first high commissioner for the western Pacific. Two or three conversations had not changed Maclay's prediction that under Sir Arthur the Fijians would be enslaved or exterminated. By 1879 he knew better. Gordon's efforts to protect Fijians and uphold traditional authority had aroused such resentment among European settlers that they petitioned for his removal. As Maclay now understood, Gordon 'did not regard a white skin as any guarantee of the lawfulness of a claim or the justice of a cause', indeed opponents complained that he treated it as prima-facie evidence of crime. Moreover, he had considerable authority over British citizens among the independent islands of the western Pacific, recently used to put down colonization schemes originating in Victoria. Shortly before Maclay appealed to him, Sir Arthur Gordon, on leave in England, had been asked to advise the imperial government on the question of annexing eastern New Guinea.

Maclay's open letter made it clear that the most desirable outcome would be exclusion of white men from New Guinea. As a minimum, he wanted a declaration that the British government, 'recognizing the rights of the natives on their own soil', would not uphold whites in conflict with those defending their land, families and possessions. Initially the measures proposed, including prohibition of guns and alcohol, were to apply to the Maclay Coast. Later, they should be extended to the rest of independent New Guinea and Melanesia.

Though newspapers assured him Sir Arthur was a kindred spirit, Maclay never quite realized he was preaching to the converted. When his plea had been forwarded to London by the governor of New South Wales, he still felt that the justice of his proposals would cause them to be ignored. But the one practical difficulty he recognized—the absence of power to enforce laws in New Guinea—would soon be removed, he believed, by annexation. Distasteful as this idea was, his one hope lay in a rule that might be a degree less evil than uncontrolled invasion.

He took it for granted that the authority would be British. In fact the imperial government, reluctant as ever to take responsibility for New Guinea, had just shelved Gordon's proposal for limited annexations. There were signs that other powers might be more interested. German officials had purchased harbours in the Duke of York group, a natural centre for trade in New Britain, New Ireland and the Maclay Coast. It was reported that three thousand men, led by Menotti Garibaldi, were organizing an Italian colony for New Guinea. There was even a rumour, said to emanate from Russian official circles, that Russia would soon occupy some Pacific island as a naval base. Imperialist and colonialist ideas were afloat everywhere, a froth upon the troubled waters of international politics. Maclay's fears concentrated on the colonies whose vessels had twice reached his coast and might easily do so again.

Fuller reports on these visits brought him no comfort. He had tried to put his friends on their guard, speaking of violence, kidnapping and enslavement, warning them to keep their distance if white men came, wear no ornaments, and hide their women and most valued possessions in the bush. Instead, they had come forward confidently, paddling their canoes out to the ships, exchanging pigs and garden produce for beads and hoop iron, offering even their weapons for barter. They had let themselves by photographed. After a week's acquaintance they had allowed their wives to meet the visitors. Without either party understanding a word the other said, friendly relations had been established between Maclay's people and their natural enemies. His country had no reliable guardian but the fever that attacked the intruders. In defiance of that, the New Zealanders meant to return. They believed these sensible natives would soon grasp the idea of trade on a commercial scale. They also claimed to have provisionally 'secured' land at Astrolabe Bay.

It was time for Maclay to return to his people, but in February 1879 he showed no sign of leaving Sydney. He spoke, it is true, of visiting Europe late that year. He enquired about the chances of the Russian Geographical Society's paying his passage to Japan. To his sister, that distant princess, handmaiden and near-stranger, he wrote of how, with Beccari's help, they would spend next New Year's Eve in a villa near Florence. But it would be 'a crime against science' to leave a country where he found so many urgent tasks. Nobody could have guessed that within a few weeks he would undertake a new voyage, as fervently convinced that his duty was to travel, not to stay.

13: Clause Two

M ACLAY'S POSITION became
intolerable early in 1879. With 'a pile of work' before him, he was
thwarted by impossible working conditions. Any gains to health from
a change of climate had been dissipated. He was sometimes so exhausted
by illness that he wanted to sleep for days on end. His nerves were in
tatters, his nasty moods nastier. For physical and mental survival, he had
to escape from the Australian Museum.

The *Sadie F. Caller*, a smart three-masted American schooner, was
loading general cargo for New Caledonia and preparing for a trading
and trepang-fishing cruise. Her route might have been planned to suit
Maclay. Her owner and skipper, Captain Webber, seemed an honest
man. The mate was a qualified shipmaster. One of the traders, an
ex-officer of the Italian army, bore the title of *cavaliere*. The accommodation was much superior to what the Royal Navy offered, a bunk in
the officers' cabin of a one-gun schooner. The captain was prepared to
aid Maclay's researches and spend at least two weeks on his coast.

'For lack of anything better', Maclay decided to sail on the *S. F. Caller*.
He needed to see more of the Melanesians to solve the basic problems of
ethnology in this part of the world. He feared that if he delayed he
might never again be able to undertake the voyage. He hinted that
'special circumstances' made the decision at once more difficult and
more urgent, and deplored the sacrifice of other plans to this. Whatever
the cost in terms of ambition and comfort, he could not allow personal
interests to overshadow the needs of science.

The cost in cash was harder to pay. He had almost nothing left, and
Captain Webber asked thirty shillings a week. Meshchersky gave a
gloomy account of the family finances. Relations with the Russian
Geographical Society were complicated by the old question of studies

in northern seas and the Society's suspicion that Maclay placed philanthropy before science. The Batavia mail put the last touch to his predicament. Ankersmit had discovered his whereabouts and begun to write dunning letters.

Maclay drew up a bill on the Russian Geographical Society and obtained £150 from William Macleay. Then he told German colleagues what he had been forced to do. His patrons, when they heard of it, could choose between prompt payment and extreme embarrassment. Released from his own 'embarrassing dilemma', Maclay concluded his bargain with Webber and bought photographic equipment.

Publicity for the voyage showed that his fellow travellers had gained prestige from his name. It also showed they attached more importance than he did to one clause of the written agreement. In return for help in his own activities, he undertook to assist the expedition by his knowledge of the islands and their inhabitants. To the syndicate this meant that Baron Maclay's experience would help them gather the 'rich harvest' of trade he predicted. They told the newspapers so, and Maclay had to write to the press, denying any part in the commercial side of the cruise. He continued to emphasize privately that no trader would receive his help in approaching New Guineans. It remained to be seen how he might reconcile the promise given Captain Webber with this promise to himself.

After I had left Sydney in March, 1879, I visited the following islands: New Caledonia, Lifu; of the New Hebrides: Tana, Vate [Efate], Tongoa, Mai [Emae], Epi, Ambrim, Malo, Vanua Lava; the Admiralty Islands; the groups Lub (or Hermit), Ninigo (Exchequer), Trobriand, the Solomon Islands, the islands at the south-east end of New Guinea, and the islands of Torres Straits.

In total, during this voyage of 409 days approximately 237 days were spent ashore or at anchor, and about 172 days at sea.

The language of duty and scientific reticence disguised from strangers the feelings with which Maclay returned to his tropical homeland. Only letters to Olga revealed his delight in 'these parts of our *joyless* planet where it is still bearable to live'.

Noumea was not such a place, a dull little official town, dominated by the prison that explained but did not excuse its existence. As the scene of a recent native uprising, with bloodshed and brutality on both sides, New Caledonia was nevertheless useful subject-matter for articles he had promised a St Petersburg newspaper. He saw the governor and obtained the use of an official steam launch. He visited the prison of Île Nou and the settlement of *communards*, favourably impressed but finally bored by these 'institutions for exiles'. He met one 'very interesting man', the Marist Père Xavier Montrouzier, who had been attempting to evangelize these islands when Maclay was born. Their conversations apparently did not reveal the attitude of that embittered priest towards the people who had rejected his message yet denied him martyrdom. Like most casual acquaintances, Maclay met only the observant, well-informed gentleman with a great taste for science, ever ready to aid a fellow naturalist.

While the *Sadie F. Caller* unloaded essentials of civilization—everything from flour and sugar to newsprint, rifles and sewing machines—Maclay sought what was native and unspoiled. His darkest fears were confirmed. People who hardly differed physically from his New Guinea friends had surrendered their dignity to an assortment of European garments. Their huts, no longer built in native style, contained chairs and tables and cheap religious prints. The second-hand decorum of villages under mission control was still a shade less degraded than scenes at a plantation whose owner especially tried to please a famous guest. In despair, Maclay watched half-drunk natives cavorting to the thunder of kerosene tins in a 'caricature' of traditional dance. Heartsick, he retreated to measure heads beneath the eyes of the Virgin and saints. He did not leave empty-handed. Besides buying weapons and utensils, he had managed to steal some interesting skulls.

From the south coast anchorage where she rode out bad weather, the schooner was sent on her way at last by news that a group of convicts had escaped. Through days at sea, heading towards the Equator, Maclay sketched the realm of islands. Rounded humps of coral rock, palm-fringed shores and sharp backbones of volcanic peaks, islands like broken spires and islands with the profiles of pancakes—his sketch book gathered them all into a group portrait. With no island in sight, he read and wrote in his cabin, improving his reports of past journeys, explaining his intentions, ranging over all his scientific and humanitarian concerns. But he spent most of May and June ashore in the Loyalty group and New Hebrides, while the vessel collected workers for trepang fishing and supplies for about fifty men.

Sometimes as guest of missionaries, Maclay lived for two days or a week in villages, inspecting and measuring the people and drawing their portraits. His pencil caught the martial stance of an Efate warrior in full array, the minimal aprons and elaborate tattoos of women on Tongoa, an Epi man in dance-costume, like a hut on legs, and a boy ingeniously dressed in one piece of string. On Tongoa and Ambrym he found groups of vertical slit gongs, standing like sacred groves among the trees. He walked on coral beaches, landed on two-tree islets and scrambled on the mountain sides of Vanua Lava. He enjoyed better health than he had for years. Life was bearable, as long as he stayed ashore.

North of Vanua Lava, he was condemned to a life afloat. The *Sadie F. Caller* sailed swiftly for the isolated Duff group, but found no reef suitable for trepang fishing. She retreated to the Santa Cruz Islands, where Maclay expected an interesting stay in a practically untouched field of research. But they found no safe anchorage; natives appeared in such numbers, so obviously hostile, that even Maclay thought a landing inadvisable. The voyagers came to rest in the lagoon of the Candelaria or Roncador reef, some 160 kilometres east of the Solomons and as remote from Maclay's interests as a crater on the moon.

For a month the schooner lay at anchor within a loop of rock and coral that almost disappeared at high tide. Fifty men worked like demons, gathering and preserving leathery creatures like half-animated cucumbers. Day and night an iron smokehouse on deck palpitated with the output of two stoves, blasting more heat into the over-charged air so that dried and cured sea-slugs might fetch large sums at market and make soup for gourmets in China. This crazy inferno in the middle of the ocean was almost too much for Maclay. He might have borne smoke and heat, the stench in the cabins, drinking water that must be filtered and boiled. He could not endure being caged in a 'human menagerie', among these 'nonsensically chattering, drinking, whistling, singing *bipeds*'. And he saw no escape short of jumping overboard. When the reef reappeared at low tide, no boat was available for excursions. He was virtually a prisoner in the cabin, where at least he found space, light and privacy.

He sketched stray birds that alighted on the vessel. Lories unknown to science were caught in the rigging. The men hauled in a shark he believed to be new. For most of his waking hours he struggled to read and write, often wondering why he bothered. Already on this voyage he had rediscovered letters months old, read them through and asked, '*Why* did I write this?', a question almost guaranteeing that the missive would never be sent. He had sat pen in hand, asking 'For what? What about?', and received no answer but groans from timbers and rigging and the smack of waves against the hull. Even Olga, the one person whose sympathy he had always relied upon, might no longer wish to read his 'uncouth' messages. 'I so little know my Olga of the year 1879', he confessed, 'that at this very moment there appears the question: "Why do I write these lines?" Their meaning, perhaps, will either remain half-understood or lead only to misunderstandings . . .'. Yet he continued to write, without faith in communication, deserted and forgotten by those who counted in his life. He added to the hundreds of letters that would never be answered, polished reports begun in New Guinea, drafted notes on Australian native customs for publication in Berlin and described the 'new' shark for William Macleay. Some day these communications might be sent, but he did not know how.

During the frustrating weeks at Candelaria Reef, Maclay was also occupied with the western Pacific's most burning problem, the 'labour trade' carried on between the islands of Melanesia and plantations in Queensland, Fiji, Samoa and New Caledonia. He could not expect to say much that was new about activities that had been denounced for almost twenty years. The so-called 'free labour trade' was already abhorred by missionaries, naval officers, administrators and unofficial humanitarians in Britain and the colonies. It stimulated a stream of revelatory books, pamphlets, reports and newspaper correspondence exposing the crimes committed for money by Europeans in the South Seas. The traffic continued, and Maclay meant to add his voice to the many that condemned the 'blackbirders' and their customers.

It was not that he actually witnessed kidnapping, violence, or the purchase of islanders from their chiefs and relatives. On labour vessels in the New Hebrides, he had seen nothing that could be treated as an illegal act. Government agents who accompanied Queensland vessels, though too ignorant and badly paid to be 'above suspicion', could not be shown to permit abuses. Natives who described crimes committed in the past could not give names or dates. White informants withheld details about offenders who might retaliate. Rather than questioning those with most to tell, the returned labourers, he had tried to avoid them, finding them 'very often impudent, more inclined to lie and cheat, ... far less to be trusted than others who never had intercourse with whites'. The most he could say with certainty was that many islanders collected by labour vessels were too young for plantation work, and that a chief's son who had shipped on a Sydney steamer a year before had not returned to his island.

Dearth of new facts did not shake Maclay's resolve to expose a traffic long equated with the slave trade. Iniquities existed, and his could be an influential voice in campaigns against them. He had gained a general view of disruption and hardship caused by the departure of young men from their villages and of damage done to native character and customs. He had learned how recruits were collected, and saw nothing to choose between kidnapping and the engagement of people fleeing famine and war. Whether they were handed over by bribed chieftains or deserted their people to follow the lure of adventure, all the recruits were too ignorant and gullible to be free agents. But recruiting formed only part of the story Maclay meant to tell.

Everything he heard about was noted, from the lies and violence of blackbirders to the price a white man charged for a box of matches, from the impudence of former labourers to the murder of 'wealthy' returned workers by their covetous kin. It would all have its place in his indictment of the European in the South Pacific.

He had found one opportunity for intervention. The *Sadie F. Caller* was equipped to collect and carry the largest possible quantity of trepang, turtle and pearlshell. Her accommodation and her long, complex route ruled out a human cargo. But she needed many hands, needed them for an indefinite time, and had to find them where recruits were already scarce. Even at Lifu and Tanna, islands policed by missionaries, the doings of John Leeman the mate had alerted Maclay. At Efate, the mate had brought Captain Webber an offer from a Noumea recruiter ready to sell a few men. After refusing the deal, the skipper was frank or foolish enough to tell his passenger.

Another visitor to Efate was a man with a professional interest in such matters—the new commodore of the Royal Navy's Australia station, making his first inspection tour and harrying wrongdoers wherever he found them. When Maclay reported the *Sadie F. Caller*, Commodore Wilson would gladly have taken strong action. Unfortunately, an American ship and an American captain escaped his jurisdiction. He could not find that Leeman, a British subject and of bad repute, had committed any punishable offence. At best, the Commodore could note the information and perhaps deliver a warning.

Maclay was not disheartened by failure to cause positive action. He was feeling his way, becoming familiar with restrictions that hampered justice in the Pacific. His meeting with John Crawford Wilson also had personal value. Thenceforth he counted on the friendship of a 'good and just man' who wielded immense power. The few opinions they did not share—like Maclay's belief that naval officers were unfit to administer justice to natives, and Wilson's conviction that the 'vindictive and treacherous' islanders were 'the most degraded people under the sun'—never intruded on what became a long and useful association.

It was uncertain how the incident affected Maclay's position aboard the schooner. Without it, he lived on bad terms with his fellow travellers. He still talked with Webber, a knowledgeable Yankee businessman whose sharp practice at sea was no worse than what others did respectably in cities. He hardly exchanged two words a day with other 'specimens of the rabble', and never spoke to some of them at all. But there was no escaping their raucous presence at Candelaria Reef. He vaguely remembered and heartily endorsed Doctor Johnson's last word on shipboard life: 'A man in jail has more room, better food and commonly better company'. When the anchor was raised, towards the end of July, he had decided to leave the *Sadie F. Caller*.

Captain Webber tried to free his prisoner. For a week he struggled towards the Duke of York group, where Maclay hoped to find a vessel for Australia. Contrary winds and currents always thrust them back. Maclay had to release the captain from his promise and resign himself to revisiting the Admiralty Islands. Among islands previously unknown to him, there had been no question of his helping the expedition. No other man aboard had visited the Admiralty group, and clause two of his agreement bound Maclay to give the syndicate the benefit of his knowledge.

He took pride in piloting the schooner to an anchorage at Andra. When islanders came aboard he made a speech in few words and much pantomime, explaining what the traders wanted and what they would give. He held another meeting in the village men's house, delighting his audience by reading out the names of people he had met there three years before. Dispensing beads and scraps of ribbon to women and children, he exercised a repertoire of charms. The natives soon recognized an old friend who would do them no injury. As for the trading, he was sure they knew he had nothing to do with it.

Trepang and pearlshell started piling up on deck at daybreak. Scores of canoes plied between schooner and shore. Captain Webber shook hands with himself, and vowed to take the last sea-slug from the reef. Visits by trading vessels, Maclay realized, had robbed life on Andra of its 'primitiveness', its soothing monotony, replacing it with trashy new desires and the pursuit of gain. He was saddened to see how the people competed for beads, red cloth and hoop iron, angry to see how little they got. The shouting and outwardly cheerful bustle gave him both headache and heartache. But he need not regret having introduced the traders to people who were already corrupted. A lovely girl-child took his head on her knees and massaged his headache away. Captain Webber gripped his hand and thanked him for bringing the syndicate to Andra.

When the smokehouse began to fume, crammed with first-class trepang, Maclay moved to the village. Shady nooks offered him peace. Freshness and innocence survived among the children splashing in the shallows and the giggling women who examined him as he inspected them. A gang of youngsters accompanied his walks, waiting on him hand and foot. When he went to bathe, dressed only in short Malay trousers, the white skin and long hairs of his chest caused a sensation. While he lolled in the warm, transparent sea, women and children waited to give him a freshwater shower from large seashells. A German steamer called, the vessel Maclay had hoped to meet at the Duke of York Islands, but he did not take the opportunity to leave with her.

Despite friendly relations and the avalanche of trade, Webber was anxious, repeatedly summoning his passenger back to the ship. Maclay sent reassuring messages and refused to go. He openly dismissed the skipper's worries as 'groundless'. He privately spurned the weakness of 'putting too high a value on this fine existence'. Sometimes he reminded the captain of clause four in their agreement, which provided that if Maclay were killed by natives no punishment would be attempted. 'In my opinion', he explained to a scientific colleague, 'the guilt of the whites in their relations with the islanders ... is *so* enormous that this so-called "punishment" only increases the number of attacks against them'. As he saw it, the islanders would never of their own accord attack visitors. They merely responded to European crimes. If he died, it would be as another victim of white men.

By Maclay's reasoning, Andra was unlikely to produce an exemplary death. Recent murders of whites in that locality—those of traders left by the *Sea Bird* in 1876—had gone unpunished. The *S. F. Caller* syndicate was not inviting destruction. In any case, Maclay relied on his own tact, good faith and knowledge of native ways, and the islanders' perception that he was not like other white men.

Disturbing incidents occurred. He was sure his silver-mounted knife had been stolen, but neither enquiries nor offers of reward brought it back. Noting this first instance of theft among these people—he did not count the pillage that followed the murder of traders—he sensed the decay of native morality. He felt it again when the villagers rented his accommodation to Captain Webber for use as a smokehouse. Maclay made the best of it, refusing to be ruffled by eviction or tricked into returning to the ship. The incident did cast doubt on his ascendancy.

The islanders nevertheless thought much of the white man who lived ashore. The traders paid for their whoring, and after hasty fumblings in dark huts they found their gifts decorating scrawny arms and wrinkled necks. On his first night in an old friend's house, Maclay was visited free of charge by a succession of temptresses, from a 'rather old' woman to a girl of ten. Though he showed them all the door, he was next night offered two beauties at once, one of them the young girl with the pain-removing fingertips.

By then, Webber had noticed many canoes gathered in an inlet of the main island. The Italian ex-officer had found the exits from the village blocked by thorny barricades. Maclay made light of the skipper's fears, declined to retreat to the schooner, dismissed the Cavaliere Bruno's pictures of ambush as products of 'fevered imagination'. Only the appearance of the temptresses convinced him a trap was prepared.

Despite Maclay's hints that he was not wanted, Bruno insisted on staying ashore with several Lifu men and a small arsenal. But at the crucial moment Maclay took charge. A drum in the darkness announced the arrival of canoes. Villagers raised the cry of 'Enemy!' Maclay would not allow the firing of a signal flare. 'Let the skipper sleep', he told the *cavaliere*. 'We'll manage without him. I'll tell you what to do.'

At his orders the sailors built up the fire. The village square, with its hushed crowd, was lighted like a stage set. In the centre stood Maclay, grasping a flaming torch.

'The enemy are coming!' he shouted. 'Maclay and the men from the schooner need light—lots of light—so they can see who to shoot. Tell

'Tamate-tambuna', skull shrine and ancestral figure, Solomon Islands, 1879

The Reverend James Chalmers, London Missionary Society

The yam house at Tume, Trobriand Islands, 1879

Tupislei village, south-eastern New Guinea, 1880

Kalo village, south-eastern New Guinea, 1880

the women and children to get out of the huts! Maclay is going to burn them!'

Perhaps he mangled the language; he had spent, in all, less than ten days on Andra. But the villagers understood the intention. Bruno and his men grasped it too, arming themselves with firesticks. Some of the people hastily rescued their valuables. Others ran to warn the 'enemy'. The leading men surrounded Maclay, begging him not to fire the huts—the enemy was a long way off and might never come. By the time he let himself be placated, the barricades had been cleared away. Dawn was breaking and a boat full of armed men had left the schooner, too late to be needed.

When he thought things over, Maclay found himself calling his old friends 'the enemy'. As he later confirmed, a strong alliance had been formed to kill the visitors living ashore. There had even been talk of seizing the ship. He did not believe the Andra people had much stomach for fighting. He pictured them standing aside, then rushing in to finish off the victims and share the plunder. But his impression of their cowardice and treachery was mixed with affection. They had paid a kind of compliment by treating him as the main obstacle. They had given him the satisfaction of detecting their plot and springing a more powerful trap. Through them, he had again experienced those moments when inspiration told him how to dominate men for their own good and win a bloodless victory.

Still, they had shown themselves unworthy of trust. Maclay moved out of Kochem's hut—his old friend had been a ringleader—and pitched a tent on the outskirts of the village. Fascinated Andrans still watched his every movement. One faithful boy remained to attend him. The other children only appeared when they wanted something, and he never again saw the girl with the healing fingertips.

Otherwise, everyone seemed inclined to forget the episode. The crew went on boiling and curing trepang. Maclay collected artefacts and continued his research. He soon had his fill of 'primitiveness'. An old man's death unleashed a tumult of mourning that made Maclay feel he was living a fantastic dream. He had never before witnessed such a display of Melanesian passion and ritual. He noted it all, powerful symbols and petty competition, theatrical posturing and quiet grief. He could not watch without nausea the self-laceration of the widows. In interludes of general exhaustion he saw women and children gnawing human bones. His head whirled and throbbed to the frenzy of the dance, the howling of women, the ceaseless thunder of drums. He had to take morphia in order to sleep.

In the quiet morning, the warriors assembled for their last duty to the dead man, an expedition to compensate for his death by taking a life in another village. Refusing an invitation to join them, Maclay found himself involved in a minor incident of the one-day war. At a well in the centre of the island, he surprised a group of women engaged in beating two female neighbours who happened to have been born in the 'enemy' village. He strode into the melée, fired over their heads and doused the most obstinate with water until the regiment of women fled. By some miracle their husbands, returning from a 'martial comedy' in which nobody was hurt, decided to overlook the incident.

Maclay found other opportunities to do good on Andra. He prevented one of the sailors from teaching the natives to make and use the deadly Lifu slingshot. Inspecting the metal blades with which they replaced the traditional shell or obsidian, he tried to explain the difference between iron and steel and the reasons why they should prefer the latter. He had no time to see them perform the Lifu dance he proposed as a substitute for the weapon, or to hear them ask the traders for steel knives and axes. The islanders had become too absorbed in their own affairs to keep up the supply of trepang and pearlshell. After eleven days in which Maclay seemed to have lived years, the *Sadie F. Caller* raised anchor.

They spent some time in the Ninigo or Exchequer group, a Micronesian outpost where the people so feared strangers that during his previous visit Maclay had seen only one inhabitant. Returning eastward, they called at the Hermit Islands, where his experience could again be useful. Early in October some days were lost in attempts to shape a course for New Guinea, in the teeth of the south-east trades. Webber eventually settled for Sori in the Admiralty group, whose emissaries had promised vast quantities of sea-produce.

The British expedition in H.M.S. *Challenger* had investigated this island five years before, but Maclay expected to find plenty of work left for him. He would live ashore, 'afraid neither of fatal (?) fever nor of treacherous, cruel savages', more likely to learn significant details than gentlemen who probably never left their ship. In the event he suffered nothing worse than difficulty in finding suitable lodgings and food acceptable to his upset stomach. But the study of native life proved far from easy. Its most noticeable feature now was the islanders' taste for trade with Europeans and the skill and self-interest they brought to it. Maclay could not collect so much as a vocabulary without paying a small fee in beads for each ten words. And that abruptly ended. The traders and islanders quarrelled. Captain Webber did not try to impose the white man's will. The schooner returned without delay to her old anchorage at Andra.

Maclay's private object in first taking the *S. F. Caller* to Andra had been to find a Malay deserter from the *Sea Bird*. This time he quickly learned the man's whereabouts. While the skipper was 'rubbing his hands with delight' over the trading, Maclay slipped away in a native canoe to the dark and dangerous mainland.

Negotiations for release of the ex-sailor were tedious, and the ransom high. Maclay was buying more than a man's freedom and pathetic gratitude. Back on the schooner, he eagerly questioned the Malay, sure that an intelligent person who had lived three years among the islanders must be fully informed about their customs.

Ahmad the runaway had not been badly treated, but a man kept in semi-slavery and constant fear among people he considered treacherous savages was not the best possible observer. His thoughts were of safety and clothing. Maclay nevertheless found out something about native polygamy, the purely private administration of justice, the exercise of power in a society with no formal system of authority. Like Maclay, though for different reasons, Ahmad had been interested in cannibalism. He could tell how often the natives ate human flesh and how they cooked a dish they preferred to pork. He knew how it was obtained, usually by the slaughter of women and children from the mountains who visited the coast to collect shellfish. He also knew where the islanders drew the line. The disgust with which they mentioned the flesh of light-skinned people had always been a comfort to him.

For this reason the people farther south had been unable to use the trader Paldi. His body had been prepared for cooking, but when it came to the point, nobody wanted to eat it. Maclay learnt nothing more about the murder. He had to fall back on his old theory that the Italian's hot southern blood, ignorance of native ways and stock of attractive goods made such a death inevitable.

He was on surer ground in explaining the death of the other trader from the *Sea Bird*. O'Hara had often been drunk. He had lived with a native woman. His over-familiarity with the Andra people had alternated with rage or obvious fear before their increasing aggressiveness. Following every possible blunder and offence, his fate clearly belonged to the class of deaths that Maclay summed up as 'one worthless white man the less'. The strange and inspiring thing was that someone had valued O'Hara for being human.

Maclay sought out the aged native who in the face of ridicule and abuse had sheltered the wretched white man. When presented with gifts in memory of O'Hara, old Mana-Salayaoo was deeply moved. Perhaps he wept for his solitary condition and the death that could not be far away. Perhaps he simply mourned a friend. To Maclay he was proof that 'compassionate people are to be found even among cannibals', the one just man who redeemed all the rest.

No just man redeemed the *S. F. Caller* syndicate. After seven months of their singing, whistling and inane chatter, Maclay flinched from mere signs that they were alive. He was irritated by curiosity and advice about his own doings. He had long before passed judgement on their drinking and whoring and rapacity in trade, and knew that such men were unfit to meet the Maclay Coast people. He desired only to escape from 'these beasts' and return to Sydney.

Webber himself proved reluctant to violate the Maclay Coast. He hesitated to take his ship through poorly-charted waters. He pointed to the dangers of sharp squalls alternating with sudden calms. With secret relief, Maclay released him from the obligation and agreed to be set down at the south-eastern tip of New Guinea.

They sailed away from idyllic Andra, where prisoners taken in recent fighting worked as slaves while waiting to be eaten. They left behind the mountainous bulk of the main island, where the Andran captives had already been eaten. Returning on her old route, the schooner ploughed southward along the east coast of New Ireland, surrounded at every anchorage by swarms of canoes. Webber was making for the Louisiade Archipelago, hoping to add new assets to his stake in the guano business.

They landed nowhere on New Ireland. At the little-known Trobriand Islands, wild weather prevented trepang fishing. Maclay had only three days to savour life in the single village of Tume and sketch its elaborate yam houses. Early in December the schooner joined battle with high winds and seas in an attempt to reach the rumoured guano.

She ended up more than 500 kilometres north-east of her destination, at Simbo or Eddystone Island in the Solomons. Maclay spent twenty days ashore while the crew repaired the damage.

Despite boisterous winds, pelting rain and attacks of fever, he enjoyed Simbo. He never tired of viewing and sketching the island which within six kilometres contained two mountain regions linked by a low isthmus. There were hot springs, fumaroles and solfataras to inspect. Volcanic peaks and glistening beaches, broad reefs and exuberant vegetation— this gemlike isle encapsulated all that delighted him in the South Seas. Even after half a century's contact with white men, its inhabitants were sufficiently numerous and unspoiled to maintain their own versions of religion, witchcraft and war.

Maclay's pencil was busy with views of the Simbo mountains, human ears pierced and distorted for ornament, the intricately-carved prow boards of canoes. Drawings of skull houses and shrines caught something of the power these objects held for his imagination. He visited nearby islands and saw enough of the people to form conclusions about their general 'habitus' and affinities. But he abandoned an impulsively-formed plan for spending several months in the Solomons. Early in 1880 he reached the islands off south-eastern New Guinea with the *Sadie F. Caller.*

He spent the end of January and half of February aboard a very different vessel. At Wari he rejected the chance of a quick passage to Queensland and joined the London Missionary Society steamer *Ellangowan* for a leisurely voyage to Port Moresby.

'The company of the missionaries', he noted, 'formed a great contrast to the company to which I had to resign myself on the schooner'. The trip itself was uncomfortable enough, with the tiny *Ellangowan* already overcrowded by missionaries and crew. At the first port of call they picked up two of those unsaved white men who were almost as dear to the reverends as their native charges. Maclay slept on deck, sometimes suffering from fever, as part of a 'human menagerie' almost comparable with that of the *Sadie F. Caller*.

The sense of imprisonment was gone. A few days were lost at sea or at anchor off uninhabited shores while the steamer, pitching and rolling, took on loads of wood as fuel. Maclay passed most of his time among the natives, taking photographs, measuring heads and copying the patterns of profuse tattoos. He inspected pile villages built out from the shore, sketched their spindly outlines and walked their paths, wondering if babies were lost by falling through holes in the floor. He tested a fish-trap and found it worked well, tasted snake meat and pronounced it good. To gauge the pain involved, he acquired two small tattoos, disappointing several female artists who wished to display their skill on a larger scale. His language was that of duty; he still had to prove he never wasted time. A certain holiday spirit nevertheless crept into his account of the voyage.

The missionaries were on an inspection tour, assessing progress and bringing supplies and moral support to the teachers at outlying stations. Maclay sometimes accompanied them and made his own inspection.

He was a critical observer of activities that perverted native life and destroyed its customs. Moreover, the exchange of European goods for food, a necessity in his own case, looked like trading 'under disguise' when practised by missionaries. He learned to make an exception for the L.M.S. people, with whom he was to have a warm and lasting association. But all missionaries, willy-nilly, 'prepared the way for the trader'. They would never have his help or approval in contacting New Guineans. He had never quite faced the fact that the missions, established in southern New Guinea and neighbouring islands, could reach the Maclay Coast without his help.

In the Loyalty Islands and the New Hebrides he had learned much about the work of missions. Now he saw, in the island he called 'my country', the crowds assembled to greet the white men, the trust and respect granted the Melanesian and Polynesian teachers. He saw little boys who knew the alphabet, formed their letters well, and were learning to read from the first book printed in a New Guinea language. To copy tattoos worn by a young girl, he had to enlist the influence of a missionary.

There were cheering moments. He noticed that few men attended church services. While a teacher delivered a boring sermon, members of the congregation yawned, giggled and winked at each other. When the missionaries were absent, women almost besieged Maclay, eager to exchange a view of their tattoos for sticks of tobacco. Some of them were 'not at all prudish' when the doors of the mission house were shut. In some respects, the mission seemed to have 'great success'. In others, the people held their own. As Maclay hinted to the Reverend James Chalmers, some Buddhist teacher, visiting that coast after a few hundred years, might find 'traces of Christian mythology' mixed with native legends.

Chalmers readily adopted Maclay as a great scientist and a personal friend. This large man, whose expansive manners made him seem larger than life, was no more made to the measure of ordinary people than his visitor. He was restless, moody, explosive, a lover of danger and strong sensations. With his eccentricities and taste for disreputable company, he fitted nobody's idea of a typical missionary. Many people, black and white, instinctively found in him their ideal of the legendary hero or demi-god.

He had ambitions to match. He wanted to be the first white man to reach the summits of the Owen Stanley Range. He wanted to follow the Fly River beyond the point reached by D'Albertis. He wanted not only to thrust deeper than any other European into the interior of the great island but to cross its ultimate mountains and descend to the shores of Astrolabe Bay. He also knew what he wanted from men. When he rejected ideas of returning to Europe, it was not merely because he felt himself becoming 'a sort of savage', unfit for civilised society. He could see James Chalmers in England—'nobody—lost—unknown'. In New Guinea, he could become 'a king with great power—far more than any other'.

As long as they avoided the subject of Christian missions, he and Maclay were natural allies. Both regarded themselves as New Guineans. Though they interpreted it differently, both placed the welfare of the natives first. So they had the same enemy. During the voyage and his visit to Port Moresby, Maclay came to know the missionary as a man to be relied upon in any fight to protect New Guineans from Europeans.

When Maclay decided to stay at the principal mission station, it was not from admiration for the surroundings. Approaching Port Moresby, he received a 'far from favourable impression'. Parched brown hills, coarse grass, a sprinkling of stunted gum trees—this landscape too

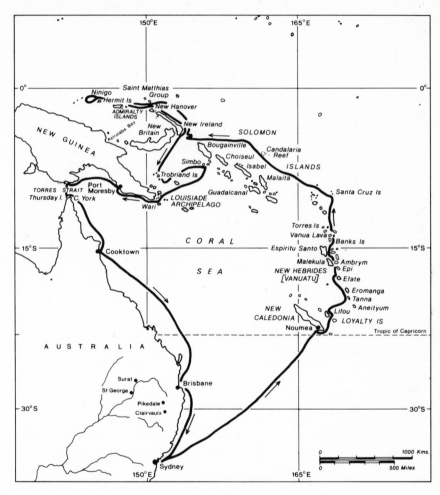

Maclay's travels, 1879–80

clearly resembled the continent that pleased him least. But he showed
no revival of interest in the hypothesis that had helped bring him to the
Pacific. If not a remnant of lost Lemuria, this corner of earth remained
primitive enough to be bearable. Maclay saw it as a base for further trips
with the *Ellangowan* and expeditions into the mountains with horses left
by departed gold-seekers.

Instead, he spent three weeks at the mission house, immobilized by
fever. Between bouts, he drafted a report of his voyage. He visited
Hanuabada, the complex of pile villages on the shore. With the help of
a girl the missionaries considered a 'lost sheep', he made considerable
additions to his records of decorative art—she was tattooed all over.
Tired of sketching people whose features were less comely than their
decorations, he relaxed by examining a large and interesting frog, the
brain of a Goura pigeon, wallabies that might be new to science or the
beautiful little sugar gliders whose piercing screams diminished their
charm. When the *Ellangowan* went back along the coast for timber,
Maclay seized the chance to rid himself of fever by a sea voyage. It was
also with the *Ellangowan* that in April he left New Guinea for the fourth
time, returning to Australia after more than a year among the islands.

14: *The Hairless Australian*

LADEN WITH INFORMATION about native life in half a dozen island groups, Maclay landed at Thursday Island late in April 1880. Again he had confirmed, in the face of 'difficulties and sacrifices', that even the briefest personal observation produced 'truer opinions about the natives of Melanesia than repeated study of all the literature'.

He had satisfied himself that, contrary to the reports of other travellers, no distinct race of light-skinned people lived in south-eastern New Guinea. He had seen many skins much lighter than the 'Papuan' norm. In some areas most of the population had curly rather than frizzy locks, and a few heads of hair were 'definitely straight'. Considered in relation to language and tattoos, these traits bore 'undoubted witness' to a non-Papuan presence. But he had always rejected the careless description of these people as a 'yellow' or 'Malay' race. He ascribed their origins to a relatively small influx of Polynesians.

The largest of his problems was that raised by his old insistence that the negritos of the Philippines and the Malay Peninsula were 'Papuans' or 'Melanesians'. Despite some observations published in 1874, eminent men in Europe still doubted his contention that tribes he had described as brachycephalic should be classified with a people generally regarded as dolichocephalic. Maclay granted no final authority to head form, but felt the need for more evidence. Now he had the answer. Measurements taken during the voyage, supported by authentic skulls, showed that broad heads had 'a far greater distribution in Melanesia than hitherto believed'.

After visiting several Torres Strait islands with the mission vessel, Maclay had felt ready to return to Sydney. As the steamer *Corea* made her way south, accumulating mishaps that made her the subject of a marine board enquiry, he saw no need to hurry back.

No Tampat Senang awaited him; those left in charge during his absence had failed to raise the money. He had long contemplated a journey in Queensland to obtain brains of lungfishes and Australian Aborigines. After inspecting those who hung about the hopeless settlement of Somerset, at the tip of Cape York Peninsula, he wished to meet the Aborigines in regions where they were comparatively numerous. And an acquaintance of Johor Baharu days, Arthur Hunter Palmer, stood high in the Queensland government. He had, it was true, a bad record of opposing reform in the labour traffic. His influence in other respects promised irresistible opportunities.

The first opportunity came because three men were to be hanged. If Maclay waited in Brisbane, he could claim for science the brains of a Chinese, a native of the Philippines, and an Australian Aborigine.

In advocating internal anatomy as a better guide in the study of race than mere comparison of outward traits, Maclay gave priority to the brain. 'The investigation of the brains of representatives of different races of men', he claimed, 'shows that there occur peculiarities of by no means trifling import, which one cannot regard as individual variations'. From preliminary studies, he predicted that science would some day establish 'definite types of cerebral convolutions corresponding to the principal varieties of mankind'. Proof or disproof called for an enormous amount of research. He hoped that his findings on the criminal population of Queensland would encourage other anatomists to work in the same field.

He enjoyed 'instructive and pleasant company' as guest of Augustus Charles Gregory, former surveyor-general of Queensland and an eminent explorer. This courtly old bachelor combined wide scientific knowledge with mastery of the roughest forms of travel. Even political opponents found him disarmingly nice. And in Gregory's house Maclay never met the 'democrats' who made him uncomfortable in Sydney. His host, instinctively and rigidly conservative, opposed majority rule and any kind of social reform. But he showed, as explorer and as member of the Aborigines Commission, a sympathetic interest in the natives. When threatened by Aborigines in the wilds, he had always tried to do them as little harm as possible. Though he insisted that Melanesian labourers were essential to Queensland's tropical industry, he believed in treating them well. He much preferred them to the white working class.

Gregory was a trustee of the Queensland Museum, which had acquired a new home in the most extravagant blend of architectural styles. Maclay easily obtained a room in the old building as a laboratory. The government as readily gave him access to photographic facilities, and the help of the colony's analytical chemist. He still found himself handicapped, but he could begin the most pressing work.

When Jimmy Ah Sue was hanged, at the end of May, the body was beheaded and the brain removed and photographed from six different angles. The Cantonese brain and head were preserved, the first for dissection and study, the second as a test of a new preservative fluid. Three weeks later the same procedure was followed with the head of Maximus Gomez, the descendant of Tagalog head-hunters. There were almost two months to wait for Johnny Campbell, the Australian. Having 'sacrificed' two spiny ant-eaters he had kept under observation, Maclay undertook his first long journey in the colonies.

In Europe he had read a vague account of 'hairless' Aborigines living in the Australian interior. At the Sydney museum he had found a portrait of a scared-looking youth who had been brought to town many years before. There was talk of a tribe of bald, yellow-skinned people, so different from others that normal Aborigines fled from them. The only certainty was that the young man in the photograph had been inspected and pronounced 'hairless'. Nobody remembered whence he came or the name of the squatter who had introduced him to science.

Almost everyone Maclay consulted in Brisbane had something to say about 'hairless blacks'. Some claimed to have seen them; others had merely heard reports. Often a whole tribe was mentioned, sometimes a single family. The question of their whereabouts received many answers, but this difficulty was settled by a friend who wrote a few letters. If Maclay travelled some 400 kilometres north-west, then 150 kilometres south-west, he would reach a sheep station whose owner would help him find him the hairless Australians.

With a free pass presented by the colonial government, he spent a day on the train between Brisbane and the temporary terminus of the advancing railway. A vehicle of sorts carried him by 'road' through the townships of Surat and St George to Gulnaber station on the Balonne River. Though it was not a particularly arduous journey for its time and place, he travelled three and a half days to see a mountain turn into a molehill.

In the district where these almost-legendary people had been known from birth, nobody claimed more than a single hairless family, of which one man and woman remained alive. Maclay found the woman at Gulnaber, photographed her and satisfied himself that she had no hair. His real interest was in her brother Aidanill, the man whose youthful likeness he had seen in Sydney.

Aidanill was on holiday, about a day's journey up the Maranoa River, and native messengers failed to entice him to Gulnaber. All his life he had provided a freak show for blacks and whites. In middle age he never took off his hat if he could help it. Hearing that someone had come from Brisbane to see him, he preferred to stay where he was.

At length the station-owner went up the Maranoa to bring back the man whose name meant 'Go back'. In the doctor's surgery at St George, Aidanill underwent rigorous examination. Every possible measurement was taken. His hand grip was tested with the dynamometer. The colour of his eyes was noted and skin colour in all parts of the body compared with the standard scale. He was washed with soap and water and eau de Cologne and inspected from head to toe with the lens. Apart from a few rudimentary eyelashes and four short hairs in the left nostril, he had not a hair. The only other feature distinguishing him from the Aboriginal onlookers was a smell that left the investigator lost for words.

Aidanill endured it, protesting only when his tormentors wished to take a sample of his skin. The history of the family remained rather uncertain, since he contradicted an informant Maclay thought more reliable. As to the future, it seemed that the hairless family must disappear. The sisters had married and produced well-thatched off-spring. Aidanill would never have children, his grinning countrymen explained. No woman wanted the hairless man.

A few shillings from Maclay allowed Aidanill to drink himself senseless. Finding him in that state, Maclay regretted his promise not to take any of the hairless skin. Neither promise nor integument was broken, but Maclay arranged that when Aidanill died, or suffered a wound requiring medical attention, a piece of his skin would be preserved.

Maclay was in Brisbane by mid-August, to receive Johnny Campbell's body and make this 'specimen of *Homo australis*' useful to science. Finally the body, with brain and digestive tract removed, lay in a bath of preservative, to be observed for a while before despatch to Europe. The press took a jocular interest in the idea of the late bushranger as 'the Baron's close companion'. He was not a bad companion at that—admirably quiet, easily kept down by acupuncture. His cerebral convolutions, Maclay announced, showed he had possessed considerable 'intellectual capacity'.

Maclay never intended to stay so long with Johnny Campbell. An exhibition was being organized in Melbourne, and he had seen in this an opportunity to examine specimens of *Homo australis* otherwise beyond his reach. He did not propose to assemble 'a crowd of blacks who would put on a corroboree for the entertainment of white Australians'. What he suggested was that families from all regions of the continent should be collected in Melbourne, studied and photographed, and displayed complete with scientific descriptions.

This did not sound like much joy for anyone but the anthropologist. Arthur Palmer responded with the usual colonial formula—Queensland would assist if the other colonies did. The exhibition commissioners thought long and hard and replied that they could not afford it. Maclay, ready to go to Melbourne to compile the necessary descriptions, resigned himself to the fact that he would never see natives of central and Western Australia.

By then, Johnny Campbell had been sent to Professor Rudolf Virchow in Berlin, where in due time he was hailed as a great rarity, perfectly preserved. Maclay had enough other company to feel the need of a place where he could work undisturbed. He was saved by an invitation to revisit Jimbour station on Darling Downs, where he had spent a few days on his way back from the Balonne.

This famous pastoral property was an ancient fief with a history of almost forty years. Its owner, Joshua Bell, was a kindly man of patrician outlook, regularly returned to parliament by the constituency he practically owned. He had been a minister in several conservative governments, and in 1880 was acting as administrator of the colony. His great sandstone mansion, fully six years old, ranked as 'Mecca of Civilisation' in those parts, but Maclay spent a fortnight in perfect peace, revising his travel notes and catching up on correspondence. There and in the township that lay at the station's feet, he collected information about the Aborigines.

Much of this was of the 'curious' kind, intended for those who appreciated notes on the position assumed by Aboriginal couples in coitus, or an account of sexual intercourse between men and pre-pubescent girls. He learned more about the operation by which inland tribes supposedly prevented weak males from becoming fathers. From a traveller who had heard it from a man who had lived with the blacks, he obtained some facts on the creation of female 'eunuchs' to provide sexual satisfaction for young men without the risk of unwanted children. He hoped in time to get photographs illustrating the physical effects of such operations.

From Jimbour he moved to Pikedale station near Stanthorpe, where he completed and annotated the report of his island journey. His new host Donald Gunn then invited him to Clairvaulx, near Glen Innes in northern New South Wales. In both localities Maclay sought material for work on the marsupial brain. The necessary animals proved rather elusive, but he obtained the brains of kangaroos, wallabies, wallaroos and koalas. With less trouble he found remains of their predecessors— *Diprotodon*, *Nototherium*, and the giant extinct wombats and kangaroos.

Pikedale, Clairvaulx and their like were a far cry from Buitenzorg, but Maclay found something of the same repose there. He sketched the modest architecture and bare paddocks of Australian homesteads with a hint of the ethnographic interest he brought to studies of dwellings in the Pacific islands. He drew out elements of grace in a bouquet of native flowers on his table, or the unformed profiles of young ladies at Clairvaulx. When he accepted as scenery a line of insignificant hills or a bend in a near-dry creek, he seemed half-reconciled to Australia.

He remained at Clairvaulx for Christmas and New Year's Day, enjoying a style of life not hopelessly far removed from the simplicity and monotony that appealed to him in primitive villages. He was full of praise for the kindness and hospitality of the squatters. But life in the bush could not go on indefinitely. On 19 January 1881, nine months after he had decided to spend a few days at Brisbane, Maclay took ship for the south.

He carried with him more than bottled brains, fossil bones and the heads of Jimmy Ah Sue and Maximus Gomez. Throughout his stay, he had gathered materials for reports on the labour traffic and proof that the colonists were unfit to have any say in the future of New Guinea. There had been no need for him to witness atrocities against Aborigines and slavery on plantations, or even to question his friends. In their newspapers, parliamentary proceedings and official reports, these people constantly condemned themselves.

Much had changed in Sydney, but not much of interest to Maclay. The entrance to the city was now dominated by the building that had housed an enormously successful and exhausting international exhibition. Steam trams plied the streets, frightening the horses and endangering the lives and clothing of pedestrians. Telephones began to appear, trailing poles and wires that would soon become an eyesore. And these fanatics of progress had many pipe-dreams. There were schemes for a high-level bridge across the harbour. The law courts were mentally housed in a new building that, if completed, would be stupendous. The visionary home of the library and art gallery would be, if possible, more so. They were still considering an old project for a combined parliament house and government office block, the size of a small town, incorporating elements of the Mother of Parliaments, the Doges' Palace, Moorish towns and Gothic cathedrals. Nobody was building a twelve-room zoological station.

Neither Maclay nor his project had been forgotten. Publication of articles completed before his departure had jogged the memories of fellow scientists. He had managed to send back letters and scientific notes during his travels. Any scrap of news about him had been picked up by the press. And it would be unfair to say that nothing had been done about the zoological station. The land had been surveyed and granted. Parliament had voted a grant in aid. Trustees had been appointed, plans drawn up and tenders called. Circulars soliciting funds had been issued and the press in Australia and England had provided a fair amount of publicity. Yet the combined efforts of colonial and English scientists had not collected enough to secure the government grant. Early in 1881 only two-thirds of the necessary £300 had been subscribed.

Maclay thought bitterly of the time he had lost and was losing for want of a suitable workplace. He lamented the useless passing of those hours when an investigator, 'in the mood most suitable for work', was thwarted by the distance between dwelling and laboratory. He was determined not to leave Sydney before this situation had been rectified. The zoological station was to be his memorial in Australia, and he wanted it erected within three months.

Two months after his return, subscriptions still lagged behind the government grant. For whatever reasons, Sydney would not pay for its own zoological station. Late in March he left for Melbourne, to appeal to the rival colony.

With official authorization, he inspected Victoria's public institutions, perhaps intending to describe them for the Russian press. Apparently at the suggestion of the New South Wales government mineralogist, he made a quick trip to Stawell, to measure temperatures in the Magdala shaft, the continent's deepest mine boring. At a hastily-organized special meeting of the Royal Society of Victoria, he found the *savants* ready to raise subscriptions among themselves. The press was not optimistic about contributions from outsiders. There were too many local demands, too little interest in science 'as apart from education'. The Royal Society itself had just lost its small government subsidy.

Victoria, Queensland and England eventually contributed. Fear of odious comparison with the sister society helped enlist the Royal Society of New South Wales. To appease botanists, the zoological station became a biological station. The land proved too steep for economical building, and another small area had to be added. The architect drastically revised Maclay's plan. But in two months or three months or six the station would be ready for occupation.

The premier of New South Wales, Sir Henry Parkes, arranged for Maclay to have a cottage in the exhibition grounds, not the place Maclay would have chosen but tolerable as a 'temporary zoological station'. He was living there in April, with his research on mammalian brains begun. For the first time since leaving the Maclay Coast, he enjoyed peace and independence, with some convenience in his work.

Or so it appeared on the surface. In reality it was not clear how he lived. The New Guinea missionaries and his hosts in Queensland had not charged for board and lodging, and travel in those parts had cost him nothing. Meshchersky and the Geographical Society had launched a public subscription in Russia, raising about 6000 roubles. Yet this sum did not reduce Maclay's debts or give him security. It had been absorbed, he explained, by travelling expenses incurred before he got it. The subscription left him worse off in a way. Thanks to publicity given the

Russian efforts, the scientific world and much of the general public knew that his debts were large and unlikely to be paid.

For more than two years he had known that the family finances had collapsed in 'almost complete catastrophe'. His patrons' uneasiness about his doings, and their wish that he should return to Russia, had been conveyed to the world at large. In June 1881 he depended on men he despised—there could be no more ostentatious 'democrat' than Sir Henry Parkes. He lived alone in an uncongenial society, behind a façade of urbane self-sufficiency that surely took effort to maintain. The strain might almost be measured by the impulse that made him pour out his feelings to Grand Duke Nikolai Mikhailovich.

This royal amateur, interested mainly in obtaining specimens for his butterfly collection, had sweetened requests for unpaid service with a few remarks that indicated personal sympathy. In return, Maclay confided the pent-up bitterness of eleven years. From the 'very cold reception' at St Petersburg in 1869 to his present precarious situation, from the first insulting suggestions that he should study 'Russian puddles and ponds' to recent 'one-sided' comments on his wanderings, he traced the history of injustice and neglect. He looked forward to nothing better. To the grand duke's prediction that he would be warmly greeted in Russia, Maclay replied 'Not so'. He half expected 'the coldest of welcomes'.

The explanation provided the consolation. He would suffer as one of the true scientists who 'go forward on their own road, *not* paying attention to the opinions of the crowd to right and left'. He knew that he had carried out his project 'as far as circumstances permitted and as far as strength sufficed'. 'I did this', he explained, 'for the sake of science itself and *for it alone*; all sympathy, praises or censure, the hopes of some or misgivings of others, could not change the programme I set up for myself after unbiassed discussion of the tasks'. This conviction, and belief that competent people must judge him right, would sustain him in the future as in the past. With a grim exposition of his financial difficulties, and a word of respect and gratitude for the young grand duke, he resumed his many-sided activities in Sydney.

At the first meeting of the Linnean Society after his return, he had presented a brief, well-illustrated report on his travels, and exhibited pictures of the hairless people as well as photographs, dissections and drawings of the brains of the spiny ant-eater, several marsupials, the Chinese, the Tagalog and the Australian Aborigine. In May he described the method of preserving Johnny Campbell's body, and gave results for temperature measurements in the Magdala shaft. For June his principal subject was 'The Practice of Ovariotomy by the Natives of the Herbert River, Queensland', followed by remarks on the brain of the dingo compared with that of the New Guinea dog. In July he made his last

A family group,
St Petersburg,
1882: Maclay
(right), his
brother Mikhail,
their mother and
a small relative

The biological station, Laing's Point, Sydney

Vladimir Miklouho as a shipwrecked sailor, 1882

Prince A. A. Meshchersky and his daughter

Sir Arthur Hamilton Gordon

Vice-Admiral N. Kopitov: memento of the voyage of *Skobelev*, 1883

Maramai of Bilbil

Maclay at St Petersburg, about 1886

Margaret Miklouho-Maclay, about 1883

Sir John Robertson, Margaret's father, about 1885

Alexander Miklouho-Maclay, the traveller's older son, St Petersburg, 1888

contribution for the year—a short paper on artificial deformation of the heads of the new-born, practised for the sake of beauty in Torres Strait, and the accidental deformation of female heads that resulted from the New Guinea habit of supporting heavy loads by a band across the head. With his travel report to the Russian Geographical Society and an article on the hairless Australians, despatched to Berlin, his list of substantial publications since his return from the islands was complete.

It was hard to see the difference between his varied subjects and those of the scientists he condemned. He was not one of those, intent on 'the largest income', who betrayed science in their scramble 'to woo the mob and its tastes', but few of his papers would have been out of place in a popular science magazine. His work was often summarized in the *Sydney Morning Herald*. His communications to Berlin regularly pleased readers who gained sexual titillation from the findings of respectable ethnographers. Some of his articles had appeared in European illustrated papers.

There was no harm in any of it, yet the total effect disagreed with his picture of the misunderstood idealist, suffering for austere principles that set him apart from others. Maclay needed to impress the grand duke, a valuable ally in any conflict with the Russian Geographical Society. More profoundly, he needed to reassure himself. Whatever he did, his motives must distinguish him from the 'journeymen' and 'charlatans' who dominated science. He had broken no promises, never deviated from his original goal. If he sank in want and obscurity, these suitors of the rabble must bear the blame.

He also needed publicity, and got it. No scientist in Australia, and few elsewhere, received more public attention. He had used his prestige in the struggle for the biological station. He intended to do more. As the long travail that taught him much about architects and contractors drew to its close, Maclay called a public meeting to lay the foundations of biological science in Australia.

The Australasian Biological Association was formed on 15 June 1881. Its objects were to 'assist in the formation and regulation of all biological stations which should in the course of time be established in Australia, Tasmania and New Zealand', and to 'combine in one organization all separate efforts of individuals in the direction of biological research in these regions'. To minimize talk, Maclay introduced a set of rules prepared in advance. A committee was elected to control the finances and general management of Sydney Biological Station and to establish principles on which future stations would be founded and run. Maclay became chairman of the committee and director of the institution for which he was already a trustee. These positions were honorary—the most optimistic could not imagine the Association paying its first director—but they offered immense possibilities.

The committee met four times in the next six weeks, and agreed upon the code of rules. Its work was done under the shadow of Maclay's imminent departure. That he would soon go somewhere was certain. His destination and the length of his absence could not be predicted.

This uncertainty arose from non-scientific concerns. Maclay tended to assume that while he travelled the rest of his world would stand still, and events had a way of conforming to expectations. During twenty two months in which he had wandered, more or less out of touch, there had been no real threat to the Maclay Coast. Soon after his return to Sydney, however, he had read a disturbing report from New Zealand. The adventurers who had visited his coast in 1878 were preparing to go there again, and meant to found a colony. They reported scented woods 'in abundance', tobacco and sugar cane under cultivation. The inhabitants showed a 'childish eagerness' for trade goods, and an encouraging readiness to work. The enterprise needed only men and money.

Maclay was in a better position to deal with New Zealanders than he had been two years before. Sir Arthur Gordon, while remaining high commissioner for the western Pacific, had become governor of New Zealand. Maclay wrote to him at once, repeating requests made in 1879—exclusion of liquor and firearms and protection of native rights over the land. He asked nothing so extreme as a ban on the expedition.

Without Maclay's prompting, Sir Arthur was anxious to stop the whole undertaking. He was about to issue regulations against sale of firearms and spirits. The correspondence nevertheless lasted some months. Sir Arthur, feeling very ignorant about New Guinea affairs, wanted Maclay to visit him for consultations. Maclay gladly promised to inform and advise the high commissioner in New Zealand or elsewhere. In advance, he suggested that a naval vessel be sent to the Maclay Coast immediately, to establish friendly relations with the inhabitants and prevent bloodshed. He indicated an intention to return to New Guinea himself, and willingness to accompany the warship.

Again, Sir Arthur had made other arrangements. A deputy commissioner had already been despatched to inspect New Guinea and New Britain. Maclay's part in the mission was limited to giving advice when this official passed through Sydney. He was not much impressed by Hugh Hastings Romilly, one of those enthusiastic young men in whose hands the British placed the welfare of thousands. He still did his best to inform the youth, providing him with suitable speeches in the Bongu dialect, the names of big-men and the right to call himself (in the native sense of the words) 'Maclay's brother'.

Romilly made the most of the acquaintance, feeling that the natives were perhaps 'more civil' to him than they would be to other visitors. He inspected their villages, appreciated their quiet life, and assured them that Maclay would soon return. His enquiries about the *Courier*'s visit gave satisfactory results. Though at least five ships had called there (four of them on Maclay's behalf), the natives seemed to say they had seen only two. Canoes had come out to H.M.S. *Beagle* at once, but Saul of Bongu assured Maclay's 'brother' that when ships came the people took to the bush. When Romilly asked whether land had been sold, he received 'a most emphatic denial'. Finding no European articles in villages where Maclay had distributed them for years, he considered this strong evidence that no land had been bought. From all the correct replies that were due to Maclay's brother, he concluded that the *Courier* had never been there.

The *Courier* had certainly visited Astrolabe Bay. Her company could not otherwise have learned by 1 January 1879 about the earlier visit of the *Dove*. But the colonizing expedition never took place. It was anyone's guess whether it collapsed under Gordon's disapproval, criticism in the newspapers, or the promoters' inability to raise cash. Maclay always felt that his intervention alone had saved the Maclay Coast.

The invitation to visit New Zealand was still open when Maclay undertook a different journey. He had returned to Australia to find newspapers carrying numerous stories about 'massacres' of white men in the Pacific. Early in 1881, the toll seemed worse than ever, the demands for action more likely to influence the authorities. Following the deaths of a Royal Navy commander and several of his crew, questions were asked in the House of Commons. Colonial writers criticized the legal basis of the western Pacific high commission and the attitudes of those responsible for its workings. The remarks of an intercolonial conference upset Sir Arthur Gordon and the commodore of the Australia station. It was time for Maclay to defend his friends. He wrote to Commodore Wilson, and published the letter in the newspapers.

The opinions he expressed in general terms were those he always held: if white men were killed it was their own fault or that of the other white men. 'Cases occur', he admitted, 'in which the natives kill the whites simply for the sake of killing'. Such apparently wanton deeds were either 'deplorable abnormalities' or an illusion produced by difficulty in ascertaining the details. The acts of islanders were but reprisals for 'kidnapping, slave trade and slavery ... and shameless spoliation which goes by the name of "trading" '.

His one specific request, 'that the Imperial Government will never permit skippers and traders taking the law into their own hands', was easily granted in theory, since imperial authorities did not knowingly permit any such thing. His desire for an international agreement to cover loopholes in British power was shared by all Englishmen concerned with law and order in the Pacific. On publication of his letter, nobody disagreed with any of this, or denied that many killings were reactions to European misdeeds.

On the other hand, no one saw much point in multiplying general accusations: 'The question is not who began the mischief, but how are the existing evils to be abated'. The demand, as always, was for a system providing justice for both blacks and whites. The alternative, as Maclay's principal critic pointed out, was for 'civilized powers' to keep their subjects right out of the islands.

Maclay might have agreed with this last solution. No other could set his mind wholly at rest. He did not bother to comment on comments. By writing to Commodore Wilson, he had performed 'a duty towards mankind'. He was preparing to place his information at the commodore's service. Meanwhile, relations with Wilson involved him in a borderline case that caused great moral confusion.

Early in March 1881 the people of Kalo, in south-eastern New Guinea, had killed ten Polynesian members of the L.M.S. mission, men, women and children. A naval officer investigated and reported, then months passed without further developments. But the missionaries themselves, while refusing to assist on this occasion, had severely criticized the navy's earlier laxity. The word went round that Commodore Wilson intended to make an example of Kalo.

Maclay believed that without his intervention great injustice would be done. He still called Wilson a just and good man. He did not hesitate to assert that the commodore was ready to burn the village and exterminate its inhabitants.

Wilson was painfully anxious not to fire a shot. As for burning the village, he would rather have burned himself. But Maclay knew nothing of this. He seemed equally unaware of enquiries and the missionaries' refusal to co-operate. When he described the interview in later years, he gave word for word a conversation in which he persuaded the commodore not to punish a thousand people for the deeds of two or three, and convinced him that the missionaries' help was essential. 'By means of the missionaries and the people of nearby villages', he explained, 'it will not be difficult to negotiate with the Kalo people, demand the names and the surrender of the guilty, and announce the punishment they will suffer if the demand is not fulfilled'. His scheme, in essence, was what the Royal Navy unsuccessfully tried to do throughout the south Pacific.

Wilson insisted that the expedition needed Maclay. According to a version written for a Russian audience, Maclay accepted for the natives' sake a proposal 'not altogether convenient' to him. At the time, he told a newspaper that his object was primarily scientific. Kalo was an especially interesting locality, he told the Linnean Society, inhabited by the mixed race. And the trip he owed to the commodore's 'kind invitation' was not an end in itself. An old acquaintance, Major-General the Honourable William Feilding, had arrived in the colonies. To give Queensland a 'land grant' railway, with vast power and profit to his syndicate, he planned to survey a line from the south-western interior of the colony to the Gulf of Carpentaria. Maclay hoped to leave H.M.S. *Wolverene* on the way back from New Guinea, join Feilding's party, visit the gulf with them, and perhaps set out on his own account for Darwin.

The departure on 10 August was majestic, *Wolverene* being temporarily included with the squadron that was taking the young sons of the Prince of Wales around the world. Accompanied by a swarm of small craft, six warships steamed down the harbour in 'single column, line ahead, close order', to lively music from their bands and storms of cheering from crowded shores. Once at sea, however, *Wolverene* left the pomp and circumstance and made a quick passage to Port Moresby.

Commodore Wilson found the missionaries as stubborn as ever. The whole affair was anguish to them. Kalo had never known traders or blackbirders or marauding sailors. Despite political explanations, the Reverends Lawes and Chalmers feared that the massacre arose from sheer blood-lust. They knew it might imperil the mission if allowed to go unpunished. Yet they resisted ideas of associating themselves with the punitive expedition. It would destroy their reputation as men of peace, and jeopardize the mission in a different way.

The commodore insisted that he needed one of them as a symbol of good will and justice, to explain his purpose and secure the instigator of the crimes. By repeating again and again that he would be 'sorry if a single shot were fired', he overcame the scruples of James Chalmers.

Maclay lost interest before discussions reached that point. Unaware that the commodore's plan was really Maclay's, the missionaries ridiculed it. Kalo would never give up its chief. Rather than interfere, the villagers Maclay nominated as intermediaries would take to the bush. The one chance of success, Chalmers maintained, was to surround Kalo before dawn and seize the chief before his men recovered their wits.

With Chalmers and the widow of a murdered teacher, Maclay accompanied a party of bluejackets who landed at night some distance from Kalo. It was a dreadful night—rainy, pitch-dark and blowing hard. Neither Chalmers nor the Samoan woman, acquainted with the district for years, could find the path to Kalo. Maclay observed the mistakes and muddle keenly, but offered no advice. They became entangled in scrub, swamps and plantations, were forced to retreat to the shore and go far out of their way to obtain a guide. When they reached Kalo, with the men nearly exhausted by nine hours of humping their equipment over rough going, it was broad morning.

There had never been a chance of surprise. The chief and a large group of warriors had been on the watch all night, and from daybreak had defied Wilson's landing party. The native force came face to face with one detachment of sailors, and attacked at once. When three bluejackets had been wounded, the order to fire was given.

The villagers were driven out. By the time they sued for peace through elders of a neighbouring community, four Kalo men had been killed, 'several' wounded and two taken prisoner. When the commodore demanded the delivery of the chief, dead or alive, it turned out that he had been the first to fall. His body was recognized by the teacher's widow. Others were identified, less reliably, as those of his son and nephew. The people returned; the chief's hut was set alight; Chalmers made a speech, explaining that events of the last two days had nothing in common with indiscriminate Papuan revenge. Maclay particularly wanted the natives to understand that white men's justice punished only the guilty.

Chalmers and the commodore more or less glossed over events in Kalo. Maclay did not describe them. It was difficult to claim that anything but accident had determined their course, equally hard to believe that the natives gained much understanding of European justice from four chance executions that occurred without a trial. The white men nevertheless congratulated themselves. Commodore Wilson, who had agonized all the way to Kalo, sent off a cheery message from the first telegraph station: 'Results of the cruise most satisfactory; parted good friends with the islanders'. The missionaries soon decided that *Wolverene*'s visit had done only good. Maclay showed no misgivings about the outcome, and forgot that he had had no part in it. 'My plan fully succeeded', he wrote. 'Instead of the burning of the village and the extermination of its inhabitants, the affair was limited to a few killed in a skirmish . . .'.

15: A Glimpse of the Kingdom

GENERAL FEILDING'S expedition was over before *Wolverene* returned to Australia. Maclay's only new inland journey was a visit to the Lakes Creek meatworks with naval officers and the mayor of Rockhampton. He was far from satisfied with scientific results when he reached Sydney towards the end of September 1881. Yet he looked back with pleasure on those seven weeks. He had formed an exceptionally close relationship with Commodore Wilson.

The biological station, fit for occupation at last, awaited him on the northern side of Laing's Point, a small promontory just inside South Head. Through the seaside resort of Watson's Bay, it was linked to the city by road and ferry. Wide views in three directions embraced most of the harbour. Half a kilometre to the east, beyond sheltering slopes of almost-undisturbed bushland, the Pacific broke against cliffs. Just to the north, the surge through the heads bore ocean creatures into tranquil Camp Cove. The glowing colours in which the location was painted for English scientists were in no way overdone.

The building was a different matter. Maclay had designed a two-storey structure, each laboratory communicating by a separate stairway with a bedroom on the floor above, so that inmates need not meet each other when moving between workplace and sleeping quarters. A commonroom was to be provided for those less adapted to permanent solitude and silence. But funds had dictated a smaller and less original creation. The six internal stairways had disappeared. Three workrooms and three bedrooms, with verandas on all sides, occupied a single floor over a basement containing another laboratory, a bathroom and a store. When Maclay moved in, only his rooms were furnished, the lower floor was unfinished and the land unfenced.

Visitors found the place 'devoid of anything like luxury—or some would say of anything like comfort'. Maclay was well content. Across little Camp Cove, it was true, he faced the colony's most extensive fortifications and biggest guns. The rugged slopes periodically sprouted tents and exploded with military exercises. But most of the time his surroundings promised a calm and fruitful mental life. His apartment was completely private, as nearly soundproof as possible. For the rest, he looked to rules drawn up long before. No resident of this building would be permitted to 'disturb any other by singing, whistling, or any other unnecessary noise'. Students and local scientists were unwelcome, and women were excluded.

These rules for a colony of scientific hermits were never tested. There was some acclaim and self-congratulation at first, predictions that scientists would hasten to Sydney to use and improve the biological station. Some might have done so if they could. T. H. Huxley would gladly have returned to Australia had he been thirty years younger. Others found themselves, if not too old, at least too poor, too busy or too far away. After the first flurry of visitors, Maclay remained sole occupant of an almost perfect Tampat Senang, where he could work, in his favourite phrase, 'undisturbed and undisturbing'.

He was settled there early in October, engaged, he told the press, in 'anatomical researches on the Australian fauna' and in sorting out records of his eleven years in the Pacific. He published nothing, devoting much time to non-scientific concerns.

One task grew out of his promise to supply Commodore Wilson with 'Notes *in re* kidnapping and slavery in the western Pacific'. He was compiling a text of more than 4000 words, with extensive footnotes, to be added to the commodore's official report.

On leaving the *Sadie F. Caller*, he had known beyond doubt that the Ambrym men who had joined the vessel for a few weeks and the Lifu sailors engaged for five or six months had been cruelly misinformed. He suspected that they would be scandalously underpaid, if paid at all, and that they might be landed far from their homes. At Simbo he had met a man, dumped there by another vessel, who for ten months work at sea had received articles that Captain Webber valued at fifteen shillings. He had seen 'very serious and neglected cases of syphilis' among workers recently returned from Queensland and ex-sailors from vessels cruising the islands. Otherwise, six of the eleven specific cases he mentioned were described from hearsay; four were stories heard about David Dean O'Keefe and others in 1876, and fell outside the sphere of the Australia station. Some concerned foreigners whom the British could not touch. Only one related to labour traffic with a British colony. The offending vessel, name unknown, was believed to have come from Fiji.

Like most compassionate Europeans, Maclay denied the islanders any ability to assess their own situation or make their own choices. Without describing how his figures were obtained, he summarized '*how* and through what means the labourers are collected'.

> About 15 per cent are taken by means of different artifices . . .; about 15 per cent are sold by relatives and chiefs; and 10 per cent are obliged to leave their islands, being pressed by victorious enemies; about 25 per cent are returned labourers who, having convinced themselves that their property was stolen by their own people, prefer to go away . . .; about 25 per cent inquisitive, mostly young people, anxious to travel, or wishing to get arms . . .; about 5 per cent pressed by want of food . . .; about 5 per cent by force.

Whoever they were, these people never understood what they were doing. Those who fled famine or war had nothing in common with the refugees of Europe. The youths in search of knowledge, adventure and gain were not like young Europeans who set out with similar motives. Always they were victims of white men's duplicity, if not violence.

Maclay had never seen conditions on Queensland plantations. His collection of newspaper articles and official reports nevertheless allowed him to indicate every abuse, from poor food and excessive working hours to the prices shopkeepers charged kanakas in the towns. He could expose the lack of medical attention and regular control of living and working conditions, because these deficiencies, and many more, had recently been described by doctors on an official inspection tour. Long extracts from their report, published by order of the Queensland parliament, were included with his submission.

He also touched on iniquities outside the scope of official reports. A newspaper cutting told how, in 1876, an employer had paid high 'passage money' for good-looking young women. A letter printed in a Noumea journal accused French planters of subjecting New Hebridean servants to the abominations of Sodom and Gomorrah. Maclay, 'sorry to say that facts confirm this statement', could not personally assert that it applied in Queensland or Fiji. He significantly linked it to remarks on the extreme youth of some recruits.

Many of the evils he described were incurable as long as the labour trade existed. Men could not be taken from the islands without disrupting native life. Though 'purchase' of recruits was illegal, it was unlikely that any could be obtained without compensation to their villages for the loss of military and economic services. Without European intervention—a solution unacceptable to Maclay—absentees would go on losing wives and property and labourers returning home would be robbed by fellow villagers. Yet after sketching a state of affairs he considered worse than slavery and the slave trade, Maclay stopped short of demanding its abolition. Four of his recommendations coincided with those of the Queensland medical men, and two were already

embodied in legislation. Two more of his 'desiderata'—higher pay and
status for government agents on labour vessels, medical inspection of
homeward-bound labourers to prevent spread of venereal disease—
appeared in the commodore's list. He had nothing further to suggest but
an 'international understanding'. It was left for the commodore to
recommend an end to the whole business.

Wilson had long before characterized the labour traffic as 'but a
legalized slave trade ... aiding to depopulate these beautiful islands,
while ... rendering more miserable the most degraded people under the
sun'. He could not imagine its being condoned by anyone with no direct
financial interest. The great necessity, in his view, was to overcome the
prejudice and fear of white working-class voters who barred the entry
of Indian and Chinese labour. Once coolies were obtained, it would be
simple to stop importation of Pacific islanders.

The commodore could do little about the cases Maclay submitted for
investigation and redress. Accusations against D. D. O'Keefe could only
be referred to the China station. In the one case that gave the
commodore grounds and facts enough for enquiries within his
jurisdiction, the accused was already dead. Wilson felt grateful, all the
same, for Maclay's 'independent evidence'. He esteemed Maclay as 'a
gentleman of great scientific knowledge and research'. As their friendship grew on the basis of shared opinions, it was natural for Maclay to
seek Wilson's advice on plans he had been considering for some time.

He always envisaged returning to his coast, to live there permanently
and shield the natives from predatory Europeans. He no longer thought
entirely in terms of keeping white men out. As he had told the Russian
geographers in 1879, he believed that through patience, tact and a true
understanding of both sides he could prevent destruction of the
Papuans. At the same time, whites might benefit from his mediation.
Accepting the general belief that Europeans were unfit for heavy work
in a tropical climate, it followed that colonists would need help from
'the fully acclimatized dark race'. With an unconscious echo of a famous
cynicism, he described extermination of the islanders as 'not merely a
ruthless injustice but an inexcusable blunder in politico-economic
respects'. In plain words, blacks should be kept alive to work for whites.

In his country they would work only for a few whites, a humanitarian élite whose first concern would be native welfare. Through
October and November 1881, he drafted his 'Maclay Coast Scheme',
devised to raise the level of their civilization and to allow them, 'without
being taken advantage of, to be brought into contact with the white
visitors'.

The scheme had something in common with one for 'agricultural
missions', suggested by Luigi D'Albertis. In some respects it resembled
a French scientific-agricultural-commercial colony lately founded in

Sumatra. Vastly more ambitious, it did not depend on public philanthropy or endowments from scientific societies. Its first step would be
formation of a company by 'philanthropically-minded capitalists ...
who will not only look for large returns but also be pleased to render
a great service *to humanity*, in widening the path of civilization'.

With £15 000 to £30 000 put up by the company, plantations of
coconut palms, sugar, sago palm, coffee and cotton would be established,
and sawmills, a brickworks and a sago refinery would eventually come
into operation. While plantations were maturing—a process for which
Maclay allowed four to seven years—the company was to function as a
trading concern. Its steamer would regularly visit other islands and other
parts of New Guinea, exchanging all kinds of trade goods (except
firearms and liquor) for pearlshell, copra, bêche-de-mer, sago and
turtleshell. Shipped to Queensland ports, these products would form
'the basis of a remunerative export trade'.

With the trading venture established and agricultural development
well under way, it would be time for social and political development.
Through work in company enterprises, the natives would have
acquired 'habits of greater industry', with knowledge allowing them to
raise their own standards of agriculture. Through Maclay's influence and
the shared experience of work and trade with the company, villages
hitherto isolated or at war would be ready to unite 'for the common
purpose of mutual interest and judicious legislation'.

Maclay believed political progress must be based upon existing
institutions, but he had difficulty in defining these. He knew that
hereditary or elected chiefs were rare in Melanesia and that the people
of his coast had none. During village discussions he had formed the
impression that anyone could have a say. Still, there were the big-men,
with an indefinite stratum of people who were respected for age or
intelligence, or obeyed because they shouted louder than the rest. He
easily imagined each village with an 'existing Tamo-Council' in whose
hands purely local matters could be left.

The next tier of government would be entirely new. Each important
village would send its most influential man to a 'Great or Tamo-boro
Council', modelled on the aristocratic great council of Fiji, and this body
would decide matters of general consequence. Maclay would act as
adviser and arbitrator to the Great Council, with personal control over
all dealings with foreigners, including relations with New Guineans
outside the Union of the Maclay Coast.

He accurately described this as 'a vast plan'. The political entity he
defined had more than 240 kilometres of mainland coast, included
numerous islands, and ran 80 to 95 kilometres inland. He had never set
eyes on half the territory. Apart from neighbours at Port Konstantin
and Bilbil, few of its estimated twenty thousand inhabitants had seen

him more that once. Yet he fearlessly undertook to develop the country, 'raise the people to a higher level' and form 'a very important centre of tropical agriculture and other suitable industry', depending on no authority but his own.

The position he chose for himself was fraught with moral difficulties. On one hand he would serve the company, working for 'large returns'. On the other, he would represent, protect and rule the people whose labour was basic to economic success. He evidently felt that conflicts of duty might arise. He suggested that the capitalists, as well as paying his salary for directing affairs, might have 'a representative of their own' on the spot.

One weakness overshadowed all others in his plan for combining native interests with those of a plantation and trading company. Garagassi, Bugarlom and the islet of Uremu (Airu on Bilbil was a mere house site) were inadequate for the quantity and variety of cultivation he had in mind. Yet his convictions seemed to make it impossible for the company to acquire more land. He had repeatedly told Sir Arthur Gordon that land on the Maclay Coast was 'entirely owned by different communities engaged in tilling a soil which has been under cultivation for centuries', that all natural products of land and sea had recognized owners. To repel invasion from New Zealand, he had summed up the position with regard to land and its transfer:

> As the natives of the Maclay Coast have no hereditary chiefs . . . and the chiefs de facto . . . have only an influence over others derived from their personal character . . . a sale of land is a difficult matter. A general consent to a sale of land to the intruders is a very unlikely event, and even should it take place . . . each member of the community has a right to claim his own share of the payment for it.
>   Again, the natives do not understand parting with their land absolutely. (For this reason I never considered it right to attempt, myself, the acquisition of a freehold property on this coast.)

The fact remained that under the Maclay Coast Scheme the inhabitants must part with large parcels of land for plantations, factories, stores and wharves. Maclay did not mention the need, and his estimate of capital costs made no provision for land dealings.

Another certainty was that the Maclay Coast people would need all their new 'habits of greater industry'. They were to work the company's plantations and industrial enterprises, but unlike plantation workers elsewhere they would not be fed by their employers, so they must continue their gardening, hunting and fishing. They would work to pay an 'adequate tax' for public expenses. They would work '*pro bono publico*', to build schools for their children and the roads, bridges and wharves that were needed only by the company. On top of all that, they would work abroad.

The Maclay Coast was planned as an expanding power. Maclay expected his trading steamer to find uninhabited islands with useful coconut groves, guano or sulphur deposits. He proposed to take possession of such places and develop their resources. It was not clear whether they would belong to the Union of Maclay Coast Papuans or to the company, but exploitation of uninhabited islands presupposed one thing: the introduction of workers. Despite Maclay's conviction that no New Guinean would willingly leave home for long, his people faced an exciting future as pioneers of empire.

Everything depended on the spirit of the enterprise, which Maclay meant to be the very highest. He recognized the need for 'patient treatment' and 'a certain tact' in introducing such changes. The key word in his thought was always 'justice'. When he pleaded the case for Pacific islanders generally, he demanded 'neither pity nor sympathy, but *justice*'. It almost went without saying that Maclay Coast people would be employed 'at a reasonable remuneration and under fair treatment'. Everything then depended on what was meant by 'reasonable' and 'fair'.

Since he did not state how many natives would be employed in the first year (about a hundred seemed a likely minimum), nothing definite could be concluded from the £250 allowed as total payment for their work. The scale of wages for foreign employees gave a clearer idea.

Maclay hoped to pay his debts from this undertaking and find means to provide for the future. He could not expect to become rich on an idealist's salary of £400 per annum. Idealism would be necessary all down the line. The lowest paid of four European tradesmen (probably the blacksmith) would have £75, about three-quarters the wage of his counterpart in Queensland, but unlike the Australian he could not expect his 'keep'. Javanese assistants, required to maintain themselves on £15 a year, would be far behind the experienced kanakas on Queensland canefields, who received £26 with 'all found'.

Maclay described these wages as 'fair but not very high'. Their effect was to be partly offset by a 'co-operative store', indistinguishable from the less progressive 'company store' of other enterprises, where employees would buy their needs at 'reasonable' prices. His proposal that the foreigners' incomes be increased only by bonuses from profits suggested that the natives were going to work harder, to give their overseers a living wage.

Secure in his purity of motive, Maclay saw no dangers in such ideas. He did not shrink from sacrificing his advocacy of the Papuans' undisturbed possession of their land, or his belief that European trade destroyed native values. The objects of the enterprise were too great to be hampered by minor considerations. It would show what could be done with 'the elements of now uncivilized men'. It would prove that the black man, properly treated, could become the white man's friend.

When its influence spread, 'the hitherto frequent massacres would soon become a matter of past history'.

It was to benefit Australia directly, by opening a new field of trade. And Maclay found a long-range advantage for his chosen audience. In time, he suggested, the Great Council of the Maclay Coast might solicit British protection.

He was increasingly elated as he drafted the document. The numbering of his pages became exuberant. Figure four sprouted wings. Figure five wore a festive garland. Figure eight, dominating his last page, became a variant of the ancient Ouroboros, the serpent holding its tail in its mouth, symbol of continuity, self-sufficiency and the Eternal Return. The scrawl beneath suggested the initial 'M' laid on its side, but jagged 'teeth' between the inner strokes produced a disturbing resemblance to the head of a shark.

Hints of British protection seemed superfluous at first glance. The imperial government resisted all attempts to entangle it in New Guinea. If the Maclay Coast achieved its planned political development, there could be no apparent grounds for European intervention. But Commodore Wilson had shown that he personally was ready to take responsibility for New Guinea affairs. Sir Arthur Gordon had twice despatched naval vessels on peaceful missions to the island, and tended to believe that any place would be the better for British supervision, provided he exercised it. Maclay knew both men well enough—Wilson by personal association and Gordon by repute and correspondence—to count on his proposal's having a strong attraction.

When he appealed for help to benefit 'humanity at large', blind spots in the minds of his advisers helped to hide weaknesses in his plan. Commodore Wilson advocated increased wages for Pacific islanders in Queensland. He had no interest in Javanese gardeners, and thought Australian workmen overpaid. Concerned only with native welfare, he was unlikely to relate what Maclay proposed for others to the £250 in trade goods intended to pay an indefinite number of labourers for a year's work. He knew that Maclay wanted conditions on Queensland plantations improved and the islanders' working day limited to eight hours. He had Maclay's assurance that terms of employment would be 'fair' and 'reasonable'. He neither quibbled about words nor dabbled in land questions. He gave the scheme his blessing, and undertook to present it to a suitable capitalist.

Maclay's approach to Sir Arthur Gordon called for tact. Determined to protect the weak against the strong, Sir Arthur still hoped to see Maclay in New Zealand. When he received the Maclay Coast Scheme, the visit was out of the question. It might not have done much good. Sir Arthur had too convincingly bemoaned his limited power. 'Understanding completely the difficult position of "H.M. High Commissioner of the Western Pacific" ', Maclay wrote, 'and finding that it would be a "*mistake*" (Your Excellency kindly *excuse* my sincerity! ...) to expect much help from him, and remembering *my* promise, I have decided to try *myself* to find the means to "protect" the people ...'.

From one quick reading, Sir Arthur judged the scheme fully worthy of support. What Maclay had taught him about the complex attachment of Papuans to their soil did not make him question the company's right and ability to obtain all the land it needed. He did not ask how or for whom Maclay would acquire uninhabited islands. Though he opposed recruiting of Melanesians for Fiji plantations, he saw no objection to their working guano and sulphur in places where the only authority was that of their employer.

His was an intensely aristocratic and romantic mind. The government Maclay described—the lone white idealist, guiding and civilizing unspoiled natives within the framework of their own traditions—appealed powerfully to Sir Arthur. It was what he had tried to do in Fiji, what he would do everywhere if the world were free of inimical Europeans. Besides, there were those blind spots. One had caused him to try to protect Fijians by importing Indian labourers. Another would one day allow him, as chairman of the Pacific Phosphate Company, to believe that the interests of Banabans would best be served by mining out their homeland at derisory compensation and removing them all to some happier island. If the right words were used, Sir Arthur seldom asked awkward questions about things.

He saw only two difficulties in the Maclay Coast Scheme. First, it would be hard to keep other white men out. Second, the financial interests of the founders might be bought or inherited by less idealistic people. Otherwise the scheme, 'feasible in practical execution, ... generously and justly designed', made up for his disappointment over not seeing Maclay in New Zealand. As further compensation, they might soon discuss it face to face in England.

Maclay was not going straight back to New Guinea, as his urgent tone suggested. He had begun negotiations with the Russian Geographical

Society for funds to spend two years in Europe, preparing accounts of his travels for publication. Then he meant to undertake 'a journey in the interior of New Guinea', a full-scale expedition requiring support from some geographical society. The Maclay Coast Scheme could not come to life until both these projects were complete.

Within a few days, before he handed the prospectus to Commodore Wilson, his immediate future had been decided. Five Russian warships were crossing the Pacific. On 27 December 1881 they anchored in Farm Cove.

All parts of his life seemed to come together, as in the symbolism of the Ouroboros. The phase represented by his first ten years in the Pacific was to be completed by publication of his work. He was taking the first realistic steps towards his greatest scientific object, exploration of the New Guinea interior. The vision of his ultimate kingdom was complete, ready to take material form. And here, as though planned, came opportunity to round off the past and animate the future. While Sydney inspected the Russian vessels, entertained the crews and was entertained by shipboard banquets and electrical illuminations, Maclay secured his passage and arranged his affairs for departure.

16: Apotheosis

THE RUSSIAN SQUADRON spent a fortnight at Sydney, visited Tasmania and berthed in Melbourne for another three weeks. Maclay dashed back and forth by train between the mainland cities arranging his accommodation. He was still consulting Wilson and Gordon. He had to arrange the affairs of the biological station, give the Australian Biological Association a full, formal existence. Amid all this activity, he had his biography written.

Ebbe Salvinius Thomassen was at first sight a strange choice as Maclay's biographer. A civil engineer by training, he worked for Ibbotson Brothers of Sheffield as a salesman of railway equipment. He and Maclay had perhaps met at Brisbane in 1880, when Thomassen gave evidence before a parliamentary select committee enquiring into the purchase of steel rails by the Queensland government. Or they might have been introduced later by General Feilding, who like Thomassen was a fellow of the Royal Geographical Society and concerned with railways. In any case, their respective movements prevented their acquaintance from being either long or intimate.

Thomassen had travelled widely in South America, Africa and Australia. He could discuss the beauty of Caribbean islands, the habits of Bolivian dictators, and political relations between Chile and Peru. He was in his way an idealist. He offered his wares less from the wish to make a sale than from personal duty to give the colonies the best and cheapest railways.

All the same, he seemed an unlikely biographer for Maclay. His dealings with the Queensland government were those of a tough and wily operator, adept in exploiting the letter of the law. It had been extremely difficult to bring him before the select committee. When he appeared, his evidence had told the investigators little that they wanted to know. The affair had left the public impression that E. S. Thomassen was rather slippery.

It was also surprising that he found time to write any biography. He lived in a hurry, juggling several great transactions at once, at times prostrated by worry and overwork. In Maclay, however, he found a considerate subject. Maclay supplied all essential documents, including a chronological outline of his life, published English-language summaries of his experiences on the Maclay Coast, a published translation of his account of adventures in Papua-Koviai, extracts from his New Guinea diary, copies of letters to Sir Arthur Gordon, Commodore Wilson and the governor-general of the Netherlands Indies, and the manuscript report on the labour traffic. He also provided a favourite quotation (from Boethlingk's collection of Indian sayings) which introduced Thomassen's work:

> Though the sun were to rise in the west, fire to be cold, and the lotus bloom from out of a rocky bed upon a mountain's top, that which is said by a true man will not remain an empty word.

Thomassen frankly called himself the 'compiler' rather than author of the work. He still made some apparently original contributions. Where Maclay's journal of 1871–72 described how two natives had loosed arrows towards him, Thomassen told of many occasions when Papuans surrounded Maclay 'in great numbers, discharging their arrows', or placed spear-points against his throat. Describing how they invested Maclay with 'the power and attributes of a deity', he related how once, when Maclay had rebuked them for their misdeeds, two earthquake shocks convinced them of his superhuman power to express disapproval. Where Maclay, during his Malay Peninsula travels, had complained only of obstructiveness and deceit, Thomassen hinted at enmity that placed the traveller's life 'in hourly danger'. Maclay had been well aware that the *Sadie F. Caller* was bound for trading and trepang fishing. Thomassen chose to say that his patron had joined the vessel because he knew her to be engaged in the labour traffic.

The work contained nothing to which Maclay objected. He corrected some points concerning his early life, and forbade the authorized biographer to call him 'baron'. Otherwise, he thoroughly approved the text that was hastily completed at Melbourne in February 1882.

The question was: for whom? The compiler proposed to communicate his work to the Royal Geographical Society in London. But the Society did not print extended eulogies on living explorers, and Thomassen's essay gave no account of scientific findings. On the other hand, it might recommend Maclay to the Society, in case Russia failed to support his proposed exploration of New Guinea.

It also suited another purpose. Thomassen suggested that the Maclay Coast people might in time claim a place among the nations and that from the Coast 'conscientious white settlers and traders might enter into peaceful relations also with other parts of the rich island-continent'. While preparing the biography, he sent his employers an equally eulogistic letter about Maclay. It appeared that the Maclay Coast Scheme might be laid before Ibbotson Brothers, 'Globe' Steel Works, Sheffield, a firm previously noted more for business acumen than for philanthropy.

Almost everything was in order when Maclay took a farewell meal with Thomassen and drove with him to the wharf, to board the steam corvette *Vestnik*, 'Messenger'. His professional interests had been placed upon a proper footing. Rumours that he and *Vestnik* were about to annex part of New Guinea for Russia had been squashed. He had comfortable quarters in a large new vessel, a congenial commander, and old acquaintances among the officers. Had he not been ill with fever and neuralgia when he sailed on 24 February 1882, he might have looked forward to a pleasant voyage. But he was weighed down by financial worries, the residue of the past, and among his new beginnings one formed a painfully loose end.

Maclay sometimes crossed the ridge from the biological station to Clovelly, the home of the veteran politician Sir John Robertson. He could not expect to enjoy these pilgrimages much. Sir John was a genial, earnest old man, but not very cultivated. His patriarchal dignity could give way to patriarchal wrath. His speech, impaired by a cleft palate, could be as lurid as any Maclay had heard at sea. Though he tried to be the soul of colonial honour, he bore the moral scars of thirty years in New South Wales politics, and even the principles to which he held true did not endear him to Maclay's other associates. He violently opposed pretensions to Australian aristocracy; he had fathered land laws that set the gentry by the ears; he had been foremost in securing the manhood suffrage that Sir Arthur Gordon called 'mob rule'. To cap it all, he had been premier in 1875, when New South Wales officially asked the British government to annex eastern New Guinea. More than anyone else, Sir John Robertson had caused Maclay to expect the invasion of his country and the extermination of his people.

On the other hand, 'old Sir Jack' always condemned the labour traffic. He favoured science and had taken the initiative in obtaining government funds for the biological station. And he really was a patriarch, with four sons and six daughters. More or less on a duty visit, Maclay had met Sir John's daughter Margaret. She was one 'Australian' who pleased him.

After many years in which he had been attracted only to extremely young girls, he was asking himself whether to marry a youthful but quite mature widow. Margaret Clark, née Robertson, was a woman fit to wear the crowns and coronets he designed. Her placid beauty spoke of a warm, composed nature. She was gentle, accomplished, musical, intelligent but no 'blue-stocking'. Maclay was in love as though for the first time.

He had not decided when he left Australia. The one change in his plans was that his book of travels would be written in Sydney, not in Europe, but there were good practical reasons for that.

At Singapore he had to make up his mind whether to go to China and Japan with *Vestnik* or await another warship for Europe. He was arranging for collections to be shipped to Sydney, placating creditors who had waited four years. One of them was a painful case. Mr Whampoa had died a ruined man, and his son served as clerk in another firm's office. But Ho Ah Yip did not press for the debt, and would no more charge interest than his father had. Maclay was heartened by this contrast with Europeans, who charged 9 per cent and meant to have every penny.

It did not help him much. He owed Whampoa's son only £100, while the Batavia debt alone now amounted to £1030 sterling. And an unexpected letter from his brother Mikhail, otherwise enigmatic, made one thing clear: Ekaterina Semyonovna deplored these debts and would not pay them. 'Tell our dear mother', he replied, 'that although the debts are considerable Miklouho-Maclay will find means to pay them all in time, and in full, and that he will *not* have to be ashamed of them, since he has not spent one kopeck on his own whims or person but has spent money conscientiously for scientific purposes'.

Health and money were still uppermost in his mind when the arrival of the cruiser *Asia*, bound for European Russia via the Suez Canal, decided his next destination. On the way across the Indian Ocean, he became increasingly disturbed by other questions clouding his home-coming.

Mikhail's letter, four months old and written like a riddle, gave no news of their sister. Maclay had heard nothing from Olga herself since January 1880, when a British warship off south-eastern New Guinea had delivered an outdated letter. He had never understood her 'long and stubborn' silences, yet this one seemed particularly strange. Somewhere near Ceylon, he begged her for a few lines to relieve his anxiety.

At Alexandria he had the answer from Meshchersky. Olga's faith that her brother could not die before they met again had been justified. But she herself was dead.

She was said to have died of typhus, a loss no human agency could prevent. Yet guilt permeated her brother's grief. 'It is painful, very painful', he wrote, 'to consider myself, though under duress, *partly* guilty of her death ... It is very burdensome for me to think about this'.

Had he known of the overwhelming burden placed upon Olga, he would have 'abandoned everything' and hurried home to relieve her of it. She would not have died. There would be no need to reproach Sergei and Vladimir by refraining *'for the present'* from reproaching them, or to excuse Mikhail by explaining that at twenty-four he was 'too young to be reproached'. These were the guilty—the brothers who had not saved Olga; Mikhail and their mother, who would not write a line to bring rescue. 'It is bitter, painful to me', he told Mikhail, 'that neither mother nor you informed me *in time*'.

Pathetic improbability—that any message from Russia to the South Seas could have brought him home in time to save his sister. Nor was it true that he had lived in ignorance of her distress. More than three years before, he had learnt of the burdens borne by Olga and their mother. The knowledge had not prevented his undertaking a long voyage, out of reach of letters and cables, or altered what he had to say to those he loved. He had gone on writing to Olga about an Italian villa, about his sufferings in a floating prison, about his low opinion of the human race and especially of women. He had repeatedly promised to come to Russia and change his sister's sad existence, hoped to show her lands where life was bearable. Two more years had passed without his doing anything he promised Olga. She had been warned that he would return only for a visit, because he now belonged to the tropics.

Well, as he said, he would not see Olga, but he would see Mikhail and their mother. Life goes on. Meanwhile, at Alexandria, death was closing in. By the time *Asia* reached that port, a long story of foreign interests in Egypt, an Anglo-French financial condominium, a shaky puppet Khedive, unpaid soldiers and rising nationalist feeling had come to a crisis. On 11 June 1882, under the guns of British and French cruisers, riots in the city had left fifty Europeans dead and scores wounded. The Khedive's men had 'restored order', but rebel soldiers were fortifying strongholds, installing guns that threatened the foreign fleet. *Asia* remained at Alexandria, at the disposal of the Russian consul-general.

Maclay concentrated on his own affairs. A letter from Semyonov-Tianshansky told him that the Geographical Society, unable to provide funds itself for publication of his work, was ready to negotiate for government money. He had to describe the form and character of the projected book. He had also to explain that it would be written in Sydney, not in Europe. Some reasons were those he had given the Australian Biological Association: the proximity of Sydney to his field of research, the value of its museums and library, the convenience of its

biological station as a workplace. He added another, the injurious effect
of a cold climate upon his health. He did not confess that he wanted to
marry an Australian woman.

Not to dwell upon his financial affairs, in miniature as complicated
and hopeless as those of Egypt, it could be said that Maclay told the
Russian Geographical Society almost everything on his mind. He
needed money to pay his debts, money to live while preparing his work
for publication, money to publish and money for the ultimate
expedition. He needed, in the end, a life pension like that granted
Przhevalsky the Asiatic explorer, to save him from grinding poverty or
unsuitable work. He hoped this money would be found in Russia. If
not—.

Threats ran parallel with offers and appeals. If the Russian Geographical Society paid his debts and provided living expenses for two years, he
could give them his book in Russian. Otherwise, he must accept a lump
sum from an English publisher. As a Russian he preferred to explore
the heart of New Guinea under Russian patronage. But the Royal
Geographical Society of London would probably foot the bill. All
financial problems could be solved immediately by putting into
operation 'a vast plan'. But this, the Maclay Coast Scheme, would mean
that his publication must be indefinitely postponed. The undertaking
itself would be 'accompanied by considerable personal risk'. If Maclay
died it was unlikely that anyone else could assemble his records as a
publishable, scientifically sound book. The Russian geographers must
provide for his future or lose the results of work they had sponsored.

He was writing to them again, urgently requesting a frank answer,
when the British sent an ultimatum to the Egyptian rebels. On 11 July
the naval bombardment began. As the forts of Alexandria crumbled,
Maclay wrote to Margaret Clark, asking her to marry him.

Like other non-combatants, *Asia* left Alexandria, but she had orders
to stay in the Mediterranean. After a voyage that changes of vessel and
delays in port had already stretched to nearly five months, Maclay found
himself revisiting his beloved Italy. Transferring at Genoa to the
'ironclad' *Peter the Great*, he had time to visit Florence, where Beccari
directed the museum and Meshchersky was temporarily anchored.
When *Peter* retraced the course of *Asia*, Maclay stayed a few days with
Anton Dohrn at the zoological palace in Naples. It was time well spent,
and so was his time at sea. As the cruiser moved out of the
Mediterranean and homeward via Cadiz, Lisbon, Brest and Cherbourg,
he prepared lectures to be given in Russia.

This Russia to which he was returning after almost twelve years
could hold no surprises. In their hostile way, Australian and British
newspapers had kept him informed about his country's affairs so far as
these appeared on the surface. Six months with Russian naval officers

and consuls had given him the news that did not reach print. He knew he was going home to an atmosphere of repression deeper than that he had left.

Since the assassination of Alexander II in March 1881, a quiet that some described as that of the grave had descended upon Russia. The new tsar had proclaimed his loyalty to the God-given duty of upholding autocracy. The liberal ministers had resigned. People no longer talked about some form of representative national government and a kind of constitution the late tsar was said to have had in his pocket. The bomb that shattered Alexander II had also shattered the revolutionary movement. The people had recoiled in horror. Ex-revolutionaries had betrayed their comrades. Besides, there were more police, more spies, more and better surveillance at every level. Emergency laws provided vast powers to imprison without trial, confiscate property, suppress publications, close schools. University students were under stricter discipline. The powers of local representative bodies were being curtailed. As Maclay approached St Petersburg, harsher censorship was being imposed. The despotism, as ever, was tempered by incompetence and bribery, but he could not expect to find Russia a happy place.

It had 'improved', if that was the word, in ways that were no more likely to please him. The cities were bigger and busier, with more people making a living there or somehow staying alive without a living. More business was done. There were more factories, roads, railways. More bureaucrats drudged or yawned in more offices and more soldiers paraded around more barracks. There was more, in short, of everything he hated and fled in modern Europe. It would take very great personal success to make life in Russia bearable for Maclay. He intended to stay no longer than two months.

There had never been any danger of the cold welcome he predicted. At the first lecture the meeting room of the Geographical Society was crowded out. People stood straining their ears in the corridor and an adjoining room. For three subsequent talks the Society rented the large city lecture hall, and still the gatherings overflowed. The morning after each lecture, Maclay attended the Geographical Society's rooms, to converse with the public and explain drawings and ethnological specimens on display.

Everywhere applause was tumultuous, admiration complete. Those who did not attend his lectures read long, inaccurate accounts of them in the newspapers. He was the talk of a city much given to enthusiasms. People talked about his adventurous journeys, his endless endurance and fortitude, his fascinating sketches of primitive life. They were intrigued by the slow, hesitant speech of one who had almost forgotten his own language and by his shy, retiring personality, accentuated by years among savages. They were moved by the change that sickness and hardship had wrought in this handsome, still-young man. He did not look quite as old as the Singapore correspondent of the *Voice* had led them to expect, but he was painfully worn. His clothes hung loose on an emaciated frame.

His compatriots came to know him as the Papuans did, as the divine *Kaaram-tamo* whose word could always be trusted, whose medicine always cured, whose authority had stopped the wars that ravaged the Maclay Coast. He was the bold captor of the robber chief of Papua-Koviai. He was the watchful humanitarian who warned his people against slave-traders, fought for the defenceless throughout the Pacific, and prevented an English commander from exterminating two thousand people. In a Russia that badly needed examples, he was the perfect hero.

St Petersburg was therefore indignant to hear that he could not obtain a paltry 15 000 roubles to complete his work. Knowing that the Geographical Society could not provide, he had concluded his report with a plea to the Society for funds. In publicly expressing gratitude and admiration, Semyonov-Tianshansky had been forced to explain the position. It made a shocking contrast to Maclay's detailed account of the help he had received elsewhere. The Society was nevertheless applying to the government on Maclay's behalf. Public indignation, though premature, might have a good influence on the finance minister.

While this phase of the campaign went forward, Maclay arranged to be presented to Alexander III. At the request of the empress, he gave a talk to the imperial family and household at Gatchina palace. He went to Moscow, to lecture to an audience of more than seven hundred, to be honoured by scientific societies and by the dignitaries of church and state. On his return to St Petersburg, he learned that the government would grant 20 000 roubles to cover his debts and support him for two years in Sydney. The cost of his publication, estimated at 6000 roubles, was to be met by the emperor personally. While the government subsidy was kept rather quiet, Alexander's generosity was well publicized, immediately increasing his popularity.

The tsar needed an improvement of public esteem, but he never acted from such motives. Nor was he noted for concern with intellectual matters, appreciating the practical uses of science rather than the pure pursuit of knowledge. Some romantic streak in his outwardly stolid nature perhaps responded to Maclay. More probably he gave for the honour of Russia. Rumour had reported that if Maclay could not obtain his necessities from the fatherland he would find them in some other country.

Within the usual limitations of human benevolence, the tsar could be good to those he liked. His government's official benevolence extended only to those who respected the ruling power and served it loyally.

Though no obvious strings were attached to the gifts, Maclay was prepared to serve.

As well as lecturing to the family at Gatchina, he had attended a secret conference there, in which the other participants were the tsar and the minister for the navy. They had decided that shortly after his return to Australia a warship would pick him up at Sydney. On a cruise of the islands he would help in selecting a site for a naval station. He naturally favoured his greatest New Guinea discovery, the fine harbour just north of Astrolabe Bay. After much consideration, he had named it in honour of the tsar's huge, handsome brother Alexei, grand admiral of the Russian navy but more interested in women than in ships.

The New Guinea question was becoming urgent towards the end of 1882. Besides the British and their Australian colonists, Italy was considering official claims. German interests in other islands threatened to expand to the nearest New Guinea coast. On 27 November the influential Augsburg *Allgemeine Zeitung* printed a long article urging German annexation of the New Guinea mainland. Considering the status of the press under Bismarck, this suggestion might have higher origins than it showed. Maclay, who would visit Germany, England and Italy on his way back to Australia, might find opportunities to look into all this.

His crowding concerns left little time for Ekaterina Semyonovna, who had been told that he was staying two months purely for her sake. Still, she was an undemonstrative mother, more than once accused of not caring whether he returned. In the same dreary old apartment she attended to his simple diet and helped preserve the routine that saved him from boring social occasions. They had posed for family photographs. He had sent his love from Moscow. He had been willing to escort her to Kiev if she had consented to go. She was probably content to know that his health was not as bad as the newspapers made out and that his debts were being paid by an unbreakable bank. She also knew that his future might be more settled.

Maclay meant to do great things for his family. He would gladly have transported all his brothers to the South Seas, to establish their kingdoms in Celebes, on Palau, at Sarimbun and on the Maclay Coast. But the older brothers were as independent and uncommunicative as ever. Sergei Miklouho, a judge at Kiev, showed signs of restlessness and discontent, but nobody really knew his feelings and intentions. Vladimir belonged completely to the navy. He was capable of returning to Russia after shipwreck, staying in Odessa without visiting his family, and sailing again for Vladivostok without letting them know. He had never responded to larger ambitions, and now he was married.

There remained Mikhail Miklouho-Maclay, who had become almost what was required. He had qualified as a mining engineer and prepared for further studies in geology and mineralogy. He had learned German as his brother insisted. Almost finished his military service, he could ride and shoot fairly well. From the time Maclay reached Alexandria on his homeward way, Mikhail had obeyed a stream of instructions concerning his brother's affairs. In St Petersburg he attended to everything from the covering of suitcases to correspondence with newspaper editors on Maclay's behalf. Despite the heavy beard that had surprised his famous brother, he was small, quiet, biddable and had not made up his mind about the future. He must learn English, French, topography, drawing and photography. He must be cured of smoking, wasting time and those habits of 'social lying' that Maclay had always scorned and had completely forgotten among primitive peoples. Then he would do very well as a right-hand man. He was offered a choice of Celebes, Palau or the Maclay Coast, with time to decide.

Maclay's time in St Petersburg was extended by neuralgia and rheumatism as well as professional concerns, fêtes and affairs of state. He had not meant to stay so long even if Olga had been there. It was well into December, the season he had dreaded, before he managed to leave for western Europe.

At Berlin he renewed old acquaintanceships, attended scientific meetings and made propaganda for the Sydney biological station. The press noted the interest German scientists took in the subject of New Guinea, but Maclay could have no difficulty in discovering that this interest had not risen to the top. Germany had powerful overseas trading companies, with plans and wishes of their own. It had societies devoted to the modern faith that colonies guaranteed national greatness and that no truly civilized country could refrain from civilizing others. Prince Bismarck still thought colonies a preposterous swindle, expensive and troublesome in themselves and likely to complicate international affairs. He was well content to see other powers embroiled with remote countries and peculiar peoples while Germany grew strong at home.

At Antwerp Maclay reached an arrangement with Hendrick-Jan Ankersmit, who promptly passed out of his life for ever. His next stop was Paris.

It was no accident that St Petersburg rumour had mentioned France as the country most likely to support his future and publish his book. He still sent ethnographical papers to Berlin. Like most Europeans, he had become more pro-French and anti-German since 1870. The Paris geographers had followed his adventures with acclaim, and the French anthropologists gladly published the one article he sent them. Paris also had the largest and most influential Russian expatriate community in western Europe. Ivan Turgenev and the friendly geographer M. I. Veniukov were members. So was the anthropologist Joseph Deniker, prepared to interpret Maclay's work for French readers. An important point was that Prince Meshchersky, never much at home anywhere, felt most at home in Paris. Maclay's ground had been prepared by a man whose marriage made him a remote connection of Meshchersky, the historian Gabriel Monod.

Though his father-in-law, the aristocratic Russian socialist Alexander Herzen, had thought it a comedown to be connected with an 'honest conservative' of middle-class origin, Monod met the prevailing standards for a good liberal and ardent humanitarian. He detested all excesses of Right or Left. He believed in rational liberty, with stricter censorship and greater powers for the police. He believed in tolerance, but as a leading Protestant and member of the party of order he could not tolerate militant atheism and bloodthirsty socialism. His loathing of war was balanced by distrust for pacifism and admiration for schoolboy soldiers who would some day recover Alsace and Lorraine. His sympathy for the working class excluded 'democratic and levelling sentiments'. As an educationist he railed against 'the chimaera of equality'. The same sense that the human world was naturally divided into superior and inferior marked his attitude to peoples who resisted European rule. When it seemed to him good that England should defeat the Mahommedan world in Egypt, he felt it a strange injustice that English liberals, instead of approving French expansion, should practically cheer for Madagascans and Tonkinese.

Yet he might have been waiting for Maclay. The mind that welcomed Islam's humiliation by Christian arms deplored 'fanatical missionaries' let loose on Pacific islands. The patriot who wanted France to increase her trade and self-esteem by conquests in Asia and Africa condemned the violent, greedy traders of the South Seas. His comfortable life included a nostalgia for a simpler world, free from 'the excessive development of wants and appetites . . . the outcome not only of a democratic form of government but of modern life itself'. All around he saw 'intellectual and moral anarchy', government paralysed by petty rivalries, society disintegrating in crime, godlessness and unrest. Literature was a deluge of filth, dominated by Zola's obscene 'realism'; the theatre abdicated its duty to elevate the spirit; in painting he faced 'the puerilities of the Impressionist school', with its vulgar human types and trivial subjects. Only in science did he find the health and order he craved. Maclay came from science and a cleaner world, bearing truth, nobility, salvation.

How and when they first met was not clear. While *Peter the Great* lay at Brest and Cherbourg, Maclay might easily have visited Paris. The article Monod had published in the *Nouvelle Revue* nevertheless depended heavily on Thomassen's compilation. It retold the same stories, sometimes improving on them. It summarized Maclay's research and adventures and paid tribute to his 'lofty, ... austere conception of the duties of science'. But Monod did not disguise his belief that the man was more important than the work.

The man was not the Maclay who had seemed eternally familiar to others after a few hours' acquaintance, the lively conversationalist who captivated Odoardo Beccari, or the bold enthusiast who entertained Luigi D'Albertis with accounts of revolver play. Yet Monod, too, felt he intimately knew this 'exceptional being'. He knew Maclay's 'horror of the first personal pronoun', his imperturbable coolness and 'searching knowledge of character'. He recognized, as though he had always known it, 'this patience, this gentleness, this slowness in his movements, gestures and speech, this frail appearance, this absence of all outward manifestations of passion'. He understood how the people of the Maclay Coast, recognizing spiritual power, had been raised in the social and religious scale to the extent of making Maclay their ruler and their god.

Monod nevertheless realized that he spoke of a man, to be brought within the compass of ordinary readers. Maclay was neither a seeker of glory nor a victim of tragic experience, choosing hardship and danger as a refuge from the past. He did not represent the pessimist's revolt against 'civilization's vanities and the illusions of life'. Nor did he share the eighteenth century's will to find in modern savages the primitive innocence of mankind. In all his actions the first motive was 'a faith, a *creed* of science' that supported him in unprecedented trials. His other great support came from the philosophy of Immanuel Kant. In sickness and discouragement he solaced himself with the critique of pure reason and practical reason. In solitude and pain he contemplated 'those two things which Kant declared the sublimest that the world contained—the star-crowned heaven above his head and the sentiment of duty at the bottom of his heart'.

In Paris it seemed expedient to point out that Maclay's background in German culture had not made him German. The professor, an Anglophile, detected something English. But Maclay remained 'one of the most remarkable types of the Slav race', loving science not as westerners did but with 'an almost mystic love', fatalistic not as an Englishman might be but with a Russian's 'undeceived, inexhaustible resignation, and a passive, joyless heroism'.

'This man who has elected to live among savages ...', Monod testified, 'is the sincerest man of ideals and the most consistent one it has been my fortune to meet. At the same time this gentle and patient idealist is a man of indefatigable activity. Idealist and man of action—is that not the definition of a hero? M. de Maclay is a hero in the noblest and broadest sense of the word'.

It strongly resembled the description of a hero that Maclay had written fourteen years before, defining for the infatuated Auguste

Seligman everything that he was not. He did not repudiate it now, for if it were not true of him he would have lived in vain. Nor did he speak up for those who were discounted in his praise. He did not draw attention to his German great-grandfather, the prominent physician. He did not object when his New Guinea friends were described as somehow 'incomplete' human beings, or as a 'childish people, used to deceit and trickery'. He established close relations with Monod, and kept copies of the article for future use.

The visit was too hurried for him to address the Paris geographical and anthropological societies. He did give an informal talk to the *Cercle Saint-Simon*, the club of Professor Monod's newly-founded *Société Historique*, delighting an audience that might well have included such thinkers as Ernest Renan and Hippolyte Taine. He also called on Ivan Turgenev, who remembered the young explorer who had visited him at Weimar in 1870.

It was a sad occasion, as Maclay recalled it. They sat in one of the small, cluttered rooms the old writer occupied in the home of his long-beloved Pauline Viardot and her husband. Conversation flagged when Turgenev had asked about Maclay's travels and plans and recounted details of his own illness. But then, Turgenev felt he could neither stand nor walk. He was facing surgery for neuroma. It seemed cruel for Maclay to ask him what was the best time of life—youth, maturity or old age. It seemed crueller still, when poor old Ivan Sergeevich had talked about it and about, and reached the expected conclusion, for Maclay to remind him that Schopenhauer had said that same thing more concisely.

Maclay did not want to be old, not even to escape the terrible Russian 'spleen' that Ivan Sergeevich claimed to have left behind. As he walked back along the Rue de Douai, he was returning to a life too full to welcome the fateful acceleration of personal time that Turgenev allegedly preferred to the long, unemployable hours of youth. He did not expect to enter for many years that tranquil harbour without desires that Turgenev, or Schopenhauer, or Plato, or the eastern sages equated with happiness. He had many desires, and expected to have more when those were satisfied. His desires were taking him now to England, for the most demanding part of his journey.

17: White Ants

THE TSAR'S INSTRUCTIONS made no difference to what must be done in England. There might never be a naval station in New Guinea. In any case, to avoid arousing British suspicion, Maclay must act as though the Gatchina conference had never occurred.

His fame as scientist and humanitarian placed him personally above suspicion. He had friends in organizations devoted to colonial questions and the welfare of aboriginal peoples. He was known as an associate of Sir Arthur Gordon and Admiral Wilson, both then in London. His letters to the high commissioner had made his name and opinions familiar to the Colonial Office. The real danger to his mission lay in the Australian colonists and ex-colonists who might happen to be in London, the noisiest exponents of the foreign threat to New Guinea. But even among these natural enemies he had friends and admirers.

One thing that might have alarmed some Englishmen, had they known it, was that Maclay had attracted the notice of Madame Olga Novikov. This charming idealist, acting in London as representative of what she called 'unofficial Russia', had an emotional attachment to Russian tradition and prestige. Her efforts to reconcile Liberal England and autocratic Russia usually led to the conclusion that the interests of Britain and the world were best served by existing Russian policies. But her humanitarian interests were too wide for anyone to be surprised when she took up the cause of the Pacific islanders. Both friends and enemies believed she had great influence with Gladstone. She had promptly sent the prime minister a copy of Gabriel Monod's article. He had read it with much interest, regretting only that he missed in Maclay the Christian element that he himself prized above all. Still, there was a 'brotherhood' between Maclay and the martyred Bishop Patteson.

Gladstone reciprocated by sending Madame Novikov a biography of the bishop, and that was all she got for the moment.

Early in 1883 suspicious English minds concerned about New Guinea were not preoccupied with Russia. They had hints of what Italy was thinking. Though the private ambitions of 'New France' had failed disastrously in New Ireland and elsewhere, and its founder sat in an old French gaol, many still feared official French initiatives in Melanesia. What most alarmed the Royal Colonial Institute was the propaganda in Germany, especially that of the *Allgemeine Zeitung.*

By 4 January the secretary of state for colonies could assure the agitators that there was no danger of German action. About the same time, he assured Maclay that Britain planned no annexations in the Pacific, a fact as pleasing to Lord Derby as to his visitor.

Maclay pursued his plans with all his disciplined calm. As well as visiting scientific colleagues, he contacted people who might take an interest in the Maclay Coast Scheme. In London the most important of these was a friend and brother-in-law of Professor Monod.

Alexander von Glehn, by origin a nobleman from one of Russia's Baltic provinces, was an Englishman by adoption. As a practical humanitarian he had faced difficulty and danger to take medical aid to the wounded during the Franco-Prussian war. As treasurer of the French Protestant relief society in London, he had made sure that the wounded received copies of the gospels and appropriate tracts. In less troubled times, he was an energetic businessman, interested in the market for tropical produce. He entered wholeheartedly into Maclay's plans and became a useful informant on their commercial prospects.

The really challenging visits were paid at the Red House, Ascot, where Sir Arthur Gordon awaited a new appointment after two unhappy years in New Zealand.

Maclay and Sir Arthur had exchanged many letters. They had exchanged photographs, as Maclay always did with those who were important in his life. For almost eight years they had not met. In 1883, after all Sir Arthur had suffered from colonists, naval officers and unappreciative officials, a meeting with Maclay was like that of twin souls long kept apart.

They sat in the study of the Red House, two slight, intense men, talking about the distant Pacific. Sir Arthur's one fear was that the Maclay Coast Scheme might be born too late. Everyone knew that Maclay would spend two years writing a book sponsored by the highest authority in Russia. But he should not delay in visiting his people, to give them moral support and advice on how to protect themselves against whites until his permanent return.

Maclay could truthfully say he meant to do exactly as Sir Arthur advised. It was never necessary to tell this sympathetic, admirable man that he would be returning to New Guinea to help choose a Russian naval station.

That was just as well. Sir Arthur detested the Australian colonists, who offended him morally, socially and politically. He imagined no worse fate for any coloured people than that of being handed over to 'the tender mercies of the Australian mob', with its 'pothouse politicians'. He nevertheless agreed that the presence of a hostile power in New Guinea would be dangerous for colonial trade and communications and none too safe for the colonies themselves. Regarding British control of the island as undesirable but almost inevitable, he favoured establishment of a crown colony, ruled, if possible, by someone like himself. If Britain continued to reject full responsibility, the next best solution was a British protectorate ruled by someone like himself.

Recognition of Baron Maclay as someone like himself made it impossible for Sir Arthur to doubt the humanitarian success of the Maclay Coast Scheme. He did not dislike commercial and industrial concerns in themselves. Controlled by men of inborn principles and power, all human activities could be turned to good. Consequently his well-founded fear of subjecting native peoples to the selfish, ignorant, financially-interested oligarchies of Australia was balanced by faith in the protective and civilizing mission of business enterprises run by titled gentlemen. He had already suggested officially that the western Pacific could be administered on Britain's behalf by a chartered company. In retirement from official duties, he would reappear as chairman of the Pacific Islands Company, seeking, in conjunction with a firm whose vessels had engaged in violent and notorious blackbirding, to obtain a 'joint domination over the Pacific'. Thwarted in attempts to turn the Solomon Islands into 'a small sort of British North Borneo', administered by his company, he would concentrate on doing good to the Banabans by taking the ground from under their feet. Sir Arthur's brilliant, idealistic mind contained chasms which swallowed the weaknesses and dangers of Maclay's proposals.

Uncertainty clouded their joint future. Sir Arthur was too disgusted, and too unpopular, to return to New Zealand. The government of his close friend Mr Gladstone had no Pacific colony available for him to rule. For the time being he remained titular high commissioner, with a hope of divorcing that office from any governorship and expanding its power. He could promise no lasting official collaboration with Maclay.

What he had to give sufficed for the present. Maclay had business with a man in Aberdeen. He could go there with enthusiastic support from a brother of the earl.

The heart of William Mackinnon, the capitalist before whom Admiral Wilson had placed the Maclay Coast Scheme, was fixed on far places and vast, romantic enterprises. As a young man, he had escaped from a merchant's office to become a trader about the Bay of Bengal. Within ten years he had founded the steamship line that had grown into the British India Steam Navigation Company. He would never go out there again, but he befriended those who went and dared mightily.

He had collaborated with 'Chinese' Gordon in obtaining a huge Zanzibar concession that the British government refused to sanction. He assisted the formation of the British North Borneo Company, which was not doing very well. Mesmerized by H. M. Stanley's name, he had subscribed capital for King Leopold's International Association of the Congo, which was doing worse in ways that would have horrified William Mackinnon. Early in 1883 his enthusiasm centred on plans for a canal from the Mediterranean to the Gulf of Aqaba.

This grey, lonely little sixty-year-old Scot, educated by the Bible and the village elementary school, was intensely moral. When famine struck in India, and other carriers charged famine prices, young Mackinnon had lowered his rates. When fellow bank directors contemplated a fiddle, old Mackinnon resigned from the board. Politically, he was an innocent. On the personal level, he could support a disloyal hypocritical spendthrift for years, without becoming embittered or wiser. His ideal business enterprise would abolish slavery, eliminate trading monopolies and ensure equal rights for all peoples. It was hard to say which presented the greater marvel, his ability to make money or his ability to keep it.

It was a pity the Maclay Coast Scheme said nothing about religion. Mackinnon always hoped his enterprises would help bring people to Christianity. It was clear, too, that the company must be a strict monopoly, but this perhaps mattered less in a country that as yet had neither trade nor government. A vast plan for preventing evil and civilizing God's untaught children, with profits to be gathered on the way, might have been made especially for William Mackinnon. Add the allure of beautiful, savage places that he would never visit. Add the personality of Maclay, the great man with a great cause, through whom Mackinnon could live noble adventures and wield benevolent power. As he had expected, Maclay came away from Aberdeen almost sure he could count on William Mackinnon.

He paid other satisfactory visits. When he left London in mid-January, he carried a letter from Sir Arthur Gordon, asking the new commodore of the Australia station to provide a passage to the Maclay Coast if a warship was going that way. He had arranged, through the Russian ambassador, for the British government to 'introduce' him officially to the governors of all Australian colonies. Lord Derby promptly sent off a circular despatch to secure the highest consideration for Maclay in Australia.

Maclay's affairs in England had been conducted with all the *sang froid* and 'searching knowledge of character' that Gabriel Monod admired. He had not suggested to the English, as he had to Russians, that the scheme would be dangerous for him, a distressing interruption to his scientific work, and an unsuitable, money-making business equivalent to 'becoming a planter'. He was breaking no promises. His hint of a future British protectorate was too much qualified to count as a promise. He had told no lies. Nobody had asked him anything that required a false answer. Knowing that it went against his nature to speak falsely or evasively, he could not attempt to lie. If awkward questions arose in the future, his answers would exercise the enquirer's imagination, like those he gave the inhabitants of the Maclay Coast. Or they would amount, like his response to Russians who mentioned the Sea of Okhotsk, to an implicit challenge to prove that his words and actions had ever meant what they seemed to mean.

Of course nothing was settled. Maclay had a wonderful group of players studying prospective roles. The backer in St Petersburg might decide upon a completely different show.

On his way east, Maclay stayed a few days with an occasional correspondent, the Marquis Giacomo Doria of Genoa. The Marquis, a generous patron of Beccari and D'Albertis, had founded a splendid museum that Maclay wished to see. He also stood at the centre of Italian colonial ambitions, but in Genoa Maclay heard nothing to cause apprehension.

At Naples he boarded a French ship for Port Said, where luggage forwarded from Russia awaited him. Only the luggage was going direct to Australia. Maclay's passage had been booked on another vessel for Batavia.

St Petersburg had decided that the choice of a naval station should not be delayed. Further consideration also showed that for a warship to collect Maclay at Sydney would be unnecessarily expensive and conspicuous. In Batavia nobody would ask questions, and the corvette *Skobelev* was expected to be there when the Queensland mail steamer *Chyebassa* arrived.

These revised orders suited Maclay. On the *Chyebassa* he had a good cabin to himself, with the Russian navy paying all additional expenses. Collections kept in hock at Batavia for nearly eight years could be inspected and sent to Sydney. After six years of neglect he could do something about the Celebes land. The new plan delayed his reunion with Margaret Clark, who had promised to marry him, but he might visit his friends on the Maclay Coast much earlier than English friends expected. He consulted the Kantian rules of conduct and cheerfully did his duty to his people and Alexander III.

His spirits rose with the temperature. He had endured a European winter that even in Italy made him appreciate the furs brought from Russia. As the *Chyebassa* neared the Equator, he exulted: 'It's warm, *glorious* ... I feel at home!' 'Here in the islands, in the tropics', he told Mikhail a month later, 'it is *so good* that you, brother, will never regret it if you follow my example'.

By then he was halfway to New Guinea, under the pennant of Vice-Admiral Kopitov, on a vessel that proved to be none other than the old *Vityaz*, remodelled and renamed. His transfer had not been entirely smooth sailing. Maclay was to tell how he had unexpectedly learned of a Russian warship's presence, hurried aboard and persuaded the admiral to go to New Guinea. As the admiral saw it, Maclay had at first seemed eager to join the cruise that headquarters had ordered. Then he had raised difficulties about urgent private affairs and the cramped conditions aboard a warship. Dumbfounded at this reluctance to accede to 'the highest command', Kopitov had used all his powers of persuasion to snare this strange bird. However it was in reality, each was satisfied that the other knew nothing about the arrangement that brought them together.

To obtain the space and privacy he had been promised, Maclay slept in a temporary shelter on deck, convincing himself that life in bivouac increased his well-being. He could not but feel some mental discomfort. He had tried to instil in his young brother the absolute truthfulness essential for a Miklouho-Maclay, pointing to the example he set. Now he must pretend to find himself 'quite unexpectedly' aboard *Skobelev*, and warn Mikhail to tell nobody but their mother.

He always enjoyed marking his letters 'Confidential' or 'Secret'. At times he had done so without apparent need. Now he could be mysterious in earnest and with a clear conscience; everything would be explained to Mikhail some day. In other quarters, he adopted a different policy.

His visit to Batavia was no secret. He had already advised English scientists of this change, mentioning the need to look after his collections. On the way to Makassar he had realized the futility of further secrecy. He had left a mail steamer full of 'Australians' and their parish-pump curiosity. They would discover his transfer to *Skobelev* and promptly embark on suspicions and rumours. Then there were the Dutch, who naturally knew the corvette's route through the islands and were making themselves useful on the way. They might not care where the Russians were going, but they could not be forced to keep quiet about it. Hemmed in by the human weakness for gossip and surmise, Maclay decided to be frank. He took out his monogrammed, coroneted paper and wrote direct to Admiral Wilson.

The discussions in London had convinced him he should lose no time in informing his people of his plans. He was sure Wilson would be glad to hear of the 'happy chance' that took him to New Guinea for a few days. If Wilson would pass on the news, Sir Arthur Gordon would be equally pleased. Maclay could not write much—the new engines and screw shook the old *Vityaz-Skobelev* abominably—but the cheerful simplicity of his note, and his memories of their weeks together on H.M.S. *Wolverene*, showed he had nothing to hide from Wilson. It was even true, in a way. Kopitov himself had been surprised. Not informed of Maclay's change of route, and considering a chance meeting almost impossible, the Russian admiral had been about to visit New Guinea without his famous passenger.

The Bam volcano was erupting, as when Maclay left his coast in 1877, but Port Konstantiñ was not shaking when *Skobelev* anchored late in the afternoon of 17 March 1883. Otherwise, too, the arrival of the *tamo-Russ* was quiet. The vessel's smoke had surely been watched for miles, yet there was no beating of slit gongs, no rush of people to the beach. Maclay went ashore, met a few Gumbu acquaintances, and ordered provisions for the ship. Afraid of fever, he returned to the corvette before dark.

The atmosphere was strange next morning, when he landed near Bongu with Admiral Kopitov and several officers. The people who appeared were friendly in a casual way, asking questions, giving news, complaining about earthquakes. Their joy fell far short of Maclay's expectations. Nothing quite matched the scene he had pictured. The village was smaller, with half its former area overgrown by jungle and the remainder looking neglected. Nearly all the young men, the most decorative part of the population, were attending a feast at Bogadjim. Those who stayed home reminded Maclay of Europeans in rags. White visitors since 1877 had found the natives making the usual brave show to impress their small world. Warned of Maclay's coming, his people had faithfully carried out the only ritual he had taught them. The young women were hidden in the bush. The men who met the Russians were unarmed, unkempt, undecorated.

And they were unfamiliar. Maclay saw young faces that meant nothing to him, adult faces to which he could attach no names. His nation of friends seemed reduced to a few old people who wept as they recited the names of the dead. One of the names was 'Tui'.

With Kopitov looking on, Maclay presented the natives with Malay bush knives, red cloth, beads and mirrors, purchased by the navy in Hong Kong and Makassar. He announced his own gifts—new plants, a young bull, a heifer and three goats, also paid for by Russia. Then he visited Bugarlom. He had left a large house, containing many articles he would need on his return. He considered this a test of his people's honesty and friendship as well as their belief in his magic. As he had learned from an account of the *Dove* expedition, the house had stood intact for at least ten months after his departure, guarded by villagers who seemed proud to look after it. His authorized biography and his St Petersburg lectures had cited this result.

Now nothing remained but a few house-stumps in the overgrown plantation. Building materials, household utensils, furniture, tools— everything had vanished.

Maclay had 'no time for reflection'. To reassert ownership, he had some ground cleared and seeds planted. When he paused, other thoughts crowded out the question of what had happened at Bugarlom. He pondered the lack of any 'friendly demonstration' on his arrival, and the fact that he himself expressed no particular pleasure. There was the sadness of familiar paths choked by jungle, the sight of ruined Gorendu, a desolation from which he fled back to the ship. He never asked what had become of his property. No doubt 'white ants' had eaten the house. But termites do not eat pots and pans and metal tools. It would have been easy to blame the European visitors who figured in old Saul's rambling stories, the people Maclay had long before likened to white ants. Maclay did not attempt it.

Throughout his crowded day at Bongu, he alternated between feeling 'at home' and a sense of loss and disintegration. There were so many unknown faces where every tree was like an old friend, so many huts with bushes pushing through collapsed roofs. At times his last visit seemed 'only yesterday', but he no longer understood the situation. He could not find out where the Gorendu people had gone. When he tried to engage an interpreter for the northern islands, he discovered that Bongu was not on friendly terms with the Contented Men and did not know their dialects. There was too much happening for him to analyse his feelings or to re-experience the tranquillity that formed his dearest memory. He concentrated on distributing seeds, telling the villagers how to plant them and how to care for the frightening new animals.

He witnessed much excitement and comedy provided by the sailors, the natives and the cattle brought from Ambon. When the pledges of Russo-Papuan friendship had finally escaped into the jungle, Maclay stood alone in the dusk, contemplating the empty yard. It was impossible to say how long the goats would last—the Papuans refused to touch the milk. He could not be sure that Saul would give the coffee beans to the right people or that the mountain men would plant them. He was leaving a hastily-cleared, unfenced garden that the pigs would probably root up. He had given the people further instructions on how to behave if the *tamo-Inglis* came. He had told them, no doubt, that he would return to live among them. He did not record their response.

Skobelev slipped away at dawn, without a farewell. Kopitov was anxious to leave a coast that had a dreadful reputation among those concerned with the health of Russian sailors. Maclay had to convince him that to be sure of avoiding bloodshed among the Contented Men it was necessary to find an interpreter. He had to emphasize that obtaining a linguist from Bilbil would take no more than an hour.

It took less. Bilbil greeted the Russians with all the enthusiasm that had been missing at Bongu. A crowd shouted greetings as Maclay's boat approached. But he did not land among them. He awaited the canoes coming out to meet him. Kain was there with his friend Hassan, who had accompanied Maclay on those memorable cruises in 1877. With no time for 'superfluous conversation', Maclay suggested that they all follow him back to the ship to get tobacco and nails. Kain scrambled into the boat, bursting with talk, but Maclay had no time to answer his questions.

On deck, the Bilbil men were worried by the crowd of sailors and the noisy engines. Most of them took their presents and left. Maclay only needed Kain and Hassan; he had to put up with Maramai, who failed to go home with the rest. These three, he assured himself, really wanted to accompany him to Sek.

Yet when the ship began to move he had to hang on to Kain. Hassan took advantage of the struggle and leapt into the sea. The only one to take it calmly was Maramai, who seemed not to understand what was happening.

Maclay had warned his people against white men who would lure them aboard ships, hold them by force and carry them off against their will. But the spirit and motive of his actions assured him he did no harm. His friends seemed to cheer up as *Skobelev* steamed north. Passing Uremu, they pointed it out and repeated what he had told them six years before: 'Maclay's island. Maclay's coconuts. Maclay will come and build a house on Uremu'. They particularly wanted the ship to take the narrow channel between Graged and the mainland, where it would be easy to swim ashore, but the admiral thought it too risky.

The Bilbil men stayed quietly aboard the corvette when Maclay and some officers went to examine the harbour. They waited until the steam launch was out of sight. They waited for a canoe to approach. Then they jumped overboard. The canoe picked them up and made for Sek.

Annoyed by the news on his return, Maclay was determined to get hold of some native. He cruised about in the steam launch until a canoe with two men appeared. Somehow the vessels were brought together. One of the islanders escaped. The other was dragged aboard the launch and carried to *Skobelev*.

A man who spoke only dialects that Maclay did not understand was useless as an interpreter. In taking him prisoner (a fact he never tried to disguise), Maclay hoped to make the Bilbil men return to the ship. It looked as though the Sek people would have to give up Kain and Maramai in exchange for their fellow villager. But Maclay's third night at home was approaching. Further action had to wait. While the Sek man was fêted and guarded by the crew, Maclay admired the magnificent sunset over mounts Kant and Schopenhauer.

Exploration next day revealed another deep anchorage and a river navigable for some distance from its mouth. The survey went ahead quickly and peacefully. But no canoes came out. The few natives seen were alarmed, kept their distance and disappeared quickly. When Maclay took his prisoner to Sek village, he found that the people had gone in a hurry, leaving valuables in open huts. Somewhere in the jungle, Kain and Maramai and the man who had escaped from the captured canoe were telling their experiences.

Keeping the prisoner obviously did more harm than good. He was set free on the beach, but presents and pampering had so won him that he loitered for hours near the boat that had brought him home. On the way to the ship, Maclay's boat fell in with several canoes. He tried the men in the Bongu dialect; they seemed to understand part of what he said; they understood what he expressed in tobacco, cloth and beads. At night he had the pleasure of seeing the home fires burning on Sek.

When Maclay went alone to the village its inhabitants soon appeared. Kain was among them, happily pressing Maclay's arm and explaining that only fear of being without Maclay had made him desert. Now he would go anywhere Maclay wished. So they visited a cannibal village on the mainland, learned more about the use of human flesh, and bought some native weapons for Grand Duke Alexei. They did not meet Maramai. He was perhaps a little slow, but once an idea got into his head it stayed there.

The Bilbil men were not invited back to the ship. They could find their own way home, and *Skobelev* was bound in the opposite direction. Determined to leave, Kopitov resisted Maclay's contention that a Russian ship should chart the whole harbour. High winds delayed their departure just long enough for Maclay to acquire another uninhabited island.

Sometimes he felt the Sek people gladly gave him the island of Malaspena. Sometimes he believed they never claimed it. Either way, he adopted the place and delighted them by promising to return and settle there. He did not warn the Contented Men that their home stood a chance of becoming a military objective in European wars. The possibility had no place in his vision.

Kopitov believed that, hydrographically, nothing better for their purpose could be found. Such a harbour would be considered splendid anywhere. The weather was fine throughout their visit. Maclay's

account of the small, scattered island communities, speaking different
languages and constantly at war with the mainland people, suggested
that Europeans could easily take over. The admiral predicted vast wealth
in sea produce, timber, minerals. He was assured that no government or
trading company had any interest in this coast. He nevertheless thought
Port Alexei unsuitable as a naval station. It was too remote from
shipping routes and places inhabited by Europeans. Though *Skobelev*
remained free of sickness so far, the climate was undoubtedly one of the
hottest and unhealthiest on earth. The people were totally savage,
unable to supply the ship with any food but coconuts. In any case, the
admiral had no authority to raise the flag. His instructions required him
to inspect several other places mentioned by Maclay.

On the way north, they visited the Admiralty Group and assessed a
large anchorage that the *Challenger* expedition had surveyed. They
investigated the Hermit Islands. They called at Palau. There were solid
objections to all the potential naval stations. With nothing definite done,
the trip had been rather a disappointment to Maclay. Yet the unsatisfactory outcome had its compensations. He would not be returning to
Sydney as the man who had helped Russia annex north-eastern New
Guinea, but the question apparently remained open. He could hope that
Papuan cultivation of new food plants, and the multiplication of cattle
and goats, would benefit his friends, prove his country's suitability for
agriculture and stock, and make it more attractive as a naval station.
Besides, the voyage produced another important friendship, leading to
exchange of signed photographs.

Their conversations had given Kopitov the highest opinion of
Maclay's knowledge and enterprise. He was indebted to Maclay for
information about the islands and their inhabitants, black and white. He
gladly acknowledged Maclay's services as interpreter and general
co-operation in the mission. And he was thoroughly imbued with
Maclay's opinions. Maclay had convinced him that attacks by islanders
on Europeans almost invariably resulted from the violence, greed and
fraudulent dealings of the whites. As firmly as Maclay, he condemned
the hasty, unjust 'punishment' inflicted by British, German and American warships. He too wished to do his part in protecting the weak against
the strong.

In Admiral Kopitov's case, however, 'the weak' primarily meant
Russia, while 'the strong' evoked thoughts of England, the arrogant,
implacable enemy. He brooded particularly on the unjust and inhumane
effect of international laws that closed neutral ports to the warships of
belligerents, giving further advantages to the power with the most ships
and colonies. Though this injustice could not be removed without
changing international law, he had ideas for circumventing its effect.

No speck of land, however remote and savage, should be dismissed as useless to Russia. Wherever possible, Russians should set up as planters and traders, secretly maintaining provision depots, coaling stations, even strongholds and assembly points for the fleet. They could do it in the Admiralty and Hermit groups and the Palaus, perhaps in Spain's neglected Philippines or in isolated parts of the East Indies, where the Dutch made land available to any European. If they were attacked, well and good: it would make a precedent for Russian attacks on the private property of enemy subjects. Maclay's acquisitions of land had shown the way. Kopitov hoped to see many enterprising Russians sent out to emulate and develop the example. He already knew of one potential helper, the Polish naturalist Jan Kubary, resident in the Palau Islands and regarded by Maclay as a trustworthy man.

Whoever owned these ideas in the first place, they became common property. Maclay and the admiral agreed about almost everything they were free to discuss. One exception was the secrecy of their mission, which Kopitov believed had been maintained. Maclay still feared that something would go wrong, and while waiting at Hong Kong for a ship to Australia he was able to say 'I told you so' to an admiral. On 4 April an obscure police magistrate, sent by the Queensland government, had raised a flag at Port Moresby and proclaimed eastern New Guinea a possession of Great Britain.

Virtually sure that Lord Derby, that sincere, high-minded man, would not abuse his trustfulness, Maclay concluded that this move originated entirely in Queensland. His predictions were equally reasonable: Britain would repudiate the annexation at first, but after a while would agree to it. 'I believe', he wrote to Kopitov, 'that the English government will not wish to fall out with the Australian colonies over New Guinea and that by and by it will consent . . ., on the pretext that it cannot allow another power to assert itself so close to Australia'.

He underestimated London's reluctance to assume responsibility for New Guinea. He overestimated his own influence when he attributed the whole *contretemps* to his change of vessel at Batavia. Without knowing what lay behind Queensland's action, he felt vaguely injured by prejudice and rumour. He did not renounce his plans or retreat to silence and obscurity. As well as reporting to Grand Duke Alexei, he vigorously resumed interventions with British officialdom.

Sir Arthur Gordon needed no reminder of his pledge to exclude firearms and liquor from New Guinea, or of what he had said on the right of natives to their land. Maclay's despairing reference to himself as 'a voice crying in the wilderness', and his description of Sir Arthur as 'a Friend of Justice . . . not afraid to take the part of the weak', came too late to influence events. At the first news of the Queensland action, Sir

Arthur had protested officially to Lord Derby. Privately, he had overwhelmed Gladstone with strongly-worded arguments against giving Queensland its way. From the dangers of allowing a colony to force the imperial hand to the threat of conflict with a non-existent Dutch administration in western New Guinea, from the brutal and rapacious nature of colonists to the fear that they would involve England in crippling expense, Sir Arthur left no question of politics, morality or finances untouched. He could not endure the thought that Gladstone, architect of generous plans for India and Egypt, might hand over the millions of New Guinea to 'those who will despise—use—and destroy them'. Without a word from Maclay, Sir Arthur had never felt more strongly or deeply on any question.

Newspapers announced Sir Arthur's appointment to Ceylon, a post suiting his style of government and one he saw as a necessary step in becoming viceroy of India. Maclay still hoped rather hopelessly that he was not lost to the Pacific. In a further monogrammed, coroneted letter he approached Sir Arthur confidentially about more South Seas affairs.

David Dean O'Keefe was to be arraigned before a British naval court, charged with innumerable crimes against islanders. Maclay showed no knowledge of this. Somewhere he had met an unfortunate Englishman who wanted to submit written evidence against O'Keefe and had chosen Maclay as a channel to authority. Maclay now forwarded these documents, with his personal endorsement of their contents. 'It is not a pleasure to me', he assured Sir Arthur, 'but I believe *it is my duty*, because *no one* seems to take up the part of the weak in the Pacific'. He did not offer to give evidence—his informant would provide more than enough—but he hoped to see the career of '*a most notorious Buccaneer and Slaver*' brought to an end.

He also took issue with British officialdom. Long before, a merchant vessel wrecked in the Palaus had been looted by natives. An investigating naval commander had blamed people of the federation ruled by Maclay's old friend the *reklai*. A fine in native produce had been imposed, and when this was not paid another warship had inflicted heavy-handed punishment, burning huts and confiscating property.

During *Skobelev's* visit, the *reklai* had assured Maclay that his subjects had taken no part in the looting. They had been slandered, denied time to pay the unjust fine, then plundered by English sailors. It was all the doing of their enemies in Koror, particularly a West Indian negro named Gibbons who acted as a kind of foreign minister. Koror always did this if it could—laid false charges and set foreigners against the *reklai's* people.

Maclay had no opportunity to enquire in Koror. In 1876 he had become indebted to James Gibbons, a valuable informant of Palau customs and tradition. But he knew what he owed the *reklai*, uncle of little Mira and principal vendor of the land at Komis and Oraberamis. Besides, if Russia established a naval station in the Palaus, it would be in the *reklai*'s domain. He wrote to the commodore of the Royal Navy's China station, demanding the return of the confiscated rifles, trepang pots and stone money and the punishment of the real culprits.

The naval authorities were beginning to realize that all foreigners in the Palaus became weapons in the conflict between the native federations. When a warship visited the islands some months later, the chiefs were summoned aboard and made to sign a peace agreement. War ceased, and with it the rituals of head-hunting. Maclay had unintentionally helped to overthrow the foundations of Palauan life.

His other specific attempt to get justice had its effect later. David Dean O'Keefe was tried several times. Perhaps the most influential witness was Jan Kubary, recommended by Maclay as a reliable informant, who testified that O'Keefe's dealings with the natives were a credit to him. James Gibbons of Koror, personally on bad terms with the defendant, supported that opinion. A judicial commissioner ultimately found that D. D. O'Keefe, provoking jealousy by his profitable relations with the natives, had been maliciously wronged by unsuccessful rivals.

That was all in the future. At Hong Kong in May 1883 Maclay proved his dedication to humanitarian causes. He demonstrated belief that the British had the authority and will (if not the knowledge and judgement) to do right by the islanders. He reasserted his duty to defend New Guinea, 'not simply as Maclay but as ... the *representative of the natives, understanding* their language and customs'. He did much for Pacific islanders, and quite as much to dispel uneasiness caused by his voyage. Wherever the rumours had travelled, evidence of his frankness and disinterested pursuit of justice would catch up and overwhelm them.

18: Among Savage Tribes

U NDISTURBED AND UNDISTURBING, Maclay again occupied the biological station. For company he had Jan, an Ambonese servant engaged during the voyage of *Skobelev*, and a monkey picked up in the course of the same journey.

He needed three flannel shirts, a leather jacket and a good fire to help him through another winter. Otherwise, he could not complain of a chilly welcome. Associates showed none of the suspicion he suspected. He reappeared at meetings of the Linnean Society, to exhibit specimens of marine life brought from Naples and discuss preservative fluids used in Berlin. He was elected to the Australian Club. The newly-formed Geographical Society of Australasia introduced him as its first honorary member. There was applause for the news that he would spend two years in Sydney preparing his book, most applause for his offer to advise the Society in planning an expedition to New Guinea. His first advice applied equally well to his position in Australia:

> ... above all, try to impress the natives' minds with the fact that you have come for a special purpose, and that you will not interfere with them; they may then leave you alone.

He saw no immediate need to interfere with colonial ambitions. Nothing had changed in New Guinea. In Australia the first ugly triumph had died down. Colonial statements on the Papuans' right to their land, security and way of life might have been written by Maclay himself. In London the objections he might have raised already formed part of public and official thinking. Like the annexationists, he awaited developments at the real centre of power.

The imperial government soon repudiated the 'annexation' as illegal and unnecessary. Maclay still believed the colonies would have their

290

way. Meanwhile, he followed in newspapers the twists and turns by which the English reached foregone conclusions. In a society where almost everything affecting public events was made public, he could study the reassuring history of the affair.

Asked to explain their fear of foreign designs, colonial governments could report only 'general rumours' about Germany and Italy, an article in the Augsburg *Allgemeine Zeitung*, the movements of a German warship. As Lord Derby put it, there were rumours about 'the intention of some power—nobody knew what power—to seize upon part— nobody knew what part—of New Guinea'. With the imperial government satisfied that such fears were groundless, the colonists looked contemptibly foolish. They looked more foolish when despite sarcasm and assurances they persisted in their fears. As far as Maclay was concerned, they were welcome to their fantasies. Talk circled round Germany, Italy, France—never a word about Russia.

He might have lived peacefully but for the problems of taking a wife. He had never foreseen such 'troubles, unpleasantness and obstacles'. His betrothed had known marriage, and could be presumed to know her own mind. She had chosen a man of internationally acclaimed achievements and principles. He belonged to the nobility; he owned large though remote and undeveloped lands; he provided for marriage by securing ground in Sydney and designing a house. Yet her family, with one voice, opposed the match.

No doubt they raised conventional objections. Maclay had money for the present, but no guarantee of more, and his proneness to debt was common knowledge. His weak nerves and ill health had caused concern for years. If he lived, his wife-to-be still faced a kind of widowhood. He did not disguise his wish to live in New Guinea, or his belief that it was no country for a white woman.

He had experimented with opium, and there was no telling where that might lead. He wrote articles that no daughter of a good Presbyterian family could read without embarrassment. He lived with a strange servant and a monkey that rattled its cage at night. He was the delightful terror of local children. Usually they found him 'very nice'. Sometimes he hung cherries over his ears and performed amusing antics. But when he chased the boys off his territory they were never quite sure whether his eyes gleamed with fun or fury. Then there had been gossip from St Petersburg about his 'unaccountable antipathy towards the fair sex', his supposed declaration that 'the sight of a woman made him ill'—newspaper talk, no doubt, but hard for prospective in-laws to forget.

The biography had come out during his absence, privately printed in Brisbane but at first sight rather like a publication of the Royal Geographical Society. Apart from some confusion about his name and academic standing, its contents were wholly admirable. Yet men who had known him for years, and served with him as trustees of the biological station, handled this pamphlet with comical precautions. It was passed around with the inscription, '*Something* about Maclay (*very confidential*)', a silent witness to the colonists' mistrust.

Where old acquaintances made a mystery of his authorized biography, Maclay need never hear what they thought of recent additions. Everyone knew that a lucky accident had taken him back to his coast. But the regrowth of colonial suspicion did not date from his disappearance at Batavia. Before the *Chyebassa* reached that port, the governor of New South Wales had written urgently to London on the New Guinea question. Among other things, he mentioned a report that 'proposals have been lately made to the Russian Government by a certain Baron Maclay-Miklouho . . . to annex New Guinea, and to establish a naval and coaling station in the vicinity of Torres Strait'.

Lord Augustus Loftus, a reserved old diplomat with eight years experience as ambassador at St Petersburg, must have felt uncomfortable when this crude rumour crossed in the mail with Derby's despatch recommending Maclay to friendly attention. There would be laughter in London, where many thought Lord Augustus a blockhead, and everyone knew the Russians had treated him as a spy. His predicament paled beside that of Margaret Clark's father. Sir John was no longer acting premier. The government in which he collaborated with Sir Henry Parkes had fallen. But it could safely be said that nothing reached the governor without being heard by Sir John Robertson.

Nobody opposed Margaret's marriage more strenuously. She believed in the lover who was both hero and saint. She dearly loved the unsaintly father who begged her not to marry this man. At times she wavered between Maclay and old Sir Jack.

When he considered the trumped-up objections that complicated 'such an *apparently* simple matter', Maclay had reason to envy his New Guinea friends. He had seen what seemed to be the purchase price handed over by a youth's relatives. He had watched a child-bride standing before her future dwelling, while the bridegroom's father lectured on wifely duty and emphasized each point by pulling her hair. He had always liked the naturalness of societies in which women were firmly subordinated and relations between the sexes were free of impractical sentiment.

But he could not pay a so-called 'bride price' or avoid civilization's artificial fuss. Emotionally, he had fallen into the gap between sound principle and the practice of an individual European. Courtship went on—playful notes, flowery pages for an album, discoveries that must be shared, hours counted until the next meeting. The couple had private names. While everyone else called her 'Maggie', she was 'Rita' to her future husband. To her, he was not 'Nikolai' or 'Kolya' but 'Nils'. They formed a united front against the world.

In November 1883 he had not begun the book he owed the tsar. On the other hand, he had contributed to the scientific annals of his fiancée's tribe. He resumed collaboration with William Macleay in work on sharks. He presented findings on the body temperature of the spiny ant-eater. He described an Aboriginal skull brought in by the government mineralogist, and another from the Australian Museum, the narrowest human headpiece ever measured. It was the first of three years in which Maclay, apart from a report to the Russian Geographical Society, published only in Australia.

The politics of getting married perhaps accounted for his appearance on the platform when fifty Presbyterians met to influence the British empire. Listening to prayers and hymn-singing, with speeches in favour of sweeping annexations, might help him with Rita's family. It did no harm to other interests. The Presbyterians sought to maintain their influence in the New Hebrides, coveted by the French. Their attempts to save scores of islands from slavers, beachcombers and Roman Catholics helped frighten the imperial government and complicate negotiations over New Guinea. Maclay neither opposed such useful blunders nor spoke in their favour. His conspicuous presence nevertheless seemed to endorse a call for annexation of 'the New Hebrides, New Guinea and the intervening islands'.

In view of the political situation, Mikhail was to spend some time developing the Palau Islands instead of going straight to New Guinea. Renewed demands for British annexations gave the Palaus their own significance. 'If England extends her colonial possessions', Maclay explained, 'Russia will necessarily take up the question of naval stations . . . Then, in my opinion, the Palau Islands may become important for Russia and for us . . .'.

By then his struggle had become more demanding. In October he had read that Sydney land speculators had bought 15 000 acres in southern New Guinea. True, the newspapers said that James Chalmers had informed the Queensland government, but Maclay dared not trust colonial authorities. Sir Arthur Palmer lost time collecting information, having letters copied and drawing up a proclamation against such dealings. Maclay sent off his own warning to London, a full week before the official one.

A still more urgent duty arose a few days later. News of a colonizing expedition proposed by 'General' MacIver, a Scottish soldier of fortune, had reached Australia early in September. Latest cables mentioned a specific place—Port Konstantin. Lord Derby promptly condemned the scheme. The Aborigines Protection Society, Sir Arthur Gordon and the Queensland agent-general helped to dispose of it. On the evening of 27

October, when all Sydney knew of MacIver's defeat, Maclay cabled London: 'Maclay Coast natives claim political autonomy under European protection'.

His intervention had its effect, producing great confusion. Some people, including Lord Derby, assumed that 'European protection' meant British protection. The letter eventually received from Maclay strengthened that impression. Hardly mentioning MacIver, it described Maclay's relations with his people, his recently-renewed promise to protect them. It asked that land should not become 'the property of the Crown, or of the Government which should protect or annex'. It insisted upon preservation of native institutions. Throughout, it implied that responsibility belonged to Britain.

English humanitarians recognized Maclay as 'the best and most impartial authority' on this question. As a prominent Australian assured the Royal Colonial Institute, Baron Maclay's statements could be implicitly trusted. This request, if request it was, from a man who represented some New Guineans, weakened one objection to a protectorate—that the natives had never asked for protection. Yet Maclay might not speak for all eastern New Guinea. It was hard to imagine him an annexationist. While idealists debated the meaning and authenticity of the message, alarmists had no doubt. To them, a Russian's intervention vividly underlined 'the danger of New Guinea coming under other than British influence'.

Maclay tried to prevent misunderstanding by giving the *Sydney Morning Herald* the text of his cablegram. More misunderstanding. A sarcastic leader-writer asked how the Maclay Coast people had learned of the annexation proposal, grasped its significance and authorized this message. 'But even this is less astonishing', the editorialist claimed, 'than the demand for political autonomy from men whose ideas of national independence are generally considered to be limited by the boundaries of their own petty towns and districts'. Maclay's telegram would frighten English taxpayers with visions of 'complications with powerful chiefs and numerous savage warriors', confirming distaste for moves essential to Australia's safety.

As early as 1871, Maclay explained in reply, he had assembled the chiefs of his coast, warned them of coming dangers, and undertaken to act on their behalf. During his latest visit he had told them 'a protectorate of white men was indispensable'. Again they had begged him to stay with them, or send someone to protect them. He could have asked for the Russian flag to be raised immediately. He had preferred not to saddle Russia with a 'useless burden', when geography suggested that British protection would be more effective. Now, forced to request a necessary evil, he hoped for a protectorate that would leave native

A dancer at a feast in Gumbu, Maclay Coast

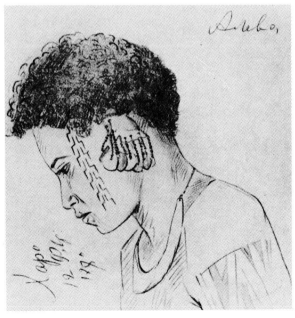

A girl of Hula village, south-eastern New Guinea

A sculpture on an axe head from the Maclay Coast: this piece, in Maclay's collection, is apparently the only known example of such ornamentation

A flute player, Bongu, Maclay Coast

institutions intact and save the people from being treated like 'a mob of cattle'.

The newspaper still doubted the New Guineans' understanding of 'political autonomy', and Maclay's ability to discuss complex ideas in all the requisite languages. He did seem to be asking British protection. Reassured for the moment, the colonial spokesman let the matter drop.

Maclay did nothing of the kind. As he told Lord Derby, his people knew too little about Europeans to ask the help of any particular country. They had left him to decide the form of protectorate and who should grant it. While he wrote to the *Herald* he heard them saying, 'Maclay knows it better'. He also heard an intercolonial conference resolving to ask for widespread British annexations. The affair would not be easy, he warned his brother, but he was sure a handful of determined men could 'save a few islands for Russia'. Without being too patriotic, he did his part. He hoped Mikhail would not be backward in the task. He was writing to ask the tsar's protection for the Maclay Coast.

Should both empires accept, there was nothing to fear. If they reached agreement, he might achieve the ideal—protection by two great powers whose mutual jealousy restrained their interference. If their claims were irreconcilable, he had a way out. Messages to London committed him to nothing. What he said to silence a colonial newspaper counted no more in international politics than his appearance at a Presbyterian prayer-meeting. Nor need he suffer any sense of personal bad faith. Playing all sides to preserve Maclay Coast interests, he acted like any ruler of a small, weak state.

The world now allowed him little peace. He soon learned that an adventurer named Wilfred Powell—the very man who had read out the cablegram before the Royal Colonial Institute—proposed to lead an expedition touching at Astrolabe Bay. Maclay had to gather information against the would-be explorer, enlist E. S. Thomassen to help warn the Royal Geographic Society against the scheme.

Then persecution by newspaper spread to Russia. The St Petersburg *New Times* learned of his appeal on behalf of his coast, and chose to imagine he had offered a possession to Britain. It accused him of lacking patriotism, made remarks about his un-Russian name and possible British ancestry. He was suspected of being dubbed 'baron' in return for services to England.

The article merely demonstrated the paper's notorious misrepresentations and 'rude mockery of everything out of the common'. The St Petersburg correspondent of the *Sydney Morning Herald* deplored the affair. An English friend, who knew about Maclay's Scottish grandmother, defended him publicly by suggesting that loss of two brothers in the Crimea war gave him 'no reason to love the English'. The worst of the muddle was that English allies and Russian detractors all assumed he wanted British protection, and Maclay could not reveal his approach to the tsar. He protested briefly against 'unjust and unfounded' accusations, and promised his compatriots a full account of his dealings with Britain.

He translated past correspondence that told the public everything and nothing. Rumours that he would soon return to New Guinea had to be contradicted. He gave the Sydney press copies of his letters to Lord Derby. He encouraged English supporters, requested clippings of news items about himself and the islands to which he was dedicated. Though the New Guinea missionaries were well able to present their own complaints and fears, Maclay made doubly sure that their views reached London. His prestige and responsibilities had never been greater. In England everyone recognized that he acted only from the highest motives. When the examinable charges against Wilfred Powell turned out to be false, the Royal Geographical Society's strictures fell on E. S. Thomassen.

At the same time, Maclay and Thomassen collaborated in a kind of publicity campaign. The biographical sketch, 'revised by Baron Maclay himself', appeared in several instalments in the Sydney *Daily Telegraph*. Maclay offered an English publisher, free of charge, the book that was nominally Thomassen's work. It seemed a durable partnership, with complete identity of interests, and Thomassen was introduced to Maclay's most influential friends as another friend. Armed with power of attorney, he would soon be going to England to look after arrangements for the Maclay Coast Scheme.

More respectable people than MacIver and his kind made plans for New Guinea. Sir Arthur Gordon repeatedly suggested a chartered company. Chalmers devised a scheme whereby New Guineans would grow cash crops for sale to a government that handled all trade and land dealings. Unlike these, Maclay's project never became public, yet it somehow attracted would-be participants. He could pick and choose, he told Sir Arthur Gordon, among applicants eager to join an enterprise of which they knew nothing. He would be able to carry out his work on any scale he wished. The advantages of having time to perfect arrangements and choose associates almost outweighed his regret that for the moment he could not act in his people's defence.

In reality he was uncertain how much time he had. Russia remained unresponsive. The British government's statements on New Guinea alternated between what sounded like firm refusal and hints that a protectorate might be established. Hugh Hastings Romilly, who reappeared in January 1884, was not alone in wishing the statesmen would 'make up their minds about that place'. Romilly nevertheless expected to become resident commissioner at Port Moresby, a move that might herald a formal protectorate. Unable to make out whether his country was under British protection or not, Maclay faced the dangers of sharing power.

He wrote to Admiral Wilson and Sir Arthur Gordon. In person and in writing, he put his case to Sir William Des Voeux, the new high commissioner. He stressed his influence over the Maclay Coast people. He pointed out what confusion the appearance of another authority must cause among the natives, the 'false and difficult position' in which both he and a resident commissioner would be placed. Sir William knew nothing about the British government's intentions. Again the question must be referred to London.

These cares and uncertainties left little time for scientific and literary work. Maclay had found enough to insist upon marriage. Rita's family, desperately clever at 'inventing obstacles', capitulated at last. The wedding took place at Clovelly on 27 February 1884. The newlyweds moved to the opposite side of the city. When the news came out, the bride was voted the prettiest specimen of natural history the baron had collected.

The von Glehns thought it splendid that he had married a colonial girl who loved her country, not some Englishwoman who would fret to go home. Admiral Wilson called him 'a happy man'. Maclay did not contradict assumptions that Australia was central to his interests. 'You are perfectly right when you call me a happy man', he confided to the admiral. 'Indeed I realize now that a woman is able to bring real happiness into the life of a man who never could believe that such a thing existed in this world.' Yet apprehension tinged his rapture. He hoped that science would not suffer. In correspondence with his brother, his marriage made one belated sentence in a postscript. At times, the conquest of obstacles seemed to have been more important than the happiness it secured.

Two months later some of his fears had come true. His work advanced too slowly. The pleasant home at Snails Bay was too far from the biological station. He wondered how to maintain a household in this expensive city. Convinced that a scientist should not marry without a secure position, he had married when the tsar's gift, his one sure resource, was more than half expended. 'I never regret my action', he assured Mikhail and himself, 'never torment myself by thinking, "It would have been better if I had done this or that, if that had been otherwise and this hadn't happened"'. He rejected absolutely these thoughts that led nowhere and soured the person who entertained them. The fact remained that they had occurred to him.

No doubts and fears were allowed to disturb his wife, whose first child would be born towards the end of November. Rita had married the Christlike hero described by Professor Monod. She daily witnessed a life she revered as holy. Her own life, apart from domestic happiness, was enlarged and intensified by his. She affectionately greeted a distant family who represented a deeper, richer tradition. Through her husband's friends in Paris, people like Natalie Herzen, the eldest daughter of the famous Russian writer, she had links with intellectual and humanitarian Europe. And she had risen in a world that valued symbols of distinction. In Australian society, and in her husband's letters to English friends, she was Lady Maclay.

Everyone who counted confirmed her faith in his worth and standing. The most respected missionaries had his help in bringing their views before the British government and people. When he spoke out against kidnapping and slavery, his charges became important news. His report on the labour traffic and his letters on behalf of the Maclay Coast people appeared in British blue-books and colonial parliamentary papers. Sir Henry Parkes mentioned him as a guardian of New Guinea. The local press praised him for efforts bringing 'great benefit to the South Sea islanders'. His reputation had reached its zenith in the report of the royal commission that had recently investigated the workings of British authority in the western Pacific.

Rumours that Maclay had 'given evidence' in London were not strictly true. The commission had held no formal inquiry. But through talks with Sir Arthur Gordon and Admiral Wilson, its most active members, Maclay perhaps contributed to findings that devastated Australians. 'No more disparaging description' of colonial morals had been published. It was felt that by depicting colonists as a very bad lot, as unfit to govern themselves as to govern blacks, Sir Arthur had fully revenged himself for criticisms received. But the report proved that he recognized worth. Condemning any idea of Australian influence in New Guinea, the commission insisted that Baron Miklouho-Maclay's influence must be preserved.

This seemed to answer, once and for all, a paragraph that slipped into another blue-book, the rumour spread by Lord Augustus Loftus. Maclay had been able to quote the commission's opinion in his letters to British officialdom. Lord Derby assured him that the imperial government would always bear in mind the overriding value of an influence that 'ought not to be in any way weakened'. Still there was no guarantee of freedom from British interference. Nor had Maclay won perfect trust in Sydney. Despite his years in Australia and a marriage that tempted some to claim him as 'an Australian colonist', the slightest misunderstanding could endanger his position.

His long account of correspondence with British officials confused Russians as much as Englishmen. Knowing the *New Times* charges only from English summaries, he could not answer in detail. Nor could he publicly refute complaints that he had never been engaged to find a naval station. His appeal to Lord Derby, translated into Russian, could still be read as inviting British protection. His comments nevertheless suggested this had been a temporary expedient, cancelled by MacIver's defeat. Emphasis on the absence of a formal British claim counterbalanced his belief that Britain would eventually take charge of eastern New Guinea. As far as he knew, his coast remained open to the moral and strategic enterprise of any power equal to the challenge.

He sketched a broad, forward-looking strategy. Outside the Panama Canal Company, the world believed that Ferdinand de Lesseps's second great undertaking would be completed within five years. Frenchmen in New Caledonia predicted that the new waterway, with island annexations, would make France 'mistress of Oceania'. Australian representatives in London pointed to it when urging 'consummation of England's supremacy in the Pacific'. Maclay easily adapted such ideas to his own. 'The opening of the Panama Canal', he concluded,

> will lead not only to considerable communication among the islands but also to trade with this part of the world, and make its produce and manufactures far more important ... Russia, possessing three thousand miles of coast on the Pacific ..., must necessarily take timely measures to secure her place ... Thus, one must hope, she will think in good time about the acquisition of a few suitable naval stations for our fleet ...

Whatever it meant to Russians, London correspondents chose that point for cables to Sydney. Maclay had to explain that his advice, inspired by French and German activities, related only to the north Pacific, that he had never urged Russian annexation of all available islands for naval purposes. Again his enemies had alarmed themselves by their crude misinterpretations.

Accustomed to outface and outmanoeuvre all kinds of opponents, he could live with any residue of suspicion. Resolve, worthy purpose and a sense of perfect integrity formed his armour. With these, and the self-control that had brought him through the testing time on the Maclay Coast, he could listen to speeches, soothe fears and tolerate attempts to adopt him, never renouncing his determination to thwart colonial greed and save a few islands for Russia.

One or two Russian newspapers took up the case for strengthening Russia in the Pacific. Maclay had no positive official response. On the British side, the situation discouraged analysis, let alone action. Early in June 1884 Australia learned that Lord Derby was willing to establish some kind of protectorate over some part of New Guinea. Without much notion of what they were paying for, the colonies agreed to provide £15 000 for the first year's upkeep. Then the question sank back into obscurity. Confronted by English muddle and inertia, the colonists' grumbling impotence, rumours of something wrong with the Panama Canal, Maclay saw no need for haste. While writing occasionally to the Russian foreign ministry, he privately felt that his plans would not 'become urgent' for a few years.

Since *Skobelev*'s visit, no white men had disturbed north-eastern New Guinea. Communications remained precarious for the half-dozen European residents at Port Moresby. Gold-seekers no longer troubled the island with their misdeeds or misfortunes. Journalists had gone in search of fresher copy. The first advertised 'excursion' carried a solitary tourist. It might be impossible, as Sir Henry Parkes said, to 'put a ring-fence around New Guinea', but a kind of charmed circle seemed to be drawn.

Outside the island, some developments might have disarmed Maclay. A new reforming government in Queensland moved towards abolition of the labour traffic. Meanwhile, it tightened control over all aspects of islander employment, and prohibited recruiting in New Guinea and neighbouring groups. Existing prohibitions on the sale of alcoholic drinks were extended. To the great annoyance of Melanesian workers, sale of firearms to islanders, inside and outside Queensland, was made illegal. The Queensland flag-raiser of 1883 had warned people around Port Moresby not to sell land to white men; the intercolonial conference had declared that no land purchases would be recognized. H. H. Romilly himself, staunch defender of islanders and bonny hater of white colonists, detected a genuine will to do right. And signs of quickening public conscience accompanied official action. Few days now passed without newspaper articles castigating the slavers.

Maclay was in the position of an accuser who sees all his denunciations adopted by the accused. Men who predicted misery and ruin for Queensland demanded an end to the labour traffic. His thesis that the islanders only reacted to European evil had become established doctrine. He refused to believe in such changes, or indeed to notice them. He ignored colonial proclamations against land-grabbers. On the labour question, he felt no more confidence in a ministry that included ardent humanitarians than in that graced by his old patron, Arthur Palmer. While it rained editorials in Sydney, and hailed prohibitions, inquiries and punishments in Brisbane, he went on reporting to higher authorities. Such faith as he had depended on those who had faith in him, a British government and humanitarian public that saw protection of New Guinea primarily as protection against Australians.

Settled in a happy marriage, Maclay could concentrate again on science. Not that everything went smoothly. With the biological station to himself, he suffered from lack of space. He lost more than two hours daily in travel between home and workplace. He had mislaid part of his New Guinea diary, and made but slow progress in revising the rest. He nevertheless believed that in 1885 he would return to Europe to arrange and superintend the printing. At the height of his optimism he worked on parallel texts for a book to appear in both Russian and English.

Material still accumulated for the 'purely scientific' part of his publication. He figured and described New Guinea mammals—a bandicoot from Garagassi, a wallaby obtained from another collector on the south coast, two 'new' wallabies that had been sitting, stuffed but uncelebrated, in William Macleay's museum. He studied marsupials whose coats appeared to contradict the Darwin-Wallace opinion that the direction of hair formed an adaptation against rain. A platypus contributed by William Macleay proved to have a body temperature close to that of the spiny ant-eater, establishing the relative 'cold-bloodedness' of animals whose egg-laying habit, just discovered, seemed to place them closer to reptiles than to mammals. Turning to larger phenomena, Maclay set out observations on sea temperatures along the Australian east coast, apparently the first such records to be published. He described seismic and volcanic activity in north-east New Guinea, and integrated his notes relating to coastal uplift.

In comparative anatomy of the human brain, he began with a handicap. During his absence, fire had destroyed the great Sydney exhibition building. Along with the assets of various scientific societies, the flames had carried off items from Maclay's collections, including an Aboriginal brain important to his theories. But his notes and drawings were safe. A new specimen revealed the same feature, known only from a single case among Europeans but present in two of the four Australian brains he had studied. Not enough to prove anything, the discovery tended to support his belief that the brains of different human varieties might be anatomically different.

Varied researches plunged him into voluminous reading—everything from treatises on extinct marsupials and the human brain to Admiralty charts and nautical almanacs—and involved consultations with many colleagues. William Macleay found new species in the small collection of Maclay Coast insects. A malacologist examined molluscs collected alive in New Guinea and from worn and broken seashells corroborated Maclay's observations on recent coastal uplift. A chemist analysed the substance coating badly-preserved bones; a geologist gave an opinion on the clays of Bongu; a dentist extracted the tooth of a dead kangaroo. All Sydney's scientific and technical facilities were at Maclay's disposal. His undertakings stimulated others. The Australian Biological Association seemed to have died of neglect, but its founder remained a force in Australian science.

Scientific visitors brought him contact with the larger world. A fellow countryman appeared, an expert sent out by the Russian government to study the Australian mining industry. Maclay exchanged visits with him, requesting help to find Mikhail a temporary job in Siberia. Members of a French scientific mission dropped in after visiting Borneo and investigating effects of the Krakatoa eruption, and one of them helped Maclay to counteract claims that the East Indies government tolerated anything like the Queensland slave trade. From the purely scientific point of view, there was no more important newcomer than Dr Robert von Lendenfeld. Exactly the kind of person for whom the biological station had been built, this Austrian *savant* settled elsewhere. He produced a stream of scientific papers as varied as Maclay's, and publicly lectured on all aspects of biology. So far as he specialized, he concentrated on sponges and coelenterates, the groups of animals whose hypothetical affinity had first brought fame to Miklouho-Maclay. In Sydney he undertook a complete investigation of Australian sponges. Maclay confidently gave his unpublished material on these animals to Dr von Lendenfeld.

An even more congenial visitor turned up in August 1884. Dr Otto Finsch had once belonged to a class condemned by Maclay, those who wrote about New Guinea and its people without having been there. He had since redeemed himself by visits to New Britain, New Ireland and south-east New Guinea. A distinguished ornithologist who turned more and more to ethnography, he had been admiringly familiar with Maclay's work when they met at Berlin in 1882. Now he appeared at a meeting of the Linnean Society just in time to support Maclay's opinion about a bandicoot found on the Maclay Coast. He did not need the biological station. He was leaving within a fortnight, for a scientific cruise in the central Pacific.

When Finsch sailed on the German steamer *Samoa*, cleared for the Phoenix Islands, Maclay had another reminder of the surrounding jealousy and mistrust. If ever a writer should have scorned colonial suspicions, it was the missionary whose newspaper articles on European crimes had sometimes been useful to Maclay. Yet the same man, under another pseudonym, suggested that the *Samoa* was on the way to establish German dominion over any number of Pacific islands, including New Guinea. Many observers in Sydney held the same opinion. Someone spoke to the commodore, who informed the governor, who wrote to London. Two months later, Lord Derby referred the matter to the Foreign Office.

Maclay did not join the alarmists. Germany had certainly embarked on a colonial policy, or at least a policy of protecting German commercial interests. A traveller had raised the German flag in south-west Africa. Bismarck had outlined businesslike principles of colonization. Gladstone himself, sincerely or not, had publicly welcomed these developments and wished Germany success. As to the Pacific, Germany gave no assurances like those obtained from France. Her national press advocated annexation of New Guinea. Germans who formed a company to colonize the island got nothing like the rebuff that English adventurers could expect from Lord Derby. Thus far, apart from London's hint that a British protectorate over New Britain and New Ireland might be inadvisable, nobody in Australia had real evidence of German imperial interest in any island.

Maclay could not fail to notice that Germany had attained great moral influence. German labour recruiters operated unrestrained in the south-west Pacific and no kind of regulation hampered German employers. German traders freely sold the islanders firearms and liquor. When a German ship was burned and its crew killed by natives of New Ireland, a gunboat inflicted severe punishment. But Bismarck and his press denounced the greed of English colonists and the arrogance of Australian governments. The chancellor was said to have declared that 'the machinations of colonial authorities must be prevented', a sentiment shared by all right-thinking men. When Fiji and Queensland recruiters encroached on German labour preserves, Germany had formally protested to London. When natives were kidnapped and German property destroyed in the Laughlan Islands, Germany had exacted compensation. While punishing whole communities for killing Germans, her naval officers laid the blame squarely on 'English' blackbirders, making the colonies squirm. Now, although the area had been closed to Queensland recruiters, warships watched over German interests in the islands north of Australia.

The purported cablegram about a German-sponsored league to protect independent territories from British imperialism was a hoax. The supposed recipient, the premier of Victoria, promptly denied having any such message. Maclay, however, had written immediately to Bismarck, urging a combination of the powers not merely against 'English aggression' but in defence of natives against 'the shameless injustice and cruel exploitation (kidnapping, slavery, etc. etc.) ... of *all the whites*'.

More than three months must pass before he could expect Berlin's reply to his proposal for an international agreement preserving the rights of South Sea islanders. British protection for parts of New Guinea was now imminent. But though the Australians remained uncertain what Britain would do in the island, they understood that they must do nothing. With these predators restrained by an unwritten edict of 'Hands off!', Maclay felt fairly secure about the rights of man on the

Maclay Coast. In official letters he subscribed himself as 'of the Maclay Coast of New Guinea'. He wrote confidently of the day when his brother, armed with the English language and experience on Russian goldfields, would accompany him to their kingdom.

The British protectorate came with a rush and a tumble. Instructions were sent to the commodore on 8 October 1884; the flag went up on 6 November. Despite the sudden haste, the terms announced were everything Maclay could wish.

There was to be no injustice, strife and bloodshed in New Guinea, no 'pretence of legitimate trade and intercourse' that could rob the people of their rights. The natives' property and families would be protected. Nobody would be allowed to occupy their country, or take them away from their homes. 'Bad and evil-disposed men' were warned that attempts to harm New Guineans would be promptly punished. Australians were notified, again, that all forms of settlement were prohibited and that no land acquisition would be officially recognized. For their part, the people must reject firearms and liquor, immediately reporting anyone who offered such things. They should restrain the impulse to 'inflict punishment' on whites, and take their complaints to Her Majesty's officers. There was no suggestion that Papuans might of their own accord harm whites or incur punishment. No imperial action had ever been conceived in a purer spirit.

British officialdom fully understood the need to preserve Maclay's power and rights. He could assume that the peremptory dismissal of land claims would never apply to his. He might have managed to co-exist with Romilly, sole present British representative in New Guinea. Yet the protectorate gave him nothing. It covered only the southern shores of eastern New Guinea, with nearby islands. It did not mention the Maclay Coast.

The colonists had reconciled themselves to the exclusion of some part of the north coast from the protectorate. They had never imagined this feeble affair, without so much as a defined northern boundary. London vouchsafed no reasons. The public tended to hope that the 'unfinished' look meant the protectorate would soon cover all eastern New Guinea. Only one voice had given any other plausible explanation. A Prussian journal, regarded as semi-official, stated that the protectorate had been limited by arrangement between Britain and Germany.

For weeks it had been suspected that Britain was 'dictated to by Germany'. If not Germany, then some other power—even Russia was mentioned. London cables hinted at something of the kind. Lord Derby had found it necessary to tell the House of Lords that England should risk European jealousy rather than Australian resentment. But Derby's colleagues cared nothing for colonial pique. Having decided to give the colonies half of what they wanted, Britain asked for twice as much as they had expected to pay.

The long-desired event thus brought the colonists bitterness and fresh alarms. Now they considered themselves excluded from New Guinea, Maclay almost believed they feared hostile neighbours. He could not dispute the argument that non-British blackbirders and land-grabbers were free to attack New Guinea's north coast. He realized that the question of expense weighed heavily with Britain. Within a few days he worked out a solution that promised to appease all interests, if only the political world stood still.

Correspondence with St Petersburg had convinced him that he could not hope for a straightforward Russian protectorate. As 'spokesman for the natives', he now asked the British to recognize the independence of the Maclay Coast. The example of Samoa, for which he gave credit to Germany, suggested that by acknowledging native autonomy a European government could at least 'hinder' annexation by other powers. By doing the same for his coast, Britain would 'grant an act of justice', reassure the Australians, save money and 'prevent possible trouble with the natives'.

As he told Derby, he had written in 'similar' terms to Russia. Similar, but not the same. Russia naturally cared nothing for Australians. His best hope was that the tsar might save the Papuans if it cost nothing. He never regarded Russia's future position as identical with that of other powers recognizing the Papuan state. His administration of an independent Maclay Coast might have 'on occasion, great importance for Russia'.

He apparently did not pursue plans for similar appeals to France and Germany. Perhaps two great powers seemed enough. Perhaps it struck him that if Russia turned her humanitarian charge into a naval base one enemy might be more manageable than three. International rumour and jealousy continued to rumble. For the time being he had done everything within his power.

He had more urgent concerns than what the papers called 'The Scramble for the World'. On 14 November 1884 his first son was born, into a household increasingly pressed for money. Only a remittance from Ekaterina Semyonovna had rescued Maclay from financial crisis. He had no idea how he would manage in the immediate future, let alone in six months time. He nevertheless resolved on several expensive projects.

First came a domestic migration, to save his time and leave his wife close to her family during his future absence. Early in December, worrying about furniture and crockery and how to pay for it, they moved to a house at Watsons Bay, named 'Aiva' after Maclay's lost paradise in Papua-Koviai. Next he meant to visit Melbourne, to discuss

New Guinea plants with Baron Ferdinand von Mueller, Australia's leading botanist. Then he would prepare for Europe.

Before going to Melbourne, he appeared at a splendid gathering. The Reverend W. G. Lawes, an old friend who believed in 'New Guinea for the New Guineans', had arrived from the island. The Pitt Street Congregational Church overflowed with people eager to welcome the beloved missionary. Baron Maclay sat on the platform with the governor, the commodore, the chief justice, a crowd of clergymen, officers and parliamentarians.

He could endorse the eulogies on Mr Lawes, who always understood that he wanted 'a very different kind of annexation from that desired by the Australian colonies'. He could enjoy the groans and hisses that greeted references to labour vessels. He could tolerate glorification of the missions, and a choir singing 'O Praise the Lord, all ye Heathen'. But speeches by civil and naval authorities revealed the English at their self-glorious worst. Cheers for the islanders' physical and spiritual salvation had ironic overtones. While orators lauded Britain's gift of civilization and Christianity, each day made it clearer that London and Berlin were negotiating over New Guinea.

Maclay was one of the first people in Melbourne to meet Major-General Peter Scratchley, the newly appointed special commissioner for New Guinea. He was possibly the angriest. While his latest proposals were on the way to Europe, while Britain shuffled papers at the conference table, Germany had seized the Maclay Coast.

By January 1885 the time for rumours and denials was past. Maclay refused to notice the German warships, the raising of flags and reading of proclamations, followed by official confirmation from Berlin. He saw only the furtive Otto Finsch, scuttling along the coast, pretending to buy land from natives. And he approached the special commissioner with fresh alarm. Newspapers reported that Britain would cede Heligoland if Germany relinquished north-eastern New Guinea. By discussing this, Britain would recognize German pretensions. An agreement would create a British claim, endangering Maclay Coast independence and future Russian privileges.

General Scratchley knew Maclay by reputation. Before he left London, the Aborigines Protection Society had approached him with complaints based on Maclay's reports. On the way out, he had conferred with Sir Arthur Gordon in Ceylon. Sympathy for the natives made him listen respectfully now, but he could neither explain the rumour of territorial exchange nor comment officially on German claims. If anything, their correspondence and interview enlightened Scratchley rather than Maclay.

Everyone who counted in London had believed Maclay wanted British protection. The boundary orginally chosen had included the Maclay Coast. The region's status had been an important point in negotiations, Britain maintaining that almost her chief reason for granting a protectorate was the wish expressed by the spokesman of Maclay Coast natives. Now Maclay seemed to fear the British protection that would follow an exchange of territory. Though he mentioned his plea for 'political autonomy', his arguments put too much stress on Russia's prior rights. As former imperial adviser on Australian defence, General Scratchley did not prefer Russians to Germans.

Any intelligent Englishman could say that Britain, as matters stood, would not object to Russia's recognizing an independent Maclay Coast. Nothing was surer to cause Russo-German discord, a desirable thing for Britain. General Scratchley, however, had no authority to pronounce on foreign policy. When Maclay imagined a promise that London would follow St Petersburg's lead, he heard a dangerously deceptive voice in his own head.

He at once sent this prophecy to the Russian minister for foreign affairs. On behalf of the Maclay Coast people, he petitioned the tsar for 'Russian protection, *with recognition of their independence*'. The foreign minister was asked to sponsor Maclay Coast autonomy 'under a general European (international) protectorate'.

Statesmen might not find these two proposals identical. There was a basic inconsistency between the equal responsibility of powers in an international protectorate and the undefined advantages Maclay offered Russia. But he acted in haste, 'solely in the name of humanity and justice, to counteract the spread . . . of abduction, slavery and the most shameless exploitation of the natives'. The diplomats could iron out difficulties.

In his anger, he still hoped to gain something from the anger raging around him. He gave the Melbourne press an account of his letter to General Scratchley, though not of the commissioner's alleged promises. He published further detailed objections to the German claim, with reasons why a Russian claim should take precedence. With the mayor of Melbourne and a string of parliamentarians, aldermen, barristers, journalists and trade union leaders, he appeared at a protest meeting in the town hall. And he did not neglect the most direct action. He sent off a cable to Bismarck: 'Maclay Coast natives reject German annexation'.

'This', a journalist remarked, perhaps tongue-in-cheek, 'will be a staggerer for the man of blood and iron'. Not at all. Bismarck faced an important Reichstag debate, with much questioning of his colonial policy and projected expenditure. He already had complaints that British subjects undermined German authority in Africa. He had just received news that the king of Samoa petitioned for British protection. Maclay's cablegram, emanating from Melbourne and signed with an 'English' name, exactly suited the chancellor's hand. He included a distorted version in his speech. He suggested that any New Guinean opposition must be fomented by England or her Australian colonists. The result was the greatest outburst of anti-British feeling ever seen in Germany.

By then, Maclay was back in Sydney. His letter to General Scratchley had reminded some Melburnians of suspicions harboured since 1871. Newspapers had headlined his arguments against Germany with what they thought the most significant point: 'Russian Claim in New Guinea'. At the great public meeting, he had endured talk of valuable timber in New Guinea and the duty to civilize the savages. One speaker had called New Guinea 'as much a portion of the Australian territory as the Isle of Wight and the Orkneys are of Great Britain'. The imperial government, whose aid Maclay still wanted, had been denounced for selling out the colonies and allowing the Russians to reach 'the gates of Kabul'. Prolonged cheers had greeted the declaration that 'neither Germany nor any other foreign power can have any foothold in New Guinea'.

Misery had made strange bedfellows in Melbourne. Maclay did not let it happen again. Sydney's protest came and went, a disorderly affair, blatantly organized to attack the rather passive New South Wales government. It found its hero in 'General' MacIver, who for six months had been trumpeting to the colonists about German designs on New Guinea and 'Russian spies in our midst'. Maclay appeared only at the Protestant Hall, where he moved the vote of thanks to W. G. Lawes for a lecture given under the auspices of the Y.M.C.A.

Yet the colonists refused to leave him alone. When they learned how Berlin interpreted his message, some were not content merely to remind each other that Baron Maclay was a foreigner who fought 'for his own hand'. Maclay had a long explanation ready, describing his humanitarian motives without a word about Russia. They slapped him in the face by printing his new statement below his earlier letter, all under the headline 'Russian Claim in New Guinea'.

Willy-nilly, he also had to notice their politics. In early 1885 he developed a lasting interest in the possibility that these old enemies might break loose from England and embark on some dangerous course of their own. But the anger and excitement produced only verbal tempests. The real centre of power remained where it always had been. Maclay again approached General Scratchley, with a plain demand that Britain withhold recognition of German pretensions while his negotiations went on. A month later, cables about German activities sent him back to the special commissioner. Scratchley understood Maclay's wish to place his coast under international protection. He approved of Maclay as a 'civilizing agent'. He refused to talk politics. With unfailing courtesy he transmitted another memorandum to London, to the Colonial Office, to the Foreign Office . . .

Maclay had reason to share the colonists' feeling that trust betrayed made the heart sick. He had trusted Britain to shelter his coast until he made other arrangements. For years he had cultivated these important Englishmen, only to find them half-hearted or powerless in his cause. He had said all there was to say about his duties towards the natives, his fears for their future, his hopes for a time when the rights of black men would be respected. He had worn himself out exposing the flimsiness of German claims and the evil deeds of Germans in the Pacific. Everyone must know by now that his only aim was to protect his people and raise them to a higher level of civilization. He was running out of words and patience. His last appeal to London was very brief, and the cry of the dispossessed broke forth:

> . . . kindly inform the British Government that I maintain my right to the Maclay Coast . . .

19: The Island of M

AFTER USING the Maclay Coast protest in his war of nerves, Bismarck ignored it. North-eastern New Guinea—'Kaiser Wilhelm's Land'—was entrusted to a chartered company, the consortium for which Otto Finsch had acted. Neu Guinea Kompagnie employees, with shiploads of stores and building materials, set out for the island. Britain washed her hands of the embarrassment and began negotiations over a common border for the new dependencies. Australians themselves, tired of abusing distant enemies, admitted that New Guinea was effectively 'Bismarcked'.

Maclay lived in a different world, with unique imperatives. He had imagined Anglo-Russian co-operation when everyone knew the two powers were dangerously at odds. Now the last messages from London—an oblique confession that Britain was helpless, advice to address his complaints to Germany—could not discourage him. His hopes again rested on the tsar and the response to long letters in Russian newspapers. He chose the Maclay Coast's representative at St Petersburg, a friend of his schooldays.

For Maclay's policy to succeed, Bismarck's must fall to pieces. Every power needed German good will or indifference on delicate questions. Britain was now the special object of German animosity, reduced to helplessness in matters more important to her than New Guinea. Russia, assured of German neutrality in case of war with Britain, had a free hand where she wanted it most. By mid-March 1885, Anglo-Russian disputes in Central Asia had reached crisis, thrusting aside all other British troubles. German diplomatic aid in keeping British warships out of the Black Sea did more to prevent war and secure Russian gains than any negotiations between the antagonists. Maclay hardly needed letters from the Russian foreign ministry. The facts rained on him from newspapers, in communications that seemed almost addressed to him.

'It cannot suit the Russian government to set itself against the colonial politics of Germany at this moment', the St Petersburg correspondent of the *Sydney Morning Herald* explained, 'and no representations as to the rights of Russia upon the Maclay Coast have as yet been made'. Many believed that coast belonged to Russia, 'by reason of a Russian subject having discovered and taken possession of it'. But Russia honoured Maclay as scientist, not as 'chief of a savage tribe'. His talk of international arrangements had robbed the matter of interest for a nationalistic and literal-minded public. In short, his pleas had met with 'utter indifference', and Russia had 'no present intention' of claiming the coast. The correspondent evidently expected Australian readers to share his regret.

Maclay's appeal to the Russian public also reached Australia, through a London newspaper associated with Olga Novikov. His attacks on Germany were sure to be well received. Though inconsistent with native autonomy, an international protectorate guaranteeing equal rights to missionaries of all religions and traders of all nations held attractions for Europeans. Yet he again emphasized that Russia had 'a stronger claim than any other power'. He left open the possibility of her announcing it.

Russian sympathizers imagined Maclay so 'wounded and offended' by his government's attitude that he might not return to Russia. He never despaired of stirring pride and conscience. Even published news from St Petersburg included the diplomatic niceties, the 'as yet' and 'no present intention' that preserved freedom of action. When politics wore a different face, Russia might save the Maclay Coast. Maclay assured Australians he was 'perfectly satisfied' with Russian mediation. He left them in the dark about what was being negotiated.

At the same time, he refrained from calling off private negotiations in England. Despite the fall of the Gladstone government, Thomassen went on wielding his power of attorney. This loyal follower, for one, never doubted Maclay's ability to protect his 'dusky brethren'. Without 'commissioners, governors, judges', the Maclay Coast Scheme would raise its beneficiaries 'so high' that ideas of placing them under a European flag became absurd.

International politics hardly allowed breathing space that year. With new imperialisms on the move, empires that had slumbered for centuries were forced to look after their rights. Maclay learned that the Palau Islands came under an ancient and nebulous claim by Spain. Instead of offering Russia a naval station there, he needed diplomatic assistance to secure his property. But this caused only trifling annoyance by comparison with another threat to territory.

At the height of the Anglo-Russian dispute, while their much-abused mother country prepared for war, Australians had worried about their own defence. General Scratchley, again acting as military adviser, insisted on works he had recommended long before. The military authorities applied for resumption of the land occupied by the biological station.

No one could call the institution vital to science in general. In three and a half years, only Maclay had used it. On the other hand, the soldiers had managed just as long without a house for the commandant. Maclay's Russian friends quickly heard of his plight. They readily believed that some 'sudden change' in the attitude of the New South Wales government was causing his eviction from a sanctuary he actually owned. They assumed he had fallen victim to the political situation. In St Petersburg a small current of indignation began to flow.

No doubt some colonists were ready to persecute. Military minds probably felt uncomfortable with an 'enemy alien' next door to their principal installations, overlooking arrangements for harbour defence. Ambiguous statements on New Guinea, and a thoughtless hint from St Petersburg that he acted in some 'official' capacity, did nothing for colonial peace of mind. But while international tension rose and fell, bureaucratic delays kept him 'unmolested' at the biological station. He meant to stay until the last possible moment.

One project might have taken him away from Sydney. The snarling of imperialist dogs over colonial bones had produced an international declaration that claims to territory would be recognized only on the basis of proven occupancy. Advised from St Petersburg to put his claim upon a proper footing, Maclay saw that words and rights were not enough. He must demonstrate 'the *fact* of *actual* possession'. His brother Mikhail and a former Russian naval officer were summoned to Australia, to be established as Maclay's representatives in New Guinea.

He informed the Russian government of these intentions, again provided details of the territory to be protected. The urgent plan never went into effect. Mikhail, an unsatisfactory correspondent, proved equally unreliable and evasive in action. He had neither gained experience on goldfields nor visited England as his brother ordered. Now he contemplated marriage, and no longer wished to leave Europe.

This alone could not thwart Maclay, who claimed to have other men ready for New Guinea. Paying for stores and a ship might defeat even his ingenuity. Above all, messages from St Petersburg, official or 'inspired', did not encourage an expensive and risky expedition. Whatever Russia might do in the future, she offered no present hope for the kind of protection that Germany gave Germans.

The blight that fell on almost everything that year did not spare scientific work. Political anxieties and the threat of eviction disrupted Maclay's time and thoughts. He nevertheless described and figured the only wallaby obtained on his coast. Specimens lent by William Macleay yielded two apparently 'new' wallabies from southern New Guinea, to be named after their owner and Odoardo Beccari. He rediscovered, discussed and figured the brain of a dugong, obtained on a Torres Strait island five years before, and continued to examine sharks. Otherwise he concentrated on revision and expansion of earlier work, turning out old papers and specimens in preparation for his book. The process reminded him of a problem he had overlooked for years.

No discovery had excited him more than the phenomenon he called 'macrodontism', first observed in the Admiralty Islands in 1876. Where almost all human front teeth were large, many were stupendous. In some men, the blackened incisors protruded from closed mouths. Maclay satisfied himself that the condition was not pathological. It had probably originated in some unknown peculiarity of diet. The result seemed to be a 'hypertrophy', now 'so deep-rooted that it had become hereditary'.

During his sojourn in New Guinea, preliminary accounts of these findings had appeared in Russia and Germany, in the English scientific magazine *Nature* and its French counterpart, and in a Swiss illustrated paper. Back in civilization, he sent fuller reports. Macrodontism had made a fascinating subject for the first scientific paper he presented in Sydney. And he continued the investigation. Returning from the voyage of 1879–80, he had listed among the most valuable results his success in learning more about macrodontism. As late as 1884, after a fourth visit to the islands, he had promised to describe 'cases of macrodontism' in his book.

Meanwhile, other cases had come to light. In 1881 an investigator had looked into mouths in the Nicobar Islands. The results, published like Maclay's in the proceedings of the Berlin anthropological society, had reached even such outposts as Sydney. Chemical analysis showed that the huge teeth of the Nicobarese owed much to a thick crust of tartar.

Rudolf Virchow left open the possibility that the phenomenon described by Maclay might be different in its nature. Maclay already knew better. As early as 1879 he had realized that Admiralty Islands teeth did not show 'hypertrophy'. Specimens revealed a hard black incrustation, removable by means of a scalpel. In one example, a quite normal tooth came out of its coating 'like a kernel from a nutshell'. Maclay hardly needed a dentist to confirm that 'macrodontism' was actually an enormous accumulation of tartar, increased and stained by the chewing of areca nut and betel with lime.

Greater scientists had made bigger mistakes. For all his incontestable standing, Virchow figured in history as the man who found the Neanderthal skull to be that of a modern idiot, deformed by bone disease and blows on the head. Huxley and Haeckel had discovered the fundamental form of life in what turned out to be an artefact produced by preserving marine sediment with alcohol. Maclay's error did not, like these, touch basic positions in biology's greatest controversies. But that did not make it easier to confess.

Criticism of his early work on sponges and the fish brain had never noticeably upset him. The 'macrodontism' embarrassment struck at what meant most to the mature scientist, his reputation as anthropologist and ethnologist. He took pride in gathering precise facts, without speculation or hasty conclusions. He found himself betrayed by the theory he could never resist. Belief in the inheritance of acquired characteristics had more than once tempted him into remarks that proved the wisdom of avoiding speculation. Now it had helped to land him in the greatest difficulty of his scientific life.

He admitted the error, with such detachment that it might have been made by someone else, pointing out the obstacles to forming a 'decided opinion'. He explained how the first specimen obtained had been lost by a careless traveller on the way to Europe. He made it clear that he himself had been first to determine the true nature of the phenomenon, discarded the term 'macrodontism' and substituted the new word 'odontolithiasis'. He did not explain why, fully aware of the mistake, he had waited six years before correcting it.

It was an unpleasant note on which to end a year's scientific contributions, but fit for its place in that difficult time. Events drifted on tortuous and uncertain currents that undermined everything he had built up. He still stood alone against the forces of inhumanity, with only words and strategy to defend his people from 'violence, slavery and perhaps total extirpation'. In Australia, where he had spent more of his adult life than in any other country, he remained an object of suspicion. Public service to the colony had brought only disillusionment. The organization devised as a framework for colonial science was moribund or extinct, and the institution he had founded as a personal monument was bound for oblivion. He thought with greater yearning than ever of the one country in which he felt at home, the one people that knew how to value him.

Late in February 1886 Maclay sailed from Brisbane on the mail steamer *Merkara*. With barely enough money to take him to Odessa, he could not afford the company of his wife and two little sons. His health was deteriorating quickly, his hair quite grey above sad, wandering eyes in a deeply lined face. His whole presence spoke of hardships in what admirers called 'fifteen years residence among savage tribes'. Yet he had never been more resolved, or readier for action. He meant to recapture lost ground, and hold it so firmly that it could not be snatched away.

As soon as he fairly set foot in Russia, he went to Livadia, the tsar's Crimea residence. He distrusted N. K. Giers, the foreign minister, a man of suspect background, too zealous about Russo-German friendship.

Alexander III, almost entirely German by descent, was believed to be truly Russian in outlook. Maclay had much to tell the emperor personally.

He twice had audience, studied that heavy face and listened to the voice that ruled Russia. Beyond his sense of the tsar's kindness and interest, he had considerable faith in this huge embodiment of absolute power. In a week at Livadia some of his hopes were realized. On the most important subject he failed to explain all the emperor should know. Settlement of the Maclay Coast question must await further discussion in St Petersburg.

He spent a few weeks at Malin, about 100 kilometres north-west of Kiev, his first visit to the family home that had cost so much struggle and grief. Late in June he was in the capital, living in the flat of the nominated Maclay Coast *chargé d'affaires*. Negotiations with Germany had begun, supervised by Osten-Sacken. Maclay still hoped to rescue the whole coast, 'from Cape Croisilles in the west to Cape King William in the east, from the seashore on the north-east to the highest mountain ranges in the south-west'. His conception of its future had changed.

Intending to engage trustworthy people to look after properties in the Pacific, he had approached a friendly newspaper. Left to put the positions-vacant advertisement in his own words, the editor had obtained astonishing results. All St Petersburg believed that Maclay proposed to found a Russian colony in New Guinea.

Reporters came for interviews. Letters poured in requesting information. Early in July about sixty people gathered at his headquarters to hear about the future colony and conditions of life on the Maclay Coast.

Those attracted by Maclay the explorer heard that he did not want men for scientific expeditions. Job-seekers were warned that settlers, apart from his employees, must find their own livelihood and shelter. Fellows in threadbare overcoats learned that capital would be as necessary as work. Among the army uniforms and Russian shirts, long faces greeted the news that the colony would be strictly teetotal. While two young women of doubtful respectability laughed until tears ran down their cheeks, many listeners recoiled from advice that New Guinea was no place for European wives and children.

The attractions outweighed all warnings. Maclay spoke of his country's beauty and fertility, its agreeable climate and its handiness to Australia and intercontinental trade routes. For those who took precautions, the fever was not nearly so bad as might be imagined— Maclay had suffered only slightly. Nor was there much danger from human hostility. The good-natured, hospitable natives, already under Maclay's authority, fought only among themselves. The rifles and land-mines to be provided were unlikely to be used.

No swindles could be tolerated, but ample land was available at little or no cost. On unused tracts between villages, settlers would find soil capable of yielding three harvests of maize a year and root crops all year round. Unattended, eight kinds of bananas bore loads of fruit. Rice and the coffee shrub would thrive. The climate and terrain invited cattle-farming. Fine timbers abounded. Coral rock and excellent brick clay provided the best of building materials. With prolific vegetables, rich hauls of fish, and a whole day's sustenance obtainable by half an hour's hunting, existence would cost next to nothing. 'The only difficulty', Maclay predicted, 'will be that of having on hand not merely a sufficiency but an overabundance of food'.

Above the call of paradise his followers heard that of patriotism. They saw a map covered with 'exclusively Russian names'. They learned how the Maclay Coast had been placed under the Russian flag in 1871. They were called to sweep aside the Germans' paper claim and transform this splendid country into 'the first Russian colony in Polynesia'.

This was no time to recall the sickness and hardship that formed part of Maclay's legend. No naval officer cared to mention that the flag raised in 1871 had been that of the merchant marine, an ensign without implications of sovereignty. Nobody disputed Maclay's statement that he had from the first established himself at Port Alexei. That offered an incomparably better harbour than Port Konstantin, and there was again talk of a naval station.

Criticism emerged, produced by feuds between newspapers rather than sincere opposition to Maclay, too obviously spiteful and ignorant to influence anyone. It floundered in the facetiousness that hacks mistook for wit. It never seriously threatened a man who enjoyed the tsar's esteem, indeed Maclay seemed unconscious of 'the fun going on at his expense'. The one gibe he noticed was the old rumour that he had offered a protectorate to Britain. Rejecting this as offensive to a Russian, he was not yet free to explain all circumstances.

He became the hero of the day. The stream of letters from all over the country swelled to an overwhelming flood. He had to announce his inability to give individual answers. When detailed plans were worked out, he would call a meeting of future colonists. He had already requested the tsar's authority to found a colony 'at Port Alexei on the Maclay Coast, where the Russian flag was raised fifteen years ago'.

Even admirers felt he underestimated the difficulties. Germany would not meekly give up what was represented as the best part of New Guinea, in the middle of her new possessions and occupying one side of a strait whose control she thought essential. Britain, reconciled to the existing situation, would surely oppose the replacement of Germany by Russia. The Balkans were in crisis; all Europe talked of war; Russia faced a multitude of enemies. Well-informed people said from the beginning that the government would not help Maclay.

With faith in absolute power, he made one concession to facts. He suggested to the tsar and the foreign minister that the first Russian colony might be formed on some Pacific island other than New Guinea. For that, he believed, he had 'the highest permission'.

Meanwhile, he saw no harm in rattling the Germans. He had already accused them of using slave labour in New Guinea. Addressed to a Reichstag deputy of the Alsace Protest Party, his revelations had caused embarrassment in Germany, with anxious expectation that he would publish 'reports'. No matter how they denied the charges, even defenders of the Neu Guinea Kompagnie never doubted that he had seen north-eastern New Guinea since it became German.

The same general ignorance of his recent whereabouts helped his cause in Russia. When he reappeared, Europeans assumed that he came from the country with which he was identified. Admirers attributed his power over the natives to 'fifteen years ceaseless striving'. Those who called him 'the King of the Papuans' easily believed that while he visited Australia to be married the Germans had taken advantage of his absence to seize his realm.

It was spiritually true, for a man to whom New Guinea had become a country of the mind. To Maclay, the nine years in which he had spent a few unsatisfactory days on his coast were devoid of meaning or reality. He still called himself 'the white Papuan', still spoke of himself as normally living 'among Papuans'. In any case he saw no need to correct misunderstandings that influenced public opinion. Nor did he neglect the feelings he found in existence. Regardless of official policy, millions of Russians hated Germans. They blamed Bismarck for international decisions that had spoiled their victory of 1878. Instead of thanking him for manoeuvres that paralysed the English, they held him responsible for all Russian misfortunes. Behind the bitterness of world events there lay the animosity between true Russians and those persons of German descent who held too many powerful positions in Russia. This had come to a head among the educated classes when the Imperial Academy of Sciences failed to elect the great chemist Mendeleev. The common explanation of this scandal, the one that had reached Maclay in Australia, was that German academicians had conspired to keep a true Russian out.

Maclay, too, had grievances against the Academy of Sciences. He intended to display his collections on the Academy's premises, then present them to the institution as a token of 'gratitude to the Russian government'. But the thirty boxes brought to St Petersburg by the royal train still lay at the goods station. He pictured them thrown into the street or auctioned by the railway management. The Academy, he told the public, refused him any kind of accommodation. It evidently wished to confirm its 'reputation of existing only for Germans'.

Pressure from above helped the Academy to overcome its problems.

The collections were taken in and stored, space made available for their eventual exhibition. Sympathy for Maclay as victim of Germans then centred on the Academy's failure to offer him membership.

Not that the passions aroused did much good. A German flag raised in the Caroline Islands had caused a Madrid mob to destroy the German embassy. Nothing of the kind seemed imminent in St Petersburg. Nor could the tsar's government assert a claim by the Spanish method of threatening to collapse. Russian public opinion, once an excuse for war, had become an implausible scarecrow under Alexander III.

Maclay seemed to forget that efforts to awaken Russia could sound alarms elsewhere. The German public at first imitated its government's calm. Commentators predicted that Maclay's scheme would harm only the Russians who joined it. But if he persisted—. When he did persist, Germans became quite angry.

Reports of his intentions might have made no public stir in London but for the shock they gave E. S. Thomassen. This faithful henchman realized that Russia might claim rights over the Maclay Coast, just enough to protect the natives against 'German adventurers or other white intruders'. He had never imagined this as a threat to his interests. On his own behalf as much as Maclay's, he explained through an agitated letter to *The Times* that the news was false. Maclay's standing as scientist and humanitarian, the admiration of men like Professor Monod, the confidence high British authorities placed in his 'rectitude and *savoir-faire*'—all these set him on 'too high a pedestal to be affected by the German snarls'. His Australian sons and his friendships with colonists guaranteed 'to a certain extent' that he would not offend Australia. English capitalists and Australian friends could rest assured that Maclay 'never desired Russia to have any colony in New Guinea'.

When Maclay wrote to *The Times*, most readers assumed that he denied the reports. He told no such lie. He merely dismissed the news as 'rumour', described the unforeseen effect of his advertisement for employees, and explained that work on his book prevented his undertaking anything else 'for the present'.

It might have satisfied the English and the Australians to whom it was promptly transmitted. But the St Petersburg correspondent of *The Times* felt he was living in Wonderland. On one side he saw Maclay, constantly talking about a project discussed in all Russian newspapers. On the other stood Maclay and his agent, apparently denying its existence. The man from *The Times* kept London well informed.

That disposed of the English, the Australians and E. S. Thomassen. The Germans quietened down. The St Petersburg *New Times* had published a quite serious piece, pointing out the political difficulties, the absence of Russian commercial interest in New Guinea, the amount of land available in Russia. Reprinted without comment in the *Journal de Saint*

Pétersbourg, which amounted to endorsement by the foreign ministry, this article persuaded Germans that Maclay had no official support.

Maclay knew better on every count. He had support to which all others must bow. The emptiness of eastern Russia was irrelevant, since he acted 'to preserve for Russia several convenient points in the Pacific', the naval stations he always kept in mind. The Muscovites who were forming a 'Pacific Ocean Association' would soon provide the commercial interests. And he could laugh at reminders that inducing the tsar's subjects to emigrate constituted a crime. The soil of his colonies was to be as Russian as Russia.

When he petitioned the tsar, 320 people wished to go to the Pacific. Within a few days, the total had reached '500 odd'. New applications came every day. He went about with pockets full of unread letters. When he no longer granted interviews, those thirsting for New Guinea accosted him in the street. All Russia rang with his name. The fame of his undertaking spread until in little Montenegro, Russia's only ally, a hundred families offered to join. But he had to answer vaguely. He did not feel 'the ground firm under his feet'.

The ardour of Russia's statesmen never matched that of her people. Maclay supplied the arguments—the flag raised in 1871, surveys by Russian naval vessels, his promises to protect the natives and his success in keeping out British adventurers. The diplomats had made some play with his humanitarian right to develop the coast for the benefit of its people. They did not openly press for Russian sovereignty. When it came to the point, they merely asked for recognition of Maclay's titles to land on the basis he indicated, the German legal principles of 'the right of the first occupant' and 'the right to possession of neglected or abandoned things'.

He consulted Grand Duke Alexei and Konstantin Konstantinovich, son of the old patron who was said to be living under police supervision. Both discouraged further provocation of Germany. They certainly were not sending a warship to the Maclay Coast as he had hoped. Wait a while, they advised; the moment was unfavourable for positive action. But there was no turning back. The tsar took one of his plunges and appointed a special committee to examine Maclay's proposals.

The *Sydney Morning Herald* correspondent got the job of convincing Australians that a Russian naval station would be good for them. Russia had long contemplated such an establishment. It obviously suited Australia that no 'chauvinist' should be in charge. Maclay was 'half an Australian by this time, . . . bent on defending English colonial interests'. His English appearance and manner, his freedom from the 'narrow-mindedness' of Russian ultra-patriots, and his boundless indignation against Germany, all showed that Australia would have a congenial neighbour. The journalist ignored the position of chauvinistic naval commanders with orders from Vladivostok. He made no attempt to explain what purpose the station could have if it did not threaten Australian shipping. The best news for his readers was his belief that the thing would never come off.

Maclay's task was harder still. The foreign ministry's arguments had practically demolished the idea of settling on the Maclay Coast. After publicizing New Guinea, he had to choose some other island. And material difficulties were not the only ones. Different people had heard his proposals in different ways. His most ardent supporter, Professor V. I. Modestov the classicist, could almost see Plato's ideal republic arising in the southern hemisphere. Or it might be a collectivist community, embodying the Fourierist or Saint-Simonian principles that Russian idealists had favoured early in the century. It had no place for the great 'Pacific Ocean Association' that Maclay was quietly encouraging, much less for the naval base that was freely discussed.

The Utopian thinkers perhaps deceived themselves, as so many others had done in interpreting Maclay. His preliminary 'Draft Rules' did not suggest that colonists would own and work the land in common, or that all would share in managing the enterprise. Certainly the profits would be divided each year, in accordance with work performed, but some participants would always be more highly rewarded by virtue of their positions. Maclay spoke as though his followers were employees who could be summarily dismissed from their jobs. The great difference was that they would have no fixed remuneration. For the first year he undertook to provide food from local sources. 'Rewards for labour' could be decided only after six months work. It was not at all clear what would happen if the colony failed to make a substantial profit in its first year.

One certainty was that the enterprise would tolerate no trouble-makers. Participants must pledge themselves to obey all the rules and decrees to be promulgated before their departure from Europe. Anyone who failed in this duty would face 'prompt dismissal from his position'. Once in the colony, the dissatisfied or recalcitrant could not count on a passage back to Europe or transfer to another island, and any crime would be punished by 'prompt expulsion'. If a criminal returned and sought to disrupt public order, the death penalty could be imposed.

While the project was embryonic in his own mind, Maclay received a number of official queries. Giers, the foreign minister, wanted to know what arrangements would be made about land if the chosen island happened to be inhabited. He was curious about the colony's 'internal structure', and its prospective communications with the closest important European settlements. He raised all kinds of questions that modified the thinking in Maclay's 'Draft Rules'.

The minister seemed worried about 'financial means', so it was evident that the colony must be founded on the capital of its members. Maclay decided that every intending colonist must have at least enough money to pay for the outward passage, food supplies, basic outfit and a possible return to Russia. These changes in turn affected the other arrangements he had had in mind, but he dealt easily enough with the problem of 'internal structure'. His reply to the minister suggested nothing like employer-employee relationships. Nor did it foreshadow the kind of tightly-organized socialist community that had interested him in his youth. But he wanted no easygoing South Seas Arcadia. He imagined his colony maintaining trade and communications, providing for defence, collecting taxes, policing 'social behaviour'. He foresaw litigation to be decided locally. Instead of being simply expelled or executed, criminals would be delivered to the nearest Russian authorities. In general, this orderly dominion must obey the Russian government, its members retaining the rights and duties of Russian citizens.

It could not be exactly like Russia. As he described them to the correspondent of the Sydney paper, his followers nearly all had money and 'a position in life'. They were nobles, army officers, professional men, including 'persons of very considerable rank and fortune'. He had to devise a commonwealth for the élite.

An imperial statute was to guarantee all benefits of self-government, including power to impose taxes and legislate on local concerns. In one respect the settlement offered advantages over British self-governing colonies. Comparatively few in number, not too widely dispersed, its inhabitants could be assembled 'as far as necessary' to adopt decrees and regulations. A council elected annually would decide routine matters, and elect a premier for each three years. The premier or 'elder', immune to changes in the council, would act as sole 'responsible' representative, directly supervising all colonial affairs. The political system thus combined direct democracy with a powerful presidency, all under the wing of an autocratic emperor. Maclay, who would be first premier, was drafting comprehensive laws.

Whatever he intended to do for them, the natives who might become Russian subjects did not figure in the system he described. He mentioned them only to reserve 'relations with the natives' among the subjects for colonial law. One thing was clear, though never spoken. Formed mainly of people unused to manual work, the European colony must depend on native labour for the products to be exported.

The foreign minister had asked, first of all, *which* island Maclay had in mind. Maclay saw the place—an island with good climate and water supply and fertile soil, not claimed by any foreign power, either unoccupied or 'voluntarily ceded' by the inhabitants. It had a safe

harbour, easily fortified. It was neither hemmed in by foreign possessions nor completely isolated, since he proposed to annex further
territories.

But where was it? The name might later be whispered in the
minister's ear. In writing, Maclay sometimes mentioned 'the island of
M'.

The South Seas had many islands beginning with 'M', all controlled
in some way by European powers. Maclay could claim none but
Malaspena, off Port Alexei, the uninhabited sliver of land where he had
spent a few hours in 1883. But Malaspena and its neighbours formed
part of Kaiser Wilhelm's Land. A surreptitious attempt to gain a Russian
foothold there would have grave international consequences.

The name of the island was not the only thing unknown when
representatives from the ministries for finance, war, internal affairs and
the navy met under the foreign minister's chairmanship in the great,
warren-like building of the general staff. They had several questions to
ask Maclay, and thought of more in the course of the evening, but he
was not treated like a shady speculator face to face with Lord Derby.
This committee met 'at the highest command', to examine a proposal
officially put forward by an eminent traveller and humanitarian. The
questions, though searching, were always polite, and Maclay was not
forced to answer those he found inconvenient. He gladly gave the
committee members an idea of the numbers, social status and nationality
of his followers. He felt confident that if only one per cent of the
colonists had sufficient means and energy the enterprise must succeed.
He saw no difficulty about defence in a colony of Russian citizens, liable
to universal military service and plentifully endowed with officers. But
he could not predict how much money each settler must lay out.
Though his name guaranteed that slavery would never arise, he could
not say beforehand what occupations and working conditions the
settlers could expect. The dignitaries never found out to what extent
the colony would control its members' capital, or the basis on which
land would be allocated. Nor did they discover the name of the island.

Official Russia was asked to provide legal charter for a settlement in
an unnameable but certainly distant place which might or might not be
already inhabited. While seeking to annex in the tsar's name, Maclay
demanded independence from the start, a combination of requirements
unknown in the history of colonization. No doubt he could be trusted
not to embroil the settlers with hostile natives or foreign powers. He
might give the empire some kind of cost-free asset. It had probably been
insulting to ask what he meant to do with other people's money. But as
N. K. Giers had already pointed out, nothing could absolve Russia of
responsibility for the fate of her citizens in a colony authorized by
Alexander III, and responsibility implies control. Quite apart from the

fact that ideas of elective government for Russians must stink in the nostrils of the tsardom's servants, Maclay was again asking what no sane rulers would give.

The committee sat, discussing something. Maclay remained the national hero, the man who proclaimed Russian colonization the great aim of his life. Day to day, he lived precariously. While he undertook to claim an empire, he had to vacate the borrowed flat. While his imagination expanded throughout the South Seas, he sought a home to share with his newly-married brother. He came to rest in a bare, servantless apartment, in a building where his family had lived twenty-four years before. From one of his two chairs, he dictated his book and drafted laws for a commonwealth.

At the same time he prepared the ethnological collection for display in the large conference hall of the Academy of Sciences. The exhibition opened to scientific societies on 20 October, brilliant with state counsellors, senators, diplomats, admirals. Two days later, three thousand members of the general public wandered among the stone axes, weapons, ornaments, cooking and eating utensils and musical instruments.

Maclay's speeches touched on the scope and aims of his travels, the gift of his collection to the nation, his hope to see an ethnological museum established in St Petersburg. But this collection, he told the public, was far less important than Russian colonization. He described the lawless acts of Germany, the oppression and slavery suffered by those who had fallen into German hands. When he revealed that fifteen hundred men had volunteered to secure Russia's place in the Pacific, a ripple of excitement went round the hall.

He spoke again at the exhibition, inspiring university and high school students with ambition to travel. He was preparing a series of lectures, to reach their climax in the unveiling of plans for colonization. But before the lectures could be arranged he heard that the committee had rejected his proposals.

He admitted no more than a 'postponement'. The tsar had not signed the committee's report. The papers had gone to the ministers for further consideration. 'I do not abandon hope of a favourable outcome ...', Maclay told one of the naval grand dukes, 'nevertheless I am sure that no decision of the committee, not even a refusal from the highest authority, will affect my determination to settle on an island of the Pacific Ocean'.

The seven lectures, given to raise money for his support and scientific work, attracted audiences that some reporters thought select rather than large. There were the usual complaints about his slow, hesitant delivery, the difficulty in speaking Russian that marked him as either a 'white Papuan' or 'half an Australian'. He only became animated when he described his people, the kind, courteous, peaceful inhabitants of the Maclay Coast. Again he dwelt on that generous land where men never struggled for the means of existence, where expressions of bitterness, spite and anger were unknown, where there were 'neither rich nor poor ... no envy, no stealing, no violence'.

His tone was elegiac, for he again spoke of what must disappear. Traders were inciting his people to greed and competition. Slavers bought or kidnapped the young men and girls. As everywhere in the Pacific, the debased survivors of slave raids and infectious diseases would burn for revenge. He foresaw the time when his 'Islands of Contented Men', under German rule, would become 'Islands of Murderers'.

Considering the South Seas as a whole, he predicted that most of the natives would be 'forced to leave the scene'. Vast profit was obtainable from such products as copra and trepang. Russia too must seek a place in the sun. Resolved to live on some Pacific island, he still meant to settle eighteen hundred Russians under their own flag.

An irony hung over the pioneers, for their colony apparently had no future unless it ceased to be Russian. Maclay believed that whites could populate the tropics only by interbreeding with native races. He foresaw the occupation of the Pacific region by 'a modern *mixed* race'. And the European heritage might disappear. Another people had come upon the scene, better adapted to the climate, more patient, industrious and prolific than whites. If his confusing remarks meant anything, his colonists were called upon to uphold both Europe and Melanesia by founding a mixed race capable of withstanding the Chinese.

Perhaps the hint was never seriously intended. In this last lecture he seemed ready to say anything that entered his mind. What emerged clearly was that he would never relinquish his aim. 'I do not withdraw from an affair once I have undertaken it', he insisted. He was a patient man, prepared to wait for decisions so important to Russia. His followers too must have patience. He could not yet answer their questions.

They waited all through January 1887 and into February, while Maclay received still more messages from people dreaming of a South Seas island. He himself was said to be awaiting publication of his book as well as the final word on the colonization scheme. Regardless of either, he had to visit Sydney. He could not maintain two households. His wife was ill, perhaps exposed to unpleasantness on his account. The only solution was to bring the family to Russia. He hastened passport formalities, cabled Sydney about his imminent arrival, and remained in wintery St Petersburg, incapable of packing his bags.

He awaited nothing, hoped for nothing but an end to pain. For days he lay moaning, his existence a round of hot-water bottles, tooth extractions, injections, mouth rinses of vodka and opium, drugged sleep.

He swallowed every concoction the doctors prescribed. He was prepared to visit a quack who advertised electrical treatment for syphilis. Still the pain raged in his swollen face and rheumatism tormented his body.

Beaten down by distress, he became unnecessarily humble. When he sought some analgesic to make his journey bearable, he hoped only that the eminent doctor would find time to instruct a secretary to write a few words. Once he had warned his brother not to whistle, warble or entertain too many visitors in their shared flat; on the grounds that his work required it, he had taken the best of their four rooms; now he wanted Mikhail's forgiveness for the long, involuntary stay that cramped the young couple's living quarters. And it had become easier to confess failure. Both the Maclay Coast business and the plans for other colonies, he told Sergei, had ended in 'almost complete fiasco'.

He was too exhausted to react strongly, at first 'not much grieved' by a rejection that allowed more time for his book. His statement to the press, advising that the founding of a Russian colony could not at present take place, conveyed no regrets to the two thousand followers who expected his call. He seemed prepared to bow to 'circumstances entirely beyond my control'.

Such humility and resignation could not last long in a man who believed in his rights and his ability to 'tame destiny'. He inwardly rejected the verdict. As the injustice came home to him, he looked for someone to blame.

He would never know how emphatically the tsar's last word had cancelled all 'promises'. Like any Russian thwarted in great plans, he heard that his disappointment was not the doing of the emperor, the strict but just father who wished to give his children everything they deserved. Too shrewd to receive this without reservations, he still could not entertain hostility towards the tsar. His anger concentrated on Nikolai Karlovich Giers, the autocrat's most self-effacing servant. Criticism of the tsar's mouthpiece amounted to criticism of the tsar, but Maclay expressed his feelings to a visitor who was sure to put them into print.

The Danish literary critic, Georg Brandes, had a gift for making interesting people fashionable. Cynics who claimed it was his way of magnifying himself did him an injustice, for he truly and rather naively loved the distinguished, the original, even the eccentric. In Maclay he found the perfect example of originality ill-used and suppressed by the Russian state and society.

The explanation of a strange object that caught his eye—the skull forming a lamp-base was that of a girl whom Maclay the medical student had loved and nursed—moved Brandes to delight. He accepted without question the information that Maclay, as 'king of the Australasian island which bears his name', was entitled to exactly one hundred and forty-seven native wives. He swallowed whole the proposition that the seizure of this island had made Maclay a German subject against his will. Beyond the exotic fascination, Brandes recognized the king in this pain-racked, prematurely-aged man with 'a splendid head and young eyes'. He saw Maclay reigning peacefully over his primitive, happy subjects until the fatal raising of the German flag. He shared Maclay's contempt for the foreign minister who had supinely surrendered to Bismarck, and sympathized with the explorer's long struggle to bring his realm into the Russian empire. That such a man as Maclay desired this was enough for Georg Brandes.

Before the year was out, Brandes would be the apostle of Friedrich Nietzsche, upholding a morality of 'self-preservation, self-development and development of power' against the cult of self-sacrifice and compassion for the weak and wretched. He would not forget Maclay, a worthy addition to his collection of superior beings, forerunners of the Superman. For the scientist, Brandes was a mere passer-by. Maclay had entered the sphere of a master who represented the opposite of everything Brandes sought.

In general, Count Leo Tolstoy held a low opinion of science. He had long taken a quite different interest in Maclay's career. Sick in bed in September 1886, reading the publications Maclay had sent him, he recognized the master-disciple he vainly sought among the pilgrims of Yasnaya Polyana. He felt instinctively that for such a man scientific research formed a mere 'pretext' for a far greater work. And he did not see that greater purpose in extending the Russian empire. He seemed to be the only person in the country who knew nothing of the scheme. Maclay's aim, as interpreted by Tolstoy, was to show the necessity and practicability of true Christian pacifism.

In New Guinea he had demonstrated the unnaturalness and senseless-ness of violence. He must complete his service to mankind by telling the whole story, or rather by 'leaving out everything but relations with people'. As Tolstoy indicated, this should prove that man is everywhere 'a good, friendly creature, with whom one can and should enter into association only with truth and goodness'.

Maclay never underestimated the importance of his relations with people. The pamphlets Tolstoy had read were full of that subject. But it was difficult to limit the account to what the great writer desired, the picture of the lone pacifist triumphing 'with reason instead of bullets and bayonets'. In applying reason to human relations, Maclay had used his own reason to benefit from misunderstandings and mystery. To maintain his safety and ascendancy, he had fertilized imagination by every available means. Though he never found himself guilty of a lie, he had not depended on 'truth' in the sense intended by Tolstoy.

wood carving, Suou Island, south-eastern
w Guinea, January 1880

Carved ornaments from islands north of New
Guinea

'Tambuna', skull house, Solomon
Islands, 1879

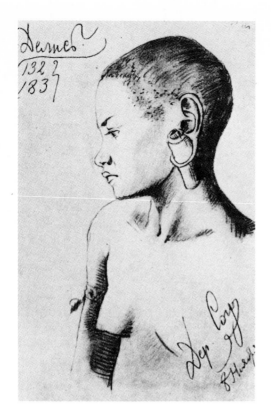

A girl of the Admiralty Islands

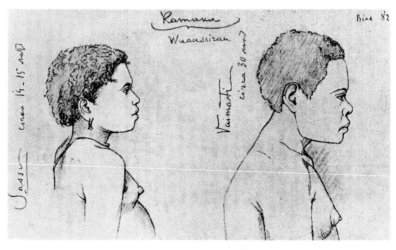

Vuoucirau women of the Kamaka Mountains, south-western New Guinea, 1874

In his complete self-portrait, the wily Ulysses co-existed with the man of perfect probity, the gentle humanitarian lived peaceably beside the man with a gun. Sometimes, it was true, he had described himself as 'alone and unarmed' when surrounded by well-armed servants. But both his survival and one side of his self-esteem had always relied on a considered willingness to use violence. When he appealed to the reason of men who threatened his life or authority, it had been by arousing a reasonable fear that he would kill them.

He did not despair of reconciling all interests. He had never encouraged misunderstandings unless they contributed to his safety and success. Except when imposing discipline, he had never been first to offer violence. Superior tactics had always allowed him to prevail without shedding blood. In any case, the master who read Maclay's 1882 report through the lens of Tolstoyan principle would probably do the same with the book. Tolstoy's desire for 'observations about the nature of man' had nothing to do with the shortcomings of Will Olsen, which Maclay intended to describe in detail. By 'relations with people', Tolstoy did not mean the management of Malay sailors, or the situation in which a European might force an insolent but unarmed Chinese to choose between obedience and death. 'People' were those who responded naturally to Maclay's influence, the uncorrupted inhabitants of the Maclay Coast.

When Tolstoy's advice arrived, Maclay had already dictated the record of sojourns on his coast. Taking 'the risk of appearing rather too subjective and speaking too much of my own personality', he had revised the manuscript to include episodes 'characteristic of my relations with the natives' and possibly illustrative of Tolstoy's beliefs. He cared nothing for readers who might 'distrustfully shrug their shoulders'. They would do so only because they did not know him. 'I am sure', he told Tolstoy, 'that the most severe critic of my book, its truth and honesty in all respects, will be myself'.

By March 1887 the manuscript had been corrected and copied. The volume was not ready to print. Illustrations must be chosen and placed. It was to be equipped with appendixes, including extracts from Tolstoy's remarks to show the principles on which it was written. Then there still stretched ahead a second volume of travels, and the purely scientific part. Two-thirds of the task remained to be done.

Despite Gabriel Monod's impression that mystical love of science made him indifferent to publication, Maclay cared intensely for seeing his work into print. When he thought of his declining strength he could not fail to regret time lost in pursuit of the colonization mirage. He never blamed this for the delay, and certainly not the changes suggested by Tolstoy.

He could not visit that disconsolate visionary, hungry for communion with the one person who lived Tolstoyan beliefs. When

Maclay dragged himself upright it was to catch the train to the south, the steamer to Port Said, the North German Lloyd liner to the Pacific. The usual rumour went round the world—that he was returning to New Guinea. He planned nothing but a few days in Australia. His one hope was that a passage through the tropics might relieve his pain.

Aboard the *Neckar* he quitted the tropics as he had entered them, tortured day and night by rheumatism and neuralgia. In all the comfort of modern travel, he endured the most unpleasant voyage of his life, an unrelieved physical distress, with 'enormous waste of time'. Yet as the ship followed the southern coast of Australia, into another winter, he had to work for the least congenial purpose, the getting of money. For the first time he travelled as a journalist with a definite mission.

The *New Times* was a reactionary rag. Its millionaire publisher and real editor, Alexei Suvorin, was hated by liberals. Its 'humorists' had put dreadful words into Maclay's mouth—'I hate Jews' . . . 'Oh, it isn't that I call myself Baron. Others call me so, though being so very absent-minded I may have signed myself so' . . . 'Oh dear! That was all my deplorable absent-mindedness. I wished to write about the protectorate to Mr Giers but wrote to Lord Derby instead'. They had pilloried him as 'ex-King of the Papuans', claimed that he offered to handle commercial agencies in New Guinea. But the *New Times* had long favoured annexation of the Maclay Coast. Its quarrel was less with Maclay than with the paper that supported him. At the height of the bombardment the editor had sent a note begging him not to take offence at a few harmless jokes. When the tsar's wishes seemed clear, opposition had turned into the discreet support Maclay wanted. And Suvorin's businesslike methods included prompt and fair payment to contributors. To earn 'a few extra kopecks', Maclay had offered to satisfy the paper's long-standing interest in Australia.

He tried to gather up-to-date views about Australian defence and relations with Great Britain. He noted opinions from the 'extreme democratic camp' as well as those of the 'more reasonable' majority. He listened to both the peacefully inclined and the 'warlike' colonists who wished to be able to defend themselves. He collected information on the management of timber resources and Australia's battle with rabbits, subjects sure to interest a large rural readership. News from Tonga gave him illustrations of the evils caused by European intrusion into the Pacific, the abuses committed in the names of 'enlightenment' and 'Christianity'. He had nothing to say of the Queensland slave trade; a date had been set for its termination. The great evil in Australia now was the ill-treatment of Chinese, and Maclay's recent special version of the 'yellow peril' did not weaken his indignation.

He suffered no personal unpleasantness, beyond the worries of dismantling his household. His arrival naturally made news. His name headed the passenger list. People asked whether he was going to New Guinea. But the newspapers had printed reports from St Petersburg without comment, and the colonists were careful to let nothing show. His worst enemies could not claim he had deceived them. They had always known, in their bones if not in their brains, exactly where his actions would lead.

It was a hard time for his wife to leave her homeland. Her self-effacing mother was ill. Her father, putting up a brave show in public, was inwardly despondent, suffering from injuries sustained while working in his new 'national park'. But her husband and his cause came first. Her idea of fidelity was simple and complete: she must believe nothing ill of him, even if she heard it from his own lips; she must never forsake him by one thought. So nothing had shaken her faith—neither the news that he was organizing Russian colonies nor the news that he denied it, neither the sketch of paradise for the well-to-do nor talk of naval stations that could frighten her relatives and friends. While she learned how he was lampooned and persecuted, St Petersburg reports had evoked his presence—broad mind and universal sympathies, eyes that seemed to reflect an unsullied world. When he returned to her, sick, disappointed, but steadfast as ever in his fight for humanity, she was ready to follow him anywhere.

The house was abandoned; possessions acquired eighteen months before were sold. The family sailed for Europe on the vessel by which Maclay had arrived. Some people in Sydney had the impression that he would return once his book was published. But he would never again live in that alien colony. He might see it once more on his way back to lands where life was bearable.

They left the *Neckar* at Genoa and took the shortest route through the heart of Europe, pausing in Vienna to be married by the rites of the Russian church. Maclay had hoped to spend summer at Malin, but by mid-July 1887 they were in St Petersburg, Maclay 'in bivouac' in an almost-empty flat, while bills for his family's accommodation mounted at the Hôtel d'Angleterre.

Greetings and news came from his brothers, but no money. There was no money for setting up house, not even the deposit for the flat. He had to obtain an advance from Suvorin for articles he had been unable to write. Crippled by rheumatism, desperate for time, he had to cope with domestic purchases and the engagement of servants on behalf of a wife who spoke no Russian. The children fell ill. There were 'many worries of different kinds', in a world where he found it increasingly 'hard to get along'. He thought of the door in the wall surrounding the family graves, and for the first time wanted the key.

He did not imagine himself dying. He had plans—for scientific consultations and for study of his anatomical collection; for publication of his book in Russian, English and possibly French; for completing his work by founding a Russian colony. In a short autobiography contributed to a history of Russian science, he spoke almost as definitely of the future as of the past. He believed in his power to survive a year or eighteen months in Europe and set out again for the blessed tropical lands.

The remainder of summer slipped away, the only time he had thought possible for work. In the fine early-autumn weather, he felt the breath of terrible winters that made him ill. Each day he dragged himself halfway across this city of excessive distances, for hydropathic treatment and massage. When time and the state of his hands allowed, he wrote—not the book that had been so many years in the making, but articles for newspapers. His life was consumed by old hotel bills, rent, medical expenses, the wages of servants.

He wrote his way through the winter of 1887–88—articles on Australia, accounts of his visit to the Admiralty Islands in 1879, his brief trips to New Guinea on British and Russian warships in 1881 and 1883, his last conversation with the much-mourned Turgenev. He fought a ladylike censorship that bleached 'local colour' from descriptions of South Seas sexual behaviour. Angered by those who criticized the Russian expression of the 'white Papuan', he retorted with a favourite quotation from Goethe:

> And when you earnestly mean what you say,
> What need to hunt for words along the way?

But few of the articles were published. St Petersburg was full of desperate men writing for newspapers. If all his output had reached print, the earnings would have made little difference. Poorer than some of those who huddled in tenements, he had to support a style of life fit for people of station, in one of the best parts of town.

Over the years he had offered protection and guidance to thousands. Now those needing help clung to him. Would-be settlers bothered him about the colony. A famous entrepreneur wanted advice about buying land in the Pacific islands. Meshchersky, from a distance, wanted assistance in business matters. The whole Miklouho family lived in the Kiev district, but people seeking aid for Nikolai Ilich Miklouho's destitute 'sister' in Kiev applied to his famous son. Day in, day out, he had before his eyes the most dependent of them all, the trustful wife and tiny, oblivious children.

After six months of distress, other people thought Rita 'as well and cheerful as on her arrival'. In fact she was ill and depressed, tormented by inability to help her husband. She bore the whole burden of nursing. She sometimes dealt with foreign correspondence. With a great effort—Maclay could not bear her looking sad—she could fulfil the wifely duty laid down by Schopenhauer, to provide her husband with cheerful solace. But she could neither lighten the task of writing for newspapers nor live within his means. She and the children needed servants and a certain standard of comfort. She felt lonelier and more discouraged without her music, and when a little money came to hand it seemed natural to hire a piano. Thinking once of what men sacrificed to women, Maclay had quoted Molière's *School for Wives*: 'In this world, all is done for these very creatures'. He had never changed his views on women, particularly the useless, artificial European woman. But when the rest of the world had failed him, his wife offered devotion that approached worship. He refused her nothing but her desire to work for money.

In spite of herself, she sometimes felt injured. With the pain at its worst, he lost all self-control. He misunderstood her best and purest motives. He could become scathingly impatient, and forget to spare her in front of others. But she knew this was the illness, not the man. When unbearably sad, she read over his letters, and realized again that no one else understood her as he did, or made such allowance for her faults. She longed only to make herself worthier, of him and of the god she believed they shared. When she took account of his suffering, each day confirmed her sense of witnessing a 'holy, noble life'.

So did his look. Gaunt cheeks bounded by deep lines spoke of pain and endurance, but the high clear brow, accentuated by grey hair worn long in the style of his student years, affirmed a lofty, untroubled spirit. His sad but forgiving eyes revealed a man reconciled to many things.

He reproached no one, now, for Olga's death. Ekaterina Semyon-ovna, a sick old lady, no longer the arbiter in financial matters, was an object of gentle concern. Vladimir's off-hand ways no longer excluded him from affectionate interest. It did not matter whether Mikhail smoked or idled, whistled or sang, shirked the truth or made mistakes in grammar; his one defection, irrelevant in the end, was nothing beside the loyalty that shaped his whole career. Sergei, the unsympathetic elder whom Maclay had once erased from his thoughts, had drawn closer through his interest in the colonization scheme. Just as it had become easier to confess failure to Sergei, it was possible to accept him as head of the family and controller of purse-strings, even to imagine sharing a home with him. Physical distance separated them. Emotional reticence still gave their communications a businesslike tone. In Maclay's mind they were all united around him, as he had always wished. He wanted to rescue the hitherto-unknown aunt, if she really was his father's sister, and gather her into the family. He proudly described his ancestry as what it was: Russian, German and Polish, with never a trace of the Scot. Once, when the distant past reclaimed him, he called himself simply 'Miklouho'.

He was reconciled to some losses in the part of the world that meant
most to him. He no longer worried about the Palaus, and had virtually
forfeited the Celebes land. After one attempt to make it profitable, he
had to forget the island of Sarimbun. He clung only to New Guinea and
the problematic archipelago in which he meant to found the first
Russian colony. As long as he lived, he would not forgive the Germans
or abandon hope of freeing his country.

Few reports from the Pacific could reach him in St Petersburg. He
might have learned that a Russian warship had visited New Guinea. But
it had called for purely touristic purposes, on the wrong side of the
island. Having shaken up Port Moresby, the visitors departed for
Singapore.

Though it ate his food, drank his whisky and 'squeezed the place quite
dry', the Russian invasion did good to H. H. Romilly. Events had left
the deputy commissioner again sole British representative in New
Guinea, devoured by boredom and the sense that a man aged very
quickly here. Every day he looked out for a ship with supplies, letters,
orders that might justify his presence. He almost wished for physical and
legal power to stop native warfare. He almost wished colonial villains
would appear, so that he might protect the natives. Though he disliked
Germans, he almost wished himself in the German colony. They must
be living more interesting and effective lives over there.

On the other side of New Guinea, the newcomers found the climate
enervating, the fever remorseless, boredom inescapable. The territory
that Otto Finsch had described in a salesman's loving phrases was
beautiful but forbidding. After two years a few small plantations existed,
one of them run by reliable Jan Kubary at Port Konstantin. The settlers
they were meant to impress never arrived. The whole idea of Kaiser
Wilhelm's Land had been a mistake.

With all the money it poured into this bottomless pit, the company
could neither exploit nor administer its domain. In Berlin Adolph von
Hansemann, the banker, ruled the colony between breakfast and his
departure for the office. Administrators on the spot were ground
between the director's sanguine orders and the realities of an overwhelming task. Missionaries and their families, the largest group of
European residents, resigned themselves to insult and wondered how to
make the natives understand. Young officials cursed the country and
their employers, tangled themselves in red tape, drank, loafed,
quarrelled, gambled and died. The fastest-growing results of German
imperialism were the Neu Guinea Kompagnie's deficit, piles of
impossible instructions from Berlin, and the cemetery at Finschhafen.

From the humanitarian point of view, not everything thus far was
bad in German New Guinea. Maclay's people were not being exterminated or evicted wholesale from their land. They were not harshly ruled;

the company had no physical power to assert its 'sovereign rights and duties' over a fragmented population in a vast and difficult territory. They would not shoot each other or be degraded by drink; inter-racial trade in firearms and alcohol was forbidden. The company was not organized for extensive trade with people who in any case had little to sell, so they were not being ruined by commerce. Recruiting of labourers for foreign plantations was prohibited, and the company had neither means nor will to recruit them forcibly for its own. Considering New Guineans too untamed for steady work, the Germans employed Javanese. Local people worked when it suited them, just long enough to get what they wanted.

So far, Kaiser Wilhelm's Land had imported the minimum of European evil. Its sole export was knowledge. While British New Guinea was sketchily investigated by private initiative, the Germans sent out well-equipped official expeditions. The scientists had no chance of fulfilling grandiose instructions for exploring the interior. They learned much about the great Sepik River that entered the sea 200 kilometres north-west of Astrolabe Bay, and the brilliant culture that flourished on its banks. They gained an idea of the lie of the land and the principal river systems. They mapped coastal districts, measured heights, amassed materials in botany, geology and ethnology.

Everywhere, they saw evidence of Maclay's presence. They glimpsed his cattle, running wild. Near the mouth of the Sepik, Otto Finsch had seen sweet corn, a few tiny kernels decorating the owner's hair, and surmised it had come from that introduced by Maclay. Around Port Konstantin, the gardeners enjoyed more orthodox benefits from Maclay's plants. They produced all kinds of European articles, from uniform buttons to tools, and explained that these had come from Maclay. In communicating with Papuans, Finsch had found a smattering of Russian almost as useful as the few Bongu words and signs he had learned from his predecessor.

The people remembered Maclay perfectly—all he had said and done and all he might have said and done. Apart from historical interest, this was important to the Germans. Against all his expectations, they were identifying his property, so that he might enjoy the rights of a foreign landowner in German territory.

In January and February 1888 he had the strength and spirit to enquire about anthropological papers that had remained unpublished for years, to rail against censorship, to defend himself against English publishers who wanted to take the translation of his book out of his hands. He wanted books, scientific information, Leo Tolstoy's photograph, all the vital ties and interests. Except in the matter of morphia—he often could not sleep without it—he followed doctor's orders as though they could secure eternal life. There was no truth in rumours that he was 'mending', or preparing his book for the press. The proofs he corrected were those of an article for the *Northern Herald*. Week after week he was 'no better', 'definitely no better'.

His distinguished visitors, including Grand Duke Nikolai Mikhailovich, brought kind words but no help. Mikhail was working in the museum of the Mining Institute, visiting frequently, able to run messages and make small emergency loans. Vladimir turned up late in January, and donated enough for immediate needs. Maclay could count on no one else but his wife. Sometimes afraid to leave him alone, she did not believe that he could be taken from her. It still seemed impossible when in February the doctors decided he was unfit to remain at home, much less to leave for the Crimea. He lay in the Baronet Wylie Clinic, an up-to-date institution attached to the Military Medical Academy, on the other side of the Neva.

He gave the address carefully, 'Building 11, bed 29', as though he already felt lost among sick and dying men. But he was not one of those for whom a bed in this place meant the end of all struggles. He was working on his second article for the *New Times*, anxiously awaiting corrected proofs of the first. He described himself as 'still very weak', as though he expected to grow strong.

Nobody could believe now that he suffered only from rheumatism and neuralgia, intensified by the winter rigours of a city he had always hated. Sometimes he had mentioned 'gout'. Fearsome headaches perhaps contributed to a story of a brain tumour. Many naturally thought him a martyr of science, succumbing to the long years of hardship in the tropics. The most definite report—'dropsy, originating in disorders of the lungs and kidneys'—might indicate renewal of illnesses from his youth, the final results of recurrent malaria, or protracted heavy dosing with half-a-dozen drugs.

His wife almost ceased to care about the causes as she watched through the end of March and the first weeks of April. When she first heard the words 'inflammation of the lungs', spring had touched the factories, railway yards, barracks, arsenals and gaols that surrounded the Wylie Clinic. The Neva ice was breaking up. Behind their sealed double windows, the well-to-do thought of summer cottages, murmuring streams, parasols. The poor again faced the season of floods, epidemics and officially-undrinkable water. In the grim, noisy hospital, there were only hopeful arrivals, and the secretive departures of those who would know no more seasons. It did not matter now whether Maclay fell victim to the mysterious malignancy of countries he had loved or to Peter's improbable city, founded on swamps and corpses. Visitors were becoming intruders, the doctors mere conscientious torturers. Hemmed in by everything he had tried to escape, he existed alone on the final island of M.

Holding him close, as though she might infuse her own strength, his wife lived for the periods of consciousness, when he spoke to her. He was able to speak a few words of pity when the children were brought to his bedside. He spoke quite often on 13 April, and again next day. She heard only endearments, no message for anyone but herself. All was summed up in the last painful breath he drew on the evening of 14 April. In the agony of loss and the fears of survival, she had the consolation that he had died in her arms, calmly, as nobly as he had lived.

When Maclay had made his last journey, across the city to the great Volkhov cemetery, on the south-eastern outskirts, to be buried beside his father and sister, his widow remembered the duty he had left her. It must have gone sorely against her feelings. Every memento, every word written by or about him, was sacred to her. He had asked her to burn his papers, all of them, and she had to make a beginning.

Another version has her driven less by obedience than by frenzied grief. Instead of limiting the havoc to the personal papers he mentioned, she burns everything she does not understand—travel journals, scientific notebooks, diaries, her husband's monument and the heritage of her sons. She does it in sheer distraction, because she cannot read Russian or appreciate the significance of drawings and dates. She does it alone, without seeking advice, in a city of linguists, where two powerful scientific societies and the sovereign have an interest in the literary remains. Within a few days of her husband's death, she destroys his work as though determined to extirpate his memory. The holocaust goes on until Mikhail and the geographers hear of it and persuade her to stop.

Amid her anguish, which was of the benumbed rather than the frantic kind, it all seemed quite different to Rita. Of course she meant to obey her dead husband's instructions, though not straight away. But the day after the funeral she had to start sorting papers. His brothers and some friends were coming that very evening to examine the manuscript of his book. He had never allowed anyone to enter his study; she would not allow it now. When they wanted the private diaries that he had told her to burn, she refused. She would no more let them probe his intimate thoughts than she had let the heartless doctors cut up his body.

Expecting help from a woman friend who knew several languages, she quite soon made a start in arranging the papers. Then came an alarming telegram from Vladimir, warning her to secure all private writings. Men from the Geographical Society were on the way. They might want to examine anything and everything. She had to rush through the painful task she had meant to spread over weeks. For one whole day she burned letters and papers she identified as private. Her eyes were sore; her head felt ready to burst; but she was sure of doing right. No stranger should see these documents that Maclay had always kept to himself.

She spent another evening, just as miserable but more leisurely, destroying many letters. Still she could not bear to part with all. She felt justified in keeping for herself some letters in English. Though she burnt most of those in Russian, she wanted to save a few. And she could not decide about the diaries. She only knew that no one else should read them first. To those who wanted to see them, she replied '*nyet*' and again '*nyet*'.

No men from the Geographical Society turned up. Instead there was difficulty with the family. Vladimir's wife seemed offended when Rita frankly considered her incompetent to handle the literary legacy. Rita's choice of a person for this work—a man recommended by a *savant* who had known her husband—was quickly overruled. Finally Mikhail and a stranger from the university went through the papers. Vladimir helped the widow with what remained. Her wretchedness was solaced by her husband's diaries, kept safe from prying eyes. Every word assured her of his deep, true love.

In the future, many compassionate excuses would have to be made for Margaret Maclay. Her action in burning some papers nevertheless had one useful result. Whenever gaps appeared in the record of Maclay's life and work, it would be possible to point to the destruction wrought by his widow. If her shoulders seemed inadequate for so much guilt, it was permissible to suggest other losses of records, in the great fire at the Sydney exhibition building in 1882, or some other mysterious fire in Sydney. Whatever was lost had been destroyed by an Australian or in Australia.

A good deal was saved. The original New Guinea diaries disappeared (a fragment of one of them reappeared much later, in Russia) but the definitive version, almost ready to print, was rescued intact. Though the journal of the second Malay Peninsula expedition never came to light, that of the first was untouched. The Papua-Koviai record, partly revised for publication, miraculously escaped destruction. Future scholars would miss the original accounts of the voyages of 1876 and 1879, but substantial extracts had already been published. There were piles of unpublished notes, hundreds of drawings, sheaves of letters—a considerable legacy from a man who had lived less than forty-two years, precariously, in many different places. It all belonged to science and to Russia.

The widow kept what no one else wanted. She took the passport with which he had left Russia in 1870, and the portfolio, with monogram and coronet, which had later contained his drawings. She gleaned early sketches of European scenes, pictorial records of travels in the Canary Islands, Morocco and about the Red Sea. Hers were the photographs of the young adventurer in Arab dress, pictures of ships on which he had travelled, signed portraits of personages like Leo Tolstoy and Admiral Kopitov, whom she had never met. She kept a terse exchange of telegrams in German with Rudolf Virchow. She treasured the certificate of honour awarded by the Moscow Imperial Society of Lovers of Natural History. She quite as carefully preserved the Victorian Government's authorization to inspect public institutions.

She might once have indiscriminately burned all papers in Russian. Now she indiscriminately kept everything—a pamphlet reprint of her husband's 1882 report, an address of welcome from students, with all the signatures, a nineteen-page letter explaining Maclay's dealings with Great Britain and recommending the establishment of Russian naval stations. Unable to read them, she preserved long newspaper cuttings about people she had probably never heard of, and short ones about a table game called 'Maclay' and the availability of electrical treatment for diseases of the sexual organs.

She naturally kept a larger miscellany in English—correspondence with Sir Arthur Gordon and Lord Derby, a translation of a letter to Bismarck, materials her husband had used in his humanitarian struggles, and papers concerning his property in various islands. One set of letters apparently went up in smoke, those in which Maclay and his associates discussed the Maclay Coast Scheme. She did keep the draft and a fair copy of the prospectus, and Sir Arthur Gordon's comments, items that Sir Arthur preferred not to keep.

One way or another, she secured enough to build her altar to Maclay on more than personal memories. It had to be built elsewhere. Her worried, ailing parents needed her. In Russia her children were nearly always ill. Though she loved Ekaterina Semyonovna, and won the empress's favour, too much in this country besides the language disturbed and baffled her. As soon as possible she packed her mementoes and returned to Australia. She left at least one durable memorial of her stay. With some difficulty, she had obtained a simple inscription for her husband's grave. It gave his name and the dates of his birth and death in Cyrillic lettering, with an English text that satisfied her belief without insulting his unbelief: 'Well done, thou good and faithful servant . . .'.

She had found him faithful in all things, worthy to rule over all. He had left only plans for a kingdom, only sketches for a crown, but she kept them.

Epilogue

WHILE MACLAY PREPARED his book, copyists had transcribed excerpts from publications in several languages, intended to supplement his final text. Most of them concerned the Pacific Islands and the inhabitants, but one quotation, in his own handwriting, evidently had a more personal significance. It referred to William Dampier, the explorer whose maps first showed the existence of Astrolabe Bay:

> Of this eminent seaman and traveller, though little more than a century can have elapsed since his death, no one now is able to tell how the evening of his life was spent, when he died, or where he was buried ...

Maclay, who had often felt the world's neglect, perhaps expected a similar fate to overtake his own memory. But his life had left its mark in too many ways and in too many places to be forgotten. When it ended without an evening, in an age of daily newspapers and abundant scientific communication, the telegraph services went to work.

Not all the tributes were free from the irony of circumstance. The most detailed and appreciative came from Otto Finsch. After Maclay's long fight against European 'white ants' in unspoiled countries, Anton Chekhov could think of him as driven partly by faith in 'Christian civilization'. Russian admirers and the St Petersburg correspondent of *The Times* stressed his dedication to founding Russian colonies, while the authors of garbled Australian obituaries preferred to omit the last phase of his career. The Russian physical scientists mentioned 'services to his country' rather than scientific or humanitarian work. On the other hand, the death of one who had tried to give his fatherland advantages in war was felt as a loss by the Peace Society.

As in his lifetime, people made him what they wished. There seemed no danger of his being forgotten. Chekhov confidently named him as one whose story was 'known to every schoolboy', a legend in the countries he had travelled, an inspiration to Europe, an antidote to the sickness of the times. He figured in the recollections of men whose records would be important in the future, remembered as the Peace Society summed him up: 'one of the bravest, purest and most successful of modern explorers'.

His place in science seemed equally secure. The journals of eight cities preserved his writings. Animals and plants had been named in his honour. He had been friend or colleague of famous men; honorary member, corresponding member or associate member of seven scientific organizations. The sense of his devotion and self-sacrifice made it natural to feel that his discoveries must have enriched every field of science. His actual achievement was never so easy to define.

In general, his ambitious early work was not destined to last. Later workers failed to confirm his first published discovery, the possible rudimentary or vestigial swimbladder in shark embryos, and changing opinion eventually robbed it of its original significance. Over the years the title of his book on the fish brain sometimes appeared in comprehensive bibliographies, but its contents had advanced science only by stimulating opposition. Though the 'coelenterate theory of sponges' held its shaky position for many years, Maclay's contribution was often forgotten in the ramifying controversy. As one authority pointed out in 1887, his theories always had too little foundation. Specialists also developed an ambiguous attitude towards the extreme variability that had seemed the most important quality of his 'new' sponges. In describing his much-discussed *Veluspa polymorpha*, he had lumped together specimens of at least three known genera. But in one way or another several of the names he conferred survived the confusion and upheavals of sponge classification. His first discovery, the tiny *Guancha blanca*, probably did more than any other sponge to preserve his memory in science. As *Clathrina blanca* it eventually became a favourite subject of study.

The bulk of his zoological publications in Australia did less to keep his fame alive. The wallaby he thought no other European had seen was finally placed with a species described from islands west of New Guinea in the eighteenth century. The Garagassi bandicoot on which he founded a new sub-genus was assigned, after several revisions, to a fifty-year-old genus that he had dismissed as established on insufficient grounds. Only one of his seven 'new' marsupials retained the specific name he gave it. The wallaby *Dorcopsis macleayi*, found badly preserved among specimens sent to William Macleay, seemed so anomalous that a later systematist was ready to think it an inter-generic hybrid. Another specialist reconsidered the question thirty years later. Renamed *Dorcopsulus macleayi*, the new species became the first of a new genus.

Maclay's mature work in neurology, never made known, may have produced important discoveries. He had briefly mentioned the detection of errors in earlier descriptions of marsupial and monotreme brains, but since he did not specify them the state of knowledge remained unchanged. His paper on the dugong made no lasting impression. One study saved this side of his activity from being a barren exercise in which many animals died for no gain to science. His modest comparison of the dingo's cerebral convolutions with those of the New Guinea dog survived to figure in the bibliography of a comprehensive late twentieth-century treatise.

These investigations threw off a by-product that was arguably his most important contribution to zoology. In measuring the body temperature of echidna and platypus, he did not discover the monotremes' incomplete thermal regulation, as his countrymen later believed. He announced only that two sleepy echidnas and one dying platypus showed temperatures far below those reported for advanced mammals. He probably did well to find no more. The monotremes' reputation as poor temperature regulators did not stand the test of closer investigation. Maclay's research, however, had a secure place as the first in the field, and he was apparently the first naturalist to suggest in print that echidnas undergo a partial hibernation.

In this second phase of his career as a zoologist, his nearest approach to commitment on questions of evolution was his proof that the Port Jackson shark was closely allied to some fossil forms, a relationship that no one doubted. Alone among his published papers, his study of 'reversed' hair tracts in some marsupials raised the question of adaptation. He suggested that observation of these animals might test the Darwin-Wallace opinion that the direction of hair formed a protection against rain. Even so, he avoided both positive commitment and a more controversial point. Darwin's real message was that the useless, upwardly directed hairs on the human forearm might point to a time when apelike ancestors sat in the rain with their hands over their heads.

Maclay had clearly admired the young Darwin, the observant traveller. His attitude to the great theorist was harder to discern. His early research had temporarily bolstered hypotheses that might have supported Darwin, but Maclay himself made no such specific connection. During his travels, he had glanced at many subjects treated in Darwin's works; he had mentioned Darwin the theorist only twice, in each case to cast doubt on Darwin's opinions. Never did he touch upon the central tenet of Darwinism, 'the origin of species by means of natural selection'. In short, a question mark hung over his position in the great scientific movement of his time. In most respects he behaved like a man burnt by theory, determined never to touch it again. Any general ideas derived from his zoological research after 1870 remained in his notebooks, where they could not affect the progress of science.

To concentrate on the study of primitive peoples, he had renounced two possible sources of fame—large collections and the general description of animal life. He never gave up his two vast zoological undertakings, potentially more important than his painstaking attempts to establish new species. The fact that after fourteen years of research he had published little on the brain, and nothing on marine zoogeography, suggested less a voluntary sacrifice than a failure to discover anything significant. With all allowance made for illness, insecurity and time-consuming political action, it appeared that as zoologist he had also fallen victim to his own insatiability. In constant upheaval and expectation of early death, he had gone on amassing materials as though he looked forward to a long and tranquil life. In the result, zoology had gained surprisingly little from his toil.

The man who clung so long to the hope of penetrating the New Guinea interior, and meditated upon the world's neglect of Dampier, had undoubtedly wished to be remembered as an explorer. When twenty years went by without the appearance of his journals, a historian of New Guinea discovery could think of him as one whose fame had passed, 'as quickly extinguished as a will o' the wisp'. He had in fact communicated little about the regions he investigated—scattered remarks on Astrolabe Bay and Port Alexei, reports on weather, earthquakes and coastal uplift, a few place names that appeared on an English map in 1884. He wrote more fully of Papua-Koviai and added some details to existing maps. Everything else was too long saved up for a final great publication. His place in the history of exploration also suffered by the fact that he could not really travel alone, or remain for long the only traveller in his country. Before he could report on his first New Guinea sojourn, published charts from *Vityaz* had filled in the principal blank in the outline of his coast. *Basilisk*'s running survey left him little to add from his eastward voyage of 1877, and *Skobelev* annexed the honour of charting Port Alexei. By the year of his death, his unpublished geographical observations had lost all novelty.

His manuscripts reached the Russian Geographical Society in such disorder that for many years potential editors declined the task of bringing out his record of travels. When Professor D. N. Anuchin undertook it, twenty more years were to pass before publication. Then the Russian text, inaccessible to most of the foreigners who might have welcomed it, had to wait another thirty years for any translation. Yet it could not be truly said that Maclay's fame as a traveller was extinguished outside his fatherland. The Dutch always gave him due credit for the discovery of Kamaka-Walla lake. Though he had meant to keep secret his geogaphical findings in the Malay Peninsula, the English quite early learned enough details to be able to honour him for throwing 'much light' on the interior of Pahang and Kelantan. Germans cited his remarks in their books on New Guinea, and from scanty information tried to preserve his geographical names. But their inquiries among the people elicited a name for part of his coast, or that of Rai village, or a local word for 'water'. Early in the twentieth century, the idea arose that the inhabitants called this coast 'Rai'. The Australians, who replaced the Germans after 1914, still spoke of the 'Maclay Coast' in the 1920s and '30s, but the place name that meant most to Maclay eventually disappeared from the maps.

Sharing the broad interests of a generation to which Alexander von Humboldt had been a living legend, steeped in the contents of *Cosmos*, Maclay had wished geographers to remember him by more than a name on maps. The trouble was that his time made it increasingly difficult for the lone traveller to contribute anything memorable to the scientific study of the physical world. Four measurements of deep-sea temperatures made him a pioneer, in that no one else had obtained readings at those points. The first of them was mentioned in an early review of the subject. Otherwise his findings on sea temperature disappeared in a mass of data credited to ships rather than men. On land, too, many questions in physical science had either passed out of the lone researcher's province or been reduced to routine. His meteorological records of north-eastern New Guinea, valued as the first from that region, were obtained by following printed instructions. Even in Australia, he could not be first to measure temperatures beneath the earth's surface, and his investigations of the continent's deepest mine basically supported what the government geologist had found in a lesser shaft. The achievement could not win either of them more than a place in a list.

In New Guinea itself it was difficult for Maclay to be first in reporting the larger phenomena, for Dutch naturalists had already described the island's earthquakes and coastal uplift. The subjects he had studied least, geology and botany, nevertheless gave him claims to fame, recognized when the state of knowledge was reviewed. He had withheld his general collection of rocks, but his report on coastal uplift, and the sub-fossil shells and Bongu clays he submitted for examination, won him a place in the annals of Australasian geology. When it became possible to chronicle activity along the Bismarck Sea volcanic arc, the infrequency of earlier sightings of Manam placed his description high on the list. Though he could give no more than a general impression of New Guinea vegetation, his small collection included two new species to be named in his honour, and one of them, the wild banana *Musa maclayi*, later aroused interest as a probable ancestor of cultivated varieties. In one department he stood alone. A hundred years later he was still the principal authority on plants used by the inhabitants of the Astrolabe Bay area, frequently cited in the most comprehensive work on New Guinea vegetation.

His readiness to turn his hand to everything was typical of scientific travellers in his time. At all times, his real fame rested upon his reputation as observer and friend of primitive peoples.

The sense that he had published only preliminary reports made it natural to feel that his early death deprived anthropology and ethnology of important truths. Maclay himself had never proposed more than the re-investigation of doubtful points. His last communications of results had added little to the first, and nothing suggested a fresh overall view of any problem in human evolution, migrations or social development. At the close of his career as at the beginning, he had discussed his studies in terms of opinions that had long been current.

As anthropologist he showed his usual reluctance to link his findings with any theory, priding himself on the presentation of uninterpreted facts. Coming after similar arguments from several eminent biologists, the central thesis of Darwin's *Descent of Man* had been quite calmly received. Maclay used the book as a mine of details to supplement his observations; for all his interest in 'atavisms', it could never be said that he pronounced definite views on the descent of man. Nor did he take a firm position on the other great question agitating nineteenth-century anthropology, that of the common or diverse origin of human races. He presumably believed, with all the clergymen and at least half the scientists, that mankind formed one species. He nevertheless observed and recorded without apparent regard for such implications.

Racial distinctions rather than similarities formed the object of his search—more constant and profound characteristics than those revealed by measurement and external inspection. When he failed to pronounce certain sounds in New Guinea languages, he concluded that Papuan vocal organs differed fundamentally from those of Europeans. His announcement that he had found significant differences in the brains of various races was a gift to 'polygenists', who saw the great divisions of mankind as distinct in origin and innate abilities. Either side of the controversy could take comfort from his observations on mixed races. The changes he thought he saw among Negroes in Brazil suggested the flexibility of a common human stock under changed conditions. The opinion he most consistently expressed—that each race had been formed by a specific climate, hence that an entirely European lineage could not survive in the tropics—was a basic tenet of polygenism.

He had provably set himself one great task: to determine the distribution and anthropological relationships of 'Papuans'. Without clearly stating conclusions, he apparently ended by accepting the old idea of these people as the first inhabitants of their region. Despite their variability and uncertain origin, they formed a unique race, only slightly blurred around the edges. He thought of the northern negritos as Papuans, not of a possible negrito strain in New Guinea. Though he noted Malayo-Polynesian affinities in their languages, he firmly separated his people from all others. He could never entertain the view that eventually prevailed. A century later, anthropologists debated the origin, size and sequence of migrations, and the racial blending that might have occurred before any group reached the New Guinea region. They agreed in the end that Melanesia contained a basic Australoid or Negrito-Australoid population, amalgamated with relative newcomers from all points of the compass. As his standard of the pure and primeval, Maclay had chosen one of the most mixed peoples on earth.

He was not alone in his day, and in his principal line of research he largely supported earlier views. He revived the oldest opinions about the negritos, confirmed rather than discovered a Polynesian influence in the New Hebrides and a Papuan strain in the Palau Islands. Contrary to his own opinion, he never penetrated the interior far enough to prove that one race occupied all New Guinea, but he established what no one denied, that widely separated coastal populations exhibited the same range of types. Science paid him tribute for two wholly new observations on the distribution of races: a general idea of the area inhabited by negritos in the Malay Peninsula, and the discovery that Micronesians occupied the Ninigo group, just north of New Guinea.

Often frustrated by impatient or suspicious 'subjects', he had tried to fulfil the latest requirements for more numerous and exact cranial measurements. He was among the first to use standard tables for assessing skin and eye colour. He tirelessly measured the diameter of curls and studied hair in microscopic section. He was also guided by a list of questions on artificially distorted heads and flattened noses, the length of big toes and the size of teeth. He had to pay attention everywhere to the dimensions of penises and the form of female external genitals, the adiposity of buttocks and the shape of breasts. He bore in mind the prevailing interest in operations on the sexual organs, and such phenomena as the 'Hottentot apron'. This approach met the requirements of the 1870s and '80s. It might not in itself have assured his place in the history of science.

To be first with these investigations in any particular place was a matter of increasing difficulty. He could add little to the voluminous data on the Polynesians. In the Philippines, two investigators had recently preceded him. Before he reached Yap and the Palaus, long-term visitors had published substantial reports, and the *Challenger* expedition was ahead of him in the Admiralty Islands. In Australia, he was practically forced to seek the 'curious', even at second or third hand.

Inspection of Australian Aborigines from Cape York to Victoria gave him nothing new to report but the occurrence of unusually long legs among Australian women.

Whatever the circumstances, he had tried to complete perennially inadequate knowledge and provide a check on his predecessors' findings. Though others had inspected the Philippines negritos, he was first to measure their heads. His results (queried) were included in an important textbook. In Micronesia he was again first to use the craniometer, and again his average figures appeared in later publications. His 'small but important work' on the Palauans was frequently cited in elaborate volumes that resulted from German research early in the twentieth century. Successors who failed to confirm some of his statements, found one or two exaggerated, and felt compelled to disagree with others, were never ungenerous in mentioning his work.

After 1876, however, the bulk of his anthropological results had been reserved for an ultimate fully-illustrated book. In his time and for many years more, the study of mankind gained nothing from his second sojourn on the Maclay Coast, little from his last long voyage and his investigations in Australia. His proof of widespread brachycephaly among Melanesians never really established their racial identity with negritos. Anthropologists who eagerly accepted his passing statement on neurological differences discovered in several races never learned anything substantial about his findings. His one publication on the Australian brain lost its apparent significance when the same rare feature was found in substantial percentages of Europeans and Chinese. His hearsay notes on subincision, still cited in the 1890s, disappeared in mounting evidence that the operation he believed to be a contraceptive measure was actually an important socio-religious rite. Late in the twentieth century, two contributions to Australian anthropology helped to maintain his fame. A treatise on race summarized his study of the hairless man. And one of the two Australian skulls he described remained the narrowest on record.

His work in the Malay Peninsula, highly valued by his colleagues, was not permanently remembered for the discoveries that at first seemed most exciting. Where Maclay's portraits of typical negritos included what contemporaries called 'a real chimpanzee profile ... the highest degree of prognathism possible in a human being', his successors in the field saw only a slight protrusion of the jaws. It had to be admitted that his *camera lucida* had 'somewhat exaggerated' that startling profile. Another remarkable feature he reported as typical—a foot like that 'found in many kinds of apes'—was more easily explained. Some negritos could bend the outer three toes inwards, one beneath the other, and Maclay had caught them doing it.

Like his discovery of 'macrodontism', these instances of too much zeal in seeking atavisms never affected his good reputation as an observer. Students of the Malay Peninsula appreciated the 'new impetus' he gave to research that had been at a standstill for twenty years. He had provided the first measurements of negrito and Jakun heads, the first general information on the distribution of tribes. His notes on customs, ornament and language were useful for thirty years and more. Criticism nearly all related to his too-exclusive concentration on negritos as 'Papuans'. But critics were never really hard on Maclay. There was too great an admiration for his courage and self-sacrifice, too deep a regret that he had not lived to publish more than preliminary reports, always a sense that he was the hero of a unique exploit, Maclay of the Maclay Coast.

A great successor, Bronislaw Malinowski, once thought of him as a 'new type' in the history of anthropology. He was in fact the first scientist to achieve what became the anthropologist's dearest ambition—to settle among people who had never seen a white man. He was apparently first to form the purpose of living so close to the natives that he could become 'almost one of themselves'. For much of his career, however, circumstances kept him far from this ideal. In island voyages he had been perforce the scientific visitor, arriving with a disruptive shipload of strangers, never staying long enough to think of entering into native life. His progress through the Malay Peninsula had resembled that of an African explorer, with a crowd of followers and an urgent need to keep moving. Wherever possible, he had wielded official authority. Moreover he was often forced, like all travelling naturalists, to fill out his observations with secondhand information. Determined as he was to believe nothing he heard from Malays, they were the only possible source of some remarks on the Malay Peninsula peoples. In Polynesia and other places where he did not know the language, missionaries helped him out. In Yap and the Palaus he had to resort to the traders, one of whom supplied notes accumulated over several years. Even in New Guinea, the land that shaped his reputation, necessity overrode the ideal. An awe-inspiring arrival left no hope of unobtrusive 'joining-in'. A certain physical and psychological distance always seemed essential for safety and power. Frustrated in attempts to explore the interior, Maclay had remained both scientific traveller and laboratory worker, largely occupied with studies remote from the natives. In the result, his reports dealt almost exclusively with visible facts, differing from the observations of other naturalists in quantity rather than kind.

He had answered many questions suggested by advisers or listed in published instructions to travellers. Those who came after him quoted his population estimates and descriptions of Papuan physical characteristics. He was the first authority on arts and crafts in the Astrolabe Bay area, gardening, fishing and methods of obtaining salt, Papuan hairdressing, the position in squatting and the habit of sleeping uncovered above a smouldering fire. His long visits allowed him to describe weddings, funerals and seasonal festivals, events rarely witnessed by ethnographers in his century. He was first to report the use of a *kava*-like drink in New Guinea, first to record the prevalence of malaria among the inhabitants. From observation he described the position of women, relations between parents and children, and the physical and moral training of the young. He gave Europeans a clear impression of how these people spent most of their time, as sympathetically viewed from the outside. What was missing from his work was not greatly missed, in his day or for many years thereafter.

Yet he had hoped to provide much more, to be truly a new type of investigator, acquainting himself intimately with all aspects of native life and thought. And this ideal had obviously proved more difficult than he expected. In some cases he had simply been unlucky: no initiations took place while he was in residence. Sometimes his demands as European and explorer had conflicted with thorough research: by insisting that the Bilbils convey him when and as he wished, he renounced the chance of studying the trade system he discovered. Though he always regarded the position of *Kaaram-tamo* as an advantage, the feigned indifference it entailed closed the way to many inquiries, and other questions were silenced by fear of misleading answers. Even so, he had often seemed strangely incurious.

He had noticed possible clues to social structure, apparently without following them up. Aware that long discussions preceded arrangements of marriage, he ignored all questions of who might marry whom and what obligations were assumed. He observed the position of 'big-men', and never discovered how it was attained. In a department where 'fanciful' and fragmentary answers were perfectly welcome—the collection of myths and legends—he had nothing to report. He noted magical performances related to weather and disease, but went through the agricultural year three times without mentioning garden magic. Once he had suggested that only stringent standards of proof prevented his writing a treatise on Papuan beliefs. At the end of a long association he had concluded that his people had no religion apart from a few superstitions and some ideas about himself.

His failure to explore the less visible sides of Papuan life was not necessarily a matter of choice. From the start he had seen a command of native languages as vital to his aims. The struggle to acquire it brought him a useful knowledge of his neighbours' tongue, wordlists from two dozen villages, and honour in the history of New Guinea linguistics. With 350 Bongu words on his list, he had estimated that he knew one-third of the dialect. But to the end he could not discuss sorcery or understand a conventional speech. It appeared that his investigations might have been limited less by policy than by inability to ask the necessary questions.

Nobody actually asked how far Maclay and his people understood each other. His writings in general implied that after the first months of struggle and frustration he readily conversed on any subject. He had written, after all, for readers who would happily accept his description of a Bilbil orator haranguing a Singor crowd in the Bongu dialect. And that account would still be accepted a century later, when many must have recognized its improbability. Neither his specific references to language difficulties nor the omissions that ethnologists later regretted in his work could touch the foundations of his fame.

For his influence was always primarily a moral one. The story of how he had won the love and trust of a primitive people, entering deeply into their lives, was permanently imprinted on the mind of Europe. With his defence of the oppressed, his years of sacrifice and suffering, and what many considered a martyr's death, it formed a great legend, embodying the highest ideals. Rooted in the eternal struggle between good and evil, such a legend could only grow, yielding whatever meanings were most desired.

Since all human beings need courage, that characteristic came first in every picture of Maclay, exemplified in all its forms. Then there were his gentleness and modesty, his strict adherence to his word, his unflinching service to truth, justice and human welfare. And beyond these qualities on which all could agree there was almost limitless personal choice. For Gabriel Monod there had been the patience and self-control, the psychological penetration and the mystic love of science. For Professor Modestov, the legend's hero was the seeker of ever wider possibilities in human thought and action, the possessor of an iron will to which 'nothing seemed impossible'. Developing his religion of non-resistance, Leo Tolstoy often thought with love and reverence of Maclay the Christian pacifist. When he identified sexuality as the greatest of evils, he saw as deep a lesson in Maclay's chastity. Even poor weak Peter Tchaikovsky could sharpen his self-disgust on the memory of that extraordinary man who had never needed the comfort of alcohol. No man who was not morally dead failed to find in Maclay an example of something to be admired if never attained by others.

For Maclay's contemporaries, other meanings had often been over-shadowed by the figure of the white man who became the ruler and god of a primitive people. A heavy emphasis fell on what Gabriel Monod called Maclay's 'incredible ascendancy', the smiling indifference and wise reserve that kept the Papuans at a respectful distance and taught them they were dealing with 'a being of superior race'. Tolstoy himself could not resist the appeal of a relationship in which savages not only adored Maclay but *submitted* to him. In Monod's interpretation, Maclay's people were rather often on their knees, imploring his mercy and forgiveness.

These images could not survive the decades in which, for increasing numbers of Europeans, the pride of dominion collapsed into revulsion and remorse. The abolition of war and cannibalism, cited by Monod as perhaps Maclay's greatest achievement, was less esteemed when anthropologists pointed to the destruction of such customs as an important factor in the decay of primitive societies. The whole idea of a civilizing mission became deeply suspect. Even the picture of Maclay as 'a father among his children' lost its simple charm. Yet the legend could always accommodate changing modes of thought. No images of kneeling Papuans appeared in Maclay's own writings. He had emphasized his determination not to interfere with native customs, claiming only to have prevented an unspecified number of wars. Arising from apparent defencelessness rather than strength, reluctantly adopted for the common good, his power in no way resembled the crude domination that had made the history of Europe abroad an inerasable infamy. And there was abundant evidence that he had concentrated his moral influence upon those who needed it. His own time had honoured his efforts to civilize white men. As empires were dismantled, in guilt and recrimination, his story became ever more potent as example and reproach.

The appearance of his New Guinea journals, five years after the Russian revolution, had trimmed many inharmonious elements from the legend. It did turn out that some events contributing to his supernatural reputation had been less accidental than previously supposed. In the light of his detailed record, it could no longer be imagined that he had lived in New Guinea without weapons, or that his means of defence had remained unknown to the Papuans. But a special quality set his actions apart from those of others. No suggestion of trade or barter touched the European goods he had given the Papuans, while the land, food, services and ethnological specimens he accepted never undermined the sense that he had done good and asked nothing in return. If he demonstrated his gun, it was to prove his ability to protect his friends. If he set off flares and burned alcohol, these were not attempts to overawe the natives, as in the case of Luigi D'Albertis, but contributions to knowledge of Papuan psychology. Established on a plane where action and effect escape from ordinary scrutiny, the legend absorbed all cases.

By the early 1950s, when his *Collected Works* appeared, Maclay was an official hero of the new Russia, revered as scientist, humanitarian, patriot and revolutionary thinker. In science he was an ardent Darwinist, with the requisite belief in the power of environment and the hereditary transmission of acquired characteristics. From his exemplary family background and lifelong devotion to Chernyshevsky to his sufferings as victim of capitalism and reaction, he satisfied every political requirement. Above all, there was his long fight against slavery and imperialism, his sacrifice of life itself in this cause. It became clear that he had dedicated himself not only to defending Pacific islanders but to refuting racist theories. In time it was found that he had scientifically proved the unity and equality of all human races.

The brilliance of this image made it impossible to see Maclay, gun in hand, confronting a Malay seaman who was too much afraid of a storm, or a Chinese sawyer who insufficiently feared a white man. The proof that Papuan hair was distributed like that of Caucasians completely overshadowed the announcement of significant differences discovered in the brains of various races. Where silence was impossible, bold dialectic transformed difficulties into gains. And in fact nothing now could seriously unsettle a conception that symbolized the Soviet struggle for the rights of oppressed peoples. Research in the naval archives fundamentally revised one episode long cherished as typical of Maclay, the story of how his urgent wish to see his people and improve their lot had persuaded an admiral to make for New Guinea instead of Vladivostok. The legend sailed on, as smoothly as the corvette *Skobelev*.

Russians condemned the tsarist government that had abandoned the Papuans and denied support to Maclay's colonization project. Otherwise the story was wholly a source of pride. Maclay was a favourite hero of schoolchildren, an inspiration to the whole Soviet people. Streets were named for him, societies founded, awards established. To mark the centenary of his arrival in New Guinea, the ethnological institute of the Soviet Academy of Sciences was named in his honour. It was Russia's duty and privilege to ensure that the world gave him his due and remembered that he was Russian.

Outside his fatherland, the legend had perhaps its most significant effect among those who owed him a kind of atonement. Early German travellers and missionaries in New Guinea had honoured him as a philanthropist, 'heart and soul for "his" natives', admiring his civilizing influence and the humane efforts that saved his people from the Australians. They had cited his fatherly treatment of Papuans as an example and reproach to their countrymen, but without evincing any sense of national guilt. In the second half of the twentieth century, when recognition of German guilt extended to the history of the lost colonies, Maclay's story again emerged as example and accusation. Scholarship rediscovered his fruitless appeals to German conscience and his revelations of slavery in Kaiser Wilhelm's Land. It exposed Bismarck's attempts to discredit him with St Petersburg by representing him as a political undesirable and an English agent. Some Germans, at least, realized how deeply their country had wronged both Maclay and New Guinea, and began to make historical amends.

In the other country that figured prominently in the legend as an enemy of mankind and Maclay, the march towards penitence was halting and confused. Having written their cautious obituaries, Australians seemed inclined to forget their famous visitor. His name appeared occasionally in scientific publications. He was commemorated by the collections that his widow had donated to William Macleay's museum. Australia possessed the materials for at least an outline of his life, but for more than half a century no Australian took up this promising subject.

The situation changed in 1944, with the appearance of Frank S. Greenop's *Who Travels Alone*. Many important publications, including Maclay's travel journals, remained unknown to the second Australian biographer. With great perseverance and the co-operation of Maclay's sons, he nevertheless put together a coherent story fully expressing his enthusiasm. Reviewers agreed that Maclay had been unjustly neglected; over the years magazines published a few articles about him; the national broadcasting service produced a radio programme; a biographical entry appeared in the *Australian Encyclopaedia*. In the 1960s his character and career were briefly but appreciatively described in several books popular with the general reader. The story of his Scottish descent persisted, as did the punctilious use of the title 'baron'. Australians readily believed that he had discovered New Guinea's tree-climbing kangaroos, animals known to science before he was born. Some imagined him first to recognize the island's strategic importance, the real instigator of British annexation. They admired his efforts to protect his people from the Germans. For all the vagueness and misapprehension, there was a strong sense of his moral significance. Once he had examined anthropologically two Papuans brought to Sydney by a missionary; on a visit to Port Moresby he had renewed acquaintance with one of them. Eighty years later, Australians had a moving tale of a kidnapped Papuan taken to Sydney and exhibited as a wild man, abandoned when no more money could be made from him, finally rescued and returned to his homeland by Maclay. Absurd in itself, such a story at least showed that the descendants of Maclay's oldest enemies were ready to accept him as example and reproach. When his name disappeared from the map of New Guinea, his legend won a subtle victory: many Australians decided that the name of the Rai Coast represented the native pronunciation of 'Maclay'. Yet Russians visiting Sydney discovered with surprise that the former biological station was not a national monument. Most Australians still knew remarkably little about its founder.

In the 1970s they were given another chance to make amends. The centenary of Maclay's first landing in New Guinea saw the beginning of efforts by his grandsons, distinguished men in their own right, to obtain historical justice for him in Australia. Four years later, the publication of C. L. Sentinella's translations in New Guinea, coinciding with that country's independence, for the first time allowed Australians to read Maclay's journals in English. In 1978 the centenary of his arrival in Sydney was celebrated by an exhibition. To carry on the spirit of that occasion, the Miklouho-Maclay Society of Australia was formed in the following year, devoted to spreading Maclay's fame throughout the nation, evolving an Australian contribution to knowledge of his life and work, and fostering his ideals in science and international understanding.

Eminent Australians enthusiastically supported the undertaking. Research by members established the Society as the authoritative source of information on Maclay, publishing its own newsletter. The old biological station, still army property, was at last marked by a commemorative plaque. The legend began to make a fresh impression among the few concerned with social responsibility in science and the many who looked back with shame and outrage upon the colonial past and Australia's dealings with native peoples. In a time of guilt and doubt, when criticism has demolished many humanitarian reputations, Maclay stands almost alone, untainted by paternalism, religious zeal or assumptions of racial superiority. To retain that symbol of hope and redemption, some Australians are prepared to do and believe a great deal. But the nation as a whole is notoriously poor soil for hero-worship, and the cult of Maclay, like all great enthusiasms, sometimes tends to claim too much. Only time can reveal the extent of its success.

However Maclay's spirit might regard campaigns to make him a national hero in Australia, he could feel only satisfaction in viewing the country with which he identified himself. For many years his people preserved his relics, and showed the white men his land, held sacred for the day of his return. They told how he could fly, control the weather, perform innumerable superhuman deeds. The plants he had given them were permanently remembered by his name; the words he taught had entered the language. All agreed that he was a deity from the beginning of the world, returned to bring them new material well-being. On Bilbil they told how their fathers had been unable to grow food until Maclay made them throw away their useless stone axes and work the soil with his iron tools.

As white men recorded it, the New Guinea legend contained no account of punitive earthquakes and frightening magic. Where Maclay had imagined the natives afraid of his gaze, missionaries learned of the love and trust inspired by his kind eyes. When people spoke of his fatherly power to punish, the typical punishment sounded more like an improbable joke. Islanders to the north always remembered how he had carried off Kain and Maramai on his smoke ship, but the Sek prisoner did not figure in the narrative, and the story became almost an instance of Maclay's kindness and understanding. On the other side of the account there were a few lapses, like the hint that Bongu men had led Maclay on the wrong paths in the mountains, preventing him from reaching his destination. There were no tales of threats against Maclay, or of what became of the goods from his house. Gentler and more harmonious than some versions known in Europe, the New Guinea legend included nothing that sympathetic Europeans would not wish to hear.

And time constantly refined the memory. At first the Bogadjim folk had vividly recalled the coming of *Vityaz*—the idea that the end of the world was at hand, the slaughter of pigs for a last enormous feast. In Bongu they described how people dug graves and lay down in them to await the end. The drama of the twenty-one-gun salute seemed likely to be recounted for ever. Yet even this faded out of the legend as white men heard it. So did the minor personages. In outlying islands the names of Boy and 'Nimbili' were preserved for generations; at the fountainhead there was no longer any memory of *tamo-Russ* or servants, of Admiral Kopitov or the crews of schooners. All the ships became one ship; all personages blended into one. Finally Maclay stood alone as the white men imagined him, powerful, mysterious, the source of infinite benefits. Those who remained uncertain about his nature and role nevertheless called him a *tibud*, a deity or demi-god.

The sympathetic white men who sought knowledge—and through all changes and tribulation an occasional seeker appeared—were always pleased with what they learned. Though they said Maclay was not a god, they liked to hear that he had been considered one. Attention and approval came to those who could speak of him. His name in a story was magical. If people knew only that his hand had left a strange smell on those he touched, or that his tobacco looked like animal dung, the knowledge was received as precious. Whatever the white men did with this information, it was clearly of immense significance and only obtainable here. God or man, Maclay had given his people a unique heritage.

Revived by each new inquiry, the story spread fresh, exciting ripples. It moved along the coast, crossed the ranges, mingled with legends from the beginning of time and with the latest tales from the towns. Where Maclay had never been seen, they knew of his goodness and power. He was Anut the first creator, emerged from his retirement, or Kilibob the culture god, who had forgotten his anger and returned among men. He was also the first white man to learn pidgin English from the eagle who sat on a rock in the sea. His name was nowhere more potent than where it was only a name. More than one white traveller in remote places was taken for the god. In parts of the hinterland where the merest whisper had penetrated, they called all gods by their own version of 'Maclay'. It was in such a place that the myth united with the greatest story told by white men. A perceptive man saw that Maclay and Jesus must be one and the same, and a new religion was born.

It was a small religion, which like others failed to bring the cargo. It probably came too late to be revived. Having moved through legend to myth, the story was moving back to the domain of history, gaining new significance as New Guinea approached independence. In 1970 the Russians put up a modest monument at Garagassi. The centenary of Maclay's arrival was celebrated with festivities and re-enactment at Bongu, and radio dramatization spread his name into places where it had never been known. Finally citizens of independent New Guinea received his journals in English translation. When Russians visited Astrolabe Bay in 1977, his meeting with Papuans was re-enacted as he described it, including the moment when he responded to spears and arrows by falling asleep. There was no more need for myth and legend, for the people possessed the story as told by Maclay.

Instead of a god they have the white man worthy of a place in their history, the only one of his race who understood and appreciated them. From the glowing commentaries supplied by white men, they learn more than the forefathers ever knew about Maclay the defender of Papuans, spiritual father of New Guinea nationhood. Yet it remains very much a white man's story, told for white men's purposes. Maclay almost certainly never imagined his journals being studied in New Guinea high schools, and some episodes may have less charm for young New Guineans than for Russians or Australians. Whatever Europeans say, New Guineans will also be the ultimate judges of how much their country lost through Maclay's inability to shape its future. But while increasing knowledge may modify their estimate of what he meant to do for his people, they cannot doubt what his people did for him. The inhabitants of his coast, always uncertain of his literal immortality, secured for him at least a fame that would never die.

Abbreviations

BL	The British Library
BSG	*Bulletin de la Société de Géographie, Paris*
CGC	*Cosmos di Guido Cora*
Greenop	F. Greenop, *Who Travels Alone*
Izv.IRGO	*Izvestiya Imperatskogo Geograficheskogo Obshchestva*
JAI	*Journal of the Anthropological Institute*
JEA	*Journal of Eastern Asia*
Jena. Zeitschr.	*Jenaische Zeitschrift für Medizin und Naturwissenschaft*
JMBRAS	*Journal of the Malayan Branch, Royal Asiatic Society*
JPH	*Journal of Pacific History*
JRAHS	*Journal of the Royal Australian Historical Society*
JSBRAS	*Journal of the Straits Branch, Royal Asiatic Society*
ML	Mitchell Library, Sydney
NGD	Miklouho-Maclay, *New Guinea Diaries*, trans. C. L. Sentinella
NTNI	*Natuurkundig Tijdschrift voor Nederlandsch Indië*
PGM	*Petermann's Geographische Mitteilungen*
Proc. LSNSW	*Proceedings of the Linnean Society of New South Wales*
Proc. RGS	*Proceedings of the Royal Geographical Society*, London
SMH	*Sydney Morning Herald*
SS	Miklouho-Maclay, *Sobraniye sochineniy* (Collected Works)
ZE. Verhl.	*Zeitschrift für Ethnologie: Verhandlungen der Berliner Gesellschaft f. Anthropologie, Ethnologie und Urgeschichte*

Notes

To limit the number of notes, it has been necessary to restrict the references to those for quotations, new material and selected points which might be found controversial.

Details of publication are given only for works which do not appear in the Bibliography. Where the same work is cited several times in close succession, the full title is given only in the initial reference.

1: The Search for Solitude

1. 'Here I can say . . .', *SS*, IV: 10.
2. Inspector's report, *SS*, I:xii.
3. 'To me, everything is indifferent', *SS*, I:2.
5. Suggestion that Miklouho investigate sponges, E. Haeckel, 'On the organization of sponges . . .', *Ann. Mag. Nat. Hist.* (Ser. 4), 5:4 (trans. from *Jena. Zeitschr.*, 5:207-54).
   Haeckel reached the tropics in 1882, when he spent some months in Ceylon.
8. 'the point of departure . . .', 'the origin . . .', *SS*, III pt 2:12 (from *Jena. Zeitschr.*, 3:448).
   The sharks are not now considered a 'primitive' line. Modern authorities regard the swimbladder as a highly-specialized organ, evolved from a more lunglike structure.
   Fear of the sea, *SS*, II:175.
   'an extraordinary person . . .', 'a tiresome egoist . . .', *SS*, IV:14.
9. 'Maclay': from the beginning the name was spelt thus, showing that it was meant to have Scottish connotations. Had it been transliterated from Russian, 'Maklai' would have been the appropriate form. For the former family tradition in Australia, see F. Greenop, *Who Travels Alone*, pp. 20-1. For the version Maclay gave British contemporaries, see G. A. Musgrave to editor, *The Times*, 24 Jan. 1884. Modern scholars have more or less abandoned attempts at explanation. See B. O. Unbegaun, *Russian Surnames* (Oxford, 1972), p. 410; T. D. Ilyina and V. N. Fedchina, 'Mikhail Nikolaevich Miklukho-Maklay', *Dictionary of Scientific Biography*, 15:427-8.
10. The Meshcherskys were of Tartar origin. The most distinguished bearer of the name was probably the poet-diplomat Prince E. P. Meshchersky (1808-44). Alexander Herzen, a great-grandson of Prince Boris Meshchersky, gives vivid pictures of the older generation in his memoirs.
    'the kind of person . . .', *SS*, IV:17.

11. There were three views of the possible phylogenetic position of sponges:
    1. that they formed a separate phylum;
    2. that they belonged with the phylum Coelenterata (jelly-fish, corals and their allies);
    3. that they were colonies of protozoa.
    View (1) is now generally accepted.
12. Position in July–August 1868, *SS,* IV:15–18.
13. Disconcerting evidence on sponges, *SS,* III pt 2:354.
14. 'many peculiarities', *SS,* IV:93.
    Ideas for zoological stations, A. Dohrn, 'The foundation of zoological stations', *Nature,* 5:277–80; Maclay to Dohrn, 28 Apr. 1875, *Nature,* 12:332–3; 'Proposed zoological station for Sydney', *SMH,* 31 Aug. 1878; *Popular Science,* 77:209–25.
    'the ridiculous aspect ...', 'even if all the universities ...', *Nature,* 5:277.
15. 'He who risks ...', *SS,* IV:21.
    'none too pleasant ...', to Sergei, 21 Mar. 1869, *SS,* IV:23.
    'As to the way ...', *SS,* IV:23.
    'almost entirely uninvestigated ...', *SS,* IV:22.
    'probably the last ...', *SS,* III pt 2:200.
    On the zoogeographical effect of the Suez Canal, see G. J. Vermeij, *Biogeography and Adaptation: Patterns of Marine Life* (Cambridge, Mass., 1978), pp. 247–8, 250–2; E. C. Pälou, *Biogeography* (New York, 1979), pp. 169, 283, 286, 287; F. S. Russell and M. Yonge, *The Seas* (London, 1975), p. 262.
16. Ignorance of Arabic, *SS,* IV:22. Maclay later claimed 'some acquaintance with the language' (*SS,* III pt 2:354).
    Preparations for journey, *SS,* III pt 2:354.
    'all the abominations ...', *SS,* IV:23.
17. 'Travelling in these parts ...', *SS,* IV:23.
    'I in no way expected ...', *SS,* IV:24.
    'good people ...', 'very comfortably ...', *SS,* IV:24.
    'not sick ...', *SS,* IV:24.
    'clearly see the luxuriant ...', *SS,* III pt 2:281.
    'immobility and apathy', *SS,* III pt 2:360.
    'only preparatory ...', *SS,* IV:27.

2: The Sea of Okhotsk

18. Miklouho-Maclay's relations with his older brother appear from the tone of his correspondence; see particularly *SS,* IV:16–20, 163–4, 174.
    Establishment of Miklouho-Maclay family, *SS,* IV:36, 174.
19. Views on academic life, *SS,* IV:32–3, 92, 108.
    First proposal for scientific travels, *SS,* IV:26–8.
20. 'a tiny nervous man ...', P. Kropotkin, *Memoirs of a Revolutionist* (reprint, New York, 1971), p. 229.
    Malaria was still prevalent in many parts of Europe. The last European pandemic was actually in progress and lasted until 1872.
    'uproar and singing ...', *SS,* IV:29.
21. Negotiations with Russian Geographical Society, *SS,* IV:30, 32–5.
    The varieties of *Veluspa polymorpha* are now assigned to at least three different genera.
    The Lake Baikal sponges are now classified with several freshwater genera and species.
    'the imprint of the Arctic', *SS,* III pt 2:193.
    'Russian puddles and ponds', *SS,* IV:196.
22. 'In the presence of great ...', *SS,* IV:35–6.

'on the quiet . . .', *SS*, IV:36.

Visit to London, *SS*, IV:39–41, 44; Huxley to Dohrn, 30 Apr. 1870, L. Huxley, *Life and Letters of Thomas Henry Huxley*, I:332–3; A. R. Wallace, *My Life*, II:34–5.

Bad news from home, *SS*, IV:37–8.

23. Lord Clarendon, *SS*, IV:40, 44.

'for these investigations . . .', *SS*, IV:44.

Memorandum to Sir Roderick Murchison, *SS*, IV:45. The Royal Geographical Society has no record of correspondence or discussion concerning this proposal.

24. 'a little old pavilion . . .', *SS*, IV:43.

Social difficulties in Jena, *SS*, IV:88–9.

Financial negotiations, *SS*, IV:48–9.

25. Until 1845 all Russian commissioned officers, and all civil servants above the seventh grade in the 'Table of Ranks', had automatically become hereditary nobles. In spite of attempts to limit it, the class continued to grow, and for the majority of members the distinction of belonging to it was negligible.

'decided repugnance to all stages . . .', *Nature*, 12:332–3 (26 Aug. 1875).

Advice to Olga, *SS*, IV:58.

26. Passport, Papers of N. de Miklouho-Maclay, A2889, vol. 1, item 1, pp. 1–23 (ML).

'this fine existence', *SS*, IV:188.

'indifference to life', quoted from Maclay's New Guinea diary, E. S. Thomassen, *A Biographical Sketch of Nicholas de Miklouho Maclay* (Brisbane, 1882), appendix, vii–viii.

'a large quantity of quinine . . .', *SS*, IV:188.

'grandiose plan', *SS*, IV:51.

27. 'Proposed programme of researches, to be carried out during travels on the islands and coasts of the Pacific Ocean', *SS*, III pt 1:7–24.

Explanation of decision to go to New Guinea, *SS*, I:3–10.

'I know of no part of the world . . .', J. B. Jukes, *Narrative of the Surveying Voyage of H.M.S. 'Fly' . . . 1842-46*, I:291.

28. 'the greatest *terra incognita* . . .', A. R. Wallace, *The Malay Archipelago* (reprint, New York, 1962), p. 440.

'Lemuria' hypothesis, E. H. Haeckel, *The History of Creation* (trans. E. Ray Lankester, London, 1876), I:361, II:325–6 and appended map of hypothetical migrations; A. R. Wallace, *The Geographical Distribution of Animals* (London, 1876), I:76–7; O. Peschel, *The Races of Man and their Geographical Distribution* (London, 1876), pp. 32–3. For modern opinion see P. J. Darlington, *Zoogeography* (New York, 1957), pp. 590–1, 602.

Wallace on New Guinea and Australia, *The Malay Archipelago* (reprint), p. 445.

'a unique country . . .', 'by its position . . .', *SS*, I:7. In the nineteenth century the term 'Polynesia' was often used in all-inclusive fashion.

'with permission . . .', *SS*, IV:28.

SS, I:3–10.

30. 'single primaeval home', Haeckel, *History of Creation*, II:325–6 and end map.

'these races . . . because of collision . . .', *SS*, I:3.

31. 'the discovery of tailed men . . .', Haeckel, *History of Creation*, II:359.

Some examples of European doubt are discussed by J. B. Bury, *The Idea of Progress* (London, 1920), pp. 332–3, 344.

32. 'chastity, honesty, cleanliness . . .', 'a people deemed by us . . .', George Busk, Presidential Address to the Anthropological Institute of Great Britain and Ireland, 1873, *JAI*, 3:508, 509.

'foul play is unknown . . .', Lieut. Musters, 'On the races of Patagonia', *JAI*, 1:193–207. Many similar quotations might be accumulated from anthropological literature and the reports of travellers.

The Guanche are now regarded as a people of Cro-Magnon stock, who possibly migrated from southern and central Europe by way of North Africa.

'Man is the wicked animal . . .', *SS*, IV:172; *SS*, III pt 1:466. Miklouho-Maclay had not necessarily read Gobineau; the quotation appears in Schopenhauer.

'joyless planet', *SS*, IV:182.

3: To the Blessed Isles

33. 'somewhere into the distance', Fragment of original New Guinea diary, *SS,* IV:402.
34. '*Au revoir* ...', *SS,* IV:55.
    German colonial aspirations, *PGM* 15:401-6 (1869); M. E. Townsend, *The Rise and Fall of Germany's Colonial Empire 1884-1914* (New York, 1930), p. 57.
    'worthy, practical persons', *SS,* IV:57.
35. English letters of introduction, T. H. Huxley to Gerhard Krefft, 15 Dec. 1870, ML Autographs A26, p. 37; Sir Charles Nicholson to Sir William Macarthur, 14 Jan. 1871, Macarthur Papers, vol. 43, p. 5, A2939 (ML).
    England, *SS,* IV:60, 126-7; *SS,* II:446.
    Change of plan, *SS,* IV:61-2, 63.
36. 'My health ...', *SS,* IV: 63.
    Relations with officers, *SS,* IV:65, 69.
37. Observations in Brazil, *SS,* I:14-21. Miklouho-Maclay's expectations were stimulated by J. C. Prichard, *The Natural History of Man* (London, 1855), I:79 and II:650. For the history of this notion, see W. R. Stanton, *The Leopard's Spots* (Chicago, 1960), pp. 3-14; M. Harris, *The Rise of Anthropological Theory* (London, 1969), pp. 86-7. The complexity of the African element in Brazil is discussed by Gilberto Freyre, *The Masters and the Slaves* (trans. S. Putnam, New York, 1946), particularly pp. 298-307, 376-7.
38. 'I am alive ...', *SS,* IV:66.
    Punta Arenas, *SS,* I:21-42.
39. 'half civilized ...', Darwin, *The Voyage of the Beagle* (reprint, New York, 1962), p. 233.
40. Australian and Dutch reaction, *Argus,* 23 Mar., 15, 17 Apr., 29 May, 16, 23 June 1871; *SMH,* 31 Mar., 4, 22 Apr., 23 May 1871; *Nature,* 4:150 (June 1871).
    'complete examination ...', *SMH,* 23 May 1871.
    'up and doing ...', 'Ubiquity' to editor, *Argus,* 15 Apr. 1871.
    'startled out ...', *Argus,* 16 June 1871.
41. Bill drawn on Meshchersky, *SS,* IV:69.
    'the exhaustless delight ...', Darwin, *Voyage of the Beagle,* p. 498.
    Vladimir to come to New Guinea, *SS,* IV:71.
    'I will come soon ...'; 'Keep your diary ...'; 'Write more to me ...', *SS,* IV:72.
    Bastian's requirements, *SS,* III pt 1:11; *SS,* I:51.
42. Rapanui, *SS,* I:45-57; Officer's account, *SS,* I:341-3.
43. Officer's account of Pitcairn, *SS,* I:343-6.
    Mangareva, *SS,* I:58-68; *SS,* IV:72.
45. For opposite motives, both the Church and Dutroux-Bornier tried to have Rapanui taken under French protection. The island was eventually annexed by Chile.
    Tahiti, *SS,* I:70; Officer's account, *SS,* I:350-3.
46. *Kohau rongorongo, SS,* I:52-4; Jaussen, *L'Ile de Pâques. Historique-Ecriture* (Paris, 1893). Gift of specimen: Jaussen says (op. cit.), '*J'en ai donné une au navire de guerre russe "Vitias"* '. Maclay did not mention either tablet in his reports to Europe. For the later history and supposed provenance of the specimens, see A. Piotrowski, 'Deux tablettes, avec les marques gravées ...', *Rev. d'Ethnographie,* 6:425-31; Lanyon-Orgill, 'A catalogue of the inscribed tablets ... from Easter Island', *Journ. Austronesian Studies,* 1(2):24-5.
47. Boy as 'guide', *SS,* IV:74.
    Boy's ignorance of languages, Letter from P. N. Nazimov, *BSG* (6 Sér.), 5:107. Maclay did not state what language he used to communicate with Boy.
    Officer's account of Samoa and Rotuma, *SS,* I:353-9.
48. New Ireland, Nazimov, *BSG* (6 Sér.), 5:108; Officer's account, *SS,* I:359-61.
    Uncertainty regarding destination, *SS,* IV:75.
49. 'high, unbroken wall', 'piled up ...', *SS,* I:75.

4: First Contact

Except where otherwise indicated, all material for this chapter is drawn from Miklouho-Maclay's New Guinea diaries as printed in *SS*, I:73–314. References to this source, with corresponding references to the English translation by C. L. Sentinella, are given only for quotations and selected points.

50. 'Sacrifice'; impression that threats had repulsed Maclay; commander's expedition: P. N. Nazimov, *BSG* (6 Sér.), 5:107–8; 'Lettera di un guardia marina della "Vitiaz"', *CGC*, 2:285.
53. Papuans aboard *Vityaz*, Nazimov, *BSG* (6 Sér.), 5:108–9; 'Lettera di un guardia marina', *CGC*, 2:286.
    Papuans not armed, Extracts from Nazimov's report, *SS*, I:339.
    Second visit of Papuans to *Vityaz*; procession with gifts, Nazimov, *BSG* (6 Sér.), 5:109; 'Lettera di un guardia marina', *CGC*, 2:286.
54. Change in natives' attitude, Nazimov's report, *SS*, I:339; Nazimov, *BSG* (6 Sér.), 5:109; *CGC*, 2:286.
    Choice of dwelling place, Nazimov, *SS*, I:338–9.
    Work on Maclay's house and land, Nazimov, *SS*, I:338; *BSG* (6 Sér.), 5:112.
    Desertion of villages, Nazimov, *SS*, I:339.
56. Tui's behaviour, 'Lettera di un guardia marina', *CGC*, 2:286.
    Installation of mines, *SS*, I:88; *NGD*, 25; Nazimov, *BSG* (6 Sér.), 5:112; Officer's account, *SS*, I:375.
    Boat, Nazimov, *SS*, I:339; *BSG* (6 Sér.), 5:112; Officer's account, *SS*, I:375; *SS*, IV:72.
57. Food supplies, Officer's accounts, *SS*, I:375–6; *CGC*, 2:286–7.
    Flag of merchant marine, Nazimov, *BSG* (6 Sér.), 5:112; Officer's account, *SS*, I:375.
    Burying papers, *SS*, IV:110.
58. 'energy, work …', *SS*, I:90; *NGD*, 26.
    Olsen's fever, Nazimov, *SS*, I:339.
59. N. I. Miklouho: N. A. Butinov, 'N. N. Miklouho-Maclay, a biographical sketch', *SS*, IV:480; 'Baron Maclay—Pt I', *Daily Telegraph* (Sydney), 15 Jan. 1884.
60. Darwin distributed his questionnaire while gathering material for *The Expression of the Emotions in Man and Animals*. Maclay obtained a copy and included all the questions in his programme.
62. 'insolence', *SS*, I:128; *NGD*, 63.
    Decision to stay at home, *SS*, I:127–8; *NGD*, 62–3. Though Maclay stated clearly that he remained at home, he often wrote as though he constantly visited villages. The final version of the journal shows confusion due to rewriting, and includes incidents which could not have occurred at this time.
63. Language studies, *SS*, I:127, 132, 141, 152; *NGD*, 62–3, 67, 73, 84; *SS*, III, pt 1:90–4.
64. 'forever on one's guard', *SS*, I:140; *NGD*, 73.
65. 'complete detachment', *SS*, I:114; *NGD*, 49. More accurately: 'I live and look upon all circumstances exactly as though they do not concern me'.
    'contemplation of the magnificent …', *SS*, I:113; *NGD*, 48.
66. 'a regular hospital', *SS*, I:106; *NGD*, 41.
    Advantages of the veranda room, *SS*, I:110; *NGD*, 45.
67. 'tied to these two …', *SS*, I:109; *NGD*, 44.
    'uninvited, inquisitive …', *SS*, I:122; *NGD*, 57.
71. 'test of impressionability', *SS*, I:149; *NGD*, 80.
    Maclay's acquaintance with writings of George Keate, *SS*, III, pt 1:277, 278, 298, 300, 306, 308.
72. 'some kind of supernatural being', *SS*, I:152; *NGD*, 84.

5: Prospero's Island

See explanation preceding notes to Chapter 4.

73. New Year celebration, Fragment of original New Guinea diary, *SS*, IV:383.
    Showing himself to the natives: *SS*, IV:391; Manuscript in English by Miklouho-Maclay, held by Royal Australian Historical Society, Sydney, quoted Greenop, p. 85.
    'indifference to life', quoted from English version of diary, E. S. Thomassen, *A Biographical Sketch of Nicholas de Miklouho Maclay*, appendix, pp. vii-viii.
74. 'noisy people ...', *SS*, I:171; *NGD*, 102.
    Mystical experiences: Fragment of original New Guinea diary, *SS*, IV:399.
75. 'no pleasure ...', *SS*, I:125; *NGD*, 60.
    'the mistrusting nature ...', English version, quoted Greenop, p. 83.
    'a kind of dreadful dream', *SS*, I:116; *NGD*, 52.
77. Digging up buried papers, *SS*, IV:110.
    Neighbours wish to own him, English version, quoted Greenop, p. 82.
79. Belief that his prestige saved his neighbours: Report finished at Ternate 3 Feb. 1873, *SS*, I:320; Account by officer of *Izumrud*, *SS*, I:383; *SS*, II:636-7.
    'the life of savages ...', *SS*, I:193; *NGD*, 123.
80. M's wish to take Tui's son away, Fragment of original diary, *SS*, IV:400.
82. 'never returning ...', *SS*, I:172; *NGD*, 103.
    'not the natives ...': description of fever, English version, quoted Greenop, p. 84.
85. 'cheerful and obliging', *SS*, I:153; *NGD*, 85.
    'ready to collapse ...', *SS*, I:138; *NGD*, 71.
    Olsen complains that he is gaining nothing, *SS*, I:153; *NGD*, 85.
    'endless anecdotes ...', *SS*, I:125; *NGD*, 60.
    Olsen as intruder, *SS*, I:171; *NGD*, 103.
    Olsen starves Maclay, English version, quoted Greenop, p. 85.
86. 'almost superfluous', *SS*, I:171; *NGD*, 103.
    Olsen's concerts, *SS*, I:119, 216, 283; *NGD*, 54, 140, 197.
87. Tui as Olsen's guest, *SS*, I:237; *NGD*, 155.
    'not to see or hear ...', *SS*, I:266; *NGD*, 181.
88. Jests and cannibalism, *SS*, I:104; *NGD*, 39; English version, quoted Greenop, p. 79.
    Defecation near dwellings, 'Remarks about the circumvolutions of the cerebrum of Canis dingo', *Proc. LSNSW*, 6:625.
89. 'Note on the "kéu" of the Maclay Coast, New Guinea', *Proc. LSNSW*, 10:690-3.
    Attitudes to sex, 'Ethnological remarks on the Papuans of the Maclay Coast', *SS*, III pt 1:83-4; *NTNI*, 35:294-333.
    'distinguished by strict morality', *SS*, III pt 1:77; *Nature*, 14:137 (summary by J. C. Galton).
    Sex ratio: Maclay's first impression was that women were fewer than men (*SS*, III pt 1:46). During his second visit (1876-77) he found that women were in the majority (*SS*, III pt 1:156).
    'number two of the human race', Schopenhauer, *Parerga und Paralipomena*, II, section 265; quoted by Maclay, *SS*, II:271; *SS*, IV:172. In his observations on Papuan women, Maclay did not refer to Schopenhauer. The parallels between his views and the contents of a work that he frequently quoted are too close to be accidental.
90. Additional material from 'Ethnological remarks on the Papuans of the Maclay Coast', *SS*, III pt 1:72-3, 77-110; *NTNI*, 35:66-93; 36:294-333; Summaries by J. C. Galton, *Nature*, 14:107-9, 136-7; 21:204-6.
    Women's indifference to art, *SS*, III pt 1:97.
91. Smallpox and influenza, *SS*, III pt 1:45-6.
    Impression that natives thought themselves the only people, *SS*, I:322; *SS*, IV:80.
92. Hopes for progress in art: *SS*, III pt 1:96.
94. 'Go away ...', *SS*, I:255; *NGD*, 172-3.

95. Myth of Kilibob and Manup: P. Lawrence, *Road Belong Cargo*, pp. 21-4, 65; R. McSwain, *The Past and Future People*, pp. 24-8, 84, 171, and Preface by P. Lawrence. See also P. Lawrence, 'Religion', *Encyclopaedia of Papua and New Guinea* (ed. P. Ryan), II:1001-10. Tentative identification of Maclay with Kilibob: Hoffmann, 'Sprache und Sitten der Papua-Stämme an der Astrolabe Bai', *Verhandlungen des Deutschen Kolonialkongresses 1905*, pp. 128-39; J. McAuley, 'We are men—What are you?', *Quadrant*, vol. 4, no. 3, p. 74.
96. 'quite extraordinary being', SS, I:260; *NGD*, 176.
    Maclay's change of attitude, SS, I:228, 260; *NGD*, 149, 176.
    'wouldn't mind sharing . . .', SS, I:248; *NGD*, 165.
97. 'such little things . . .', SS, I:255; *NGD*, 173.
    '*Kaaram-tamo*': This title does not appear in Maclay's New Guinea diary as prepared for publication. The earliest extant reference to it seems to be that in a report completed at Ternate in February 1873 (SS, I:323). His definitive explanation was given in a lecture of 1882, SS, II:635-6.
    'European, scientist . . .', SS, II:637.
98. Invitation from Bogadjim, SS, I:250; *NGD*, 185.
    'strange request', SS, I:283; *NGD*, 197.
99. Hope of moving to mountains, and decision to stay at Garagassi, SS, I:320-1, 323.
100. Visit to islands of Contented Men, SS, I:321-2.
101. 'bride inspection', SS, I:296; *NGD*, 206-7.
    Shortcomings of Papuan women, SS, I:181; SS, III pt 1:32, 36, 81, 82.
    Beauty of boys, SS, I:245, 301; *NGD*, 163, 212.
    Maclay's determination that Papuans should not enter his hut, SS, II:148-9, 405-6, 529 (note).
    'many years . . .', SS, I:299; *NGD*, 210.
102. State of the clearing, Officer's report, SS, I:378.
    Olsen's shopping, SS, I:298; *NGD*, 209.
103. 'getting ready to die', 'pretending . . .', SS, I:300, 305; *NGD*, 211, 216.
    Maclay advises suicide, SS, I:301, *NGD*, 212.
105. Events aboard *Izumrud*, Officers' accounts, SS, I:376-8, 382-3.
    Alarms about Maclay, Anniversary Address by Sir Henry Rawlinson (27 May 1872), *Proc. RGS.*, 16:356; Officer's account, SS, I:376; *CGC*, 1:7 (note).
    The Russian Geographical Society also appealed to the French government.
    'a real Robinson Crusoe', Officer's account, SS, I:377.
    'the sound of voices . . .', SS, I:309; *NGD*, 219.
106. 'way of thought . . .', SS, I:306; *NGD*, 217.
    Maclay's inability to understand a speech, SS, II:332; *NGD*, 246 (1876-77 journal).
    determination to return, SS, I:310; *NGD*, 221.
107. How Maclay gained trust, Officer's account, SS, I:383; Report finished at Ternate, SS, I:320; SS, II:636-7.
    Russo-Papuan relations, Officers' accounts, SS, I:378-81, 384.
108. Officers' comments on Olsen, SS, I:378, 383-4.
    Promise to return 'in due time', SS, I:311, 314; *NGD*, 221, 223.
    Vityaz Strait. Contrary to modern belief, this channel was not discovered by *Vityaz*. Its existence had been known since Dampier's day. The first report on its suitability for shipping was apparently that published in 1841 by R. L. Hunter of the *Marshall Bennett* (*Nautical Magazine*, 10:743-5). The few captains who subsequently used the strait never thought to give it a name, regarding it as the western arm of Dampier Strait.
109. Maclay Coast, Report finished at Ternate, 3 Feb. 1873, SS, I:325, footnote. At this point the name covered only Astrolabe Bay and the coast and islands immediately to the north. It was to be greatly extended.

6: Sans Souci

110. 'strong-nerved, elastic ...', *SS*, IV:79.
     'A Russian begins well ...', *SS*, IV:79.
111. 'Sultan Maclay ...', *SS*, IV:82.
     Meeting with A. B. Meyer, *ZE*, 7: *Verhl.* 47.
     'Are these negritos ...', *SS*, III pt 1:14.
112. 'the same race ...', 'customs, attitude ...', Maclay to K. E. von Baer, *CGC*, 2:291-2.
     Papuans as 'most primitive', *SS*, IV:80.
     'the most vigorous ...', *SS*, IV:81.
     'most welcome guest', *SS*, IV:85.
113. 'lay 11 months sick', to A. Petermann, 11 Mar. 1873, *PGM*, 19:192.
     Magic as accident, *SS*, II:636; Thomassen, *Biographical Sketch*, p. 8.
     Power of Maclay's gaze, *SS*, I:223.
     '*Kaaram-tamo*', '*Tamo-boro-boro*', *SS*, I:323.
     'entered deeply ...', 'In spite of five long months ...', to A. Petermann, 11 Mar.
     1873, *PGM*, 19:192.
     'My destiny ...', *SS*, IV:83.
114. Requests for money, *SS*, IV:79, 80-1.
     Opium experiment, *SS*, IV:412-15.
115. 'simplest and most remote ...', *SS*, IV:87.
     'a man of justice ...', *SS*, IV:108-9.
     'the role of king', 'more absolute power ...', *SS*, IV:86, 91.
117. 'Inborn laziness ...', 'almost without mistakes', *SS*, IV:111.
     John Charles Galton, a former lecturer at Charing Cross Hospital and surgeon
     at Darmstadt, had published a translation of an important German work on the
     brain. His meeting with Maclay in December 1873 began an association that lasted
     for several years.
     Maclay's expectation of criticism, *SS*, IV:99, 110-13.
     'quiet and sedentary ...', *SS*, IV:111.
118. 'the price ...', *SS*, IV:88.
     Evenings at Buitenzorg, *SS*, IV:88, 91, 93.
     'My health has suffered ...', *SS*, IV:92.
     'the rotten air ...', *SS*, IV:90.
119. '*Tengo una palabra*', *SS*, IV:116. Maclay frequently quoted this motto.
     'take a look ...', 'Nature, air and conditions ...', 'independent and comfort-
     able ...', 'demands and caprices', 'Well, I shall settle ...', *SS*, IV:92.
     Italian villa, *SS*, IV:89, 92, 93.
     'This would be a glorious surprise ...', *SS*, IV:93.
     'near them ...', *SS*, IV:92.
     'intractable thing', *SS*, IV:95.
120. 'the blood-thirstiness ...', *SS*, IV:97.
     'one there doesn't need ...', *SS*, IV:95.
121. 'Really, they are forcing ...', *SS*, IV:99.
     'not worth thinking about', 'Whatever is to come ...', *SS*, IV:96, 99.
     Advance of funds, *SS*, IV:100.
     'utterly indifferent ...', *SS*, IV:88.
     'He who knows well ...', *SS*, IV:95.
     'this dear, peaceful ...', *SS*, IV:100.

7: Pray Tomorrow

Unless otherwise indicated, all material in this chapter is drawn from Maclay's journal of the expedition, *SS*, II:13-113. Precise references to that source are given only for quotations and selected points.

123. 'decided otherwise', *SS*, II:21.
    Meeting with Beccari, *SS*, II:21-2; Beccari to Doria, 26 Dec. 1873, *CGC*, 2:4-5; Beccari, *Nuova Guinea, Selebes e Moluccha, Diarii di Viaggio* (Florence, 1924), pp. 271-2.
    'silly, ignorant letters', *SS*, II:22.
125. Choice of men from different communities, *SS*, II:649.
    Conflicting statements on intentions regarding vessel and crew, *SS*, II:31, 38-9.
    James Bruce, 'Travels in Abyssinia', in R. Cochrane (ed.), *The English Explorers* (London, 1877), p. 143.
    'You can pray ...', *SS*, II:37.
    'accustomed to obey', *SS*, II:94.
127. Landing at Namatote, *SS*, II:41.
128. 'And of course ...', *SS*, II:48.
129. 'I myself am convinced ...', *SS*, II:54.
130. 'troubles of daily existence', *SS*, II:59.
    'I have been ...', *SS*, II:59.
132. please 'the most exacting ...', *SS*, II:61.
133. 'not the best ...', *SS*, II:75.
    Preparation to repel attack, *SS*, II:76.
135. Maclay's apportionment of guilt, *SS*, II:81.
    Raja Aiduma's absence from Aiva. Maclay's revised journal does not explain Raja Aiduma's whereabouts at the time of the attack. It shows, however, that Aiduma was with Maclay on 23 March and 3 April 1874. Between those dates there is no mention of Aiduma's leaving the *urumbai*. Maclay makes the following statements bearing on Aiduma's whereabouts:
    'the headman and the majority of the men were not at the settlement', *SS*, II:79.
    'Raja Aiduma, who was absent', *SS*, II:79.
    'during the temporary absence of the chiefs and part of the men', ('Incidents of travel in Papua-Koviai', *Proc. RGS*, 19:518).
    'Here [at sea, apparently after 10 Apr.] I met the Raja Aiduma ...', ('Incidents of travel ...', p. 519). The revised journal mentions no such meeting. The date implied in 'Incidents of travel ...' contradicts the journal statement that Aiduma was with Maclay on 3 April.
    'the wife and little daughter of Raja Aiduma, the old man I had taken with me as guide and interpreter', (Report printed in St Petersburg, 1882, *SS*, II:654).
    The 1882 statement, apparently Maclay's last word on this subject, suggests that Aiduma had been with him all the time. A further point is Maclay's statement (*SS*, II:89) that the child's body remained in his hut. Had Raja Aiduma been at Aiva between 28 March (the supposed date of the attack) and 3 April, it is unlikely that he would have left his child unburied.
    Aiduma's reproaches, 'Incidents of travel ...', *Proc. RGS*, 19:519.
    Size of the attacking force, 'about one hundred', *SS*, II:80, 82; 'more than two hundred', Report printed in St Petersburg, 1882, *SS*, II:654.
    Maclay's losses, *SS*, II:83, 109, 423.
136. Visits to Aiva. In the revised journal, the presumable time of these visits is represented by a gap of three days. The present account is drawn from 'Incidents of travel ...', *Proc. RGS*, 19:519, retrospective remarks in the journal, *SS*, II:89, and the report printed in St Petersburg, 1882, *SS*, II:654. The report Maclay wrote immediately after the expedition refers only to his *wish* to return.
137. Letter requesting help, *SS*, IV:102.

138. Life at Umburmeta: Journal account supplemented by report finished at Kilvaru, 13 May 1874, *SS*, II:110-12.
     'Fear has big eyes ...', *SS*, II:85-6.
     'irksome and tiring', *SS*, II:111.
139. Absence of Raja Namatote. Maclay did not explain why he had not arrested Raja Namatote aboard the *urumbai* on 3 April.
     'one of the leading ...', *SS*, II:88.
     Decision to kill Kapitan Mavara. C. L. Sentinella's translation ('The Papua-Koviai Expedition of Mikloucho-Maclay', ML MSS 2913, pt 1, p. 43) makes this phrase 'capture or kill'. The Russian text (*SS*, II:89) unambiguously says 'capture *and* kill'. 'Incidents of travel ...', *Proc. RGS*, 19:520, also makes it plain that on capturing Mavara Maclay meant 'to launch him into eternity'.
140. 'looted everything ...', *SS*, II:90.
     'interesting anthropological object' and its provenance, *SS*, II:90-1; 'Incidents of travel ...', *Proc. RGS*, 19:519.
     Kapitan Mavara's wife, *SS*, II:91.
141. Attack on Namatote and Bicharu Bay, 'On the political and social position of the Papuans of Papua-Koviai', Memorandum presented to the governor-general, *SS*, III pt 1:204; 'The social-political position of the population of Papua-Koviai', *SS*, III pt 1:212.
     Death of Raja Namatote, Note in Maclay's handwriting in detached copy of 'Incidents of travel ...', National Library of Australia, MS3375.

8: Disillusion

142. Voyage to Kilvaru, *SS*, II:93-4, 91-2. These are two separate accounts which in some respects conflict. That mentioned first is the original diary, while that in *SS*, II:91-2 forms a conclusion to the Papua-Koviai journal as partly revised for publication.
     'as a last resort', *SS*, II:94.
     Stay at Kilvaru, *SS*, II:94-101; 'On the Papuan-Malay racial mixture', *SS*, III pt 1:196-201.
143. Escape of Kapitan Mavara, *SS*, II:95.
     'Talking very confusedly', Statement to governor-general, *SS*, IV:103.
     Appeal to governor-general, *SS*, IV:102-3. In thus going over the resident's head, Maclay showed mistrust of that official's competence or integrity.
     Persistence of *hongi*, *SS*, III pt 1:206, 212.
     Slavery and ill-treatment of Papuan children, *SS*, II:99; *SS*, III pt 1:207.
144. Maclay at Ambon, *SS*, II:102; *SS*, IV:106.
     Visit from officers of *Basilisk*, *Nature*, 10:294; *SS*, II:118; J. Moresby, *Discoveries and Surveys in New Guinea and the D'Entrecasteaux Islands*, p. 293; Maclay to editor, *SMH*, 23 Nov. 1883.
     Statement to governor-general re Kapitan Mavara, *SS*, IV:102-4.
     'permitting' murders, *SS*, II:90 (Journal, 23 April 1874).
     Maclay's first account of Mavara's behaviour on arrest, *SS*, II:89-90.
145. Sangil, *SS*, II:41, 45, 54, 62, 90; *SS*, IV:104.
     frequently 'robbed ...', 'salutary example', Memorandum presented to the governor-general, *SS*, III pt 1:204.
     Fate of Kapitan Mavara, 'Incidents of travel in Papua-Koviai', *Proc. RGS*, 19:521; *SS*, II:92.
     Recommendation for settlement, *SS*, III pt 1:205-6.
146. 'humane and sympathetic feelings', to Russian Geographical Society, 10 Nov. 1874, *SS*, IV:109.
     Respect of the natives, *SS*, II:104-5.
147. Offer to rule Papua-Koviai, Letter to Russian Geographical Society, 10 Nov. 1874, *SS*, IV:109.

148. 'a sure and simple way ...', SS, III pt 1:214 (footnote).
  'starving, plundering and killing ...', SS, IV:109.
  Enquiry about action in St Petersburg, to Osten-Sacken, 8 Dec. 1875, SS, IV:127.
  'alone and unarmed', SS, II:105.
  Later stories of arrest, SS, II:112; 'Incidents of travel ...', Proc. RGS, 19:520-1. In these versions, Maclay's only assistant was Moi-Birit the Papuan.
  Exchange of promises, SS, II:123.
  'placed under the necessity ...', 'It is even possible ...', SS, IV:106.
149. Purchase of estate, SS, IV:99, 106.
  'to turn it ...', 'Approximately when ...', 'My tasks ...', 'I ask you ...', SS, IV:108-9.
  Olga's response, SS, IV:355-6 (note 2 to letter 97).
150. 'not as a gift ...', 'I have already said ...', SS, IV:105.
  Osten-Sacken's reaction, SS, IV:355 (note 3 to letter 96).
  Plans for Malay Peninsula expedition, SS, IV:105; SS, II:216; 'Ethnological excursion in Johore', Journal of Eastern Asia, July 1875.
  'not thinking much ...', SS, IV:106.
151. Will made 20 November 1874, SS, IV:418.
  Bitterness of Buitenzorg, SS, II:122, 126.
  'Don't become attached ...', SS, II:126.
  No further information about the Buitenzorg episode is available. Maclay possibly discussed it in a letter to his sister (SS, IV:114), but censorship has been at work.

9: Pages from an Old Book

152. Singapore and Johor Baharu, SS, II:116-22, 217, 218.
  'respectable members ...', SS, II:121.
153. 'constantly more ...', SS, II:121.
  British ignorance of Malay Peninsula, D. D. Daly, 'Surveys and explorations in the native states ... 1875-82', Proc. RGS (n.s.) 4:393; Sir Andrew Clarke, in discussion of preceding paper, Proc. RGS (n.s.) 4:410; F. Swettenham, British Malaya (London, 1948), p. 113.
  Meeting with D'Albertis, SS, II:122; D'Albertis to Doria, CGC, 3:96. D'Albertis had the impression that friction between the sailors and the natives had caused the attack. Maclay's complaint, originally, was that 'friendly relations' between the Ceramese and the Papuans had resulted in a conspiracy against him, SS, II:82, 110.
  Maclay's plans for more visits to New Guinea, D'Albertis to Doria, CGC, 3:96; SS, II:147.
155. Predicted difficulties of expedition, SS, II:122, 218.
  Journey through Johor, SS, II:122-99.
156. White tuan's immunity to Malay disputes, SS, II:165.
  Retrospective accounts, 'Ethnological excursion in Johore', Journal of Eastern Asia, 1(1):3; SS, II:219; SS, IV:117-18.
157. 'But in the jungle ...', SS, II:188.
  'perfectly well ...', SS, II:189.
  Obtaining assistance, SS, II:146, 150, 155.
  Respect for Europeans, SS, II:181.
  Obtaining research material, SS, II:123, 129, 143, 147, 155, 160, 183.
159. 'quiet pleasant faces', SS, II:134.
  Imposing discipline, SS, II:128, 136, 150, 154.
  'What next ...', SS, II:138.
  'these backwoods', SS, II:150.
  Truant Jakun, SS, II:146.
  Shelter ablaze, SS, II:181.
160. Desertion of the Jakun, SS, II:187-91.
161. Encounters with Chinese, SS, II:198.

162. Maclay's observations on border dispute, SS, II:164, 165, 170-2, 175, 176, 177-8, 183, 187. On official knowledge of the situation, see W. Linehan, 'A History of Pahang', *JMBRAS*, 14:90-1, 101.
    'an interesting old book ...', 'Ethnological Excursion in Johore', *NTNI*, 35:250; *Journal of Eastern Asia*, 1(1):3.
163. Bangkok, SS, II:212-15, 220-1.
164. Trials of the Villa Whampoa and Johor Baharu, SS, II:222-3.
    Poison experiments, SS, II:673; 'Ethnological excursions', *JSBRAS*, 2:213.
    'absolute necessity', 'quiet sanctuary', SS, II:223.
    'Tampat Senang', Maclay to Dohrn, 28 Apr. 1875, *Nature*, 12:332.
165. Abu Bakar's change of mind, Maclay to Dohrn, 9 June 1875, *Nature*, 12:333.
    White men and white ants, G. F. Hose, Inaugural Address, *JSBRAS*, 1(5):9-10.
    Improved account of Papua-Koviai, 'Incidents of travel in Papua-Koviay (New Guinea)' (trans. W. Feilding), *Proc. RGS*, 19:517. A separated copy in the National Library of Australia (MS 3375) bears a note in Maclay's handwriting stating that the original letter was addressed to Baroness von Rhaden.
166. Mkal, SS, II:166-9.
167. The journal of the second expedition is not available. C. L. Sentinella suggests (*NGD*, 231) that for political reasons Maclay kept no journal. Maclay himself stated (to Russian Geographical Society, 2 Oct. 1875, SS, II:233) that he 'kept a careful diary the whole time'. His intention to publish it is mentioned in 'Ethnological excursions in the Malay Peninsula', *JSBRAS*, no. 2:206.
    Letters from British governor. Maclay to Russian Geographical Society, 2 Oct. 1875, SS, II:234, reveals that he had such letters. In a report presented in St Petersburg, 1882, he said that he 'deliberately took no letter or recommendation from the governor in Singapore', SS, II:669.
    Reception in Pekan, SS, II:230, 670-1.
168. Ahmad's information about the interior, W. Linehan, 'A History of Pahang', *JMBRAS*, 14(2):94.
    'almost European', SS, II:218, 666.
    'the pure Malay ...', SS, II:397.
    Departure from Pekan, SS, II:232, 671; W. Linehan, 'A History of Pahang', *JMBRAS*, 14(2):102.
169. Travels in Pahang and Kelantan, SS, II:232, 671-2; 'Ethnological excursions in the Malay Peninsula', *JSBRAS*, no. 2:206-21.
    'Malay laziness ...', SS, II:670.
    'pure-blood Papuan tribe', SS, II:232. In papers written after the expedition, Maclay began to describe these people as 'Melanesian'.
170. Rate of progress. Dates for Maclay's presence at various places are provided by letters and dated drawings.
    'how people live ...', SS, II:670.
    Presentation of letters, SS, II:234.
    'no little anxiety ...', SS, II:670.
    'great suspiciousness ...', SS, II:234.
171. Advantages of being Russian, SS, II:232, 238. Malay ideas of Russian status, SS, II:154; SS, IV:128 (footnote); A. R. Wallace, *The Malay Archipelago* (reprint, New York, 1962), p. 283.
    'peace-loving, friendly ...', SS, II:232.
    'definite and satisfactory ...', SS, II:232.
172. Travels in Siam, SS, II:233, 675; 'Ethnological excursions ...', *JSBRAS* no. 2:207.
    Study of Siamese society and politics, SS, II:233.
173. Summing-up of Malay character, SS, II:234.

10: Return to Paradise

174. Life in Java, *SS*, II:238-40; *SS*, IV:126; *NTNI*, 36:52-4.
'on the marine fauna ...', 'And we regret ...', Semyonov-Tianshansky to Maclay, *SS*, IV:457-8. Maclay could not have received this letter until he returned from his first expedition in Johor, 2 Feb. 1875.
Rejection of funds, *SS*, IV:127.
'patriotically-inspired men', *SS*, IV:126.

175. Dyak sexual customs. Maclay had not visited Borneo. His information was obtained from other travellers in 1874 and examination of Dyak penises preserved in the Batavia museum.
Zoological stations and land purchases: *NTNI*, 36:64; 'Proposed zoological station for Sydney', *SMH*, 31 Aug. 1878.
Varying plans, to Olga, Dec. 1874, *SS*, IV:115; to Russian Geographical Society, *SS*, II:228; to Anton Dohrn, 9 June 1875, *Nature*, 12:333.
'large accumulation ...', to Olga, Dec. 1874, *SS*, IV:115.
'waste time ...', '*Mein Cadaver* ...', to Osten-Sacken, 8 Dec. 1875, *SS*, IV:126.
Intention to revisit New Guinea, D'Albertis to Doria, 18 Dec. 1874, *CGC*, 3:96.
Russians 'in Astrolabe Gulf', Moresby at meeting of Royal Colonial Institute, 16 Mar. 1875, *Proc. R. Col. Inst.*, 6:140-1.
Deputation to Secretary of State for Colonies, *Proc. R. Col. Inst.*, 6:189-204.
Russian protection for New Guinea. Maclay's first letter on this subject, 24 May 1875, is not available. Its date and contents are shown by later appeals to Semyonov-Tianshansky, 28 Oct. 1875 (*SS*, IV:122), 14 Feb. 1876 (*SS*, IV:131) and 29 Jan. 1878 (*SS*, IV:152).

176. 'not as a Russian', '*my* country', etc., to Semyonov-Tianshansky, 28 Oct. 1875, *SS*, IV:122-3.
Promise to return, *SS*, I:311, 314; to Meshchersky, 17 Mar. 1876, *SS*, IV:132; *CGC*, 3:344-5.
'I attained ...', to Semyonov-Tianshansky, *SS*, IV:123.
'their true interest ...', '*too disastrous* ...', to Meshchersky, 17 Mar. 1876, *SS*, IV:133; *CGC*, 3:344-5.
'that the *Papuan Union* ...', to Osten-Sacken, 26 Mar. 1876, *SS*, IV:137.

177. 'tactless policy ...', *SS*, IV:128 (footnote).
'to withhold their confidence ...', 'a true understanding ...', 'the invasion ...', *SS*, IV:128; *SS*, II:237-8.
'irreconcilable future enemies', *SS*, IV:134.
Earlier intention to return to Java, *SS*, II:220; *SS*, IV:115, 125.

178. Substitution of 'English' for 'Dutch', *SS*, IV:128; *SS*, II:238. The early, unfinished version of the letter is that in *SS*, IV:127-8. The second version, *SS*, II:237-41, as well as being complete, reveals an interest in Perak which is not apparent in the first.
'Whatever the contents ...', to Semyonov-Tianshansky, 14 Feb. 1876, *SS*, IV:131.
Efforts to ensure support, *SS*, IV:131, 132-3.
Request for finance, *SS*, IV:131.
Appointment for Ankersmit, *SS*, II:241; *SS*, IV:157.

180. Maclay's agreement, *SS*, II:243.
D. D. O'Keefe: *Pacific Islands Monthly*, Sept. 1952, pp. 68-70; Jan. 1953, pp. 68-9; F. X. Hezel, 'A Yankee trader in Yap', *More Pacific Islands Portraits* (ed. D. Scarr), pp. 59-74. O'Keefe was the subject of a slightly biographical novel (Lawrence Klingman and Gerald Green, *His Majesty O'Keefe*, Aust. ed., Sydney, 1950).
Voyage to the Carolines, *SS*, II:242-4, 246-9.
'the public opinion ...', *SS*, IV:133; *CGC*, 3:345.
'only weakness ...', *SS*, IV:136.
'the *profit and progress* ...', *SS*, IV:137.
Approach to mother, *SS*, IV:134.

181. Yap, *SS*, II:252-3; *SS*, III pt 1:252-68. Maclay's informants exaggerated the power and formality of the Yap empire. The point here is the impression he received.
     'on the path ...', *SS*, III pt 1:264.
182. 'interesting, as showing ...', *SS*, III pt 1:266.
     'the melancholy old truth ...', *SS*, III pt 1:267.
     Palau Islands, *SS*, III pt 1:268-313.
     'all ruses ...', 'A woman can bear ...', *SS*, III pt 1:310.
     Palauan character, *SS*, III pt 1:306-9.
     'carefree spirit', *SS*, III pt 1:308.
183. 'All these useful ...', *SS*, III pt 1:308.
     White men as gods, *SS*, III pt 1:307-8. Maclay's basic ideas on this were derived from George Keate's *Account of the Pelew Islands* (London, 1788). The men of the wrecked Indiaman *Antelope* had been honoured largely because they lent their firepower to their hosts' side in the everlasting war. Keate, a London littérateur, had written up the captain's account in line with the prevailing nostalgia. For the effects of this, see Bernard Smith, *European Vision and the South Pacific, 1768-1850* (Oxford, 1960), pp. 96-9, 119, 129, 130; H. N. Fairchild, *The Noble Savage* (New York, 1961), pp. 112-17.
     Purchase 'of land, to N. K. Giers, 30 Oct. 1885, *SS*, IV:284; 25 Jan. 1886, *SS*, IV:285.
184. Position of foreigners in the Palaus, F. X. Hezel, 'The role of the beachcomber in the Carolines', *The Changing Pacific* (ed. N. Gunson), p. 261.
     Maclay as target, *SS*, III pt 1:311 (footnote).
     Girls of the *pai* (*bai-bai*), *SS*, III pt 1:257-8 (Yap); 287-9 (Palau).
     'temporary wife', to Meshchersky, 3 July 1876, *SS*, IV:140.
     'waiting their turn', *SS*, III pt 1:289.
     Mira, *SS*, IV:140; to Olga, 20 Dec. 1878, *SS*, IV:174-5.
185. 'a man of cruel ...', *SS*, II:314; *SS*, IV:138-9.
     Voyage to Admiralty Islands, *SS*, II:252-93, 314-15.
     Ideas for fresh field of research or for leaving *Sea Bird*, *SS*, II:315; *SS*, IV:138-9.
186. 'so much human ...', *SS*, II:262.
     Hermit Islands, *SS*, II:294-312.
     'very low class', 'the impudence ...', *SS*, II:295.
     'last reserves ...', *SS*, II:315.
     Maclay's letters were duly delivered, some of them with polite and informative covering letters from O'Keefe. See, for example, *Nature*, 15:149 (reprinted from St Petersburg *Golos*).

11: No Ships Call

Basic material is drawn from three sources:
1. The rather scanty revised version of Maclay's journal, *SS*, II:316-83 (translation by C. L. Sentinella, *NGD*, 235-88).
2. A report written in October 1877 and revised July 1879, *SS*, II:388-409.
3. 'Some supplementary material about my second stay on the Maclay Coast of New Guinea 1876-1877' (From a letter to A. A. Meshchersky), *SS*, II:410-34.
References to these sources are given only for selected points.

187. Need for native labour, *SS*, II:411.
     Size of estate, Maclay to Osten-Sacken, 4 July 1886, *SS*, IV:290-1.
     Decision to go to Europe, Maclay to Russian Geographical Society, 3 July 1876, *SS*, IV:139, 140.
     'a very fair Bordeaux ...', 'My daily life and relations with the natives', *SS*, II:385. This short article, apparently written much later, and left unfinished, presents a happier picture of Maclay's situation than that given in the longer accounts.

188. Control of the natives, SS, II:405-6.
     Maclay as the 'only white man', SS, II:389-90, 404.
     Difficulties over land, SS, IV:291.
     'Secretiveness ...', SS, II:391.
     Reasons for not exploring the interior, SS, II:387-8.
     Trying out the natives, SS, II:413-14.
189. Mission to Maragum, SS, II:413. Presumably another quarrel had occurred in Maclay's absence, since he had reported peace established in June 1872.
     Difficulties of expeditions, SS, II:393, 414-15.
190. 'completely useless', SS, II:414.
     'rather tiresome', SS, II:393.
     'coaxing and persuading', SS, II:415.
191. routine, SS, II:384.
     'beneficial to the character', SS, II:398.
     Saleh, SS, II:385, 413.
     Mebli, SS, II:413, 414, 422.
     'laziness and malingering', SS, II:420.
     Mira, SS, II:413. The 'official' records of this sojourn in New Guinea never mention Mira by name or indicate that the younger Palauan servant was a girl. A letter from Maclay to his sister (20 Dec. 1878, SS, IV:174-5) gives a little information about Mira and shows that his original diary contained an account of her.
193. Requests for ships, SMH, 27 July, 22 Nov. 1876.
194. Slow progress in research, SS, II:385, 389-91.
     'melancholy thoughts', SS, II:399.
     ugliness of faces, SS, II:331; NGD, 245.
     'so remote ...', to Rudolf Virchow, Feb. 1877, SS, III pt 1:216.
195. Conversation with Paldi, SS, II:528-9 (footnote).
     Continuing reservations about safety, SS, II:354; NGD, 266.
     Advantages of godlike position, SS, II:404-6.
     The *bulu-ribut*, SS, II:336-8; NGD, 250-2. In some parts of Melanesia, the inhabitants themselves built arrangements like the *bulu-ribut*, R. H. Codrington, *The Melanesians*, p. 340.
196. 'to interfere as little ...', SS, II:385.
     'good men' and 'bad men', SS, II:324; NGD, 239.
     Summoning workers, SS, II:420.
     Maclay's fears for the Papuans, SS, II:408-9, 423-4.
197. 'opportunity to observe ...', SS, II:421.
     'There are many things ...', SS, II:408.
     'a member of the commercial classes', SS, II:407.
198. 'quite convenient ...', SS, II:343-4; NGD, 257.
     'a considerable depth ...', 'deep enough ...', SS, II:346, NGD, 259.
199. Threat from Gorima, SS, II:352-4; NGD, 264-6.
     Maclay undoubtedly slept '*badly*' at Gorima. He used the word '*plokho*' (SS, II:357), which cannot be translated otherwise. At least two translators, however, have thought it more dignified for him to sleep 'well'.
200. Mira's presence on voyage. Maclay states (SS, II:395) that he took two servants. One of them was Saleh (SS, II:358) and Mebli remained at Bugarlom (SS, II:372).
     Kain's story of people with clothes and metal tools, SS, III pt 1:149.
     Demonstration of power in Singor, SS, II:365; NGD, 274.
     'They will kill', 'Maclay is one ...', SS, II:368; NGD, 276.
201. Limits of authority, SS, II:370; NGD, 278; SS, II:387-8.
     Objections to war, SS, II:400-1.
     Previous prevention of war, SS, II:399-400.
202. Request for an earthquake, SS, II:376; NGD, 283.
203. 'limited knowledge ...', and other reasons to avoid discussion of sorcery, SS, II:378; NGD, 284; SS, II:390, 402.

204. 'We wanted to beat ...', *SS*, II:403; *SS*, II:379; *NGD*, 285.
     'quite typical', *SS*, II:404.
205. Saul's enquiries, *SS*, II:342; *NGD*, 256.
     Test of immortality, *SS*, II:381-2; *NGD*, 287-8.
206. Earth tremors, *Proc. LSNSW*, 9:965.
207. Relations of Maclay's servants with Papuans, *SS*, II:337, 376-7; *NGD*, 252, 383.
     'the earthly origin ...', *SS*, II:404. Earlier in the same report (*SS*, II:390), Maclay
     remarks:

     > My being the only white man who has lived among them ... contributes no
     > little to my success ... In the absence of other whites, the natives have no
     > standard of comparison to guide them in assessing their relationship with any
     > individual white man.

     Mebli's ghosts, *SS*, III pt 1:280 (footnote).
     Thefts by servants, *SS*, II:382-3; *NGD*, 288.

12: Descent into Hell

209. Illnesses, *SS*, IV:151, 154, 166.
     Financial difficulties, *SS*, IV:151-2.
210. Arrangements for return to Russia, *SS*, IV:150, 153.
     'chronic catarrh ...', *SS*, IV:154.
     'extreme nervous irritability', 'almost constant...', 'frequent, sudden ...', 'almost
     hysterical...', *SS*, IV:166.
     'for the *worst*...', *SS*, IV:157.
     Lack of comfort or care, *SS*, IV:154, 156.
     Residence with medical friend, E. S. Thomassen, *A Biographical Sketch of Nicholas
     de Miklouho Maclay*, p. 26.
     Attendance of doctors, *SS*, IV:167.
     Mebli and Mira, 'Notes *in re* kidnapping and slavery in the Western Pacific',
     appended to the report 'Labor trade in the Western Pacific', by Commodore
     Wilson, R.N., Vic. Leg. Assby. Papers, no. 31 of 1882, p. 10.
     Borrowings, *SS*, IV:214.
     War talk, *SS*, IV:155.
     Sarimbun, 'Proposed zoological station for Sydney', *SMH*, 31 Aug. 1878.
     Beccari, 'List of plants in use by the natives of the Maclay Coast', *Proc. LSNSW*,
     10:346.
     Volcanic eruption, *Proc. LSNSW*, 9:965.
     Honorary membership, *JSBRAS*, no. 1 (July 1878), p. *v*.
     Ankersmit 'incensed ...', *SS*, IV:157.
     Plans, *SS*, IV:152, 153, 155.
211. Reasons for going to Australia, to Russian Geographical Society, 28 Oct. 1878,
     SS, IV:167. Maclay had in fact always intended to visit that continent.
     'a devoted martyr ...', *Cooktown Herald*, 13 July 1878, reprinted, *SMH*, 27 July.
     Life at Australian Club, *SS*, IV:167.
     Proposal for zoological station, *SMH*, 30 July 1878. (Linnean Society meeting
     of 29 July).
212. Supposed connection between Macleay family and Miklouho-Maclay, D. S.
     Macmillan, *A Squatter Went to Sea*, p. 62 (note). Many Australians still believe this.
     W. Macleay on Darwinian theory, Address to Linnean Society, 21 Jan. 1876,
     reprinted, Ann Mozley Moyal (ed.) *Scientists in Nineteenth Century Australia*
     (Melbourne, 1976), p. 197.
213. Life at Elizabeth Bay, *SS*, IV:161, 164.
     'Regulations, traditions, ...', *SS*, III pt. 2:344.
214. Campaign for zoological station, *SMH*, 30 Aug. 1878, 1 Oct. 1878; *Proc. LSNSW*,
     3:161-3.
     Title of 'baron'. Maclay confused the issue by telling his biographer that this

'stupid' error originated in Jena (E. S. Thomassen to Editor, *Argus*, Melbourne, 27 Mar. 1882). For use of the title in Singapore and Johor, see: Sir A. H. Gordon (Lord Stanmore), *Fiji: Records of Private and of Public Life, 1875-1880*, I:100, 102. Maclay's explanation is given in 'The Maclay Coast and protectorate', draft letter (in Russian) to St Petersburg *Novosti*, April 1884, Papers of N. de Miklouho-Maclay 1863-1888, vol. 1, item 1, A2899 (ML).

There was no Russian title of 'baron'. Some Russian citizens used it by virtue of descent from the old German nobility of the Baltic region.

Special writing paper. The earliest example seems to be that used for a letter to T. H. Huxley from Johor Baharu, T. H. Huxley Papers, 1846-1878, vol. 22, microfilm FM4/216 (ML).

Various styles of coronet and monogram appear on letters to British officials (and some private persons) between 1878 and 1883.

Visiting card, Papers of N. de Miklouho-Maclay 1863-1888, vol. 1, item 1, A2899 (ML).

215. 'saved from close ...', *SS*, IV:172.
    'the white Papuan', *SS*, IV:162, 172.
    Beccari and New Guinea annexation, John Goode, *The Rape of the Fly*, p. 214.
    'unpleasantness' in Sydney, *SS*, IV:162.
    'Papuan Union', *SMH*, 1 Feb. 1877.
216. Disappointment with Russia, to Semyonov-Tianshansky, 29 Jan. 1878, *SS*, IV:152.
    Sydney as observation post. Daniil Tumarkin suggests (N. Miklouho-Maclay, *Travels to New Guinea*, p. 30) that Maclay came to Australia primarily to keep watch on Australian activities and fight for the rights of Pacific islanders. If this was so, he expected a quick victory. He consistently told family and friends that he would return to Russia late in 1878 or early in 1879 (*SS*, IV:156, 162, 164, 174; *SS*, II:445).
217. Disadvantages of staying with W. Macleay, to Virchow [early 1879] *SS*, III pt 2:345; to Sergei, 30 Aug. 1878, *SS*, IV:164.
    Horrors of the Australian Museum, to Virchow, *SS*, III pt 2:345-6.
    'these democrats', *SS*, IV:172.
218. Sponges, E. Haeckel, *Die Kalkschwämme* (Berlin, 1872), I:25-7, 461 (footnote).
    Fish brain, T. H. Huxley, 'On *Ceratodus forsteri* ...', *Proc. Zool. Soc. London*, 1876 pt 1:30-1; F. M. Balfour, *A Monograph on the Development of the Elasmobranch Fishes* (London, 1878), p. 182; E. Ehlers, 'Die Epiphyse am Gehirn der Plagiostomen', *Zeitschr. f. Wissenschaftlich Zool.*, 1878, vol. 30 (Suppl.), p. 630; E. Ray Lankester, preface to Gegenbaur, *Elements of Comparative Anatomy* (London, 1878), pp. xii-xiii; *SS*, III pt 2:419-21 (notes by I. I. Pusanov).
219. 'of no moment ...', 'every friend ...', 'a good test ...', *Proc. LSNSW*, 4:104-5.
    'popular instruction ...', W. J. Stephens, Annual Address to Linnean Society of New South Wales, *SMH*, 8 Feb. 1879.
    Moves on zoological station, *SS*, II:438-9.
220. Return of *Courier*, *SMH*, 1, 27, 30 Jan. 1879.
    'murder and war ...', Maclay to Gordon, 23 Jan. 1879, G.B. & I. Parl. Papers, *Further Correspondence Respecting New Guinea*, C-3617, pp. 108-9.
    a 'just adversary', *SS*, II:442.
    Acquaintance with Gordon, Sir A. H. Gordon, *Fiji: Records of Private and of Public Life, 1875-1880*, I:100, 102.
    'did not regard ...' *SS*, II:441-2.
221. Gordon in Victoria, *SMH*, 22 July 1878.
    Gordon to be consulted about New Guinea, *SMH*, 10 Aug. 1878.
    'recognizing the rights ...', to Gordon, 23 Jan. 1879, G.B. & I. Parl. Papers, *Further Correspondence ...*, C-3617, pp. 108-9.
    German purchase of harbours, *SMH*, 7 Feb. 1879.
    Projected Italian expedition, *SMH*, 19 Mar. 1879.
    Rumour of Russian naval base, *SMH*, 25 Feb. 1879.
    Expeditions of *Dove* and *Courier*, *SMH*, 24 Jan., 30 Jan., 4 Feb. 1879.
222. 'crime against science', *SS*, IV:179.

13: Clause Two

223. 'a pile of work', *SS*, IV:179.
　　　State of mind and health, *SS*, III pt 2:345-6.
　　　Ideas for travelling with the Royal Navy, *SS*, II:446.
　　　Advantages of the *S. F. Caller, SS*, II:447-8; *SS*, IV:188.
　　　'For lack ...', *SS*, II:559.
　　　Motives, *SS*, II:444-5, 559.
　　　'special circumstances', *SS*, II:445.
　　　Family finances, *SS*, IV:198.
224. Ankersmit, *SS*, II:445.
　　　Obtaining funds, *SS*, II:446. Apparently the first news of this reached the
　　　Russian Geographical Society in a *copy* of a letter Maclay had sent to Rudolf
　　　Virchow.
　　　Undertaking to assist *S. F. Caller, SS*, II:448.
　　　Unpleasant publicity, 'To New Guinea Again', *Evening News* (Sydney), 27 Mar.
　　　1879; *The Echo*, 28 Mar. 1879. Maclay's denial, *SMH*, 29 Mar. 1879.
　　　'After I had left ...', Paper read to Linnean Society, 23 Feb. 1881, *SMH*, 26 Feb.
　　　1881.
　　　'In total ...', *SS*, II:568.
　　　'these parts ...', *SS*, IV:183.
　　　Noumea, *SS*, II:449-56.
225. Theft of skulls, *SS*, II:452-3.
　　　Loyalty Islands, *SS*, II:457-8.
226. Voyage to Candelaria Reef, *SS*, II:559-60.
　　　'human menagerie', 'nonsensically chattering ...', *SS*, IV:187, 188.
　　　'Why did I write ...', 'For what ...', 'I so little know ...', *SS*, IV:182-3.
227. Observations on the labour traffic, 'Notes *in re* kidnapping and slavery in the
　　　Western Pacific', *Labor Trade in the Western Pacific*, Vic. Leg. Assby Papers, no. 31
　　　of 1882, pp. 9-13. This communication, appended to a report by Commodore
　　　Wilson, also appeared in the parliamentary papers of New South Wales and
　　　Queensland.
228. Report to Wilson at Efate, *Labor Trade in the Western Pacific*, Vic. Leg. Assby Papers,
　　　no. 31 of 1882, pp. 4, 10.
　　　'good and just man', *SS*, II:511.
　　　John Crawford Wilson entered the navy in 1847. He had seen some service in
　　　war, but had been more concerned with the naval training of boys. He arrived to
　　　take charge of the Australia station in December 1878.
　　　'vindictive and treacherous', 'the most degraded ...', Report from Commodore
　　　J. C. Wilson, 5 July 1879, Confidential printed papers, 2/8095.3, Archives of New
　　　South Wales.
　　　'specimens of the rabble', *SS*, IV:188.
　　　Attempt to leave the schooner, *SS*, II:561.
229. First visit to Andra, *SS*, II:459-510. These extracts from Maclay's journal were
　　　rewritten in 1887 for magazine publication.
　　　'putting too high ...', *SS*, IV:188.
　　　'In my opinion ...', *SS*, II:448 (note).
230. Observations by Webber and Bruno, *SS*, II:494, 495. Cavaliere Bruno was said to
　　　have had a good deal of experience in the islands. He had been associated with the
　　　so-called 'Garibaldian' scheme for settlement in New Guinea.
　　　'Let the skipper sleep ...', *SS*, II:497.
　　　'The enemy are coming ...', *SS*, II:497-8.
232. Sori, *SS*, II:511-17 (rewritten in 1887); *SS*, II:561-2.
　　　'afraid neither of ...', *SS*, IV:188.
233. Second visit to Andra, *SS*, II:519-33 (rewritten in 1887).
　　　O'Hara, *SS*, II:485-6, 527-8, 530.
　　　'one worthless white ...', *SS*, II:491.
　　　'compassionate people ...', *SS*, II:528.

234. 'these beasts', *SS*, IV:189.
	Reasons for not visiting Maclay Coast, *SS*, II:562.
	Voyage to New Guinea, *SS*, II:562-4.
235. Travels in south-east New Guinea, *SS*, II:535-8 (rewritten); *SS*, II:564-7.
	'The company of the missionaries...', *SS*, II:537.
	Trading 'under disguise', 'prepared the way...', *SS*, II:423.
236. 'not at all prudish', *SS*, II:546.
	'traces of Christian mythology', *SS*, II:545.
	'a sort of savage', R. Lovett, *James Chalmers*, p. 242.
	'nobody—lost...', 'a king...', quoted by Gavan Daws, *A Dream of Islands* (Brisbane, 1980), p. 194.
	Port Moresby, *SS*, II:552-8, 565-6.

14: The Hairless Australian

239. 'difficulties and sacrifices', 'truer opinions...', *SS*, II:570.
	'a far greater...', *SS*, II:568.
240. Earlier ideas for visiting Queensland, *SS*, IV:170-1.
	(Sir) Arthur Palmer, E. S. Thomassen, *A Biographical Sketch of Nicholas de Miklouho Maclay*, p. 33; O. W. Parnaby, *Britain and the Labor Traffic in the Southwest Pacific*, pp. 85, 89.
	Internal anatomy in ethnological work, Maclay to Virchow, 9 Dec. 1876, *SS*, IV:142.
	'The investigation of the brains...', 'definite types...', *Proc. LSNSW*, 6:171-5.
	'instructive and pleasant...', *Proc. LSNSW*, 6:171-5.
241. Identification of men hanged, Greenop, pp. 175-6.
	Hairless Australians, *ZE*, 13:*Verhl*.143-9.
242. 'specimen of *Homo australis*', *Proc. LSNSW*, 6:577.
	Maclay and Johnny Campbell, *Queenslander*, 2 Oct. 1880.
	Proposal for exhibition of Aborigines, to F. von Mueller, Aug. 1880, *SS*, IV:191-2; to Virchow, 3 Nov. 1880, *SS*, III pt 1:393.
244. Progress of zoological station, Archives of New South Wales, CSIL, 86/8461; N.S.W. *Govt. Gazette*, 10 June 1879; *Nature*, 20:506-7; *SMH*, 16 Dec. 1879, 19 Feb. 1881.
245. 'in the mood...', *Proc. LSNSW*, 4:105.
	'temporary zoological station', *SMH*, 19 Feb., 30 July 1881.
	Financial position, *SS*, IV:198-9; *Nature*, 21:22.
	Public subscription, *SS*, IV:197-8; *Nature*, 21:22; 23:44. Possibly the Russian Geographical Society expected the debt to William Macleay to be paid out of this sum.
246. 'almost complete catastrophe', *SS*, IV:198-9.
	Maclay to Nikolai Mikhailovich, 10 June 1881, *SS*, IV:196-9. The grand duke, a nephew of Alexander II, was twenty-three at the time. He interested himself in several branches of science and scholarship. Eventually he became a serious historian, author of a valuable 'life and times' of Alexander I.
247. 'to woo the mob...', *SS*, IV:197.
	Australasian Biological Association, *SMH*, 18 June, 30 July 1881.
248. New Zealand colonization project, *SMH*, 29 Mar. 1881 (from *Lyttelton Times*).
	Offer to Gordon, 1 May 1881, Stanmore Papers, British Library, Add. ms. 49239.
249. Official visit to Astrolabe Bay, H. H. Romilly, *The Western Pacific and New Guinea*, pp. 220-30.
	After a disastrous voyage, the *Dove's* company unexpectedly ended up in Japan. Consequently their adventures remained unknown in the colonies until late in January 1879.
	'Cases occur...', 'kidnapping, slave trade...', 'that the Imperial Government...', to Wilson, 8 Apr. 1881, *SMH*, 18 Apr. 1881, reprinting Melbourne *Argus*.

250. For general diffusion of 'retaliation only' theory, see for example leaders in *SMH*, 29 Sept., 30 Nov. 1880; *Daily Telegraph*, 7 Dec. 1880; 'South Sea Massacres', *SMH*, 3 Apr. 1881. The idea is discussed by D. Shineberg, *They Came for Sandalwood*, pp. 199–214.

British desire for an international agreement, O. W. Parnaby, *Britain and the Labor Traffic in the Southwest Pacific*, pp. 176–8; J. M. Ward, *British Policy in the South Pacific*, pp. 229–30, 261, 284.

'The question is not...', *SMH*, 18 Apr. 1881 (leader).

Kalo incident, *SMH*, 29 Mar. 1881, 30 Mar. (leader), 8 Apr. (Letter from T. Beswick, New Guinea missionary).

Attitude of missionaries, J. Chalmers, *Pioneering in New Guinea*, p. 157; M. E. Turvey, 'Missionaries and imperialism', *JRAHS*, 65:99.

Wilson's approach to Kalo, Chalmers, *Pioneering in New Guinea*, p. 158; W. G. Lawes, Journal, 1881–82, pp. 48–50, 63, CYA388 (ML). Maclay was perhaps over-impressed by the fact that the Royal Navy, legally, could only proceed by 'act of war'. In reality, the Admiralty urged officers to avoid the kind of action Maclay feared.

251. Maclay's decision to go to Kalo, *SS*, II:573; *SMH*, 30 July 1881 (Linnean Society meeting, 28 July); *SMH*, 11 Aug. 1881.

Ideas for joining Feilding's expedition, *SMH*, 30 July 1881. Maclay apparently met Feilding at Singapore in 1875 (Sir A. Gordon, *Fiji: Records of Private and of Public Life*, I:96, 97). The association developed further when Feilding translated for the Royal Geographical Society Maclay's account of adventures in Papua-Koviai.

Discussions with missionaries, Chalmers, *Pioneering in New Guinea*, pp. 157–8; W. G. Lawes, Journal, 1881–82, pp. 48–50, 63, CYA388 (ML); *SS*, II:576.

According to one account, the Kalo chief had wished to emulate a neighbour who had gained wealth and prestige by killing foreigners. In another version the chief's wife, resenting the wife of the leading teacher, had incited the massacre. Without explaining why, Maclay accepted the latter version.

252. Events in Kalo, *SMH*, 5, 6, 29 Sept. 1881; Chalmers, *Pioneering in New Guinea*, p. 158.

'Results of the cruise...'. *SMH*, 5 Sept. 1881.

'My plan...', *SS*, II:581.

15: A Glimpse of the Kingdom

253. First plan for biological station, *Nature*, 20:506–7.

Final structure, *Sydney Mail*, 14 May 1881; *Nature*, 24:246, 313; *SMH*, 30 July 1881 (Linnean Society meeting 28 July); *SMH*, 7 Feb. 1882 (Australian Biological Association).

'devoid of anything...', W. J. Stephens, Australian Biological Association, *SMH*, 7 Feb. 1882.

254. Rules of biological station, *Proc. LSNSW*, 3:161–3.

'anatomical researches...', *SMH*, 12 Oct. 1881.

'Notes *in re* kidnapping and slavery in the western Pacific', appended to report by Commodore Wilson, *Labor Trade in the Western Pacific*, Vic. Leg. Assby Papers, no. 31 of 1882. This report was also printed in the parliamentary papers of Queensland and New South Wales, and summarized in several newspapers.

'very serious and neglected...', 'Notes *in re* kidnapping...', p. 10. Maclay offered no suggestions about control of venereal disease among sailors on inter-island vessels.

255. '*how* and through what means...', 'Notes *in re* kidnapping...', pp. 10–11.

Maclay apparently took it for granted that the nice-looking young women were required as concubines or prostitutes. Island girls, however, had been engaged as housemaids and nursemaids in some of north Queensland's 'best' homes and such employers preferred good-looking servants. Mainly as a result of white working-class agitation, the employment of islanders in domestic service had been prohibited by 1881.

256. The Pacific Island Laborers Act of 1880 (Queensland) raised the legal age for recruiting and provided for the establishment of district hospitals for islanders. Despite Maclay's conviction that the law would remain a dead letter, the hospitals were actually built. They were not a success.

'but a legalized slave trade ...', Report from Commodore Wilson, 5 July 1879, no. 128, Confidential printed papers, 2/8095.3, Archives of New South Wales.

The skipper of the *Loelia*, accused by Maclay of cheating a sailor, had been killed with some of his crew on New Britain late in 1880, a fact well known in Sydney.

'independent evidence', 'a gentleman of great ...', Wilson report, *Labor Trade in the Western Pacific*, Vic. Leg. Assby Papers, no. 31 of 1882, p. 8.

'not merely a ruthless ...', *SS*, II:440.

257. Maclay Coast Scheme, Papers of N. de Miklouho-Maclay, 1863-1888, vol. 1, item 1, A2889, pp. 36-52 (ML). All quotations are drawn from this document unless otherwise attributed.

The proposal for forming a company was not mentioned until Maclay reached the seventh page of his draft. His plan for government and social progress was placed well ahead of first steps.

'a vast plan', to Semyonov-Tianshansky, 29 June 1882, *SS*, IV:214.

258. 'entirely owned ...', 'As the natives', to Gordon, 23 Jan. 1879, G.B. & I. Parl. Papers, *Further Correspondence Respecting New Guinea*, C-3617, pp. 108-9.

Schools were clearly a project for the distant future. Maclay said nothing about engaging teachers or devising an educational system for a scattered population with many languages.

259. Maclay's belief that New Guineans preferred to stay home, Maclay and Chalmers to Lord Derby, 1 June 1883, *SMH*, 5 Jan. 1884; G.B. & I. Parl. Papers, *Correspondence Respecting New Guinea and Other Islands*, C-3863, p. 5.

'neither pity nor sympathy ...', to Wilson, 8 Apr. 1881, *SMH*, 18 Apr. 1881.

Hope of paying debts, *SS*, IV:214.

Lists of comparable wages can be found in *SMH*, 16 Aug. 1884.

261. Maclay to Gordon, 25 Jan. 1882, Stanmore Papers, p. 102, British Library Add. ms. 49239.

Gordon's response, 13 Feb. 1882, N. de Miklouho-Maclay, Papers, 1863-1888, vol. 1, item 2, pp. 13i (1-3), A2889 (ML).

Gordon (Lord Stanmore) and Pacific Phosphate Company, D. Scarr, *Fragments of Empire*, pp. 270-8.

262. Maclay's plans, *SMH*, 25 Jan. 1881; *SMH*, 7 Feb. 1882 (Australian Biological Association); to Semyonov-Tianshansky, 9 Nov. 1881, *SS*, IV:204, and 29 June 1882, *SS*, IV:211-15.

16: Apotheosis

263. Only three of the warships called at Melbourne.

Australian Biological Association, *SMH*, 7 Feb. 1882. The term 'Australasian' had been dropped.

E. S. Thomassen, *A Biographical Sketch of Nicholas de Miklouho-Maclay*, Brisbane (privately printed), 1882.

On Thomassen, see Queensland Legislative Assembly, *Votes and Proceedings*, 1880, vol. 2, 'Contract and correspondence relating to supply of steel rails' and 'Proceedings of Select Committee, July-Oct. 1880'; *SMH*, 13 Nov. 1880 (Brisbane letter).

264. 'Though the sun ...', also quoted in Maclay to Meshchersky, 20 Nov. 1873, *SS*, IV:95.

'in great numbers ...', Thomassen, *Biographical Sketch*, p. 7. The story of almost daily attempts at murder had, of course, begun with Maclay. By December 1873, when J. C. Galton heard it, the natives were pressing their spears against Maclay's teeth, forcing his mouth open (*Nature*, 9:328). The most hair-raising version of all was that purveyed by H. H. Romilly (*The Western Pacific and New Guinea*, p. 18), in which Maclay was tied to a tree, had spears forced down his throat, and 'nearly died of his injuries'. Even the mildest of the accounts authorized or approved by Maclay are inconsistent with that given in the final version of his New Guinea journals.

'the power and attributes...', Thomassen, *Biographical Sketch*, pp. 18–19.

Maclay's supervision and approval of text, Thomassen, *Biographical Sketch*, p. 46 (postscript); Thomassen to editor, *Argus*, 27 Mar. 1882; Maclay to Unwin, 29 Apr. 1884, *SS*, IV:269; *Daily Telegraph* (Sydney), 15 Jan. 1884, pp. 3, 5.

'communicated to the Royal Geographical Society': Several writers assume that this phrase on Thomassen's title page referred to an organization in Brisbane. At the time, however, Brisbane had no geographical society. The archivist of the Royal Geographical Society, London, can find no evidence of the biography's being 'communicated' in the usual sense.

265. 'conscientious white settlers...', Thomassen, *Biographical Sketch*, p. 44.

Thomassen to Ibbotson Brothers, *Biographical Sketch*, Appendix, vii–viii.

Farewells in Melbourne, Thomassen to editor, *Argus*, 27 Mar. 1882.

According to family tradition, as recounted by F. S. Greenop, Maclay first met Margaret Clark in December 1881. The inscription on a photograph in the Mitchell Library, however, shows that the love affair was well established in July of that year.

266. 'Tell our dear mother...', to Mikhail, 23 Apr. 1882, *SS*, IV:207.

267. Response to news of Olga's death, to Mikhail, 17 June 1882, *SS*, IV:209.

Previous knowledge of Olga's plight, to Grand Duke Nikolai Mikhailovich, 10 June 1881, *SS*, IV:198.

Promises to Olga, *SS*, IV:175, 178–9, 187, 189. Warning, *SS*, IV:183.

268. Reasons for living in Sydney, *SMH*, 7 Feb. 1882 (Australian Biological Association); to Semyonov-Tianshansky, 29 June 1882, *SS*, IV:211–12.

Financial affairs, *SS*, IV:212, 213–15, 216.

Royal Geographical Society: Maclay told the Russian geographers (*SS*, IV:215) that the English society had invited him to present an account of his travels and given him reason to hope for support. The archivist of the Royal Geographical Society advises that the organization had no communication with Maclay in the relevant period.

'accompanied by considerable...', *SS*, IV:214–15.

270. Negotiations over funds, *SS*, IV:222–3, 227; *SS*, II:682 (conclusion of report given in St Petersburg); Autobiography written in 1887, *SS*, IV:432.

Relations with imperial family, *SS*, IV:225.

Assistance from government and tsar, L. S. Berg, 'Nikolai Nikolaevich Miklouho-Maclay', in *Otechestvennie fiziko-geografy i puteshestvenniki*, p. 275; *SS*, IV:432; *Proc. RGS* (n.s.) 5:47; *Nature*, 27:92; *SMH*, 18 Nov. 1882; 14 Feb. 1883.

271. Commission to help choose naval station, B. A. Valskaya, 1959, 'The struggle of N. N. Miklouho-Maclay for the rights of the Papuans of the Maclay Coast', *Strany i narody Vostoka*, I, pp. 135–6; Valskaya, 1970, 'The project of N. N. Miklouho-Maclay for the establishment of a free Russian colony on an island of the Pacific Ocean', *Avstraliya i Okeaniya (istoriya i sovremennost')*, p. 38; Sentinella, *NGD*, pp. 295, 345 (note 13).

272. Mikhail's faults, *SS*, IV:209, 240.

Rumours about France, *SMH*, 3 Feb. 1883 (St Petersburg letter).

273. Gabriel Monod's views on politics and social issues are best revealed in articles written for the English *Contemporary Review*, vols 42 and 44, from which the quotations used here are drawn.

274. G. Monod, 'La Nouvelle-Guinée. Les voyages de M. de Miklouho-Maclay', *La Nouvelle Revue*, t. 19, no. 2, 15 Nov. 1882, partly reprinted in *Bull. de la Soc. Historique*, 1883, pp. 103–12.

Visit to Turgenev, *SS*, IV:421–3.

17: White Ants

276. Gladstone to Olga Novikov, 5 Dec. 1882, Gladstone Papers, BL Add. ms. 44546, f.43.
277. Derby's assurances, Maclay to *Novosti* [April 1884], Papers of N. de Miklouho-Maclay 1863-1888, vol. 1, item 1, p. 135, A2889 (ML).

Alexander von Glehn, *SS*, IV:252; *The Times*, 9, 24, 26 Sept. 1870; von Glehn to Maclay, 26 Oct. 1884, Papers of N. de Miklouho-Maclay, vol. 1, item 1, pp. 194-9, A2889 (ML) (printed by Greenop, pp. 225-6, but without a rather significant postscript on business matters).

Visits to Sir Arthur Gordon, Maclay to Wilson, 27 Feb. 1883, Stanmore (Sir A. H. Gordon) Papers 1873-1912, f.234, BL Add. ms. 49239; ML microfilm FM4/2721; to Gordon, 2 Apr. 1884, BL Add. ms. 49240, f.34; to Editor, *SMH*, 23 Nov. 1883.
278. 'the tender mercies...', 'pothouse politicians', quoted by J. K. Chapman, *The Career of Arthur Hamilton Gordon, First Lord Stanmore*, p. 302.

Gordon and Pacific Islands Company, D. Scarr, *Fragments of Empire*, pp. 264-6.
279. Approach to William Mackinnon, Maclay to Gordon, 25 Jan. 1882, BL Add. ms. 49239, ff.102-3; to Gordon, 2 Apr. 1884, BL Add. ms. 49240, f.34; to Wilson, 27 Feb. 1883, BL Add. ms. 49239, f.234, ML microfilm FM4/2721.

The archivist, School of Oriental and African Studies, University of London, advises that the papers of Sir William Mackinnon contain no correspondence or documents concerning the Maclay Coast Scheme.

Request to Royal Navy, Maclay to Wilson, 27 Feb. 1883, Stanmore Papers, BL Add. ms. 49239, f.234; ML microfilm FM4/2721.

Introduction to colonial governors, Sec. of State to Governor of New South Wales, 31 Jan. 1883, no. 5, Archives of New South Wales, 4/1376.
280. Personal disadvantages of Maclay Coast Scheme, to Semyonov-Tianshansky, 29 June 1882, *SS*, IV:214-15.

'becoming a planter', to Osten-Sacken, 6 July 1882, *SS*, IV:216.

Maclay in Italy, *SS*, IV:232; *SMH*, 2 Apr. 1883.

Change of plans, Sentinella, *NGD*, pp. 295, 345 (note 13); Maclay to Mikhail, 24 Jan. 1883, *SS*, IV:235; to Kopitov [Apr. 1883], *SS*, IV:244.
281. 'It's warm, *glorious* ...', *SS*, IV:239.

'Here in the islands ...', *SS*, IV:242.

Voyage to New Guinea, *SS*, II:582; *NGD*, 295-6. This account, rewritten late in Maclay's life, maintains the fiction that his meeting with *Skobelev* was accidental.

Meeting at Batavia, Kopitov's report, in B. A. Valskaya, 1972, 'Unpublished materials ... on the voyage of the corvette *Skobelev* ... 1883', *Strany i Narody Vostoka*, 13(2), p. 20. (Russian).

Maclay's fear of Australian suspicion, to Kopitov, *SS*, IV:247.

Information to English scientists, *Nature*, 27:371.
282. Letter to Admiral Wilson, 27 Feb. 1883, Stanmore (Sir A. H. Gordon) Papers, BL Add. ms. 49239, f.234; ML microfilm FM4/2721.

Kopitov's previous intentions, report in Valskaya, 1972, p. 20.

Visit to Maclay Coast, *SS*, II:583-95; *NGD*, 296-306.

Purchase and presentation of gifts, Valskaya, 1972, p. 26.
283. Articles left in house, *SS*, II:383; *PGM*, 24:407-8.

Preservation of Maclay's property, Thomassen, *Biographical Sketch*, p. 45; *SS*, II:644.

Discovery that house and goods were gone, *SS*, II:584-5; *NGD*, 297-8.
284. Need for interpreter, *SS*, IV:243.

Obtaining Bilbil men, *SS*, II:589; *NGD*, 301-2.

Capture of canoe, *SS*, II:590; *NGD*, 302-3.
285. Malaspena, *SS*, II:594; *NGD*, 305-6; to Osten-Sacken, 4 July 1886, *SS*, IV:291.

Kopitov on Port Alexei, Valskaya, 1972, pp. 27-9.
286. Kopitov on Maclay, Valskaya, 1972, pp. 20, 32, 37.
287. Kopitov's views on settlement of Russians in the Pacific and establishment of

naval stations, Valskaya, 1972, pp. 29-30, 31, 32, 33-7.

Maclay's trust in Lord Derby, to *Novosti* [Apr. 1884], Papers of N. de Miklouho-Maclay 1863-1888, vol. 1, item 1, p. 135, A2889 (ML).

Prediction of British response, to Kopitov, 3 May 1883, *SS*, IV:247.

'a voice crying ...', 'a Friend of Justice ...', to Gordon, 2 May 1883, Stanmore Papers, BL Add. ms. 49239, f.235; ML microfilm FM4/2721.

Gordon's reaction to Queensland annexation attempt, Gordon to Gladstone, 20 Apr. 1883, printed in P. Knaplund, 'Sir Arthur Gordon on the New Guinea question', *Hist. Stud. A. & N. Z.*, 7:329-31; anonymous article in *The Times*, 15 May 1883 (comparison with the letter to Gladstone and other writings shows this article to be by Gordon).

288. Information against O'Keefe, to Gordon, 3 May 1883, Stanmore Papers, BL Add. ms. 49239, f.237; ML microfilm FM4/2721.

289. Defence of Palauans, to Commodore of China Station, 29 Apr. 1883, *SS*, IV:245.

Royal Navy's dealings with Palau, F. X. Hezel, 'The role of the beachcomber in the Carolines', N. Gunson (ed.), *The Changing Pacific*, p. 261.

Trials of D. D. O'Keefe, F. X. Hezel, 'A Yankee trader in Yap', D. Scarr (ed.), *More Pacific Islands Portraits*, pp. 66-8.

Recommendation of Kubary, to Commodore of China Station, *SS*, IV:246.

'not simply as Maclay ...', to Gordon, 3 May 1883, Stanmore Papers, BL Add. ms. 49239, f.237; ML microfilm FM4/2721.

18: Among Savage Tribes

290. 'above all, try to impress ...', quoted by E. Marin La Meslee at meeting of Geographical Society of Australasia, *SMH*, 23 June 1883. Maclay's advice had no discernible effect upon the expedition which took place two years later.

291. 'troubles, unpleasantness ...', to Mikhail, 1 Nov. 1883, *SS*, IV:256.

Maclay and local children, Greenop, pp. 216-18, 222.

'unaccountable antipathy ...', *SMH*, 3 Feb. 1883 (St Petersburg letter).

292. '*Something* about Maclay ...', note on cover of Mitchell Library copy of Thomassen's *Biographical Sketch*.

'proposals have lately been made ...', Loftus to Derby, 19 Feb. 1883, G.B. & I. Parl. Papers, *Further Correspondence Respecting New Guinea*, C-3617, pp. 123-4.

'such an *apparently* simple matter', to Mikhail, *SS*, IV:256.

293. Presbyterian meeting, *SMH*, 15 Oct. 1883.

'If England extends ...', *SS*, IV:256.

Land speculation, *SMH*, 14 Oct. 1883; Maclay to Derby, 17 Oct. 1883, G.B. & I. Parl. Papers, *Correspondence Respecting New Guinea and Other Islands*, C-3863, p. 56; Palmer to Derby, 24 Oct. 1883 (with copy of letter by J. Chalmers and articles from newspapers), *Correspondence Respecting New Guinea ...*, p. 71. The complaint did not actually concern Queensland. It came to Palmer only because the Queensland premier had asked Chalmers to report anything objectionable.

'General' MacIver, *SMH*, 5 Sept., 18, 20, 23 Oct. 1883.

Derby's action, *SMH*, 27 Oct. 1883.

294. 'the property of the Crown ...', Maclay to Derby, 28 Oct. 1883, G.B. & I. Parl. Papers, *Correspondence Respecting New Guinea ...*, C-3863, p. 85; *SMH*, 5 Jan. 1884.

'the best ... authority', *Pall Mall Gazette*, reprinted *SMH*, 5 Jan. 1884.

Discussion in London, *Proc. R. Col. Inst.*, 15:24-5, 35, 36; *SMH*, 16, 19 Nov., 27 Dec. 1883, 2, 5 Jan. 1884.

'the danger of New Guinea ...', *SMH*, 16 Nov. 1883.

Attempt to prevent misunderstanding, Maclay to editor, *SMH*, 6 Nov. 1883.

'But even this ...', *SMH*, 19 Nov. 1883.

295. Maclay to editor, *SMH*, 23 Nov. 1883. Editorial response, *SMH*, 28 Nov. 1883.

'Maclay knows ...', to editor, *SMH*, 23 Nov. 1883.

Request for Russian protectorate; 'save a few islands ...', to Mikhail, 27 Nov. 1883, *SS*, IV:257.

In his campaign against Wilfred Powell, Maclay wrote to the Royal Geographical Society on 31 December 1883. Thomassen followed suit on 9 January 1884. Their intervention had no effect on the proposed expedition, which fell through for lack of funds. Since both asked that their letters be treated as 'privileged' or 'confidential', the Society destroyed these communications. The archives, however, contain the supporting letters Maclay obtained from others and copies of the Society's replies. The Society has kindly made photocopies of this material available.

The article from the St Petersburg *New Times* (*Novoe Vremya*), 7 Jan. 1884, is partly reproduced in Miklouho-Maclay, *Travels to New Guinea*, p. 506. It was accurately summarized in *The Times*, 21 Jan. 1884. Maclay reacted to the first brief cablegrams in Sydney papers.

Indignation on Maclay's behalf, *SMH*, 22 Apr. 1884 (St Petersburg letter); G. Musgrave to editor, *The Times*, 24 Jan. 1884. Maclay's protest [22 Jan. 1884], Papers of N. de Miklouho-Maclay 1863-1888, vol. 1, item 1, pp. 191-2, A2889 (ML).

296. 'revised by Baron Maclay ...', *Daily Telegraph*, 15 Jan. 1884, p. 5. The biography began under the title 'Baron Maclay' on p. 3 of the same issue. The newspaper file being incomplete, it has not been possible to see all instalments, which appeared at approximately weekly intervals. In those seen, the revisions did not in any way alter the character of Thomassen's work.

Power of attorney, Thomassen to editor, *The Times*, 26 July 1886.

Applicants for Maclay Coast Scheme: to Gordon, 2 Apr. 1884, Stanmore Papers, BL Add. ms. 49240, f.34.

297. Attempts to find out about British protectorate: to Wilson, 4 Mar. 1884, Papers of N. de Miklouho-Maclay, vol. 1, item 1, pp. 175-7, A2889 (ML); to Gordon, 2 Apr. 1884, BL Add. ms. 49240, f.34; to Des Voeux, 22 Apr. 1884, G.B. & I. Parl. Papers, *Further Correspondence Respecting New Guinea*, C-4273, p. 2.

'You are perfectly right ...', to Wilson, 4 Mar. 1884.

'I never regret ...', to Mikhail, 23 Apr. 1884, *SS*, IV:267.

298. Sir Henry Parkes on Maclay, *SMH*, 15 Mar. 1884 (reprinting *Pall Mall Gazette*).

'great benefit ...', *Illustrated Sydney News*, 15 Mar. 1884, p. 3.

Rumour of Maclay's giving evidence, *SMH*, 26 May 1883 (Fiji news).

'No more disparaging', *SMH*, 19 Apr. 1884 (leader).

Anxiety to preserve Maclay's influence, 'Report of the Western Pacific Royal Commission', London, 16 Oct. 1883, reprinted in Queensland Legislative Assembly, *Votes and Proceedings*, 1884, vol. II.

'ought not to be ...', Derby to Des Voeux, 25 June 1884, G.B. & I. Parl. Papers, *Further Correspondence Respecting New Guinea ...*, C-4273, p. 3.

'Australian colonist', *Illustrated Sydney News*, 15 Mar. 1884, p. 3.

Maclay's reply to Russian critics, 'Maclay Coast and Protectorate', letter to St Petersburg *Novosti* [Apr. 1884], Papers of N. de Miklouho-Maclay 1863-1888, vol. 1, item 1, A2889 (ML).

299. English reaction, *SMH*, 5 June, 22 July 1884.

Maclay explains motives, *SMH*, 6 June 1884.

300. 'become urgent', to Mikhail, 10 Aug. 1884, *SS*, IV:271.

301. The 'Garden Palace' was totally destroyed on 22 September 1882. It is frequently stated that most of Maclay's ethnological collection and many of his papers were lost in this fire. No contemporary evidence for this has come to light. Maclay's only reference to his losses is apparently that in *Proc. LSNSW*, 9:579, where he mentions only brains.

302. Maclay on East Indies and Queensland, *SMH*, 10 Sept. 1884 (Geographical Society of Australasia). Maclay's remarks were already out of date. They are interesting as an example of the way in which he ignored public knowledge and government action to emphasize his own.

Suspicion of O. Finsch: 'German Policy in the Pacific', *SMH*, 26 Sept. 1884; G.B. & I. Parl. Papers, *Further Correspondence Respecting New Guinea ...*, C-4273, pp. 19, 26. The author of the *SMH* article is identified by a reference in a later article under his usual pseudonym.

303. 'the shameless injustice . . .', to Bismarck, 1 Oct. 1884, Papers of N. de Miklouho-Maclay, vol. 1, item 1, p. 193, A2889 (ML). This English translation was apparently intended for Lord Derby.

305. Reasons for seeking recognition of Maclay Coast independence. In a brief autobiography written during the last months of his life, Maclay says:

> Convinced by correspondence with the Russian ministry for foreign affairs of the impossibility of obtaining a Russian protectorate . . ., N. N. addressed himself to the Russian and English governments with a proposal for recognition of the independence of the Maclay Coast under his administration (*SS*, IV:433).

This appears to be his definitive explanation of his actions.

Maclay to Derby, 10 Nov. 1884, G.B. & I. Parl. Papers, *Further Correspondence Respecting New Guinea . . .*, C-4273, p. 56.

The situation in Samoa was not what Maclay imagined. The consuls of Germany, Britain and the United States exercised virtual joint control. Equilibrium was temporarily maintained by each power's treaty rights, reluctance to rule the islands directly, and opposition to any attempt by the others to do so. German commitment to what remained of Samoan sovereignty amounted to 'willingness' to recognize the islands' independence provided they were run in accordance with German interests.

'*on occasion*, great importance . . .', Maclay to Giers, 9 Jan. 1885, *SS*, IV:281. The letter written about the same time as that to Derby is not available, but Maclay's views on Russia's future position probably did not change greatly inside two months.

306. Welcome to W. G. Lawes, *SMH*, 12 Dec. 1884.

'very different kind of annexation . . .', Lawes to editor, *SMH*, 17 May 1884.

Approach to special commissioner, Maclay to Scratchley, 5 Jan. 1885, Miklouho-Maclay, *Travels to New Guinea*, p. 486; *Argus*, 6, 7 Jan. 1885.

Britain actually was prepared to cede Heligoland, desired by Germany for defence of the projected Kiel Canal. New Guinea, however, did not figure in the proposed deal. The alarming report originated in the speculations of a London newspaper.

307. Maclay Coast in negotiations between Britain and Germany, Scott to Hatzfeldt, 19 Sept. 1884, G.B. & I. Parl. Papers, *Correspondence Respecting New Guinea . . .*, C-4273, pp. 11–12. At that date, the British were still running on their previous misapprehensions, which Maclay had never plainly corrected.

Maclay's idea of what he heard from Scratchley, Maclay to Giers, 9 Jan. 1885, *SS*, IV:280–1.

'Russian protection . . .', to Alexander III, 9 Jan. 1885, *SS*, IV:280.

'under a general European . . .', to Giers, 9 Jan. 1885, *SS*, IV:281.

Communications to the press, *Argus*, 6, 7 Jan. 1885.

Protest meeting, *Argus*, 8 Jan. 1885.

Cable to Bismarck and its effects, *Argus*, 10 Jan. 1885; *SMH*, 10, 12 Jan. 1885; *The Times*, 12 Jan. 1885; Cutting from unidentified English newspaper in Latrobe Library, Melbourne, Pacific Islands Historical Pamphlets, vol. 7, SLt 990, p. 11. There was possibly an element of genuine confusion in Bismarck's attack. Communications to London show that the Germans mixed up 'Maclay' and 'Macleay' and believed some Australian interest was involved.

308. 'for his own hand', *SMH*, 13 Jan. 1885 (leader).

Maclay's statement, *Daily Telegraph* (Sydney), 13 Jan. 1885; G.B. & I. Parl. Papers, *Further Correspondence Respecting New Guinea . . .* C-4584, pp. 81–2.

Appeals to Scratchley, *Further Correspondence . . .*, C-4584, pp. 116, 127.

309. 'kindly inform . . .', to Scratchley, 6 Mar. 1885, *Further Correspondence . . .*, C-4584, p. 127.

19: *The Island of M*

311. Response in Russia, 'St Petersburg letter', *SMH*, 29 Apr. 1885.
   A translation of Maclay's appeal to the Russian public appeared in the *Pall Mall Gazette* and in *SMH*, 26 May 1885.
   Russian impression that Maclay was offended, 'St Petersburg letter', *SMH*, 28 Aug. 1885; Maclay's reply, *SMH*, 3 Sept. 1885.
   Thomassen's expectations, *The Times*, 26 July 1886.
   The Palaus came into prominence when the German flag was raised in the Carolines.
312. Resumption of biological station: Archives of New South Wales, CSIL, 86/7500; *Royal Soc. NSW, Journ. & Proc.*, 20:19; 'St Petersburg letter', *SMH*, 28 Aug. 1885; Maclay to editor, *SMH*, 3 Sept. 1885.
   'Official' standing, 'St Petersburg letter', *SMH*, 22 May 1885.
   Intention to install representatives in New Guinea: Maclay to Mikhail, 24 Mar. 1885, *SS*, IV:281-2; to Sergei, 27 Mar. 1885, *SS*, IV:283; to Giers, 31 Mar. 1885, *SS*, IV:283. On this subject Maclay had written N. K. Giers, the Russian foreign minister, at least one previous letter (no. 7, 25 Mar. 1885) which is not available.
   The ex-officer Maclay proposed to send to New Guinea was A. A. Rakovich, who had been with *Vityaz* and *Izumrud* and had published interesting accounts of those voyages.
313. 'macrodontism': for the earliest observations, see *SS*, II:271, 284, 299, 304; *SS*, III pt 1:234, 330; *Nature*, 26 July 1877; 'On macrodontism', *Proc. LSNSW*, 3:169-73. For further observations see 1879 diary extracts (revised in 1887), *SS*, II:173-4; Report of 16 Nov. 1880, *SS*, II:570; 'A short resume of the results of anthropological and anatomical researches ...', *Proc. LSNSW*, 6: 171-5 (also published in *SMH*, 26 Feb. 1881 and *Nature*, 24:157); Maclay to H. N. Mozeley, 7 Apr. 1884, *SS*, IV:265. Final account: 'A second note on "macrodontism" ...', *Proc. LSNSW*, 10:682-5 (read 28 Oct. 1885).
314. 'fifteen years residence ...', *SMH*, 11 Sept. 1886 (St Petersburg letter).
   Livadia interview: Letters to brothers, *SS*, IV:288; brief autobiography, *SS*, IV:427-34.
315. Extent of Maclay Coast, Maclay to Giers, 31 Mar. 1885, *SS*, IV:283.
   Advertisement, Maclay to Giers, 27 June 1886, *SS*, IV:293; to Alexander III, *SS*, IV:293; to editor, *The Times*, 4 Aug. 1886.
   Meeting of prospective colonists: Articles from *Peterburgsky Listok* (approved by Maclay), reprinted in *SS*, IV:470-7; 'St Petersburg letter', *SMH*, 11 Sept. 1886.
   Maclay told his followers that he had never used alcohol, which he considered 'one of the worst poisons'. Up to 1879, however, his supplies had normally included wine, and he had found rum a fine drink on expeditions. In 1886 the temperance movement was officially encouraged in Russia.
316. Port Alexei: Article from *Peterburgsky Listok* (approved by Maclay), *SS*, IV: 470; Maclay to Alexander III, *SS*, IV:293.
   Fun at Maclay's expense, 'St Petersburg letter', *SMH*, 18 Sept. 1886.
   Relations with British, *SS*, IV:471.
   Public response, Maclay to *Novoe Vremya*, *SS*, IV:291; to *Novosti*, *SS*, IV:294.
   Political considerations: Germany had also annexed New Britain, and control of both sides of the Dampier-Vityaz Strait had been represented as a vital precaution against British interference with German colonial communications.
317. 'The highest permission' was claimed in the autobiography mentioned in notes to p. 314. It was allegedly given at Livadia. In an interview with the correspondent of the *Sydney Morning Herald* (*SMH*, 18 Sept. 1886), Maclay spoke of 'important promises' received from the tsar.
   Accusations against Germans: Klaus-J. Bade, 'Colonial missions and imperialism', in J. A. Moses and P. M. Kennedy (eds), *Germany in the Pacific and the Far East, 1870-1914*, pp. 329-30.
   European ideas of Maclay's whereabouts, *Nature*, 34:41 (13 May 1886); 'St Petersburg letter', *SMH*, 22 May 1885, 11 Sept. 1886; *The Times*, 4 Aug. 1886

(reporting interview given by Maclay to St Petersburg *Herold*). Such misunder-standings had persisted for several years.

'white Papuan', to Tolstoy, [Feb. or Mar.] 1888, *SS*, IV:334.

Living 'among Papuans', *SS*, IV:471.

318. Academy of Sciences, Maclay to *Novoe Vremya*, *SS*, IV:291; 'St Petersburg letter', *SMH*, 11, 18 Sept., 1886; Maclay to Academy, *SS*, IV:307.

German reactions, *The Times*, 23 July, 28 July, 31 July 1886.

Thomassen to editor, *The Times*, 26 July 1886.

Maclay's 'denial', *The Times*, 4 Aug. 1886; *SMH*, 6 Aug. 1886; *Age* (Melbourne), 27 July 1886.

Reports by St Petersburg correspondent, *The Times*, 19 July, 4 Aug., 12, 26 Oct., 4 Nov. 1886, 3 Feb. 1887. These reports were summarized in cables to Australia.

319. *Novoe Vremya* article and its effect in Berlin, *The Times*, 31 July 1886.

Preserving convenient points, to *Novoe Vremya*, *SS*, IV:291.

Response of public and grand dukes, 'St Petersburg letter', *SMH*, 18 Sept. 1886 (interview with Maclay), and 21 Oct. 1886.

Negotiation with Berlin, to Osten-Sacken, 22 June 1886, *SS*, IV:289-90; to Giers, 22 July 1886, *SS*, IV:295-6 (mentions hope of going to New Guinea with a warship); Russian note to Berlin, quoted by D. Tumarkin, in Miklouho-Maclay, *Travels to New Guinea*, p. 49.

320. Communication to Australia, 'St Petersburg letter', *SMH*, 18 Sept. 1886. The correspondent (not an Englishman) was apparently not Russian, but he had lived more than twenty years in Russia and claimed to have high sources of information. He sometimes acted as channel for 'inspired' reports.

Impression that Maclay was developing a socialist experiment, Valskaya, 1970, 'The project of N. N. Miklouho-Maclay for the establishment of a free Russian colony on an island of the Pacific Ocean', *Avstraliya i Okeaniya*, p. 40 (Russian); D. Tumarkin in Miklouho-Maclay, *Travels to New Guinea*, pp. 50-1.

Maclay's 'Draft Rules for those wishing to settle on islands of the Pacific Ocean' are given in full by Valskaya, 1970, pp. 43-4.

Inquiries received from Giers, Valskaya, 1970, pp. 46-7.

321. Official proposal for colony, to Giers, 9 Aug. 1886, *SS*, IV:297-9; *The Times*, 12 Oct. 1886 (summarizing *Petersburger Zeitung* interview with Maclay).

Standing of prospective settlers, 'St Petersburg letter', *SMH*, 18 Sept. 1886 (interview with Maclay).

322. Malaspena: This suggestion is made by C. L. Sentinella (*NGD*, p. 318) and appears to be the only possible one. Maclay apparently did not designate the other islands to be annexed.

First meeting of special committee, and Maclay's replies to questions, Valskaya, 1970, pp. 49-50.

323. Speeches at exhibition, *The Times*, 26 Oct. 1886; 'St Petersburg letter', *SMH*, 29 Dec. 1886; *Revue d'ethnographie*, 5:479.

Rejection of colonization scheme, *The Times*, 4 Nov. 1886; *SMH*, 8 Nov. 1886; Maclay to grand duke [Nov. 1886], *SS*, IV:305.

Lectures, to Kraevsky, 3 Nov. 1886, *SS*, IV:305; to Suvorin [Nov. 1886], *SS*, IV:306; 'St Petersburg letter', *SMH*, 27 Jan. 1887; *SS*, III pt 1:464-74.

324. Chinese, *SS*, III pt 1:473.

325. Maclay's health and state of mind, *SS*, IV:309, 312, 313, 314, 315, 316; advertisement from unidentified Russian newspaper, Miklouho-Maclay Papers, vol. 1, item 1, p. 251, A2889 (ML).

Failure of colonization scheme, *SS*, IV:311, 314.

326. Georg Brandes, *Impressions of Russia*, (trans. S. C. Eastman), reprint (New York, 1966), p. 118.

Maclay to Tolstoy, 19 Sept. 1886, *SS*, IV:303-4; Tolstoy to Maclay, 25 Sept. 1886, *SS*, IV:464-6 (also *Tolstoy's Letters*, trans. and ed. R. F. Christian (London, 1978), II:406-7); Maclay to Tolstoy, [Feb. or Mar.] 1888, *SS*, IV:334.

328. Relations with *Novoe Vremya* (*New Times*), Maclay to editor, 25 June 1886, *SS*,

IV:291; to Suvorin [Nov. 1886], *SS*, IV:306; 'A somnambulist's visit to Baron Maclay', *SMH*, 23 Aug. 1886 (trans. from *Novoe Vremya*); 'St Petersburg letter', *SMH*, 18 Sept. 1886; articles contributed by Maclay, *SS*, II:618-28. A report in *The Times*, 4 Aug. 1886, explains how Maclay became a victim in a newspaper 'war'.

329. Margaret Maclay's definition of fidelity is given on the first page of her 1888 diary, Fisher Library, University of Sydney, microfilm XT 79.
'many worries ...', *SS*, IV:325.

330. All memories of Turgenev, who had died in 1883, were precious to Russians. In setting his down, Maclay was perhaps influenced by Meshchersky, who had been present at Turgenev's death and had published an account of the novelist's last hours.
'as well and cheerful ...', *SMH*, 17 Mar. 1888 (St Petersburg letter).

331. Margaret Maclay's diary, 1888, entries for 6, 11, 18 Jan., 10 Mar. (Julian calendar).

332. Attempt to make use of Sarimbun, Papers of N. de Miklouho-Maclay 1863-1888, vol. 1, item 1, p. 205, A2889 (ML).
Russian visit to New Guinea, H. H. Romilly, *Letters from the Western Pacific and Mashonaland*, p. 299. The corvette *Rynda*, with a grand duke aboard, had paid a courtesy call at Sydney during the colony's centenary celebrations.

333. Kaiser Wilhelm's Land: S. Firth, *New Guinea under the Germans*, pp. 4-6, 21-9; S. Firth, 'German firms in the Pacific Islands, 1857-1914', in J. A. Moses and P. M. Kennedy (eds), *Germany in the Pacific and the Far East, 1870-1914*, pp. 13-15; S. Firth, 'The New Guinea Company', *Hist. Stud.*, 15:364; M. Jacobs, 'German New Guinea', *Encyclopaedia of Papua and New Guinea* (ed. P. Ryan), pp. 486-7; I. Moses, 'The extension of colonial rule in Kaiser Wilhelmsland', *Germany in the Pacific ...*, pp. 288-312; P. Biskup, 'Foreign coloured labour in German New Guinea', *JPH*, 5:85; G. Souter, *New Guinea: The Last Unknown*, pp. 71-8.
Traces of Maclay, O. Finsch, *Samoafahrten. Reisen in Kaiser Wilhelmsland und Englisch-Neu-Guinea*, (numerous references); 'Explorations in German New Guinea', *Proc. RGS.* (n.s.) 10:33-4.
Finsch certainly did not ask Maclay for information. His journey to New Guinea was strictly secret, and any such request would have aroused Maclay's suspicion. Much of the knowledge Finsch displayed could have been obtained from newspaper publication of H. H. Romilly's reports.

334. The Baronet Wylie Clinic was named after Sir James Wylie (1768-1854), founder of the Military Medical Academy and medical attendant to three tsars.
'dropsy ...', *The Times*, 17 Apr. 1888 (St Petersburg telegram). Maclay had mentioned 'gout' to Georg Brandes. It has not been possible to trace the origin of the 'brain tumour' story that crops up from time to time.

335. Margaret Mikluho-Maklai—Diary 1888, Fisher Library, XT 79, entries for 7, 8, 12, 13, 15, 18, 22, 28 April, 2, 3 May (Julian calendar). The fate of Maclay's private diaries remains unknown.

336. The suggestion that journals were lost in the Sydney fire of 1882 is refuted by one fact: early in 1887 Maclay estimated that his travel account would fill two substantial printed volumes, a prediction he could not make if any original journal had been destroyed. In his reports to the Russian Geographical Society, he did not mention loss of any manuscript.

337. Inscription for Maclay's grave, Papers of N. de Miklouho-Maclay, vol. 2, pt 3, p. 156, A2889 (ML).
St Matthew 25:21: 'Well done ... thou has been faithful over a few things, I will make thee a ruler over many things: enter thou into the joy of thy lord'. Only the first and last sentences were used in the inscription.

Epilogue

338. Notebook of extracts, N. de Miklouho-Maclay Papers, vol. 2, pt 1, pp. 1–127, A2889 (ML).

'Of this eminent seaman . . .', extract from *Lives and Voyages of Drake, Cavendish and Dampier*, p. 5 of notebook mentioned above.

Tributes to Maclay: O. Finsch, 'Nikolaus von Miklucho-Maclay', *Deutsche Geogr. Blätter*, 11 (3–4); A. Chekhov, *Sobraniye Sochineniy*, 10:389–90 (Obituary on Przhevalsky); *The Times*, 17 Apr. 1888; *SMH*, 18 Apr. 1888; letter of condolence from Russian Physico-Chemical Society, N. de Miklouho-Maclay Papers, vol. 1, pt 3, p. 14, A2889 (ML).

339. 'one of the bravest . . .', cutting from unidentified Peace Society publication, N. de Miklouho-Maclay Papers, vol. 1, p. 268B, A2889 (ML).

Memberships of scientific societies: Imperial Russian Geographical Society (associate member); Berliner Gesellschaft für Anthropologie, Ethnologie und Urgeschichte (corresponding member); Royal Society for Natural Sciences, Batavia (foreign corresponding member); Royal Asiatic Society, Straits Branch (honorary member); Linnean Society of New South Wales (honorary member); Philosophical Society of Queensland (honorary member); Geographical Society of Australasia (honorary member).

Swimbladder, T. W. Bridge, *Fishes* (*Cambridge Natural History*, vol. 7, pt 1, London, 1904), p. 298; E. S. Goodrich, *Studies on the Structure and Development of Vertebrates* (London, 1930), p. 578; E. C. Olson, *Vertebrate Paleozoology* (New York, 1971), p. 98.

Fish brain, see notes to p. 218.

Sponges, E. Haeckel, 'On the organization of sponges . . .', *Ann. Mag. Nat. Hist.* (ser. 4), 5:12; Haeckel, *Die Kalkschwämme*, I:27; *Zoological Record*, 7:503; H. J. Carter, 'A description of two new Calcispongiae . . .', *Ann. Mag. Nat. Hist.* (ser. 4), 8:1–27; G. C. J. Vosmaer, *Porifera* (Bronn's *Klassen und Ordnungen des Thiers-Reichs*, vol. 2), 1887, pp. 78, 83–4.

Present names of marsupials described by Maclay, E. M. O. Laurie and J. E. Hill, *List of Land Mammals of New Guinea, Celebes and Adjacent Islands*, British Museum (Natural History) 1954, pp. 11, 24, 25, 28.

340. *Dorcopsulus (Dorcopsis) macleayi*, O. Thomas, *Catalogue of the Marsupialia and Monotremata in the Collection of the British Museum (Natural History)*, 1888, p. 92; Laurie and Hill, *List of Land Mammals . . .*, p. 25.

Body temperature of monotremes, M. Griffiths, *Echidnas* (London, 1968), pp. 14–18; H. Burrell, *The Platypus* (Adelaide, 1974), pp. 56–9; J. Bligh, *Temperature Regulation in Mammals and Other Vertebrates* (Amsterdam, 1973), pp. 314–15.

341. 'as quickly extinguished . . .', A. Wichmann, *Entdeckungsgeschichte von Neu Guinea*, I(2):325.

Maclay's manuscripts, Wichmann, *Entdeckungsgeschichte*, I(2):325.

D. N. Anuchin (1843–1923), geographer and anthropologist.

342. Malay Peninsula discoveries, A. M. Skinner, 'Geography of the Malay Peninsula', *JSBRAS*, 1878, no. 1, pp. 53, 60–2.

Name 'Rai Coast', G. Höltker, 'Tapa-Mäntel und Schambinde, Schwirrholz und Häuserschmuck von der Rai-Küste . . .', in *Festschrift Alfred Bühler*, ed. C. A. Schmitz and R. Wildhaber (Basel, 1965), pp. 197–8. The name actually appeared in German publications of earlier date than the earliest reference given by Höltker.

Maclay's measurement of deep-sea temperature, *PGM*, 17:315.

The neglect of Maclay's work on sea-temperatures along the Australian coast perhaps had its good side. His observations in 1883 were made a month earlier than shown in his table of results.

Temperature measurements in Magdala shaft and findings of C. S. Wilkinson, *SMH*, 27 May 1881 (Linnean Society meeting). Wilkinson was interested in the then-unproven theory that the distance per degree rise in temperature increases with depth beneath the earth's surface, but he apparently had too little confidence in his results to publish them formally, and neither his observations nor Maclay's were mentioned in reviews of the subject. For the state of knowledge at the end of the 19th century, see J. Prestwich, *Collected Papers on some Controverted Questions of Geology* (London, 1895).

Geological work, R. L. Jack and R. Etheridge, *The Geology and Palaeontology of Queensland and New Guinea* (Brisbane, 1892), pp. 690, 695; E. R. Stanley, 'Report on the salient geological features ... of the New Guinea Territory', Austr. Parliament, *Accounts and Papers* (Territory of New Guinea), Report 1921-2, App. B, p. 92.

Report on volcanism, W. D. Palfreyman and R. J. S. Cooke, 'Eruptive history of Manam volcano, Papua New Guinea', in *Volcanism in Australasia*, ed. R. W. Johnson (Amsterdam, 1976), p. 121.

343. Plants of Astrolabe Bay area, J. H. Powell, 'Ethnobotany', in *New Guinea Vegetation*, ed. K. Paijmans, pp. 107, 122, 124, 134, 135.

Papuan vocal organs, *SS*, III pt 1:91; A. H. Keane, *Ethnology* (Cambridge, 1896), pp. 193-4.

Announcement of discovery of neurological differences between races, *SS*, II:680; *Nature*, 27:185; Keane, *Ethnology*, p. 47.

344. Distribution of races, R. Martin, *Die Inlandstämme der Malayischen Halbinsel*, p. 160; Keane, *Ethnology*, p. 288.

Karl Semper and A. B. Meyer had preceded Maclay in the Philippines, Semper and Kubary in Yap and Palau.

345. P. Topinard, *Anthropology* (London, 1878), p. 327.

A. Kramer, *Palau*, Part 1, p. 149; Part 2, pp. 141, 298, 302, 303, 304, 305, 306; Part 3, pp. 32, 34-7, 229, 275, 277, 308; Part 5, p. 3.

J. R. Baker, *Race* (London, 1974), pp. 280, 296.

'a real chimpanzee profile ...', H. H. Giglioli, quoted by A. H. Keane, *Ethnology*, p. 259; cf. W. W. Skeat and C. O. Blagden, *Pagan Races of the Malay Peninsula*, vol. 1, p. 44; I. H. N. Evans, *The Negritos of Malaya* (Cambridge, 1937), p. 41; R. Martin, *Die Inlandstämme der Malayischen Halbinsel*, p. 388.

Foot 'found in many kinds of apes', Miklouho-Maclay, 'Ethnological excursions in the Malay Peninsula', *JSBRAS*, no. 2, p. 211; Keane, *Ethnology*, p. 259; W. H. L. Duckworth, *Studies from the Anthropological Laboratory* (Cambridge, 1904), p. 254; Martin, *Die Inlandstämme*, pp. 276-7.

346. Comments on work in Malay Peninsula, Martin, *Die Inlandstämme*, pp. 160, 186, 243, 276-7, 304, 326-7, 362-3, 388, 407-8, 664, 667, 696, 704-6, 773, 785, 786, 973-4, 1004-5, 1012; Skeat and Blagden, *Pagan Races*, vol. 1, pp. 27, 32, 75, 79-80, 201, 252, 254, 264, 529-30; vol. 2, pp. 36, 40-1, 56, 78, 281-2, 284-5, 388, 414, 487-8.

Maclay as 'new type', B. Malinowski, *A Diary in the Strict Sense of the Term* (London, 1967), p. 155.

'almost one of themselves', A. R. Wallace, *My Life*, II:35.

Assistance from traders, *SS*, III pt 1:274.

347. Papuan religion, *SS*, III pt 1:88-9, 102-6, 450-6; 'La Nouvelle-Guinée et les Papous', *Bull. de la Société Historique*, 1883, no. 2, p. 117.

Maclay's contribution to New Guinea linguistics, B. A. Hooley, 'A brief history of New Guinea linguistics', *Oceania*, 35:26; D. C. Laycock, 'A hundred years of Papuan linguistic research: Eastern New Guinea area', in *Papuan Languages and the New Guinea Linguistic Scene* (*New Guinea Area Languages and Language Study*, vol. 1, ed. S. A. Wurm), Canberra, 1975, p. 45.

Maclay on his knowledge of Bongu dialect, *SS*, III pt 1:90-4; *SS*, II:332, 378; *NGD*, 246, 284. According to Gabriel Monod, Maclay still estimated after his second visit that he knew 'one-third of the language'. His list of 350 Bongu words (*SS*, III pt 1:159-68) included names for twenty-seven animals, the numbers from one to ten, terms for various conditions of the coconut, six different kinds of yams, details of dress and ornament and almost every part of the human body. The only complex ideas expressible with his fifty-four verbs and parts of verbs were those of deceiving and forgetting.

348. Modestov on Maclay, quoted by D. Tumarkin, N. Miklouho-Maclay, *Travels to New Guinea*.

   Tolstoy's remarks on Maclay are collected by B. Putilov, 'Lev Tolstoy and Miklukho-Maklai', *Soviet Literature*, 1978, no. 8:95-102.

   G. Monod, 'La Nouvelle-Guinée', *Nouvelle Revue*, 19(2):223; *Bull. de la Société Historique*, 1883, no. 2:103-12.

350. The belief that Papuan hair grew in separate tufts is frequently cited as an example of the racist ideas that Maclay demolished. The earlier writers who had given this idea currency, however, did not regard it in that way; see G. W. Earl, *The Native Races of the Indian Archipelago. Papuans*, pp. 1-2. Anthropologists were interested mainly in the supposed resemblance of Papuan hair to the 'peppercorn' hair of Hottentots and African Bushmen (Pruner-Bey, 1864, 'On human hair as a race character', *Anthropological Review*, 2:5, 6). Contrary to modern statements, Maclay was not the first to refute this notion. It had been contradicted in 1865 by an amateur anthropologist working in the New Hebrides (W. T. Pritchard, 'On the Caroline Islanders', *Anthropological Review*, 4:165). Beccari, D'Albertis, A. B. Meyer and Gerard de Rialle all published similar observations at about the same time as Maclay, but some years passed before the correction was incorporated into textbooks.

   'heart and soul ...', B. Hagen, *Unter den Papua's*, p. 134.

351. Many persistent Australian misapprehensions about Maclay appear in an article by C. Dawson, *SMH*, 8 May 1971.

   Tree-climbing kangaroos, P. Stanbury, 'Baron Nikolai Nikolaivitch Miklouho-Maklai', in *100 Years of Australian Scientific Exploration*, ed. Stanbury, p. 18. Maclay's first impulse, when he saw no tree-climbing kangaroos in New Guinea, was to deny that such creatures existed. After study of specimens in the Australian Museum he revised this opinion.

   Legend of Maclay and the kidnapped Papuan, Olaf Ruhen, *Mountains in the Clouds* (Adelaide, 1963), p. 33.

352. The history of the Miklouho-Maclay Society of Australia is given in early issues of the Society's *Newsletter*.

   Legends of Maclay in New Guinea, N. A. Butinov, 'Papuan recollections of Miklouho-Maclay', *SS*, II:739-50; O. Finsch, *Samoafahrten*, p. 65; Miklouho-Maclay Society *Newsletter*, 1(2):2 (address by Professor P. Lawrence); 4(2):3, 8; B. Gammage, 'Maclay comes to Gorendu', *Oral History*, 4(1):64-72; R. McSwain, *The Past and Future People*, p. 188, note 14; P. Lawrence, *Road Belong Cargo*, pp. 64-6; P. Lawrence, 'Statements about religion ...', in *Anthropology in Oceania*, ed. Hiatt and Jayawardena, p. 149.

Bibliography

Since it would be impossible to list all the books that have contributed to the making of this one, this Bibliography is necessarily selective. It includes no general accounts of European or Australian history, and only a few of the biographical works devoted to Miklouho-Maclay's associates. Numerous scientific works consulted are not listed here, but references to those directly relevant are given in notes to the text.

The Bibliography is arranged in six sections:
1. Manuscript sources
2. Principal published works of Miklouho-Maclay
3. Works on Miklouho-Maclay
4. Contemporary non-Russian periodicals and newspapers
5. Works on regions visited by Miklouho-Maclay
   (i) Melanesia, including New Guinea
   (ii) Pacific islands generally
   (iii) South-east Asia, Indonesia and the Philippines
6. Biographical works on persons associated with Miklouho-Maclay.

In the fifth section, asterisks indicate publications which influenced Miklouho-Maclay and those which contain substantial references to him.

Manuscripts

Huxley, Thomas Henry—Papers, 1846-1878. Originals in Unwin Library of City and Guilds College, South Kensington. Selected items available for reference, ML microfilm FM 4/216.

Miklouho-Maclay, Nicholas de—Papers, 1863-1888. Original mss. and printed papers; drawings and photographs. Two boxes. ML A2889^{-1}, A2889^{-2} (Issued as Xerox copy, CYA2889^{-1}, $^{-2}$).

Miklouho-Maclay, Nicolaus de, Baron—Correspondence 1884-1886 with Sir William Macleay re entomological specimens. Originals in possession of

Professor T. G. Vallance, University of Sydney. Photocopies, ML DOC 3023.

Miklouho-Maclay, Nicholas de, Baron—Papers, consisting of letters and memoranda, 1875-1935. Originals in possession of Mr K. A. Miklouho-Maclay, Sydney. Available for study on ML Microfilm FM3/480.

Miklouho-Maclay, Nicholas de, Baron—Papers, 1873-1881. Typescript, carbon typescript and photocopies of translations by C. L. Sentinella of Miklouho-Maclay's travel journals.
Item 1 The Papua-Koviai expedition 1873-74.
Item 2 Journeys in the islands of the Pacific, 1873-1881.
Item 3 Journeys in the Malay Peninsula, 1874-75.
Available for reference ML MSS 2913.

Miklouho-Maclay, N. N.—Notebook, containing photographs, newspaper cuttings and drawings, 1886. Available for reference. National Library of Australia MS 3375.

Mikluho-Maklai, Margaret—Diary 1888. Fisher Library, University of Sydney Microfilm XT79.

Stanmore, First Lord (Sir Arthur Hamilton Gordon)—Selected papers 1873-1912. Originals in The British Library. ML Microfilm FM4/2717-2722.

Principal published works of N. N. Miklouho-Maclay

An almost complete bibliography of Miklouho-Maclay's publications is given in the Russian *Collected Works* (*Sobraniye Sochineniy*, IV:436-46, listed under 1950-1954, below). The present listing omits reprints and some very slight reports, and includes translations or summaries only where these are likely to be useful to English-speaking readers.

1867-1869

'Über ein Schwimmblasenrudiment bei Selachiern,' *Jena. Zeitschr.*, 3:448-53.
'Beiträge zur Kenntnis der Spongien', *Jena. Zeitschr.*, 4:221-40.
'Beitrag zur vergleichenden Anatomie des Gehirnes', *Jena. Zeitschr.*, 4:553-69.
'On a sojourn on the coasts of the Red Sea' (from minutes of meeting), *Izv. IRGO*, 5(1):279-87 (Russian); *SS*, III pt 2:353.

1870

'Researches on marine sponges and on the freshwater sponge of Lake Baikal', *Izv. IRGO*, 6(1):218 (Russian); *SS*, IV:33.
Beiträge zur vergleichenden Neurologie der Wirbelthiere. I. Das Gehirn der Selachier. II Das Mittelhirn der Ganoiden und Teleostier, Leipzig, Endlicher.
'Bemerkungen zur Schwammfauna des Weissen Meeres und des Arktischen Oceans', *Bull. de l'Acad. des Sciences de St Pétersbourg*, sér. 7, 15:203-5.
'Eine zoologische Excursion an das Rothe Meer', *PGM*, 16:124-6.
'Über einige Schwämme des Nördlichen Stillen Oceans und des Eismeeres', *Mém. de l'Acad. des Sciences de St Pétersbourg*, sér. 7, 15(3); *SS*, III pt 2:197.
'Programme of researches in the Pacific Ocean', *Izv. IRGO*, 6:258-72 (Russian); *SS*, III pt 1:7.

1871-1872

'On investigation of deep-sea temperatures', *Izv. IRGO*, 7(2):149-57 (Russian); *SS*, III pt 2:313.

'On measurement of deep-sea temperatures', *Izv. IRGO*, 8(2):33-42 (Russian); *SS*, III pt 2:323.

'Islands of Rapanui (Easter), Pitcairn and Mangareva', *Izv. IRGO*, 8(2):42-55 (Russian); *SS*, I:45.

'Über die "Kohau rogo-rogo", oder die Holztafeln von Rapanui', *Ztschr. der Gesellschaft für Erdkunde zu Berlin*, 7:79.

1873

'Mijn verblijf aan de Oostkust van Nieuw-Guinea in de jaren 1871 en 1872', *NTNI*, 33:114-26.

Letters to Russian Geographical Society, *Izv. IRGO*, 9(1):156; 9(2):94, 203-7 (Russian).

'On the Papuans of the island of Luzon', *Izv. IRGO*, 9(2):368-71 (Russian); *SS*, II:7.

'Anthropologische Bemerkungen über die Papuas der Maclay-Küste in Neu-Guinea', *NTNI*, 33:225-50. Summarized by J. C. Galton, *Nature*, 9:328-9.

'Notice météorologique concernant la Côte Maclay en Nouvelle Guinée', *NTNI*, 33:430-1.

'Schädel und Nasen der Eingeborenen Neu-Guinea's', *ZE*, 5:*Verhl.*, 188-9.

1874

'On the use of the "kéu" drink by the Papuans in New Guinea, *Izv. IRGO*, 10(2):83-6 (Russian); *SS*, III pt 1:125.

'Further remarks on some ethnologically important customs of the Papuans of the Maclay Coast', *Izv. IRGO*, 10(2):147-9 (Russian); *SS*, III pt 1:146.

'Second journey to New Guinea', *Izv. IRGO*, 10(2):309-17. Translated as 'Meine zweite Excursion nach Neu-Guinea, 1874', *NTNI*, 36:148-79.

'Über Brachycephalität bei den Papuas von Neu-Guinea', *NTNI*, 34:345-7. Translated as 'Brachycephality among Papuans', *JEA*, 1(1), 1875.

1875

'Ethnological questions on the Malay Peninsula'. *Izv. IRGO*, 11(2):231-6 (Russian).

'Ein Opiumrauchversuch (Physiologische Notiz)', *NTNI*, 35:243-9.

'Ethnologische Excursion in Johore', *NTNI*, 35:250-8; in English, *JEA*, 1(1), 1875.

'Ethnologische Bemerkungen über die Papuas der Maclay-Küste in Neu-Guinea. I.', *NTNI*, 35:66-93. Summarized by J. C. Galton, *Nature*, 14:107-9, 136-7.

'Incidents of travel in Papua-Koviay in New Guinea', *Proc. RGS*, 19:517-21 (translated by W. Feilding from a letter to Baroness von Rhaden).

1876

'Ethnologische Bemerkungen über Papuas der Maclay-Küste in Neu–Guinea.
II', *NTNI*, 36:294-333. Summarized by J. C. Galton, *Nature*, 21:204-6, 226-9.
*Einiges über die Dialecte des Melanesischen Völkerschaften in der Malayischen
Halbinsel* (Zwei Briefe an Otto Böthlingk), Batavia. Translated as 'Dialects
of the Melanesian Tribes in the Malay Peninsula', *JSBRAS*, no. 1 (July 1878),
pp. 38-43.
'Sprachrudimente der Orang-Utan von Johor', *Tidjschr. v. Indische Taal- Land-
en Volkenkunde*, 23:303-12.
'Ethnologische Excursionen in der Malayischen Halbinsel', *NTNI*, 36:3-26.
Translated as 'Ethnological excursions in the Malay Peninsula', *JSBRAS*, no.
2 (Dec. 1878), pp. 205-21.
'Über die künstliche *perforatio penis* bei den Dajaks auf Borneo', *ZE*, 8:*Verhl.*,
22-4.
'*Perforatio glandis penis* bei den Dajaks auf Borneo und analoge Sitten auf
Celebes und auf Java', *ZE*, 8:*Verhl.*, 24-6.
'Über eine anomal-frühzeitige starke Behaarung der Schamgegend und des
Perinaeums eines Knaben von Ceram', *ZE*, (8):*Verhl.*, 70-1.
'Travels to the islands of western Micronesia', *Izv. IRGO*, 12(2):367-8, 429,
502-5; *SS*, II:246 (Russian).
'Über die grosszähnige Melanesier', *ZE*, 8:*Verhl.* 290-1.
'The island of Yap', *Izv. IRGO*, 13(2):76-89; *SS*, III pt 1:247 (Russian).

1878

'The Palau Archipelago. Sketches of travel in western Micronesia and northern
Melanesia', *Izv. IRGO*, 14(2):257-97; *SS*, III pt 1:268 (Russian).
'Anthropologische Notizen, gesammelt aúf einer Reise in West-Mikronesien
und Nord-Melanesien im Jahre 1876', *ZE*, 10:*Verhl.*, 99-118.
'Admiralty Islands. Anthropological-ethnographical sketches of travels in
western Micronesia and northern Melanesia', *Izv. IRGO*, 14(2):409-55; *SS*,
II:252 (Russian).
'The Agomes (Hermit) Islands. Sketches of travels in Western Micronesia and
northern Melanesia', *Izv. IRGO*, 15(2):25-43; *SS*, II:294 (Russian).
'Reise in West-Mikronesien, Nord-Melanesien und ein dritter Aufenthalt in
Neu-Guinea, von Februar 1876–Januar 1878', *PGM*, 24:407-8.
'Über vulkanische Erscheinungen an der nordöstlichen Küste Neu-Guinea's',
PGM, 24:408-10.
[Geographical notes on Malay Peninsula] published in A. M. Skinner,
'Geography of the Malay Peninsula', *JSBRAS*, no. 1:60-2.
'Vestiges de l'art chez les papouas de la Côte de Maclay en Nouvelle Guinée',
Bull. de la Soc. Anthrop. de Paris, 3 sér., 1:524-31.

1879

'Proposed zoological station for Sydney', *Proc. LSNSW*, 3:144-50.
'On macrodontism', *Proc. LSNSW*, 3:169-73.
'Plagiostomata of the Pacific. I.', *Proc. LSNSW*, 3:306-17 (with W. Macleay).
'Anatomical remarks. On the dentition of the Heterodonti. On the external
genital organs of the male *Heterodontus phillipi*', *Proc. LSNSW*, 3:318-34.

1880

'Second sojourn on the Maclay Coast in New Guinea (from June 1876 to November 1877)', *Izv. IRGO*, 16(2):149-70; *SS*, II:386 (Russian).

'Sojourn in Sydney (from August 1878 to March 1879)', *Izv. IRGO*, 16(2):416-24; *SS*, II:435 (Russian).

'The proposed zoological station at Sydney', *Proc. LSNSW*, 4:103-6.

'Travels to the islands of Melanesia in 1879', *Izv. IRGO*, 16(2):425-9; *SS*, II:444 (Russian).

'Uber die Mika-Operation in Central-Australien', *ZE*, 12:*Verhl.*, 85-7.

'Stellung des Paares beim coitus und das Ausschleudern des Sperma's vom Weibe nach demselben', *ZE*, 12:*Verhl.*, 87-8.

'Geschlechtlicher Umgang mit Mädchen vor der Geschlechtsreife derselben', *ZE*, 12:*Verhl.*, 88-9.

'Langbeinigkeit der Australischen Frauen', *ZE*, 12:*Verhl.*, 89-90.

'Einige Worte über die sogennante "gelbe Rasse" im Süd-Osten Neu-Guinea's' *ZE*, 12:*Verhl.*, 90.

1881

'Travels in the islands of Melanesia and fourth visit to New Guinea', *Izv. IRGO*, 17(1):131-42; *SS*, II:559 (Russian).

'Leichnam eines Australiers', *ZE*, 13:*Verhl.*, 94-6.

'Haarlose Australier', *ZE*, 13:*Verhl.*, 143-9.

'A short resumé of the results of anthropological and anatomical researches in Melanesia and Australia (March 1879–January 1881)', *Proc. LSNSW*, 6:171-5.

'A solution for preserving large vertebrata for anatomical examination', *Proc. LSNSW*, 6:576-9.

'Temperature of the rock in the Magdala shaft, Victoria', *Proc. LSNSW*, 6:579-80.

'On the practice of ovariotomy by the natives of the Herbert River, Queensland', *Proc. LSNSW*, 6:622-4.

'Remarks about the circumvolutions of the cerebrum of *Canis dingo*', *Proc. LSNSW*, 6:624-6.

'Cranial deformation of new-born children at the Island Mabiak, and other islands of Torres Straits, and of women of the S.E. peninsula of New Guinea', *Proc. LSNSW*, 6:627-9.

1882

'Communication concerning travels', *Izv. IRGO*, 18:296-347; *SS*, II:631 (Russian).

1883

'La Nouvelle-Guinée et les Papous', *Bulletin de la Société Historique*, no. 2, pp. 112-17. Talk given to Cercle Saint-Simon, 28 Dec. 1882; preceded by extracts from article by G. Monod.

1884

'Remarks on a skull of an Australian Aboriginal from the Lachlan district', *Proc. LSNSW*, 8:395-6.

'On a very dolichocephalic skull of an Australian Aboriginal', *Proc. LSNSW*, 8:401-3.

'Temperature of the body of *Echidna hystrix*, Cuv.', *Proc. LSNSW*, 8:425-6.

'Plagiostomata of the Pacific. II. *Heterodontus japonicus*', *Proc. LSNSW*, 8:426-31 (with W. Macleay).

1885

'On a new species of kangaroo (*Dorcopsis chalmersii*) from the south-east end of New Guinea', *Proc. LSNSW*, 9:569-77.

'On a complete debouchement of the *sulcus Rolando* into the *fissura Sylvii* in some brains of Australian Aboriginals', *Proc. LSNSW*, 9:578-80.

'Notes on the zoology of the Maclay Coast in New Guinea. I. On a new sub-genus of Peramelidae, *Brachymelis*', *Proc. LSNSW*, 9:713-20.

'Note about the temperature of the sea-water along the eastern coast of Australia, observed in July 1878 and 1883', *Proc. LSNSW*, 9:887-90.

'On two new species of *Macropus* from the south coast of New Guinea', *Proc. LSNSW*, 9:890-5.

'On volcanic activity on the islands near the north-east coast of New Guinea and evidence of rising of the Maclay Coast in New Guinea', *Proc. LSNSW*, 9:963-7.

'Notes on the direction of the hair on the back of some kangaroos', *Proc. LSNSW*, 9:1151-8.

'On the temperature of the body of *Ornithorhynchus paradoxus*', *Proc. LSNSW*, 9:1204-5.

1886

'Notes on the zoology of the Maclay Coast in New Guinea. II. On a new species of *Macropus, Macropus tibol*', *Proc. LSNSW*. 10:141-4.

'On two new species of *Dorcopsis* from the south coast of New Guinea', *Proc. LSNSW*, 10:145-50.

'Note on the brain of *Halicore australis*', *Proc. LSNSW*, 10:193-6.

'List of plants in use by the natives of the Maclay Coast, New Guinea', *Proc. LSNSW*, 10:346-54.

'Plagiostomata of the Pacific. III (Fam. Heterodontidae)', *Proc. LSNSW*, 10:673-8 (with W. Macleay).

'A second note on "macrodontism" of the Melanesians', *Proc. LSNSW*, 10:682-6.

'Note on the *kéu* of the Maclay Coast, New Guinea', *Proc. LSNSW*, 10:687-95.

Catalogue of Objects in the Ethnological Collection from Islands of the Pacific Ocean, St Petersburg, 'Novosti', (Russian).

1887-1888

'A few days in Australia (from travel notes)', *Novoe vremya*, 13 Oct. 1887, 22 Mar. 1888; *SS*, II:596 (Russian).

'The island of Andra (from diary of 1879), *Severniy vestnik*, Dec. 1887, no. 12, pp. 153-75; Jan. 1888, no. 1, pp. 199-230; *SS*, II:459 (Russian).

Works posthumously published

Apart from the first publication of Miklouho-Maclay's travel journals, separate publications of material contained in the Collected Works are not listed. The only translations included are those in English.

Puteshestviya (Travels), 1923, edited and introduced by D. N. Anuchin, Novaya Moskva, Moscow.

Sobraniye sochineniy (Collected Works), 1950-54, Akademiya Nauk SSSR, Moscow-Leningrad. With much additional material, biographical essay and discussion of Miklouho-Maclay's work, and extensive annotation.

Vols I, II   Journals and reports of travels.
Vol. III pt 1,   Articles on anthropology and ethnology.
Vol. III pt 2,   Articles on zoology, geography, meteorology and organizational questions.
Vol. IV   Correspondence.
Vol. V   Illustrations (drawings by M-M and photographs of objects in his ethnological collection).

New Guinea Diaries, 1871-1883, 1975, translated, with biographical comments and notes, by C. L. Sentinella, Kristen Press, Madang.

Travels to New Guinea, 1982, Progress Publishers, Moscow. With introduction and notes by D. D. Tumarkin.

Works on Miklouho-Maclay

Anuchin, D. N., 1923, 'Miklouho-Maclay, his life and travels', in N. N. Miklouho-Maclay, *Puteshestviya*, Novaya Moskva, Moscow (Russian).

Berg, L. S., 1959, 'Nikolai Nikolaevich Miklouho-Maclay', in *Otechestvennie fiziko-geografy i puteshestvenniki*, Moscow (Russian).

Butinov, N. A., 1953, 'N. N. Miklouho-Maclay (Biographical Sketch)', in N. N. Miklouho-Maclay, *Sobraniye Sochineniy*, IV, Akademiya Nauk SSSR, Moscow-Leningrad (Russian).

Butinov, N. A., 1971, *N. N. Miklouho-Maclay—A great Russian scientific-humanist*, Leningrad (Russian).

Chub, D., 1981, *New Guinea Impressions (In the Footsteps of Myklukho-Maklay)*, Lastivka, Melbourne.

Chukovskaya, L. K., 1952, *N. N. Miklouho-Maclay* (ed. N. N. Baransky), Gosudarstvennoe Izdatel'stvo Geograficheskoi Literatura, Moscow (Russian).

Dawson, C., 1971, 'He asked Russia to claim New Guinea', *Sydney Morning Herald*, 8 May, p. 6.

Deniker, J., 1883, 'Les Papous de la Nouvelle-Guinée et les voyages de M. Miklouho-Maclay', *Revue d'Anthropologie*, 2 sér., 6:484-501.

Finsch, O., 1888, 'Nikolaus von Miklucho-Maclay, Reisen und Wirken', *Deutsche Geographische Blätter*, 11(3-4).

Fischer, D., 1955, *Unter Südsee-Insulanern: das Lebens des Forschers Mikloucho-Maclay*, Koehler and Amelang, Leipzig.

Ford, E., 1963, 'Nicolai Nicolaevitch de Miklouho-Maclay, 1846-1888',

Papuan and New Guinea Scientific Society Annual Report and Proceedings, pp. 8-18.

Gammage, B., 1976, 'Maclay comes to Gorendu', *Oral History*, 4(1):64-72.

Germer, E., 1961, 'Miklucho-Maclay und die koloniale Annexion Neuguineas durch das kaiserliche Deutschland', *Beiträge zur Volkerforschung Hans Damm zum 65 Geburtstag*, Akademie-Verlag, Berlin.

Greenop, F., 1944, *Who Travels Alone*, K. G. Murray, Sydney.

Grumm-Grzhmailo, A. G., 1939, 'N. N. Miklouho-Maclay against the contemporary background of his time', *Izvestiya Gosudarstvennogo Geograficheskogo Obshchestva*, 71(1-2) (Russian).

Izvestiya Gosudarstvennogo Geograficheskogo Obshchestva, 1939, 71(1-2). Issue devoted to life and work of Miklouho-Maclay (Russian).

Kolesnikov, M., 1961, *Miklouho-Maclay*, Moscow (Russian).

Levin, M. G., 1960, *Sketches from the History of Anthropology in Russia*, Akademiya Nauk SSSR, Moscow (Russian).

Mamaev, O. I., 1957, 'Miklouho-Maclay as oceanographer', *Izvestiya Gosudarstvennogo Geograficheskogo Obshchestva*, 89:255-9 (Russian).

Markov, S. N., 1975, *Tamo-rus Maklai*, Moscow (Russian).

Miklouho-Maclay Society of Australia, *Newsletter*, 1(1), Jan. 1980 to 5(1) Feb. 1984.

Mikluho-Maclay, R. W. de, 1974, 'Nikolai Nikolaevich Mikluho-Maklai', *Australian Dictionary of Biography*, vol. 5, Melb. Univ. Press, Melbourne.

Mikluho-Maclay, R. W. de, 1974, 'Nicholai N. Mikluho-Maklai (1846-1888), pioneer educator in New Guinea and Melanesia', *Educational Perspectives in Papua New Guinea*, Australian College of Education.

Minakov, A. A., 1939, 'The life and work of N. N. Miklouho-Maclay', *Izvestiya Gosudarstvennogo Geograficheskogo Obshchestva*, 71(1-2) (Russian).

Monod, G., 1882, 'La Nouvelle-Guinée. Les voyages de M. de Mikluho-Maclay', *Nouvelle Revue*, 19(2):223, partly reprinted in *Bulletin de la Société Historique*, 1883, no. 2, pp. 103-12.

Putilov, B., 1978, 'Lev Tolstoy and Miklukha-Maklai', *Soviet Literature*, no. 8:95-102.

Roginsky, Ya. Ya., and S. A. Tokarev, 1950, 'Miklouho-Maclay as ethnographer and anthropologist', *Sobraniye Sochineniy*, II, Akademiya Nauk SSSR, Moscow-Leningrad.

Sentinella, C. L., 1972, 'N. N. Miklouho-Maclay', *Journ. of the Papua and New Guinea Soc.*, 6(2):43-4.

Sentinella, C. L., trans., 1975, *Mikloucho-Maclay: New Guinea Diaries*, Kristen Press, Madang. Biographical sections and notes by the translator.

Sokolov, V., and J. F. Faivre, 1947, 'Un centenaire: Mikloukho-Maklai', *Journal de la Société des Océanistes*, 3(3):94.

Stanbury, P., 1975, 'Baron Nikolai Nikolaivitch Miklouho-Maklai, or the complete nineteenth century international explorer and scientist', in *100 Years of Australian Scientific Explorations*, ed. P. Stanbury, Sydney.

Thomassen, E. S., 1882, *A Biographical Sketch of Nicholas de Miklouho Maclay the Explorer*, privately printed, Brisbane.

Tumarkin, D. D., 1963, 'A great Russian scientific-humanist', *Sovyetskaya etnografiya*, no. 6 (Russian).

Tumarkin, D. D., 1977, 'The Papuan Union (from the history of the struggle of N. N. Miklouho-Maclay for the rights of the Papuans of New Guinea)', *Rasy i narody*, 7, Nauka, Moscow (Russian).

Tumarkin, D. D., 1982, Introduction and notes to N. N. Miklouho-Maclay, *Travels to New Guinea*, Progress Publishers, Moscow.

Valskaya, B. A., 1959, 'The struggle of N. N. Miklouho-Maclay for the rights of the Papuans of the Maclay Coast', *Strany i narody vostoka*, 1, Nauka, Moscow (Russian).

Valskaya, B. A., 1970, 'The project of N. N. Miklouho-Maclay for the founding of a free Russian colony on an island of the Pacific Ocean', *Avstraliya i Okeaniya (istoriya i sovremennost')*, Nauka, Moscow (Russian).

Valskaya, B. A., 1972, 'Unpublished materials on the preparation of N. N. Miklouho-Maclay's expedition to New Guinea in 1871 and on the voyage of the corvette *Skobelev* to that island in 1883', *Strany i narody vostoka*, 13(2), Nauka, Moscow (Russian).

Worsley, P. M., 1952, 'N. N. Mikloukho-Maclay, Pioneer of Pacific Anthropology', *Oceania*, 22:307-14.

Contemporary periodicals and newspapers

The following non-Russian publications contain numerous reports on the activities of Miklouho-Maclay.

Scientific journals:

Bulletin de la Société de Géographie, Paris.
Cosmos di Guido Cora
Das Ausland
Globus
Nature
Petermann's Geographische Mitteilungen
Proceedings of the Royal Geographical Society, London
Zeitschrift für Ethnologie

Daily newspapers:

Age, Melbourne
Argus, Melbourne
Daily Telegraph, Sydney
Sydney Morning Herald
The Times, London

Works on regions visited by Miklouho-Maclay

Standard texts are not listed unless they have had a direct bearing on the present book.
Publications that influenced Miklouho-Maclay, and those containing significant references to him, are indicated by asterisks.

Melanesia, including New Guinea

★ Badner, M., 1979, 'Admiralty Island "Ancestor" figures?', in *Exploring the Visual Art of Oceania*, ed. S. M. Mead, Honolulu, pp. 227-37.

★ Baer, K. E. von, 1859, 'Über Papuas und Alfuren', *Mémoires présentés à l'Académie Impériale des Sciences de Saint Pétersbourg*, 10:271-346.

Berndt, R. M., and P. Lawrence, eds, 1971, *Politics in New Guinea*, Univ. of Western Aust. Press, Nedlands.

Biskup, P., 1970, 'Foreign coloured labour in German New Guinea', *JPH*, 5:85-107.

★ Bodrogi, T., 1953, 'Some notes on the ethnography of New Guinea', *Acta Ethnographia Acad. Sci. Hungariae*, 3:91-184.

★ Bodrogi, T., 1959, 'New Guinea style provinces. The style province "Astrolabe Bay"', in *Opuscula Ethnologica Memoriae L. Biró*, eds T. Bodrogi and L. Boglar, Budapest.

★ Burridge, K. O. L., 1960, *Mambu: A Melanesian Millennium*, Methuen, London.

Capell, A., 1969, *A Survey of New Guinea Languages*, Sydney Univ. Press, Sydney.

Chalmers, J., 1887, *Pioneering in New Guinea*, Religious Tract Society, London.

Chalmers, J., 1895, *Pioneer Life and Work in New Guinea, 1877-1894*, Religious Tract Society, London.

Codrington, R. H., 1891, *The Melanesians*, Oxford, Clarendon Press.

Comrie, P., 1877, 'Anthropological notes on New Guinea', *JAI*, 6:102.

Corris, P., 1968, '"Blackbirding" in New Guinea waters, 1883-84: an episode in the Queensland labour trade', *JPH*, 3:85-105.

Corris, P., 1970, 'Pacific Island labour migrants in Queensland', *JPH*, 5:43-64.

Cranstone, B. A. L., 1961, *Melanesia, a Short Ethnography*, British Museum, London.

D'Albertis, L. M., 1879, 'New Guinea: its fitness for colonization', *Proc. R. Col. Inst.*, pp. 43-68.

D'Albertis, L. M., 1880, *New Guinea: What I did and what I saw*, 2 vols, Sampson Low, London.

Docker, E. W., 1970, *The Blackbirders. The Recruiting of South Seas Labour for Queensland, 1863-1907*, Angus and Robertson, Sydney.

★ Earl, G. W., 1853, *The Native Races of the Indian Archipelago. Papuans*, Bailliere, London.

★ Finsch, O., 1865, *Neu-Guinea und seine Bewohner*, Müller, Bremen.

★ Finsch, O., 1888, *Samoafahrten: Reisen in Kaiser Wilhelmsland und Englisch-Neu-Guinea in den Jahren 1884 und 1885*, Hirt, Leipzig.

Firth, S., 1972, 'The New Guinea Company', *Hist. Stud.*, 15:364.

Firth, S., 1982, *New Guinea under the Germans*, Melb. Univ. Press, Melbourne.

Gibbney, H. J., 1972, 'The New Guinea gold rush of 1878', *JRAHS*, 58:284-96.

Girard, J., 1872, 'Les connaissances actuelles sur la Nouvelle-Guinée', *Bull. de la Soc. de Géographie*, Paris, 6 sér., 4:451-79, with map.

★ Girard, J., 1883, *La Nouvelle-Guinée*, Paris, reprinted from *L'Exploration*.

Gordon, D. C., 1951, *The Australian Frontier in New Guinea, 1870-1885*, Columbia Univ. Press, New York.

Great Britain and Ireland, Parliamentary Papers:
  1876, *Correspondence Respecting New Guinea*, C-1566.
★ 1883, *Further Correspondence Respecting New Guinea*, C-3617.
  1883, *Further Correspondence Respecting New Guinea*, C-3691.
  1884, *Further Correspondence Respecting New Guinea and Other Islands*, C-3839.
★ 1884, *Correspondence Respecting New Guinea and Other Islands*, C-3863.
  1884, *Further Correspondence Respecting New Guinea*, C-4217.
★ 1885, *Further Correspondence Respecting New Guinea and other Islands in the Western Pacific Ocean*, C-4273.
★ 1885, *Further Correspondence Respecting New Guinea . . .*, C-4584.

★ Haddon, A. C., 1916, 'Kava drinking in New Guinea', *Man*, 16:145-52.

★ Hagen, B., 1899, *Unter den Papua's*, Kreidel, Wiesbaden.

★ Harding, T. G., 1967, *Voyagers of the Vitiaz Strait. A Study of a New Guinea Trade System*, Univ. of Washington Press, Seattle and London.

★ Hoffmann, Revd, 1906, 'Sprache und Sitten der Papua-Stämme an der Astrolabe Bai', *Verhandlungen des Deutschen Kolonialkongresses 1905*, Berlin.

Hogbin, H. I., 1939, *Experiments in Civilization*, Routledge, London.

Hogbin, H. I., and P. Lawrence, 1967, *Studies in New Guinea Land Tenure*, Sydney Univ. Press, Sydney.

Hollrung, M., 1887, 'Verzeichnis von einer Untersuchung längs der Astrolabe Bai', *Nachrichten aus dem Kaiser Wilhelmsland*, 3:135-43.

Hollrung, M., 1888, 'Kaiser Wilhelms-Land und seine Bewohner', *Verhandlungen der Gesellschaft für Erdkunde*, 15:298-314.

★ Hooley, B. A., 1964-65, 'A brief history of New Guinea linguistics', *Oceania*, 35:26-44.

Jacobs, M. G., 1951, 'Bismarck and the annexation of New Guinea', *Hist. Stud. A. & N.Z.*, 5(17):14-26.

Jacobs, M. G., 1952, 'The Colonial Office and New Guinea, 1874-1884', *Hist. Stud. A. & N.Z.*, 5(18):106-18.

★ Jukes, J. B., 1847, *Narrative of the Surveying Voyage of H.M.S. Fly . . . during the Years 1842 to 1846*, 2 vols, Boone, London.

Knaplund, P., 1956, 'Sir Arthur Gordon on the New Guinea question', *Hist. Stud. A. & N.Z.*, 7:329-33.

★ Kolff, D. H., 1840, *Voyages of the Dutch Brig of War 'Dourga' . . . along the Previously Unknown South Coast of New Guinea, 1825-1826*, Madden, London.

★ Kops, G., 1852, 'Contribution to the knowledge of the north and east coasts of New Guinea', *Journ. of the Indian Archipel.*, 6:312-18.

★ Lawrence, P., 1964, *Road Belong Cargo. A Study of the Cargo Movement in the Southern Madang District, New Guinea*, Melb. Univ. Press, Melbourne.

Lawrence, P., and M. J. Meggitt, 1965, *Gods, Ghosts and Men in Melanesia: Some Religions of Australian New Guinea and the New Hebrides*, Oxford Univ. Press, Melbourne.

★ Lawrence, P., 1971, 'Statements about religion: The problem of reliability', in *Anthropology in Oceania, Essays presented to Ian Hogbin*, eds L. R. Hiatt and

C. Jayawardena, Angus and Robertson, Sydney, pp. 139-54.

Legge, J. D., 1949, 'Australia and New Guinea to the establishment of the British protectorate', *Hist. Stud. A. & N.Z.*, 4(13):34.

Lewis, A. B., 1951, *The Melanesians*, Chicago Nat. Hist. Museum.

Löffler, E., 1979, *Papua New Guinea*, Hutchinson, Melbourne.

★ McAuley, J., 1960, 'We are men—What are you?', *Quadrant*, 4(3):74.

★ McSwain, R., 1977, *The Past and Future People. Tradition and Change on a New Guinea Island*, Oxford Univ. Press, Melbourne.

★ Marin La Meslée, E., 1883, 'Past explorations of New Guinea and a scheme for the scientific exploration of the great island', *Proc. Geogr. Soc. Australasia, N.S.W. & Vic. Branches*, 1:5-26.

★ Meyners d'Estrey, Dr Count, 1881, *La Papouasie ou Nouvelle-Guinée Occidentale*, Paris and Rotterdam.

★ Modera, J., 1830, *Verhaal van eene Reize naar en langs de Zuid-West Kust van Nieuw-Guinea gedaan in 1828*, Loosjes, Haarlem.

★ Moresby, J., 1876, *Discoveries and Surveys in New Guinea and the D'Entrecasteaux Islands*. Murray, London.

★ Moseley, H. N., 1877, 'On the inhabitants of the Admiralty Islands', *JAI*, 6:379.

★ Muller, S., 1857, *Reizen en Onderzoekingen in den Indischen Archipel*, 2 vols, Amsterdam.

★ Muller, S., 1857, 'Contributions to the knowledge of New Guinea', *Proc. RGS*, 2:181-5.

Oram, N. D., 1976, *Colonial Town to Melanesian City. Port Moresby 1884-1974*, Aust. Nat. Univ. Press, Canberra.

★ Powell, J. H., 1976, 'Ethnobotany', in *New Guinea Vegetation*, ed. K. Paijmans, Aust. Nat. Univ. Press, Canberra.

Primrose, B. N., 1968, 'Other factors in the annexation of south–eastern New Guinea', *University Studies in History*, 5(2):51-118.

★ Romilly, H. H., 1886, *The Western Pacific and New Guinea. Notes on the Natives, Christian and Cannibal, with some Account of the Old Labour Trade*, Nutt, London.

Romilly, H. H., 1889, *From my Verandah in New Guinea*, Nutt, London.

Romilly, H. H., 1896, *Letters from the Western Pacific and Mashonaland*, Nutt, London.

★ Rosenberg, C. B. H. von, 1875, *Reistochten naar de Geelvinkbai op Nieuw-Guinea in de Jaren 1869 en 1870*, 'sGravenhage.

Rowley, C. D., 1965, *The New Guinea Villager*, Cheshire, Melbourne.

★ Ryan, P., ed., 1972, *Encyclopaedia of Papua and New Guinea*, 3 vols, Melb. Univ. Press, Melbourne.

Sahlins, D. M., 1963, 'Poor man, rich man, big-man chief', *Comparative Studies in Society and History*, 5:285-303.

Scarr, D., 1967, 'Recruits and recruiters: a portrait of the Pacific islands labour trade', *JPH*, 2:5-24.

★ Schmitz, C. A., 1959, 'Zur Ethnologie der Rai-Küste in Neuguinea', *Anthropos*, 54:27-56.

Shineberg, D., 1967, *They Came for Sandalwood*, Melb. Univ. Press, Melbourne.

Shutler, M. E., and R. Shutler, 1967, 'Origins of the Melanesians', *Archaeology and Physical Anthropology in Oceania*, 2(2):91-9.

★ Souter, G., 1963, *New Guinea: The Last Unknown*, Angus and Robertson, Sydney.

Stuart, I., 1970, *Port Moresby, Yesterday and Today*, Pacific Publications, Sydney.

★ Turner, W. Y., 1878, 'The ethnology of the Motu', *JAI*, 7:470-97.

Turvey, M. E., 1979, 'Missionaries and imperialism: Opponents or progenitors of empire? The New Guinea case', *JRAHS*, 65:89-108.

★ van der Sande, G. A. J., 1907, *Résultats de l'Expedition Scientifique Neérlandaises à la Nouvelle-Guinée en 1903. Ethnography and Anthropology, Nova Guinea*, vol. III, Brill, Leiden (in English).

Wallace, A. R., 1859, 'Notes on a voyage to New Guinea', *Proc. RGS*, 3:358.

Wallace, A. R., 1862, 'On the trade between the eastern islands and New Guinea', *Proc. RGS*, 6:43.

★ Whittaker, J. L., Gash, N. G., Hookey, J. F. and Lacey, R. J., 1975, *Documents and Readings in New Guinea History, Prehistory to 1889*, Jacaranda Press, Brisbane.

★ Wichmann, A., 1910, *Nova Guinea. Entdeckungsgeschichte von Neu Guinea*, 2 vols, Brill, Leiden.

Pacific islands generally

Alkire, W. A., 1977, *An Introduction to the Peoples and Cultures of Micronesia*, Cummings, Menlo Park, Calif.

Bach, J., 1968, 'The Royal Navy in the Pacific islands', *JPH*, 3:3-20.

Barnett, H. G., 1949, *Palauan Society*, Univ. of Oregon, Eugene.

Beaglehole, J. C., 1934, *The Exploration of the Pacific*, Black, London.

Bellwood, P., 1979, *Man's Conquest of the Pacific. The Prehistory of Southeast Asia and Oceania*, Oxford Univ. Press, New York.

Brooker, J. I., 1941, *International Rivalry in the Pacific Islands*, Univ. of California Press, Berkeley.

Bühler, A., Barlow, T., and Mountford, C. P., 1962, *Oceania and Australia: The Art of the South Seas*, Methuen, London.

★ Cheyne, A., 1852, *A Description of Islands in the Western Pacific Ocean*, Trubner, London.

Churchill, W., 1912, *Easter Island. The Rapanui Speech and the Peopling of Southeast Polynesia*, Carnegie Inst. Washington Publ.

Coon, C. S., and J. M. Andrews, eds, 1943, *Studies in the Anthropology of Oceania and Asia*, Papers of the Peabody Museum, vol. 20, Cambridge, Mass.

Davidson, J. W., and D. Scarr, eds, 1970, *Pacific Islands Portraits*, Aust. Nat. Univ. Press, Canberra.

Dodge, E. S., 1971, *Beyond the Capes. Pacific Exploration from Captain Cook to the 'Challenger', 1776-1877*, Little, Brown, Boston.

Fitzhardinge, V., 1966, 'Russian naval visitors to Australia, 1862-1888', *JRAHS*, 52:129-58.

Force, R., 1968, *Leadership and Culture Change in Palau*, Fieldiana, vol. 50, Chicago Nat. Hist. Mus., Chicago.

Freeman, J. D., and W. R. Geddes, 1959, *Anthropology in the South Seas*, Avery, New Plymouth (N.Z.).

★ Gana, I. L., 1870, 'Descripción científica de la Isla de Pascua' (official report of the commander of the Chilean corvette *O'Higgins*). Reprinted in *La Isla de Pascua*, ed. L. Ignacio Silva, Santiago, 1903.

Grace, G. W., 1961, 'Austronesian linguistics and culture history', *American Anthropologist*, 63:359-68.

Gunson, N., ed., 1978, *The Changing Pacific*, Oxford Univ. Press, Melbourne.

Harding, T. G., and B. J. Wallace, eds, 1970, *Cultures of the Pacific*, Free Press, New York.

Howells, W. W., 1973, *The Pacific Islanders*, Reed, Wellington.

Jaussen, T., 1893, *L'Ile de Pâques. Historique–Ecriture*, Leroux, Paris.

Jennings, J. D., ed., 1979, *The Prehistory of Polynesia*, Harvard Univ. Press, Cambridge, Mass.

★ Keate, G., 1788, *An Account of the Pelew Islands*, London.

Kennedy, P. M., 1974, *The Samoan Tangle*, Univ. Queensland Press, Brisbane.

★ Kramer, A., 1919, *Palau* (*Ergebnisse der Südsee-expedition 1908-1910*, ed. G. Thilenius, II Ethnographie, B Mikronesien, Band 3), 2 vols, Hamburg.

Langdon, R., 1968, *Tahiti: Island of Love*, Pacific Publications, Sydney.

★ Lanyon-Orgill, P. A., 1956, 'A catalogue of the inscribed tablets and other artifacts from Easter Island', *Journ. Austronesian Studies*, 1(2):20-35.

★ Lesson, A., 1880-1884, *Les Polynésiens*, 4 vols, Leroux, Paris.

McArthur, N., 1967, *Island Populations of the Pacific*, Aust. Nat. Univ. Press, Canberra.

McCall, G., 1981, *Rapanui. Tradition and Survival on Easter Island*, Allen and Unwin (Aust.), Sydney.

Maude, H. E., 1968, *Of Islands and Men. Studies in Pacific History*, Oxford Univ. Press, Melbourne.

Mead, S. M., ed., 1979, *Exploring the Visual Art of Oceania*, Honolulu.

Metraux, A., 1951, *Easter Island* (trans. M. Bullock), Scientific Book Club, London.

Moorehead, A., 1966, *The Fatal Impact. An Account of the Invasion of the South Pacific 1767-1840*, Hamish Hamilton, London.

Morrell, W. P., 1960, *Britain in the Pacific Islands*, Oxford Univ. Press, Oxford.

★ Moseley, H. N., 1879, *Notes of a Naturalist on the 'Challenger'*, Macmillan, London.

Moses, J. A., and P. M. Kennedy, eds, 1977, *Germany in the Pacific and Far East 1870-1914*, Univ. of Queensland Press, Brisbane.

Oliver, D. L., 1951, *The Pacific Islands*, Harvard Univ. Press, Cambridge, Mass.

★ Palmer, J. L., 1869, 'Observations on the inhabitants and the antiquities of Easter Island', *Journ. Ethnol. Soc. London*, 1:371-7.

★ Palmer, J. L., 1870, 'A visit to Easter Island, or Rapa Nui, in 1868', *Journ. RGS*, 40:167-81.

Parnaby, O. W., 1964, *Britain and the Labor Trade in the Southwest Pacific*, Duke Univ. Press, Durham, N.C.

★ Piotrowski, A., 1925, 'Deux tablettes, avec les marques gravées, de l'île de Pâques', *Revue d'Ethnographie et des traditions populaires*, 6:425-31.

Scarr, D., 1967, *Fragments of Empire: A History of the Western Pacific High*

Commission 1877-1914, Aust. Nat. Univ. Press, Canberra.

Scarr, D., ed., 1978, *More Pacific Islands Portraits*, Aust. Nat. Univ. Press, Canberra.

Valentine, C. A., 1963, 'Social status, political power and native responses to European influence in Oceania', *Anthropological Forum*, 1:3-55.

Vayda, A. P., ed., 1968, *Peoples and Cultures of the Pacific*, American Museum Nat. Hist., New York.

Ward, J. M., 1948, *British Policy in the South Pacific*, Australasian Publ. Co., Sydney.

South-east Asia, Indonesia and the Philippines

Bickmore, A. S., 1868, *Travels in the East Indian Archipelago*, Murray, London.

Brandt, J. H., 1961, 'The Negritos of peninsular Thailand', *Journ. of the Siam Soc.*, 49:123-58.

Buckley, C. B., 1902, *An Anecdotal History of Singapore in Old Times*, 2 vols, Fraser and Neave, Singapore.

Carey, I., 1976, *Orang Asli: the Aboriginal Tribes of Peninsular Malaysia*, Oxford Univ. Press, Kuala Lumpur.

Cole, F. C., 1945, *The Peoples of Malaysia*, Van Nostrand, New York.

Cowan, C. D., 1961, *Nineteenth-Century Malaya: The Origins of British Political Control*, Oxford Univ. Press, London.

Daly, D. D., 1882, 'Surveys and explorations in the native states of the Malayan Peninsula, 1875-82', *Proc. RGS* (n.s.), 4:393-412.

de Klerck, E. S., 1938, *History of the Netherlands East Indies*, 2 vols, Rotterdam.

Evans, I. H. N., 1937, *The Negritos of Malaya*, Cambridge Univ. Press, Cambridge.

Favre, P., 1865, *An Account of the Wild Tribes Inhabiting the Malayan Peninsula . . . with a Journey in Johore . . .*, Imperial Printery, Paris.

Hall, D. G. E., 1955, *A History of South-East Asia*, Macmillan, London.

* Hervey, D. F. A., 1881, 'The Endau and its tributaries', *JSBRAS*, no. 8:93-124.

Krieger, H. W., 1942, *Peoples of the Philippines*, Smithsonian Inst., Washington.

Lebar, F. M., ed., 1975, *Ethnic Groups of Insular Southeast Asia*, 2 vols, Human Relations Area Files Press, New Haven.

Lebar, F. M., Hickey, G. C., and Musgrave, J. K., 1965, *Ethnic Groups of Mainland Southeast Asia*, Human Relations Area Files Press, New Haven.

Linehan, W., 1926, 'The bendaharas of Pahang', *JMBRAS*, 4(3):334-8.

Linehan, W., 1936, 'A history of Pahang', *JMBRAS*, 14(2):1-256.

Makepeace, W., ed., 1921, *One Hundred Years of Singapore*, London.

* Martin, R., 1905, *Die Inlandstämme der Malayischen Halbinsel*, Fischer, Jena.

Mills, L. A., 1925, 'British Malaya, 1824-1867', *JMBRAS*, 3:1-340.

Parkinson, C. N., 1960, *British Intervention in Malaya, 1867-77*, Univ. of Malaya Press, Singapore.

Reed, W. A., 1914, *Negritos of Zambales*, Philippines Dept of the Interior, Ethnological Survey Publications, vol. II, pt 1, Bureau of Printing, Manila.

Reid, A., 1969, *The Contest for North Sumatra. Atjeh, the Netherlands and Britain*, Oxford Univ. Press, Kuala Lumpur.

Ridley, H. N., 1892, 'Expedition to the Tahan district, Malay Peninsula', *Proc. RGS* (n.s.), 14:533.

Robequain, C., 1958, *Malaya, Indonesia, Borneo and the Philippines*, trans. E. D. Laborde, Longmans, London.

Sadka, E., 1968, *The Protected Malay States, 1874-1895*, Univ. of Malaya Press, Singapore.

Schebesta, P., 1927, *Among the Forest Dwarfs of Malaya*, Hutchinson, London.

* Semper, C., 1869, *Die Philippinen und ihre Bewohner*, Würtzburg.

* Skeat, W. W., and C. O. Blagden, 1906, *Pagan Races of the Malay Peninsula*, 2 vols, Macmillan, London and New York.

* Skinner, A. M., 1878, 'Geography of the Malay Peninsula', *JSBRAS*, no. 1:53.

Swettenham, F., 1929, *British Malaya: An Account of the Origin and Progress of British Influence in Malaya*, 2nd ed., Allen and Unwin, London.

Turnbull, C. M., 1980, *A Short History of Malaysia, Singapore and Brunei*, Cassell Aust., Melbourne.

Vella, W. T., 1957, *Siam under Rama III, 1824-1851*, New York.

Vlekke, B. H. M., 1946, *The Story of the Dutch East Indies*, Harvard Univ. Press, Cambridge, Mass.

Williams-Hunt, P. D. R., 1952, *An Introduction to the Malayan Aborigines*, Government Printer, Kuala Lumpur.

Winstedt, R. O., 1932, 'A history of Johore (1365-1895)', *JMBRAS*, 10(3):1-167.

Biographical works on persons associated with Miklouho-Maclay

Australian Dictionary of Biography, ed. D. Pike, vols 3-5, ed. B. Nairn, vol. 6, Melbourne University Press, 1969-76. Articles on: Joshua Bell, J. W. Brazier, J. Chalmers, J. C. Cox, L. M. D'Albertis, O. Finsch, A. C. Gregory, W. A. Haswell, J. S. Kubary, W. Macarthur, W. Macleay, F. McCoy, G. Masters, J. Norton, A. A. Onslow, A. H. Palmer, E. P. Ramsay, J. Robertson, G. W. Rusden, P. Scratchley, W. J. Stephens, C. S. Wilkinson.

Boelsche, W., 1906, *Haeckel: His Life and Work* (trans. J. McCabe), T. Fisher Unwin, London. See also *Dictionary of Scientific Biography*.

Boveri, T., 1912, 'Anton Dohrn', *Science*, 36:453-68. See also *Dict. Scientific Biogr.*

Chapman, J. K., 1964, *The Career of Arthur Hamilton Gordon, First Lord Stanmore*, Toronto Univ. Press.

Cumpston, J. H. L., 1972, *Augustus Gregory and the Inland Sea*, Roebuck, Canberra.

Curinier, C-E., 'Gabriel-Jacques-Jean Monod', *Dictionnaire National des Contemporaines*, Paris [1899-1906].

de Graaff, S., and D. G. Stibbe, eds, 1918, *Encylopaedie van Nederlandsch-Indië*, 2nd ed., 'sGravenhage and Leiden. Article on James Loudon.

de Leone, E., and M. A. Cappelletti, 1965, 'Odoardo Beccari', *Dizionario Biografico degli Italiani*, Rome.

Dictionary of Scientific Biography, ed. C. C. Gillispie, Charles Scribner's Sons, New York, 1970-1980. Articles on: A. Dohrn, H. Fol, C. Gegenbaur, E. Haeckel, T. H. Huxley, Mikhail Miklukho-Maclay, P. P. Semyonov-Tyan-Shansky, R. Virchow, K. E. von Baer.

France, P., 1968, 'The founding of an orthodoxy. Sir Arthur Gordon and the doctrine of the Fijian way of life', *Journ. Polynesian Soc.*, 77:6-32.

Galbraith, J. S., 1972, *Mackinnon and East Africa 1878-1895*, Cambridge.

Goode, J., 1977, *The Rape of the Fly*, Nelson, Melbourne. Adventures of D'Albertis and Beccari.

Heath, I., 1974, 'Toward a reassessment of Gordon in Fiji', *JPH*, 9:81-92.

Huxley, L., 1900, *Life and Letters of Thomas Henry Huxley*, 2 vols, London.

Langmore, D., 1974, *Tamate—A King*, Melb. Univ. Press, Melbourne. Biography of James Chalmers.

Laracy, H. M., 1970, 'Xavier Montrouzier, a missionary in Melanesia', in J. W. Davidson and D. Scarr, eds, *Pacific Islands Portraits*, Aust. Nat. Univ. Press, Canberra.

Lovett, R., 1902, *James Chalmers: His Autobiography and Letters*, Religious Tract Society, London.

Macmillan, D. S., 1957, *A Squatter Went to Sea*, Currawong Press, Sydney. Biography of William Macleay.

Stanmore, Lord (Sir A. Gordon), 1897-1912, *Fiji—Records of Private and of Public Life 1875-1880*, privately printed, Edinburgh.

Stead, W. T., 1909, *The M.P. for Russia*, 2 vols, London. Activities of Olga Novikov from a friend's point of view.

Tepito, J., 'Mgr Jaussen, premier évêque de Tahiti (1815-1891), *Les Contemporains*, no. 387, Paris, n.d.

Vetch, R. H., 1905, *General Sir Andrew Clarke*, London.

Wallace, A. R., 1905, *My Life*, 2 vols, London.

Index

407